Building the Next American Century

Building the Next American Century

The Past and Future of

American Economic Competitiveness

Kent H. Hughes

Published by
Woodrow Wilson Center Press
Washington, D.C.

Distributed by
The Johns Hopkins University Press
Baltimore

EDITORIAL OFFICES

Woodrow Wilson Center Press
Woodrow Wilson International Center for Scholars
One Woodrow Wilson Plaza
1300 Pennsylvania Avenue, N.W.
Washington, D.C. 20004-3027
Telephone: 202-691-4010
www.wilsoncenter.org

Order from

The Johns Hopkins University Press
Hampden Station
P.O. Box 50370
Baltimore, Maryland 21211
Telephone: 1-800-537-5487
www.press.jhu.edu/books

2 4 6 8 9 7 5 3 1

Library of Congress Cataloging-in-Publication Data

Hughes, Kent H.
  Building the next American Century : the past and future of American
economic competitiveness / Kent H. Hughes.
    p.   cm.
  Includes bibliographical references and index.
  ISBN 1-930365-16-0 (cloth : alk. paper) — ISBN 1-930365-17-9 (pbk. : alk. paper)
    1. United States—Economic policy—1981–1993.   2. United States—Economic
policy—1993–2001.   3. United States—Foreign economic relations.   4. United
States—Commercial policy.   5. Competition—United States.   6. Competition,
International.   I. Title.
HC106.8.H84   2005
330.973—dc22
                                                            2004022446

ABOUT THE CENTER

The Center is the living memorial of the United States of America to the nation's twenty-eighth president, Woodrow Wilson. Congress established the Woodrow Wilson Center in 1968 as an international institute for advanced study, "symbolizing and strengthening the fruitful relationship between the world of learning and the world of public affairs." The Center opened in 1970 under its own board of trustees.

In all its activities the Woodrow Wilson Center is a nonprofit, nonpartisan organization, supported financially by annual appropriations from the Congress, and by the contributions of foundations, corporations, and individuals. Conclusions or opinions expressed in Center publications and programs are those of the authors and speakers and do not necessarily reflect the views of the Center staff, fellows, trustees, advisory groups, or any individuals or organizations that provide financial support to the Center.

To my wife Ginny and my children, John, Jeff, and Krista, who patiently suffered with me through the late evenings and lost weekends that seem to come with the writing of every book.

Contents

Preface

This book is about America's economic future and its economic past. The book traces the history of how a competitiveness strategy that started to form in the late 1970s became national policy in the 1990s. The book also seeks to provide a framework for future prosperity. It describes the ideas that drove economic policy and the political and private-sector leaders who transformed ideas into a politically viable, economically successful set of policies.

The story starts in the late 1970s in the midst of a troubled American economy. The seemingly assured growth and prosperity of the two decades following the end of World War II gave way to a 1970s economy that suffered two oil shocks, rising prices, recessions, and stagnant productivity growth. By the end of the decade, Americans were talking about stagflation, signaling an economy that combined rising prices and no growth. During the same decade, the United States was facing rising international competition from Germany and Japan.

The troubled economy touched off a search by political leaders for a new set of policies that would control inflation, stimulate productivity growth, and effectively respond to international competition. The present volume focuses on a set of policies targeted at long-term productivity growth that developed under the general umbrella of a competitiveness strategy. The strategy, emphasizing the synergy of public and private investment, stressed the importance of opening markets around the world, and it advocated a technology policy that was linked to an economic climate encouraging rapid commercialization and an education policy that included investments in training and lifelong learning.

The advocates of a long-term competitiveness strategy adopted as a test for competitiveness the definition advanced in the 1985 report of the President's Commission on Industrial Competitiveness, better known as the Young Commission after John Young, its chairman, who was then the chief executive of Hewlett-Packard. The Young Commission saw the ultimate goal of a competitive economy as the ability to "meet the test of international markets while simultaneously *maintaining or expanding the real income of its citizens*" (emphasis added).

The development of a national competitiveness strategy was the product of an extensive search for new ideas and new policies that would put America on the path to sustained economic growth. This book is about that search and the key individuals whose imagination, dedication, and willingness to take risks turned those ideas first into proposals, then legislation, and then national policy. Some of the key figures are well-known political leaders: former senator and Treasury secretary Lloyd Bentsen, former House speaker Jim Wright, and Senator (and former Senate majority leader) Robert C. Byrd. President Bill Clinton's campaign was partially built on a competitiveness strategy for long-term growth, and he would pursue that strategy throughout his eight years as president.

A small band of House Democrats played an early leadership role. The late U.S. representative Gillis Long of Louisiana, in his role as chair of the House Democratic Caucus; former representative and senator Tim Wirth; and former House majority leader Dick Gephardt crafted an early version of a competitiveness strategy in the House Democratic Caucus report *Rebuilding the Road to Opportunity*.

The private sector also played a vital role in influencing public policy, as well as in changing private-sector strategy. John Young played a unique leadership role. His efforts at building corporate and national competitiveness were supported by a host of fellow chief executives, union leaders, and university presidents, and by thousands of other concerned Americans.

The present volume focuses on the development of public policy and those who made it. The focus on the public sector and public life reflects my own background. My analysis of three decades of economic policy draws on my personal experience, as well as research, reading, and interviews. In social science terms, I was a participant-observer at many points in the development of a national competitiveness strategy. I worked on economic ideas, publications, and legislation from several vantage points on Capitol Hill, in presidential campaigns, as president of the private-sector

Council on Competitiveness, and as associate deputy secretary in the Clinton administration's Commerce Department. At times, I was one of the staff people who proposed policies, turned academic thinking into the stuff of legislation, or drafted key documents.

Acknowledgments

As with so many ventures, I am thankful of the support and tolerance of my family for what I thought would be a relatively brief project and that instead stretched over a number of years. Ginny, my wife, not only saw many mostly-work weekends but also provided very helpful editorial guidance through more than one draft.

I am very grateful for all the support offered by the Woodrow Wilson Center. My special thanks go to its associate director, Samuel F. Wells, who first brought me to the Center as a public policy scholar. I owe a considerable debt to the Center's president and director, Lee Hamilton, who not only supported my effort but also asked me to stay at the Center to direct the new Project on America and the Global Economy, recently renamed the Program on Science, Technology, America and the Global Economy. Michael Van Dusen, the Center's deputy director, was equally generous with his support and encouragement. Three others at the Center made it possible for me to meet a host of commitments and still finish *Building the Next American Century*. As part of managing the entire U.S. Studies Division at the Center, Susan Nugent kept her eye on my project. Without the generous, volunteer support of Jane Mutnick, neither the book nor the Project on America and the Global Economy would have made it much beyond the stage of wishful thinking. Lynn Sha not only managed the events and publications for the Project on America and the Global Economy but also provided invaluable editorial suggestions on several parts of the book. Joseph Brinley, the director of the Woodrow Wilson Center Press, gave me useful guidance at several stages of the book's development that touched on everything from length to interviews to format. I will always owe a debt of gratitude to the economics faculty at Washington University in Saint Louis. In particular, I thank Murray Weidenbaum, the Mallinckrodt Distinguished University Professor, and David Felix, professor emeritus, who helped push me down the path toward economics and economic policy.

I also owe many thanks to friends and colleagues who reviewed different sections of the book. My wife, Ginny, belongs at the top of the list of people who helped streamline the early drafts and made many important substantive suggestions as well. Warren E. Farb, a former colleague at the U.S. Department of Commerce, gave generously of his time in making sure there were not too many errors in the economic aspects of the discussion in chapters 13 through 17. He brought a sharp mind as well as a sharp pencil to the endeavor. Carol Ann Meares of the Technology Administration of the U.S. Department of Commerce, and Kelly Carnes, former assistant secretary of technology at Commerce, gave me valuable suggestions for chapters 15 and 16 on strengthening the American innovation system and building an American learning system. Wilson Center senior fellows John Sewell and William Krist added thoughtful suggestions to chapter 17 on global engagement. Many thanks to Kelly Carnes, Warren E. Farb, Carol Ann Meares, and Jeri Jensen-Moran for helpful suggestions on the timeline that is at the end of the book. The remaining sins of commission or omission are, of course, entirely mine. Finally, I want to express my appreciation to Graham (Rusty) Mathews, who helped ensure that I had the politics as well as the economics right. Rusty was a constant source of advice, inspiration, and support.

Many people were generous in giving me time for interviews on different aspects of the competitiveness movement. John A. Young gave generously of his time on more than one occasion. I am doubly indebted to John, who hired me as the president of the Council on Competitiveness that he had founded and who helped keep my own thinking and energies focused on national competitiveness. Former House speaker Jim Wright was not only patient with his time but also saw that I had access to his archives at Texas Christian University. Many thanks to Norma Ritchson, who made the arrangements for my visit, and to Glenda Stevens, the university archivist who helped locate the material I needed in the speaker's archive. A special thanks too to J. Nelson Hoffman, who was kind enough to send me extensive background material on the summits on competitiveness he helped organize in 1991 and 1992.

For a book that spans two decades of economic policymaking, the list of interviews is long and yet, if anything, should probably be longer. Many thanks to the following, who found time to sit through many questions:

John M. Albertine, Bruce R. Bartlett, David Barram, Erich Bloch, Donald L. Bonker, Harry G. Broadman, D. Alan Bromley, Daniel F. Burton, Jr., Steve Charnovitz, C. Richard D'Amato, Stephen J. Entin, Sally Ericcson, George M. C. Fisher, Warren E. Farb, Alvin (Al) From, Martin Frost, Eric Garfinkle, Paul E. Gray, Victoria Hadfield, Robert Hamrin, Edwin L. Harper, Christopher T. Hill, J. Nelson Hoffman, James Jaffe, Jeffrey Lang, Jack Lew, Robert Liberatore, Alan H. Magazine, Robert Maher, Rachel McCulloch, Egils Milbergs, Sybil Mobley, Ellis Mottur, Thomas J. Murrin, Arnold Packer, Mark Policinski, Michael E. Porter, Roger Porter, Perry Quick, Edward V. Regan, Howard Rosen, Howard D. Samuel, Susan C. Schwab, Robert Shapiro, James H. Turner, Thomas Uhlman, Patrick Windham, Timothy E. Wirth, Jim Wright, Jr., Rufus Yerxa, John A. Young, and John Zysman.

With regard to sources, in writing this volume, I have not relied on any one preceding book to shape my approach. Herbert Stein's *Presidential Economics: The Making of Economic Policy from Roosevelt to Reagan and Beyond* provides a detailed picture of how new economic ideas mixed with economic reality and political pressures to produce a new approach to fiscal and monetary policy. Otis Graham's *Losing Time: The Industrial Policy Debate* also looks at the interplay of ideas and politics in shaping the congressional debate over industrial policy and the broader question of the government's role in the economy. In his 1995 *Rethinking America,* Hedrick Smith explored some of the ways that the private and public sectors were meeting the challenge of global competition. I have also reviewed the extensive literature on the complex interaction of a changing economy, ideas, and economic interest groups that affect policy decisions. In particular, I have looked to I. M. Destler's *American Trade Politics,* Susan Schwab's *Trade Offs: The Omnibus Trade and Competitiveness Act of 1988,* and my own *Trade, Taxes, and Transnationals: International Economic Decision Making in Congress.*

No one can write about competitiveness without recognizing a significant debt to a wide range of scholars. Bruce R. Scott and George C. Lodge of the Harvard Business School were early and significant contributors to competitiveness thinking. Laura Tyson, Steve Cohen, John Zysman, and the entire Berkeley Roundtable on International Economics played and continue to play an important role in shaping the development of the nation's competitiveness strategy. Anyone writing on competitiveness owes a special debt to Harvard Business School professor Michael E. Porter. From his seminal *The Competitive Advantage of Nations* to his recent work on the Innovation Index for the Council on Competitiveness, Porter has been a giant in his impact on competitiveness-related thinking in the United States and around the world.

In bringing together the elements of the competitiveness strategy, I have drawn on a wide variety of publications. From the public sector, I relied on a series of key congressional reports, the report of the Young Commission, and a number of administration reports, including several from the Department of Commerce and the work of the Competitiveness Policy Council. These reports are important for their ideas and also because they reflected a growing consensus in Congress and the country on the direction policy should take. Many private-sector studies were also important, particularly those of the Council on Competitiveness. Specific private-sector reports also spoke to a growing private consensus about the desired direction of public policy as well as pointing to needed private initiatives.

Finally, there were years of experience on Capitol Hill, directing policy in a presidential campaign, serving as president of the private-sector Council on Competitiveness, and as associate deputy secretary of Commerce in the Clinton administration.

Abbreviations and Acronyms

AFL-CIO	American Federation of Labor–Congress of Industrial Organizations
ARPA	Advanced Research Projects Agency, U.S. Defense Department
ATP	Advanced Technology Program
CPC	Competitiveness Policy Council
COC	Council on Competitiveness
FOMC	Federal Open Market Committee, United States
GATT	General Agreement on Tariffs and Trade
GDP	gross domestic product
IMF	International Monetary Fund
JEC	Joint Economic Committee, U.S. Congress
MEP	Manufacturing Extension Partnership, United States
MITI	Ministry of International Trade and Industry, Japan
NACS	National Advisory Commission on Semiconductors, United States
NEC	National Economic Council, United States
NSF	National Science Foundation, United States
OMB	Office of Management and Budget, United States
OSTP	Office of Science and Technology Policy, United States
PCIC	President's Commission on Industrial Competitiveness, United States
USTR	Office of the U.S. Trade Representative

Building the Next American Century

Introduction: Meeting the New Economic Challenge—Forging an American Dream for the Twenty-First Century

In the first decade of the twenty-first century, America is rediscovering the need for a national competitiveness strategy. After a decade of rising prosperity in the 1990s, the United States has struggled through three years of bust beginning in 2000. The country also faces new competitors and a new form of global competition. Established competitors such as Germany and Japan have been joined by emerging economic powers such as China, India, and parts of the former Soviet empire. The determination of China to become an economic power, India's shift toward international markets, and the collapse of the Soviet Union have essentially added 2.5 billion people to the world labor supply. The Soviet Union had always emphasized the importance of preparing students for scientific and engineering careers. China and India are now investing heavily to develop a scientifically trained workforce that can compete for sophisticated manufacturing and services. The combination of digital technology and the spread of the Internet have created a whole new kind of global competition. Any task that can be digitized —from financial analysis to chip design to reading X-rays—can now be performed anywhere in the world.

Thirty years ago, the United States faced another period of economic troubles. By the late 1970s, its economy was mired in a mix of seemingly intractable inflation, declining productivity growth, and rising international competition. This economic challenge eventually brought a national response that led to a new set of public policies focused on long-term productivity growth. Clustered under the broad umbrella of a national competitiveness strategy, these new policies would eventually play a critical role in driving America's economic success in the late twentieth century. The same broad

1

strategy provides the outlines for long-term economic strength in the twenty-first century.

From the start, the search for a competitiveness strategy was linked to the American Dream of greater individual opportunity and a rising standard of living for all. The strategy, born at the end of the 1970s in the midst of the Cold War, was also based on the premise that economic strength supported American leadership abroad. The Cold War was, after all, not just a struggle of military might but also a contest of values and economic systems. While Germany and Japan remained key allies in containing the Soviet Union, their rise to economic prominence in the 1970s and 1980s challenged the industrial and technological foundation that had given the United States a military edge. Neither Germany nor Japan emphasized the classic American virtues of largely unfettered free markets or limited government support for industry. In a fundamental sense, they posed a challenge to vaunted American values and to the superiority of the U.S. economic system.

The national competitiveness strategy was the product of an extensive search for new ideas and new policies that would put America on the path to sustained economic growth. *Building the Next American Century* is about that search for new ideas and the policies that followed and their contribution to long-term growth. Policymakers were critical to the effort, but so were private-sector leaders, academic specialists from a variety of disciplines, and the policy community in Washington.

In public hearings and private-sector reports, the advocates of an activist national competitiveness strategy forged various policy elements into a strategic whole. They stressed the impact of monetary and fiscal policy in creating a climate favorable to public and private investment. To the existing national commitment to basic research, they added an emphasis on basic technology, technology policy, and an economic climate that fostered rapid commercialization. By the end of the 1980s, the initial emphasis on education and training had become a call for lifelong learning to keep skills fresh and opportunities alive. In addition to the long-standing U.S. commitment to international trade, the competitiveness strategy put added emphasis on export promotion and access to closed markets overseas.

As the 1980s progressed, there emerged the outlines of what I call a "New Growth Compact" that depended on growth-supporting public policies and private-sector initiative. During the same period, the country became ever more a "Partnership Nation," as colleges, businesses, labor unions, and a host of other institutions formed a web of partnerships. In the development of technology, in education and training, and in opening markets abroad, the public and private sectors often formed partnerships with each other.

With the fall of the Berlin Wall in 1989 and the collapse of the Soviet Union in 1991, the United States entered the 1990s as the world's sole military superpower. As the U.S. economy raced forward in the 1990s, economic difficulties slowed growth in Germany and Japan. By the mid-1990s, the United States had regained its standing as the world's preeminent economy.

As the country moves through the first decade of the twenty-first century, however, it faces a new set of challenges—a global war on terrorism, the rise of new competitors, and the emergence of worldwide digital competition. The broad outlines of the competitiveness strategy pursued in the 1990s must now be adapted to new economic circumstances and shifting geopolitical realities.

The Outlines of a National Competitiveness Strategy

The broad elements of the competitiveness strategy will be familiar to students of economic growth or growth accounting. But it took the courage and imagination of leaders in the public and private spheres to forge a set of ideas that ultimately achieved legislative success, secured private-sector involvement, and gained broad public support.

The Great Depression had ended with World War II, and civilian prosperity returned in the two decades after the end of the war. But the searing memory of unemployment and widespread economic failure was still very much a part of the national memory. The Employment Act of 1946 established the president's Council of Economic Advisers and the congressional Joint Economic Committee to focus on the policies that would lead to full employment. Well into the 1970s, much of the public policy debate focused on stimulating and eventually fine tuning the national demand for goods and services to ensure that the economy was operating at its full potential.

When demand management failed to restore productivity and income growth in the 1970s, political leaders looked for a new set of policies. The group that developed the competitiveness strategy shifted from an exclusive focus on demand management to an emphasis on fiscal and monetary policies that also created an economic environment fostering public and private investments. As it developed in the 1980s, the specific emphasis was on a mix of tighter fiscal policy and more expansive monetary policy to create lower, investment-supporting, long-term interest rates.

The shift to encouraging long-term productivity growth threw an added spotlight on the importance of public investments in research and development, education, training, and infrastructure. The composition of public spending or fiscal policy had an importance separate from how much stimulus it might provide to the economy.

The rapid economic growth of Germany and Japan had a powerful impact on both public- and private-sector thinking. By succeeding in the American market with different public policies and private practices, Germany and Japan forced America to rethink its own public policies, corporate strategies, and educational philosophy. Although the United States, Germany, and Japan devoted similar shares of their total economic output (i.e., gross domestic product) to research and development, much of the U.S. total was dedicated to military-related research. Not only did Germany and Japan focus most of their research dollars on the civilian economy, but they often seemed to bring new products to market more rapidly than their U.S. counterparts. The response of the competitiveness advocates was to call for a public commitment to basic technologies as well as basic science and to emphasize the importance of policies that created a climate that allowed companies to bring products to market rapidly.

At different points in the post–World War II period, America had focused its attention and concern on its education system. Parents in the 1950s were already asking *Why Johnny Can't Read,* when, in 1957, the Soviet Union's Sputnik became the first artificial satellite to enter space.[1] There was a national reaction that emphasized science, mathematics, and foreign languages at virtually all levels of formal education. In 1983, the Reagan administration's *A Nation at Risk* report shocked the nation by claiming that if a foreign power had created our then-current elementary and secondary school system we would have viewed it as an act of war.[2]

In terms of mathematics and science, the number of engineering graduates, and performance on international tests, in the 1980s the United States was lagging behind its major international competitors. In *The Japanese Educational Challenge,* Mary White suggested that the average Japanese high school graduate had the equivalent of an American bachelor's degree.[3] Students of the Japanese economy also noted that they spent more on training and included front-line workers rather than concentrating on upper management and technical specialists, the more common American practice.

The developers of the competitiveness strategy included an early emphasis on education, including computer literacy, and training. The spread of

Toyota's idea of lean production depended on the improving skills of front-line workers as well as management. The pace of innovation and the adoption of new technologies were eliminating the idea of resting on a college degree or the mastery of a particular skill.

Instead of turning away from global competition, the competitiveness strategy focused on the need for public policies and private practices that would make American institutions, companies, and workers competitive on the world stage. Instead of turning toward protecting domestic markets, the competitiveness strategy emphasized opening markets overseas, effective export promotion, and streamlining Cold War policies that restricted the export of many high-technology products.

The competitiveness strategy was not simply a set of isolated policies. The policies were mutually reinforcing and created a competitive whole much greater than the sum of its individual parts. Today's innovation was tomorrow's export, and added sales abroad helped generate the profits that fueled the next generation of research spending. Education, training, and lifelong learning created the scientists and engineers that performed the research and produced a more highly educated workforce that would speed the introduction of new products and processes. Public funding for research, national laboratories, and early purchases by federal agencies all supported private-sector innovation. A low-interest-rate macroeconomic policy made public and private investments more attractive, including investments in research facilities and in the capital equipment that embodied a host of innovations.

Nor was the spotlight only on public policies. A national competitiveness strategy needed a national effort—innovative companies committed to research and training and an education system that encompassed elementary and secondary schools, community colleges, and advanced research universities. The 1980s brought sharpened awareness that national economic growth and strength depended on both public and private sectors, on the government and the market. It was this shift in thinking that created the outlines of a New Growth Compact, whereby (in summary terms) the federal government helped set the stage and the private sector, local schools, and other institutions put on the play.

As it developed in the 1980s, the competitiveness strategy put more emphasis on partnerships, many of them between the public and private sectors. Companies might shy away from investing in a basic technology for fear that they might not be able to adequately capture the benefits—in effect, that their investment would subsidize domestic or international competitors. In other cases, technologies and great innovative capacity had been isolated in national laboratories or research universities. Over the course of the 1980s, the federal government took a series of steps that encouraged public–private cooperation in pursuit of more rapid innovation. Companies, recognizing their need for an educated workforce, often became effective partners in seeking to improve the elementary and secondary education system. The spread of partnerships started the country on the path to becoming a Partnership Nation, in which national prosperity drew on an often intricate web of partnerships involving a mix of government, universities, schools, unions, and private businesses.

A Short History of the Competitiveness Movement

The story starts with the expectations bred by the economic success of the 1950s and 1960s. After a decade of economic depression and the rationing of the war years, the rapid economic growth of the early post–World War II years was an almost intoxicating change. Americans came home from World War II, trained under the GI Bill, and started moving to the suburbs. America fulfilled a campaign pledge from an earlier era—there was not only a car in every garage but a good deal more than a chicken in every pot. In the 1950s, the General Electric Company caught the ethos of the times with its slogan "Progress Is Our Most Important Product."[4] By the end of the 1960s, Americans had lived through a quarter-century of largely uninterrupted growth and higher incomes. For Americans and most business leaders, the quarter-century of growth took place in a world in which the United States was the leading industrial power. The era bred an assumption of endless American economic dominance and ever rising prosperity.

The economic turmoil of the 1970s changed that reality and even challenged America's confidence about the future. Persistent inflation, periodic recessions, and stagnating incomes eroded American confidence in the ability of the government to provide economic leadership and prosperity. National anger and national concern set policymakers, business leaders, and prominent academics looking for answers to the challenges posed by the 1970s. They were not alone. Americans responded much as they had in the 1950s, when the Soviet Union beat America into space with its Sputnik satellite. All across the country, engineers, schoolteachers, leading academics, presidents of community colleges, labor unions, think tanks in Washington and around the country, professional societies, thousands of businesses, and local elected officials took individual steps that helped define a new strategy and lay the basis for long-term economic growth.

In Washington, there was a search for new ideas and policies that met the new economic reality and also promised electoral success. By the late 1970s, several ideas were contending for national prominence. As the international economy grew in importance, some focused on boosting exports, and others sought to restrict imports.

In the late 1970s and early 1980s, a number of academics, some prominent business leaders, and many Democrats in Congress developed proposals for an active industrial policy. Initially, the focus was on improving the standing of established, traditional industries. Later, the emphasis shifted to so-called sunrise industries that were based in Silicon Valley and other emerging high-technology centers around the country.

At much the same time, a small group of journalists, congressional staff, and one future Nobel Prize winner built a strategy on the idea that reducing marginal tax rates (the tax one pays on the last dollar of earnings), would induce Americans to save more, invest more, and work harder. Representative Jack Kemp (R-N.Y.) and Senator William Roth (R-Del.) turned this idea into legislation and, by 1980, it had become a key element in Ronald Reagan's successful bid for the presidency.

Building the Next American Century traces the development of a third set of ideas that emphasized national competitiveness and long-term productivity growth. The economic challenge posed by Germany and Japan forced policymakers and private-sector leaders to reconsider their respective roles. Closer ties between the public and private sectors in Germany and Japan prompted a new appreciation of how public policy and private initiative were both necessary for long-term productivity growth. Without any formal agreement, many policymakers and private-sector leaders began to think of a New Growth Compact. In other words, government investments in basic science and technology complemented private research and innovation, and public and private spending on aspects of innovation became part of the same value chain. The same was true of government spending on education and training.

Important parts of the American business community turned to Washington for policies that would support American business in its effort to match international competition. Some companies sought traditional protection through tariffs, quotas, or negotiated limits on foreign exports (generally known as voluntary export restraints or market-sharing agreements).

But a growing number of firms pushed for government policies that complemented their own efforts to become more productive and innovative. Where there was a shared interest in innovation or training, the government and the private sector often found themselves forming a variety of public–private partnerships. Federal laboratories formed cooperative research and development agreements with private companies to foster the development of new technologies. Companies turned to community colleges to help provide specialized education that would strengthen their workforce.

Cooperation with the private sector was not new. Many of the business leaders had lived through World War II, the national reaction to Sputnik, and the continuing challenge of the Cold War—all national challenges that called forth an effort from all Americans. These challenges had all forged close ties between the federal government and a variety of industries. What was new was the widespread use of partnerships in areas outside the confines of traditional national security. The federal approach was part of a broader trend of partnerships formed at the state and local levels, between universities and the private sector, and among private firms themselves. It was this move to broad-based cooperation that marked the emergence of a Partnership Nation that will influence the pace of innovation, investment, and economic growth well into the twenty-first century.

The 1990s: Competitiveness Strategy Becomes National Policy

As the country entered the 1990s, President George H. W. Bush and his administration took some steps in the direction of a national competitiveness strategy. His decision to deal with failed savings and loans institutions, coupled with an increase in taxes, helped lay the basis for fiscal policy under President Bill Clinton. Bush's White House Office of Science and Technology Policy issued its first-ever white paper on technology policy and, despite some initial reluctance, the administration did seek funds for the technology programs created by Congress in 1988. Bush also renewed the push for improved education by holding only the third-ever summit with the nation's governors. The result was a call for national standards and new initiatives that would draw on collaboration with the private sector.

But with the election of President Clinton in 1992, competitiveness came center stage as national policy. Clinton had run on a broad competitiveness platform that emphasized public and private investment. He was the first modern president to make technology policy a plank in his presidential platform. His principal campaign document, *Putting People First,* emphasized education, training, and research, and he endorsed international trade, adding the slogan "Compete Not Retreat" to his campaign vocabulary.

Clinton entered office with an economy that was recovering from a recession and still burdened with slow employment growth. Fiscal deficits were already large and expected to grow in the future. The Federal Reserve had lowered short-term interest rates, but long-term rates had remained stubbornly high. In a meeting with Federal Reserve Chairman Alan Greenspan, Clinton became convinced that by attacking the federal deficit he would reduce fears of future inflation, lower long-term interest rates, boost business confidence, and trigger added investment. Deficit reduction in the face of a slow economy ran against standard advice and past experience, but it worked in the circumstances of the early 1990s.

Throughout his presidency, Clinton worked to implement a technology policy designed to increase innovation and growth in the civilian economy. He continued President Bush's work in pushing for national educational standards and successfully proposed a number of programs and tax incentives to support higher education and to upgrade the skills of workers already on the job. To programs and policies, he added his frequent use of the bully pulpit to stress the reality of a changing world that would force all U.S. workers to improve their skills.

The Clinton administration was also active in the arena of international trade. The administration finished the Uruguay Round of multilateral trade negotiations that had started under President Reagan and largely been completed by President Bush's chief trade negotiator, Carla Hills. President Bush had also initiated and signed the North American Free Trade Agreement, encompassing Canada, Mexico, and the United States. At some considerable political cost, President Clinton successfully steered approval of the Uruguay Round and the North American Free Trade Agreement through Congress. Later in his term, Congress granted permanent normal trade relations status to China, a major step that paved the way for China to join the World Trade Organization in December 2001. To trade agreements, Clinton added an aggressive approach to opening foreign markets and promoting U.S. exports. In a post–Cold War era, the Clinton administration felt much freer in following the European and Japanese practice of using top officials to advocate major trade deals.

Like its early creators, the Clinton administration saw the competitiveness strategy as a reinforcing whole. The administration did not pursue international trade in isolation but saw it as part of a process of creating better paying export-related jobs, opening new markets to American innovations, and stimulating innovation at the same time. Education and training made a direct contribution to long-term growth and, at the same time, helped prepare people for higher-skill jobs in export and other industries. By limiting the ability of companies to raise prices, international trade also encouraged corporate innovation and gave the Federal Reserve more room to pursue a growth-supporting monetary policy.

Clinton and his team viewed their economic policies as being part of a national competitiveness strategy in which the private sector played a powerful role. For Clinton and his administration, there was a clear sense that rapid growth and flexible markets could be a powerful force for achieving national goals including social welfare. Where they made sense, the Clinton administration did not hesitate to seek and encourage public–private partnerships.

September 11: New Reality, New Competitors, and New Competition

As the United States enters the twenty-first century, the geopolitical and global economic landscape has shifted once again. In 2001, its economy slipped into a recession lasting three quarters. The subsequent economic recovery in 2002 and the first half of 2003 was tepid and halting. And the economy carried the extra burden of the September 11, 2001, terrorist attacks on the World Trade Center and the Pentagon and a series of corporate scandals that started with the collapse of Enron in late 2001. The long bull market of the 1990s ended in March 2000, as the air began to come out of the stock market bubble and ushered in three consecutive years of decline. Individual investors, major pension funds, foundations, and university endowments suffered a collective loss of trillions of dollars. Investment slowed and fell to near-depression levels in the information-technology and telecommunications sectors.

The September 11, 2001, attacks on the World Trade Center and the Pentagon brought the post–Cold War era to an end. President George W. Bush called America to a global war on terrorism. Only months later, the country sent its troops halfway around the world to a rapid victory over the terrorist-harboring Taliban regime in Afghanistan. In his 2002 State of the Union address, the president spoke of an "axis of evil" that encompassed Iraq, Iran, and North Korea. In the spring of 2003, the U.S. military scored a rapid victory over Iraqi forces. The fighting, however, is not over. Insurgent-led conflict and almost daily death continue, while the United States and its coalition partners work to bring stability, democracy, and renewed prosperity to Iraq. Homeland security became more of a national priority than at any time since the emphasis on civil defense in the 1950s. In 2002, Congress created a new federal agency, the Department of Homeland Security, to coordinate national efforts to provide domestic security. National leaders began to prepare the country for the risk of another terrorist attack.

With the focus on national security and recovery from a faltering economy, concern about long-term growth largely disappeared. The lessons of the competitiveness strategy, the possibilities of a New Growth Compact, and the growing importance of public–private partnerships received little public attention.

Yet questions are again surfacing about the long-term competitiveness of the American economy. The sense in the 1990s that globalization was inevitable and almost always part of a "win–win" outcome has faded in the early twenty-first century. At times, advocates for trade as an isolated engine of growth overlooked the need for institutions, sound governance, adequate infrastructure, and a host of other elements. Thinking has changed in light of the 1997 Asian financial crisis, the difficult search for prosperous democracies in the former Soviet Union, and a growing acceptance that there are significant short-term losers as well as many winners as the world experiences ever deeper economic integration.

At home in the United States, there will be continued efforts to build on the Trade Act of 2002 by further extending trade adjustment assistance to include service workers. Faced with accelerating change driven by trade and technology, the country must move toward supporting even greater flexibility by making pensions, health care, and other benefits universally available and universally portable.

The interdependence that has come with globalization has brought many benefits but also created added risks. In two recent years, the global supply chain of parts and products was disrupted by the threat of terrorism, the eruption of Severe Acute Respiratory Syndrome, and a West Coast longshoreman's strike. Managing dependence has become a national imperative. The focus on fighting terrorism, the ongoing conflicts in Iraq and Afghanistan, and the global security interests of the United States will almost surely lead to a Cold War–like era in which geopolitical considerations will come at the cost of the domestic economy. At the same time, the United States faces a growing number of new competitors and new, global, online competition.

To meet these new challenges, the country must develop national policies that recognize shifting global economic patterns, the development of new technologies, and the growth strategies of major economic competitors. In effect, the United States must develop a capacity for geoeconomic strategy that matches its commitment to geopolitics. Where foreign policy penalizes a domestic industry, leaves intellectual property rights unenforced, or foreign markets unopened, the United States will need to take offsetting action to compensate an industry or add funds for research to maintain its long-term economic strength.

In the early twenty-first century, the country faces a new geopolitical challenge, rising new competitors, and a new form of competition. As Mark Twain once said, "History does not repeat itself . . . but it rhymes." Like the Cold War, the United States is again engaged in a global struggle, this time against terrorism, failing states, and the spread of weapons of mass destruction. Instead of focusing on Germany and Japan, national attention has shifted to the rise of China, the loss of jobs to India, and Brazil's leadership of a new bloc of countries in international trade relations.

And again, private voices are joining those of government leaders in calling for improved education; increased funding for advanced technologies, and a faster pace of innovation. In a 2004 op-ed article in the *Wall Street Journal,* Carly Fiorina, the chief executive of Hewlett-Packard, looks back at the President's Commission on Industrial Competitiveness as a guide for responding to today's economic challenges.[5] On July 22, 2004, Senator Joseph Lieberman (D-Conn.) introduced the Commission on the Future of the United States Economy Act (S 2747), which was inspired by the 1983 President's Commission on Industrial Competitiveness (the Young Commission).[6] The Computer Systems Policy Project—chaired by Craig Barrett, the chief executive of Intel, a leading semiconductor firm—calls for greater innovation and investment to drive future productivity growth.[7] The private-sector Council on Competitiveness is on the move again with a major National Innovation Initiative cochaired by Samuel J. Palmisano, the chairman and chief executive of IBM, and G. Wayne Clough, the president of the Georgia Institute of Technology.[8] Mary Good, the 2000 president of the American Association for the Advancement of Science and President Clinton's first undersecretary for technology policy, chairs the Alliance for Science & Technology Research in America (ASTRA), a new organization pushing for increased funding for the physical sciences.[9] In the early twenty-first century, many of the nation's concerns and some of the proposed answers are beginning to rhyme with some of the most important verses from the 1980s.

The broad outlines of a twenty-first-century competitiveness strategy grow readily out of the experience of the 1990s. The emphasis on public and private investment, a recognition of how public and private sectors complement each other, and the continued importance of public–private partnerships are not just artifacts of yesterday but also important guideposts for the future. These policies helped generate rapid growth in the 1990s, creating tight labor markets that opened up new opportunities for all Americans, including those still struggling to develop twenty-first-century skills. The central role played by innovation and technology policy also suggests creative ways to combine the goals of economic growth, energy security, and an improved environment. While the experience and success of the 1990s contain the broad outlines of a growth strategy for the twenty-first century, individual policies must be adapted to a shifting geopolitical reality, a new set of challenges, and changed economic conditions.

The need for a mix of long-term strategy and policy adaptability was very effectively made by John Rollwagen, the candidate to be deputy secretary of commerce at the beginning of the first Clinton term. As the former chief executive of Cray Research, then the leading supercomputer company in the United States, Rollwagen used stories about Cray founder Seymour Cray to teach key management lessons. Rollwagen would periodically take a group of Cray employees to visit different university researchers and Cray suppliers. As Rollwagen told the story, the group would always start with a visit to Seymour Cray, who would spell out a detailed, five-year vision of the future. At the end of one tour, the group had time for a second visit with Cray. Again, he spelled out a detailed five-year vision of the future, but one that was slightly different from the vision of just a few weeks before. Competitiveness strategists need to think in similar terms—a long-term vision, and a strategy that adjusts to changing circumstances. In describing the past, *Building the Next American Century* seeks to help shape the future.

Chapters 1 through 4 of this book set the economic and political context of America in the 1970s and describe the search for a new growth policy that involved looking overseas as well as to the country's past. Chapters 5, 6, and 7 discuss the congressional initiatives and the response of the Reagan administration that culminated in the Omnibus Trade and Competitiveness Act of 1988. Chapter 8 points to some of the parallel developments in the states and in the private sector.

The book then moves to describe the George H. W. Bush administration and its partial embrace of a competitiveness strategy (chapter 9) and the focus on competitiveness in the 1992 presidential campaign (chapter 10).

Subsequent chapters explore the adoption of competitiveness as national policy (chapter 11), briefly examine the 1994 Gingrich revolution and the Clinton comeback (chapter 12), and assess the relationship of the strategy for competitiveness to 1990s prosperity (chapter 13).

The book also looks forward to sketch the outlines of a competitiveness strategy for the twenty-first century. Building on the twentieth-century experience, the twenty-first-century strategy would encourage public and private investment (chapter 14), strengthening the innovation system (chapter 15), and building an American learning system (chapter 16). The United States will need to move beyond the emphasis on international trade to a policy of global engagement focusing on the flows of capital and technology, growth in the developing world, international environmental goals, the construction of adequate social safety nets, and the protection of labor rights (chapter 17). Chapter 18 summarizes the past contributions and future direction of a national competitiveness strategy and concludes with thoughts about the American Dream in the twenty-first century.

Notes

1. Rudolf Flesch, *Why Johnny Can't Read, and What You Can Do about It* (New York: Harper & Row Perennial Library, 1955).

2. The text of the report, *A Nation at Risk,* which was issued by the National Commission on Excellence in Education, can be found at http://www.ed.gov/pubs/NatAt/Risk/html.

3. Mary White, *The Japanese Educational Challenge: A Commitment to Children* (New York: Macmillan, 1987).

4. For a brief description of the General Electric Theater that helped make the GE slogan famous, see "General Electric Theater," at http://www.museum.tv/archives/etv/G/htmlG/generalelect.htm.

5. Carly Fiorina, "Be Creative, Not Protectionist," *Wall Street Journal,* February 13, 2004.

6. See Senator Joseph I. Lieberman, *Congressional Record,* July 22, 2004 (Washington, D.C.: U.S. Government Printing Office), S8731–33.

7. "Choose to Compete: How Innovation, Investment and Productivity Can Grow U.S. Jobs and Ensure U.S. Competitiveness in the 21st Century," Computer Systems Policy Project, Washington, January 7, 2004. The report can be viewed at http://cspp.org/reports/ChoseTOCompete.pdf.

8. A summary of the National Innovation Initiative can be found at http://www.compete.org/nii/.

9. For information on ASTRA, see http://www.aboutastra.org/.

Chapter 1

From Effortless Growth
to the Era of Stagflation

In the 1990s, the United States enjoyed a record economic expansion and prosperity that, by the middle of the decade, was raising the standard of living for all Americans. It was a decade of peace as well as prosperity. The collapse of the Soviet Union in 1991 left America as the world's only military superpower. American power, American political values, and the American way of doing business were on the march around the world. Germany and Japan, which had posed such a challenge to the American economy in the 1980s, were struggling with limited growth and high unemployment. The absorption of the former East Germany had added a new burden to the German economy, and the bursting of Japan's financial and real estate bubbles in the early 1990s slowed Japanese growth to a crawl.

As the United States entered the twenty-first century, it encountered new challenges. On September 11, 2001, two hijacked planes slammed into the World Trade Center; a third plane crashed into a wing of the Pentagon; and a fourth plane, reported to have been headed for the Capitol Building, fell and burned in rural Pennsylvania. The post–Cold War era had come to end. In a matter of days, President George W. Bush announced a global war on terrorism. Again, America was engaged in a worldwide struggle.

In retrospect, the 1990s seemed a golden economic age. Low inflation, low interest rates, and low unemployment had been coupled with rapid growth and sharply improved productivity. By the end of the decade, it was referred to as the "Goldilocks" economy where everything, like Goldilocks's preferred porridge, was just right. The porridge began to cool in 2000 and became a bit chilly in 2001 as the economy slipped into a shallow recession for three quarters of the year. The financial markets peaked in early 2000, with the Dow Jones Industrial Average at 11,723 and the technology-heavy

Nasdaq at 5,048.62. Declining markets were staggered by the attack of September 11 and then roiled by a series of corporate scandals that exposed deceptive accounting, lax corporate governance, and what Federal Reserve Chairman Alan Greenspan termed "infectious greed."[1] From their highs in early 2000, the stock markets entered into a protracted bear market.

Despite the sharp change in circumstances, America remains the world's sole superpower, an economic powerhouse, and cultural force. Within months of the September 11 attacks, American troops were deployed halfway around the world in a successful effort to defeat the Taliban regime in Afghanistan. Despite the egregious failures of American accounting, corporate governance, and regulatory oversight, the U.S. economy's flexibility and ability to innovate continue to command respect around the world. The drop of many stock indices into bear-market territory has not triggered any talk of an American climacteric or the coming eclipse of American influence. The 1990s resurgence of the American economy did not happen by accident. American economic strength had grown out of public policies and business practices adopted during the preceding decade. American investments and innovations had given America a new, global competitive edge.

In 1992, President Bill Clinton and his election team reminded the country and each other that "it's the economy, stupid." By the end of the decade, public opinion was focused on other issues—the country's values, the strength of families, improving education, and creating livable communities. In the 2000 election, prosperity was almost taken for granted.

It was not always that way. Twenty years earlier, the country was struggling with stagnant incomes, persistent inflation, and a sharp increase in global competition. Since the early days of World War II, the United States and its economy had been on the march to a new era. The specter of the Great Depression made the early post–World War II years seem all the brighter. Brief recessions were surrounded by years of steady growth. In the early 1960s, the country started down the path to 106 months (almost nine years) of unbroken prosperity. By the middle of that decade, Americans were debating everything from civil rights to the war in Vietnam. Growth had slipped from the national agenda. Growth was simply taken for granted.

Three decades of rising incomes, low unemployment, and steady growth did not prepare the country for the economic roller-coaster of the 1970s. After the 1973 oil embargo, America started a decade of intermittent inflation, recession, and stagnating productivity growth. The oil embargo highlighted U.S. dependence on imports for energy and a host of other critical raw materials. American economic turmoil coincided with the economic recovery of Europe and Japan. Rising international competition was beginning to threaten America's sense of industrial dominance. Suddenly, the vaunted American prosperity machine was struggling at home and under attack abroad.

The economic challenges of the 1970s triggered a search by political and business leaders for policies and practices that would restore national prosperity and private-sector profitability. The search was not a modern-day version of the Lewis and Clark exploration of untracked territory. Instead of a tight team with a clearly defined mission, there was the clash of new ideas and established interests. Political parties and political leaders struggled to find practical policies that would bring power as well as prosperity. American business fought to respond to domestic and international competitors. In foreign firms, American business often saw a double challenge—superior business practices and a supportive foreign government acting as a kind of silent partner. The battle of ideas involved the academic world and the policy community. But it was not a dispassionate debate. Ideology often blended with ideas, and analysis lapped over into advocacy.

The American response took a thousand forms. Individual businesses struggled to meet the challenge of Japanese quality and rapid innovation. Community college presidents responded to the business call for a more skilled workforce. Labor unions added training programs to their collective-bargaining agreements. Local school boards put renewed emphasis on the basics of mathematics, science, reading, and writing. State governors developed their own strategies to respond to global competition, technology-driven growth, and the pressure for improved education. Universities forged partnerships with the private sector to improve education and speed the commercialization of university research. Step by step, Congress and the executive branch adopted laws or pursued initiatives to help the private and public sectors respond to the challenges of an emerging "new economy" based on information technology and global competition. The complicated, decentralized, often entrepreneurial American system helped put the country back on the road to economic growth.

America as No. 1: The Era of Endless Prosperity

As in so much of political and economic life, the concerns of the 1970s were a combination of objective changes, prevailing expectations, and the reigning ideas about how the world worked. American expectations and economic thinking were both heavily influenced by post–World War II prosperity and the Great Depression that dominated the 1930s. After World War II, the United States entered an era of rapidly growing prosperity. Rising wages and family incomes pulled millions of Americans into the ranks of the middle class. Adjusting for inflation, Americans' disposable income (what a person has to spend after taxes) almost doubled between 1945 and 1973.[2]

Underlying the rise in average income was the rapid rise in production and productivity growth. The Great Depression had slowed consumption and production. In some years, 25 percent of the workforce went jobless. Production and employment recovered during World War II, but large percentages of the nation's income were being channeled into the war effort. By 1944, the nation was spending more than 40 percent of its national income on defense.[3] The Great Depression also slowed private-sector investment and hence the introduction of new technologies into the civilian economy.[4] That trend continued as World War II emphasized the development and application of technologies that would contribute to the war effort. But the war's industrial demands also significantly added to the stock of technologies with a potential for use in the civilian economy.

By the end of World War II, two generations had struggled through economic hard times and then the global threat of fascism. The soldiers coming home and the millions of civilians working for the war effort were ready for better economic times. There was an enormous pent-up demand for consumer products and an array of technologies ready to help produce them.

As the country entered the 1950s, public policies and private initiative combined to give American prosperity a new look. The 1950s were not simply a more prosperous version of the 1930s, but were also filled with different products and expanding opportunities. Federal policies fostered home ownership through mortgage insurance, and American industry filled these homes with labor-saving devices. Prosperity made a near reality out of Herbert Hoover's 1928 campaign slogan, "A chicken in every pot and a car in every garage."[5] Combined with a national commitment to road building, the automobile made the suburbs accessible. An ever-restless America was on the move.

America Meets All Challenges

American confidence was not just based on higher wages. In the 1950s, the Great Depression was still a vivid memory. From the vantage point of the widespread, almost universal prosperity of the twenty-first century, it is easy to forget how poor America was in the 1930s. Although the New Deal did not banish the Great Depression—it took the mobilization for war to put all of America back to work—it did help transform rural areas through development, electrification, and agricultural support. When people flooded into defense and later civilian production, they left poverty behind. But the memory lingered and added luster to the prosperity of the 1950s and 1960s.

The American military and American industry had combined to defeat first Germany and then Japan. The war had taken a terrible toll on European and Japanese industry. Industrial complexes and whole cities had been severely damaged, while established markets and trade networks were seriously disrupted. The story was dramatically different in the United States. In America, new investments and technology had significantly strengthened the country's industrial base. At the end of World War II, America "commanded fully half the entire planet's manufacturing capacity and generated more than half the world's electricity. America owned two-thirds of the world's gold stocks and half of all its monetary reserves."[6] At the same time, America was a largely self-sufficient economy that did not yet depend on imports of energy or other raw materials. In the late 1940s, America was even a net exporter of petroleum. America entered the war still struggling with the Great Depression. America left the war as the dominant global economic power.

In looking to the future beyond World War II, America and the industrial world had learned some clear lessons from the economic mistakes made between the two great wars. In place of the ruinous economic conditions imposed by the Versailles Treaty on a defeated Germany, there were the International Bank for Reconstruction and Development (commonly known as the World Bank) and the American Marshall Plan to help rebuild Europe. During the interwar period, countries had tried to gain an economic advantage by devaluing their currencies or raising tariffs—both designed to boost domestic production and employment at the expense of their competitors. To guard against competitive devaluations, the United States and the United Kingdom worked to establish a system of exchange rates that were fixed in terms of dollars and gold. To support this system (known as the Bretton Woods system after its founding conference at a New Hampshire resort hotel), these same two countries took the lead in creating the International Monetary Fund to help countries that encountered temporary balance of payments difficulties. To limit competition through tit-for-tat increases in tariffs, the United States helped to create the General Agreement on Tariffs and Trade, whose structure was used for a series of global trade negotiations that eventually led to today's World Trade Organization.[7]

America had fought and won a "Crusade in Europe."[8] The euphoria of victory, however, quickly gave way to the global Cold War, which presented its own set of challenges. Soviet troops occupied much of Eastern and Central Europe and brought communist governments with them. In 1947, the Soviets tested their first atomic bomb, breaking the American monopoly on atomic weapons. The arms race had begun.

The contest in space left a particularly strong imprint. Both the United States and the Soviet Union were intent on developing advanced missiles that could extend the reach of atomic weapons and exert control over space. When the Soviets became the first in space with their 1957 launch of Sputnik,[9] America was stunned. It was a potential threat to American national security, and an even greater shock to America's technological pride.

America responded. The most visible response was President John Kennedy's commitment to land a human on the moon before the end of the 1960s. In July 1969, Neil Armstrong took that first "step for man and a giant leap for mankind." Twelve years after Sputnik challenged America with its steady beep, America had put the first human on the moon.

Less well remembered was how the entire nation responded to the challenge of Sputnik. Local school boards demanded more science and mathematics in high school curricula.[10] Congress was shocked by Sputnik and the apparent weaknesses in America's commitment to teaching science and mathematics. The result was the National Defense Education Act of 1958 (NDEA).[11] A generation of graduate students in everything from energy to economics benefited from NDEA's provisions. Some of the graduate fellowships combined an academic discipline with a foreign language— America, after all, was engaged in a worldwide struggle. When Americans entered college in 1958, many of them chose to study Russian. It was important to know the enemy.

America responded to Sputnik with ambitious goals, federal programs, individual decisions, and local initiative. In many ways, that complicated, many-layered response anticipated the way America would respond to the competitiveness challenge more than two decades in the future.

Measuring Success: Are You Better Off Today?

Much of American thinking revolves around the idea of individual success and national progress. Americans generally measure that success relative to other countries, relative to the country's past performance, and relative to their widely shared expectation of continued progress. It was that past performance that Ronald Reagan had in mind when he asked American voters in 1980 if "they were better off today than they were four years" before.

As Americans entered the 1970s, they had a very positive answer to the "are you better off today" question. Expectations for the economic future were also high—built on almost three decades of rising prosperity and the high-growth, low-unemployment economy of the 1960s. Despite the turmoil in Vietnam, America still felt very much in control of its economic destiny. There was a broadly shared confidence in American industry and American economic policies. *Time* magazine reflected the contemporary confidence in economists and their policies by featuring John Maynard Keynes on its December 31, 1965, cover. It was the "first time a person no longer living was so honored. The point of the article was that the New Economists had learned to apply Keynesian theory in a way that would maintain high employment and steady growth without inflation."[12] America was not sure how they did it, but their magic seemed to work. By the end of the decade, there were already warnings of inflation, nagging balance of payments difficulties, and a growing trade challenge. But, for most Americans, continued prosperity made it easy to ignore the early signs of changing economic times.

Foreign competition was only beginning to appear on the national radar screen. Europe and Japan had suffered from the global impact of the Great Depression and the much greater devastation of World War II. Although, by 1970, Europe and Japan had largely recovered from the war, they were just beginning to be a force in global markets. The Volkswagen Beetle had made a dent in the U.S. auto market, and Toyota was working hard to establish an American presence. But for most Americans, Europe and Japan were political allies and not economic rivals. The post-Stalin spurt in Soviet growth had faded, and with it the fear that central planning might have had some advantages over American reliance on private markets.[13]

America had problems, but the economy was not one of them. In 1970, the Gallup Poll rated campus unrest as the biggest national concern (at 27 percent of the respondents), with the Vietnam War second (at 22 percent). The focus was on military challenges abroad and political turmoil at home. The economy simply did not register. Five years later, 60 percent of Americans rated the cost of living as the single most important issue, with 20 percent putting unemployment second.[14]

When the Economic Future Darkened

At the beginning of the 1970s, many prominent economists, political and business leaders, and much of the American public thought that the country had the economic knowledge and policy tools to maintain steady economic growth. Ten years later, America was searching for new ways to foster growth, control inflation, and meet rising global competition.

Even in the 1960s, there were some early warnings of future economic troubles. For much of the decade, the United States was struggling to bring its international payments position into balance. Fixed exchange rates and higher inflation in the United States created two problems. The United States was committed to redeem major foreign currencies in gold at a fixed dollar price. By the end of the decade, potential foreign claims were outpacing the size of U.S. gold reserves. The same fixed exchange rates and rising prices combined with industrial recovery overseas to create competitive pressures for specific American industries.

At the same time, America was becoming ever more dependent on imported energy. Warnings about the growing dependence on imported energy and raw materials went unheeded by political leaders as well as the general public. Although inflationary pressures began to build in the 1960s, there was relatively little public outcry. Economic advisers urged a tax increase to limit the impact of government demand on prices, but fearing a popular questioning of his two wars (in Vietnam and on poverty), President Lyndon Johnson rejected their advice until it was too late.[15]

Although the public mood remained confident, the gradually changing international economic fortunes of the United States had already begun to have a political impact. In the 1960s, virtually all major American economic interests supported the adoption of the Kennedy Round of international trade negotiations. Ten years later, organized labor had broken with the free trade coalition. Instead, labor was backing comprehensive legislation that would have slowed imports and imposed limitations on the outward flow of capital and technology.[16] President Richard Nixon's modest Trade Act of 1969 emerged from the House Ways and Means Committee with quotas to protect the U.S. textile and shoe industries.[17]

For President Nixon, rising international competition, domestic inflation, and the gradual slowing of the American economy posed political as well as economic problems. He responded with decisive action. On August 15, 1971, more than fifteen months before the next election, he shocked the international economy by ending the Bretton Woods system of fixed exchange rates and imposing a temporary surcharge on a wide range of imported goods. To tame inflation, he imposed comprehensive wage and price controls.[18] This combination of initiatives was designed to defuse an emerging trade issue, slow inflation, and allow for the kind of faster domestic growth that would help assure prosperity and reelection.

Nixon's international strategy was partially successful. By closing the gold window, he unilaterally eliminated the potential threat to the U.S. gold supply. The move from fixed to floating exchange rates also reduced near-term competitive pressures on American industry. The shift in America's trade fortunes helped limit congressional and political opposition to Nixon's trade initiatives. In 1974, he succeeded in securing congressional approval for a new round of trade negotiations.[19] The import surcharge did not have any lasting effect on the trade deficit. It was best understood as a political tool that conveyed seriousness of purpose to U.S. trading partners and demonstrated presidential concern and a commitment to American workers and industry.

Over the longer term, however, floating rates did not return the United States to an era of trade surpluses. A decade later, President Reagan was faced with growing international competition, an overvalued dollar, and domestic pressures to take action on the trade front. Like Nixon, Reagan turned to a kind of dollar diplomacy. On September 22, 1985, Secretary of the Treasury James Baker forged an agreement with the finance ministers of the other major industrial powers to coordinate a gradual decrease in the international value of the dollar.[20] With a more competitive currency, the share of exports in domestic production rose from 14.8 percent in 1984 to 23.1 percent in 1990. Imports as a share of domestic production continued to grow but at a slower pace, rising from 25.8 percent in 1986 to 26.5 percent in 1987 and then to 28.3 percent in 1990 (figures are in real 1982 dollars).[21] The deficit continued to rise, but at the pace of a slow snail. Reagan did avoid any congressional action to impose trade restrictions, but he did not slow the congressional drive for a more active trade policy and a comprehensive competitiveness strategy—a drive that culminated with the Omnibus Trade and Competitiveness Act of 1988.[22]

Nixon's inflation strategy was never an economic success. Although inflation remained at 3.4 percent in 1972, it leapt to 8.8 percent in 1973 and to more than 12 percent in 1974.[23] Inflationary pressures dated to the 1960s, but a powerful inflationary force was building overseas—starting with yet another war in the Middle East. With Arab armies suffering a swift and decisive defeat at Israeli hands, the Arabs turned to a different weapon: oil. By imposing an oil embargo on the United States, Middle Eastern oil exporters posed an added challenge for Nixon's price controls.[24] At much the same time, a major Soviet grain purchase increased the domestic cost of foodstuffs. Even without the oil shock, the Nixon controls faced an uphill battle. The World War II experience with wage and price controls proved difficult to transfer to the 1970s. The economy itself had become considerably more complex and more difficult to control. In place of a shared sense of national urgency, the country was split over the Vietnam War and the culture clashes of the 1960s. Under Nixon, price controls passed from Phase I to II to III and were abandoned in 1974.

Much the same success met Nixon's June 1973 attempt to limit inflation by imposing short-supply export controls on American soybeans. The Nixon policy had little impact on inflation, shocked Japan—a major market for American soybeans—and helped stimulate the development of the Brazilian soybean industry. The economic damage, however, lay in the future.[25]

Although an economic failure, Nixon's efforts to control inflation were probably a short-term political success. He had shown concern and taken action in response to a major economic problem. The presence of price controls may have given Arthur Burns, the chairman of the Federal Reserve Board, the confidence to increase the growth of the money supply.[26] Faster money growth contributed to near-term economic growth, and thus, indirectly, helped improve President Nixon's reelection chances over South Dakota senator George McGovern, the Democratic nominee.

Despite the growing reality of both international competition and the presence of inflation, the economy was not the issue in the 1972 campaign. In searching for a winning theme, the early Democratic front runner, Edmund Muskie, had focused on fairness—spreading the wealth more equitably, not creating more of it. For McGovern, it was his cry to "Come home America" and his call to end the Vietnam War. After the election, America was still focused on the war in Vietnam and would soon begin to follow allegations about the president's involvement in a break-in at the Democratic Party headquarters in the Watergate complex.

Then, suddenly, the economy moved center stage. The 1973 Arab oil embargo had shocked America out of its assumptions of almost effortless economic prosperity and economic independence. As the decade progressed, inflation posed a seemingly insurmountable economic and political challenge for policymakers. The oil shock of 1973 also coincided with a drop in the rate of productivity growth. The country was beginning to suffer from the worst of two worlds—rising prices and stagnating growth. The era of stagflation was born. In 1979, a second oil shock staggered the national economy by adding further fuel to the fire of already rising prices. Individuals and businesses began to adapt their behavior to the expectation of persistent inflation. By the end of the 1970s, published statistics showed productivity growth slowing and then disappearing altogether. The slowing productivity growth, in turn, gradually brought to an end the rapid increases in wages and incomes that Americans had come to expect.

Even before the oil shock, the United States had begun to take steps to limit the impact of inflation on the purchasing power of incomes. In 1972, Congress adopted cost-of-living increases for Social Security and other federal retirement programs.[27] The cost-of-living adjustments were meant to protect recipients from inflation while slowing the congressional practice of adding to the number of Social Security benefits. Major private-sector employers in steel and automobiles sought labor peace by accepting similar cost-of-living adjustment clauses in their collective-bargaining agreements. For most working Americans, neither their wages nor their taxes were automatically adjusted for inflation. As the decade progressed, many found themselves squeezed between stagnant wages, rising prices, and increased tax bills. The seeds of the tax revolts of the late 1970s were sown by the inflationary forces of the 1960s and early 1970s.

Neither President Gerald Ford nor President Jimmy Carter proved adept at dealing with inflation. Ford's policies did not go much beyond his famous WIN (Whip Inflation Now) buttons. By the time Carter assumed the presidency, the authority to invoke price (or wage) controls had lapsed. With the controls' lack of success under President Nixon, it is unlikely that they would have been adopted in any case. Carter did attempt a voluntary incomes policy, and he later invoked credit controls and appealed for Americans to cut up their credit cards. Many Americans responded to the president's use of the bully pulpit with thousands sending their credit cards to the White House. Inflation, however, raged on.

The old answers did not work. President Nixon had declared himself a Keynesian just as the country entered an era that demanded a broader set of policies. The Keynesian touch that had earned Keynes a spot on the cover of *Time* seemed to have lost some of its magic.[28] The economy no longer yielded the expected trade-off between rising prices and falling unemployment. Key policymakers were fumbling for economic guidance that the experts seemed unable to give. It was time to look for a new set of answers.

Notes

1. Greenspan used the phrase in his July 16, 2002, *Federal Reserve Board's Semiannual Monetary Policy Report to the Congress,* before the Senate Committee on Banking, Housing, and Urban Affairs.

2. Council of Economic Advisers, *1980 Economic Report of the President* (Washington, D.C.: U.S. Government Printing Office, 1980), table B 22, p. 229. These figures are calculated in 1972 dollars.

3. See Council of Economic Advisers, *1980 Economic Report of the President,* chart B 1, p. 203.

4. Lester V. Chandler, *America's Greatest Depression, 1929–1941* (New York: Harper & Row, 1970), 131–32. In the early 1930s, investment in producers' durable equipment initially fell to 30 percent of its 1929 level. It did not reach its 1929 level until 1941. The story was even more dramatic in terms of nonresidential private construction, where the falloff in investment was sharper and the recovery slower.

5. Thomas A. Bailey, *The American Pageant: A History of the Republic* (Boston: D. C. Heath, 1956), 805.

6. David M. Kennedy, *Freedom from Fear: The American People in Depression and War, 1929–1945* (New York: Oxford University Press, 1999), 857.

7. The General Agreement on Tariffs and Trade (GATT) was essentially the commercial portion of a much more ambitious proposal to create an International Trade Organization (ITO). The Havana (after the site of the negotiations) Charter would have included the GATT. The House Ways and Means Committee rejected a resolution supporting the ITO on March 18, 1948. While avoiding the ITO debate during the 1948 campaign, Truman sought congressional action in 1949 and again in 1950. The outbreak of the Korean War in June 1950 and significant Republican gains in the midterm elections sealed the ITO's fate. Buried in a December 1950 State Department press release, the Truman administration announced its intention not to resubmit the treaty. See Steve Dryden, *Trade Warriors: USTR and the American Crusade for Free Trade* (New York: Oxford University Press, 1995), 24–32.

8. *Crusade in Europe* was General Dwight David Eisenhower's account of World War II in Europe. See Dwight David Eisenhower, *Crusade in Europe* (New York: Doubleday, 1949).

9. "Sputnik" means "fellow traveler with a traveler." Sancho Panza was a "sputnik" in Don Quixote's orbit.

10. This is from a conversation between the author and Stuart Auerbach, a reporter for the *Washington Post.* Auerbach's first assignment as a cub reporter was covering local school boards in Massachusetts shortly after the Soviet launch of Sputnik. In Auerbach's words, the local boards felt that it was their patriotic duty to increase mathematics and science education to keep America ahead of the Soviets.

11. For a brief discussion of the act, see Garrett Moritz, "From Sputnik to NDEA: The Changing Role of Science in the Cold War," at http://www.gtexts.com/college/papers/j3.html.

12. Herbert Stein, *Presidential Economics: The Making of Economic Policy from Roosevelt to Reagan and Beyond,* 2nd rev. ed. (Washington, D.C.: American Enterprise Institute, 1988), 113.

13. Following Stalin's death, there was a burst of growth in the Soviet economy. At

first, it was not clear whether the Soviets had found a formula for truly rapid growth or were merely benefiting from eliminating the worst inefficiencies of the Stalin period. As growth slowed, it became clear that "eliminating inefficiencies was the answer." In economists' terms, the Soviets suddenly moved closer to their production possibility frontier rather than rapidly growing the frontier itself.

14. "What's the Problem?" *New York Times,* August 1, 1999. The article reported Gallup Poll results for several years between 1950 and 1999.

15. Herbert Stein, *Presidential Economics: The Making of Economic Policy from Roosevelt to Reagan and Beyond,* 2nd rev. ed. (Washington, D.C.: American Enterprise Institute, 1988), 118–22.

16. For a discussion of the AFL-CIO's changing position on international economic policy, see Kent H. Hughes, *Trade Taxes and Transnationals: International Economic Decision Making in Congress* (New York: Praeger Publishers, 1979), 17–23.

17. Hughes, *Trade Taxes and Transnationals,* 2, 21.

18. See Stein, *Presidential Economics,* 176–80. See also Daniel Yergin and Joseph Stanislaw, *Commanding Heights: The Battle between Government and the Marketplace That Is Remaking the Modern World* (New York: Simon & Schuster, 1998), 60–64.

19. Hughes, *Trade Taxes and Transnationals,* 197. For a brief discussion of the act, see I. M. Destler, *American Trade Politics,* 2nd ed. (Washington, D.C.: Institute for International Economics with the Twentieth Century Fund, 1992), 142–45.

20. For a discussion of the agreement reached by Secretary Baker, see Yoichi Funabashi, *Managing the Dollar: From the Plaza to the Louvre* (Washington, D.C.: Institute for International Economics, 1989); see particularly 9–41.

21. See Destler, *American Trade Politics,* 201. All figures are calculated from data found in Council of Economic Advisers, *1991 Economic Report of the President* (Washington, D.C.: U.S. Government Printing Office, 1991), tables B7 and B21.

22. For a description of the politics surrounding the Omnibus Trade and Competitiveness Act as well as a detailed description of its trade provisions, see Susan C. Schwab, *Trade-Offs: Negotiating the Omnibus Trade and Competitiveness Act* (Boston: Harvard Business School Press, 1994).

23. Statistics are for the consumer price index, Council of Economic Advisers, *1984 Economic Report of the President* (Washington, D.C.: U.S. Government Printing Office, 1984).

24. Stein, *Presidential Economics,* 176–87.

25. I. M. Destler, *Making Foreign Economic Policy* (Washington, D.C.: Brookings Institution Press, 1980), 50–64. See also Stephen D. Cohen, *The Making of United States International Economic Policy: Principles, Problems and Proposals for Reform* (New York: Praeger Publishers, 1977), 99–100.

26. Stein, *Presidential Economics,* 184.

27. A brief history of the Social Security system can be sound at http://sss.gov.

28. There is still some debate among economists about the specific causes of the productivity slowdown that occurred in the United States and in much of the industrial world after the 1973 oil shock. Yet another group of economists saw the post-1973 decline in productivity growth as a return to a more normal, historical trend from the sharp productivity rebound that occurred during and after World War II. See, for instance, William J. Baumol, Sue Anne Batey Blackman, and Edward N. Wolff, *Productivity and American Leadership: The Long View* (Cambridge, Mass.: MIT Press, 1989), 68–71.

Chapter 2

The Search for a New Growth Strategy: The Policy and Politics of Prosperity

The American prosperity machine had run into trouble. Brief recoveries followed recessions, but productivity and income growth had stalled. The hoped-for trade-off between inflation and unemployment had disappeared, to be replaced by slow growth and rising prices. Economists in the 1970s called it "stagflation."

The global economy was posing an added set of challenges. In 1971, the United States registered its first trade deficit since World War I. A few political leaders and some Americans began to worry. The 1973 oil shock awakened the public and policymakers to the realities of global interdependence. By the end of the decade, European and Japanese industry were challenging the position of major American industries in the United States and around the world.

No one found the right policy combination in the 1970s. President Richard Nixon had taken an activist approach to restoring growth, controlling inflation, and responding to international pressures. In economic terms, he was largely unsuccessful. Mandatory wage-price controls proved a complicated failure. Expansive monetary policy did stimulate growth, but only at the cost of increasing pressure on the very controls meant to limit inflation. Nixon's break with the Bretton Woods system of fixed exchange rates reduced political pressure for trade restraints but did not prove a long-term antidote for persistent merchandise trade deficits.[1] Presidents Gerald Ford and Jimmy Carter struggled with inflation but failed to control it. Carter turned to credit controls, developed his own approach to industrial policy, and finally turned to the Federal Reserve Board. The overall economy continued to sputter.

Searching for New Policies: Meeting the Three Challenges

By the end of the 1970s, policymakers and the broad policy community were wrestling with three clusters of economic challenges: How to bring back an economy that combined steady growth and stable prices? How to restore more rapid productivity growth that would allow wages and incomes to rise? And how to respond to international competition that was forcing painful adjustments in one American industry after another?

An increasingly anxious country was looking to Washington for answers. The questions came not in neat packages but in a variety of public and private settings. There were town meetings where voters expressed their anger at falling behind the pace of rising prices. Some workers had already lost their jobs to foreign competition. Many more worried that their jobs would follow. Major economic interests expressed their own concerns. Organized labor had already broken with the free trade coalition, and as the 1970s progressed, labor's concerns began to find some sympathy among leaders of traditional manufacturing firms.

Virtually every sector of society was engaged in the search for new policies. Academics played an important role, as did the think tanks and policy analysts who are active participants in forming national policy. Business and union leaders proposed their own sets of answers. The proposals fell into four broad and often overlapping groups. First, the rise in international competition spawned a series of trade-related proposals. Some in this first group called for limiting access to the American market, others focused on opening overseas markets, and still others emphasized export promotion. The competition with Germany and particularly Japan forced political leaders, business executives, and the academic world to think anew about the workings of the international economy.

A second group focused on the impact of slow growth and international competition on specific industries. Established manufacturing industries were particularly vulnerable. The efforts of individual industries and their unions to seek policy support helped stimulate thinking about a national approach to an industrial policy that would respond to industry as a whole. The thinking quickly moved beyond troubled or "sunset" industries to add the "sunrise" industries that were thought to define the economic future.

A third group formed under the banner of the "supply side." The various international trade schools and industrial policy advocates did not, for the most part, develop comprehensive strategies that promised to control inflation, foster investment, and stimulate overall growth. The supply-side school thought they had the answer to all the economic challenges of the 1970s. Cuts in marginal tax rates were at the heart of their program. Lower marginal tax rates would spur people to work hard and save and invest more. By stimulating growth, supply would catch up to demand and reduce inflationary pressures. To control inflation, they also advocated tightening monetary policy. They were influenced by the views of Milton Friedman, the University of Chicago economist who favored a monetary policy that targeted the money supply rather than one that adjusted course in response to changes in interest rates or other economic conditions.

Most economists and business leaders agreed that a restrictive monetary policy would control inflation, but only at the cost of slow growth or an actual recession. To keep the promise of rapid growth with lower prices, the supply-side advocates turned to a third strand of economics, which is generally referred to as "rational expectations." Once they announced a credible, inflation-fighting monetary policy, the supply-siders argued that rational individuals could be expected to immediately change their inflationary ways, interest rates would fall, and supply-side incentives would take hold. They were promising tight money without tears.

Finally, there were the early seeds of a fourth group that emphasized productivity growth and international competitiveness. For this group, macroeconomic policy became part of a long-term growth strategy as well as a critical element in bringing short run economic stability. The competitiveness school emphasized public and private investments in science and technology as well as education and training. Advocates of the competitiveness approach emphasized opening markets and export promotion but also saw trade as an integral element in fostering and stimulating innovation.

From this welter of ideas and interests, political leaders sought to craft a set of policies that would spur economic growth and bring electoral success. The search for public policies and improved private-sector practices would eventually lead to a New Growth Compact between government and the private sector and a proliferation of public–private partnerships.

The Economy Goes Global: Washington Battles over Imports and Exports

American history is full of disputes over international trade and trade policy. In nineteenth-century America, the level of tariffs had often been a matter of regional conflict, second only to the fight over slavery. In these earlier, often bitter battles the focus was largely on the economic impact of tariffs and the gains and losses to different sections of the country. In post–World War II America, however, trade policy took on an added sensitivity. As the United States emerged from the war, policymakers and the policy community looked back at an interwar period that was marred by a destructive economic competition among nations. The protectionist policies of the major trading nations were blamed, in part, for the Great Depression, the rise of fascism, and the onset of World War II. Trade policy was no longer discussed in the simple economic terms of costs to consumers or profits to protected industries. Trade protectionism was now linked to the horrors of the Holocaust and the devastation of war.

After World War II, the United States helped lead the world in a sharply different direction. America pressed for reconstruction, not reparations. International trade, stable exchange rates, and economic development were to be the pillars of postwar prosperity and security. With the advent of the Cold War in the late 1940s, trade became a diplomatic tool that helped cement military alliances. Trade policy, trade agreements, and even the tolerance of overseas protectionism became important elements in securing America's national security.

Trade theory and policy also occupied a place of privilege among academic economists. In the early nineteenth century, the philosopher and economist David Hume developed the doctrine of comparative advantage to show how countries could gain from trade. His key insight was to emphasize comparative, not absolute, advantage. At the time, he used the example of trading British cloth for Portuguese wine. Even if Britain used fewer resources to produce wine or cloth than did Portugal, Britain would still gain from trading with Portugal because it was much more efficient at producing cloth than it was wine. That is, its *comparative advantage* lay in producing cloth.

Hume's insight became a bedrock of international economics and is routinely taught in today's introductory classes in economics and, in a more elaborate fashion, in advanced classes in international economics. In the view of Paul Krugman, now a professor of economics at Princeton University, comparative advantage has become one of the defining marks of the economics profession.[2] When Congress transformed Herbert Hoover's modest proposal for higher agricultural tariffs into much broader industrial protection, more than a thousand professional economists urged the president to veto the bill. Although they were unsuccessful, it remains a revered public moment for the profession.[3]

In effect, in the post–World War II era, trade protectionists were seen as ignoring morality, national security, and economic science. In a phrase, they bordered on being depraved, disloyal, and dumb.

Prelude to Action: The 1960s

Global competition became a national concern in the 1970s. But pressures were building on America's international standing throughout the 1960s. An increasingly overvalued dollar threatened the U.S. gold stock and contributed to competitive problems for some large American industries.

The Dollar: No Longer Good as Gold

Under the Bretton Woods system of fixed exchange rates, the dollar acted as the world's key reserve currency. The dollar in turn was backed by gold, with the United States committed to exchange gold for dollars at a fixed rate. As recovery proceeded in Europe and Japan, their dollar holdings gradually came to exceed the U.S. stock of gold. At much the same time, the market price of gold began to exceed the fixed rate established by the United States. In theory, foreign holders of dollars could have exercised their claim to U.S. gold and left Fort Knox with nothing to guard.[4] Gradually the United States responded. There were efforts to raise short-term U.S. interest rates to keep financial capital in the United States combined with efforts to keep long-term rates low so as not to discourage capital investment. There were also modest upward revaluations of the German mark and the Dutch guilder. Despite all these efforts, the United States was still wrestling with a payments imbalance and the strictures of the Bretton Woods system as it entered the 1970s.[5]

Saying No to Global Competition

The combination of 1960s inflation, essentially fixed exchange rates, and overseas recovery put a number of American industries at a competitive disadvantage. Some industries responded by seeking trade protection. American textile and apparel interests successfully sought short- and long-term restrictions on imports from a revived Japanese textile industry. There were also growing complaints from the shoe, specialty steel, and consumer electronics industries.

By the end of the 1960s, rising concern about competitive imports stalled efforts to launch a new round of international trade negotiations. The Kennedy Round of trade negotiations (concluded in 1967) had left some unfinished business. U.S. trade negotiators had agreed to eliminate the practice of basing tariffs for certain products—especially benzoid chemicals—on the American price rather than on the actual price paid for imports. Congress had refused to make the needed change in the law. When President Lyndon Johnson proposed to make the agreed-to change in his Trade Expansion Act of 1968, the proposal did not even leave the House Ways and Means Committee.[6]

In the Trade Act of 1969, President Nixon introduced a similar measure. What emerged from the House Ways and Means Committee, however, was Chairman Wilbur Mill's Trade Act of 1970. In addition to some of the changes proposed by Nixon, Mills added explicit quotas on textiles and shoes and included a provision for quota or tariff relief that could be triggered by a combination of import penetration and injury. In part, Mills may have been influenced by his own presidential ambitions. New Hampshire, the site of the first presidential primary, was home to many import-competing shoe and textile firms. But the Mills bill also indicated the beginnings of a more fundamental break with the broad coalition that had supported the Trade Expansion Act of 1962. Although the Mills bill foundered in the Senate, it was a warning of battles to come.[7]

The AFL-CIO Breaks with the Free Trade Coalition

As the 1960s progressed, the AFL-CIO and a number of major industrial unions expressed growing concern about U.S. trade policy. By the end of the decade, they no longer saw international trade as a plus for their members. Andrew Biemiller, the AFL-CIO's chief lobbyist, spelled out the new labor position in his 1970 testimony to Congress on President Nixon's proposed Trade Act of 1969. Biemiller mentioned the recovery of overseas economies and the impact of the Common External Tariff in Europe and then went on to fundamental concerns:

> The basic causes are major changes in the world economic relationships during the past 25 years, which accelerated in the1960s. Among these changes are the spread of government-managed national economies, the internationalization of technology, the skyrocketing rise of investments of U.S. companies in foreign subsidiaries and the mushrooming growth of U.S.-based multinational corporations.[8]

In 1971, the AFL-CIO threw its weight behind the Foreign Trade and Investment Act of 1971, better known as the Burke-Hartke Bill after its lead Democratic sponsors, Representative James Burke of Massachusetts and Senator Vance Hartke of Indiana. Burke-Hartke proposed comprehensive import quotas on goods that competed with American-made products. Ball bearings would have had a quota, but bananas would not. In addition, the bill sought to slow down the mobility of capital and technology that had been identified in Biemiller's testimony. The president would be granted the power to stop any overseas transfer of capital or technology that could cause a net reduction in U.S. employment. Burke-Hartke also proposed changes in the taxation of overseas income that would make overseas investment much less attractive. The proposal was viewed as punitive by virtually every United States–based multinational corporation.[9]

For the most part, Burke-Hartke's provisions did not find their way into 1970s trade legislation, but the bill did have a lasting impact on the debate over international trade and the global economy. Multinationals responded to Burke-Hartke's tax provisions by sharply increasing their lobbying presence in Washington. The mid-1970s saw a host of studies on what multinationals meant for the U.S. economy. The Burke-Hartke debate also stimulated new academic work on international trade that sought to incorporate multinationals, intrafirm trade, economies of scale, and other factors. Thinking about these added factors was one element leading to the development of the "strategic trade theory" that influenced the 1980s debate over U.S. competitiveness in a variety of ways. The same could be said for Burke-Hartke's focus on technology. In the 1980s, technology policy emerged as a key element in the debate over U.S. competitiveness and has become central to the competitiveness strategies being pursued by state governments, the federal government, and many governments around the world.

Burke-Hartke is often described as the high water mark of post–World War II protectionism in the United States. Since its introduction, there has been no comprehensive proposal for trade protection. In another sense, however, Burke-Hartke was ahead of its time. As the global economy has developed during the past two decades, the importance of technology and capital mobility has become more and more apparent, as has the role of multinational corporations in both developing and diffusing innovations. Nations, states, and provinces are all engaged in a competition to attract the global investment and innovation dollar. The emphasis is on modern carrots rather than Burke-Hartke's sticks (or controls), but the questions are surprisingly similar.

Nixon Acts: A Global Strategy for Domestic Growth

At almost the same time as Senator Hartke and Representative Burke were seeking a sharp change in the direction of American trade policy, President Nixon acted to reduce the international challenge and boost the domestic economy at the same time. After a weekend of debate, Nixon and his economic team came down from the mountain (or in this case, Camp David) with a bold new set of policies.[10]

On August 15, 1971, President Nixon broke with the Bretton Woods system. The United States would no longer redeem dollars in gold. Nixon took the added step of imposing a temporary surcharge on virtually all imports (see chapter 1). Both measures reduced the pressure for legislation restricting international trade. Nixon also moved to impose wage-price controls in the hope that he could bring down prices while stimulating employment-generating growth.

The wage-price controls did not work and, after two other phases, were abandoned. In terms of their impact on future policy, the controls fit under the heading of lessons learned and mistakes not to be repeated. Their failure, however, did not mark the end of a search for less painful ways to control inflation.

The break with the Bretton Woods system had a more lasting impact. The formal adoption of floating rather than fixed exchange rates is still a feature of today's international economy. The shift in exchange rate policy did reduce some of the competitive pressures on politically important industries and helped Nixon clear the path for the Trade Act of 1974 and the Tokyo Round of trade negotiations.

Responding to Imports: One by One or a Noah's Ark?

As international competition grew, more and more industries sought relief from import competition. This process started with protection for cotton textiles in the form of a Short-Term Arrangement in 1961.[11] Protection was soon extended to human-made fibers and evolved into the 1973 Multi-Fiber Arrangement, which controlled the import of most textiles.[12] Over the course of the 1960s, the shoe industry, specialty steels, and consumer electronics all sought protection from imports. In the 1970s, color television sets, steel, automobiles, and other products joined the list for which manufacturers demanded import relief.

Some industries sought relief under U.S. trade laws that offered protection from products that benefited from foreign-government subsidies or were sold or dumped in the United States below their cost of production overseas. Starting in the 1970s, the integrated steel companies sought and often secured antidumping duties on foreign steel. International rules and U.S. trade law also allowed temporary protection against fairly traded imports. U.S. law, however, made it difficult to secure temporary protection, and international trading rules required that compensation be paid by a comparable lowering of tariffs on some other products. To avoid both problems, the United States worked with overseas exporters to achieve voluntary limits on their exports. Because the limits were, in theory, voluntary, the usual limitations of U.S. trade law or international trading rules did not apply.

Throughout the 1970s, there were bitter battles over import relief. While industries and their employees saw unfair tactics and domestic economic damage, the U.S. administration saw economic benefit or foreign policy gains. Responding to the growing trade pressures, in 1979 President Carter proposed shifting responsibility for administering the unfair trade laws from the Treasury to the Department of Commerce. Advocates of the change argued that Commerce was more knowledgeable about industry and less likely than Treasury to emphasize foreign policy or dollar diplomacy. Responding to much the same pressures, Congress agreed.[13]

The industry-by-industry protection sought or secured in the 1970s did not have much direct influence on the emergence of a national competitiveness strategy or the development of a new growth compact between government and business. The industry-by-industry efforts in the 1970s did, however, have an indirect impact on the public debate and on private-sector behavior. The debate initiated more systematic thinking about everything from the nature of Japanese competition to the importance of a diversified manufacturing base. At times, it also fostered closer cooperation between industry and labor as both sides saw their profits and wages at risk.

Discovering Exports

Policymakers wanted to respond to the global economic challenge, but most were unwilling to turn to import protection. Many were also unwilling to embrace the other economic alternatives that developed in the course of the 1970s—industrial policy or supply-side economics. Instead, they turned to exports. By the late 1970s, bipartisan export caucuses or task forces were active in both the Senate and the House.[14]

Focusing on exports allowed policymakers to have an active trade agenda while avoiding the political and economic stigma that was widely attached to protectionist policies. An aggressive agenda favoring exports garnered the support of major export industries without alienating key constituencies. Organized labor took the lead in pushing for import constraints, but it had no objection to policies that favored exports. Some industrial unions were active in supporting the U.S. Export-Import Bank, which helps finance exports of capital equipment—equipment that was often made by union labor.[15]

The emphasis on exports shifted the trade debate from its exclusive focus on imports and led to a number of specific legislative initiatives. Export-related provisions would form an important part of the massive Omnibus Trade and Competitiveness Act of 1988 (which will be treated in detail in chapters 7 and 8) and continue to appear on the congressional calendar.[16] Emphasizing exports not only added a global dimension to national economic thinking but also turned the global economy into an opportunity as well as a challenge.

Looking at economic policy through the prism of exports helped refocus policymakers and, to some extent, policy analysts on the basics of macroeconomic policy and the economic fundamentals that contribute to productivity growth. If your interest was exports, you had to be concerned about the exchange rate or the price of dollars in other currencies. In both the short term and the long term, the exchange rate was powerfully influenced by domestic monetary and fiscal policies.

Lowering the exchange rate was like lowering the price on all exports and raising it on all imports. Cutting prices is one thing. Making a profit is another. The higher productivity growth in America's major trading partners gave them a price advantage unless there was a steady decline in the U.S. exchange rate. In other words, the United States could meet foreign competition only by continuing to lower its prices, the value of its wages, and its overall standard of living. Dollar wages might stay the same, but with the higher price of imports they now bought less. To boost exports, reduce the trade deficit, *and* raise the standard of living required a set of public policies and private practices that would boost productivity growth. That broader perspective on exports contributed to the definition of competitiveness later adopted by President Ronald Reagan's Commission on Industrial Competitiveness, which still very much functions today. In the commission's words, "Competitiveness for a nation is the degree to which it can, under free and fair market conditions, produce goods and services that *meet the test* of the *international market* while simultaneously maintaining and *expanding the real income* of its citizens" (emphasis added).[17]

Exports and export policy also became one way in which the United States could respond to the industrial strategies of its trading partners. During the 1980s, policymakers and the private sector saw Japan using profits generated in a protected, domestic market to gain an edge in international competition. The export focus put an emphasis on market access that improved opportunities for U.S. manufacturers and, at the same time, reduced or eliminated any edge gained from economic "sanctuaries" overseas.[18] As technology and technology policy moved center stage in the 1980s, exports came to be viewed as an important part of the overall innovation chain. For many manufacturers, today's innovation was tomorrow's export. Added exports not only helped fund the next generation of research but also forced the domestic manufacturer to meet world-class standards.

At first, the academic community put little stock in export promotion. It was particularly skeptical of claims linking exports to jobs. For most academic economists, employment was largely a function of fiscal and monetary policies. In the midst of a recession, exports could add jobs, but that was often viewed as exporting a domestic problem along with specific goods or services. The trade balance itself was seen as largely determined by the imbalance between savings and investment (or domestic spending and domestic production). In this view, export programs or initiatives in a full-employment economy were little more than rearranging the deck chairs on the *Queen Elizabeth 2*. If you helped one industry, you were hurting another.

In the 1970s, most academic economists viewed exports as a way of paying for imports. Export subsidies by an American trading partner were viewed as a gift to the American consumer. In this view, the Japanese approach to using export subsidies to increase world market share was an exercise in mercantilist irrationality. The academic view began to become much more complex in the early 1980s with the emergence of strategic trade theory.

Washington, Japan, and the Development of Strategic Trade Theory

If there was little academic support for an active export promotion policy, there was even less for any efforts to restrain imports—whether they were categorized as fair or unfair under U.S. trade laws. What policymakers heard from the academic world was essentially a continued emphasis on the market. For most academic economists, the only action needed was a further dismantling of U.S. barriers to trade. In this view, changing trade patterns were a function of shifting comparative advantage driven by market forces. Import restrictions were a costly way of penalizing consumers in an attempt to provide an off-budget subsidy to one industry or another.

None of these answers helped policymakers respond to the questions raised by business leaders and organized labor about Japan. By the late 1970s, many policymakers believed that Japan's growth strategy involved intervention in the domestic economy to favor particular industries, restrict imports, and promote exports. Yet Japan was growing rapidly, its productivity growth was considerably above that in the United States, and it was successfully challenging one American industry after another. While the United States was experiencing persistent trade deficits, Japan was generating significant trade surpluses. The policymakers asked: Why was Japan growing so rapidly? Was Japan irrational in discouraging manufactured imports and in encouraging manufactured exports? Or was there some method to what many economists saw as Japanese madness?

Into this seeming policy conundrum stepped the National Science Foundation (NSF), which was created after World War II as part of the national commitment to support scientific research. In the fiscal 1981 budget, Congress and the executive branch both supported what the NSF termed an "experimental effort" to develop a long-term analysis of the international economy. The analysis was to be specifically directed to the policymaking community. Following this mandate, the NSF commissioned a number of papers as a prelude to a colloquium held in Washington on October 3 and 4, 1980.[19]

Three leading scholars—William Branson, of Princeton University; Gary Hufbauer, then of Georgetown University and currently at the Institute for International Economics; and Robert Stern, of the University of Michigan —summarized the current state of international economic understanding, pointed to areas that needed research, and discussed possible policy options. Economists usually explained the patterns of international trade by pointing to the differing factor endowments (how much capital, labor, land, and so forth) in each trading nation. Stern noted that the standard (Heckscher-Ohlin) trade model did not explain how a country developed its factor endowment or how that endowment might change through time.[20] Sumiye Okubo of the NSF compressed Stern's language in providing a summary of his views: "The most significant gaps [in theoretical analysis] concern the dynamics of factor accumulation and endogenous technological change, the determinants and impact of international factor movements, monopoly power and cartels, and the role and impact of changes in government policy."[21] In other words, when it came to the hard issues before Washington policymakers, the academic world could not offer policy advice that was based on theoretical insights.

Following the colloquium, the NSF sought to stimulate new thinking with a classic American tool—competition. In the field of international trade (there was a separate competition for international finance), it asked academic specialists to form separate teams. The NSF committed to funding an initial round of research and promised additional research funding for the winning team. This was not, however, to be a strictly academic exercise. As part of their funding grant, each team had to consult with the Washington-based policy community. In practice, that meant talking with senior administration officials and key congressional staff. The NSF wanted to make sure that the academic and policy communities talked with and listened to one another.

When the academic trade teams came to Washington, they were still inclined to emphasize the value and importance of traditional international economic theory. It may not explain everything or some of the newer questions that were coming to the fore, but it had powerful insights into international economic behavior and, in policy terms, pointed to open borders and free trade—a policy that virtually all academics thought took the country in the right direction.

In meeting with senior administration officials and key congressional staff, the academics were not dealing with elected officials. They were talking with lawyers, economists, and political scientists who served elected officials. In a number of cases, the administration officials and congressional staff had graduate degrees in international economics or a related field. A few were ex-academics. In sum, they were aware of current economic thinking but often found it lacking. In a very stylized sense, the academic–key staff discussion went something like this: The Washington-based staff would say that "we are facing a series of international economic challenges." The academics' first response would be to stress the need to "think about comparative advantage." And the Washington staff would provide a virtual chorus of "But what about Japan?"

The combination of Japan's overseas success and U.S. domestic stagnation had led a number of administration officials and congressional staff to question the almost routine dismissal of European and Japanese policies as "irrational," "counterproductive," or simply "providing a subsidy" for the American consumer. Japan, in particular, began to look like an economic rival that had an effective, long-term growth strategy that included the goal of dominating key, high-technology sectors. Where Americans used fiscal and monetary policy to maintain overall demand, the Japanese approach seemed to focus on using macroeconomic policy tools to support public and private investment that was itself part of a broader growth strategy. Comparative advantage was not something fixed or subject to the vagaries of market forces. It, too, was a matter of national policy. At a subsequent NSF-sponsored gathering, one of the congressional staff members suggested that "only God can make a tree but any government can make a comparative advantage."[22]

The Academic Response

This was not, however, to be a proverbial dialogue of the deaf. In fact, the combination of prodding by the policymaker community and academic reflection contributed to a new way of thinking about international trade. The prodding came at a propitious moment. In fact, some serious academic work was already under way. Paul Krugman, who became a leading architect of the new trade theory, traces its beginnings back to 1978. The development of new theories in the field of industrial organization, the renewed interest in economic geography, and the impact of accidents of history on national economies all contributed to the new thinking.[23] The ability of Krugman and his colleagues to express their new ideas in concise, mathematical form made them a new force in professional circles.[24]

In his *Peddling Prosperity,* Krugman sketches the impact of historical accident on the pattern of trade. In an economist's term, the economy was "path dependent." That is, where you are depends, in part, on where (and when) you started. Krugman and others also pointed to the aircraft industry. The decision to locate Boeing in Seattle was not a function of the market. Boeing might have been someplace else. Silicon Valley might have started in another location. But once started, clusters of industries built on one another.

Economies of scale also mattered. So did external economies—the ways in which similar firms benefited from a skilled labor pool, innovations, and shared infrastructure. International economists began to weave these ideas into their thinking about why and how countries trade. In this new approach to trade, companies could no longer be thought of as small firms simply reacting to market prices. Governments took on the character of potential business partners, which could help elements of a nation achieve a global presence or even dominance. Strategy mattered in the sense that it could affect the pattern of international trade. Just as fundamentally, strategy could lead to profit.

The new group of strategic trade theorists expanded their theories and sought to apply them to specific industries. James A. Brander and Barbara J. Spencer were early and active contributors to strategic trade thinking. They showed that by supporting a national champion or a few national firms with some degree of monopoly power, government policy could increase the share of global profits flowing to the national firms and hence to the national economy. In a sense, they made a theoretical case for the European or Japanese subsidies to major firms that had previously been dismissed as irrational.[25] Brander and Spencer also demonstrated how early government support for domestic production may translate into a subsequent advantage in international competition.[26] Again, Brander and Spencer were articulating a version of the world that was already being sketched by business leaders, administration officials, and congressional staff.

Strategic trade theory was soon applied to specific cases. In some instances, intervention provided positive results; in others, not. For instance, Krugman and Richard Baldwin looked at both the semiconductor industry producing sixteen-kilobyte random access memory chips and the example of Airbus, the European consortium formed to compete for the global airplane market. In their analysis, Japanese protection was critical in establishing the global Japanese semiconductor industry, but only at excessive costs to the Japanese.[27] In other words, strategic trade worked, but it did not pay. They also looked at policy alternatives—free trade or trade war—and found that everyone was better off under free trade.[28] Their study of Airbus, however, led to different results. In this case, their model pointed to a successful intervention that not only created an industry but also translated into lower consumer prices for aircraft.

It is fair to say that the development of strategic trade theory with its implications for government intervention ran against the grain of academic economics, which was in the midst of a twenty-year shift toward emphasizing the power of markets and free competition. The suggestion that protectionism pays was even more unsettling—a little like suggesting that Willy Sutton's years of robbing banks had been an effective way of maximizing lifetime earnings. The economists developing strategic trade theory were persistently concerned that their results would be misused by special interests and policymakers to justify old-fashioned protectionism. Their fears were not groundless. When *Fortune* magazine profiled some of the strategic trade theorists, the headline read "The New Case for Protectionism."[29]

The National Bureau of Economic Research (NBER) had emerged as the winner of the first round of NSF-sponsored research. As the NBER entered a second round of research, it added many of the prominent participants from the other teams. It also continued to include key congressional staff and administration officials in its deliberations.

The NSF and the NBER fostered a fruitful dialogue in which trade negotiators, government economists, trade lawyers, and congressional staff were able to challenge academic thinking with real-life complexities that may not have been included in one economic model or another. The academics pushed the Washington participants to put particular problems in a broader context that weighed short-term and long-term economy-wide costs as well as the benefits to a particular industry. Even more important, the strategic trade theorists developed an analytic framework that policy-makers could use to better understand the policies of America's economic competitors as well as designing America's own international trade policies. Where Krugman and Baldwin considered two cases—free trade or trade war—Washington could pursue a variety of strategies that might mix export promotion, research and development support, and the threat of retaliation. Without putting it in economic terms, many of the trade negotiators and key congressional staff thought that theory was an academic specialty while policy was their comparative advantage.

It did not take long for the strategic theorists to have an impact on thinking in the public policy arena. The NSF requirement that the competing trade (and finance) teams talk to key administration and congressional staff members brought the political world unusually close to new developments in international economic thinking. There was not, of course, a one-to-one translation of theory into practice, nor were the specific policy implications of a particular study taken as gospel. There was, rather, a general sense that the pattern of Japanese protecting and targeting industries coupled with a persistently high growth rate had something to do with one another.

Lasting Impact

Strategic trade theory would have a lasting impact on the development of a national competitiveness strategy. It added intellectual heft to the demands that U.S. trade (and other) policies take account of the initiatives of U.S. trading partners. The suggestion that import protection could create new competitors added to the importance of an export policy that would reduce or eliminate overseas sanctuaries. Government could create the conditions for growth if the private sector was aggressive and effective in turning innovations into competitive products. The idea that government and industry could collaborate in a way that served the national interest was one of many forces that would lead to a new, informal growth compact and the widespread use of public–private partnerships.

Strategic trade theory continued to stimulate policy research throughout the 1980s. In December of 1989, C. Fred Bergsten, the director of the Institute for International Economics (IIE), "launched a study on 'The Managed Trade Option.'" Because IIE was generally viewed as having a decidedly internationalist or free trade slant, for it to look at managed or strategic trade was something of a departure.

IIE asked Laura D'Andrea Tyson to conduct the study. At the time, Tyson was the research director of the Berkeley Roundtable on the International Economy (BRIE) at the University of California, Berkeley, and a visiting professor at Harvard Business School. The study led to Tyson's 1992 book, *Who's Bashing Whom? Trade Conflict in High-Technology Industries.*[30] After looking at a series of trade conflicts in high-technology industries, Tyson concluded that a "cautious activist" policy was an appropriate guide for government action. The Council on Competitiveness reached a similar conclusion in its 1993 publication *Roadmap for Results: Trade Policy, Technology, and American Competitiveness.*[31]

Policy Initiatives

Over the course of the 1980s and 1990s, strategic trade theory contributed to a number of key policy initiatives. The federal government intervened in a variety of ways to protect, support, and stimulate the U.S. semiconductor industry when it was seriously challenged by Japanese producers in the mid-1980s. Several features of the Omnibus Trade and Competitiveness Act of 1988 reflected the influence of strategic trade thinking.

When President Bill Clinton took office, he brought strategic trade thinking and strategic trade advocates with him. For chair of the Council of Economic Advisers, he selected Laura D'Andrea Tyson, who had returned to her position as professor of economics at the University of California, Berkeley. Tyson's "cautious activist" position on trade policy "made her less than a purist in the trade debate, and controversial among the economic mandarins, but Clinton was looking for people who would cut through the old debates, find a 'third way.'"[32]

The academic community continued to be nervous about the possible misuse of its new creation. Paul Krugman, in many ways the godfather of strategic trade theory, was particularly concerned that he had made the political world an offer that it would not refuse. In the mid-1990s, Krugman downplayed the importance of the international economy to overall American prosperity and expressed the fear that an emphasis on national competitiveness could lead to trade protectionism, fiscal deficits, and a focus on the short rather than the long run.[33]

Krugman's fears were real and reasonable. In practice, however, the focus on national competitiveness had just the opposite effect.[34] In part, Krugman understated the importance of the international economy. The linking of capital markets has made every small businessperson and home builder more aware of financial developments in Asia, Europe, Latin America, and the Newly Independent States of the former Soviet Union. Krugman also understates the importance of the international economy to manufacturing. Virtually all American manufacturing and a growing array of services face international competition. Manufacturers provide an important market for business services and are also a critical element in commercial activities that combine manufacturing and services. For instance, early in the Clinton presidency, textile and apparel firms joined together with wholesalers and retailers in an attempt to make the entire value chain more efficient. Under the title AMTEX, they formed an umbrella Cooperative Research and Development Agreement with the national energy laboratories to develop new, systemwide technologies.[35]

By focusing on the economic successes of U.S. trading partners, the competitiveness perspective helped drive quality and innovation. By emphasizing comparative rates of productivity growth, competitiveness policies favored investment in new equipment, training, and technology. Open markets at home became one of several ways of stimulating the kind of domestic competition that leads to innovation as well as efficiency. Access to overseas markets forced domestic firms to be more competitive, eliminated sanctuaries that could put American firms at a competitive disadvantage, and provided added sales that would help fund future rounds of research.

Industrial Policy: Sunset to Sunrise

Industrial policy concerns arose in the 1970s as troubled large institutions sought help from the federal government. Then, in the 1980s, some policymakers put forward a view of industrial strategy that would help young, growing industries gain more resources. This section reviews these developments and goes on to analyze American and foreign successes and challenges—along with the questions of protectionism and of a broader form of industrial policy.

Industrial Policy for Struggling Industries

Stagflation and slowing productivity growth were not the only economic problems that faced policymakers and the policy community in the 1970s. If the economy was in trouble, some institutions were threatened with out-right failure. Over the course of the decade, three major institutions came to Washington for financial help. In 1971, Lockheed, a major defense contractor, was planning on using Rolls-Royce engines on its new, commercial aircraft. When Rolls-Royce declared bankruptcy, Lockheed was left with a serious disruption in delivery and a resulting financial squeeze. It sought and received federal loan guarantees. In 1975, New York City itself had stumbled into near bankruptcy. Again, Washington responded.

Lockheed and New York, however, were both seen as special cases. Although Lockheed's difficulties were concentrated in its civilian operations, as a major defense contractor, Lockheed was one of America's tools in fighting the Cold War. As the nation's largest city, New York was too large, too economically important, and too distinct to be easily taken over by the State of New York, let alone private creditors.

Then, at the end of the decade, Washington was faced with the prospective failure of another major industrial enterprise. In 1979, Lee Iacocca, chief executive of the Chrysler Corporation, first broached the question of the federal government helping Chrysler through financial assistance and regulatory relief.[36] The economic and political stakes were large. Chrysler was, at the time, the third largest American manufacturer, with hundreds of thousands of employees located in a number of states. The hundreds of companies that formed Chrysler's supplier chain were also at risk.

The Chrysler "bailout," as it came to be called, triggered a major congressional debate. Opponents feared such overt intervention in a marketplace where Chrysler had apparently failed. Others cited the potential precedent of adding manufacturing to the scope of federal loan activities. Still others were willing to act but feared that a resurrected Chrysler might tip Ford Motor Company into economic difficulties. In the end, however, both houses of Congress approved "$1.5 billion in federal assistance at the heart of a $3.5 billion infusion of capital."[37]

The size of Chrysler, the extent of its financial need, and its eventual request for direct financial assistance did set it apart. Chrysler was also acting alone rather than on behalf of a larger industry group. But, it was far from being the only large entity seeking economic assistance from federal action. When he looked back over his years as the assistant to President Carter for domestic affairs, Stuart Eizenstat remembered a president who was "called upon regularly by powerful interests to make sectoral decisions."[38] Eizenstat was frequently "confronted with decisions on orderly marketing arrangements, tariffs and quotas on color television sets, shoes, specialty steel, nuts and bolts, and even mushrooms, and Mexican tomatoes, as well as economic development programs and agricultural price and production decisions."[39] The pattern of responding to trade or other economic pressures did not start or end with the Carter administration. Earlier administrations had granted trade relief for textiles and apparel, steel, automobiles, meat, and sugar that went "well beyond the technical confines of the statutory system."[40]

Most of these decisions had an ad hoc quality. The size of the industry was important, and so was its political influence in terms of geographic dispersion. Timing could count, as did the vagaries of the congressional seniority system. There was not, however, any clear set of economic criteria to choose one industry over the other or any effort to anticipate problems before they became serious. When private firms seek bankruptcy protection, they either contemplate an orderly sale of assets to satisfy creditors or develop a credible plan to return to operating profitability. By way of contrast, the ad hoc federal approach to industry support often came with few strings attached.

Washington's search for a more coherent approach to troubled industries led to thinking about an industrial policy that would encourage the flow of resources to specific sectors and industries. In searching for answers, Washington looked to the experience of a Europe also struggling to adjust to Japanese competition and to Japan's approach to its own troubled industries.

Washington also looked to America's past. The institution that garnered the most attention and stimulated the most controversy was the Reconstruction Finance Corporation (RFC). From its creation during the Hoover administration, the RFC went through three distinct phases before being abolished by Congress in 1953. It came to prominence in the New Deal by providing critical support to the financial sector and to the railroads. During World War II, the RFC played a major role in financing capital investments in defense industries and securing critical materials for the war effort. Following the war, the RFC "entered its most aggressive lending period . . . with poorly defined objectives and little accountability."[41] Students of the bank have generally praised its performance in the Great Depression and during World War II, but they have been considerably less positive about its later years.[42] The 1950 Fulbright investigation of the RFC found that in its final phase, the bank had invested in "snake farms, movie houses, a rainbow trout factory and a roulette room in a Nevada hotel."[43]

Advocates of a more active industrial policy were also drawing lessons from the country's recent experience in responding to troubled institutions and industries. Both the Municipal Assistance Corporation, which had been established to restore financial solvency to New York,[44] and the Chrysler Loan Guarantee Board required concessions on the part of workers, creditors, and other interested parties. The general idea was that where troubled or declining industries were involved, "an industrial finance agency . . . could enforce the mutual sacrifice necessary on the part of management, labor and suppliers."[45]

The idea of linking government assistance to conditions carried forward into the 1983–84 House debate over an industrial financing bank. The legislation, drafted by Representative John J. La Falce (D-N.Y.), would have expanded "the government's Chrysler Corp. loan guarantee program to entire classes of industries with conditions to be attached as the price of government help."[46]

The question of linking assistance to conditions also became part of the debate over temporary import relief from fairly traded imports. The broader philosophy of shared sacrifice for shared gain became more prevalent as the federal government developed more public–private partnerships. The combination of federal assistance and company resources would become a common feature in the Clinton administration's technology and, to some extent, training programs.

Sunset to Sunrise: An Answer to Renewed Productivity Growth

The debate over industrial policy was not limited to dealing with troubled industries. Early on, other voices stressed the need to help emerging or "sunrise" industries. Over time, analysts began to develop an industrial strategy that consciously fostered the flow of resources from the "sunset" to the "sunrise" industries as an answer to slow productivity growth. A number of academics with a policy bent adopted this approach. The Massachusetts Institute of Technology professor Lester Thurow,[47] and also Robert Reich and Ira Magaziner in their 1982 *Minding America's Business,* were prominent exponents of this view. They (and many others, including Thurow) also saw industrial policy as a way of easing "society's adjustment to structural changes in a growing society."[48] But they were decidedly not in favor of trying to freeze today's industrial structure and were critical of federal policies and programs that "retarded the flow of capital and labor" to more productive uses.[49]

American Successes

Advocates of industrial policy had searched America's past for how to deal with troubled industries. As the industrial debate broadened to include the sunrise industries, they looked again at the American past for successful government efforts to establish one industry or another.

U.S. agriculture emerged as a prime example of a successful American industrial policy. Productivity growth in agriculture reduced the farm population from about 50 percent of the total at the end of the nineteenth century to about 3 percent in the early 1980s. Fewer people were growing more food in greater variety at a lower cost than virtually anywhere on Earth. Government policy had played several different roles. Going back to the 1862 Morrill Act and the creation of the land-grant colleges, the U.S. government helped fund agricultural research and educated future farmers in new techniques.[50] An agricultural extension service brought new innovations and a variety of other information to farms across the country. In more recent years, the government also shared the cost of opening new export markets for American agricultural products.

Critics of American agriculture pointed to everything from trade restraints to supporting farm incomes by stabilizing prices. But whatever the failures in agricultural policy, there was general agreement that government programs had played a positive and important role in agriculture's economic success.

Industrial policy proponents also pointed to a number of high-technology industries that had received federal assistance. Computers, semiconductors, telecommunications, aircraft, and a host of other products trace their start to the changing national security needs of the military.[51] In some cases, government intervention had been extensive, long lasting, and effective.

For instance, following World War I, the Navy was concerned about America lagging behind in the developments in radio technologies. The Navy's answer was to create a new company. The government provided significant capital, and the Navy actually owned a substantial portion of the company's shares. Thus was RCA (now owned by the General Electric Company) born. America's lead in pharmaceuticals and the emerging biotechnology industry builds on government-funded research and, in part, on the large health care market created by the government Medicare program.

There were other government initiatives that did not figure extensively in the debate. Government successfully supported broader home ownership through the creation of savings institutions and mortgage guarantees. Some would argue that the federal highway system (initially justified on national security grounds), coupled with tax support for oil exploration, helped develop the automobile industry by stimulating car ownership.

Foreign Successes

First proponents and then opponents of an industrial policy looked to Europe and East Asia for examples of what worked and what did not. Two leading economies—Germany and Japan—quickly became the focus of the debate. German industry had a closer relationship with government, extensive ties with strong unions, and very different relationships with large banks. But it was Japan that garnered the most attention. In addition to providing general support for manufacturing industries and industrial exporters, the Japanese government actively worked with its private sector to encourage the development of specific industries. Proponents of an American industrial policy saw a string of Japanese success stories. Opponents saw a very different Japan. In their view, growth stemmed from strong fundamentals (high savings rates, good education, and a strong work ethic), not government policies. Where intervention occurred, they contended that it had little impact or was as likely to be a failure as a success.

The Japanese rise to economic prominence triggered a voluminous literature attempting to explain the keys to Japanese growth. The debate over who saw the real Japan continues to rage to this day. In *Japan: The System That Soured—The Rise and Fall of the Japanese Miracle*, Richard Katz records the early successes of the Japanese model but also Japan's failure to shift direction as its economy has matured and the world around it has changed.[52] At Japan's instigation, the World Bank did its own assessment of the so-called East Asian miracle. In *The East Asian Miracle: Economic*

Growth and Public Policy, the bank opted for language that could be read as either an endorsement of the Japanese approach or an affirmation of Western economists' current skepticism toward industrial policy and government intervention.[53] In a more recent assessment of East Asia, *Rethinking the East Asian Miracle,* the World Bank staff wrote a volume of essays that pointed to some of the flaws in the East Asian approach and the need for change in everything from the banking sector to the nature of government–business ties.[54] The Japanese Ministry of Finance recently entered the fray with a study critical of the Ministry of International Trade and Industry's (MITI's) efforts to guide the Japanese economy.[55]

In my own view, the latest World Bank study and the views of Japan's Ministry of Finance ignore the challenge facing Japan after World War II and the role MITI played in fostering growth. The Japanese economy was in ruins, Tokyo was rubble, and the occupation forces of the United States were working to remake Japanese industry and institutions. Growth required energy, and, except for limited coal deposits, Japan had to depend on imports. MITI was charged with allocating scarce foreign reserves and in effect determining who could import energy.

MITI's record is certainly far from flawless. Its early but unsuccessful effort to consolidate the Japanese automobile industry could have slowed the innovation that made Japan such a formidable competitor on the world market. It guessed wrong on how long it would take to develop digital television and put too many eggs in the analog basket. MITI would describe its own role as changing with Japan—more advice and less guidance. As the 1990s became a decade of slow Japanese growth, the Japanese government became the target of widespread criticism from Japanese and overseas economists. Yet the spray from a burst financial bubble should not obscure the way business and government cooperated in Japan to foster the rapid industrialization that led to the Japanese prominence in key high-technology industries that persists to this day.

The Foreign Challenge

Whether or not foreign intervention made for economic success, it could still have a significant impact on American industry, the composition of American manufacturing, and the level of manufacturing employment. The prospect of facing the combined force of a foreign company and a foreign government could easily deter an American company or entire industry from investing in the next generation of research or acquiring the latest equipment. Proponents of an American industrial policy argued that the United States had to respond to foreign government support for targeted industries or risk having an industrial base that was the shrinking residual of other countries' industrial strategies.

Avoiding Protectionism

Proponents of an industrial policy often pointed to the on-again, off-again protection provided to occasionally troubled American industries. In their view, a forward-looking industrial policy would help create new industries, restore to health industries or portions of industries with a long-run comparative advantage, and, where unavoidable, manage the orderly decline of sectors that could no longer meet global competition.[56]

Design versus Serendipity

In the late 1970s and early 1980s, when the industrial policy debate raged, the Internet existed only as a creature of the Defense Department's Advanced Research Projects Administration (ARPA). The National Science Foundation was just beginning to bring the American research universities into what was then called the ARPA-net.[57] Widespread civilian use was fifteen years in the future. But the Internet makes the serendipity point—can the country count on the good fortune and good timing that has given us an information technology industry that is transforming the way we work, live, and learn? It also makes the counterpoint. Could we have foreseen that investments in linking 1960s computers would lead to such spectacular results thirty years in the future? What would emerge from the debate over design or serendipity was some combination of the two. What was to become the national competitiveness strategy would emphasize investments in innovation and the conditions that favored rapid commercialization but make little effort to create specific marketplace winners.

The broader view of industrial policy did respond to some of the challenges posed by the economy of the 1970s. Higher productivity growth promised a rising standard of living and would also create an environment in which inflation could more easily be controlled.[58]

The broader form of industrial policy also offered Democrats distinct political advantages. It promised action in response to rising international competition, potential relief to workers in declining industries, and the promise of restored national growth. The emphasis on sunrise industries added traditional American confidence and a sense of the future. The sunrise element was particularly important to the 1974 post-Watergate Congress, with many members representing suburban districts built on a high-technology industrial base.

The debate finally reached the floor of the House in 1984. The focus was on a bill drafted by Representative John La Falce, a Democrat from the Buffalo–Rochester area of upstate New York. La Falce proposed an industrial advisory board to help set national policy and a federal financing facility that would have helped emerging as well as declining firms, and sunrise as well as sunset industries. In the end, however, the push for an industrial policy failed to garner enough votes to establish either an industrial bank or a new advisory structure.[59] There proved to be enduring political resistance to putting additional, systematic power in the hands of the federal government. As one observer put it, the debate shifted from "a discussion of policy instruments to seemingly balanced or neutral institutional arrangements."[60]

Although the proposals for a formal industrial policy were not successful, the debate over foreign competition and the economic fate of specific industries continued. At the very least, the debate over industrial policy helped sharpen America's response to international competition. The debate also helped prepare the way for later federal support for sunrise industries, which were viewed as critical for national security as well as the country's economic future.

The Allure of the Supply Side

By the end of the 1970s, Washington policymakers were wrestling with a rapidly changing economic and political landscape. The Great Depression had left a generation of policymakers, policy analysts, and academic economists in the United States and in much of the world focused on the failures of markets and the limits of capitalism.[61] In the aftermath of World War II, many leading American economists adopted the ideas of John Maynard Keynes, who preached the need for active monetary and fiscal policies to counteract a depression.[62] Keynes also described the risk of what he termed a "liquidity trap,"[63] where uncertain consumers and hesitant investors would not borrow and spend, even at very low interest rates. To beat the trap, Keynes turned to fiscal policy—in the case of a depression that meant added spending or tax cuts.

The Keynesian emphasis on fiscal policy came at a time when Americans had great confidence in their government. In the late 1940s, Americans could look back at two decades of government leadership that had fought the Great Depression and won World War II. Historians would be quick to point out that President Franklin Roosevelt's New Deal did not provide a cure for the Great Depression. In 1940, unemployment still stood at 14.6 percent of the workforce.[64] But the New Deal did provide direct employment for many Americans, developed an economic safety net, and restored a national sense of confidence. In World War II, as the United States armed the allies and defeated fascism, unemployment fell sharply, reaching a low of 1.2 percent in 1944.[65] After the war, a confident America worked to create a new international economic system, helped rebuild Europe and Japan, and started on what would be a forty-year effort to contain Soviet communism.

In the 1960s, academics and policymakers had relied on an apparent trade-off between inflation and unemployment. By the end of the 1970s, however, the economic, political, and intellectual climate had changed. Modest adjustments to fiscal and monetary policy no longer seemed to keep the economy on an even keel. Now policymakers were left with the worst of both economic worlds—stagflation, which combined rising prices with a stagnant economy. Popular opinion had also become less supportive of governmental activism. The Vietnam War and Watergate had eroded Americans' trust in governmental institutions. Stagflation raised questions about the government's ability to deliver an effective economic policy. Many Americans came to see the 1960s war on poverty as a costly failure, while some critics even saw it as making a bad situation worse. The uneven application of environmental and workplace regulations adopted in the 1970s led many parts of the business community to question the government's regulatory competence. The emergence of persistent trade deficits and rising international competition raised added questions about the efficacy of federal policy.

When policymakers looked to the academic world for policy advice, they found little that would justify an activist agenda. Academic economists who questioned Keynes and the whole idea of an active fiscal or monetary policy had gained prominence. Other academics continued to offer policy advice from a Keynesian perspective but did not have many new proposals to deal with stagflation.[66]

Neither President Carter nor President Ford seemed to find the right combination of fiscal and monetary policies to control inflation and return steady growth. Productivity growth rates declined throughout the decade. Herbert Stein, who served as chair of President Nixon's Council of Economic Advisers, characterized the 1974–80 period as one of "ad hoc pragmatic fine tuning." In Stein's view, the "dissatisfaction with the results of such a strategy . . . led to a movement in a more conservative direction . . . in the last years of Carter."[67] The stage was being prepared for what came to be called supply-side economics.

The Supply-Side View

Popular coverage of political disputes over economic policy often speaks in terms of Republican or Democratic policies. There is a tendency to compress the views of thousands of politicians and millions of supporters into a single voice. In practice, both parties are complex coalitions that include individuals or groups that may differ over questions of the economy, social policy, and national security. In developing an economic strategy, the major parties need a set of policies that help bring their respective coalitions together. Both parties will generally look at the distributional consequences of policies—who gets what—as well as their impact on overall growth. With a shared interest in political office, they also need an approach that will appeal to independents and members of the other party. Because the economy imposes a reality test for any set of policies, they must also pay attention to how well and how quickly their policies will work.

The mid-1970s created a complex challenge for any party. How to restore growth and control inflation? What to do about productivity growth and stagnating real (adjusted for inflation) wages? How can we respond to the interests of our core supporters in a way that commands a broader, national constituency? Could any party do all this and still serve the central philosophy of the party? Starting in the mid-1970s, a small band of Republican insurgents hammered together a strategy that they contended would control inflation, avoid recession, stimulate growth, reward their core supports, appeal to American optimism, and still pay homage to long-standing Republican verities.

The Republican strategy was not driven by academic ideas, although it drew on important currents that had come to academic prominence. Representatives, congressional staff, a well-placed journalist, and a leading professor of economics were at the core of the new thinking. They came be to known as supply-siders. Instead of focusing on using monetary policy or fiscal spending to stimulate demand, their strategy was to increase work, saving, and investment.

The term "supply side" was first used in a paper presented by Herbert Stein in April 1976.[68] Stein had actually used "supply side fiscalists" in describing a group that "concentrated on the effects of taxes, expenditures and deficits on the total supply of output." [69] Another economist, Alan Reynolds, passed on the phrase to Jude Wanniski, a member of the *Wall Street Journal* editorial board. Wanniski dropped the "fiscalists" as "awkward and misleading." "Supply-side economics" it became.[70]

In his *The Seven Fat Years and How to Do It Again,* Robert L. Bartley tells much of the supply side story.[71] Bartley himself contributed to supply-side thinking and was an active participant in many of the discussions that gave rise to the supply-side effort. He was also the major publicist for the movement. As director of the *Wall Street Journal* editorial page for three decades (1972–2002), he provided an important and widely read forum for supply-side ideas.

As Bartley tells it, three groups were independently developing supply-side thinking. In addition to the New York group, Bartley mentions John Rutledge, a California-based economic consultant and president of Claremont Economics Institute, who was developing a new model of the economy. He also points to a third group in Washington that included Norman Ture and Paul Craig Roberts.

In recounting the story as he saw and lived it, Bartley focuses on the New York group that gathered for dinner at Michael I, just "thirty steps south of the American Stock Exchange on Wall Street."[72] In describing the eclectic group that helped develop supply-side economics, Bartley focuses on three regulars—Jude Wanniski, Robert Mundell, and Arthur Laffer.

Wanniski was a journalist who had worked in Washington for the *National Observer.* In Washington, he met Laffer, who was then working as an economist in the Nixon administration. Bartley brought Wanniski to New York to write for the *Wall Street Journal*'s editorial page.

The other two were professional economists. Robert A. Mundell had taught for many years at the University of Chicago and then for a period at Waterloo University in Canada before joining the faculty of Columbia University in New York. He had already achieved considerable prominence for his work in international economics. His theory of optimal currency areas is often used to justify (and at times criticize) the European Union's adoption of a common currency, the euro. His views on the conduct of fiscal and monetary policy in the face of flexible exchange rates are still very much part of leading textbooks on international economics.[73] Mundell would later be awarded the 2001 Nobel Prize in economics for this path breaking work.

At Michael I, however, the focus was not principally on international economics but on an alternative approach to domestic policy. Mundell had been developing his own alternatives to an economic orthodoxy that revolved around the thinking of Keynes's *General Theory.* For Mundell, the Keyneisan approach relied on "a *short run* model of a *closed* economy, dominated by *pessimistic* expectations, and *rigid* wages" (emphasis in original).[74] In his 1971 *Monetary Theory,* Mundell reversed many of these assumptions to develop a model that would better describe a growing economy wrestling with inflation rather than one mired in depression. Mundell emphasized a mix of tight money and stimulative fiscal policy that would fit well with the emerging supply-side consensus in favor of large tax cuts through reductions in marginal tax rates and tighter monetary policy to control inflation.

The other professional economist dining at Michael I was Arthur Laffer, at the time a professor of economics at the University of Southern California. Unlike Mundell, Laffer had Washington experience and connections. He had worked as an economist in Richard Nixon's Office of Management and Budget and had already garnered a national reputation for his optimistic estimate of growth in the domestic economy. He would become one of the best known of the supply-siders.

Even today, Laffer is often associated with the curve that bears his name. Laffer noted that at some level government tax rates would become so high that people would start working less. At that point, higher rates would yield lower revenues. The corollary could also be true—that is lower rates could actually increase revenue. To make his point, Laffer drew a curve on a paper napkin that illustrated the relationship between taxes and government revenues. There is some controversy as to exactly when and where Laffer drew his famous curve. In *Seven Fat Years,* Bartley accepts the version that the curve was drawn in Washington at the Two Continents restaurant (located across the street from the U.S. Treasury Department) when Laffer was conversing with Richard Cheney, then the deputy chief of staff to President Ford.[75] In any case, the Laffer curve and the napkin have become embedded in the lore of Washington policymaking.

Laffer was not speaking only from theory. He had spent some time looking at how to help individuals move from dependence on poverty programs to the world of work.[76] Many analysts had looked and continue to look at barriers in terms of their lack of skills, inadequate transportation, the disappearance of low-skilled manufacturing jobs, and other factors. Laffer focused on the high marginal tax rate involved in leaving a series of government programs for entry-level employment. In many cases, the sacrifice of losing welfare payments, rent subsidies, food stamps, and health care more than offset the income from low-skilled work. In other words, the individual faced a marginal tax rate of more than 100 percent. In this situation, the strictly rational individual might well chose welfare over work.[77]

So far, so good. Virtually everyone could think of a tax system so confiscatory that it simply did not pay to get up in the morning. But Laffer and his colleagues had no idea what the Laffer curve actually looked like or any indication that the country had reached the point where a cut in income tax rates would lead to a dramatic increase in tax revenue.[78] The supply-siders eventually assumed a relationship between marginal tax rates and work, savings, and investment that was neither grounded in theory or experience.[79]

Washington and the Supply Side

While Bartley and the others were meeting just off Wall Street, another group was meeting and working in Washington to not only define supply-side thinking and but also shape it into legislative form. In *The Supply-Side Revolution: An Insider's Account of Policymaking in Washington,* Paul Craig Roberts recounts supply-side history from the viewpoint of a Washington insider who was very much involved in the battle over ideas and legislation.

Roberts's book is ambitious. The introduction starts by saying that "this is the story of a revolution in economic policy from its origin in Representative Jack Kemp's (R-N.Y.) office in the summer of 1975 through the first thirty months of the Reagan administration. . . . It was a revolution brought about by the unstinting efforts of a few people."[80]

Roberts was certainly one of those people. In the course of a few years, he worked for Jack Kemp, served on the House Budget Committee, and served on the staff of Senator Orrin Hatch to help with his work on the Joint Economic Committee. Roberts is also generally credited with drafting the Kemp-Roth Bill, which served as a broad outline for President Reagan's tax bill that was enacted in 1981. At that time, Roberts was a member of the Reagan administration, serving as assistant secretary for economic policy in the Treasury Department.

Roberts was not alone. He notes the contribution of a number of other congressional staff members, including three who served on the Joint Economic Committee—Bruce Bartlett, Steven Entin, and Mark Policinski. They all pointed to the influence of the late Norman Ture, who later served as an undersecretary of the Treasury during Reagan's first term.

Like many of the supply-siders, Entin had ties to the University of Chicago, where he had taken classes with Friedman and Mundell. Laffer was then a professor at the University of Chicago Business School. Entin was lured to Washington when a friend called and said there was an opening for a tax economist on the staff of Ohio senator Robert Taft. After Taft left Congress, Entin stayed on to work for Senator Robert Griffin, a Republican from Michigan, and then developed a proposal for indexing the tax code for inflation for Senators Bob Dole (R-Kans.) and Robert Packwood (R-Ore.).[81]

For Entin, the example of the Kennedy tax cut loomed large. John Kennedy's Council of Economic Advisers generally saw the tax cut as stimulating demand and helping put idle resources back to work. They were speaking from a Keynesian point of view. Entin and the other supply-siders emphasized Kennedy's cuts in marginal tax rates. In their view, it was the change in relative prices caused by the marginal tax cut that made all the difference.[82]

Mark Policinski came to Washington in much the same kind of accidental way as Entin. In the mid-1970s, Policinski was studying for a master's degree in economics and working in college administration at Western Kentucky University. Representative Clarence J. "Bud" Brown Jr. of Ohio, a senior Republican member of the Joint Economic Committee, had secured an additional staff position on the committee. A friend from Western Kentucky who was already working in Washington called Policinski. He came to town, interviewed for twenty minutes with Representative Brown and, in 1976, joined the staff of the Joint Economic Committee.[83]

How did he become part of the supply-side band? Policinski traces it to a lunch with Entin. Asked whether President Ford should raise taxes, Policinski argued that higher taxes would simply make things worse. At that point, Entin introduced Policinski to Bruce Bartlett, Paul Craig Roberts, and the few other congressional staffers working on the supply-side approach.

Unlike Entin and Policinski, Bartlett was already in Washington. But he had come to study American diplomatic history at Georgetown, not the state of economic theory or the current condition of economic policy.[84] When Bartlett abandoned academic life for Capitol Hill, he joined the staff of

Representative Ron Paul (R-Tex.). He was attracted by Paul's conservative views (Paul had billed himself as being to the right of Barry Goldwater), not by a concern over marginal tax cuts. Paul was defeated in the next election, and Bartlett was looking for another position when a friend called to say that Jack Kemp was looking for an economist—Paul Craig Roberts had departed for the House Budget Committee. In his interview with Kemp, Bartlett remembers being asked "Are you a supply-side fiscalist?" At the time, Bartlett had no idea what that meant, but he managed to find the right answer and got the job.

There were links between the Washington band and the New York contingent that gathered at Michael I. There were occasional lunches with Laffer and dinners that included Laffer and Wanniski. But, in Roberts's telling, he emphasizes the early initiative and independence of the Washington group.

There may have been only a handful of supply-siders in New York and Washington, but they had a promising idea at the right time. Bartley and Wanniski remained powerful voices for the supply-side view at the *Wall Street Journal.* Representative Jack Kemp and Senator William Roth (R-Del.) turned the supply-side approach into a legislative vehicle that would, if enacted, cut marginal tax rates by 10 percent in each of three years. By September 1977, the Kemp-Roth Bill had been endorsed by the Republican National Committee.[85]

The option of marginal tax cuts promised a number of political as well as economic benefits. First, at least for the supply-siders, tax cuts promised the growth that had been an on-again, off-again reality in the 1970s. Second, the prospect of cutting taxes and stimulating so much growth that government revenues might rise allowed them to appeal to Republicans who favored tax cuts but who also supported deficit reduction and balanced budgets. For those more skeptical about the impact of marginal tax cuts on growth, there was at least the possibility that tax cuts would slow the growth of government spending or possibly even lead to actual budget cuts. In political terms, across-the-board cuts in marginal tax rates promised significant benefits to upper-income individuals, who tended to support the Republican Party. In addition, reductions in the marginal rates applied to personal income provided immediate benefit to small business owners who were either individual proprietorships or subchapter S corporations (i.e., firms that passed through corporate profits to individual income without any corporate tax).

In addition, the Kemp-Roth proposal included faster write-offs for investments in capital equipment, offering benefits to major businesses, another traditional constituency. In other words, the supply-siders' view of the world held out the promise of serving the national interest in a way that also rewarded key Republican constituencies.

In the supply-siders' view, tax cuts would take care of restoring growth. That still left them with the persistent and perplexing problem of inflation. Here, they relied on academic thinking confirmed by past experience. They adopted the broadly held view that restrictive monetary policy would eventually force a return to price stability. Tight money, however, generally meant recession not growth. How could the supply-siders' square that particular circle? They turned to a relatively new development in academic thinking: rational expectations theory.

In simple terms, rational expectations took the old saying that you can not fool all the people all of the time and turned it into a rigorous economic theory. As used by the supply-siders, the implication was that people would realize the economic implications of tight money. Rather than wait for interest rates, prices, and wages to stabilize after a painful period of unemployment, the rational individual, company, or bank would quickly adjust to tight money policy and turn to stable economic behavior without the need for a wasteful recession. As noted earlier, the supply-siders believed they could promise stable prices without tears.

Supply-siders felt they had met the challenge of controlling inflation and still stimulating growth. That left them with the productivity challenge and the question of the trade deficit. Their answer to these two questions was at least implicit in their view of the impact of marginal tax cuts on the volume of investment, savings, and work.

Although they did not generally dwell on the question, the supply-siders could argue that higher rates of investment would contribute to higher rates of productivity growth. The trade deficit was not a central concern of the supply-siders. But they could have argued that savings rates were expected to be high enough to fund increased investment, which would at least not increase the need to borrow internationally and hence contribute to the trade deficit. If the savings rate rose even more, that would be consistent with a declining trade deficit or even trade balance.

In the supply-siders' view, they promised high growth, rising incomes, and stable prices without government deficits or government action beyond the reduction in tax rates. It was a "Look Ma, no hands" approach to economic policy that fit traditional Republican suspicion of government, hostility to government action, and concern about deficits. "There were aspects of the supply-side story that appealed to every brand of Republican."[86] And it did it all in a way that promised immediate benefits to the constituencies that supported Republicans and funded their campaigns.

The Early Seeds of a Competitiveness Strategy

While the supply-siders took center stage and the advocates of industrial policy took the House floor, another view was beginning to emerge. It was not the product of a particular academic school. The focus was on the long term and the importance of restoring rapid productivity growth. The new approach emphasized reduced inflation but in a way that would not deter needed increases in capital investment. It shared the supply-siders' emphasis on incentives for investment but without the almost giddy optimism promised by the Laffer curve.

The 1979 and 1980 annual reports of the congressional Joint Economic Committee contain many of the early elements of this approach.[87] In addition to increasing business investment in new plant and equipment, there is an emphasis on added investment in research and development, training, and infrastructure. Foreign competition is taken seriously but met with an emphasis on exports, overseas market access, and a competitive dollar. The 1979 and 1980 reports were harbingers of an approach that increasingly characterizes the long-term growth strategies of industrial countries around the world. The following chapters trace the development of that strategy in the United States and its emergence as national policy in the 1990s.

Notes

1. At the time, many economists and policymakers saw trade deficits correcting themselves through lower exchange rates that would, in turn, increase the deficit country's exports. As capital flows came to dominate international markets, the emphasis shifted to the imbalance between a country's saving and investment. To invest more than it saved, a country could borrow overseas. The borrowing would be reflected as a surplus on the country's capital account. Because actual investments require tangible resources, the capital inflow was matched by an inflow of goods (or services) that was reflected in the trade deficit.

2. See Paul Krugman, *Peddling Prosperity: Economic Sense and Nonsense in the Age of Diminished Expectations* (New York: W. W. Norton, 1994), 241. In Krugman's words, "Because comparative advantage is a beautiful idea that it seems only economists understand, economists cling to the idea even more strongly, as a kind of badge that defines their professional identity and ratifies their intellectual superiority."

3. The bulk of the economics profession opposed the passage of the Smoot-Hawley Tariff of 1930. "A petition objecting to the act containing 1028 signatures was presented to President Herbert Hoover." Richard E. Caves, Jeffrey A. Frankel, and Ronald W. Jones, *World Trade and Payments: An Introduction,* 9th ed. (Boston: Addison Wesley, 2002), 23. For the context of the times, see Charles P. Kindleberger, *The World in Depression: 1929–1939,* rev. and enlarged ed. (Berkeley: University of California Press, 1986), 123–27.

4. Herbert Stein, *Presidential Economics: The Making of Economic Policy from Roosevelt to Reagan and Beyond,* 2nd ed. (Washington, D.C.: American Enterprise Institute, 1988), 164.

5. Robert Solomon, *The International Monetary System: 1945–1981* (New York: Harper & Row, 1982), 47, 48, 51.

6. For a brief discussion of the Johnson proposal see Kent H. Hughes, *Trade Taxes and Transnationals: International Economic Decision Making in Congress* (New York: Praeger Publishers, 1979), 18.

7. For a further discussion of the Nixon and Mills trade proposals see Hughes, *Trade Taxes and Transnationals,* 21–22.

8. Andrew J. Biemiller, Statement before the House Ways and Means Committee, *Tariff and Trade Proposals,* Hearings, part 4 (Washington, D.C.: U.S. Government Printing Office, 1970), 1001. As quoted in Hughes, *Trade Taxes and Transnationals,* 21.

9. For a more detailed discussion of the Burke-Hartke bill, see Hughes, *Trade Taxes and Transnationals,* 23–35.

10. For a description of the Camp David negotiations over Nixon's New Economic Policy, see Stein, *Presidential Economics,* 167, 176–80.

11. Raymond J. Waldman, *Managed Trade: The New Competition between Nations* (Cambridge, Mass.: Ballinger, 1986), 104.

12. Steve Dryden, *Trade Warriors: USTR and the American Crusade for Free Trade* (New York: Oxford University Press, 1995), 190.

13. Dryden, *Trade Warriors,* 252–53.

14. The House Export Task Force was founded in 1978.

15. Author's interview with Edmund Rice, president, Committee for Employment through Exports, 2002.

16. The details of the export provisions of the Omnibus Trade and Competitiveness Act of 1988 can be found in U.S. Congress, *Omnibus Trade and Competitiveness Act of 1988: A Conference Report to Accompany HR 3* (Washington, D.C.: U.S. Government Printing Office, 1988), under title II, subtitle B, pp. 234–55.

17. President's Commission on Industrial Competitiveness, *Global Competition: The New Reality* (Washington, D.C.: U.S. Government Printing Office, 1985), vol. 1, 6.

18. See, for instance, the statement by Robert W. Galvin (then chairman of the board and chief executive officer of Motorola) before the U.S. Senate Foreign Relations Committee, September 14, 1982. (I relied on a reprint from Motorola generously provided by Sue R. Topp, manager of the Motorola archives.)

19. The commissioned papers and the proceedings of the colloquium are contained in National Science Foundation, ed., *International Economic Policy Research: Papers and Proceedings of a Colloquium held in Washington D.C., October 3, 4, 1980* (Washington D.C.: National Science Foundation, 1980).

20. Robert M. Stern, "Changes in U.S. Comparative Advantage, Issues for Research

and Policy," in *International Economic Policy Research,* ed. National Science Foundation, III-84.

21. Sumiye Okubo, "Introduction and Summary" of the session on "Changes in Comparative Advantage," in *International Economic Policy Research,* ed. National Science Foundation, III-10.

22. It was the author's comment.

23. Krugman, *Peddling Prosperity,* 221–34. See also Paul R. Krugman, *Rethinking International Trade* (Cambridge, Mass.: MIT Press, 1990), 1–8.

24. "Since economics as practiced in the English-speaking world is strongly oriented toward mathematical models, any economic argument that has not been expressed in that form tends to remain invisible." Krugman, *Rethinking International Trade,* 3.

25. Gene M. Grossman and J. David Richardson, *Strategic Trade Policy: A Survey of Issues and Early Analysis,* Special Papers in International Economics 15 (Princeton, N.J.: International Finance Section, Department of Economics, Princeton University, 1985). For a brief summary of Brander and Spencer's analysis, also see Krugman, *Rethinking International Trade,* 248–54. Krugman uses a stylized example of government-influenced competition between Boeing and Airbus to make the Brander-Spencer point. See Krugman, *Peddling Prosperity,* 235–39.

26. Grossman and Richardson, *Strategic Trade Policy,* 21.

27. Centre for Economic Policy Research, "Strategic Trade Policy: Is There a Case for Intervention?" *Bulletin,* February 19, 1987, 4. The *Bulletin* was reporting on a January 30, 1987, workshop on strategic trade.

28. Paul R. Krugman and Richard E. Baldwin, "Market Access and International Competition: A Simulation Study of 16K Random Access Memories," in Krugman, *Rethinking International Trade,* 199–225.

29. Sylvia Nasar, "The New Case for Protectionism," *Fortune,* September 16, 1985, 33–38.

30. Laura D'Andrea Tyson, *Who's Bashing Whom: Trade Conflict in High-Technology Industries* (Washington, D.C.: Institute for International Economics, 1992).

31. Eric Garfinkle, *Roadmap for Results: Trade Policy, Technology, and American Competitiveness* (Washington, D.C.: Council on Competitiveness, 1993).

32. Elizabeth Drew, *On the Edge: The Clinton Presidency* (New York: Simon & Schuster, 1994), 26.

33. Krugman, *Peddling Prosperity,* 284–91. Krugman's argument first appeared in his "Competitiveness: A Dangerous Obsession," *Foreign Affairs,* March–April 1994.

34. Krugman's criticism of competitiveness and at least the rhetoric if not the policies of the Clinton administration brought forth a number of responses. E.g., see Benjamin M. Friedman, "Must We Compete?" *New York Review of Books,* October 10, 1994. Among other points, Friedman notes that Clinton pushed for congressional approval of the North American Free Trade Agreement and to reduce the deficit—just the opposite of the fears expressed by Krugman.

35. AMTEX is discussed briefly in Daniel Roos, Frank Field, and James Neely, "industry Consortia," in *Investing in Innovation: Creating a Research and Innovation Policy That Works,* ed. Lewis M. Branscomb and James H. Keller (Cambridge, Mass.: MIT Press, 1998), 411. See also National Science and Technology Council Committee on Civilian Industrial Technology, *Technology in the National Interest* (Washington, D.C.: U.S. Government Printing Office, 1996), 56.

36. Otis L. Graham Jr., *Losing Time: The Industrial Policy Debate* (Cambridge, Mass.: Harvard University Press, 1992), 33.

37. Graham, *Losing Time,* 34.

38. Stuart E. Eizenstat, speech at the *Business Week* Corporate Planning 100 Senior Planner's Roundtable, Phoenix, November 18, 1982, 6.

39. Eizenstat, speech, 7.

40. Gary Clyde Hufbauer and Howard Rosen, "Managing Comparative Disadvantage," revised draft, photocopy, Institute for International Economics, Washington, D.C., January 6, 1984, 7. Hufbauer and Rosen follow Richard Cooper in characterizing the more politicized trade decisions as high-track cases, in contrast to the "low-track" cases that were handled within the existing trade laws that provide for import relief from unfairly and fairly imported goods.

41. Graham, *Losing Time,* 128.

42. This was essentially the view taken by an unpublished Carter administration Treasury Department's review of the RFC. "The Question of whether a useful role was served by the RFC's activities is generally 'yes'—both regarding its cushioning role for the economy during the Depression years and its private-to-public reallocation role during the war years. The RFC's effectiveness after World War II ended was considered doubtful enough that Congress voted in 1953 to terminate its activities." Office of Corporate Finance, U.S. Treasury Department, *Federal Credit Programs: An Overview of Current Programs and Their Beginning in the Reconstruction Finance Corporation* (Washington, D.C.: U.S. Government Printing Office, 1982), 10, as cited in Eizenstat, speech, 12.

43. Graham, *Losing Time,* 128. The quote was used by Reagan Treasury official Paul Craig Roberts in his testimony before the Joint Economic Committee. See Joint Economic Committee, *Industrial Policy, Economic Growth, and the Competitiveness of U.S. Industry: Part I,* 98th Congress, 1st session (Washington, D.C.: U.S. Government Printing Office, 1983), 92, 24–30.

44. See Felix Rohatyn, "The Coming Emergency and What Can Be Done about It," *New York Review of Books,* December 4, 1981; and "Reconstructing America," *New York Review of Books,* March 5, 1981.

45. See a brief discussion in Congressional Budget Office, *The Industrial Policy Debate* (Washington, D.C.: U.S. Government Printing Office, 1983), 68.

46. Richard Corrigan, "Smokestacks and Silicon: The Debate Over U.S. Industrial Policy Continues," in *Smoketacks and Silicon: Regaining America's Edge* (Washington, D.C.: National Journal, 1984), 9.

47. Lester C. Thurow, "The Case for Industrial Policies," photocopy, Center for National Policy, Washington, D.C., January 1984; e.g., see 18.

48. Ira C. Magaziner and Robert B. Reich, *Minding America's Business: The Decline and Rise of the American Economy* (New York: Harcourt Brace Jovanovich, 1982), 6.

49. Magaziner and Robert B. Reich, *Minding America's Business,* 5.

50. For current examples, see National Science and Technology Council, *Technology in the National Interest,* 20–21.

51. National Science and Technology Council, *Technology in the National Interest,* especially 25, 35, 72–73.

52. Richard Katz, *Japan: The System That Soured—The Rise and Fall of the Japanese Economic Miracle* (Armonk, N.Y.: M. E. Sharp, 1998).

53. World Bank, *The East Asian Miracle: Economic Growth and Public Policy* (New York: Oxford University Press, 1993).

54. Joseph E. Stiglitz and Shahid Yusuf, eds., *Rethinking the East Asian Miracle* (New York: Oxford University Press, 2001).

55. See Issei Morita, "Japanese Explode the Myth of MITI Economic Growth: Once-Revered Ministry Hindered Industrial Progress, say Finance Officials," *Financial Times* (London edition), June 27, 2002, 10.

56. See, for instance, Stephen A. Merrill, "The Politics of Micropolicy: Innovation and Industrial Policy in the United States," photocopy, Center for Strategic and International Studies, Georgetown University, Washington, D.C., February 1984. The Merrill essay also appears in *Government Policies for Industrial Innovation: Design, Implementation, Evaluation*, ed. J. David Roessner (Tarrytown, N.Y., Associated Faculty Press, 1984). In the essay, Merrill focuses on the difference between innovation and industrial policies, noting that innovation policies had been relatively uncontroversial but also largely ineffective.

57. See National Science and Technology Council, *Technology in the National Interest*, 68.

58. See, for instance, Joint Economic Committee, *Joint Economic Committee Report, 1979* (Washington, D.C.: U.S. Government Printing Office, 1979). The report does not advocate an industrial policy but emphasizes the way in which increased investment and related productivity growth could contribute to steady growth and stable prices. The cover of the report puts inflation in a large vice being squeezed by the leverage of productivity and employment.

59. Graham, *Losing Time,* provides the best overview of the industrial policy debate.

60. Merrill, "Politics of Micropolicy," 20.

61. See, for instance, Karl Polanyi, *The Great Transformation: The Political and Economic Origins of Our Time* (Boston: Beacon Press, 1957).

62. John Maynard Keynes, *The General Theory of Employment, Interest, and Money* (New York: Harcourt, Brace, 1936).

63. Many academic observers point to the 1990s Japanese economy as an example of a modern-day liquidity trap. Low or even negative interest rates (when nominal rates are adjusted for inflation) have not triggered a Japanese recovery.

64. This statistic is from the Bureau of Labor Statistics. The figures for 1929–47 include persons 14 years of age and older. The BLS data can be found at http://data.bls.gov/cgi/srgate to retrieve document LFU110001000. From 1948 onward, figures include only those 16 years and older. Lester V. Chandler, *America's Greatest Depression, 1929–1941* (New York: Harper & Row, 1970), 38, reports the total unemployed in 1940 as 9.6 percent, which excludes the number employed in public emergency work. By any measure, it was high.

65. This statistic is from the Bureau of Labor Statistics (see above at note 64).

66. Stein, *Presidential Economics,* and Krugman, *Peddling Prosperity,* both provide useful overviews of the academic questioning of Keynesian economics. Krugman goes on to discuss the reemergence of Keynesian academic thought in the 1980s.

67. Stein, *Presidential Economics,* 210.

68. Stein, *Presidential Economics,* 241. The paper is "The Doctrine of the Budget-Balancing Doctrine or How the Good Guys Finally Lost" (March 25, 1976). His paper was later published in *Fiscal Responsibility in a Constitutional Democracy,* ed. James M. Buchanan and Richard E. Wagner (Boston: Martinus Nijhoff, 1978).

69. Stein, *Presidential Economics,* 241.

70. Robert L. Bartley, *The Seven Fat Years and How to Do It Again* (New York: Free Press, 1992 and 1995), p. 44; the citation is from the 1995 paperback edition.

71. Bartley, *Seven Fat Years;* see especially 43–76.

72. Bartley, *Seven Fat Years,* 43.

73. See, for instance, Caves, Frankel, and Jones, *World Trade and Payments,* chap. 22.

74. Robert A. Mundell, *Monetary Theory: Inflation, Interest, and Growth in the World Economy* (Pacific Palisades, Calif.: Goodyear Publishing, 1971), 1.

75. Bartley, *Seven Fat Years,* 58.

76. In the early 1980s, I accompanied Representative Lee Hamilton (D-Ind.) on a visit to Laffer's home outside Los Angeles. During our visit, Laffer talked about his work on poverty and how it had influenced his thinking.

77. This is how Laffer described the evolution of his thinking at an early 1980s meeting with Hamilton and the author (see note 76).

78. The supply-siders' estimates of the impact of the cuts in marginal tax rates were not always so extreme. For instance, in his additional views to the *Joint Economic Report, 1979,* Senator William V. Roth Jr. (R-Del.) expected an increase in tax revenues (or reflows) of 20 percent of the tax cut in the first year and 30 percent in the second. Roth was the coauthor of the Kemp-Roth bill mentioned below. In his additional views, he also emphasizes the then-current version of his bill (Kemp-Roth II), which included strict limits on the size of federal spending relative to gross national product. See Joint Economic Committee, *The Report of the Joint Economic Committee, Congress of the United States, on the 1979 Economic Report of the President* (Washington, D.C.: U.S. Government Printing Office, 1979), 109. The 1979 report of the committee was a rare joint report endorsed by the minority Republicans as well as the majority Democrats.

79. In *Day of Reckoning* (New York: Random House, 1988), Harvard professor Benjamin M. Friedman illustrates how dramatically the economy would have had to respond in terms of work, saving, and spending to have borne out the economic projections of the supply-siders. See Friedman, "Roots of Reaganomics," in *Day of Reckoning,* chap. 10. Krugman covers similar ground in Krugman, *Rethinking International Trade,* 82–103, as does Stein in his chapter titled "The Reagan Campaign: The Economics of Joy" in Stein, *Presidential Economics,* 235–62.

80. Paul Craig Roberts, *The Supply-Side Revolution: An Insider's Account of Policymaking in Washington* (Cambridge, Mass.: Harvard University Press, 1984), 1.

81. Author's interview with Steve Entin, February 8, 2002.

82. See Norman B. Ture, "Supply Side Analysis and Public Policy" in *Essays in Supply Side Economics,* ed. David G. Raboy (Washington, D.C.: Institute for Research on the Economics of Taxation, 1982), 10.

83. Author's interview with Mark Policinski, April 5, 2002.

84. Author's interview with Bruce Bartlett, May 24, 2002.

85. Stein, *Presidential Economics,* 246.

86. Garry Wills, *Reagan's America: Innocents at Home* (Garden City, N.Y.: Doubleday, 1987), 365.

87. See Joint Economic Committee, *Report of the Joint Economic Committee on the 1979 Economic Report of the President,* and Joint Economic Committee, *Plugging in the Supply Side: Report of the Joint Economic Committee on the January 1980 Economic Report of the President* (Washington, D.C.: U.S. Government Printing Office, 1980).

Chapter 3

Looking Abroad for Answers: Pearls of Wisdom from the Global Oyster, Japan—The Samurai Surprise

From the start, the debate over national competitiveness was carried out on a global stage. The oil embargo by the Organization of the Petroleum Exporting Countries, the international challenge to some of America's traditional economic strengths, and the contrast between rapid productivity growth abroad and seeming stagnation at home forced Americans to look at foreign economies in a way they had not for many decades.

It was not only the challenge posed by global competitors. The bouts with inflation, recession, and slowing productivity growth in the 1970s were shock enough to drive the search for new economic policies. Three decades of rapid income growth had fueled expectations of continuing good economic times. American prosperity, innovation, and economic leadership were so much a part of the national fabric that the national debate could shift to questions of war and peace, the battle for civil rights, and areas of persistent poverty.

But the international dimension of the competitiveness challenge forced changes in public policy and the private economy that have had a lasting impact on the formation of an American economic strategy for the future. The international dimension of the competitiveness challenge triggered a widespread reflection on America's economic policies, business practices, and fundamental assumptions about economic growth. The questioning of America's existing policies and practices was not confined to a few business leaders, political figures, or concerned academics. University presidents,[1] engineers, schoolteachers, research directors, and a host of other Americans responded to the global challenge by taking local action as well as supporting the search for national policies.

As America looked around the world, three countries occupied most of its thinking. First, there was Japan. No country had a greater impact on late-twentieth-century American economic thinking, public policy, or business practice than Japan. That Japan's productivity was growing so rapidly was only part of the story. By the 1980s, Japan was challenging the very-high-technology industries that were meant to define America's future. And Japan was doing it with public policies and a private sector that raised doubts about established thinking in Washington and in boardrooms around the country.

Second, there was Germany. In 1945, Germany stood in ruins. Its wartime political leadership was reviled; its economy was devastated, its dictator's dreams of a global Third Reich had turned into the reality of a defeated and divided country. When America started to look at the global economy in the mid-1970s, it saw a very different Germany. By the 1970s, the German economic miracle of rapid postwar reconstruction had led to widespread prosperity. Productivity and income were both rising rapidly.

Third, there was the cautionary example of Britain. The greatest empire the world had ever known, the much envied "workshop of the world," had become a second-rate power with a troubled economy. Americans began to ask, "Could it happen here?"

Japan: The Samurai Surprise

Bit by bit, export by export, Japan came to challenge American industry, American policy, and American thinking. In the last half of the twentieth century, Japanese success drove much of American industry to sharpen its focus on quality and change its approach to business. The impact came first to manufacturing but has steadily spread to service industries as well. Japanese success also had a significant impact on American public policy. In some cases, American policy was inspired by a Japanese example. At other times, American policy was driven by attempts to counteract specific Japanese trade policies or the impact of Japanese corporate conglomerates. The greatest impact of the Japanese challenge on public policy, however, will not be found in an individual piece of legislation or negotiating strategy. Japanese success forced Americans to think about their own institutions and how they fit together to form a system that fosters long-term economic growth.

Responding to the Japanese challenge also has contributed to a new, more cooperative relationship between business and government. The political parties were both affected. Many Republicans shared the concern about the Japanese challenge and supported efforts to improve markets and secure effective market access in Japan. The impact on the Democrats was, if anything, greater. In the post–World War II era, Democrats had concentrated on fighting short-term unemployment, extending the welfare state, and sharing fairly the wealth generated by the American economy. For many, long-term growth seemed to take care of itself. When the 1970s pushed them to develop their own growth strategy, they became more aware that long-term business success was critical to employment, prosperity, and national economic strength.

The United States did not attempt any wholesale importation of Japanese institutions. Instead, Americans looked to their own past, the experience of other countries, and evolving economic and political circumstances. When Japanese policies were imported, they were adapted to American conditions and culture. In the end, the American solution looked like the proverbial wedding dress of the traditional bride—something borrowed, something blue, something old, and something new.

Growing Awareness of Japan

In the 1980s, senior policymakers and leaders of business could still remember when Japanese goods were viewed as cheap and flimsy. Three decades after World War II, the times and Japan had changed dramatically. Interest in Japan grew along with Japanese imports. To many observers, Japan was achieving stunning economic results with a startlingly different approach to economic growth. Japan protected domestic industries and subsidized exports rather than opting for a free trade policy. Japan intervened in industry with everything from direct subsidies to strongly worded advice (generally referred to as "administrative guidance"). Antitrust laws were weakly enforced or ignored altogether.[2] Business and government seemed to work closely and effectively together. Business practices themselves differed sharply from what was then the American norm. How, Americans began to ask, could the Japanese do so well, do it so differently, and do it while ignoring American assumptions about economic life?

As early as 1970, the debate over the functioning of the Japanese economy began to spill over into the American press. For instance, Boston Consulting Group's James Abegglen's term "Japan, Inc.,"[3] was taken as the title for a *Business Week* article.[4] Early observers of post–World War II Japan made similar observations, which were not viewed as controversial at the time.[5] But as Japan began to challenge American industry, the question of how Japan worked was linked to a possible change in American policy. Several important and, at times conflicting, interests were at work.

Japanese Democracy

At the end of World War II, America sought to remake the defeated Axis powers as market democracies. Some of the American architects of post-war Japan were still very much involved in the 1970s–80s Washington policy debate. To some extent, they saw Japanese democracy as an unfinished product that would be endangered by a sudden shift in Japan's economic relations with the United States.

Strategic Partner

The Cold War changed America's thinking about Japan. As communists advanced in China, America began to think of Japan as a future ally rather than as a former adversary. Japan became an important base for American troops in the Far East and a bastion in the strategy to contain world communism. In the popular press and in national security circles, Japan was at times described as an unsinkable aircraft carrier off the Chinese coast.

Economic Ties

While consumer interests and organizations were an increasingly forceful 1970s presence in questions of product safety, they were generally not well organized to express their interests in debates over trade, industrial policy, or long-term growth. For the most part, support for open trade relied on American businesses that either depended on imports or were deeply involved in global commerce.

Increased exports would benefit the overall American economy through greater economies of scale. In meeting the quality and other demands of the Japanese consumer, American companies would have to become more innovative. The added profits from export sales also help fund the next generation of research and innovation and provided an added stimulus to innovation. Leading American exporters suspected that their Japanese competitors could support low-priced exports by charging higher prices in a protected domestic market. The quality of jobs was also at stake. The shift from domestic to export production is generally associated with the creation of better-paid jobs.

Even the drive for opening the Japanese market encountered some unanticipated opposition. Companies with a strong position in the Japanese market feared disruption of current market access as the cost of a broader trade dispute. As firms began to depend more heavily on imported Japanese components, they also shied away from serious trade confrontation. In general, the 1980s shift in international commerce from trading entire products to individual parts raised the potential costs of any dispute that actually disrupted trade.[6] A loss of critical components could shut down an entire assembly line and potentially affect a range of products.

America's Worldview

Democratic capitalism, free markets, and individual initiative were usually cited as the heart of America's economic success. If Japan succeeded with a different set of policies, it suggested that America might have to rethink its philosophy or change its institutions.

There was a parallel reaction in the academic and policy communities. Adam Smith and his famous invisible hand were the foundation of American economic thinking. The idea that a highly visible Japanese hand might do as well (or even better) was a direct challenge to reigning economic thought. By the 1970s, economics had become increasingly mathematical. The growing use of mathematics added rigor, elegance, and in many instances important insights, but made it all the harder to incorporate Japanese institutional factors or business practices into the models that were coming to influence economic thought. Economic thinking had also moved away from a preoccupation with the Great Depression. The generation of economists that had focused on market failures and the near collapse of capitalism was giving way to a newer group that emphasized the myriad strengths of the market. Where government had once been seen as solution if not savior, it was increasingly seen as untrustworthy, unconcerned with the average American, and often incompetent.

As interest in Japan grew, some of the leading experts on Japan sought to downplay the differences between the Japanese and American economies. Neoclassical economists were generally skeptical of government intervention and would be expected to look for other factors to explain Japan's success. In his 1998 book *Japan: The System That Soured*, Richard Katz looks back more than twenty years to *Asia's New Giant* as a particularly influential scholarly treatment of Japan that took this point of view. Hugh Patrick and Henry Rosovsky, who edited the earlier volume, saw a Japanese economy that was very much in the American mold. Katz describes Patrick as being "of the school, which interprets Japanese economic performance as due primarily to the actions and efforts of private individuals and enterprises responding to the opportunities provided in quite free markets for commodities and labor."[7] Patrick describes the role of the Japanese government as supportive but exaggerated. Philip Trezise, a former assistant secretary of state for East Asia and another contributor to *Asia's New Giant,* shared the Patrick-Rosovsky view of the Japanese economy. As a fellow at the Washington-based Brookings Institution, Trezise was a particularly active and influential participant in Washington trade and economic circles.

Japan as Number One: The Second Sputnik

As the debate continued, however, the advocates of "Japan is just like us" lost more and more of their credibility. As the United States staggered from one oil shock to the next while wrestling with bouts of recession, inflation, and high unemployment, Japan seemed to emerge from each storm to pose yet another challenge to American industry, the American economy, and the American way of thinking. In fact, Japan along with the rest of the industrial world also had been jolted by the economic turmoil of the early 1970s. Japanese productivity did drop from the very rapid pace of the preceding two decades. Even after 1973, however, Japan continued to prosper with low unemployment, stable prices, and productivity growth at three times the American level.

In political and policy circles, there was a persistent feeling that somehow America had got it wrong and Japan had got it right. Then, in 1979, one author concentrated American thinking with a new book and a challenging title. Ezra Vogel's *Japan as No. 1: Lessons for America* caught the national mood.[8] Vogel was not an economist but rather a longtime student of Japan, a Harvard University professor of sociology, and chairman of Harvard's Council on East Asian Studies. Like many of the thinkers and policymakers involved in the competitiveness debate, Vogel would later serve in the Clinton administration.

Despite the title, Vogel was careful to qualify his appraisal of Japanese strength. As he notes, "In gross national product, standard of living, political power, and cultural influence, Japan is not number one in the world today."[9] Many of Vogel's nuances were dropped in the ensuing debate. *Japan as No. 1* seemed to say it all. A virtual flood of books, reports, studies, magazine articles, and newspaper columns followed Vogel's book. By the time of the congressional debate over industrial policy in the early 1980s, "the English-language literature on the Japanese system spanned a substantial range of interpretations, whereas four years earlier there had been essentially one view."[10] While studies continued to be published that saw the Japanese economy as open to trade and working along familiar American lines, they had less and less influence on the public policy debate in the 1980s.

Vogel's book helped focus attention on Japan's Ministry of International Trade and Industry (MITI) as one of the key governmental contributors to Japanese industrial success.[11] Soon articles began to appear about MITI's vision for building Japanese economic strength in the 1980s,[12] including strategies for overtaking the U.S. lead in semiconductors and a "worldwide strategy for the computer market."[13] At about the same time, Chalmers Johnson published his detailed and influential *MITI and the Japanese Miracle: The Growth of Industrial Policy, 1925–1975.*[14] Where Patrick and Rosovsky had put the emphasis on broad economic factors such as the national savings rate and the education level of the Japanese worker, Johnson looked at an additional array of factors that included national purpose, the relative independence of industry from shareholders, and key governmental institutions. He traces the growth of MITI from its prewar roots to its World War II role as the Ministry of Munitions, to its postwar role in helping Japan to first recover and then become a world economic power. He portrays MITI and many of its key officials as learning from prewar mistakes as well as successes. He also portrays a MITI whose powers were changing and, in many ways, declining as Japan recovered and many industries became internationally successful.

Other key books or articles also caught the eye of the public and many political leaders. Each brought a different perspective to the Japanese challenge. Each added to the understanding of the public, the policy community, and the political leaders who were trying to define an American economic strategy. But none provided a simple guide that pointed to the key elements in Japan's success or policies or practices that could be easily adapted to American conditions.

By the early 1980s, a growing number of American business leaders, academics, policy specialists, administration officials, political leaders, and congressional staff members had some firsthand experience with Japan. They noted that the price of Japanese goods in Japan was much higher than in America. Foreign goods were available—but at high prices. If the Japanese market was open, they asked, why were there no American entrepreneurs buying Japanese goods in New York and making a killing in Tokyo? At the end of the 1980s, Robert Lawrence (then of the Brookings Institution and now a professor at the Kennedy School of Government) took a systematic look at Japanese prices and came to the same conclusion.[15] Although Lawrence's study came relatively late in the debate over Japan, his respected standing as a mainstream economist gave his findings all the more weight.

From the end of the 1970s on, there was growing interest in Japanese management practices. The idea of learning something from Japan gained added support from important voices at the Harvard Business School. Early in the 1980s, Harvard Business School professors William Abernathy and Robert Hayes spoke of "Managing Our Way to Economic Decline."[16] Professors Bruce Scott and George Lodge also emerged as prominent and influential voices in the competitiveness debate. They edited an important volume that pulled together some of the then-current thinking on American competitiveness,[17] and they held an early 1980s seminar at Harvard that included key administration officials and congressional staff. At the end of the decade, Scott and Lodge also participated in the Competitiveness Summits organized by concerned members of the business community (see chapter 8).[18]

In 1984, Lodge called for a reexamination of America's individualistic culture and its impact on everything from business strategy to government policy. During the 1970s, American writers had frequently referred to the United Kingdom's economic troubles as the "British disease." Lodge's *The American Disease* immediately invoked the specter of the British economy and the fear that America was on the path to irreversible economic decline.[19] Like Vogel before him, Lodge had chosen a title that carried a symbolic significance. Lodge's title also paralleled an older title from a recent period of American economic strength—French journalist Jean-Jacques Servan-Schreiber's 1967 *The American Challenge*.[20] Servan-Schreiber saw an American economy that was everywhere on the march. He foresaw a future in which the world's third-largest economy (after the United States and Russia) would be American industry in Europe. "We are," he wrote, "witnessing the prelude to our own historical bankruptcy."[21] Just a blink of an historical eye later, and American authors were writing about Japan in very similar tones.

As the debate moved through the 1980s, two authors helped to pull together a systematic view of the Japanese government. Both were journalists. Karel G. van Wolferen, a longtime East Asia correspondent for the Dutch daily *NRC Handelsblad,* was virtually unknown in Washington until his winter 1986 article in *Foreign Affairs,* "The Japan Problem."[22] In "The Japan Problem" and his subsequent book *The Enigma of Japanese Power,*[23] van Wolferen paints a picture of strong, fiercely competitive bureaucracies surrounding a weak prime minister. As van Wolferen put it, "There is no supreme institution with ultimate jurisdiction over the others. . . . There is no place where, as Harry Truman would say, the buck stops."[24] In American governmental terms, there was no effective White House management of an interagency process to reconcile the views of conflicting agencies.

At about the same time, a young American journalist began to write and reflect on Asia. James Fallows's interest took him to a number of stops in Asia and a lengthy stay in Tokyo. Reading his articles in the *Atlantic Monthly,* Americans followed the course of Fallows's thinking about Japan. He wrote about individual differences between Americans and Japanese,[25] the influence of rice farmers on Japanese politics,[26] and the difference between an economy focused on producers (Japan) and one favoring consumers.[27]

The May 1989 issue of the *Atlantic Monthly* showed a wary world looking out at the enormous stomach of a Japanese Sumo wrestler. Pulling together his own thinking, the experience of American trade negotiators, and recent work on everything from economic theories to detailed studies of Japanese society, Fallows laid out his case for "Containing Japan."[28] His specific prescriptions for "Getting Along With Japan" came seven months later in the December 1989 issue.[29]

In "Containing Japan," Fallows brought together a number of approaches to Japan that had contributed to a seemingly contradictory set of policies. He took seriously the importance of Japan as a strategic ally and the potential damage that perpetual hectoring over endless trade disputes might do to the overall relationship. In looking at Japanese governance, he saw a structure that was focused on high-value-added industrial growth and that was difficult to change. In his article, he specifically points to Chalmers Johnson's work on MITI and several times refers to van Wolferen's recently published *The Enigma of Japanese Power.* He understood the views of frustrated trade negotiators and shared their concerns about the potential impact of trade flows on industries important to America's future economic prospects. In explaining Japanese success, Fallows also drew on the strategic trade theory developed by Paul Krugman and others.

As its title suggests, in "Containing Japan," Fallows concentrated on making the case for containment. As he saw it, the Japanese economy worked differently than America's, it was unlikely to change, and continued trade imbalances threatened everything from key industries to the broader United States–Japan relationship. In "Getting Along with Japan," Fallows starts by calling on America to "stop haranguing and negotiating with Japan, and instead act politely but firmly to defend the industries and technologies" that were important to its future.[30]

Fallows, however, was not the only voice calling for a rethinking of the American approach to Japan. By 1989, a decade of trade negotiations had begun to produce some thoughtful reflections on Japan, as well as on America's trade-negotiating strategies. None was more influential than Clyde Prestowitz's *Trading Places: How We Allowed Japan to Take the Lead.*[31] Prestowitz had worked as a businessman before joining the Reagan administration as the counselor for Japan affairs to Secretary of Commerce Malcolm Baldrige. Faced with a Japanese challenge to key American industries, Prestowitz portrayed the American response as inconsistent and often wrongheaded. Concern with preserving Japanese political ties and the grip of traditional economic theory often combined to hamstring trade negotiators' efforts to open the Japanese market or enforce existing trade agreements. Early in Prestowitz's book, he reproduced the chart from the Council on Competitiveness report *Picking Up the Pace* that showed the rise of Japan and the fall of the United States in the global market for the memory chips used in the world's computers (see chapter 8). The chart featured an ominous X that caught the warning and the spirit of Prestowitz's *Trading Places.*

As the 1980s drew to a close, other voices also caught the attention of official Washington. Daniel Burstein's *Yen! Japan's New Financial Empire and Its Threat to America*[32] not only focused attention on Japan's financial influence but also portrayed a Japan that was at once saddened at America's competitive woes and yet disdainful of America's decline. Bruce Stokes, a prize-winning reporter at the *National Journal,* conveyed a nuanced picture of U.S. trade and competitiveness policies through his balanced reporting on United States–Japan economic relations.

A series of incidents eventually forced a change in public-sector thinking. The growing success of Japan in semiconductors and sophisticated electronics was an important element in the change (see "The Challenge to Chips" below). Then, in 1987, Washington was rocked by the discovery that Toshiba Machine Tool and the Norwegian Kongsberg Vaapenfabrikk had formed a partnership to sell a highly sophisticated milling machine to the Soviet Union. With the new equipment, the Soviets were able to reduce the noise signature generated by submarine propellers, allowing them to approach American ships or targets largely undetected. The congressional reaction was swift, draconian, and bipartisan. Utah Republican senator Jake Garn took the lead in proposing comprehensive sanctions on the entire Toshiba Corporation.

In 1989, a second shock hit when Shintaro Ishihara and Sony president Akio Morita wrote *The Japan That Can Say "No."*[33] Japan saying no did not trouble Washington. What did trouble Washington was the authors' suggestion that Japan would say no by stopping sales to the United States of key semiconductors and, instead, shift its focus to selling to the Soviet Union. As Ishihara put it, "If . . . Japan sold chips to the Soviet Union and stopped selling them to the U.S., this would upset the entire military balance."[34] Americans already concerned with the Japanese challenge agreed with the general link between economic and military strength. In the paperback edition of *Trading Places* Prestowitz commented on the Morita-Ishihara volume and agreed that "industrial and financial leadership is national security."[35] John Stern, the head of the American Electronics Association office in Tokyo, saw it as "a manifesto for the new Greater East Asian Co-Prosperity Sphere," the original sphere having been a goal of Japan's World War II invasion of East and Southeast Asia.[36] Lawrence Summers, a future Treasury secretary in the Clinton administration and then a professor of political economy at Harvard, weighed in as well, noting that the Morita-Ishihara approach could even shake his economist's faith in free markets.[37] Ishihara also saw racial bias at the heart of American criticism of Japan—a theme used by some of Japan's advocates in Washington.[38]

Although the Morita-Ishihara volume was originally published in Japanese,[39] an unofficial English translation quickly surfaced in Washington and circulated widely among political leaders and their staffs working on U.S. trade and competitiveness policy. The fact that the book came from Ishihara, a frequently outspoken Japanese politician, made it noteworthy enough. But that it also carried the apparent imprimatur of Morita, the widely respected cofounder of Sony, caught people by surprise.

The debate over Japan continued to move center stage. Early in the

George H.W. Bush administration, Washington, Congress, and the administration were caught up in a bitter dispute over the proposed joint United States–Japan production of the FSX, an experimental fighter, in which it appeared that critical U.S. technology would be transferred to Japan. All the while, the United States marched from trade deficit to trade deficit, from one trade dispute to another.[40]

Certain books and key articles had a disproportionate impact on American thinking and American action. But the public and private sectors were not relying only on academics or journalists; they were pursuing their own education on things Japanese. American managers became frequent visitors to Japanese plants to see the combination of process technology and management practice that worked so well. Political leaders, trade negotiators, and key congressional staff members were visiting the same Japanese factories, exploring Japanese schools, and talking with a growing circle of Japanese and American experts on Japan. The Japanese were actively involved in the process—too much was at stake to leave things to chance. They were learning about the American political system while also educating and seeking to influence Americans.

From the perspective of 2003, Japan differs greatly from the way it looked just a decade earlier. Although Japan remains an innovative and effective competitor in many fields, its overall economy stagnated throughout the 1990s. The political constituencies that had contributed to the long-standing reign of the progrowth Liberal Democratic Party continue to act as a brake on the opening or deregulation of the economy that many Japanese and foreign observers see as necessary for Japan to regain customary levels of economic growth. Japan is changing,[41] but it has not yet developed the combination of economic and political institutions needed for it to regain the kind of growth path that was characteristic of past decades.[42]

In the 1980s, however, Japan still presented a challenge that was not well understood. Japanese growth, exports, and quality continued to set global standards. Despite the ongoing challenge of the Cold War and the improved prosperity that came with economic recovery, many Americans continued to focus on Japan. It is hard to overstate the impact Japan had on American economic thinking and the range of policies and proposals that were either inspired by Japanese practice or adopted in response to the Japanese economic challenge. In public thinking and public policy, Japan influenced America in everything from trade to technology to training, from corporate governance to effective government organization.

Trade Policy

It was trade and trade battles that triggered the early interest in Japan. The American policy response to Japanese exports dates at least to the Kennedy-era agreement limiting the export of Japanese cotton textiles. Even in the early 1970s, congressional staff members working on trade quickly found themselves enmeshed in United States–Japan economic relations.[43]

As Japanese officials and companies became more of a presence in Washington, they inadvertently fostered a growing network of American congressional staff members and administration officials concerned about trade with Japan and the much broader question of American competitiveness. Frequent Japanese receptions provided the relatively rare occasions when staff members from Senate and House committees as well as key administration officials could informally confer.

By the 1980s, Washington was awash in complaints from American economic interests struggling to respond to Japanese imports or frustrated by their inability to penetrate the Japanese market. American trade policy bent in two ways. Import protection came in the form of voluntary restraint agreements (VRAs), under which Japan "voluntarily" limited the export of first television sets, then steel, then automobiles, and finally machine tools.[44] The affected industries were large, geographically dispersed, and heavily unionized. They were able to call on representatives in both political parties and helped trigger the 1970s debate over an industrial strategy to strengthen traditional industries.

The VRAs provided some protection for American industry and workers without constituting a wholesale assault on free trade or formally violating the standards of international agreements. The higher imported prices that came with restricted quantity amounted to a kind of side payment or compensation to the Japanese exporter. The VRAs also permitted higher domestic prices, which could be used to help the domestic industry invest and adjust. In each case, the subsidy or side payment went directly from the consumer to the producer without any impact on the federal budget. In a sense, the VRAs were a very Japanese-like solution, in which short-term consumer interests were sacrificed to strengthen industry and avoid a break in international relations.

While official Washington responded to import pressures, many congressional, administration, and policy-community voices stressed the changing nature of America's strength. In economists' terms, officials argued that America's comparative advantage was shifting away from traditional industries and toward high technology. In political terms, this view came to be associated with a group known as Atari Democrats (until the Atari Company moved offshore in response to changing economic conditions). These were the Democrats who supported a "sunrise," or new-industry, approach to industrial policy.

The Challenge in Chips

As Japan continued to produce more and more sophisticated electronics, it began to challenge America's dominance in the memory chips that were an integral part of the booming computer industry. As Japanese chip production began to dominate world markets, Japanese strength also grew in the supporting supplier chain that included the production of advanced materials and the sophisticated equipment that actually made the chips.

Semiconductor manufacturers stressed the importance of memory chip production as a critical learning experience that prepared them for the next generation of semiconductors. At the time, much of Washington and the industry thought that without memory chips one could forget the future of the industry.

Washington and the industry developed a multipronged response. In 1986, industry succeeded in securing antidumping duties on Japanese chips that gave them some breathing room. Antidumping suits were a traditional remedy. Two other steps, however, were novel. First, the industry succeeded in getting greater access to the Japanese market for semiconductors, including a side letter that specified a minimum market share that would go to non-Japanese (expected to be largely American) chip makers.[45] The Americans pointed to their significant market share in third countries where the United States and Japan competed on an even footing. In Japan, their share remained negligible despite a formally open market. The Americans argued that without an assured market share, U.S. chip exports would continue to be blocked by a combination of administrative guidance from the Japanese government and the *keiretsu* (Japanese conglomerates') practice of buying from related firms.

The emphasis on what became known as "results-oriented trade" was a response to the complexities of the Japanese market rather than an attempt to borrow from Japanese practice. The second new step, however, was influenced by Japanese success in working with industry to stimulate new technologies. Leading American chip makers formed Sematech, an industry consortium, to close the manufacturing and quality gap with the Japanese.[46]

For several years, Sematech operated as a public–private partnership with costs shared equally by industry and the Department of Defense.

Although inspired by Japan, Sematech kept its American flexibility. The initial plan for Sematech was to become a world-class producer of memory chips whose product and process innovations would be shared with its members (which were all American). Even before its facilities formally opened, IBM and AT&T used Sematech as a vehicle to share some of their best process technology with other chip producers. By helping to save the American semiconductor industry, they hoped to assure a market for American semiconductor equipment and materials manufacturers.

Sematech took the first step toward production by building a chip or fabrication facility, but it quickly shifted away from chip production to focus on strengthening the American material and equipment manufacturers that formed key parts of the semiconductor industry's supplier chain. To help in this effort, Sematech created Semi-Sematech, an organization of companies in the semiconductor materials and equipment business.[47] The major Japanese semiconductor manufacturers often include equipment and material suppliers, chip makers, and the final product under a single corporate roof. By contrast, the American equipment industry was characterized by many small, innovative firms. Sematech's Austin-based fabrication facility offset the advantages of vertical integration by providing a cost-effective site for testing the viability of new equipment. Over time, Sematech helped restore the competitive position of many of the hundreds of companies that supply the industry.

Export or Die

As American manufacturers realized they had to meet Japanese standards of quality, customer focus, and speed of innovation, they looked at an array of Japanese practices. The emphasis on exports and meeting the requirements of the global consumer became part of their corporate strategy. The shift in American corporate thinking also added to the existing pressures for greater access to the Japanese market. Former Motorola chief executive Robert Galvin spoke of three critical reasons for securing access to the Japanese market: First, Japan was the second largest economy in the world. Profits earned in Japan could be substantial and would help fund the next generation of research and innovation. Second, Japanese consumers demanded high standards of quality and reliability. Meeting those standards made Motorola and other American companies more effective competitors in the United States and around the world. Third, access to the Japanese market would allow American companies to compete away the profits that Japanese companies could use to subsidize (or dump) their exports in American or other overseas markets. As Galvin put it, there could be no sanctuaries from international competition.[48]

In Washington, public attention focused on Japan's success in building international information networks and on the export success of Japan's global trading companies. The global reach of the Japanese trading companies was impressive by any standard. Would an American version of the Japanese approach work in the United States? Key political leaders in Congress thought the idea was worth trying. In the American context, the kind of export cooperation common in Japan would require an antitrust exemption. One (the Webb-Pomerene Act) already allowed a certain degree of overseas cooperation by American exporters.[49] Congress added a legal framework for what all hoped would be Japanese-style export trading companies.[50] The export trading company idea did work well. The contribution, however, has been made largely by the original Japanese firms operating in the United States. In that sense, Japan changed thinking and practice at the same time.

As the U.S. trade deficits grew in the 1970s, American business and many elected political leaders became frustrated by what they felt was the lack of State Department interest in promoting U.S. commercial interests overseas. It was no secret that the way to a career ambassadorship lay through a series of political posts. Commercial work was often viewed as an onerous, unrewarding distraction from the department's real work. Japan's success and its effective overseas representation added to the frustration over State's seeming lack of commercial interest. The frustration boiled over into action when President Carter's Reorganization Proposal Number Three shifted the responsibility for overseas commercial representation from the Department of State to the Department of Commerce. Japan did not directly cause the shift. But certainly Japan was a bale of straw on the trade camel's back.

Innovation: New Products and New Ways of Making Them

Suddenly, or so it seemed, Japan had gone from an "also ran" to setting the pace. American automobile companies were struggling to emulate the fit and finish of their Japanese competitors and match the Japanese companies' ability to bring new, high-quality models to market in a fraction of the time required in Detroit. In the 1970s, the quality (as well as the price) of Japanese consumer electronics swept away the American competition. By the mid-1980s, Japan was threatening to dominate the global market in a whole array of sophisticated electronic products.

How had the Japanese done it? How had they closed the innovation gap? How had they taken American inventions in everything from videocassette recorders to flat-panel displays and made them into a commercial success? American economists still talk about a product cycle in which an advanced industrial country develops a new product. As production of the product grows and becomes standardized, it is often more efficiently produced in a developing country. They saw a cycle in which innovation and production in the industrial world eventually led to production and trade in the developing world. Now there was still American innovation, but initial production and the ensuing profits were found in Japan.

The Japanese success with consortia and public–private partnerships did act as an impetus and inspiration for Sematech and subsequent consortia. The success of Sematech became an influence all its own—showing that U.S. industry could pull together and work with the federal government to foster innovation and competitiveness.

The glaring example of American innovations being commercialized first in Japan contributed to another institutional innovation—the Advanced Technology Program (ATP).[51] Leaders in Congress were already concerned about America's seeming inability to beat the Japanese to the market when IBM announced a stunning breakthrough in superconductivity in 1986. Without missing a beat, Japan announced a program to help commercialize this breakthrough.

Key congressional staff had been visiting Japan and studying elements of the Japanese approach that might be applied in the United States. Prodded by the announcement of Japan's intent to focus on the early commercialization of the IBM discovery, Senator Ernest F. Hollings (D-S.C.) turned to his top technology aide, Pat Windham, for an action plan. Windham worked with Jim Turner, his counterpart on the House Science Committee. The result was the ATP—a program to focus on the high-risk, high-payoff technologies that industry was increasingly unwilling to fund itself.[52] Under the ATP, the government and industry would share the cost (on roughly a 50/50 basis) of proposals that were peer reviewed for their technical merit and their eventual commercial prospects. The ATP was later added to the Omnibus Trade and Competitiveness Act of 1988, received initial funding in the Bush administration, and was made a high-priority program by the Clinton administration. The ATP continues to serve as a successful example of public–private risk sharing. Despite repeated attempts by Republican Congresses in the 1990s and then the George W. Bush administration to first limit the ATP's funding and then eliminate it altogether, it has continued to survive. As a political hot potato, however, it has fallen far short of the original funding level envisioned by the Clinton team.

In responding to Japanese competition, American political leaders also looked at the organization of the Japanese government and the way it worked with the private sector. In particular, the Ministry of International Trade and Industry loomed large in American thinking. Advocates of an industrial policy pointed to MITI's role in supporting key industries, from basic steel to sophisticated computers. Others focused on MITI's approach to international trade. In contrast to the fragmented American approach to trade policy, MITI brought trade negotiations, trade policy, and export promotion under the same large umbrella. MITI's ambit also included technology development as well as international trade.

Again, Japanese success triggered a search for an American response. Starting in the late 1970s, a variety of proposals were made to create a U.S. Department of Trade that would put trade functions under one roof. By the mid-1980s, there was a similar interest in giving more prominence to science and technology. Interested parties inside the Reagan administration helped make the call for a Department of Science and Technology the lead recommendation of the 1985 report of the President's Commission on Industrial Competitiveness (or the Young Commission).[53] Senator John Glenn (D-Ohio) became a leading advocate of a proposed department that—like MITI—would have put trade and technology together in a restructured Department of Commerce. Senator Hollings, though sympathetic to Glenn's approach, took a more modest and, he felt, more achievable path by proposing to strengthen and rename the National Bureau of Standards (NBS), a division of the Department of Commerce.

The NBS was an important but relatively obscure agency that set a variety of technical standards to help industry improve its performance. Once again, Pat Windham, Hollings's key aide for technology, played an important role. Looking for ways to respond to MITI's ability to stimulate technology development by working with Japanese industry, Windham was impressed by the effective way the NBS's Advanced Manufacturing Laboratory worked with industry to solve manufacturing problems. John Lyon, the director of this laboratory (who would later serve as the head of a renamed NBS), had already contributed to Windham's thinking on the creation of an extension service and the creation of a cooperative approach to developing basic technologies with industry. Windham thought a change of name and mission would highlight a new, more ambitious approach to technology development. Windham initially settled on the National Institute of Technology (NIT), but his House Science Committee counterpart, Jim Turner, persuaded him that NIT would be a disastrous acronym. Instead, Windham proposed the National Institute of Standards and Technology (NIST). Senator Hollings agreed, and NIST became part of the Omnibus Trade and Competitiveness Act of 1988.[54]

In technology, as in trade, Japan's challenge and its success drove both public and private sectors in the United States to change their thinking, their business practices, and their public policies. In some cases, the link between Japanese policy and the American program is relatively clear. In most cases, however, Japanese practice is one of several influences that led to a policy initiative adapted to American conditions and history.

Education and Training

Like the Soviet launching of Sputnik in 1957, Japanese success cast a harsh spotlight on much of American education. Unlike the Sputnik era, there was a similar focus on the training offered to the industrial workforce.

The formal structure of Japanese elementary and secondary education shows the influence of the post–World War II American occupation. Six years of elementary school was followed by three years of junior high school and three more of senior high school. The formal structure, however, masked significant differences. The Ministry of Education mandated a national curriculum that was taught on the same day in all parts of Japan. In Japan, a longer school day and year were only one of three aspects of the overall system. In the early years of elementary school, Japanese children start to attend *juku*, or after-school classes, which offered everything from added academics to personal enrichment.[55] They were routinely used to help slower students keep pace with their class and more ambitious students take on extra work. By the fifth grade, particularly in urban areas, most students were enrolled in *juku*. In addition, the Japanese family and particularly the mother played a critical role in education. Well educated herself, with small families that averaged fewer than two children, the Japanese mother worked hard to supplement the efforts of her children. The mother read textbooks ahead of the class so she could help with difficult assignments. There were frequent reports that a mother would even attend class to keep a sick child from falling behind.

The performance of Japanese students on international examinations, in government, and on the factory floor all had an impact on American thinking. Spurred by the dictates of global competition, leading American manufacturers have emerged as strong advocates of improved elementary and secondary education as well as lifelong learning. Before the 1980s, American companies spent less on training and concentrated their spending on the professional development of engineers or scientists and on the managerial ranks. That has begun to change. Motorola, a leading manufacturer of communications equipment and electronic components, started to provide regular training for everyone in the company. Why did Motorola make this change? Responding to the quality, flexibility, and ability to rapidly commercialize Japanese firms, Motorola saw the shift to training as a matter of simple survival.[56]

If American industry was relatively quick to absorb the importance of continually upgrading workers' skills, the impact on American elementary and secondary education was less clear and certainly less direct. In contrast to the European or East Asian approach, the American school system is very diffuse. In place of a single national curriculum, choices on classes and textbooks are heavily influenced by 14,000 individual school boards. Parents seeking improved education and businesses seeking skilled graduates, however, have combined to pressure state governments to become active on the education front. Many states have responded by requiring students to pass exams showing a degree of mastery of key subjects, in addition to imposing certain curricular standards. In some cases, states have even taken charge of persistently failing local schools.

For well over a decade, there has been a recurring debate over establishing national standards in certain core subjects. The effort started with the George H. W. Bush administration, which provided financial support for the National History Standards Project.[57] In the Goals 2000: Educate America Act of March 1994, the Clinton administration and Congress added their support for the development of national curriculum standards. National bodies of scientists, mathematicians, historians, and academics from other disciplines have developed their own recommendations for a national curriculum. Particularly in the field of mathematics and science, they have had some impact on the content standards developed by individual states. By way of contrast, the proposed history standard was immediately caught up in a swirl of controversy over what critics saw as its emphasis on individuals, groups, and civilizations—to either the neglect or denigration of Western civilization.[58]

In his campaign for the presidency, George W. Bush emphasized his active role in working to improve elementary and secondary education in Texas. As president, he has worked closely with Congress and garnered bipartisan support for educational reforms that linked federal aid to periodic testing in the states. Under the new legislation, students stuck in failing schools (as measured by the tests) would have a right to transfer to a new public school in the same district.[59]

The ferment in American education is being driven by the commitment to equal opportunity, the desire for economic growth, the needs of local corporations, and the sense of urgency among many parents. As early as Reagan's second term, the U.S. Department of Education looked overseas and went so far as to issue its own report on the Japanese elementary and secondary school system.[60] The report did not, however, appear to have a direct impact on departmental policy. The Japanese challenge helped to create the debate but Japanese practices have not, as yet, played much of a direct role.

Thinking Long Term

In the 1970s and 1980s, Japan was almost universally described as taking the long view. Japanese companies were said to focus on long-term goals rather than being consumed by measuring their performance quarter by quarter to meet Wall Street's expectations. Like European firms, Japanese firms were intent on being active institutions that would achieve a kind of secular immortality.

The Japanese government was often described in similar terms. MITI published visions defining the next decade of progress for the Japanese economy and Japanese society. A story circulated in Washington of an elderly Japanese scholar who had prepared a century-long view of future developments in Japanese science. He was reportedly criticized for taking too short a view.

For American corporations facing Japanese competition, the question of the longer view often translated into a Japanese company's tolerance for low profits (or even losses) while manufacturing experience was acquired and market share built. The challenge was often compounded for small U.S. companies facing diversified Japanese firms that could use the profits from one division to patiently nurture a newer enterprise. A pattern of cross-shareholding by major Japanese companies meant that they were essentially impervious to hostile takeovers. Patient Japanese investors seemed willing to take their dividends in rising wages and job security while accepting very low returns on their stock holdings.

Japanese firms poured money into new plant and equipment.[61] From the viewpoint of the late 1990s, it is clear that these high rates of Japanese investment in plant and equipment posed a significant challenge to American manufacturers.

The U.S. private sector responded in a variety of ways. Companies reorganized to become more innovative and efficient. The added sense of efficiency extended to their use of capital. Large public and some private pension funds began to express their concern about companies' failures to invest in the future. Edward Regan, then the head of New York State's public pensions fund, urged the Securities and Exchange Commission to require firms to report their levels of investment in plant, equipment, and research.[62] In *The Competitive Advantage of Nations* and later in *Capital Choices,* Harvard Business School professor Michael Porter proposed public policies and corporate reforms that would support needed investments in research and training as well as plant and equipment.[63] All this effort was influenced by the Japanese challenge, but little of it represented the adoption of Japanese policies or practices.

Public–Private Partnerships

Even at the height of the Japanese challenge in the late 1980s, no one really thought there was a "Japan, Incorporated," in which government initiative and corporate strategy formed a seamless whole. But, the much greater degree of cooperation between the Japanese government and Japanese corporations was widely seen and widely accepted as one of many factors that contributed to Japanese economic success.

The Japanese example had a profound affect on political leaders in both parties. Particularly for Democrats, Japan helped to introduce a new strand of thinking about how to work with business to foster growth, job creation, and innovation. In a broader sense, it contributed to the idea that the power of markets could be harnessed to a variety of national purposes.

The Japanese example was also a lesson for state and local political leaders. Public–private partnerships are now a common feature in state and local efforts to attract industry, stimulate employment, improve education, and strengthen universities. The same is increasingly true at the federal level in the fields of education, training, technology, and trade. American entrepreneurship and pragmatism deserve much of the credit. But the Japanese example played an important role.

Systemic Thinking

Japan forced the United States to think of its economy in systemic terms. Japan worked differently, and it worked well. Why? How did the pieces of its economic system fit together so effectively, even though Japan violated traditional American rules of thumb, such as open markets and effective antitrust policies? After looking at Japan, Americans thought more about macroeconomic policies as part of a long-term growth strategy as well as a tool for fighting short-term unemployment. Education, training, the national climate for innovation, and a host of other factors emerged as parts of an overall system rather than isolated pieces of the national economic landscape. American political leaders and the broader policy community began to see the interdependence of economic factors. Access to foreign markets was not just part of a trade strategy but also an often-critical aspect of an innovation system in which today's invention was tomorrow's export, in which today's export earnings fueled tomorrow's research and development. Education, training, and lifelong learning emerged as foundation stones for growth, innovation, and a dynamic way of helping to achieve income equality. In helping public as well as private America think systemically about its economy and its future, Japan had its most lasting impact.

Notes

1. As chancellor (and then president) of the University of Massachusetts, Joseph Duffey was so concerned about the state of the American manufacturing base that he introduced one of the first degrees in manufacturing to be offered by an American university. (Author's interview with Joe Duffey, 1999.)

2. See, for instance, Clyde V. Prestowitz Jr., *Trading Places: How We Allowed Japan to Take the Lead* (New York: Basic Books, 1988), 141. Also see Richard Katz, *Japan: The System That Soured—The Rise and Fall of the Japanese Economic Miracle* (Armonk, N.Y.: M. E. Sharpe, 1998), 176–77.

3. As noted in Chalmers Johnson, *MITI and the Japanese Miracle: The Growth of Industrial Policy, 1925–1975* (Stanford, Calif.: Stanford University Press, 1982), 283.

4. *Business Week,* May 7, 1970, as quoted in Johnson, *MITI and the Japanese Miracle,* 292.

5. For a useful summary of the early view, see Katz, *Japan,* 291. As its title suggests,

Katz's chapter 13, "Beyond Revisionism and Traditionalism," usefully summarizes the debate between economists and political observers who saw Japan as being a market democracy similar to the United States and those who saw a Japan that was organized quite differently in economic and political terms (pp. 289–317).

6. See, for instance, Eric Garfinkle, *Roadmap for Results: Trade Policy, Technology, and American Competitiveness* (Washington, D.C.: Council on Competitiveness, 1993), 33–34. In response to antidumping duties imposed on active-matrix flat-panel displays in 1991, significant portions of U.S. laptop computer assembly shifted offshore.

7. Katz, *Japan,* 299.

8. Ezra Vogel, *Japan as No. 1: Lessons for America* (Cambridge, Mass.: Harvard University Press, 1979).

9. Vogel, *Japan as No. 1,* 21.

10. Otis L. Graham Jr., *Losing Time: The Industrial Policy Debate* (Cambridge, Mass.: Harvard University Press, 1992), 133.

11. Vogel, *Japan as No. 1,* chap. 4, "The State: Meritocratic Guidance and Private Initiative," 53–96.

12. "Vision for the 1980s": Basic Course of MITI's Trade-Industry Policy," *Oriental Economist,* November 1979, 12–16.

13. "Japan's Strategy for the 1980s," *Business Week,* December 14, 1981, 39–120; see, particularly, "Semiconductors," 53–64, and "Information Processing," 65–87.

14. Johnson, *MITI and the Japanese Miracle.*

15. Robert Z. Lawrence, "International Trade Policy in the 1990s," in *American Economic Policy in the 1990s,* ed. Jeffrey A. Frankel and Peter R. Orszag (Cambridge, Mass.: MIT Press, 2002).

16. William J. Abernathy and Robert H. Hayes, "Managing Our Way to Economic Decline," *Harvard Business Review,* July–August 1980, 67–77.

17. Bruce R. Scott, George C. Lodge, and Joseph L Bower, eds., *U.S. Competitiveness in the World Economy* (Cambridge, Mass.: Harvard University Press, 1985).

18. "Summit 91" was held July 19–20; "Summit 92" was held on September 16–18. Both summits took place at the Broadmoor Hotel in Colorado Springs.

19. George C. Lodge, *The American Disease* (New York: Alfred A. Knopf, 1984).

20. Jean-Jacques Servan-Schreiber, *The American Challenge* (New York: Avon, 1969). The book was originally published in French as *Le défi américain* in 1967.

21. Servan-Schreiber, *American Challenge,* 31.

22. Karel van Wolferen, "The Japan Problem," *Foreign Affairs,* winter 1986–87, 288–303.

23. Karel van Wolferen, *The Enigma of Japanese Power* (New York: Alfred A. Knopf, 1989).

24. Van Wolferen, "Japan Problem," 289.

25. James Fallows, "The Japanese Are Different from You and Me," *Atlantic Monthly,* September 1986, 35–41.

26. James Fallows, "The Rice Plot," *Atlantic Monthly,* January 1987, 22.

27. James Fallows, "Playing by Different Rules," *Atlantic Monthly,* September 1987, 22–32.

28. James Fallows, "Containing Japan," *Atlantic Monthly,* May 1989, 40–54.

29. James Fallows, "Getting Along with Japan," *Atlantic Monthly,* December 1989, 53–64.

30. Fallows, "Getting Along with Japan," 53.

31. Prestowitz, *Trading Places.*

32. Daniel Burstein, *Yen! Japan's New Financial Empire and Its Threat to America* (New York: Simon & Schuster, 1988).

33. Shintaro Ishihara and Akio Morita, *The Japan That Can Say "No,"* unofficial translation, 1989.

34. Ishihara and Morita, *Japan,* 3.

35. Clyde V. Prestowitz Jr., *Trading Places: How We Are Giving Our Future to Japan and How to Reclaim It,* paperback edition (New York: Basic Books, 1989), 4.

36. David Sanger, "Seeing a Dependent and Declining U.S., More Japanese Adopt a Nationalistic Spirit," *New York Times,* August 4, 1989.

37. Lawrence Summers, "What to Do When Japan Says 'No,'" *New York Times,* December 3, 1989.

38. Morita and Ishihara, *Japan,* 13. See also Urban C. Lehner, "A Japanese Nationalist Finds a Wide Audience for His Racial Theory," *Wall Street Journal,* November 7, 1989.

39. Akio Morita and Shintaor Ishihara, *The Japan That Can Say No: The New U.S.–Japan Relations Card* (Tokyo: Kobunsha, 1989).

40. See Woondo Choi, "Japanese Bargaining Behavior and U.S.–Japan Relationship: FSX Co-Development Project," *2001 Global Economic Review* 30, no. 1. See also Prestowitz, *Trading Places* (1988), 300–1.

41. See, for instance, P. J. Pempel, *Regime Shift: Comparative Dynamics of the Japanese Political Economy* (Ithaca, N.Y.: Cornell Univesity Press, 1998).

42. See Katz, *Japan,* chap. 14, "Interregnum: Whither Japan," 318–46.

43. This was also the author's personal experience after joining the staff of Senator Vance Hartke (D-Ind.) in 1972.

44. Katz, *Japan,* 295.

45. I. M. Destler, *American Trade Politics,* 2nd ed. (Washington, D.C.: Institute for International Economics with the Twentieth Century Fund, 1992), 128.

46. Sematech is discussed briefly (pp. 406–7) in Daniel Roos, Frank Field, and James Neely, "Industry Consortia," in *Investing in Innovation: Creating a Research and Innovation Policy That Works,* ed. Lewis M. Branscomb and James H. Keller (Cambridge, Mass.: MIT Press, 1998). For a longer discussion of Sematech, see John Horrigan, "Cooperation Among Competitors in Research Consortia: The Evolution of MCC and Sematech," Ph.D. dissertation, Lyndon B. Johnson School of Public Affairs, University of Texas, December 1996.

47. SEMI (for Semiconductor Equipment and Materials International) is a private organization representing the global semiconductor equipment and materials industry. SEMI often worked closely with Sematech, but Semi-Sematech was a creature of Sematech itself.

48. See the statement by Robert W. Galvin (then chairman of the board and chief executive of Motorola) before the U.S. Senate Foreign Relations Committee, September 14, 1982, p. 6. (I relied on a reprint from Motorola generously provided by Sue R. Topp, manager of the Motorola archives.)

49. Webb-Pomerene Act, U.S. Code, title 45, chap. 2, subchap. II, soc. 61; see http://www4.law.cornell.edu/uscode/15/61/html.

50. Export Trading Company Act, U.S. Code, title 12, chap. 17, soc. 1841; see http://www4.law.cornell.edu/uscode/12/1841/html.

51. For a discussion of the Advanced Technology Program, see Christopher T. Hill, "The Advanced Technology Program," in Branscomb and Kellers, eds., *Investing in Innovation,* 143–73.

52. Author's interview with Patrick Windham, October 25, 1999.

53. President's Commission on Industrial Competitiveness, *Global Competition: The New Realtity* (Washington, D.C.: U.S. Government Printing Office, 1985), vol. 1, 51.

54. Interview with Windham.

55. For a largely sympathetic view of Japanese education, see Merry White, *The Japanese Educational Challenge: A Commitment to Children* (New York: Kodansha International, 1987).

56. In a tour of a Motorola plant that made the cells for cell phones, they explained their emphasis on training and the shift to a high-performance workplace to the late secretary of commerce, Ron Brown. After a tour of the plant, Motorola used a series of slides to brief the late secretary on workplace practices they had adopted and why they adopted them. The first slide simply said "survival."

57. For a brief history of the development of history standards for elementary and secondary schools, see National Center for History in the Schools, *National Standards for History: Basic Education* (Los Angeles: National Center for History in the Schools at UCLA, 1996). The report can be found online at http://www.ucla.edu/nchs/standards/preface.html.

58. See, for instance, Gary Putka, "Historians Propose Curriculum Tilted Away from West, Critics Worry Contribution of Europeans, Americans Will Not Get Proper Due," *Wall Street Journal,* November 11, 1994, and Guy Gugliotta, "World History Teaching Standards Draw Critics: As With American Guidelines Last Month, Dissenters Say Western Contributions Shortchanged," *Washington Post,* November 11, 1994.

59. The "No Child Left Behind Act of 2001" (PL 107-110) was signed by President George W. Bush on January 8, 2002. For details of the law, go to the Department of Education's Web site, http://ed.gov/legislation/ESEA02/.

60. U.S. Department of Education, *Japanese Education Today* (Washington, D.C.: U.S. Government Printing Office, 1987).

61. Council on Competitiveness, *Competitiveness Index 1990* (Washington, D.C.: Council on Competitiveness, 1990), 5.

62. Author's interview by telephone with Edward Regan, August 19, 2002. Regan served on both the President's Council on Industrial Competitiveness (the Young Commission) and the Capital Formation Subcouncil of the Competitiveness Policy Council, an independent federal advisory committee established by the Omnibus Trade and Competitiveness Act of 1988. At the time, Regan was the comptroller of the State of New York and in charge of the state pension fund.

63. Michael E. Porter, *The Competitive Advantage of Nations* (New York: Free Press, 1990); and Porter, *Capital Choices: Changing the Way America Invests in Industry* (Washington, D.C.: Council on Competitiveness, 1992).

Chapter 4

Looking Abroad for Answers: Rising Germany, the Specter of Britain, and the Clash of Capitalisms

In the 1970s and the early 1980s, there was relatively little focus on the specifics of the German economic miracle, the details of subsequent German economic policies, or the structure of German industry. The key point was the sharp contrast between German growth and American stagnation.

Germany's rapid recovery from the devastation of World War II was not unexpected. Germany had been a major economic power before World War II with a strong presence in a number of key industries. Achieving industrial strength was more a return to long-established patterns than an unexpected challenge to American economic might. Germany did, however, pose a broad question to political leaders in the United States. By the early 1980s, Germany managed to combine a high standard of living, rapid productivity growth, and low unemployment. If Germany could do it, why could the United States not do it?

German success was certainly a spur to American action. But it did not trigger the same exhaustive examination of American policies, business practices, and institutions as did Japan. Why? There are several plausible explanations. First, German industrial strength was spread over a broad array of products. Its export success did not depend on dominance in a few select areas. Second, much of German strength was in intermediate products. With the notable exception of German automobiles, German exports were relatively invisible to the American public. Third, German strength was often in familiar areas. The return of German machine tool, chemical, and pharmaceutical concerns was not a total surprise to their American counterparts. Finally, Germany did not emerge as a major competitor in high-technology sectors that were viewed in America as an American preserve and a key to America's industrial future. As a result, even though Germany was often the world's largest single exporter and, at times, had a larger current account surplus relative to the size of its economy than Japan, German exports—sold more to companies than consumers—remained, again, relatively invisible to the public. As a result, German exports did not become a major issue in the debate over economic policy.

The relative openness of the German economy to international trade and investment also made a significant difference. Congress heard few complaints from American exporters about access to the German market or about subsidized German exports in third-country markets. The large number of American-based multinationals successfully operating in Germany created a political force that highlighted the lack of trade and investment barriers in the German economy. In the 1970s, and early 1980s, there was no similar cluster of American companies successfully participating in the Japanese economy.

Sheer familiarity may have also played a role. More Americans trace their ancestry to Germany than to any other single country. World wars had dimmed those ties (many Schmidts became Smiths during and after World War I), but there was still a broad understanding of German culture. German institutions were reasonably well known. German banks were different —they combine commercial, merchant, and investment banking functions that were long kept separate by America's Depression-era banking laws. But even the dominant role of Germany's universal banks looked familiar to students of American business history who remembered the House of Morgan.[1]

This is not to say that German policy was totally ignored. The early search abroad for examples of industrial policies included Germany, but in general found that much strategic thinking about the overall direction of German industry was left to the market, individual firms, or the major German banks.[2] As the debate shifted from international trade to industrial policy to the broader search for a national competitiveness strategy, several elements of the German economy did influence American political leaders, their staffs and, in particular, Washington think tanks. The German system of education and training had an impact on American thinking and, eventually, policy. German support for technology development also stimulated a new approach in American policy, especially the practice of diffusing innovations to small and medium-sized enterprises. The German practice of involving union representatives in a wider range of corporate decisions was of particular interest to organized labor but did not have a major impact on business governance in the United States.

The close relationships between German banks and German industrial corporations became part of the early 1990s American debate over the pattern of investments made by American corporations. At the time, many political and business leaders argued that the pressures of Wall Street investors for quarterly results led American companies to avoid the kind of long-term, riskier investments that were critical for sustained economic success. They pointed to the close relationship between corporations and banks that allowed German (and Japanese) corporations to take a longer view of an investment's payoff.

German macroeconomic policy was also one of the keys to the German economic miracle. In particular, the Bundesbank, the German equivalent of America's Federal Reserve, acquired a reputation for probity. It was viewed as a hawk's hawk when it came to controlling inflation. In a general sense, the Bundesbank's refusal to tolerate inflation, coupled with Germany's economic success in the 1980s, probably helped strengthen the hand of the Federal Reserve in the United States. Beyond that, however, it is not clear that German spending or monetary policies had any direct influence on the development of macroeconomic policies as part of a larger competitiveness strategy.

Germany figured in the debate over industrial policy but was not central to it. In their early proposal for an American industrial policy, Ira Magaziner and Robert Reich discussed the elements of a German policy that supported industry.[3] In their view, the German government helped grow business by investing in infrastructure, science, and other areas where the "public return on investment is likely to exceed the private return."[4] They also found that German support for workers and communities reduced political opposition to economic change and that in some instances governments restructured "industries to take better advantage of growth opportunities"[5] though they indicated that "the German government . . . played a less direct role than other governments in [affecting] industrial structure."[6]

At the very beginning of the 1990s, Harvard Business School professor Michael Porter published his enormously influential *The Competitive Advantage of Nations*. Where Magaziner and Reich were focused on the question of a government's industrial policy and how it might contribute to future economic growth, Porter posed a different problem. Instead of starting with government or macroeconomic performance, he asked what made individual firms and whole industries competitive. He developed what he called "the diamond of national advantage."[7] Porter's diamond was made up of "four broad attributes of a nation":[8]

1. Factor conditions—including skilled labor and infrastructure,
2. Demand conditions—everything from the size of the domestic market to the expectations of consumers,
3. Related and supporting industries—internationally competitive supplier industries that contribute to the competitiveness of other industries, and
4. Firm strategy, structure, and rivalry—how firms are created and managed as well as the degree of rivalry or competition for firms in a particular industry.

Where Magaziner and Reich detail German initiatives that aid the adjustment of declining industries and support the development of new ones, Porter found the principal role of the German government had " been factor creation, especially in education and science and technology."[9] Porter found that "German workers and managers have a high and sustained commitment to their industry" that was "sustained [and] reinforced by the German capital markets."[10] German banks held a significant portion of the shares of German companies and played a prominent role on their boards.

These three features of the German system—education and training, science and technology, and what came to be called "patient capital"—became important aspects of the debate that led to a national competitiveness strategy.

Training for Today's Work

As Porter notes, "German factor creation mechanisms begin with the public educational system which is rigorous and of high quality."[11] At a relatively young age, German students were guided into two educational tracks. One led to the university, whereas the other led to an elaborate system of apprenticeships, combining education with hands-on business or industrial experience.

The contrast with much of the American education system was stark. Even at the dawn of the twenty-first century, many Americans still believe it is college or nothing. Vocational education—America's general answer to the German apprenticeship system—does not command the same level of respect and offers less in the way of rigorous, academic preparation.

If the vocational education programs lagged behind in terms of preparing U.S. students for the world of work, the general education courses offered to the non-college-bound too often provided even less. In his 1995 book *Rethinking America,* former *New York Times* reporter Hedrick Smith highlights the contrast between the two systems.[12] The television version of his book, *Challenge to America*, made the point in visually powerful terms. Smith followed the smooth transition of a German apprentice to the world of work and then looked at an average American high school graduate who spent several years drifting from one low-skill job to the next before settling on a more permanent direction.

The structured German approach to education for students choosing work rather than college stimulated a different approach to vocational education in many parts of the United States. Certainly by the mid-1990s, many school districts were working with companies to combine academic and workplace skills.

The German system also has had some impact on federal policy. In the early days of the Clinton administration, Congress approved legislation creating a school-to-work program in the Department of Labor. As with many Clinton administration initiatives, the scope and scale of the program were constrained by the ongoing realities of fiscal deficits and the importance deficit reduction played in the administration's overall economic strategy. The Labor Department's school-to-work office funded a number of initiatives around the country and sought to inspire many more by the force of its example. There was a clear emphasis on work as well as school. Businesses and business associations were looked to as critical partners.

The school-to-work approach continues to influence the thinking of school boards around the country. But, the program itself ran into some significant opposition. Many feared that school-to-work was just a fancy name for tracking their children into a low-skill, low-wage future. Some feared that more business-oriented curricula might demand too little and leave their students unprepared for citizenship, higher learning, or the appreciation of American culture. In many cases, teachers had chosen their profession in order to share learning, not to impart skills. When Republicans swept to power in the 1994 congressional elections, they were committed to limited government and reducing the fiscal deficit. At the time, they were intent on eliminating or limiting the Clinton administration's initiatives, and the administration itself moved on to other priorities.[13]

The shifting political winds in Washington could not, however, reduce the growing need for skilled workers. Whether directly inspired by the German example or not, American companies began to pursue their own version of school-to-work initiatives. In the 1990s, leading software companies such as Microsoft and Novell began to award certificates indicating mastery of various software applications. Though they were not linked to schools, they did provide non-college-bound students (or college graduates seeking new skills) with a structured alternative to the "learning by drift" described by Smith. In 1997, Cisco, a major provider of the hardware for the Internet, adopted an explicit school-to-work approach in its Cisco academies. High school students took an academic core curriculum during part of the day and worked on Cisco systems during the rest. In many cases, they also ran the computer systems in their local schools—adding to their learning and providing a service to the school. Graduates of the program were certified to administer a range of Cisco systems.[14]

The German and other European apprenticeship systems also contributed to the formation of the National Skill Standards Board (NSSB). Created by the National Skill Standards Act of 1994, the NSSB was initially focused on setting skill standards that would be nationally recognized—as apprenticeship training was in Germany and other parts of Europe.[15] Clear standards would help students and schools target their training on needed skills. At the same time, nationally recognized skill standards would ease the transition of workers from troubled to healthy firms and would also facilitate geographic mobility.

While the NSSB was working to develop standards, it was also gathering information on the welter of standards that were already being generated by the private sector. Like time and tide, markets, it would seem, wait for no government. Showing typical American flexibility, the NSSB turned to setting standards while, at the same time, stimulating the creation of standards in other areas. From the start, the NSSB was due to expire after a five-year life. In 2003, a successor organization, the National Skills Standards Board Institute, was created to continue the work started by the NSSB.[16]

The private and public sectors were beginning to adapt to changing economic circumstances in a way that contributed to the strength of the overall economy. Beyond the specifics of an individual public program or private initiative, the institutional adaptability of America's public and private sectors emerges as a critical American strength.

Building Technology: Government, Industry, and Universities

Germany carried into the postwar world a number of prewar patterns. There was the vaunted German commitment to engineering excellence, the habit of hard work, and a sense that national destiny was tied to economic prosperity. "'Chemistry not colonies' was a popular refrain in prewar [World War I] Germany."[17] Innovation not imperialism (though Germany sought colonies as well) was a key to raw material independence.

This German strength in science and technology reemerged as Germany rebuilt on the ruble and ruin of World War II. German industry and the German government played important and complementary roles in developing German technology. Magaziner and Reich found in Germany "the most direct government efforts to promote new products and processes."[18] They pointed to the 1972 founding of the Ministry of Technology as the point at which "Germany became extensively involved in selectively funding projects with specific commercial potential."[19] Writing almost a decade later, Porter found similar strengths. In his view, Germany had "perhaps the most effective structure for commercial research and development of any nation."[20] Porter points to shared government and industry funding of research institutes and the sponsorship of university research by company and industry associations.

Germany was particularly adept at bringing new technologies to German industry. Government and industry shared the cost of the Fraunhofer Gesellschaft, which had the mandate to "expedite the application of new technologies in German industry."[21] Japan had a different system that was also effective in rapidly diffusing new technologies to small and medium-sized enterprises.[22]

The German and Japanese examples and America's own experience with the Agricultural Extension Service led to proposals for a similar service focused on manufacturing. Senator Ernest F. Hollings (D-S.C.), an early advocate of improving America's innovation system, sponsored legislation establishing a handful of manufacturing (or Hollings) centers in the mid-1980s. The Omnibus Trade and Competitiveness Act of 1988 (see chapters 7 and 8 below) provided for additional manufacturing extension centers. President Clinton made the centers part of his overall competitiveness strategy. By the mid-1990s, the Manufacturing Extension Partnership program had formed a national system that put a center or office within easy reach of the more than 370,000 small and medium-sized manufacturers in the United States.

Although the German system of diffusing technology had the most immediate effect on America's innovation system, the emphasis on industry consortia, closer ties to universities, and the close links between training and the spread of technology all had an impact.[23] The private-sector Council on Competitiveness saw the "German system . . . as a source of ideas—ideas that, if adapted to an American context, could help maintain U.S. technological leadership."[24]

Building the Future: Patient Capital and Competitive Industries

American corporations were described as having short time horizons, with Americans in general suffering from a kind of "short-termism." America's corporate and national culture was often viewed as part of the problem. In his 1992 *Capital Choices: Changing the Way America Invests in Industry*, Michael Porter pointed to "American corporate goals . . . centered on earning high returns on investment and maximizing current stock prices," while "in both the Japanese and German companies, the dominant goal is to ensure the perpetuation of the enterprise."[25] In a mid-1980s speech, Richard Darman, a senior official in the Bush and Reagan administrations, spoke of American "Now, Nowism." In a general sense, he thought that too many Americans were following the spirit of a then-popular cereal ad—they wanted their "Maypo and they wanted it now."[26]

Broader economic circumstances also mattered. The steep recession of the early 1980s, an overvalued dollar, and a high cost of capital made many previously attractive investments uneconomic. The financial markets created their own pressures. In the midst of recession and rising international competition, American firms were faced with a wave of hostile takeovers and leveraged buyouts. A new set of investors demanded higher returns and sought to free unused or, in their view, misused capital for other purposes. High debt levels were viewed not as part of a prudent mix of capital assets but as a financial tool to force changes in management behavior. As academics and financial specialists looked back at the "Deal Decade" of the 1980s, they saw rational and often successful restructuring of "firms in slow-growing and declining industries" turn into "a fad driven by the machinery invented to facilitate the deals."[27]

Germany and Japan stood in stark contrast. Their workers' and firms' incomes and productivity were rising rapidly, both were successfully competing in the international arena, and capital was widely available and at a lower than American cost. Rates of investment were high, and there seemed to be a willingness in German and Japanese firms to look to the long run. What explained the difference? At the time, most observers—

whether from the business, policy, or academic communities—stressed the importance of the different financial structure in Germany and Japan. In Japan, the major industrial conglomerates (or *keiretsu*) had their own lead bank that provided capital and influenced management. In Germany, the major banks provided capital, influenced management, and took seats on corporate boards. By contrast, the U.S. financial system was more fragmented, with commercial banking separated from investment banking and both constrained from holding securities. Whatever their strengths, American banks were less likely to have the same detailed knowledge of an individual firm or to have such a deep financial stake in the long-term health of an enterprise.

While America did not rush to adopt the German approach, Germany forced Americans to rethink their own system, shift their focus to the longer term, and emphasize the importance of investment generally and the need for complementary investments that ranged from equipment to training and from short to long-term. Institutional investors—mutual funds, pensions funds, insurance companies, and so forth—which had increased "their holdings from 8 percent of total equity in 1950 to almost 60 percent in 1990"[28]— began to talk to corporations about their long-term performance. Some boards of directors became more active in demanding better short-term and long-term performance from managers. Competitive pressures demanding short-term results led to public policies that encouraged investment in basic as opposed to near-to-market technologies.[29] The higher cost of capital and pressure from the financial markets also forced American managers to be more effective in managing their financial resources. America looked at Germany, learned, and adapted the American system to move closer to German-like results.

The German Export Machine

The German success in exporting contributed to the shift in American thinking from largely domestic to global markets. With a much smaller economy, Germany often challenged the United States for the title of world's largest exporter.[30] In product after product, Germany offered high-quality and steady improvements.

Government policy was also supportive. Magaziner and Reich pointed to Germany's "elaborate system of incentives for overseas marketing," which ranged from export credit guarantees to encouraging investments in developing countries.[31] German institutions and practice were usually matched elsewhere in Europe and, if anything, exceeded by Japan's.

America has its own set of export-related institutions. Export guarantees are available for major capital sales through the Export-Import Bank. The Overseas Private Investment Corporation offers political risk insurance for overseas investments, and the Trade and Development Agency pays for feasibility studies in developing countries. An American company pays for such a study only if it actually wins a contract. The State Department and then the Commerce Department (after 1979) provided overseas support through commercial offices in key export markets.

For America, however, exports generally came second. For many years, market access was important, but containing the Soviet Union was the real international mission. Whereas a British prime minister might call a foreign leader to support a British firm fighting for an overseas contract, American presidents and Cabinet officials had other priorities. Bit by bit, American policy as well as industry changed in response to global competition. But the major push on export policy would wait until the 1990s, after the Cold War had ended.

In sum, German and European institutions did lead to some institutional innovation in the United States. German and European influence can be seen in education, the approach to diffusing technology, and the growing cooperation between government and industry. Their emphasis on exports, their success in export markets, and the contribution their exports made to their overall economic performance also had a lasting influence on American policy and practice.

Britain: The Fallen Titan

At various points in U.S. history, there have been fears that America was at the point of irretrievable decay. From the early nineteenth century onward, for brief periods, the specter of Rome's decline and fall haunted American thinkers. In the 1980s, it was the example of Britain's decline and fall that fed fears about America's economic future. Critics dismissed much of the writing about America's troubled competitive position as overwrought "declinist literature." The fear of decline, however, was real.

Britain was shadow before it was substance. At first, there was little attempt to explore the extensive literature on the British economy or the economic aspects of the British Empire. It was enough that what had once been the workshop of the world had slipped from the first rank of economic powers. It was enough that Britain had been great and was great no longer. In the 1970s and early 1980s, there was little focus on the complicated balancing act Britain faced at the turn of the twentieth century when it sought to maintain its military and economic superiority while faced with the rise of industrial and political rivals.

Most Americans know more about the United Kingdom than about any other foreign country. Even close neighbors Canada and Mexico do not occupy quite the same place in national thinking as does Britain. The common language, the shared political institutions, the enduring impact of English culture, and the political alliances forged in World I, World War II, and the Cold War all made Britain seem closer and more understandable.

In the 1970s and 1980s, even young congressional aides could remember when maps of the world showed a ring of British imperial red. In 1900, Britain "possessed the largest empire the world had ever seen, some twelve million square miles of land and perhaps a quarter of the population of the globe."[32] The triumphant Britain of 1945 looked back on the innovations of the war years and forward to unequaled prosperity. Britain was one of the three great powers that met to establish the borders of the new Europe. Lord Keynes and the American Treasury's Harry Dexter White took the lead in designing a postwar economic system that would contribute to peace and prosperity. "The British took it for granted that Great Britain was, and would always remain, a first rate power."[33] "It was certainly in no man's mind and certainly no man's intention that the next forty years should see Britain diminished to fourteenth place in the non-communist world in terms of Gross National Product per head."[34] Commentators and competitors began to refer to the British disease, "a combination of militant trade unionism, poor management, 'stop-go' policies by government, and negative cultural attitudes toward hard work and entrepreneurship."[35] Where once the sun had never set (on the British Empire) now, it would seem, the sun seldom smiled.

As the competitiveness debate moved into the 1990s, historians helped the policy world take a more detailed look at the relative decline of Britain's position in the world. In the competitiveness debate, three broad themes emerged from the more thorough exploration of the British economy: First, empire—or, more generally, global commitments—can slow the growth of the very economy that underpins global strength. Second, culture matters—

attitudes toward business, work, and risk taking can be critical parts of the intangible "software" that makes a national system productive. And third, comprehensive domestic investment is critical to growth—including broad-based training as well as elite education, technology as well as basic science.

The Wages of Empire

In the late nineteenth century, the United Kingdom was faced with the emergence of new geopolitical as well as economic rivals. Germany and the United States both passed Britain in terms of iron and steel production. Both economies were moving ahead in chemicals and a number of fields where British businesses had failed to take the lead. The same technological innovations that were fueling economic growth in Britain and around the world were creating added pressures on a global empire. For instance, with the spread of railroads, Russia was now in a position to threaten British interests in Afghanistan and even the jewel in the British crown, India.[36] The spread of shipbuilding and shipbuilding technologies created naval rivals in the Atlantic (the United States), in the Pacific (Japan), and especially in the North Atlantic (Germany).

In Paul Kennedy's terms, Britain suffered, as had other great powers in the past, from "imperial overstretch,"[37] in which global commitments eventually outran or even undermined domestic economic strength. After World War I, Britain moved quickly to maintain its empire and regain its economic prominence. By setting its exchange rate at a prewar level, Britain unintentionally put its manufactures at a competitive disadvantage in world markets and slowed domestic economic recovery. After World War II, Britain sought to affirm its great-power status. Again, the exchange rate was set at a level that put its manufactures at a disadvantage. Overseas garrisons and global ambitions competed for funds that might have been devoted to domestic investments. Britain did invest in research, but much of its spending was focused on national defense rather than on the civilian economy.

Was the United States making similar mistakes? It was leading the effort to contain Soviet communism while Germany and particularly Japan spent relatively little on national defense. Much of the U.S. research effort was focused on national defense rather than the civilian economy. America even seemed to have forgotten its own recent experience with the exchange rate. While President Nixon broke with a regime of fixed exchange rates to make

U.S. industry more competitive in international markets, President Reagan's initial combination of restrictive monetary and expansive fiscal policies put U.S. industry at a disadvantage by driving up the value of the dollar.

Culture Counts

British culture also came under attack. The decline of British workmanship, the elite preference for careers in government as opposed to industry, and the commitment to science rather than technology all seemed to find some rough counterpart in 1980s America. Well into the 1960s, American products had been the envy of the world. That place had now been lost to German engineering and the Japanese commitment to quality. To many observers, lawyers and investment bankers were taking the place of the engineers that had helped win the war and sent Americans to the moon. America still led the world in Nobel Prizes but seemed suddenly to lag behind its competitors in process and product innovation.

Investing in the Future

Still other observers stressed the failure of British industry and the British government to make the array of investments to ensure a competitive future. In *The Pride and the Fall*, Correlli Barnett singles out as a key error Britain's post–World War II failure to invest in broad-based technical education supportive of industry.[38] In *The Competitive Advantage of Nations*, Porter also cites the lack of investment in workers' skills as one of the crucial factors explaining Britain's relative decline as well as a key to British revival.[39]

In the nineteenth and early twentieth centuries, Britain had built much of the world's infrastructure. American railways, Brazilian streetcars, and Argentine power plants were more often than not financed by British capital. Americans who watched the steady stream of American capital and technology flowing overseas asked if Britain would have been stronger had it invested more at home.[40]

The more thoughtful reflections on Britain did have their own impact on the competitiveness debate and the policies it spawned. They supported policy ideas that had already been formed out of new analytic work, America's own economic past, or the successes of Germany and Japan. The British experience added to the growing emphasis on the need for improved education, engineering excellence, and long-term investments. But, in the end, it was Britain's relative decline that acted as both spur and specter to the Americans fighting to improve the U.S. competitive position.

Systems at War: The Competition of Capitalisms

As the United States and American companies struggled to regain their competitive footing, the question of systemic differences came more and more to the fore. It started with economic policy but eventually encompassed the whole fabric of a society. In *The American Disease,* Harvard Business School professor George C. Lodge called for a shift in American ideology and the need for a new moral basis to justify the American corporation.[41] American University professor Steven D. Cohen, a longtime student of Washington policymaking as well as United States–Japan economic relations, put a colorful label on the systemic differences in his *Cowboys and Samurai: Why the United States Is Losing the Battle with the Japanese and Why It Matters.*[42] In *The End of the American Century,* Steven Schlosstein anticipated the 1990s debate over Asian values by pointing to the East Asian emphasis on family, work, and education.[43]

The most explicit comparison of the three different systems—the Anglo-American, the Japanese, and the European—came in Lester Thurow's *Head to Head: The Coming Economic Battle among Japan, Europe, and America,* which looks at the strengths and weaknesses of Europe, Japan, and the United States.[44] After assessing the three economic giants, Thurow concludes that "future historians will record that the twenty-first century belonged to the House of Europe!"[45]

From the perspective of the early twenty-first century, Thurow looks woefully wide of the mark. Before being too quick to give your copy of *Head to Head* to the church bazaar, however, there are several points to make in defense of Thurow. First, he identifies many of the weaknesses in Europe and Japan that become even clearer from the perspective of a new century. Second, he was clearly writing for the very long term. He sees, for example, a Europe that could eventually draw on the scientific strengths of Russia. Third, his analysis of the weaknesses in American fiscal finances and elementary and secondary education were very much on target.

In *The Competitive Advantage of Nations,* Porter took a more detailed look at a number of countries. In addition to the "big three" of Germany, Japan, and the United States, he assessed the competitive advantage of

Britain, Italy, South Korea, Sweden, and Switzerland. He looked at all these countries through the prism of his diamond, in which firm strategy and rivalry, customer demands, the strength of supporting industries, and the factors of production all play a role. His work on competitive advantage and the growth potential of regional clusters or groupings of firms that build on a complementary base is now being widely used by regional and national governments around the world.

All the researchers that have emphasized the systemic differences among national economic systems have contributed to a new way of American thinking. In a very real sense, they have helped create a pattern of thought in which public policies are put into a systemic context and, like corporate practices, are "benchmarked" or compared with the best in the world. Even more than specific insights into a competitor's strengths or proposals to reform a particular American weakness, the emphasis on comparative systems has made a lasting and positive contribution to America's public policymaking.

The Decline and Fall: Sic Transit America?

One strand of thinking linked America's global commitments to its stagnating productivity growth and the growing economic strength of Germany and Japan. Into the debate over the links between the economy and national security came distinctly different perspectives. In his 1987 book *The Rise and Fall of the Great Powers: Economic Change and Military Conflict from 1500 to 2000,* the Yale history professor Paul Kennedy described a period in Western history in which one great power after another had made military commitments that eventually undermined the very economic strength that had made those commitments possible.[46] In Washington in the late 1980s, Kennedy's phrase "imperial overstretch" became common in discussions of America's economic prospects. The dust jacket to Kennedy's book carried an added warning—a drawing of Britain's John Bull stepping off the stage of world power, America's Uncle Sam moving to a lower level, and Japan's new economic man moving toward center stage.

Fearing that the idea of imperial overstretch might lead to a diminished international role for the United States, advocates of America's larger foreign policy interests were quick to respond. In *Bound to Lead: The Changing Nature of American Power,* Joseph Nye, a professor at Harvard University's John F. Kennedy School of Government, pointed out that earlier powers often carried not only a much greater economic burden in terms of military spending relative to gross domestic product but also had the added onus of occupying foreign colonies.[47]

Nye's discussion of the American economy was particularly important for the competitiveness movement. Nye cites the definition of competitiveness developed by the President's Commission on Industrial Competitiveness (or the Young Commission) and treats competitiveness as "a useful measure of America's overall international position, particularly in the manufacturing sector."[48] In his discussion of late-nineteenth-century Britain, he points to internal as well as external causes for Britain's decline. For internal causes, Nye cites as "among the most important . . . the failure to maintain that productivity of British industry, particularly in new sectors, and the nature and level of education."[49]

Looking back more than a decade after Kennedy published *The Rise and the Fall of the Great Powers,* America in the 1990s seemed twice blest. The collapse of the Soviet Union reduced the pressures of military spending on the domestic economy, and the economic challenges of Germany and Japan contributed to a positive shift in public policies and private-sector practices just as America's economic rivals encountered serious economic difficulties of their own.

Writers who made systemic comparisons among the United States, Germany, and Japan were often attacked as "declinists." The tag was firmly stuck on those who discussed Britain even more than on those who suggested an era of imperial overstretch. It was as if the declinists had given up on America and saw nothing ahead but an aging Uncle Sam gradually stepping down from his position of power and preeminence. The charge was understandable but mistaken. The competitiveness movement and most of the so-called declinists were sounding an alarm bell that, they hoped, would stir America to action, investment, and future productivity growth.

Notes

1. Ron Chernow, *The House of Morgan: An American Banking Dynasty and the Rise of Modern Finance* (New York: Simon & Schuster, 1990).

2. In *Minding America's Business: The Decline and Rise of the American Economy* (New York: Harcourt Brace Jovanovich, 1982), Ira Magaziner and Robert Reich do quarrel with the notion that Germany was a more market-oriented economy than either Britain or France. They note, for instance, that "the German government's aids to

industry have been slightly greater than those provided by the French government" (p. 261).

3. Magaziner and Reich, *Minding America's Business,* 266, 267, 272–74, 279–82, 289–91, 304, 312–14.

4. Magaziner and Reich, *Minding America's Business,* 7.

5. Magaziner and Reich, *Minding America's Business,* 295.

6. Magaziner and Reich, *Minding America's Business,* 304.

7. Michael E. Porter, *The Competitive Advantage of Nations* (New York: Free Press, 1990), 69–130. The diamond appears on p. 72. Porter covers similar ground in Porter, "The Competitive Advantage of Nations," *Harvard Business Review,* March–April 1990, 73–93.

8. Porter, *Competitive Advantage of Nations,* 77.

9. Porter, *Competitive Advantage of Nations,* 378.

10. Porter, *Competitive Advantage of Nations,* 376.

11. Porter, *Competitive Advantage of Nations,* 368.

12. Hedrick Smith, *Rethinking America: A New Game Plan from the American Innovators: Schools, Business, People, Work* (New York: Random House, 1995).

13. See Alan B. Krueger and Cecilia E. Rouse, "Putting Students and Workers First? Education and Labor Policy in the 1990s," in *American Economic Policy in the 1990s,* ed. Jeffrey A. Frankel and Peter R. Orszag (Cambridge, Mass.: MIT Press, 2002), 676–77.

14. See http://Cisco.com and http://Cisco.netacad.net/public/academy. More advanced Cisco programs are offered on a postsecondary level.

15. The National Skill Standards Act was Title V of the Goals 2000: Educate America Act of 1994, PL 103-227.

16. See http://www.NSSBI.org.

17. Porter, *Competitive Advantage of Nations,* 371.

18. Magaziner and Reich, *Minding America's Business,* 279.

19. Magaziner and Reich, *Minding America's Business,* 279.

20. Porter, *Competitive Advantage of Nations,* 370.

21. Porter, *Competitive Advantage of Nations,* 8.

22. David W. Cheney and William W. Grimes, *Japanese Technology Policy: What's the Secret?* (Washington, D.C.: Council on Competitiveness, 1991).

23. See Henry Etzkowitz, "Bridging the Gap: The Evolution of Industry–University Links in the United States," in *Industrializing Knowledge: University–Industry Linkages in Japan and the United States,* ed. Lewis M. Branscomb, Fumio Kodama, and Richard Florida (Cambridge, Mass.: MIT Press, 1999), 203–33. Etzkowitz does not cite the impact of international competition but provides a useful overview of universities' growing links to industry and economic development generally.

24. Katie Hansen and Daniel F. Burton, *German Technology Policy: Incentive for Industrial Innovation* (Washington, D.C.: Council on Competitiveness, 1992).

25. Michael E. Porter, *Capital Choices: Changing the Way America Invests in Industry* (Washington, D.C.: Council on Competitiveness, 1992), 9–10.

26. Richard Darman, "Beyond the Deficit Problem: 'Now-Nowism' and the New Balance," speech to National Press Club, Washington, D.C., July 20, 1989. See Darman, *Who's in Control: Polar Politics and the Sensible Center* (New York: Simon & Schuster, 1996), 219–20.

27. Margaret M. Blair, ed., *The Deal Decade: What Takeovers and Leveraged Buyouts Mean for Corporate Governance* (Washington, D.C.: Brookings Institution Press, 1992), 12.

28. Porter, *Capital Choices,* 8.

29. The Omnibus Trade and Competitiveness Act of 1988 created the Advanced Technology Program, which encouraged corporate investment in basic technologies by providing peer review and partial public funding. The program was implemented by the George H. W. Bush administration and significantly expanded by the Clinton administration.

30. Germany was the world's leading exporter from 1986 to 1988. The United States regained the lead in 1989 and slipped behind Germany in 1990. See Council on Competitiveness, *Competitiveness Index 1990* (Washington, D.C.: Council on Competitiveness, 1990) and the Council on Competitiveness, *Competitiveness Index 1991* (Washington, D.C.: Council on Competitiveness, 1991). Germany slipped behind the United States through the rest of the decade but again passed U.S. export totals (measured in dollar terms) in April 2003. See Thomas Fricke, Sebastian Dullien, and Nina Hardenberg, "Germany Topples US as Biggest Exporter," *Financial Times,* October 14, 2003.

31. Magaziner and Reich, *Minding America's Business,* 280–91.

32. Paul Kennedy, *The Rise and Fall of the Great Powers: Economic Change and Military Conflict from 1500 to 2000* (New York: Random House, 1987), 224.

33. Corelli Barnett, *The Pride and the Fall: The Dream and Illusion of Britain as a Great Nation* (New York: Free Press, 1986), 2.

34. Barnett, *Pride and the Fall,* 8.

35. Kennedy, *Rise and Fall of the Great Powers,* 424.

36. Aaron L. Friedberg, *The Weary Titan: Britain and the Experience of Relative Decline, 1895–1905* (Princeton, N.J.: Princeton University Press, 1988), 215–16.

37. The phrase is credited to Kennedy and his book on the great powers. See Kennedy, *Rise and Fall of the Great Powers.* For a brief discussion of the "imperial overstretch" idea and its inapplicability to the United States, see Joseph S. Nye Jr., *Bound to Lead: The Changing Nature of American Power* (New York: Basic Books, 1990), 1–10.

38. Barnett, *Pride and the Fall.* See his chapter titled "The Lost Victory" (pp. 276–304) for the clearest exposition of his views.

39. Porter, *Competitive Advantage of Nations,* 498, 720.

40. Britain liquidated much of its overseas holdings to finance the war effort in World Wars I and II. Domestic investments might not have been as liquid and thus less available to finance armament purchases and other needed war matériel.

41. George C. Lodge, *The American Disease* (New York: Alfred A. Knopf, 1984).

42. Stephen D. Cohen, *Cowboys and Samurai: Why the United States Is Losing the Battle with the Japanese, and Why It Matters* (New York: Harper Business, 1991).

43. Steven Schlosstein, *The End of the American Century* (New York: Congdon & Weed, 1989).

44. Lester Thurow, *Head to Head: The Coming Economic Battle among Japan, Europe, and America* (New York: William Morrow, 1992).

45. Thurow, *Head to Head,* 258.

46. Kennedy, *Rise and Fall of the Great Powers.*

47. Nye, *Bound to Lead.*

48. Nye, *Bound to Lead,* 209.

49. Nye, *Bound to Lead,* 59.

Chapter 5

Congress Takes the Lead

A series of Carter administration initiatives failed to bring inflation under control. By 1979, the economy was slowing, and it actually declined in 1980, while inflation raged on.[1] Americans were growing angry about the economy, frustrated with the Carter administration and concerned about foreign policy. In 1978, Howard Jarvis, a septuagenarian businessman in California, gathered a million signatures to force a statewide vote on capping property taxes.[2] In November 1979, students seized the American embassy in Tehran and took the embassy staff as hostages. In December, the Soviet Union sent 85,000 troops into Afghanistan to quell a stubborn rebellion.[3]

It was against this uncertain economic and political background that Congress continued its search for a set of policies that would ensure economic and political success. In the Republican Party, the policy tensions lay between the new "supply-side" school and the more orthodox approach of balanced-budget conservatism. After Ronald Reagan endorsed the Kemp-Roth bill that embodied the supply-side emphasis on cuts in marginal tax rates, the Republican debate was largely over.

Among Democrats, the search was on for a strategy that would, in the words of President Kennedy, "get the American economy moving again." The economy of the 1970s had left Washington policymakers groping for the right combination of initiatives to restore productivity growth, control inflation, and respond to international competition. The Democrats were split in several ways. A significant group of Democrats still looked back to the experience and lessons of the Great Depression. The English economist John Maynard Keynes developed a theory that provided a broad framework for the overall (macro) economy and that, in cases of protracted decline like the Great Depression, pointed to fiscal policy (added spending or cuts in taxes) as the needed antidote.[4]

The application of Keynes's theory in the decades following World War II led American policymakers and many American economists to develop confidence in their ability to moderate economic cycles with modest changes in fiscal policy. They counted on a kind of fiscal "fine-tuning" to fight unemployment and contribute to a more equitable distribution of income. President Carter's early proposal for a $50 tax rebate was a product of the fine-tuning school of thought. Faced with persistent economic challenges, Carter and the Democrats also wrestled with several different economic strategies.

Chapter 2 traced the debate over industrial policy as it moved from an initial focus on how to strengthen well-established basic industries to the question of how to support or stimulate the emergence of the new high-technology firms of the future. Within and outside the Democratic Party, the debate focused on three key issues: Could the government help established industries become globally competitive, or would government assistance be little more than a subsidy to the inefficient? Could an imperfect government do better than the private markets at directing investment to "winning" industries? And finally, should the government establish a bank or some other kind of credit facility that would allow it to help finance the resuscitation of old industries and the creation of new ones?

The debate over federal financing of sector-specific (or industry-specific) intervention influenced the debate over economic policy throughout the late 1970s and early 1980s. Even after the industrial policy debate had subsided, opposition to sectoral intervention lingered as part of the Reagan legacy. It appeared again in the 1990s debate on technology policy and erupted into a major confrontation between the Clinton administration and the new Republican congressional majority in 1995. Sectoral policies, however, appeared less controversial at the state level. Whether in building on their own comparative advantage or seeking to attract new industries, states were relatively free to adopt policies that were adapted to the needs of a particular industry or set of industries. The transformation of American industry, the resurgence of the American economy, and a decade of economic difficulties in Europe and East Asia have muted the question of sector- or industry-specific intervention. The debate itself, however, continues.[5]

As industrial policy was being debated, another alternative was beginning to gain ground. In his masterful *Losing Time: The Industrial Policy Debate,* Otis L. Graham Jr. marked the emergence of a competitiveness strategy in 1985. In his view,

> trade policy, moving into the vacuum left by the 1984 disappearance of the concept of Industrial Policy, could not entirely fill it. Democrats and those Republicans convinced that Reaganomics was inadequate, continued the search for an alternative framework for national economic policy. Apart from their political defects, trade and industrial policies were limited to quadrant 4 [micro-economic or small-scale steps taken by the public sector]. The concept of Competitiveness offered hope of a larger framework for discussion in Reagan's second term—a vehicle for the sense of economic urgency widely felt in business and political circles, for a crusade to produce public- and private-sector reforms amounting to a strategic response to the new competition, *but without the discomforts of targeting.* (emphasis added)[6]

By the late 1970s, some congressional leaders were beginning to look beyond industrial policy. The shift in congressional and particularly Democratic thinking can be seen in a number of key reports that were developed in parallel to the debate over industrial policy. In fact, by the late 1970s, Congress was already developing the outlines of what would become the comprehensive competitiveness strategy—or long-term strategy for productivity growth—that was eventually adopted and applied by the Clinton administration.

The Joint Economic Committee: A New Kind of Supply Side

There is seldom a single document that marks the emergence of new policy thinking. However, the 1979 and 1980 annual economic reports of the congressional Joint Economic Committee (JEC) come very close.

The JEC was established by the Employment Act of 1946 as the congressional counterpart of the President's Council of Economic Advisers.[7] There were, however, important differences between the two bodies. The three-member council is traditionally composed of professional economists drawn from the academic world for relatively brief (two- or three-year) periods. The JEC was composed of often long-serving members of the House and Senate supported by a professional staff. As the term "joint" suggests, the JEC was one of the few standing congressional bodies with a membership drawn from both houses of Congress as well as both political parties.

Under the Employment Act of 1946, the JEC was directed to provide Congress with its own evaluation of the annual economic reports of the president. It had no other official function and could not directly produce legislation. The JEC was not, however, without influence. It had the power of ideas and the ability of its influential membership to translate ideas into action.

With its responsibility to make its own assessment of the economy as well as to respond to the annual economic reports of the president, the JEC was deeply involved in the search for a response to the economic troubles of the 1970s. Two of the JEC's senior members, Senator Hubert Humphrey (D-Minn.) and Senator Jacob Javits (D-N.Y.), proposed sweeping economic reforms, which included a national planning agency.[8] The proposal for this planning agency, however, was eliminated when the Humphrey-Javits bill became the Humphrey-Hawkins bill (after Representative Gus Hawkins, D-Calif.). Humphrey-Hawkins (or the Full Employment and Balanced Growth Act of 1978) kept the emphasis on growth and unemployment by setting a national target of 4 percent unemployment.

Humphrey-Hawkins is part of the fabric of today's economic debate—there are still press references to the Humphrey-Hawkins goal of 4 percent unemployment and regular coverage of the periodic testimony by the chairman of the Federal Reserve required under the act. But the JEC was about to take a very different direction.

Bentsen Breaks with the Past

The passage of Humphrey-Hawkins came in 1978 as Senator Humphrey was struggling with terminal cancer. With Humphrey ailing, the JEC turned to Senator Lloyd Bentsen of Texas, the Democrat in line to chair the JEC when the chairmanship passed to the Senate in 1979. The prospective shift from Minnesota to Texas marked more than a change in geography. Bentsen brought a different economic philosophy and a different life experience to his chairmanship.

Bentsen had served briefly in the House before returning to Texas and a successful business career. When Bentsen returned to Washington, he brought with him a vision of economic growth that was grounded in a Texas experience that emphasized incentives for private investment and rewards for taking risks. In writing about Texas in 1983, Barone and Ujifusa found the

state "a class and culture of risk-taking entrepreneurs who seem more ven-
turesome and more aggressive than their counterparts in the Northeast or
Midwest, and rivaled in the United States only by those of California."[9] At
the same time, Bentsen was no "free market ideologue."[10] He had been
elected by a coalition that included rural, black, and Hispanic voters with
a shared interest in a stronger safety net as well as the better jobs promised
by economic growth.

Bentsen's chairmanship brought other important changes to the JEC.
John Stark, the committee's distinguished, long-serving staff director, had
decided to retire. In his place, Bentsen appointed John (Jack) Albertine, a
former professor of economics at Mary Washington College and a member
of Bentsen's personal staff. Like Bentsen, Albertine brought a somewhat
different economic perspective to the committee.

Albertine might well have been a traditional Democrat. His father and
grandfather had both worked in the anthracite coal mines of Northeastern
Pennsylvania. By the mid-1950s, he saw the coal mines shutting down as
consumers shifted from coal to gas for home heating. Living through a
vivid example of how shifting supply and demand could affect a community, it is not surprising that Albertine chose to study economics at King's
College, in nearby Wilkes Barre, Pennsylvania. Albertine had his eye on the
University of Chicago for graduate study when he received a call from James
Buchanan offering him a National Defense Education Act scholarship to
study economics at the University of Virginia. It was not Chicago, but it offered a similar outlook on the economy and on economic policy.[11]

The Joint Economic Committee Looks at Long-Term Growth

While Albertine was shifting from academic life to a position on Senator
Bentsen's staff, the JEC was undergoing an evolution in its own thinking.
The Democrats on the committee were spending more time looking at the
different elements of long-term growth. Senator Humphrey himself had
pushed down this path in the mid-1970s when he added Robert Hamrin to
the committee staff. Hamrin's work on economic growth led to a series of
hearings and committee publications that focused on elements of what would
later be called the "new economy."[12] When Representative Richard Bolling
(D-Mo.) assumed the leadership of the committee in 1977, he commissioned a Special Study on Economic Change to develop new policies for a
new era. The Bolling study, published in ten volumes in December 1980,
touched on many of the key elements of a long-term growth. Among other

matters, separate volumes covered human resources, innovation, energy, and federal finances. The final volume focused on "Productivity: The Foundation of Growth."[13]

The Joint Economic Committee on the Supply Side

Change was also taking place on the Republican side of the JEC. By the late 1970s, the supply-side view was represented on the committee in the form of Senator William Roth (R-Del.). It was even more firmly entrenched in the staff. Paul Craig Roberts had shifted from his position on the staff of Representative Jack Kemp (R-N.Y.) and his subsequent role on the House Budget Committee to work with Senator Orrin Hatch (R-Utah), a member of the committee. Bruce Bartlett had also left Kemp's staff and was now working for Senator Roger Jepsen (R-Iowa), a new Republican member of the committee. On the Republican committee staff, both Steven Entin and Mark Policinski were staunch advocates of the supply-side view.

The shift in Republican supply-side thinking can be found in the minority views contained in the JEC's annual reports for 1977 and 1978. In his account of the supply-side revolution, Roberts put particular emphasis on the 1978 report that not only emphasized the need for added production but also "noted the importance of marginal income tax rates (the tax paid on the last dollar of income earned)."[14] Roberts highlighted the minority view that it was "very likely that marginal tax rates have risen to the point where they are causing a substantial reduction in the country's growth rate."[15] The text read like a variant of the Laffer curve in more elaborate clothing.

In 1979, any new chair would have faced the problem of a troubled economy and a committee with the full spectrum of views on economic policy. But Senator Bentsen and staff director Albertine faced an added challenge: The role of the committee was being questioned. It was a pointed piece by Art Pine that caught the attention of the committee members and staff. Writing in the *Wall Street Journal,* Pine pointed to the growing impact of the House and Senate budget committees, argued that the committee no longer had a role, and raised questions about whether or not the committee should be abolished. In his article, Pine noted that the JEC's reports "brim with so many footnotes expressing members' dissents that often it's hard to detect *any consensus* (emphasis added).[16] In retrospect, Albertine thought that the Pine piece jarred the committee and made it more open to moving in a different direction.

Bentsen was intent on shifting the committee to an agenda that emphasized investment and productivity growth. The troubled economy, a search for new ideas that cut across party lines, and the possible threat to the committee's existence combined to create an opportunity to build a committee consensus around Bentsen's philosophy. Albertine saw the opportunity in the same minority views cited by Roberts. It was not the emphasis on cuts in marginal tax rates that applied to personal income—neither Bentsen nor the other Democrats on the committee were likely to accept the extreme version of the Laffer curve. Rather, it was the minority's emphasis on productivity growth and business investment. This sounded like Bentsen country.[17] Albertine suggested the idea of a *consensus* report to Bentsen. He was skeptical but agreed to let Albertine try.

The Search for a Joint Economic Committee Consensus

Albertine started the process by walking over to the office occupied by the three economists working for the JEC's Republican side. Entin and Policinski both had vivid memories of Albertine's initial proposal.[18] Albertine noted that the minority views included in the 1977 and 1978 reports had both spoken about business depreciation and business taxes.[19] Albertine wondered if they could form the basis of a consensus report? Policinski also remembered discussing several newspaper articles, including the one by Pine, that there was no longer the need for a nonlegislative body like the JEC.

What Albertine got was an initial no. Policinski remembers that he and Entin thought that the Democrats were on the run and probably worried about the presidential election. Bentsen, they thought, was also concerned about the Democratic Party. Despite the initial no, Policinski later approached Albertine to explore the possibility of a joint report. In his conversation with Albertine, Policinski stressed that the Republican members wanted tax cuts. Albertine asked if they could deliver the Republicans. Policinski said they could.

Entin saw a consensus report offering the Republicans a substantial half loaf. The Democrats would be talking about an economy in trouble with a Democrat, President Carter, in the White House. He also saw the shift from the emphasis on the demand side to long-term productivity growth as perfectly consistent with their own approach. At the time, Entin thought that monetary policy was overly tight, which would allow the Republican members to talk about a near-term loosening of monetary policy while still proposing tighter policy in the long run. In Entin's view, at least in the long run, they would be talking about tighter monetary policy and more expansive fiscal policy, very much the mix that Robert Mundell had advocated.[20]

Albertine also worked hard to forge a consensus with the JEC's Democratic members and the committee staff, to whom most members of Congress turned for advice. I had joined the committee staff in 1977 so was still a relative newcomer to the senior staff. Although my particular focus was the international economy and how it affected U.S. prospects for growth, the entire staff was concerned with policies to help move the economy to full employment. Even more than the committee members, I remember the Democratic staff looking for answers to a troubled economy. Most of the staff had gone through graduate school when the emphasis on markets of the "Chicago school" of Milton Friedman and other University of Chicago economists was contending with the Keynesian view that there was an important role for fiscal policy in managing the economy. My own thinking had been influenced by two years studying the Brazilian economy and almost a decade working on U.S. foreign economic policy—in particular United States–Japan relations. I thought then and still do today that the Keynesian framework is an important tool for analysis and policy. But it was certainly not the whole story for growth in Brazil or the rapid increase in Japanese productivity. I suspect the staff was much more open to Bentsen's emphasis on long-term growth than he may have suspected.

Chairman Bentsen was already working to forge a consensus among Democrats. In a 2002 introduction to a set of comments on the 1979 and 1980 reports, Bentsen talks of suggesting a consensus report to Bolling, the JEC's vice chair. He remembered Bolling as not only being positive about the report but as also agreeing to work with other House Democrats to gain their support.[21]

In the end, Bentsen was successful in putting forth a vision for economic growth and forging a consensus on the committee.[22] Both the 1979 and 1980 reports contain many of the elements that would later become a national competitiveness strategy. Bentsen's ideas spread. Extensive media attention to a rare unanimous report was an important factor. Influential members and an active staff carried the report's ideas into other discussions and incorporated them in other projects. The ideas found their way into other, key congressional publications and, eventually, into legislation and national policy.

Near-term inflation and high unemployment were important political and economic issues for both the JEC and Congress. However, the slow growth in productivity became the JEC's central focus and a main theme of its 1979 and 1980 reports.[23] With the emphasis on productivity growth, the JEC took a longer-run view of the economy, emphasized the importance of public and private investment, and recommended monetary and fiscal policies that were consistent with long-term growth as well as the short-term stabilization of the economy. Herbert Stein, the chair of President Nixon's Council of Economic Advisers and a respected scholar on presidential economics, noted a similar shift in the thinking of mainstream economists. "The basic change was in the new emphasis on the long run."[24]

In terms of macroeconomic policy, the JEC agreed that monetary restraint was needed to control inflation, but it feared that the use of added spending to offset the impact of tight money on employment was shifting the economy "from capital investment toward higher levels of consumption . . . [that] has contributed significantly to our sluggish productivity performance, which in turn has exacerbated our underlying rate of inflation."[25] In broad outlines, the committee advocated the same combination of tighter fiscal policy and looser monetary policy that would eventually be adopted by President Clinton in 1993.

The JEC's productivity growth strategy also included specific targets for capital investment and endorsed raising "real business fixed investment to 12 percent of real [gross national product]."[26] In addition to tax incentives to spur capital formation, the committee proposed additional tax incentives for research and development, and it identified training as a key factor in productivity growth. The committee also anticipated the current trend of relying on private-sector training and individual training grants (or vouchers).

By the time the 1980 JEC report was being written, the economy had become more troubled and the political situation had become more complex. The political tide had been running against President Carter for much of 1979, with Senator Edward Kennedy running well ahead of the president in public opinion polls. Then a mob of Iranian students stormed and took over the U.S. embassy in Tehran. In *Why Americans Hate Politics,* E. J. Dionne notes that Carter's approval rating soared in a single month from "around 30 percent to about 60 percent." Dionne includes Nelson Polsby's comment that the Carter surge was "the most dramatic rally-'round-the-flag effect ever recorded."[27]

Bentsen's introduction to the JEC's 1980 annual report made an even sharper break with the past than the 1979 report. "The 1980 Report," wrote Bentsen, "signals the start of a new era of economic thinking."[28] Instead of emphasizing the demand side, he made it clear that the JEC recommended "a comprehensive set of policies designed to enhance the productive side, the supply side of the economy."[29] Again, the committee supported tax incentives to increase capital investment and urged that at least half of any future stimulus package be focused on increasing savings and investment.

There were some new themes in the 1980 report. More attention was given to Germany and Japan—both on the challenge they might present and the possible lessons they had to offer. There was also a new emphasis on greater cooperation among organized labor, business, and government. For a precedent, the JEC pointed to the effective working relationship between the Department of Agriculture and the American farmer. The report also noted that the relative lack of adversarial relations was often cited as one element in Germany and Japan's stronger economic performance.

The consensus reports helped shift national thinking and the thinking inside the Democratic Party in a new direction. But not everyone liked the reports. Albertine remembers that Walt Rostow, the former professor at the Massachusetts Institute of Technology and aide to President Kennedy, calling from his new position at the Lyndon B. Johnson School of Public Affairs at the University of Texas. Rostow thought the report was supply-side nonsense.[30] The press, however, gave the consensus report and its ideas extensive coverage.

Supply-side advocates still see the reports as important in bringing their ideas to prominence. The reports did emphasize production, shifted from demand management to long-term growth and endorsed tax cuts—albeit to stimulate business investment. Certainly Entin and Policinski saw it as a big step in their direction. At the time of the 1979 and 1980 reports, Roberts was writing a column for the *Wall Street Journal*. Albertine remembers him being lavish in his praise.[31] In his 1984 book *The Supply Side Revolution*, Roberts even characterized the report as "Reaganomics before Reagan."[32] In his *Reaganomics*, Bruce Bartlett also points to the JEC reports—particularly Bentsen's language in the 1980 report about signaling a new direction in economic thinking.[33] Bartlett was certainly right about the new direction. But it was not Reaganomics. Bentsen and his report would start Congress and eventually the country down a much broader path than the supply-siders' emphasis on reductions of the tax rates applied to personal income.[34]

Bentsen was in a good position to leverage the ideas in his own reports. He was already a prominent and influential member of the powerful Senate Finance Committee, which controls tax, trade, Social Security, Medicare, and welfare policies. In 1980, he also chaired the Senate Democratic Task Force on the Economy, which had been established by Majority Leader

Robert C. Byrd (D-W.Va.). When the task force issued its 1980 report, it
carried Bentsen's stamp. There was, for instance, an explicit focus on productivity growth, a call for the coordination of fiscal and monetary policies,
and strong support for tax incentives to spur capital investment. The task
force report also called for "incentives to promote lagging industrial research
and development [and] to spur exports."[35]

Senator Bentsen continued to be a force in economic policy for many of
the next fifteen years. He rose to become chairman of the Senate Finance
Committee, ran for vice president in 1988 with the Democratic presidential
nominee, Governor Michael Dukakis of Massachusetts, and served as secretary of the Treasury in President Clinton's first term. Bentsen brought
with him to the Treasury and to the Clinton administration a detailed understanding of the president's competitiveness strategy, which Bentsen had
started to craft so many years before.

On to the Yellow Brick Road

While the debate over industrial policy was brewing, the House Democratic Caucus developed an alternative approach that, like the Bentsen JEC
reports, would articulate many of the elements of a long-term competitiveness strategy.

The story starts with the election of a new leader for the House Democratic Caucus, Representative Gillis W. Long (D-La.). The year 1980 proved
to be a good one for Long but not for national or congressional Democrats.
Ronald Reagan swept into the White House with a substantial margin of the
electoral college vote. The Reagan tide brought a Republican majority to
the Senate and near control in the House. In the early days of 1981, near
control often seemed like effective control as conservative Democrats joined
with Republicans to support key parts of the Reagan program, which included
the Kemp-Roth version of cuts in marginal tax rates. The Reagan revolution and supply-side economics were taking their place in the sun.

The Reagan tide was a direct challenge to traditional Democrats' thinking and a threat to their political future. For years, Democrats had held a
popular edge in being able to deliver economic growth and employment.
Now, the Democrats had just lost an election over the voters' answer to Reagan's simple economic question: "Are you better off today than you were
four years ago?"

By the beginning of the 1980s, the economic troubles of the 1970s could be seen more clearly—stagflation had become a common term, international competition was a fact of life, and slow productivity growth was recognized as the underlying cause of stagnant incomes. A series of Carter economic experiments had met with mixed economic success and clear political failure. Nor was President Reagan's economic strategy of tax cuts and restrictive monetary policy working as hoped or dreamed. While Reagan secured some stunning legislative victories, the economy soured in 1981 and 1982.

The international position of the United States also continued to deteriorate. The trade deficit grew from $25.5 billion in 1980 to $28 billion in 1981 and rose again to $36 billion in 1982. At the same time, the dollar was rising (or appreciating) against other currencies and beginning to penalize American exports. American manufacturers found themselves caught between a recession at home and dwindling export sales abroad.

In the years before Long became chair of the House Democratic Caucus, some Democratic House members were already searching for a new economic approach. Tim Wirth (D-Colo.) and Dick Gephardt (D-Mo.) were collaborating on the Budget Committee. Together with Budget Committee members Leon Panetta and Norman Mineta of California, Wirth and Gephardt formed the "Gang of Four," "a collection of neoliberals, who drafted their own version of the 1981 budget as a compromise between the Reagan plan and the Democratic leadership's budget."[36] (At some point, the gang of four became five, with William Broadhead, D-Mich., joining the gang in 1980 and Les Aspin, D-Wis., taking the fifth spot in 1981.)[37] They pointed to the state of the economy, Carter's failed policies, and the Reagan electoral juggernaut as calling for new thinking and a new approach.

A 1981 House Democratic task force on the budget, chaired by Gephardt, developed a set of Democratic principles that were eventually approved by the full Democratic caucus. The principles included an emphasis on the middle class and the long run. At an April 9 press conference, Speaker Tip O'Neill said, "The Democratic economic principles would permit middle-income Americans 'to get a college education, to own a home and to earn a decent living.'" Gephardt stressed that in the fight against inflation, a "variety of areas must be addressed if we are to affect inflation, . . . including energy, research and technology."[38]

Wirth and Gephardt were pushing the leadership to continue the search for Democratic alternatives by holding an issues conference. Speaker O'Neill was not interested in sponsoring the issue forum, while Majority Leader

Wright was prepared to pay for an issues conference but was already over-committed. Long, as the new caucus chair, stepped into the breach and offered to put the conference together.[39]

After the issues conference, Long's first step was to form the thirty-six-member House Caucus Committee on Party Effectiveness (CPE).[40] To be truly effective, Long needed to include members who represented the full diversity of the caucus. He did. In *The Neo-Liberals,* Randall Rothenberg described the committee as "a diversified group that represented such a variety of faiths and ideologies that the word 'incompatible' would be too weak a description of it."[41] Long expected this group of "incompatibles" to "develop a new direction for the Democratic Party."[42] Eventually, the CPE would do just that. After more than a year of work, the CPE would endorse an economic strategy that came to dominate national policy more than a decade later.

The next step was to flesh out these economic principles into a report that made economic and political sense. Long turned to the CPE. "In September 1981, work began on six more policy statements on the topics of crime, housing, long-term economic policy, the environment, women's issues and small business."[43] All the issues were important. In addition to economic policy, Democrats had been vulnerable to the charge of being weak on crime and national defense. But the development of a long-term economic strategy lay at the heart of the enterprise. To take on that challenge, Long chose two rising Democratic stars—Tim Wirth as task force chair with Dick Gephardt and himself as key members.

Wirth had come to Washington with the huge Democratic post-Watergate class in 1974. From the start, he was a leader with a different set of ideas.[44] Although from humble beginnings, Wirth had a sterling educational background that included Exeter, Harvard, and a Ph.D. from Stanford. Gephardt came to Congress two years later in 1976. Gephardt represented a mixed city and suburban district in Saint Louis that still had something of its original German character. Like Wirth, Gephardt had risen from humble circumstances to acquire top academic credentials at Northwestern and the University of Michigan Law School.[45]

In crafting a long-term economic strategy, Wirth, Gephardt, and the other members of the task force had to focus on the needs of the national economy in a way that would meet with popular acceptance, party approval, and the support of a voting majority of their own constituents. Members of Congress do not have the luxury of taking either a scholarly pace or a strictly academic approach to problems. They act in a world of uncertainty, competing interests, and periodic elections. Yet they knew that their economic ideas would be scrutinized by the academic community, vetted by the economic press, and weighed by political commentators. Key economic interests were looking at their work as a possible guide to future economic policy or legislation.

The members' respective staffs also played an important role in preparing drafts, suggesting new directions, and developing ideas that met the tests of good economics and sound politics. Many would later hold positions in the Clinton administration. Robert Maher from Wirth's staff would go on to serve in the Commerce Department's Technology Administration during Clinton's second term. Speaker of the House O'Neill asked three of his staff members—Sally Ericcson, Jack Lew, and S. Ariel Weiss—to work with the task force. Ericcson and Lew went on to senior positions in the Clinton administration, with Ericcson serving at the Department of Commerce and then on the White House Council on Environmental Quality, and Lew holding several positions before being elevated to the powerful position of director of the Office of Management and Budget.

Long added two key staff members of his own—Alvin From, executive director of the House Democratic Caucus, and myself from the staff of the Joint Economic Committee.[46] From had first come to Washington to work at the Office of Economic Opportunity during the last quarter of his graduate study at Northwestern's Medill School of Journalism. He decided to stay. After President Nixon's victory in 1968, From moved to the staff of Senator Joseph Tydings (D-Md.), and after Tydings's defeat in 1970 he found himself working for Senator Edmund Muskie (D-Maine) on the Senate Government Operations Committee.[47] As a key aide to Senator Muskie, From had been active in helping to craft the congressional budget process as well as working extensively on sunset legislation (i.e., adding time limits to initiatives so that they had to be affirmatively readopted).

When Muskie shifted to the Senate Budget Committee in 1978, From moved to the White House to become one of four deputies to Alfred Kahn, then President Carter's counselor on inflation. As a special assistant to Carter, he saw firsthand the inability of an older economics to deal with the 1970s. Close to the 1980 election, From received a call from Patti Tyson, a key aide to Gillis Long, who held a senior position on the House Rules Committee. At this point, Long was confident of winning the race to chair the House Democratic Caucus and was already thinking ahead to who might serve as his executive director. Robert Strauss, one of the most respected figures in the Democratic Party, had written Long a letter recommending

From, describing him as someone who hunted with the hounds. Long did not need a translation of that Texas phrase, and he asked Tyson to call From.

From met with Long, who spoke of his campaign as well as his plans for the caucus. Long confidently predicted that he would win 146 House Democrats' votes for caucus leader. After talking with Long, From checked with President Carter's congressional liaison office—and they told him that Speaker O'Neill was for South Carolina representative Charlie Rose, or possibly New York representative Matt McHugh. Still, From agreed to take the job. Long won the post with the predicted 146 votes.

From also had contacts with some of the newer, up-and-coming members of the House. He had actually covered Gephardt as a cub reporter for the *Daily Northwestern* and later worked with Gephardt and his staff on sunset legislation in the mid-1970s. Because From knew Gephardt, the Carter White House had asked From to be a bridge to him. The White House also asked From to be one of the people who spoke at the Wirth seminars— gatherings Wirth arranged for his Colorado constituents to talk about issues and meet key Washington leaders.

I came to the project after a decade of working on congressional economic policy with an emphasis on trade and other aspects of international economic policy. I had started with Senator Vance Hartke (D-Ind.), then worked at the Congressional Research Service and was serving as a senior economist on the congressional Joint Economic Committee. In mid-1978— when Representatives Long and Lee Hamilton (D-Ind.) asked John Stark, the committee's staff director, to assign a committee person to keep them informed of committee initiatives and work with them—I got the call. When Senator Bentsen crafted two consensus reports emphasizing long-term productivity growth, I had been part of the committee staff who contributed their own ideas and helped draft the actual report. Like most of the congressional staff working on international economic policy, I had been wrestling with the question of how to respond to the rising competitive challenge posed by Germany and Japan. (As an active member of the JEC, Long was very familiar with Bentsen's work.) It was at Long's request that I started to work with the House Democratic Caucus. Wirth would frequently introduce me as the Caucus economist, and during 1981–82, I essentially played that role.

To develop that broader report, a few of us met in a small room that was part of a House Energy and Commerce subcommittee chaired by Wirth. There was an early attempt to include sympathetic Senate views. Ava Feiner from the office of Senator Bill Bradley (D-N.J.) attended our first meeting.

But forging a House Democratic consensus would be challenge enough, and the project quickly became a House-only effort.

From the start, Wirth, Gephardt, and Long were looking for a new set of economic policies that would challenge the views of many within the Democratic Party. They would be accused of violating Democratic principles and ignoring the working person. Even worse, they risked being charged with abandoning the spirit of Franklin Roosevelt. The opening paragraphs of the first concept paper moved to avoid the latter charge by putting FDR's mantle squarely over our own effort. Instead of looking at the Roosevelt legacy in terms of a fixed set of programs, we portrayed Roosevelt as an experimenter and a pragmatist looking for the best way to achieve Democratic principles and broadly shared national goals. It was more important to ask what Roosevelt would do today to shape tomorrow than to emphasize what he had done yesterday.

In crafting the new approach to long-term economic policy, Wirth, Gephardt, and the rest of us faced several interrelated problems. First, we needed to have a credible response to inflation but not one that risked a severe recession. With an eye on long-term investment as a key to productivity growth, we also needed a macroeconomic strategy that would encourage long-term investment rather than focus solely on economic stability. Second, in looking to the future, we wanted to foster emerging industries without either abandoning or directly subsidizing established ones. Wirth and Gephardt also faced a political imperative. Organized labor was an important part of the Democratic coalition and represented millions of workers who had found prosperity and a ladder to the middle class in the metal-bending industries. Democrats simply could not turn their back on them or their industries. At the same time, the country as a whole was hostile to government bailouts—federal dollars rushing in where private-sector angels refused to tread. There was already a sense in the country that there was more future in silicon than in steel.

The members of Congress and the staff working on long-term economic policy were also thinking of a new relationship with the business community. And there was a growing understanding that organized labor and business were often in the same boat and could benefit from the same set of public policies. Still, many Democrats remained suspicious of or even hostile to the business community. In taking a new approach toward business, Wirth, Gephardt, and the others on the task force had to seek a formula that would draw support from often-reluctant Democrats.

Finally, Wirth and Gephardt had to craft a policy that would respond to the international challenge without adopting a protectionist stance. The document had to be economically sound, intellectually coherent, and politically compelling to a CPE that included more than thirty members who "reflected all the political philosophies" in the Democratic Caucus.[48]

In seeking a new framework for economic policy, Long faced potential obstacles within the House Democratic Party as well as the conceptual challenge of developing something new. If he veered too close to specific legislative proposals, he might invoke the ire of committee chairs, who would see the task force as threatening their own jurisdiction. With that in mind, From stressed that he and Long always kept their focus on preparations for the mid-term Democratic convention to be held in Philadelphia and not on a legislative agenda.[49]

In breaking new ground, Long also had to keep on the right side of the speaker of the House, Tip O'Neill, who was not adamantly opposed to Long's search for a new direction. Like most Democrats, O'Neill had been stunned by the Reagan electoral sweep and accepted the need for some new thinking. Nor was he averse to going outside the usual committee system to chart a new course or even to develop legislation. He had already done that in forming an ad hoc energy committee to deal with President Carter's response to the energy crisis. In his recent biography of the speaker, *Tip O'Neill and the Democratic Century,* John A Farrell termed the ad hoc energy committee solution "bold and innovative."[50] As Farrell put it, O'Neill was an old dog who could learn new tricks.[51] But there were limits. O'Neill knew that some of the new members were impatient with his leadership. Dan Rostenkowski (D-Ill.), chair of the House Ways and Means Committee, thought that the CPE and the effort to develop a new economic framework were part of a plot to dethrone the speaker.[52] Farrell notes that "throughout the 1980s, there were serious plots to challenge O'Neill."[53] Among the specific names mentioned by Farrell were Wirth and Long himself.

At one point, Speaker O'Neill appointed Representative Richard Bolling to add some oversight to Long's work on developing new ideas. As chair of the House Rules Committee, Bolling was himself a key part of the House leadership and could be expected to keep the speaker well informed. Bolling, however, was not averse to new thinking about the economy. He had spent his years (1977–78) as chair of the Joint Economic Committee looking at the economic future of the American economy and was, at the time, working with John Bowles on *America's Competitive Edge,* his own, new approach to economic policy.[54] Bolling was also close to Long and Gephardt. Long had managed Bolling's unsuccessful run for majority leader and Gephardt, like Bolling a Missouri Democrat, was something of a Bolling protégé. It was Bolling who had steered Gephardt toward membership on the powerful Ways and Means Committee rather than his first choice, Banking.[55]

Two of the speaker's staff, Ari Weiss and Jack Lew, were involved on a regular basis with the various task forces, including the Special Task Force on Long-Term Economic Policy. Sally Ericcson joined the speaker's staff after the caucus report, *Rebuilding the Road to Opportunity,* had been drafted. Her initial responsibility was to vet the report with various economic experts in and outside the academic world. The three worked for the Steering and Policy Committee, a speaker-appointed committee that held the formal power to appoint new Democratic members to the various House committees. As staff of the Steering and Policy Committee, Weiss, Lew, and Ericcson did serve "as additional eyes and ears of leadership" but also "got involved in working out problems, not just reporting them."[56]

Lew saw their role as more than just "eyes and ears."[57] In his words, they were both "clients and staff" for *Rebuilding the Road to Opportunity.* He and others on the Steering and Policy Committee staff were coordinating the work of various committees and did not want *Rebuilding* to contradict their legislative initiatives. But he also saw himself as basically an ally of the CPE effort. He worked closely with the caucus in organizing the first issues retreat and actually set up all the panels. Ericcson also remembers the speaker being supportive of a new direction—the old approach was not working economically or politically.[58]

While Long was keeping peace with the speaker and the committee chairs, a few of us were drafting and redrafting the report. In addition to From and myself, this drafting group included representatives from Wirth's and Gephardt's staffs. Jim Jaffee, then Gephardt's chief of staff, carefully reviewed the report for Gephardt. Bob Maher from Wirth's telecommunications subcommittee (of the House Energy and Commerce Committee) reviewed the drafts and helped develop a strategy to promote the report. After being cleared by Wirth and Gephardt, the drafts went to the CPE for further discussion.

As we neared a final draft, we turned our attention to suggesting the right name for the document. A few of us gathered in the offices of the House Democratic Caucus, located in what was then called House Annex No. 1 (and is now a parking lot). We were close to settling on *Regaining the Road to Opportunity* when Ross Baker, a professor of political science from Rutgers University, made a critical observation. Baker was a longtime student of Congress who was working with the House Democratic Caucus as part of his congressional studies. Baker noted that "Regaining" might easily be redubbed "*Reagan*ing." We quickly shifted to "Rebuilding" and the title became *Rebuilding the Road to Opportunity: Turning Point for America's Economy.* In the end, the CPE and the Democratic Caucus as a whole endorsed the document and its new direction. The report made its public debut in September 1982.

Solving the Economic Puzzle

How did Wirth and Gephardt find a way to meet the economic imperatives and the political requirements of a new policy? How did they solve the specific challenges that ranged from macroeconomics to foreign economic policy? How much of a break did they actually make with the past? How well received was the report in terms of press and politics? How much of a lasting impact did *Rebuilding the Road* actually have?

Macroeconomics is a critical piece of virtually any economic puzzle. It was certainly central for Wirth and Gephardt in developing an effective economic strategy as well as in meeting the demands of the profession, the press, and the broader public. Wirth and Gephardt started their discussion of macroeconomic policy under the broader heading of an "environment for investment." Like Bentsen, Wirth and Gephardt advocated fiscal and monetary policy that would contribute to controlling inflation by stimulating long-term investment and higher productivity growth.

There was a clear economic logic to the Wirth-Gephardt approach. Tighter fiscal policy (through reducing federal spending or raising federal taxes) should make more capital available for investment at a lower price (or interest rate). Increased capital investment would expand industrial capacity and, by increasing productivity growth, help offset the impact of rising prices. By eliminating the fiscal deficits, they also saw the Federal Reserve being freed to adopt a pro-investment monetary policy.

The macroeconomic policy espoused in *Rebuilding the Road* met several tests. It promised an approach that would rebuild the American Dream by promoting the productivity growth that underlies rising incomes. They also sought to match the supply-siders' optimism by controlling inflation and promoting growth at the same time.

Would tighter fiscal policy and balanced budgets mean higher taxes? In the early 1980s, Democrats were aware that they had been successfully painted as the "tax and spend" party. The report talked about balancing the budget "while limiting taxes" and rejected the idea of the federal government spending an "ever-increasing percentage of the nation's wealth." With regard to specific tax policy, *Rebuilding the Road* continued the Democratic Party's traditional focus on fairness while making significant departures in emphasizing the need to encourage saving and foster business investment. The mix of old and new can be found in a single sentence in the report's section on taxes: "We must revise our business tax laws to assure that profitable corporations cannot escape paying their fair share of taxes, to encourage productive investment and to renew the entrepreneurial spirit in our economy."[59]

And some ideas were clearly new. Under the broad umbrella of making tax laws fairer and simpler and to encourage savings, the report mentioned eliminating many special tax preferences and lower marginal tax rates—the proposal generally known as the Bradley-Gephardt bill (after Senator Bradley and Representative Gephardt). As another approach, the report mentioned a "progressive consumption tax" as a spur to savings. Both ideas have had a lasting impact on the policy debate and on policy itself. The Bradley-Gephardt bill served as one of the bases for the Tax Reform Act of 1986. Eliminating special preferences offset the cost of the tax cuts. The progressive consumption tax idea emerged again as a key element in a series of proposals developed by the Strengthening America Commission cochaired by Senators Sam Nunn and Pete Domenici in the early 1990s.[60] Since the commission reported in 1992, the question of a consumption tax has continued to be periodically debated in Congress. It is still actively promoted by the American Business Conference, an association made up of high-growth, midsize companies, and it was raised again in the *2003 Economic Report of the President.*[61]

Investing in the Future

Wirth, Gephardt, and a broad array of Democrats were looking at the federal budget as a critical element in an investment-led growth strategy. In *Rebuilding the Road,* the House Democratic Caucus recommended dividing "federal spending into investment and operating expenditures . . . to allow Congress to determine how much spending it wants to devote to long-term investments which spur economic growth."[62] In particular, the report emphasizes investments in new technologies, in people, and in public infrastructure—themes that would later be echoed in candidate Bill Clinton's campaign platform, *Putting People First.*

New technologies were already important to a group of Democrats who were frequently referred to as "Neoliberals" or "Atari Democrats."[63] In *Rebuilding the Road,* the Democrats took a comprehensive view of the national innovation chain. For Wirth and Gephardt, technology was not simply a matter of people in white coats hovering over an experiment. They emphasized the role of universities, industry laboratories, entrepreneurs, and the government.

The report's approach to investing in people is not nearly so broad. There is an almost post-Sputnik-like emphasis on science, mathematics, and technical preparation.[64] The report made specific proposals to "increase the supply of junior faculty in computer science and . . . engineering" and to bring into higher education "the new emphasis on computer literacy and language / area studies." For elementary and secondary schools, the report emphasized the importance of computer literacy and set a goal to "provide every school with access to a computer within five years and to make every student 'technically literate' in computer-era basic skills by the end of this decade." The report looked for leadership to "the National Science Foundation, which so successfully developed science and math curricula in the post-Sputnik period" and proposed incentives to attract "talented teachers in . . . science, mathematics [and] foreign languages / area studies."[65]

The Democrats were taking a decidedly new direction. Growth had joined fairness as a Democratic priority. Growth, in turn, demanded a series of policies that would encourage public and private investment. Key elements in a national competitiveness strategy were coming to economic and political prominence.

Supporting Basic and Growth Industries

In the early 1980s, it seemed that the very bastions of America's industrial strength—cars, trucks, steel, apparel, shoes, and consumer electronics—were under siege. With literally millions of union members out of work or fearing they would be caught in the recession, the unions were actively interested in an industrial policy that would provide relief, financing, and at least temporary protection for embattled basic industries.

A growing number of Democrats were also emphasizing the need to support the industries of the future. Gradually, however, industrial policy was characterized by its critics as focused on maintaining older, established industries with a combination of import protection and financial bailouts. Democrats were faced with a complicated economic choice. They could not ignore the economic importance of basic industries or the political costs of turning their policy backs on either union members or the Midwest. At the same time, they were anxious to be associated with the industries of the future.

Rebuilding the Road looked to technology as a way of responding to basic and growth industries at the same time. After cataloging a series of economic trends that afflicted America's basic industries in the 1970s, *Rebuilding the Road* points out the continuing importance of basic industries to everything from national security to opportunities for millions of Americans. The report also notes that basic industries "have been the proving grounds for a number of high technology products."[66] In other words, there was a productive synergy between basic and growth industries. As the debate sharpened during the 1980s, the links between basic industries and growth or high-technology industries became increasingly clear. Not only were basic industries important markets for high-technology products—the auto industry remains an important customer for semiconductors—but new technologies were also important in making basic industries more innovative and more competitive.

Rebuilding the Road proposed dealing with the likely impact of shrinking employment in basic industries with an emphasis on training that would allow workers to move to new, rapidly growing industries. Instead of traditional programs in which the public sector actually did the training, *Rebuilding the Road* suggested "financial incentives to private employers and labor unions . . . to help pay the costs of training and retraining."[67]

The same strategy fit the needs of high-technology industries as well. So did *Rebuilding the Road*'s approach to trade. Avoiding any call for protectionism, the report pointed to an America that remained "an unaggressive exporter" where policy was made with little thought to its implication for international trade. Instead of looking to a halcyon past, the report emphasized building on America's high-tech and small business strengths, negotiating to open markets that promised a gain for the United States, and a commitment to enforce existing trade agreements.

Looking to the Future

To help anticipate and respond to change, Wirth and Gephardt took a leaf from the Japanese book, adapted it to 1980s America, and proposed the creation of an Economic Cooperation Council (ECC). In their view, the ECC would provide a clear analysis of current and future trends, anticipate major challenges to the American economy, clarify key economic choices, and build a consensus in support of public initiatives. In sum, Wirth and Gephardt were recommending an ECC that "would combine the ability to assess future trends with a membership that would help build a partnership around solutions to future problems."

The proposed ECC had a lasting impact. It inspired the Competitiveness Policy Council (CPC) created by the Omnibus Trade and Competitiveness Act of 1988. Like the proposed ECC, the Competitiveness Policy Council included representatives from business, labor, universities, and state and local government. The CPC wound up its work in 1996, a victim of its own success, the economy's surging strength in the mid-1990s, and the emergence of the 1994 Republican majority in Congress. The National Economic Council (NEC) of the Clinton administration also can trace its roots back to the ECC. Having been established at the beginning to the Clinton administration, the NEC developed into the key economic decision-making body in the White House. While not playing quite the same central role, the NEC structure has been retained by the George W. Bush administration.

Taking the "Yellow Book" to the Party and the Public

By September 1982, *Rebuilding the Road to Opportunity* had passed the scrutiny of the broadly representative Committee on Party Effectiveness. Long, Wirth, and Gephardt were ready to unveil the report for the press and the public. Wirth and his aide Robert Maher took the lead in arranging a series of interviews in New York.

Press coverage from the New York trip was largely favorable. *Business Week* was particularly supportive in praising the general direction of the report but insistent in its call for congressional action. A *New York Times* editorial praised *Rebuilding the Road* for rising "above intraparty and even partisan rivalry to focus on long-term national goals."[68] As a measure of how much Japan was on the minds of politicians and the press, the *Times* singled out the Economic Cooperation Council as the "key proposal," characterizing it as "MITI-minus."[69] Instead of MITI's (Japan's Ministry of International Trade and Industry) "powerful hand in determining . . . public and private economic priorities," the *Times* portrayed the Democrats as seeking "some kind of vehicle for a constructive partnership between business, labor, universities and government."[70]

Press coverage around the country summarized the report's key proposals and almost always included Wirth's own characterization of the report. As Wirth put it, the Democrats wanted "to move away from a temporary economic policy of redistribution to a long-term policy of growth and opportunity."[71] Like it, as some clearly did, or not, as other chose to do, *Rebuilding the Road* marked a new direction for the Democratic Party.

Renewing America's Promise

For the House Democratic Caucus, *Rebuilding the Road to Opportunity* created broad agreement among House Democrats that influenced future legislation and publications. During 1983, the Committee on Party Effectiveness continued to meet and refine the ideas developed in *Rebuilding the Road*. In January 1984, their work led to the publication of *Renewing America's Promise: A Democratic Blueprint for Our Nation's Future*. A blue cover replaced the yellow to emphasize the idea of a more detailed blueprint to complement the broader vision of the "yellow brick road."

Renewing America's Promise followed much the same direction as the earlier *Rebuilding the Road*. If anything, *Renewing America's Promise* put even more emphasis on the development of partnerships among business, labor, and the government. The "blue book" also stressed the need for continuous training—a policy position that would come center stage in the 1990s.

The "yellow book" had called for linking domestic and international policies.[72] In much the same spirit, the "blue book" put trade policy in the context of broader economic initiatives. In the "blue book," House Democrats argued for a "strategy to combine our trade policy with other measures in a way that creates the correct foundation from which we can succeed in winning markets abroad and in staying competitive at home."[73] The "blue book" dealt with some aspects of the industrial policy debate by calling for policies that would respond to foreign industrial targeting. At the same time, the "blue book" moved well beyond the industrial policy debate to stress the importance of a broad-based investment strategy and creating an "environment for enterprise" as the keys to an effective response to the international challenge.[74]

The press coverage for the "blue book," like that for the earlier "yellow book," was national in scope. The *New York Times* and a number of other major newspapers noted that the focus on economic growth was "a significant shift in emphasis for the Democrats."[75] The *Dallas Morning News* described the actual publisher of the "blue book," the National-House

Democratic Caucus, as a "newly formed organization headed by Rep. Gillis Long, D-La., chairman of the House Democratic Caucus, and Robert S. Strauss, former party chairman. The group's membership includes 70 House Democrats and 83 other top party figures."[76]

In establishing the National-House Democratic Caucus, Long was providing a base for what eventually became the Democratic Leadership Council. At the 1984 Democratic convention in San Francisco, Long took another step in that direction. Before leaving the convention, Lindy Boggs, a Democratic representative from Long's Louisiana, recounts a meeting of "all the 'super delegates'—elected and appointed public officials." Out of that meeting, she continues, "was born an organization that became known as the Democratic Leadership Council (DLC)."[77] Boggs went on to describe how the DLC continued the kind of issues seminars initiated by Gillis Long as chair of the House Democratic Caucus.[78]

Looking ahead to 1985, Long was already thinking about the prospect of being the next chair of the Joint Economic Committee. Limited to two terms as chair of the caucus, Long intended to pursue his quest for new policies through the JEC. He had asked Al From to come with him as committee staff director and had asked me to return to committee as well. (I had left the JEC to work for Senator Gary Hart during his first presidential run in 1983–84.) We both knew that Long was ill; he had had heart trouble in the past. Then, on January 20, Long suffered a fatal heart attack in his Watergate apartment.[79] Long never lived to see the formation of the DLC or the development of his ideas into a national strategy. But a number of elected officials who had been working with Long continued his work and formally launched the DLC in early 1985. Al From was its first president and continues with DLC, as its chief executive, in 2004. Many of the rest of us helped carry Long's ideas and his vision for the country forward till we saw them translated into national policy in the 1990s.

The Senate Looks at Competitiveness

Although the House Democrats had taken the lead in developing a new strategy for economic growth, Senate Democrats were also hard at work forging their own consensus around effective and politically attractive policies to stimulate incomes and productivity growth. Minority leader Robert Byrd established a Democratic task force on the economy in February 1983 and chose Senator Edward Kennedy to chair the thirteen-member group.

Byrd turned to his staff on the Democratic Policy Committee (DPC) to help draft the task force report. At the time, Rob Liberatore, DPC staff director, remembers starting with a focus on industrial policy that over time evolved into a "proposal to facilitate the competitiveness of American Business."[80] Liberatore was also aware that the House had already issued *Rebuilding the Road to Opportunity.* Much of the thinking and drafting of the Senate task force report was done by Arnie Packer, an economist and veteran of the Carter Labor Department. When Packer took the position as chief economist of the DPC, he thought he would be developing a jobs program. But as the economy recovered in 1983, the Senate Task Force and Packer shifted their view to the longer run.[81] While working on the task force report, Packer kept in close touch with Al From about the work of the House Democratic Caucus, including their work on *Rebuilding the Road* and its successor volume, *Renewing America's Promise.* They "wanted to make sure that the [House and Senate efforts] coincided."[82]

When the Kennedy Task Force reported on November 16, 1983, Packer's close collaboration with his House counterparts showed. The Senate task force report struck many of the same themes adopted by the House Democrats.[83] In making their proposals in *Jobs for the Future,* the Senate Democrats knew that they were likely to be accused of mixing old-fashioned protectionism with a new version of central planning. They went to some lengths to avoid both charges. They focused on fostering change rather than resisting it. Temporary trade relief, if granted, would be conditioned on "a realistic, hardheaded plan for adjustment and modernization."[84] The Senate Democrats portrayed themselves as favoring "neither central planning nor aimless drift," but rather pointed to government intervention where "private incentives are weak" and where the government can "encourage competitiveness and recognize the inevitability of change."[85] With the publication of *Jobs for the Future,* there was something of a Congress-wide consensus among Democrats on the elements of a national competitiveness strategy that would stand in contrast to the supply-side approach still advocated by the Reagan administration.

Gary Hart: Policies and the Pursuit of the Presidency

When *Jobs for the Future* appeared in late 1983, the race for the Democratic presidential nomination was well under way. At the time, former vice president Walter Mondale was viewed as an overwhelming favorite for the nomination. He had the support of major Democratic interest groups, a large group of former officials from the Carter administration, and much of the Democratic establishment in Washington and around the country.

Still, Mondale faced a number of rivals, including four sitting senators— Alan Cranston from California, John Glenn from Ohio, Ernest Hollings from South Carolina, and Gary Hart from Colorado. Governor Bruce Babbit of Arizona and former Florida governor and former U.S. trade negotiator Ruben Askew were also in the race. Of the six, Gary Hart had the most lasting impact on the development of a Democratic alternative to the supply-side approach of the Reagan administration.[86]

Hart had been reelected to a second term in 1980, and by 1982, he was actively preparing his run for the presidency. In February of that year, he presented an "An Economic Strategy for the 1980s," an early version of the economic ideas that would provide important planks for his platform in his 1983–84 run for the presidency.[87] This position paper contained an emphasis on the entrepreneur, specific proposals for stimulating investments in research and skills, and a program for expanding rather than restricting trade. Hart struck many of the same themes in his speech at the June 1982 Democratic midterm convention in Philadelphia.

Hart had been working on gathering new ideas for some time. During 1981 and 1982, Hart and Texas representative Martin Frost held periodic breakfasts to take in new perspectives. Through fellow Texan and majority leader Jim Wright, Frost had secured a position on the House Rules Committee that made him a junior member of the House leadership. Frost's Dallas-based district included everything from unionized workers at major industrial plants to a healthy dose of Texas conservatives. He was looking for an economic platform that would promise long-term growth and meet the needs of his diverse district. He was also one of the young members that Gillis Long, a Rules Committee member himself, added to his Committee on Party Effectiveness. Frost was not sure who first suggested he form a partnership with Hart, but he felt the breakfasts had been a useful way to develop new ideas.[88]

In *The Neo-Liberals,* Rothenberg suggested that the "morning sessions became a meeting ground for congressional neoliberals during their early efforts" at forming a coalition.[89] The breakfasts continued into early 1983, until just before Hart became a full-time candidate for the presidency.

Hart's real passion was national security. He was an active member of the military reform caucus that, for instance, favored small rather than large aircraft carriers. But he knew that he also needed a credible set of economic ideas. To craft a legislative program, Hart turned to Billy Shore and Kathy Bushkin. Shore and Bushkin shared the duties of a legislative director while Bushkin also doubled as Hart's press secretary. As Hart moved toward a presidential run, he added new thinkers to his staff. Perry Quick, now an economic consultant, did much of the work on Hart's initial economic proposals. In 1981, Hart added Robert Hamrin to his ideas staff.

Hamrin, an economist from the University of Wisconsin, first came to Washington in 1974 to work on the Joint Economic Committee.[90] Between 1974 and 1978, Hamrin worked on the committee pursuing Senator Hubert Humphrey's interest in long-term growth. The Humphrey-Hamrin effort led to a twelve-volume series, *U.S. Economic Growth 1976–1986: Prospects, Problems and Patterns,* that included separate "volumes on technology, capital [and] human resources," as well as other factors.[91] Hamrin turned the committee's work into a book, *Managing Growth in the 1980s: Toward a New Economics,* that highlighted the information economy as the country's new economic frontier. Hamrin also worked for the President's Commission for a National Agenda for the 1980s—another exercise in looking broadly at the economic and social future of the country.[92]

By the time he joined the Hart staff in 1982, Hamrin was a veritable walking encyclopedia of new ideas about the American economy and economic policy. Hamrin brought in key economic thinkers to meet with Hart and started work on a series of papers dealing with different economic topics, with a future book a distinct possibility. Once Hart decided on a book, Bushkin coordinated the work but looked to Hamrin to develop the ideas and do much of the drafting. As he worked on the book, Hamrin drew on his JEC and presidential commission experience. He circulated the drafts for comment in the academic world, in the private sector, and on the Hill. In part, Hamrin was gathering new ideas and providing a check on his own thinking. But he was also building support for Hart's ideas and for his expected candidacy.

Hart declared his formal candidacy in 1983 on a sunny February day in Denver. I had joined Hart's staff in January 1983 to develop and coordinate the policy side of the campaign as well as his legislative initiatives. Shore and Bushkin were shifting from their shared duties to the demands of the coming campaign. Along with most of Hart's Washington staff, I had traveled to Denver to be there for the announcement. Glancing upward and commenting on the providential weather, Hart joked that he did not necessarily count the presence of such good weather as an endorsement of a higher power.

Not long after the announcement, Hart released a detailed statement of his views on the economy as well as national security in *A New Democracy: A Democratic Vision for the 1980s and Beyond.*[93] Even before his formal announcement, Hart was seeking to identify himself as the candidate of new ideas for "a new generation of leadership" by making detailed white papers available to his audiences. But not everyone was convinced that a new ideas campaign was a winning formula. Martin Schramm, then a reporter for the *Washington Post,* expressed his skepticism about the Hart strategy when he said that what Americans wanted was "red meat not white paper." But Hart persevered. Now, in *A New Democracy,* Hart had turned his various new ideas into a detailed campaign platform.[94]

In part I of *A New Democracy,* "The Path to Prosperity," Hart spelled out his ideas for long-term growth, revitalizing industry, and stimulating employment. Many of his ideas paralleled those developed by the House Democrats in their 1982 "yellow book" and 1984 "blue book." Hart's economic prescriptions also contained most of the elements that would later emerge as a national growth and competitiveness strategy in the Clinton administration. In addition to rebalanced macroeconomic policy, Hart favored added public investments in research and development, infrastructure, and education and training. He maintained his focus on expanding trade with a series of proposals for opening markets and promoting exports.

Having been inspired by the post-Sputnik National Defense Education Act, Hart proposed an American Defense Education Act to create incentives for all the U.S. school districts to improve their performance in teaching mathematics and science.[95] He also sought to update the Morrill Act, the nineteenth-century legislation that had strengthened American agriculture by establishing a nationwide system of land-grant colleges. Hart's High Tech Morrill Act would provide federal grants to match the "contributions of business and state governments to institutions of higher education that are establishing or expanding high technology instruction."[96]

Hart also saw the need for ongoing training for the incumbent workforce. Among other ideas, he promoted the "Individual Training Account (ITA) analogous to the popular Individual Retirement Account (IRA)."[97] The ITA was the brainchild of Pat Choate, a former Carter administration official who later served as a policy maven with TRW, an innovative manufacturer and major supplier of parts for the automobile industry. Choate's vision of the ITA included tax-deductible contributions by both employers and employees, with the worker able to chose any training as long as the quality of instruction had been certified by the Department of Labor.

Instead of industrial policy, Hart spoke in terms of an "industrial strategy." Like the 1982 "yellow book," he rejected the choice between sunrise and sunset industries and saw technology as a way to revitalize existing industries as well as a path to creating new ones. Where would the needed finance come from? Hart did not endorse the ideas of a national development bank. Instead, he proposed two alternatives: "easing regulations on private financial institutions and strengthening the activity of development centers in the states."[98] He saw an active role for the public sector, but it was more likely to be catalytic than programmatic.

Hart brought his ideas to added prominence during his campaigns for the Democratic nomination for president in 1983–84 and again in 1987–88. Hart's emphases on mastering rather than resisting change, on looking at national solutions and not just federal programs, and on involving private as well as public entities became the foundations of much Republican and Democratic thinking about public policy. Hart, of course, was not alone in advocating new ideas and new policies for a changing economy. But his effort helped bring many ideas into a political context, put them under a national spotlight, and give them added impetus.

Congressional Republicans Look at a Competitiveness Strategy

Congressional Republicans had played an active role in developing and promoting supply-side economics. President Reagan modeled his own tax-cutting legislation after the Kemp-Roth proposal named after Representative Jack Kemp (R-N.Y.) and Senator William V. Roth Jr.(R-Del.). Many Republican members of Congress saw the Reagan revolution as their revolution.

With the economy already weakening, however, Republicans were painfully aware that the extreme claims of the supply-side school—painless elimination of inflation, sharp increases in savings and investment, and growth so robust that increased revenues would lead to fiscal surpluses rather than deficits—had not come to pass. Then came the shock of David Stockman's public confession that he had never believed the extreme supply-side vision. In December 1981, the *Atlantic Monthly* carried William Greider's article based on a series of interviews with Stockman.[99] The article was read in many circles as an admission that supply-side economics was not only a failure but also a fraud.

The loss of twenty-four Republican House seats in the 1982 midterm election was a warning to Senate as well as House Republicans. Congressional

Republicans responded to the policy and political challenge in at least three different but complementary ways. Many did simply follow President Reagan's admonition to "stay the course." Some Republicans voted for tax increases to reduce the deficit and, in 1982, Congress adopted the Tax Equity and Fiscal Responsibility Act, at that point the largest single tax increase in the nation's history.

Starting in 1980 and continuing through 1981 and into 1982, a restrictive, inflation-fighting monetary policy drove real interest rates to near record levels. As the recession deepened in 1982, the Federal Reserve Board came under pressure to change course from several quarters—the White House, the supply-siders in the Treasury, the failure of Penn Square bank in Oklahoma, and the weakening financial position in Mexico (see below).[100] Congressional demands for a shift in policy were intense. Congressional complaints about high interest rates were hardly new, but key congressional leaders were actively questioning the independence of the Federal Reserve Board.

The Senate Democratic leader, Robert C. Byrd, had become convinced that Federal Reserve chairman Paul Volker was avoiding responsibility for the high interest rates. Like most effective Fed chairs, Volker had mastered the kind of obfuscatory speech, which allowed him to respond to congressional questioners without really answering them. Liberatore, Byrd's staff director on the Democratic Policy Committee, helped develop a proposal that would have required the Fed to set short-term rates at their historic real levels. Senator David Boren (D-Okla.) introduced the bill (the Balanced Monetary Policy Act of 1982), and it quickly gathered more than thirty cosponsors in the Senate. In an August 3, 1982, floor speech, Senator Byrd called on Congress "to wrest control of monetary policy from the hands of a tiny group of ideologues in the White House."[101] Liberatore remembers Jim Wright pursuing the idea in the House.

By the time Congress took its first legislative steps, however, Volker and the Federal Open Market Committee had already shifted toward easing monetary policy.[102] With inflation already brought under 4 percent a year, the shift in macroeconomic policy helped lay the basis for the recovery that began in late 1983. The Republicans' electoral prospects brightened along with the economy. It is seldom easy to determine which pressures led to a change in policy. Most observers agree, however, that the prospect of a Mexican default and its anticipated impact on other countries (including the United States) weighed heavily in the thinking of Volker and the Federal Reserve as a whole.[103] Still, Liberatore wonders if the pressure generated by the Democrats did not, in the end, help keep the Senate Republican. In 1984, the Democrats lost four Senate races by a combined total of 64,000 votes.[104]

In terms of developing an alternative to President Reagan's supply-side strategy, the Republicans did not play a major role. For the most part, they were content to continue with their harsh critique of Democratic industrial policy. There were exceptions. As they heard from their business constituents struggling to respond to the rigors of the global economy, the Republicans began, slowly, to propose a series of initiatives that contained some of the elements of a broader national competitiveness strategy. Eventually, the Republicans wanted to beat the Democrats and selectively join them at the same time.

In the House, Representative Ed Zschau (R-Calif.) developed a series of proposals as chairman of the Steering Committee of the Republican Task Force on High Technology Initiatives.[105] Having been elected in 1982, Zschau both represented and in many ways embodied Silicon Valley. After earning his Ph.D. at Stanford and teaching at the Stanford Business School, he went on to found and lead Systems Industries, a major producer of disc storage systems. Before coming to Washington, he had cut his political teeth by building support in the California high-technology community for the "Steiger Amendment," which reduced taxes on capital gains.

Zschau was not shy about attacking the Democrats who were themselves developing policies for the high-technology future. Quick with a phrase, Zschau defined an "Atari Democrat" as "someone who liked playing games with the economy."[106] Zschau did not just criticize but also worked to put a Republican stamp on the high-technology future. Under his leadership, the House Republicans developed a series of proposals where government policy would complement the entrepreneurial strength of the private sector. In "Targeting the Process of Innovation," the Steering Committee of the Tax Force on High Technology Initiatives recommended fourteen steps that Congress could take before adjourning in 1984.[107]

In the Senate, the Senate Republican Conference Task Force on Industrial Competitiveness and International Trade covered much the same ground. This task force, which was chaired by John H. Chafee, reported on March 16, 1984.[108] The task force spelled out a series of initiatives to improve the availability of capital resources, encourage research and development, improve human resources, and open markets for international trade.

Senate Republicans also proposed supporting innovation through tax incentives, changes in the antitrust laws, and improved patent protection.

Their task force also saw the potential for industry collaboration with the national laboratories to create "technological breakthroughs that could have revolutionary effects on older industries."[109] Without focusing on the national laboratories, House and Senate Democrats had also turned to technology as the force that could transform older industries as well as creating new ones.

In responding to the rising trade deficits, the Senate Republican task force emphasized the importance of macroeconomic policy. It specifically pointed to deficit reduction and a Federal Reserve Board policy that would "not put unnecessary pressure on interest rates."[110] Beyond macroeconomic policies to decrease the international value of the dollar, they proposed a series of measures to open markets, stimulate exports, and deal with unfair trade practices.

In a final section, the task force looked to provisions for dislocated workers and adult training as necessary components of adapting to economic change. Although the specifics may differ, the approach is similar to the one adopted by the Clinton administration.

Republicans were far from leading the charge for a long-term productivity growth strategy, but they were beginning to develop their own variant of a competitiveness policy. It was not until the 1987–88 fight over the Omnibus Trade and Competitiveness Act of 1988, however, that a majority of Republicans endorsed the new growth compact that was emerging from Democratic initiatives.

Rebuilding the Road: How Much of a Highway to Future Policy?

How much of an impact did *Rebuilding the Road to Opportunity* have on Democratic thinking, future legislation, and national policy? As a product of the Committee on Party Effectiveness and the House Democratic Caucus, it had already influenced the thinking of House Democrats and identified a growing force inside the Democratic Party. Wirth, Gephardt, and the others carried these ideas with them as they went on to influence policy in the late twentieth and early twenty-first centuries.

It is always hard to separate the influence of one document, even a consensus document designed to set a new course, from the host of factors that influence policy. *Rebuilding the Road* was an island surrounded by a swirling sea of economic trends, constituent complaints, and congressional testimony by academics, think tank specialists, and business leaders. Many of these same individuals who testified before Congress also met individually with key members of Congress or found their ideas being transported into the political sphere by a print or electronic journalist.

There are clear links between *Rebuilding the Road* and the earlier Joint Economic Committee annual reports crafted under the leadership of Senator Lloyd Bentsen. Gillis Long was an active member of the Joint Economic Committee and brought his JEC staff into the drafting of his own report. *Rebuilding the Road* made an even fuller statement of the productivity growth strategy that responded to the realities of international competition and the growing importance of technology for American economic strength. The emphasis on creating a macroeconomic environment that fostered investment was the clearest possible move from a short-term to long-term focus. The report's emphasis on investing in research and development, education and training, and public infrastructure found expression in future congressional documents and legislation. The report's emphasis on an aggressive trade negotiating and export policy also had a lasting impact.

At the time of its publication, some observers expected little in the way of a long-term impact from *Rebuilding the Road*. Writing in a January 1984 edition of the *National Journal,* Richard Cohen wondered whether the Democrat's "blue book" would be "relegated to a dusty shelf with other party reports, including the House Democrats' 1982 'yellow book,' which critics contended was longer on rhetoric than recommendations."[111] Yet, in looking at future policy developments, one can trace the ideas and many of the specific policies in *Rebuilding the Road* to a Senate Democratic Caucus report, *Jobs for the Future,* the broad outlines of the Omnibus Trade and Competitiveness Act of 1988, and the campaign documents and early governing philosophy of President Clinton. The members of Congress and their staffs who were involved in drafting *Rebuilding the Road* carried its principles and policies with them into future legislation. Many would eventually serve in the Clinton administration in key economic posts. In retrospect, *Rebuilding the Road to Opportunity* was a turning point for the Democratic Party and, eventually, for the nation.

Notes

1. Council of Economic Advisers, *1984 Economic Report of the President* (Washington, D.C.: U.S. Government Printing Office, 1984), 222.
2. Burton I. Kaufman, *The Presidency of James Earl Carter* (Lawrence: University Press of Kansas, 1993), 106.

3. Kaufman, *Presidency of James Earl Carter,* 162.

4. John Maynard Keynes, *The General Theory of Employment, Interest, and Money* (New York: Harcourt, Brace & World, 1964). *The General Theory* was first published in 1936.

5. President George W. Bush has taken a number of industry-specific steps in his first term. He has imposed wide-ranging tariffs on steel imports, agreed to sharp increases in agricultural subsidies, sought to secure congressional support to allow the Defense Department to lease (rather than buy) tankers from Boeing, and approved a post–September 11 program to provide financial assistance to commercial airlines. In 2003, the president endorsed a manufacturing initiative, which has included pressure on China, Japan, and other East Asian nations to allow their currencies to appreciate (or rise relative to the dollar). Each of the steps has proven controversial. There has been no attempt to elevate the specific initiatives to a broader theory, with even the term "industrial policy" being scrupulously avoided.

6. Otis L. Graham Jr., *Losing Time: The Industrial Policy Debate* (Cambridge, Mass.: Harvard University Press, 1992), 219. Graham's framework appears on p. 80 and bears a useful resemblance to Michael Porter's diamond. See, for instance, Michael E. Porter, "The Competitive Advantage of Nations," *Harvard Business Review,* March–April 1990, 77.

7. See 15 U.S.C. 1021. The Employment Act of 1946 was amended by the Full Employment and Balanced Growth Act of 1978, P.L. 95-523.

8. Graham, *Losing Time,* 20.

9. Michael Barone and Grant Ujifusa, *Almanac of American Politics, 1984* (Washington, D.C.: National Journal, 1983), 1115.

10. Barone and Ujifusa, *Almanac of American Politics,* 1119.

11. Author's interview with Jack Albertine on March 1, 2002.

12. Author's interview with Robert Hamrin on April 4, 2002.

13. Joint Economic Committee (JEC), U.S. Congress, *Special Study on Economic Change,* 10 vols. (Washington, D.C.: U.S. Government Printing Office, 1980). The volumes appeared between December 1 and December 29.

14. Paul Craig Roberts, *The Supply-Side Revolution: An Insider's Account of Policymaking in Washington* (Cambridge, Mass.: Harvard University Press, 1984), 60.

15. Roberts, *Supply-Side Revolution,* 60. The quotation is from JEC, *Joint Economic Report 1978* (Washington, D.C.: U.S. Government Printing Office, 1978), 98.

16. Art Pine, "JEC: Actor on Hill Seeking a New Role," *Washington Post,* April 30, 1978.

17. Interview with Albertine.

18. Author's interviews with Steve Entin, February 8, 2002, and Mark Policinski, April 5, 2002. Both thought that the third economist, Chick Bradford, was not in the office at the time. Chick Bradford had already died when I started work on this book, so I was not able to speak to him about the 1979 and 1980 JEC reports.

19. JEC, *Report of the Joint Economic Committee on the January 1977 Economic Report of the President* (Washington, D.C.: U.S. Government Printing Office, 1977); and JEC, *1978 Joint Economic Report* (Washington, D.C.: U.S. Government Printing Office, 1978).

20. Interview with Entin.

21. JEC, *The Supply Side Revolution: 20 Years Later* (Washington, D.C.: U.S. Government Printing Office, 2000), 40.

22. Barone and Ujifusa, *Almanac of American Politics,* 1119.

23. The JEC was looking at "output per hour for all persons in the private business sector of the economy"; JEC, *1979 Joint Economic Report* (Washington, D.C.: U.S. Government Printing Office, 1979), 5.

24. Herbert Stein, *Presidential Economics: The Making of Economic Policy from Roosevelt to Reagan and Beyond,* 2nd ed. (Washington, D.C.: American Enterprise Institute, 1988), 222.

25. JEC, *Report of the Joint Economic Committee on the January 1979 Economic Report of the President* (Washington, D.C.: U.S. Government Printing Office, 1979), 20.

26. JEC, *1979 Joint Economic Report,* 61.

27. E. J. Dionne, *Why Americans Hate Politics* (New York: Simon & Schuster, 1991), 137–38.

28. JEC, *1980 Joint Economic Report* (Washington, D.C.: U.S. Government Printing Office, 1980), 1.

29. JEC, *1980 Joint Economic Report,* 1.

30. Interview with Albertine.

31. Interview with Albertine.

32. Roberts, *Supply-Side Revolution,* 63.

33. Bruce Bartlett, *Reaganomics: Supply-Side Economics in Action* (Arlington, Va.: Arlington House, 1981), 8.

34. In the JEC's twenty-year retrospective, Bentsen rejected both what he saw as a Democratic emphasis on wage-price controls and deficit financing and the Republican view, which "seemed stuck on personal income tax reductions as the only policy. JEC, *Supply Side Revolution,* 40.

35. Introduction, Senate Democratic Task Force on the Economy, Senator Lloyd Bentsen, Chairman, September 1980, 3.

36. Randall Rothenberg, *The Neo-Liberals* (New York: Simon & Schuster, 1984), 161.

37. See Gail Gregg, "House Outlook Grim for Budget Conference," *Congressional Quarterly,* May 24, 1980, 1387, which refers to a "Gang of Five" and includes Broadhead; and Dale Tate, "Rep. Jones: Beleaguered Budget Chairman," *Congressional Quarterly,* June 19, 1982, 1449, which refers to a "Gang of Five" that includes Aspin rather than Broadhead.

38. Gail Gregg, "Democrats Score on Budget in House and Senate Panels," *Congressional Quarterly,* April 11, 1981, 619.

39. Author's interview with Alvin From, February 28, 2002.

40. Interview with From. See also David W. Rohde, *Parties and Leaders in the Postreform House* (Chicago: University of Chicago Press, 1991), 68; Diane Granat, "Democratic Caucus Renewed as Forum for Policy Questions," *Congressional Quarterly,* October 15, 1983, 2115. See also Barbara Sinclair, *Legislators, Leaders, and Lawmaking: The U.S. House of Representatives in the Postreform Era* (Baltimore: Johns Hopkins University Press, 1995), 112. Sinclair cites a manuscript by Ross Baker, "Short History of the Democratic Caucus." Baker, a professor of political science at Rutgers University and a longtime student of Congress, was working with the House Democratic Caucus as part of his congressional studies.

41. Rothenberg, *Neo-Liberals,* 160.

42. *Questions and Answers* prepared for a September 13 and 14, 1982, visit to New York media outlets by Representatives Martin Frost (D-Tex.), Richard A. Gephardt

(D-Mo.) and Timothy E. Wirth (D-Colo.). These representatives were in New York to present and explain a new Democratic strategy for long-term growth by the House Democratic Caucus, *Rebuilding the Road to Opportunity: Turning Point for America's Economy* (Washington, D.C.: House Democratic Caucus, 1982).

43. Sinclair, *Legislators, Leaders, and Lawmaking,* 112.

44. For instance, Wirth opposed controls on oil and gas as ineffective in the face of global markets and counterproductive in terms of spurring new exploration. His position was not totally at odds with his suburban district in an oil-producing state, but was marked by its emphasis on setting policy that recognized the power of global markets and economic incentives. See Barone and Ujifusa, *Almanac of American Politics,* 189.

45. In his *What It Takes: The Way to the White House,* Richard Ben Cramer includes a detailed portrait of Gephardt the boy as well as Gephardt the member of Congress. See Cramer, *What It Takes: The Way to the White House* (New York: Random House, 1992), chap. 18.

46. As a staff member on the JEC, the author worked closely with Representative Long and, as a result, functioned as the lead economist for the caucus.

47. Interview with From.

48. Gillis W. Long, preface to House Democratic Caucus, *Rebuilding the Road,* 1.

49. Interview with From.

50. John A. Farrell, *Tip O'Neill and the Democratic Century* (Boston: Little, Brown, 2001), 466.

51. Farrell, *Tip O'Neill;* see chapter 24, "An Old Dog Learns New Tricks," 563–606.

52. Author's interview with Jim Jaffe, April 9, 2002. When the task force was drafting *Rebuilding the Road,* Jaffe served as Richard Gephardt's chief of staff. He later worked for Rostenkowski on the House Ways and Means Committee.

53. Farrell, *Tip O'Neill,* 650.

54. Richard Bolling and John Bowles, *America's Competitive Edge: How to Get Our Country Moving Again* (New York: McGraw-Hill, 1982). In 1982, Bowles was an investment banker with Kidder, Peabody & Company and an active Democrat who was focused on developing a new economic approach for the party and the country.

55. Interview with Jaffe.

56. Barbara Sinclair, *Majority Leadership in the U.S. House* (Baltimore: Johns Hopkins University Press, 1983), 76–77.

57. Author's interview with Jack Lew, April 5, 2002.

58. Author's interview with Sally Ericcson, March 11, 2002.

59. House Democratic Caucus, *Rebuilding the Road,* 20.

60. The Strengthening America Commission was sponsored by the Washington-based Center for Strategic and International Studies (CSIS). The CSIS Commission included academics, senior businesspeople, and a number of elected officials in addition to the two senators. Senator Sam Nunn represented the state of Georgia before retiring in 1996. Senator Pete V. Domenici is the senior senator from New Mexico. The Democrat Nunn and the Republican Domenici gave the commission a bipartisan cast.

61. The American Business Conference was founded in the early 1980s by Arthur Levitt, then president of the American Stock Exchange who later served as chairman of the Securities and Exchange Commission. Their longtime and recently retired (in April

of 2002) president, Barry Rogstad, served on the CSIS Commission, which endorsed a progressive consumption tax. Jack Albertine, JEC executive director under Senator Lloyd Bentsen, succeeded Levitt as president of the American Business Conference. See also Council of Economic Advisers, *2003 Economic Report of the President* (Washington, D.C.: U.S. Government Printing Office, 2003), 185–90.

62. House Democratic Caucus, *Rebuilding the Road,* 20. The same question was raised in a meeting of the Clinton transition team. In the end, the team decided against recommending a capital budget fearing it would lead to an effort to reclassify a wide range of items as investments and undermine the effort at deficit reduction. Wirth and Gephardt wrestled with similar considerations. The report specifically states that the emphasis on investment is not intended to reduce the pressures to eliminate the budget deficit.

63. See Rothenberg, *Neo-Liberals,* 79–80, for the origin of the term "Atari Democrat." The term fell out of favor and eventually out of use as Atari shifted production overseas and ran into economic difficulties.

64. Following the Soviet Union's successful launch of a satellite in 1957, the United States reacted by adopting the National Defense Education Act (NDEA) to spur graduate education. There was also an intense emphasis on mathematics and science in elementary and secondary schools. As in *Rebuilding the Road,* there was a focus on learning foreign languages. The NDEA included National Defense Foreign Language Fellowships for graduate work that included the study of a critical language.

65. The quotes are all from "Investing in People," House Democratic Caucus, *Rebuilding the Road,* 21.

66. House Democratic Caucus, *Rebuilding the Road,* 18.

67. House Democratic Caucus, *Rebuilding the Road,* 26.

68. "The Democrats and MITI-Minus," *New York Times,* September 22, 1982. In *Neo-Liberals,* Rothenberg described a reaction in which the *Times* "gently criticized but approved of the Wirth-Gephardt proposal as a MITI-minus" (p. 232).

69. "Democrats and MITI-Minus."

70. "Democrats and MITI-Minus."

71. The quote was contained in coverage by the *Baltimore Sun, New York Times,* and *Los Angeles Times.*

72. House Democratic Caucus, *Rebuilding the Road,* 30.

73. House Democratic Caucus, *Renewing America's Promise: A Democratic Blueprint for Our Nation's Future* (Washington, D.C.: House Democratic Caucus, 1984), 40.

74. See the section on "Environment for Enterprise," House Democratic Caucus, *Renewing America's Promise,* 19–22.

75. Steven V. Roberts, "Group in House Stresses 3 Issues for Democrats," *New York Times,* January 8, 1984.

76. "Democrats Unveil Policy Manifesto," *Dallas Morning News,* January 8, 1984.

77. Lindy Boggs and Katherine Hatch, *Washington Through a Purple Veil: Memoirs of a Southern Woman,* (New York: Harcourt Brace, 1994), 343.

78. Boggs and Hatch, *Washington Through a Purple Veil,* 344.

79. Diane Granat, "Rep. Long's Death a Blow to Democratic Leadership," *Congressional Quarterly,* January 26, 1985, 145.

80. Author's interview with Rob Liberatore, June 7, 2002.

81. Author's interview with Arnie Packer, June 10, 2002.

82. Interview with Packer.

83. Senate Democratic Caucus, *Jobs for the Future: A Democratic Agenda* (Washington, D.C.: Senate Democratic Caucus, 1983).

84. Senate Democratic Caucus, *Jobs for the Future,* 7.

85. Senate Democratic Caucus, *Jobs for the Future,* 6–7.

86. The author served as Senator Hart's policy director in his Senate office during 1983 and 1984.

87. Gary Hart, "An Economic Strategy for the 1980s," photocopy, February 6, 1982.

88. Author's interview with Representative Martin Frost.

89. Rothenberg, *Neo-Liberals,* 131.

90. Author's interview with Robert Hamrin, April 4, 2002.

91. Interview with Hamrin.

92. Hamrin mentioned that the commission report was delivered to President Carter on the very day he left office.

93. Gary Hart, *A New Democracy: A Democratic Vision for the 1980s and Beyond* (New York: Quill, 1983).

94. For a sense of Hart's early campaign strategy, see Peter Goldman and Tony Fuller, *The Quest for the Presidency 1984* (New York: Bantam Books, 1985), especially 82–103.

95. The NDEA was targeted at graduate education and included provision for combining the study of strategic languages as well as specific disciplines. Hart's American Defense Education Act was targeted at the primary and secondary public schools. Hart and others had seen firsthand the massive voluntary response of America's public schools to Sputnik's challenge to America's national security and technological preeminence.

96. Hart, *New Democracy,* 93.

97. Hart, *New Democracy,* 102.

98. Hart, *New Democracy,* 55.

99. William Greider, "The Education of David Stockman," *Atlantic Monthly,* December 1981.

100. William Greider, *Secrets of the Temple: How the Federal Reserve Runs the Country* (New York: Simon & Schuster, 1987). In chapters 13 ("Slaughter of the Innocents") and 14 ("The Turn"), Greider provides a vivid overview of the pressures brought on Federal Reserve Chairman Paul Volker.

101. Greider, *Secrets of the Temple,* 512.

102. Greider, *Secrets of the Temple,* 13. See also Herbert Stein, *Presidential Economics: The Making of Economic Policy from Roosevelt to Reagan and Beyond,* 2nd rev. ed. (Washington, D.C.: American Enterprise Institute, 1988). Stein notes that "by the fall of 1982 the Federal Reserve had given up any pretense of stabilizing the growth of the money supply" (p. 404).

103. For a brief review of the Mexican situation and the steps Volker took to stem a full default, see Robert Solomon, *Money on the Move: The Revolution in International Finance since 1980* (Princeton, N.J.: Princeton University Press, 1999), 36–44.

104. Interview with Liberatore.

105. For detail on Zschau, see Barone and Ujifusa, *Almanac of American Politics,* 108–9.

106. As quoted in Rothenberg, *Neo-Liberals,* 80.

107. Steering Committee of the Task Force on High Technology Initiatives, *Targeting the Process of Innovation,* 1st ed. (Washington, D.C.: House Republican Research Committee, 1984).

108. Senate Republican Conference Task Force on Industrial Competitiveness and International Trade, "Report and Recommendations," March 16, 1984.

109. Senate Republican Conference Task Force, "Report and Recommendations," 7.

110. Senate Republican Conference Task Force, "Report and Recommendations," 8.

111. Richard Cohen, "A Party Agenda," *National Journal* 16, no. 2 (1982): 78.

Chapter 6

Reagan Responds: The President's Commission on Industrial Competitiveness

In December 1984, John Young, the chief executive of Hewlett-Packard, a leading multinational electronics firm based in Silicon Valley, walked into a meeting of the Reagan Cabinet. Young brought a world of credibility with him. Firms like Hewlett-Packard and Silicon Valley itself were widely viewed as helping to define and create the leading edge of America's economic future.

Young was there to report on eighteen months of work by the President's Commission on Industrial Competitiveness (hereafter, the PCIC, the Young Commission, or the commission), which had been formally established in mid-1983 by the Reagan administration and had a membership dominated by chief executives and other top officials of America's major manufacturing firms. Leaders from organized labor and the academic community complemented the PCIC's blue ribbon industrial membership. The commission and its staff had developed a series of recommendations for both the public and private sectors to respond to the new economic challenges facing the country.

Not every commission reports to the Cabinet. It was Malcolm Baldrige, the secretary of commerce and a former industrialist and chief executive, who had successfully pushed for the Cabinet session. Young gave the Cabinet a crisp, corporate-style briefing on an economy still suffering from slow productivity growth, insufficient investment, and the growing challenge of global competition.

As Young remembers it, his report stimulated little interest among the Cabinet members. Rather than creating a sense of urgency and direction, his presentation elicited only one or two questions. Over the next year, Young saw his work mostly gathering dust in the company of hundreds of reports from previous commissions. Aside from some international economic initiatives taken in the fall of 1985, Young could detect little in the way of administration action that could be traced to his report.[1]

The Young Commission report itself had developed a clear definition of national competitiveness, articulated a strategy for long-term American growth, and made a series of recommendations for public and private action. It built upon academic work, think tank products, and Democratic and Republican reports in Congress. The Young Commission added a powerful, blue ribbon voice to the chorus of concern about America's economic standing in the global economy. In addition to partisan advocacy or ivory tower analysis, the American public now heard a clear call from the captains of industry who were on the front line of global competition. The report was widely embraced by industry and received a warm welcome in most congressional quarters, even though the Cabinet and the Reagan administration had largely ignored it.[2]

The Cabinet's limited interest in the Young Commission report should not have come as a total surprise. The Cabinet was probably still basking in the glow of Ronald Reagan's forty-nine-state sweep in the November 1984 presidential election. Reagan's opponent, former vice president Walter Mondale, had carried only the District of Columbia and his home state of Minnesota. Reagan had run and won on the theme that America was back—prosperous at home and respected abroad. As the president's campaign commercials stressed, it was "Morning again in America." Just as important, the president had continued to run against Washington—depicting government as the problem and not the solution.

John Young was painting a very different picture. America faced a series of economic challenges at home and abroad. Slow productivity growth, stagnating incomes, and the lingering effects of the early 1980s recession were still pressing economic problems. Overseas, Germany and particularly Japan were challenging America in one industry after another. Young and his commission also saw government as a necessary part of the answer.

The Young Commission's Origins

As is the case with many Washington initiatives, the decision to launch the Young Commission involved a variety of policy and political motives. When discussions started about the commission, the economy was in the worst recession since the Great Depression, the president's popularity was sagging, and former vice president Mondale was talking about the need for an American industrial policy.[3] There were ample reasons for the president and his team to have their own counterproposal to that of an expected Mondale campaign for the White House.

It would be wrong, however, to neglect the various policy voices that were pushing the administration to develop its own set of policies. In general, the administration thought the proposal for a new industrial development bank or a resuscitated Reconstruction Finance Corporation was a bad idea. Others had been working on initiatives that could improve America's productivity performance. And still others were concerned about the state of America's industrial base and the growing challenge of Japan.

Some of the president's allies in the business community were also looking for action. Lee Morgan, the chief executive of Caterpillar, was leading a campaign to focus Washington on the damage that a highly valued dollar was doing to American industry by penalizing exports and encouraging imports. Morgan's was not a lone voice; he was speaking for the Business Roundtable, a business group made up of the chief executives of leading American firms. He wanted a change in policy. The Business–Higher Education Forum, an industry–university coalition, was calling for a series of steps to improve U.S. competitiveness (an early use of the concept in its modern sense of a national productivity-growth strategy) and strongly supported the "president's stated intention" to create a National Commission on Industrial Competitiveness.[4]

Reagan's own secretary of commerce, Malcolm Baldrige, was also concerned about American industry. Baldrige had come to Commerce after rising to become the chief executive of Scovill, a large, diversified manufacturing firm. In Reagan's system of Cabinet government, Baldrige chaired the Cabinet Council on Commerce and Trade (CCCT). Well before the idea of the Young Commission was broached, Baldrige was pushing to focus attention on the competitive position of the U.S. economy. He also had his eye on the same high-technology sector that the industrial policy advocates identified as "sunrise" industries. In December 1981, the CCCT asked for a study on the competitiveness of the United States in high-technology industries.[5] When the requested report appeared in February 1983, it found that over the previous twelve years, "there has been a decline in the international market position of U.S. high technology industries." If present trends continue, the report warned, there could be "a further decline in [their] competitive position."[6]

Nor had the president completely ignored the productivity challenge.

A month before the CCCT requested its study of high-tech industries, in November 1981, President Reagan established the National Productivity Advisory Committee.[7] In its December 1983 report to the president, the advisory committee spelled out dozens of recommendations and, in an appendix, reported on the extent to which they had already been considered or acted upon. Roger Porter, the president's deputy assistant for policy development, had been one of the voices urging early steps on the productivity front.

Porter had initially come to Washington to work as a White House fellow on the staff of then–vice president Gerald Ford. He actually arrived on the day Ford was being sworn in as president.[8] During his time in the Ford White House, it fell to Porter to coordinate the activities of the Economic Policy Board, a Cabinet-level organization created to develop economic policy. Porter used his experience as the basis of his first book, *Presidential Decision Making: The Economic Policy Board.*[9]

Before coming to Washington, President Reagan had practiced a kind of Cabinet government as governor of California.[10] As he and his transition team sought to develop a similar structure in the new administration, Porter's earlier work and his book caught their eye. Porter was invited to Washington to coordinate the economic policy aspects of the transition and then to stay on to manage the Cabinet Council on Economic Affairs, a close analog to the Economic Policy Board under President Ford.[11]

Porter was an active advocate for doing something about productivity and argued for creating what became the National Productivity Advisory Committee. Secretary of the Treasury Donald Regan provided financial support for the committee, and Porter served as its executive secretary. Chaired by William E. Simon, secretary of the Treasury under both Presidents Nixon and Ford, the committee had a blue ribbon membership drawn largely from the private sector. Michael Deaver, then assistant to the president and deputy chief of staff, was also a member.

In assessing the impact of the committee, Porter was pleased that as proposals developed they were mooted to the relevant executive-branch department so that by the time the committee reported in December 1983, it could note action or at least significant consideration of many of its specific recommendations. The focus of the recommendations, however, was generally limited to adopting added tax incentives and to eliminating or streamlining regulations. The committee's recommendations for stimulating added private-sector investment in technology were positive but relatively modest—including added patent and copyright protection, support for improved mathematics and science education, and a modification of antitrust laws to allow cooperative research. The president actually proposed such a change in the antitrust laws to Congress, and it was adopted by Congress in 1984.[12] While including a number of positive steps, the recommendations fell far short of the kind of broad-based growth strategy being developed on Capitol Hill.

While the National Productivity Advisory Committee was pursuing its work, President Reagan decided that he wanted to discuss new ideas over weekly lunches with his key White House advisers. In addition to James Baker, Edwin Meese, and Michael Deaver, the White House group now included Edwin L. Harper. Harper had served on President Nixon's domestic policy staff and returned to government to work as President Reagan's deputy director of the Office of Management and Budget. When Martin Anderson left the administration, Harper was asked to take Anderson's position as assistant to the president for policy development.

Harper had returned to government from Emerson Electric, a Saint Louis–based manufacturing firm. At the time, Japan was beginning to seem "invincible and indefatigable." America was starting to wonder if "manufacturing was part of the past."[13] For Harper, a twenty-minute videotape of a "lights out" Japanese factory (one that worked a full third shift without any onsite human intervention) made a vivid visual statement of the Japanese challenge. He had the film edited to five minutes and showed it to President Reagan and the others. Reagan responded positively, reminding his aides that as a spokesman for General Electric he had visited more factories than all of them.[14]

The problem and the policies to deal with it were very much part of Harper's concern. But he did not ignore the realities of reelection. Harper suggested that a commission looking at industrial competitiveness would be both good policy and good politics. Harper remembers arguing that a presidential commission would provide a ready answer when people asked what the president was doing about American competitiveness and the Japanese challenge. It would also preempt the movement in Congress to "plan the economy" or adopt an industrial policy. Harper got along well with the political people and talked with them about his idea for a commission.[15]

It is impossible to think that Reagan's politically sophisticated White House staff was not thinking of policy initiatives and political steps that could blunt the political damage emanating from this troubled economy. In late 1982, unemployment had hit a post–World War II high. The loss of twenty-four Republican House seats in the November congressional elections was still fresh in political minds, and the president's popularity was continuing to fall. In January 1983, Reagan's popularity would hit a first-term low of 35 percent.[16] It was in this climate that Harper, the president's assistant for domestic policy, represented the White House at a meeting of the Business Council, an organization of corporate leaders from across America that gathers annually to discuss economic and other policies of the day. Baldrige had been a member of the Business Council and may well have been instrumental in adding Harper to the program.

The conversation that eventually led to the formation of the President's Commission on Industrial Competitiveness started at a tennis match with John Young and Harper on the court.[17] Harper had been specifically invited to address the Business Council on the Reagan administration's science and technology policy. Young told Harper that he did not think the administration had one.

In early1983, Harper broached the possibility of forming a commission to take a hard look at American competitiveness.[18] Young was interested. He explored the idea with key officials in the White House and received assurances from Edwin Meese, counselor to the president, and others in the White House that the commission's work would lead to action. Young himself thought that they were anxious to head off proposals for a reborn Reconstruction Finance Corporation, which had become a key element in the debate over industrial policy. The White House, Young believed, thought that competitiveness was a private-sector problem—that the government had no role.

There were clear political advantages to the commission approach. The administration could point to the commission as its response to calls from the business community and a thoughtful approach to a national problem. If industrial policy proved to be a compelling part of a genuine challenge by the Democratic nominee for president, the administration could not only point to the commission but, if needed, could also call for the commission's preliminary results to serve as guides for immediate administration action.

Whether because of economic uncertainties, Reagan team differences over the future course of economic policy, political calculations, or the fact that commitments had been made, the president and his White House team continued down the path of forming a presidential commission. On June 28, 1983, the president made the formal announcement establishing the commission and named John Young chair.

Naming the Commission's Members

The President's Commission on Industrial Competitiveness had a blue ribbon membership. Not surprisingly, a number of the senior executives were from large industrial firms, many of which were leaders in one high-technology field or another.[19] In addition to the senior business executives, there were six individuals from the world of finance and a sprinkling of university presidents and academics. Michael Porter of the Harvard Business School, a leading student of corporate competitive strategies, also joined the PCIC and would eventually play a major role in developing the framework it used in articulating a competitiveness strategy.

Young did not have a role in determining the shape of the PCIC or its particular members. As he put it, the White House had its own candidates. Prospective members were invited to join the commission with a call from the White House.[20] Michael Porter remembers being called by Harper himself. Others had a vaguer memory of who called but remembered that it was the White House. There was at least one exception to the general rule. Edward Regan, then the comptroller of the State of New York, had been doing some work on competitiveness-related issues. Through Republican friends, he contacted the White House, interviewed with Michael Deaver, and secured a spot on the commission.[21]

Although Young did not choose the business members of the PCIC, he did insist on including at least some members from organized labor. Young himself did not have extensive labor contacts—workers at his company, Hewlett-Packard, were not represented by a union nor were most who worked in high-technology Silicon Valley. In seeking names, Young Talked with Tom Murrin, a senior executive at Westinghouse, then a manufacturing rival of General Electric.[22] As a result of Young's pressure, two labor representatives were included in the final membership of the commission—Howard Samuel, president of the Industrial Union Department (IUD) of the AFL-CIO, and Don Ephlin, vice president of the United Auto Workers (UAW).[23] Samuel had started his union life with the Amalgamated Textile Workers,[24] in the hard bargaining world of the New York garment district. Ephlin was the UAW's lead negotiator with General Motors.[25]

Two figures represented administration views on the PCIC. Harper left the administration just as the commission was being announced, but he went on to serve on the commission in his capacity as executive vice president of the Dallas Corporation. Before he left, Harper passed the White House baton to Roger Porter so the commission would still have a White House–

based champion.[26] The other administration figure on the commission, George A. Keyworth II, was the science adviser to President Reagan. He brought with him some strong ideas on science and technology policy.

Staffing and Funding the Commission

Young had been promised adequate staff and funding for the PCIC. He got both. In addition to a budget of $1.5 million, he was provided with extensive support from the Department of Commerce, starting with Egils Milbergs, his talented executive director.[27] Young also added some talent of his own. At Hewlett-Packard, Robert Kirkwood and his government affairs shop were active and effective supporters of the commission's work. Young added to Kirkwood's team by hiring Thomas Uhlman, a recent graduate of Stanford Business School who also held a Ph.D. in political science, and who brought actual Washington experience from a period spent with the Department of Education. Several members of the Berkeley Roundtable on International Economics (BRIE), a multidisciplinary team based at the University of California, Berkeley, served as frequent consultants to the commission. One of their number, Laura Tyson, became President Clinton's first chair of the Council of Economic Advisers and later served as director of the White House–based National Economic Council.

Picking the Issues

When President Reagan formally announced the formation of his Presidential Commission on Industrial Competitiveness, the country was well into a debate over what to do about established industries, emerging technologies, and the challenge of international competition. To sort through the issues, Young started with a "measles chart." His team pored through the many documents written on American industrial competitiveness[28] to identify the clusters (the measles spots) of issues that were commonly cited. Young also consulted extensively with the PCIC's members to solicit their own suggestions of what key factors should be explored.[29] What emerged from this exercise were committees focused on four key factors (which are described below) and a fifth group to develop an "analytic framework for assessing America's future competitiveness."[30]

The Commission's Report:
New Directions for the Public and Private Sectors

When John Young walked into the Cabinet room in December 1984, he brought with him a clear economic analysis, a set of specific proposals, and a vision of an economy that depended on the parallel efforts of government, educational institutions, and the private sector. Without using the term, Young and his strategy group had articulated an early vision of an emerging New Growth Compact between public and private spheres.

The Young Commission report, *Global Competition: The New Reality,* takes just over sixty pages to summarize the economic challenges facing the country and to spell out a series of steps the country needed to take to assure its long-term competitiveness. The report defined competitiveness and identified the role different sectors—public and private—must play in building a competitive economy. The call to action did not stop with the analysis of sectors but also asks "what must we all do?"[31]

Defining Competitiveness

In defining competitiveness and establishing a framework for the committee report, Young and the PCIC members drew heavily on the thinking of Michael Porter. In the past, Porter's focus had been on corporate initiatives. He had literally written the book (actually, a number of books) on corporate strategy. Thinking about government strategy and how it might affect corporate strategy or corporate success, however, was something of a new exercise for Porter. He had certainly thought about the growing importance of global markets and global competition, but, again, from a firm point of view.[32] Though he was well known for his work on the competitive strategy of firms, Porter was new to thinking through how the role of the government and the initiative of the firm worked together.

Even after the PCIC's report was issued, Porter remained unsatisfied with the analytic framework underlying its approach to competitiveness. Building on its work, he went on to elaborate his well-known diamond, in which government, the private sector, and consumers all play important and complementary roles.

The BRIE group made their own seminal contribution to the commission's thinking. BRIE had been formed in response to the urging of the semiconductor industry that was looking for analytic support. John Zysman, one of BRIE's founders, remembers a dinner at the home of Regis McKenna, who was in the marketing end of Silicon Valley—he was famous for designing the Apple logo among other creations—and was adept at bringing the right people together. The dinner included Charlie Spork, Jerry Sanders, and Bob Noyce—all giants in the semiconductor industry. At the end of the dinner, Noyce offered a check to what would become the BRIE team. BRIE was born shortly thereafter.[33]

The BRIE team had firsthand exposure to the business world of Silicon Valley, but it also had thought about government's role in the economy. Zysman and Steve Cohen, another BRIE founder, had both studied in France. Zysman had taken a scholarly look at French industry, and Cohen had studied French indicative planning. The name BRIE was in part a recognition of their French roots and, they thought, an effective way for each "cheese" joke suggested by the group's name to end up as a marketing tool. Laura Tyson, another BRIE founding member, had also thought about industry and government. Her first book was on the Yugoslav economic system when that country was attempting to move toward a market-oriented system.[34] Zysman and Tyson had both consulted with the Carter administration's Department of Commerce on industry, competition, and technology. Their collaboration led to a jointly edited 1984 volume, *American Industry in International Competition: Government Policies and Corporate Strategies,* which complemented the work of the Young Commission.[35]

In response to John Young's request, four of the senior members of BRIE (Zysman, Tyson, Cohen, and David Teece) together wrote what was originally meant to be published separately as a third volume of what was to become the two-volume PCIC report.[36] In their contribution, the BRIE team spelled out much of the definition of competitiveness eventually adopted by the PCIC and suggested important parts of the framework as well. They drew a clear distinction between the individual competitive firm and the overall competitiveness of an economy that depended on its productivity and on its "ability to shift output to high productivity activities."[37]

They concluded that "national and corporate competitiveness are analytically distinct but practically intertwined."[38] In their view, the success of the economy and the competitive firm were influenced by human resources, "the supporting infrastructure of the economy, and the policies of the nation."[39]

Others on the commission wanted to avoid a definition of competitiveness that emphasized trade performance or that focused on the idea that improved productivity performance in one industry or sector of the economy would translate into added national prosperity. Rachel McCulloch, a commission member and professor of economics at the University of Wisconsin, Madison, expressed some concern about the potential use of trade as a measure of competitiveness. She published her reservations in the *California Management Review* while the commission's work was still in mid-passage.[40]

On the commission itself, Porter was becoming more and more of an intellectual leader.[41] He had done some thinking and pulling together of ideas before the first meeting. He pressed Young on the need for an overall framework or strategy, and Young essentially asked him to pull one together for the group.[42]

The PCIC's final report wove together Porter's strategy, the BRIE analysis and perspectives, and the ideas of the various commissioners. The report articulated the definition of competitiveness that is still commonly used today: "Competitiveness is the degree to which a nation can, under free and fair market conditions, produce goods and services that meet the test of international markets while simultaneously maintaining or expanding the real incomes of its citizens."[43] The commission's emphasis on real incomes and the standard of living has become an almost universal test for policies adopted under the broad umbrella of national competitiveness.

The PCIC's strategy group went a step further by ruling out three popular but misleading measures of a country's competitiveness: the trade deficit, the level of manufacturing employment, and the viability of a single industry. One could almost read this as a response to the points raised by McCulloch in her essay for the *California Management Review.*[44] In looking at the historical record, the strategy group noted that there is no simple relationship between the trade deficit and either a country's standard of living or the growth rate of the economy. A look at U.S. economic history would make the same point. In the nineteenth century, the United States grew rapidly, eventually overtaking major European countries. In surging ahead, however, the United States ran trade deficits as it imported capital from abroad.

In terms of manufacturing employment, the strategy group made the point by drawing on the example of contemporary Japan, where rapid economic growth corresponded with a decline in manufacturing relative to the size of the overall economy. The group noted that "all industries cannot be competitive, because increasing competitiveness in one industry will allow it to bid up wages and attract resources away from others and reduce their competitiveness."[45]

At the same time, the strategy group emphasized that "both 'basic' and 'high-tech' industries can be competitive if they utilize resources productively."[46] Finally, the group stressed that "it is in the U.S. national interest to maintain a broad and diverse industrial base in which *many* industries achieve high levels of productivity" (emphasis in original).[47] In effect, the group was arguing for a large, diversified industrial base without insisting on freezing the current structure. It was decidedly not, however, ready to cavalierly abandon manufacturing for the pleasures of a service economy.

The commission's report, Porter's work on strategy, and the BRIE contribution to the thinking about competitiveness would all lead to further influential work. The BRIE team members continued to be advisers to high-technology firms based in Silicon Valley and active participants in the ongoing debate over the direction of U.S. economy policy. Their voices were heard directly through visits to Washington and work with key committees, members of Congress, and congressional staff. At other times, their ideas were articulated by others in Silicon Valley, including the Semiconductor Industry Association.[48]

Porter was still unsatisfied with the analytic basis for thinking about national competitiveness, the strategies of firms, and the impact of government policy. The eventual result was his magisterial *The Competitive Advantage of Nations,* which has become something of a General Theory of National Competitiveness. In his much-translated book, he links everything from government education and training policies to the impact of demanding customers to portray the differing competitive performance of several industrial economies. I believe that his work on the commission and his interaction with the Silicon Valley–based BRIE group stimulated and enriched his thinking about industrial clusters—usually geographically based firms that included the right mix of competitive suppliers and competitive producers of final products. He has gone on to chart the impact of clusters on the process of innovation.[49]

Focusing on Four Key Areas

In responding to President Reagan's charge to "review the means" of making U.S. industries internationally competitive, the PCIC looked at four key factors in long-term competitiveness: innovation, capital resources, human resources, and international trade. In its final report, however, the commission went well beyond making a list of policy proposals. Instead, it developed a long-term competitiveness strategy that built on key, mutually reinforcing elements. The PCIC report emphasized that "while the . . .

determinants of our competitiveness are treated separately, it is important to note that they are all interrelated."[50]

Ideas and Innovation

The PCIC recommended making "technology a continuing competitive advantage."[51] It responded to the large but fragmented federal research and development (R&D) structure with a call for a Cabinet-level Department of Science and Technology. This was a definite priority of Keyworth, Reagan's science adviser. In particular, the PCIC added the voice of high-technology industry to that of policymakers and some academics in calling for a national technology policy to complement the country's sustained commitment to basic science.

Capital Resources and Competitiveness

The PCIC called for steps to improve "(1) the supply of capital, (2) its cost to American industry, and (3) our ability to let capital flow to its most productive uses."[52] It emphasized the need to reduce the fiscal deficit that put the government in competition with the private sector for limited funds. At the same time, it linked the deficit to the need to borrow internationally, the resulting increase in the value of dollar, and the consequent loss of exports.[53]

The PCIC's Capital Resources Committee emphasized the link between investment, technology, and productivity growth. As the committee put it, "The effectiveness of R&D in raising productivity is greatly enhanced if the cost of capital is low enough so that businesses can afford to undertake more R&D and to embody R&D results more quickly in the capital stock."[54]

Human Resources

The PCIC did not look at human resources as only a question of improving education or adding new training programs. Instead, it called on the country to "develop a more skilled, flexible, and motivated workforce."[55] Although it did not use the phrase, it was, in essence, recommending a lifelong learning strategy in which governments, the private sector, and universities all played a role. It proposed a balanced tax treatment of investments in human and physical resources, the use of vocational education funds for incumbent workers, and federal funding for graduate study in engineering.

It called on the nation's business schools to "prepare managers for this new era of competition."[56] Other recommendations stressed the need for improved labor–management dialogue, plans to allow employees to share in company success, and policies that would help ease the transition of workers from one job to the next.[57]

The PCIC was equally far reaching when it came to elementary and secondary education. In a single paragraph, it called for higher standards in elementary and secondary schools and suggested that "effective use of computers in schools and the development of educational software should be supported through *federally funded proto-type research*" (emphasis added).[58]

International Trade Policy

The PCIC was looking at an American economy that was operating on a global stage. Yet it saw a highly fragmented trade policy process that involved "at least 25 executive branch agencies and 19 congressional subcommittees"[59] and was overseen by two of the Cabinet-level committees established by President Reagan in his first term. Its answer was to create a Cabinet-level Department of Trade as part of a policy that put trade on "a par with domestic and foreign policy issues."[60] It also called for reducing self-imposed limits on exports, increasing support for U.S. exporters; and strengthening the international trading system. In addition, it recommended the development of an "Omnibus Trade Law" that would help industries adjust to international competition, respond to "foreign government policies aimed at fostering specific industries," and improve the enforcement of laws against unfair trade.[61]

Reaction to the Report

Armed with the PCIC report's detailed analysis, a clear strategy, and a bevy of specific recommendations, Young was ready for the Cabinet. The Cabinet, however, did not seem to be ready for him. It should have been. Roger Porter, a key White House aide throughout the commission's existence, attended at least some of its sessions, and, given his combination of intelligence and attention to detail, must have had a good idea of its direction, findings, and recommendations.[62] Milbergs, its executive director, stressed that he wrote regular and frequent reports to the White House on its progress and its members' thinking.[63]

Young, Michael Porter, and Tom Uhlman were the three who met with the Cabinet. Knowing that time would be brief, they had boiled down the presentation to its essentials. Porter, who was used to the corporate environment, remembers being taken aback that the White House did not have a decent screen or projector for the slides that he had prepared.[64] It was, apparently, the first time that overheads had been used in a Reagan Cabinet meeting.[65]

Porter's memory was not clear as to whether or not both he and Young made the presentation or if it was just Young. In any case, the Cabinet did not have much of a response. Young remembered a question or two from Secretary of State George Shultz. Porter's memories are similar. He remembers Shultz making some points and asking questions but nothing from any of the others. The president was amiable, a bowl of jellybeans at his place, but did not ask any questions. Uhlman remembers someone writing a note—"If the U.S. is in such trouble, why are the Europeans so jealous?"— to Baldrige. Uhlman thought it was the president but was not absolutely sure.

Why was there such a limited response? Porter put it down as just a "polite hearing." Young thought the report simply did not fit the preconceived ideas of some in the White House. Putting a humorous face on the meeting, Young decided that the lack of response could be traced to Uhlman's curly hair preventing the Cabinet from actually seeing the projected graphs.[66]

Having presented its report to the Cabinet and released the report, the commission was at an end. But this did not mean that Young and the other commission members had finished their work. Young, the other members, and Milbergs testified before various congressional committees. Young felt the congressional response was positive and showed considerable interest in the PCIC's work. Here was a blue ribbon commission, heavily influenced by chief executives of high-technology companies, that identified a series of challenges facing the country that demanded public- as well as private-sector action. More than any specific recommendation, the PCIC in effect told concerned members of Congress that they were right in identifying national competitiveness as a serious problem that needed action. There was enough interest that the Senate passed a "resolution demanding that the White House respond to the PCIC report."[67]

Young believes the business community's response was also largely positive.[68] After all, businesses facing international competition had been unhappy about some elements of the administration's economic program from the very start. Although the economic recovery was well under way when Young reported in December 1984, a highly valued dollar was still penalizing exports and industries that faced import competition. Industries competing in the global market were also wrestling with a new, often effective kind of competition in which overseas industry and a foreign governments acted in tandem. While strong advocates of the "magic of the marketplace," these same companies knew they drew strength from the federal R&D enterprise, looked to public institutions to educate much of their labor force, and relied on national negotiators to develop and enforce international trading rules.

The lack of Cabinet interest was paralleled by a lack of administration action. With the 1984 election safely past, the administration was moving confidently into a second term. The president, the Cabinet, and much of the country felt that America was back. It was not just the economic recovery but also a renewed confidence in the American spirit. Carter's malaise had given way to Reagan's "Morning again in America."

Secretary of Commerce Baldrige had assembled a talented staff to help provide the PCIC with data and analysis. The staff was prepared to take the next step and help turn prescription into policy. But there was no interest. Baldrige had been a strong supporter of the PCIC and had been instrumental in arranging for Young's briefing of the Cabinet. Baldrige remained concerned about American competitiveness until his untimely death in 1987 in a rodeo accident. He did not, however, seem able to muster support within the administration for a more active approach. Shortly after the PCIC issued its report, Baldrige told the staff to close up shop and move on to other tasks.[69]

Young was not content with a well-written report, a Cabinet briefing, and a presidential thank-you. In his early conversations with Harper, Meese, and others in the White House, he had sought a commitment for action following the analysis. His fellow commissioners had much the same view. In the end, Young believed that the competitiveness agenda was so broad that a president would have to take "ownership" of it. But there was no indication that either President Reagan or his White House was moving in that direction.

By 1986, Young had tired of waiting and had gone on to found the private-sector Council on Competitiveness to pursue the broad-based competitiveness agenda. He kept the structure of the presidential commission by including labor leaders, captains of industry, and university presidents as members. Six of the PCIC members went on to serve on the private council's first executive committee, including Young as council chair. Michael Porter—who had done so much to develop a framework for thinking about and measuring competitiveness—also joined the council's executive committee. Although they did not participate in the council's executive committee, other PCIC members joined it as general members.

In forming the Council on Competitiveness, Young had the active support of Sandy Trowbridge, then the president of the National Association of Manufacturers. To help speed the council's formation, Trowbridge allowed it to use a tax-exempt 501(c)(3) organization that had already been established by the National Association of Manufacturers.

Since its founding by Young in 1986, the Council on Competitiveness and its members—building on the PCIC's work—have emphasized the critical importance of technology to everything from economic growth to national security, as well as pursuing the even broader question of national competitiveness. The council has supported considerable research on different aspects of national productivity growth and overall competitiveness. In particular, it has succeeded in making technology, technology policy, and national innovation key elements of the national debate on economic policy. The council has done much more than simply keep the competitiveness flame alive. It and its membership have joined with many others in a competitiveness movement that has eventually changed national economic thinking and national economic policy.

Notes

1. Author's interview with John Young, November 30, 1999.
2. Interview with Young.
3. See Otis L. Graham Jr., *Losing Time: The Industrial Policy Debate* (Cambridge, Mass.: Harvard University Press, 1992), 160, 165. Mondale also took a strong line on trade policy but by 1983 "de-emphasized trade restrictions." See I. M. Destler, *American Trade Politics*, 2nd ed. (Washington, D.C.: Institute for International Economics, 1992), 176–77.
4. Business–Higher Education Forum, *America's Competitive Challenge: The Need for a National Response* (Washington, D.C.: Business-Higher Education Forum, 1983), 8.
5. Cabinet Council on Commerce and Trade, "An Assessment of U.S. Competitiveness in High Technology Industries," revised draft, photocopy, October 1982.
6. U.S. Department of Commerce, International Trade Administration, *An Assessment of U.S. Competitiveness in High Technology Industries* (Washington, D.C.: U.S. Department of Commerce, 1983), iii.
7. This committee was established by Executive Order 12332. The text of the order can be found in the National Productivity Advisory Committee's report "Restoring Productivity Growth in America: A Challenge for the 1980s," submitted to the president in December 1983.
8. Author's interview with Roger Porter, April 24, 2002.

9. Roger Porter, *Presidential Decision Making: The Economic Policy Board* (New York: Cambridge University Press, 1980).

10. Lou Cannon, *President Reagan: The Role of a Lifetime* (New York: Simon & Schuster, 1991), 183.

11. Interview with R. Porter.

12. National Productivity Advisory Committee, "Restoring Productivity Growth in America," 29–43. The president proposed the relaxation of antirust laws in his National Productivity and Innovation Act of 1983 and it became law in the National Cooperative Research Act of 1984. See Lewis M. Branscomb and Richard Florida, "Challenges to Technology Policy in a Changing World Economy" in *Investing in Innovation, Creating a Research and Innovation Policy That Works,* ed. Lewis M. Branscomb and James H. Keller (Cambridge, Mass.: MIT Press, 1998), 17.

13. Author's interview with Edwin L. Harper, June 21, 2002.

14. According to Lou Cannon, during his eight years with General Electric, Reagan visited every one of General Electric's 135 plants and spoke to 250,000 General Electric employees. See Cannon, *President Reagan,* 89.

15. Interview with Harper.

16. Cannon, *President Reagan,* 274.

17. The meeting on the tennis court and much subsequent material is drawn from an interview with John Young on November 30, 1999.

18. Young thought the conversation was in late 1982 or early 1983. Harper thought the idea lunches with Reagan started in 1983, suggesting that his conversation with Young was in early 1983. Interviews with Young and Harper.

19. In addition to Young, there were Robert Noyce, coinventor of the integrated circuit and cofounder of Intel; Mark Shephard Jr., chairman and chief executive of Texas Instruments; and Dr. Ian Ross, president of AT&T's Bell Labs. Aerospace was represented by Robert Anderson, chairman and chief executive of Rockwell International; pharmaceuticals by Dr. Gerald D. Laubach, president of Pfizer; and power generation by Thomas J. Murrin, president of the Energy and Advanced Technology Group at Westinghouse. Among more traditional manufacturers, the widely respected John D. Ong, chairman, president, and chief executive of B. F. Goodrich, stands out.

20. Author's interviews with commission members Rachel McCulloch, May 1, 2002; Sybil Mobley, May 20, 2002; and Tom Murrin, April 4, 2002.

21. Author's interview with Edward V. Regan, August 19, 2002.

22. Author's interview with Thomas Murrin, April 4, 2002.

23. The IUD was the descendant of Walter Reuther's Congress of Industrial Organizations, which had merged with the American Federation of Labor.

24. The Amalgamated Textile Workers has merged with the International Ladies Garment Workers Union to form UNITE—the United Needle Industrial Trades.

25. Although the UAW had resisted calls for auto industry protection from imports in the early 1970s, it had become an ardent supporter of import restraint in the 1980s. With its backing, the House of Representatives had already passed legislation pertaining to cars sold in the United States: "The Fair Practices in Automotive Products Act, more familiarly referred to as the 'domestic contents' . . . bill . . . requires that all companies, domestic and foreign, selling more than half a million cars a year in the U.S. manufacture them with at least 90 percent American parts and labor. Companies selling 200,000 to 500,000 autos must use 75% domestic parts and labor. . . . The domestic contents bill generated more reams of editorials and analyses, pro and con, than virtually

any other single piece of domestic legislation in 1982." Randall Rothenberg, *The Neo-Liberals* (New York: Simon & Schuster, 1984), 101.

26. Interview with R. Porter.

27. Milbergs had joined the Reagan administration after a successful career at the RAND Corporation, a nationally renowned think tank with close ties to the military. His initial assignment at the Commerce Department as associate deputy secretary allowed him to form a close working relationship with the senior political leadership at the department. Author's interview with Egils Milbergs, August 5, 1999.

28. For instance, see the list of documents mentioned in the report of the PCIC's strategy group. PCIC, *Global Competition: The New Realtity,* 2 vols. (Washington, D.C.: U.S. Government Printing Office, 1985), vol. 2, 37, 52–53.

29. The membership of the PCIC was expanded from twenty-five to thirty on September 8, 1983, and to thirty-five on January 3, 1984. See PCIC, *Global Competition,* vol. 2, 246.

30. PCIC, *Global Competition,* vol. 2, xi.

31. PCIC, *Global Competition,* vol. 1, 3.

32. E.g., see Thomas M. Hout, Michael E. Porter, Eileen Rudden, and Eric Vogt, "Global Industries: New Rules for the Competitive Game," Working Paper HBS 80-53, photcopy, Graduate School of Business Administration, Harvard University.

33. Author's interview with John Zysman, April 10 2002.

34. Laura D. Tyson, *The Yugoslav Economic System and Its Performance in the 1970s* (Berkeley: University of California Press, 1980).

35. John Zysman and Laura D. Tyson, *American Industry in International Competition: Government Policies and Corporate Strategies* (Ithaca, N.Y.: Cornell University Press, 1984).

36. See Stephen Cohen, David J. Teece, Laura Tyson, and John Zysman, "Global Competition: The New Reality, Volume III," unpublished working paper of the President's Commission on Industrial Competitiveness, Washington, November 8, 1984.

37. Cohen et al., "Global Competition," 2.

38. Cohen et al., "Global Competition," 2.

39. Cohen et al., "Global Competition," 2.

40. See Rachel McCulloch, "Point of View: Trade Deficits, Industrial Competitiveness, and the Japanese, *California Management Review* 27, no. 2 (winter 1985). Although the article appeared in the 1985 issue, McCulloch sent copies to Young, Porter, and others in July 1984. See the July 16, 1984, letter from McCulloch to John Young in which she discussed the draft.

41. A number of commission members mentioned Porter's growing influence. See, e.g., interview with Regan.

42. Author's interview with Michael Porter, May 17, 2002.

43. PCIC, *Global Competition,* vol. 2, 6.

44. McCulloch, "Point of View," 142.

45. PCIC, *Global Competition,* vol. 2, 7.

46. Cohen et al., "Global Competition," 7.

47. Cohen et al., "Global Competition," 7.

48. Interview with Zysman.

49. Michael E. Porter (Harvard University), Monitor Group and the Council on Competitiveness, "Clusters of Innovation: Regional Foundations of U.S. Competitiveness," photocopy, Council on Competitiveness, Washington, October 2001.

50. PCIC, *Global Competition*, vol. 1, 18.

51. PCIC, *Global Competition,* vol. 1, 18.

52. PCIC, *Global Competition,* vol. 1, 25–26.

53. PCIC, *Global Competition,* vol. 1, 26.

54. PCIC, *Global Competition,* vol. 2, 108.

55. PCIC, *Global Competition,* vol. 1, 30.

56. PCIC, *Global Competition,* vol. 1, 37.

57. PCIC, *Global Competition,* vol. 1, 35.

58. PCIC, *Global Competition,* vol. 1, 37.

59. PCIC, *Global Competition,* vol. 1, 38.

60. PCIC, *Global Competition,* vol. 1, 41–42.

61. PCIC, *Global Competition,* vol. 1, 42.

62. This is my conclusion based on conversations with a number of commission members, who remember Roger Porter, and my interview with Roger Porter.

63. Interview with Milbergs.

64. Interview with M. Porter.

65. Interview with Young.

66. Interviews with M. Porter, Uhlman, and Young.

67. Graham, *Losing Time,* 169.

68. Interview with Young.

69. Interview with Milbergs.

Chapter 7

Congress Acts on Trade and Competitiveness

Looking at the future in January 1985, one might have expected four more years dominated by Reagan administration thinking and initiatives. It did not turn out that way. Instead, a growing national concern about trade deficits, international competition, and slow productivity growth created a new congressional coalition that forged a consensus around just those ideas that had seemed abandoned after the 1984 election.

In a remarkable four-year period, Congress moved from a focus on trade and trade deficits to craft an omnibus bill that encompassed most of the elements of a comprehensive competitiveness strategy. In crafting and then passing this complicated piece of legislation, Congress and the business community developed a new working relationship. Just as Congress developed a better understanding of the importance of business, the business community rediscovered the critical role government policy could play in its own success. Despite often-adamant opposition from the executive branch, congressional initiative and persistence were a reminder of how important America's system of dispersed governance could be. At the same time, it took leadership. There was nothing inevitable in the struggle or its outcome that, in the end, helped move the country toward a more competitive future.

Pressure Builds for Action on Budget and Trade Deficits

The Reagan administration's early promise of a balanced budget had given way to one record budget deficit after another. For 1984, the deficit approached $185 billion, and the prospects for future deficit reduction were

172

not bright. In four years, President Reagan had essentially doubled the national debt.

The budget was not the only deficit that captured political and public attention. Year by year, the country was also running one record trade deficit after another. By 1984, the merchandise trade deficit passed the $100 billion mark, with no clear prospects for improvement. Just as striking was the deterioration of the current account, a broader measure of U.S. international transactions that includes not only trade but also the sale of international services, royalties on U.S. intellectual property, and dividends from America's overseas investments. By 1984, the current account deficit had also pushed past the $100 billion level and at, $107 billion, was almost as large as the $112 billion deficit in merchandise trade.

The trade and budget deficits were widely pointed to as signs of an economy living on borrowed money and borrowed time. Without focusing on any detailed economic rationale, there was popular unease that in recording fiscal deficits, the United States was borrowing from the future in a way that was unsustainable. The trade deficits raised a similar kind of concern. Although trade surpluses were commonplace for much of the post–World War II era, from 1976 on trade deficits had become an annual reality. At times, trade deficits had been an important element in fostering long-term American growth. In the nineteenth century, trade deficits were the economic counterpart to the foreign capital that helped build the railroads and develop the country. John Young's commission had been careful *not* to focus on the trade deficit as a current measure of a country's long-term competitiveness.

In the mid-1980s, however, the trade deficit had more resonance, for several reasons. Trade and international investment had become much more important to the domestic economy. The combination of rising international competition and the very strong dollar created economic difficulties for many firms that had been very successful exporters. Most striking of all, an array of high-technology firms were facing a Japanese challenge that combined fierce competition in the American market with seemingly impenetrable barriers to its own. Trade problems could no longer be dismissed as the exclusive domain of industrial laggards. Suddenly, America's industrial future was on the line.

The trade deficit was a particularly attractive target for the Democrats. It unified a party that contained strong labor constituencies as well as more suburban Democrats focused on high technology and growth. It allowed Democrats to forge new relationships and potential alliances with key segments of the business community that found few in the Reagan administration who would listen to their concern about either the dollar or Japanese trade practices.

Some Democrats also saw trade as a way of compensating for their perceived weakness on questions of national security. Representative Tony Coelho (D-Calif.), then chair of the Democratic Congressional Campaign Committee, referred to trade as "a Democratic macho issue. We're for American strength."[1] In particular, the competitive challenge to electronics came to highlight the link between trade and national security. It was no longer a question of some overall concept of economic strength but rather of key components for weapons systems that were facing a competitive challenge.

While trade pressures on Congress grew, the Reagan administration did little to reduce them. The confident, almost cavalier dismissal of the strong dollar in the president's 1985 economic report was followed by a series of specific trade actions that fueled congressional concern among Republicans as well as Democrats.[2] The president's budget request for fiscal 1986 proposed eliminating a $3.8 billion direct loan program used by the Export-Import Bank to support U.S. exports. Whatever the merits of the president's proposal, objections were voiced by the Hill and by the business community.[3] On March 1, 1985, the president announced that he would not extend the voluntary automobile agreement with Japan.[4]

The president's next trade move came on the question of shoe imports. American law and international trading rules allow industries suffering serious injury from imports to seek temporary import protection. Under American law, industries seeking relief can petition the International Trade Commission. In this case, the commission had recommended granting temporary protection for the shoe industry. On August 27, however, the president indicated that he would not impose tariffs or quotas on imported shoes, despite the recommendation of the commission. Senator John Danforth (R-Mo.), a "shoe state" senator and a Republican leader on trade questions, was particularly outraged. He predicted "a rise in protectionist legislation."[5]

Congress Takes the Initiative

Congress was no longer willing to wait for administration action. Even before the opening of Congress in January 1985, the majority leader, Jim Wright (D-Tex.), had begun to think differently about international trade as a national concern.[6] Wright had some sense of how disruptive a shift in trade could be. He still had a vivid memory of a story his father had told him about how a decision by the Soviet Union to stop buying British textiles led to a collapse in the price of Texas cotton. Wright had been born in December 1922 and had grown up during the Great Depression. When his generation read about the Smoot-Hawley tariff (signed into law by President Herbert Hoover), it was often cited as an important cause of the Great Depression itself.

The state of U.S. international trade had also been broached at a recent issues retreat for House Democrats that featured Lee Iacocca, then the chief executive of Chrysler Corporation (now DaimlerChrysler). At the time, Iacocca spoke with enormous credibility. After securing federal loan guarantees in 1980, Iacocca had brought Chrysler back from the brink of financial collapse and repaid its federal loans. In rebuilding Chrysler, Iacocca had worked closely with his dealers and suppliers, including a manufacturer of air conditioners whose headquarters was in Wright's Fort Worth–based district. He was, Wright believed, "something of a folk hero." Wright remembered Iacocca saying that eliminating the trade deficit was as patriotic a duty as conventional defense. For Wright, Iacocca "presented the trade issue in a way he had not heard it presented before."[7]

When House Democrats again assembled at the Greenbrier Hotel in anticipation of the 99th Congress (1985–86), Wright was ready to start the House down the path of what, four years later, would become the Omnibus Trade and Competitiveness Act of 1988. On the train to the Greenbrier, Wright talked to Representative Don Bonker (D-Wash.) about the need to do something about trade and the trade deficit. Bonker remembers thinking that Wright "had a sense about the politics of trade."[8]

Wright told Bonker that when the Democrats returned from the Greenbrier, he was going to tell the speaker of the House, Tip O'Neill, that there should be a trade task force and that Bonker should head it. Bonker responded that Sam Gibbons (D-Fla.) was really Mr. Trade. As head of the subcommittee on trade of the House Ways and Means committee, Gibbons would have been an obvious choice to head a Democratic trade task force. But Wright had already decided that he needed to move beyond the confines of Ways and Means. He told Bonker that Gibbons would serve as the vice chair.

After their return, Speaker O'Neill called a meeting of committee chairs at which Wright spelled out the idea of a task force. The speaker must have known that at least some of the committee chairs would be apprehensive about a leadership task force that was operating outside the committee system. When the speaker had established an ad hoc committee to consider President Jimmy Carter's energy plan, the ad hoc body was given the power to overrule the individual committees.[9] At this meeting, the speaker stressed that no bill would go to the floor unless the committee chairs were in agreement.

The choice of Bonker was something of a surprise. At the time, Bonker was chair of the Subcommittee on International Economics and Trade of the House Foreign Affairs Committee. The committee's and subcommittee's jurisdiction was focused on export promotion and export controls. The Ways and Means Committee—with its jurisdiction over tariffs, trade negotiations, and the unfair trade laws—would have been an obvious choice to provide a task force chair. Although Sam Gibbons was not upset about serving as vice chair,[10] committee chair Dan Rostenkowski (D-Ill.) was not happy with the decision to work around the committee structure. Other committees had a strong interest as well. Under the leadership of John Dingell (D-Mich.), members of the Energy and Commerce Committee maintained an interest in trade and had an expansive view of their jurisdiction. Before energy was added to its title, the committee had been known as the Committee on Interstate and Foreign Commerce.

Wright remembers choosing Bonker because he had worked hard on the trade question and was popular with the younger members.[11] Because he was from Washington State, some of the leadership staff thought that Thomas Foley, the Democratic whip and number three in the House Democratic leadership, had pushed Bonker's nomination.[12] Foley's influence could have been at play. He had advised the younger members from Washington State and had urged Bonker to seek a position on the Foreign Affairs Committee, whose export promotion jurisdiction would fit well with the state's heavy dependence on exports. But Bonker himself did not think Foley had played a key role. Rufus Yerxa, then the chief trade counsel on the Ways and Means Committee, thought the choice of Bonker allowed Wright to avoid choosing between Rostenkowski and Dingell.[13] By choosing Bonker, Wright also indicated his preference for a broader approach to trade—one that considered exports as well as imports and involved a number of committees. By April, Wright had pulled together the membership of the task force and, at the beginning of the month, O'Neill, Wright, and the House Democrats launched a twenty-one-member Trade Task Force chaired by Bonker.[14]

While Wright was working to launch a trade task force, other Democrats were taking their own steps to open markets or restrict imports. In February 1985, even before Reagan made his decision on the automobile agreement, Representative Stanley Lundine (D-N.Y.) introduced a proposal (HR 1060) to phase out the voluntary restraint agreement with Japan rather than simply bring it to an abrupt end.[15] In mid-July, a proposed import surcharge took center stage in the trade debate. Representatives Dan Rostekowski and Richard A. Gephardt (D-Mo.) and Senator Lloyd Bentsen (D-Tex.) introduced legislation imposing a surcharge on imports from countries that "maintained both a large bilateral trade surplus with the United States and unfair barriers to imports."[16] "With subsequent revisions, the bill became a stand-alone Gephardt measure and remained a part of the Omnibus Trade and Competitiveness Act debate well into the 100th Congress."[17] (The 100th Congress was in session in 1987–88.)

As is often the case, the bill's sponsors were more important than the details of the proposed legislation. Rostenkowski was chair of the powerful Ways and Means Committee that governed tax and trade legislation as well as most of the spending on entitlements, including Social Security and Medicare. Bentsen was the ranking Democrat on the Senate Finance Committee, which had a similar jurisdictional reach. As chair of the House Democratic Caucus (he had succeeded Gillis Long), Gephardt was part of the House Leadership and was widely viewed as a rising star in the House. The bill was another signal to the White House that it was time to act on the trade front.

Bentsen was far from alone in the Senate in demanding action on trade. In late March, the Senate approved by 92 to 0 a Danforth-sponsored resolution (S. Con. Res. 15) calling on the president to retaliate against Japanese trade practices.[18] Five days later, the Senate Finance Committee, by a 12-to-4 margin, passed a bill "that would force the President to retaliate if Japan did not end unfair practices."[19] Throughout the spring, Bentsen and Danforth repeatedly expressed their concern about trade. In early March 1985, Danforth presented data detailing the trade restrictions of the European Community.[20] At the same time, Bentsen expressed his fear that "every finance minister from Kuala Lumpur to Brasilia thinks the model for development is Japan."[21] In Bentsen's view, that meant protectionism. Bentsen's comments were a clear example of how, at least in congressional thinking, Japan was beginning to emerge as a pervasive problem rather than as just the source of a series of isolated trade disputes.

As the year progressed, the trade issue took on more and more political prominence. It even emerged as a key issue in an off-year election to fill a congressional vacancy in the First District in Northeast Texas. Like much of Texas and much of the South, the First District had a long history of supporting Democrats. The first district had sent the populist Wright Patman to Congress for almost fifty years. When Patman's successor, Sam B. Hall Jr., resigned to take a federal judgeship, the national Republican Party leaders thought they saw an opportunity to make headway in what had always been a "yellow dog" Democratic district.

The Republicans threw their support behind Edd Hargett, a local rancher and engineer. Hargett brought a number of personal advantages to the race. Among other strengths, he was still remembered as the football hero who had quarterbacked the Texas A&M University "Aggies" to their last Cotton Bowl victory in 1968. In a race against six Democrats, Hargett carried a 42 percent plurality of the vote but was forced into a runoff against Democrat Jim Chapman, a former local district attorney.

Heading into the runoff, Hargett seemed reasonably well positioned. He had beaten Chapman by 12 percent (42 to 30 percent) in the primary, continued to draw on the "Aggie" network, and was again well supported by the national party. In the run-up to the runoff, observers singled out Hargett's "political amateur status" as his single biggest liability.[22] It may have been just that lack of experience that let him stumble over the trade issue. Competition from foreign steelmakers had forced Lone Star Steel to lay off workers from their First District plants. When asked about trade, however, Hargett responded that he did not "know what trade policies have to do with bringing jobs to East Texas."[23] It was the kind of response that let an opponent criticize Hargett's lack of experience and a lack of understanding of the district itself. As Chapman emphasized the trade issue, Hargett compounded his error by handing out campaign hats that were labeled "Made in Taiwan." Wright had campaigned for Chapman and remembered an even more costly political gaffe—Hargett's Fourth of July flags had also been made overseas.[24]

In the end, Hargett lost a very close contest (50.9 to 49.1 percent). The Democrats felt they had not only won a close congressional election but had also identified a winning issue. While campaigning in Texas in August, Wright had made trade and competitiveness an important part of his standard stump speech.[25] If there was a trade shot fired in Texas, it was heard in many other parts of the country. Democrats and Republicans returned from their August recess with a shared sense that trade had become a major issue. *Congressional Quarterly* described a Congress where "Members

Seek the Initiative on 'Trade Fever'" and quoted Speaker O'Neill as recognizing that the trade deficit was surpassing the budget deficit as a concern
among members.[26]

It was past time for the Reagan administration to act. President Reagan
took the first step in early September 1985, when he set a December 1, 1985,
deadline for negotiations with Japan over lowering barriers to shoe and
leather imports and with the European Union over ending subsidies for
canned fruit exports. For the first time, the president used his authority to
initiate cases against unfair trade practices rather than waiting for a petition
from industry.[27] He picked three targets: a Brazilian law limiting the sales
of imported computers, Japanese restrictions on the sale of U.S. cigarettes,
and a Korean law prohibiting the sale of life and fire insurance by foreign-
based firms.[28]

Two weeks later, the president and the administration moved more broadly
and more decisively. The dollar came first. On September 22, 1985, Secretary of the Treasury James Baker and the finance ministers of France,
Germany, Japan, and the United Kingdom agreed on the need for further
dollar depreciation. They issued the Plaza Accord, a communiqué stressing
the need for coordination in economic policies and joint intervention in currency markets to bring down the value of the U.S. dollar.[29] The following
day, President Reagan delivered a major trade policy speech, in which he
announced further trade initiatives, indicated support for major trade legislation, and established a multidepartmental trade strike force.[30]

The shift to a more competitive dollar would not bring results over night.
As I. M. Destler notes, the "decline of the dollar would bring first the hope,
then the reality of improvement in the trade balance."[31] The hope before the
decline reflects what economists refer to as the "J curve." Because currency
values change more rapidly than the underlying volume of trade, a declining currency will usually lead to an increase in the dollar size of the deficit
and then only over a year or more translate into a smaller trade deficit.

In establishing a trade strike force, Reagan opened another avenue for
the Commerce Department to be active on trade. By all reports, the strike
force was a last-minute idea. In his *Trade Warriors,* Steve Dryden credits
Don Regan with inserting the idea into the speech to "heighten the appearance of action."[32] Writing in his *Trading Places,* Prestowitz describes the
initial strike force as "only a speech writer's rhetorical flourish."[33] Whatever
its origin, the administration turned to Secretary of Commerce Malcolm
Baldrige to run it. The strike force proved particularly active in dealing with

the trade challenges faced by the American semiconductor industry. The Semiconductor Industry Association had filed a Section 301 (of the 1974 Trade Act) or unfair trade petition in July 1985 against leading Japanese chip producers. There followed antidumping (alleging below-cost sales) petitions, including one filed by the secretary of commerce himself. The battle with Japan over dumping semiconductors and access to the Japanese semiconductor market continued until a complex agreement was reached in August 1986.[34] The August agreement was not, however, the end of the story, and negotiations over semiconductors continued well into the 1990s.

Despite the attack on the dollar and the deficit, the newly aggressive stance on trade barriers, and the rhetorical nod toward fair as well as free trade, the president's program did not markedly slow congressional action on the trade front. Looking back from the perspective of 1994, Susan Schwab, the senior trade adviser to Senator Danforth, thought that "the executive branch's proactive stance probably had some impact in moderating the various trade measures being drafted in the Congress, but it was too little, too late to stop them."[35] Within two months, Democrats and Republicans in both houses of Congress had developed their own versions of omnibus trade legislation. In addition, Congress continued to press forward on individual trade measures, including the proposal to impose strict limitations on textile imports.

The House Republicans moved first, unveiling their proposal on October 8, 1985. Nine days later, Representative Don Bonker's Democratic Task Force outlined the principles for their trade legislation. In early November, Senate Democrats, led by Bentsen introduced their own comprehensive bill (S 1837). Later in November, a bipartisan group led by Republican Senator Danforth introduced a comprehensive bipartisan measure (S 1860). The next day, November 21, the House Energy and Commerce Committee approved its own answer to comprehensive trade reform (HR 3777).

The key maneuvering, however, centered on the proposal to impose quotas on imports of textiles and shoes. When finally placed on the president's desk, the legislation had been narrowed to focus on exports from South Korea, Taiwan, and Hong Kong. President Reagan vetoed the bill on December 17, 1985, while offering nothing more than a study of global trade conditions in the two industries and $100 million for retraining.[36] Instead of moving quickly to challenge the president, congressional leaders decided to hold the vote on overriding the president's veto until later in 1986 when the prospect of congressional elections might strengthen their hand.

Taxes before Trade, 1985–86

Trade and competitiveness grew in importance as the country moved into 1986. Trade and budget deficits continued to rise. The once-vaunted surplus in high-technology trade had virtually disappeared. Japanese competition continued to progress from one industry to the next in a seemingly unstoppable march to industrial supremacy.

Despite an ever louder chorus of concern in industry and growing pressure from Congress, the administration's priority was a comprehensive reworking of the tax code that promised lower marginal rates and considerable simplification. Chairman Rostenkowski and his Ways and Means Committee spent much of 1985 working on the proposed tax reform. With final passage of the House tax reform bill coming on December 17, 1985, there was less time for Ways and Means to turn its attention to trade legislation.

The pressure for action on trade, however, was building throughout 1985. Then, in early March 1986, Speaker O'Neill appointed Majority Leader Wright to coordinate the activities of House committees.[37] Wright had his hands full. The problem was not in crafting a bill. The broad outlines of legislation had been contained in the October 1985 report of the Bonker-led Democratic Trade Task Force. The real challenge was in moving legislation that cut across jurisdictional boundaries to involve several powerful House committees.

For the Democrats, trade was becoming one element in an overall competitiveness strategy. They were looking at trade in the context of exchange rates and the underlying influence of fiscal and monetary policies. Economic and political logic had given exports as much prominence as imports in their thinking. There was also growing support for new trade measures that sought to protect American intellectual property.

Although the House Ways and Means Committee was the lead player on trade legislation, other committees also had important roles. Wright used unusual—not to say extraordinary—procedures to put an overall bill together. He met with key committee and subcommittee chairs to set a clear timetable for committee action. He turned to the Rules Committee to combine the seven separate trade bills while settling as many jurisdictional disputes as possible. The Rules Committee moved quickly and successfully to turn the seven bills and the work of six committees into HR 4800, the Trade and International Economic Policy Act of 1986.[38]

What had started with a focus on trade law had evolved into an embryonic competitiveness strategy. The inclusion of bill titles on export promotion and export controls was not a surprise—these were, after all, the heart of Bonker's own trade jurisdiction. However, the addition of other pieces to the bill was less obvious. Provisions on exchange rates grew out of the work of the House Banking Committee, which had focused on the manipulation of exchange rates to gain trade advantage. At the time, there was a suspicion that Japan was buying dollars to drive down the relative value of the yen so that Japanese exports would be more price competitive on world markets.

It was the inclusion of education provisions that turned trade legislation toward a full competitiveness strategy. It was a step I helped make. At the time, I was working for Representative Don Bonker as his staff director on the International Economic Policy and Trade Subcommittee of the House Committee on Foreign Affairs. Along with the staffs of the Ways and Means Trade Subcommittee and the House leadership, I was working to help turn the broad outlines of the Bonker-led task force on trade into actual legislation. In talking with Sally Ericcson, part of Speaker O'Neill's policy team, I suggested that education and training should be part of any long-term growth strategy. Sally had been working closely with John Mack of Wright's staff in helping manage the development of the bill. Ericcson agreed on the desirability of including a title on education. We then went to talk to Rufus Yerxa who, at the direction of Rostenkowski, was also actively involved in helping to craft a comprehensive bill. He had no objection. The bigger hurdle was the Education Committee. Ericcson took the lead in talking with Susan McGuire, the key staff person, who—after considerable persuasion —agreed that adding education could be a plus.[39] The education bills could still be moved separately. At least to my thinking, adding them to the trade bill might garner some added support while giving the committee two chances to pass its legislation. With the inclusion of an education title, the bill also began to look more and more like a competitiveness bill and less and less like a traditional piece of trade legislation.

The House approved the rule on May 15 and passed the bill itself on May 22 by the margin of 295 to 115—more than enough to override a presidential veto.[40] The relative speed and breadth of House action was another measure of concern about the international economic standing of the United States and the political promise the legislation held. Wright's role and his use of extraordinary means was yet a third measure of the issue's salience. Despite a departure from the usual legislative pace and process, many representatives reacted favorably. They had responded to a complicated problem in a comprehensive and timely way.

While the House was stitching together its omnibus bill, the Senate was taking its own steps on trade. In mid-March 1986, the Senate Banking Committee approved a $300 million war chest to respond to the use of export finance subsidies by America's leading competitors. President Reagan had proposed the war chest the preceding September.[41] A week later, the Senate Judiciary Committee approved legislation allowing individuals to go into court to enforce U.S. trade law.[42] It was another sign of the broadening support for action on trade. In late April, the Senate Finance Committee narrowly rejected a resolution that would have barred the use of fast-track procedures (which barred amendments and set strict time limits for action) to implement the Canadian Free Trade Agreement on a 10-to-10 vote.[43]

Then, on June 24, the Senate passed the tax reform bill by the overwhelming margin of 97 to 3. The prospects for action and perhaps even fast action on trade suddenly seemed to brighten. Other observers cautioned that the tax bill and the tax conference might be a "complicating factor" that could slow or even derail trade legislation.[44] They proved to be right.

It was not until September 18, 1986, that the Senate Finance Committee held its first drafting sessions on possible trade legislation. The committee returned to trade on September 23, but it made no progress on a bill. Instead, the year belonged to tax reform—President Reagan signed the Tax Reform Act of 1986 on October 22. Trade would have to wait until the next Congress.

Trade Takes Center Stage, 1987

While the overall economy continued to grow, the Reagan administration did not make any progress in reducing either the fiscal or the trade deficit. If anything, the trade deficit became an even more potent symbol of an America in economic trouble. It was not just the deficit in isolation. It was the combination of the trade deficit, struggling American corporations, and the rise of international competition. The growing volume of writing on Japan was having more and more of an effect on American thinking. American business leaders pointed to the "lack of a level playing field" and the ability of Japan to compete from a strong base of protected markets. Academic articles, congressional hearings, and press reports painted a picture of a successful Japanese economy that worked very differently from its American counterpart. It was as if the vaunted American way of business itself was being called into question.

Other aspects of the Reagan economic strategy also were beginning to fray. For more than a decade, inflation had created a growing challenge to the nation's savings and loan (S&L) system. By the early 1980s, the industry was in trouble. The S&Ls turned to Washington for help. The effort to rescue the S&Ls would continue throughout the remaining two years of the Reagan presidency and on into the early years of the Bush administration. The point is not that the Reagan administration bore the sole blame for the S&L crisis. It did not. But the crisis was another example of how the administration's economic strategy, in this case an almost religious emphasis on deregulation, was running into economic difficulties.[45]

The administration found itself confronted by other challenges that had little or nothing to do with trade and competitiveness legislation but weakened its standing on Capitol Hill. By 1987, the president and the administration were attempting to explain to the American people how they ended up selling arms to Iran in return for the release of hostages held in Lebanon. Just as startling, the administration had been using some of the proceeds to fund the Nicaraguan Contras in direct violation of congressionally mandated policy. To the press and significant portions of the public, the president was not only contradicting his own policy of refusing to deal with terrorists but was also violating the Constitution.

One other incident affected the atmosphere surrounding trade and competitiveness legislation in 1987 and 1988. It started in 1986, when "a U.S. hunter submarine in the North Atlantic was zapped by the sonar of a nearby Soviet submarine—something that was not supposed to happen."[46] The U.S. Navy had spent billions of dollars so it could identify the sound signatures of every Soviet submarine before it was close enough to "bounce sound waves off U.S. hulls."[47]

How had they done it? The answer involved cooperation between the Japanese Toshiba Machine Tool Company and the Norwegian Kongsberg Corporation. Toshiba supplied a five-axis machine tool, and Kongsberg sold the computer and software to run it. The combination allowed the Soviets to mill propellers that were so quiet they could no longer be detected by then-current U.S. technology.

Congress reacted with outrage. Members principally concerned about traditional national security questions had not been leaders in the debate over American competitiveness. They were now faced with a loss of Western leadership in submarine detection that would take vast sums to regain. This would have been bad enough if the Soviets had developed the technology on their own. But it was worse because American friends and allies had sold it to them. Suddenly trade—and particularly trade with Japan—acquired a new sense of urgency.

In the Senate, Senator Jake Garn (R-Utah) took the lead in proposing legislation that would punish the 1983–84 sale to the Soviets as well as any future violations of the trade embargo against the Soviet Union.[48] In addition, Garn proposed to bar sales by the parent company as well as the subsidiaries that actually made the sale. The implications were serious for Kongsberg but promised enormous damage to Toshiba, a major Japanese conglomerate with a significant stake in the American market.[49] The prospect of across-the-board sanctions on Toshiba set off a scramble within and outside the government to see exactly who bought what from Toshiba. Among others, the Department of Defense learned how dependent America's defense industry had become on Toshiba (and other Japanese) products. The discovery may have increased Defense Department interest in supporting key American industries and lessened opposition to competitiveness-related legislation.

Congress Races Ahead

When the new Congress convened in January 1987, Jim Wright, the majority leader who had driven passage of the 1986 trade legislation, became speaker of the House. Looking ahead at the 100th Congress (1987–88), Wright planned "to oversee work on major legislation, directing various committee chairmen to play their parts in turn and speedily."[50] He made it clear that trade legislation remained a top priority. He followed words with action. On January 6, one hundred Democrats joined to introduce HR 3—essentially the same bill that had been passed by the House in 1986 as HR 4800.

Wright's views on trade were not simple. He shared the economist's view that the trade deficit was largely the product of fiscal and monetary policies but also thought that trade policy could make an independent contribution to correcting imbalances.[51] He was also adding an emphasis on long-term competitiveness to his initial emphasis on trade and the trade deficit. There were many voices around Wright that were thinking about competitiveness or long-term productivity growth. Wright was impressed with the Joint Economic Committee work of fellow Texan Lloyd Bentsen. He viewed Gephardt as something of a protégé, and he was familiar with his work on *Rebuilding the Road to Opportunity.*

Having been invited to speak at a December 12, 1986, gathering of the Democratic Leadership Council in Williamsburg, Virginia, Wright chose to address the trade issue.[52] After his speech, he had a long conversation with Lloyd Hand, a former aide to Lyndon Johnson who was then and is now a prominent Washington attorney and active Democrat. In his *Balance of Power,* Wright reports that Hand arranged for him to meet "John Young and other business leaders, who, in the past year, had conducted an intensive study of the trade problem at President Reagan's request."[53] The president may have ignored the Young report, but Wright did not.[54]

This was not Wright's first exposure to the recently formed Council on Competitiveness. On November 18, 1986, he had spoken to the council on the importance of trade and his intention to act quickly on trade legislation in the upcoming 100th Congress. But he did not stop with trade. He went to talk about a "long-term battle for the edge in productivity and competitiveness in manufacturing" that depended on the ability of a country to introduce new ideas and adopt new technologies.[55]

According to Wright, Young and the others urged him to "host a high-level, bipartisan conference on trade policy."[56] Wright agreed that the conference was a good idea and set out to make it high level and bipartisan. He spoke personally with the House Republican leader, Bob Michel (R-Ill.), and the Senate Republican leader, Bob Dole (R-Kans.), as well his Senate counterpart, Robert Byrd (D-W.Va.). They all liked the idea of a conference and agreed to issue invitations over their four signatures. A week after the invitations were issued, Michel and Dole called to withdraw their sponsorship, citing pressure from the Reagan White House.[57] Wright persisted, however, and the conference was held on January 21, 1987, as scheduled— but without the support of the Republican leadership.

While Wright was moving rapidly to reintroduce the trade and competitiveness bill passed by the House in the previous Congress, the Senate was not far behind. With the Democrats having recaptured the majority in the Senate, Byrd had an opportunity to establish a Senate agenda for the upcoming 100th Congress. As part of that preparation, Richard D'Amato, a key aide to Byrd, urged him to make trade a leadership priority. The day after Wright introduced HR 3, Byrd, now speaking as the leader of a Democratic majority, announced that "trade will be one of the Senate's top priorities."

Byrd, like Wright, planned to play a key role in speeding the legislation through the Senate. He instructed committees to report their separate work by May 1, 1987, when he would "meld the bills in one omnibus measure."[58] *Congressional Quarterly*'s Steve Pressman noted that "the trade debate also will feature discussion over improving the international competitiveness of U.S. industries and workers." Pressman suggested that Democrats thought the emphasis on competitiveness would "dampen their reputation as protectionists, while some Republicans" thought the issue might offer "common ground for the Congress and the Reagan Administration."[59]

There were other signs that competitiveness as well as trade was becoming a major congressional interest. The same day that Byrd announced trade as a Senate priority, 150 House and Senate members joined to form the bipartisan, bicameral Congressional Caucus on Competitiveness. Senators Max Baucus (D-Mont.) and John R. Chafee (R-R.I.) and Representatives Buddy MacKay (D-Fla.) and Claudine Schneider (R-R.I.) were to serve as caucus cochairs. They did not announce a specific program but stressed that "Congress must consider comprehensive solutions in areas such as *research and development, worker retraining, and intellectual property rights*" (emphasis added).[60] The same Pat Choate who had prepared a competitiveness report for the Business-Higher Education Forum and developed the individual training account idea for Gary Hart helped to create the Congressional Economic Leadership Institute to provide support for the caucus.

Congressional determination on trade and competitiveness was not lost on the administration. Even before the opening of the 100th Congress, Secretary of the Treasury Baker had indicated his interest in working with Congress on trade and competitiveness. By mid-February, the administration responded with its own 1,600-page Trade, Employment, and Productivity Act.[61] Schwab, who as the senior trade counsel to Senator Danforth was an active participant as well as keen observer of the 100th Congress, did not think the administration proposal had much influence. In her view, it was "so all-encompassing that many in the Congress simply wrote it off as a grab bag of previous initiatives on which Congress had refused to act."[62] And in fact, the administration proposal had no visible impact on the trade or competitiveness provisions that formed what would become the Omnibus Trade and Competitiveness Act of 1988.

Washington was again reminded of the potential political salience of trade when, just a few days later, Representative Richard Gephardt announced his intention to seek his party's presidential nomination.[63] Gephardt, one of the authors of *Rebuilding the Road to Opportunity,* had more recently emerged as a leading advocate of a trade policy that focused on trading partners with large bilateral surpluses with the United States and protected markets. His candidacy promised to thrust presidential politics into the ongoing effort to craft trade and competitiveness legislation.

Work progressed swiftly in the House. By mid-April 1987, House committees had finished their work, and their individual proposals had been melded together into a single bill. For the most part, the bill's trade and competitiveness provisions had broad, increasingly bipartisan support. The principal controversy revolved around the 1987 version of the Gephardt amendment. The House Ways and Means Committee and Gephardt had both added a new test—the "excess surplus" country had to have a global current account surplus (not just with the United States) as well as a bilateral surplus with the United States.[64] Secretary Baker was pursuing something of a parallel path by urging countries with large current account surpluses to grow faster and import more as a way of reducing global trade imbalances. Proponents of the House-passed bill made the point that Gephardt was actually giving added leverage to Baker in his negotiations with Japan and others.

The Gephardt amendment required the International Trade Commission to examine all major exporters (i.e., those with bilateral trade with the United States in excess of $7 billion) to determine if they had an *excess* trade surplus with the United States. Three tests were involved. The exporting country had to have: (1) a global current surplus, (2) a $3 billion trade surplus with the United States, and (3) nonoil exports to the United States that exceeded nonoil imports from the United States by more than 75 percent. The next step was to see if the *excess* trade surplus was *unwarranted*—that is, was the product of unfair trade practices. These features were also part of the House Ways and Means Committee's bill. It was on remedies that Gephardt and the committee differed. Gephardt demanded full elimination of the unfair trade practices (the committee called for substantial reduction) and, to emphasize results, added a provision requiring a 10 percent reduction per year in the trade surplus if the unfair trade practices continued. If a country continued to record an excess surplus and maintained its unfair trade practices, a further 10 percent reduction would be required up to calendar year 1992.

Gephardt and his amendment were attacked both for its substance and as a symbol. Much of the business community,[65] the White House, and free traders in Congress all actively opposed the Gephardt approach. His call for action—particularly the demand for a 10 percent reduction in the trade surplus—was the target of many attacks. For the most part, press coverage and the political discourse continued to pin the protectionist label on the

Gephardt amendment, though Gephardt himself insisted the amendment was designed to fight foreign protectionism.[66]

The controversy over the Gephardt amendment would persist until the final days of the House–Senate conference over trade and competitiveness legislation. Schwab writes that business groups focused so much energy on defeating the Gephardt amendment that they ignored a number of other measures. As a result, the "Senate bill emerged tougher than" the version adopted by the House.[67]

The Senate Adds Technology to the Mix

While the House was debating HR 3, the Senate's committees were busily working on different aspects of its own bill. The Senate Commerce Committee was the last to complete its work.[68] In finishing its portion of the bill, the Commerce Committee added technology to a bill that already ranged from macroeconomic policy to computer literacy.

As chair of the Commerce Committee, Senator Ernest F. Hollings (D-S.C.) had been at the center of the attempt to protect the American textile industry from international competition. In focusing on textiles, Hollings was very much looking after his own constituents in a state heavily dependent on the textile and apparel industries. But he also shared his colleagues' concern about America's flagging economic fortunes and the growing challenge from Japan. Hollings's focus was on strengthening America's civilian technology base. The committee also added an amendment authored by Senator James Exon (D-Neb.) that gave the president powers to limit foreign acquisition of American companies where U.S. national security was threatened.

In an earlier Congress, Hollings had attempted to strengthen the civilian economy by adding a manufacturing focus to the National Bureau of Standards. Reagan, however, had pocket-vetoed the bill in 1984, "claiming the provision would establish a framework for a federal industrial policy."[69] With the trade bill a priority in both houses of Congress, every committee chair saw an opportunity to move key legislation. Hollings was no exception.

Hollings turned to his key technology adviser, Patrick Windham, with general instructions to develop an American response to Japan's successes at developing and diffusing technology. In seeking answers, Windham was looking closely at the Japanese model. He also made use of the Young Commission's report (see chapter 6).[70]

Building on Windham's work, Hollings and his Commerce Committee proposed three important technology initiatives. First, they renamed the National Bureau of Standards as the National Institute of Standards and Technology to create an institutional base for what Hollings hoped would be a new national focus on civilian technology. Second, the Commerce Committee's legislation would also establish a "network of regional education centers to help small and medium-sized businesses modernize their production lines." [71] Third, Hollings did not fail to respond to the Japanese Ministry of International Trade and Industry's (MITI's) collaborative efforts with industry. Again building on Windham's work, Hollings and his committee created the Advanced Technology Program, "to provide research grants to small businesses and to provide 'seed' money for multi-company joint research ventures."[72]

The House Science Committee had not yet proposed its own legislation to add to the House trade bill. With a new chair, the House Committee had been slow to organize and had missed the speaker's deadline for adding measures to HR 3.[73] In drafting the Senate legislation, Windham kept in close contact with Jim Turner, a professional staff member on the House Science Committee. Windham and Turner both had Japan on their mind. Japan had 175 manufacturing extension centers, and Windham and Turner wanted 176 for the United States. By the time the trade and competitiveness legislation returned to the House, however, the House Science Committee had developed its own versions of the manufacturing extension initiative and the Advanced Technology Program.[74] On July 23, House Science adopted HR 2916 to rename the National Bureau of Standards and to create an Advanced Technology Foundation to "help industry resolve production problems."[75] Alan Rosenstein, a professor at the University of California, Los Angeles, and a high-technology entrepreneur, had been promoting the idea of a national technology foundation. Rosenstein saw it as a response to the success of Japan's MITI and the strengths of some of America's own institutions, including the National Science Foundation. George Brown (D-Calif.), the chair of the House Science Committee, liked Rosenstein's idea and turned it into legislation.[76]

Turner made a cosmetic but probably crucial suggestion that found its way into the Senate bill. As was mentioned in chapter 3 above, Windham had been thinking of changing the name of the National Bureau of Standards to the National Institute of Technology (NIT). Turner warned that NIT would be one of those Washington acronyms that brought unwanted attention. He suggested National Institute of Standards and Technology (NIST) as an alternative. And NIST it is to this day.[77]

With the action of the Senate Commerce Committee, Congress had now transformed an initial concern with trade and the trade deficit into a trade and competitiveness bill that created the framework for a long-term growth strategy. Majority Leader Robert C. Byrd made the transition official when, on June 25, he introduced S 1420, the Omnibus Trade and Competitiveness Act of 1987.[78]

On July 21, the Senate passed the Omnibus Trade and Competitiveness Act of 1987 by 71-to-27 margin. According to *Congressional Quarterly*'s John Cranford, the administration had lobbied hard for "no, but" votes, yet nineteen Republicans joined with the Democratic majority to push the yes vote well past the number needed to override a veto.[79] There were signs that the administration was modifying its view of government support for industry. As part of its effort to respond to the impact of Japanese trade practices on the semiconductor industry, the administration was considering funding Sematech, a joint industry–government collaborative effort to strengthen the semiconductor industry.[80] On July 28, just days after Senate passage of the Omnibus Act, the administration departed from its past stance on industrial policy by calling for "a coordinated government approach to ensure continued U.S. competitiveness in the field" of supercomputers.[81]

Stitching Together a Single Bill: The House and Senate Go to Conference

After passing distinct versions of similar bills, the relevant House and Senate committees routinely meet in conference to iron out their differences. The conference on HR 3, however, was anything but routine.[82] By any measure, the conference was one of the largest and most complex ever convened. By the time the conference was seriously under way in the fall of 1987,[83] it included 13 House and 8 Senate committees and a total of 199 conferees, 155 from the House and another 44 from the Senate.[84]

Persistent trade and budget deficits provided a backdrop to conference committee deliberations. The emphasis on macroeconomic fundamentals and a competitive dollar, a variety of education and training proposals, and the new technology initiatives all remained in the bill. The same was largely true of the trade provisions, which focused on boosting exports as well as responding to imports. On the export side, the bill provided for new trade negotiating authority, sought to require presidential action in response to closed foreign markets, streamlined the export control system, and strengthened export promotion programs.

While deliberations were under way, the country was rocked by a near financial panic. On October 19, 1987, or Black Monday as it came to be known, the Dow Jones Industrial (DJI) average plunged 508 points. In a single day, the DJI index lost 22.6 percent of it value—almost twice the 12.8 percent lost on Black Tuesday, October 28, 1929, an event that is widely associated with the onset of the Great Depression.[85]

As Congress returned to work in early 1988, the trade and competitiveness bill remained a top priority. For the most part, the broad elements of the competitiveness strategy fell easily into place. The conference committee, however, continued to wrestle with several controversial proposals that sought to regulate America's dependence on foreign capital and to respond to violations of the embargo on exports to the Soviet Union.

One of the investment proposals, authored by Representative John Bryant (D-Tex.),[86] would require foreign investors holding a 5 percent stake in an American company to report their holding as well as other information to the Securities and Exchange Commission. The other, authored by Representative James J. Florio (D-N.J.),[87] would allow the president to block any foreign acquisition of an American company where either the national security or "essential commerce" was involved. Senator Exon introduced a companion piece in the Senate.[88] Bryant, Florio, and Exon were all concerned about the potential impact of foreign acquisitions on American prosperity. Much of the focus was on Japan. Part of the policy and business communities were emphasizing the vulnerability of small American businesses to the financial strength of large, integrated Japanese firms that, because of extensive corporate cross shareholding, were themselves essentially impervious to foreign takeovers.

If Congress was concerned about losing key parts of its technology base and a degree of corporate control to foreign firms, the Treasury Department had its eye on a different kind of dependence. It was the large inflow of foreign capital that allowed America to combine low public (the budget deficits) and private saving with relatively low interest rates. Any sharp drop in the flow of foreign capital could disrupt investment in housing, automobiles, and capital equipment and tip the country into a recession just as the 1988 elections loomed.

Although Bryant made modifications in an attempt to garner majority support, the Bryant amendment was eventually dropped from the bill altogether. Exon-Florio, as it came to be called, remained in the bill but was narrowed to focus only on acquisitions that endangered national security. The question of "essential commerce" was left for another day. Senator Garn's amendment barring imports from Toshiba and Kongsberg was also narrowed to a time-limited ban on the importation of products from the subsidiaries that actually made the sale to the Soviet Union rather than the parent companies.

Despite the decline of Gephardt's presidential aspirations in 1988, the Gephardt amendment continued to have the backing of much of the House Democratic leadership (including the speaker), organized labor, and some businesses. Negotiations over the amendment continued until the conference was near its conclusion. At meetings that started in Gephardt's office early in the morning and finished in the Senate late in the day, the Gephardt amendment was scaled back into what became known as "Super 301." Some of the Gephardt language and approach was retained, but the focus shifted to trade barriers rather than trade deficits, and there was no prescribed formula for reducing a bilateral trade deficit.

Two other much-debated provisions remained in the bill and became the subject of considerable maneuvering. The first extended the ban on exporting Alaskan crude oil to the output of an Alaskan refinery. By forcing the shipment of Alaskan crude to another U.S. destination, it was subject to the Jones Act, which requires coastal shipping within the United States to be carried on U.S.-flagged ships.

Much more controversial was a proposal to give workers advance notice of layoffs or plant closings. This plant-closing proposal—developed under the leadership of Senate Labor Committee chair Edward Kennedy (D-Mass.)—triggered harsh opposition in the administration and a sharp reaction in the business community. At the same time, the issue of plant closings took on an added importance to the labor movement. Although not originally a labor priority, plant closings grew in prominence as labor-backed trade and investment provisions were softened or, in some cases, dropped altogether. With the prospect that HR 3's answer to the Gephardt amendment would not require reductions in bilateral trade deficits, labor leaders were left with little they could bring home to their own rank and file. They needed a visible victory.

The notification for layoffs and plant closings was strongly backed by Senator Kennedy and his Labor Committee colleagues. His staff had worked hard to build broad popular support for the bill. They met with more than a little success. At critical moments in bargaining over the provision, the nightly network television news would picture padlocked factories that had closed with no notice at all, leaving workers and their families scrambling for survival. Serendipity played its usual role. Shortly before a key vote on the bill, Lipman-Wolf, a major downtown department store in Portland, Oregon, closed its doors. The workers received pink slips rather than advance warning. Senator Robert Packwood (R-Ore.), the ranking member of the Senate Finance Committee, changed his mind about the need for plant-closing legislation.

By late April, the conference committee finished its work on the massive HR 3, which included the provision on plant closings and the restriction on the export of refined oil from the Alaskan refinery. On April 21, the House approved the conference report by a veto-proof margin of 312 to 107. Six days later, on April 27, the Senate approved the conference report by a margin of 63 to 36—three votes short of the margin needed to override a veto.

The president's veto was not long in coming. Wielding his veto pen on May 24, he emphasized his objections to the plant-closing provision. His veto message also mentioned provisions on Alaskan oil exports, the creation of a Competitiveness Policy Council, and a number of other provisions. At the same time, he kept the door open for future action by indicating that there was much to like in the bill.[89]

The House reacted within hours by overriding the president's veto. Voting after the Memorial Day recess, the Senate sustained the president's veto by a margin of 61 to 37.[90] A week later, on June 15, Speaker Wright announced his decision to reintroduce the trade bill (most of HR 3 reemerged as HR 4848) but to leave the provision on plant closings to a separate bill. The congressional leadership decided to have the Senate take the first step on the plant-closing provision. By June 22, the Senate debate on S 2527, the freestanding plant-closing legislation, was under way. On July 6, the Senate approved the plant-closing bill by a margin of 72 to 23—enough to override a veto with votes to spare.[91]

A week later (on July 13), the House approved the Senate-passed plant-closing bill and HR 4848, the Omnibus Trade and Competitiveness Act of 1988, minus the provisions on Alaskan oil and plant closings. Although House approval (286–136) fell slightly short of an assured veto override, observers felt that calling on members who had been absent for the vote would assure ultimate passage.[92] The president and his team arrived at a similar assessment. On August 2, he announced that he intended to allow the plant-closing bill to become law without his signature—a mild and largely symbolic form of protest.[93]

The House passed HR 4848 by an overwhelming 376-to-45 margin—more than 80 votes beyond the total needed to override a presidential veto.[94] The Senate followed suit on August 3 with an equally strong 85-to-11 vote.[95] On August 23, President Reagan signed the Omnibus Trade and Competitiveness Act of 1988.[96] It was now the law of the land. The journey that had started with the economic turmoil and troubles of the 1970s had, some ten years later, resulted in the legislative expression of a comprehensive competitiveness strategy.

National Concern Meets Congressional Action

In 1986, when what would become the Omnibus Trade and Competitiveness Act began its legislative journey, a diffuse congressional structure offered many opportunities for an active president or a determined interest group coalition to slow or stop congressional action. The more complex the legislation, the more committees involved, the more interests affected, the more likely it was that a proposal would fail.

The opponents of the Omnibus Act did not fail for want of trying. Following the complicated course of the Omnibus Act from the early days of 1986 to President Reagan's signature in 1988 would amount to a graduate course in congressional procedure. The proponents also took unusual steps. Wright's actions in opting for an omnibus structure, setting deadlines for House committee action, and pressuring strong committee chairs to reach agreement were rare if not unprecedented. Byrd's decision to follow a similar omnibus course was all the more remarkable in a body that demands comity and consensus. Where the House uses a majority vote to pass a rule governing amendments and debate, the Senate counterpart is a unanimous-consent agreement negotiated with all 100 senators on the nature of amendments and the length of debate.

Then there was the House–Senate conference. Although not technically the largest conference ever, the conference on the Omnibus Act was enormously complicated. During its course, the *Wall Street Journal*'s Washington bureau called congressional offices for stories on how the size and complexity of the conference were leading to inaction.[97] The real and remarkable story was that the conference was moving ahead.

Almost as surprising was the way that partisan politics did not get in the way of the Omnibus Act. Although the ups and downs of the presidential primaries may have affected the level of interest in the Gephardt amendment, they did not affect the progress of the bill itself. When Senator Bentsen was asked to join the Democratic ticket as the vice presidential nominee, his absence, the partisan furor of the presidential conventions, and the continuing reservations of the Reagan White House failed to derail the bill. The Republicans were sensing many of the same pressures as the Democrats. The business coalition that was often viewed as reliably Republican was working closely with Democratic leaders in fashioning the Omnibus Act. This was more than political survival or interest group politics. Democrats and Republicans alike shared a concern for the future of the country. And they both wanted action.

Many Streams and a Powerful River

The Omnibus Trade and Competitiveness Act was the product of myriad influences. The policy and business community's emphasis on a broad-based investment strategy was there. Many of the act's trade provisions—particularly those focused on overcoming closed markets—were responding to East Asia in general and Japan in particular. Japanese influences could be seen in a number of other parts of the bill. Japanese policy helped show the way to thinking of macroeconomics as part of an investment strategy as well as critical to a competitive exchange rate. The Japanese and German influence could also be seen in some of the act's technology proposals. The act's emphasis on partnerships and cooperation drew not only on America's own past experience but also on policy and practices in Germany and Japan.

The evolution of academic thought also provided a context for the Omnibus Act. The development of strategic trade theory suggested that government–industry cooperation could pay national dividends. By providing a rationale for Japan's combination of import protection and export promotion, strategic trade theory also gave general support to those who pushed for access to the Japanese market. As former Motorola CEO Robert Galvin noted (see chapter 3, pp. 82–83), greater access meant added sales to fund future research, the quality that came with responding to the demands of the Japanese consumer, and eliminating a protected sanctuary for Japanese industry. Academic discussions of America's potential decline added to congressional fears that, without a national response, the United

States might go the way of Britain rather than returning to its position of global economic leadership.

There were even some faint echoes of the industrial policy debate. In easing access to temporary import relief, Congress expected industries to develop a strategy for returning to international competitiveness. There was an emerging concern about specific industries that were critical for national security as well as the economic future. While Congress did not create the Cabinet-level department on science and technology recommended by the Young Commission, it did create the National Institute on Standards and Technology on the base of the old National Bureau of Standards. Later in the year, with administration support, Congress added a new Technology Administration to the Commerce Department to provide a policy structure for an emerging focus on civilian technology.[98]

Toward a National Strategy for Competitiveness and Long-Term Growth

Much of the discussion of the Omnibus Trade and Competitiveness Act has centered on its trade provisions. Schwab's excellent 1994 book *Trade-Offs: Negotiating the Omnibus Trade and Competitiveness Act* provides a detailed insider's look at crafting the Omnibus Act with a clear emphasis on its trade aspects.[99]

The trade provisions are an important part of the story. They accounted for a bit more than half the pages in the Omnibus Act and a great deal of the controversy. The grant of trade-negotiating authority to the president and the renewal of fast-track authority (i.e., allowing expedited consideration of trade agreements by precluding congressional amendments and limiting congressional debate) were critical to completing the Uruguay Round of multilateral trade negotiations that had been launched in 1986.

The importance of the trade-related provisions, however, should not obscure the broader and longer-lasting impact of the added provisions that turned a trade bill into a major piece of legislation that helped develop a comprehensive competitiveness or growth strategy for the country. It was an important case of the whole being a great deal more than the sum of its individual parts. In passing the Omnibus Act, Congress was putting key elements of a growth strategy into a systemic whole.

An emphasis on broad-based investment runs through the entire act. Although it did not have a specific macroeconomic chapter, reducing the budget deficit and adopting a more accommodating monetary policy was a likely path to a more competitive dollar. Reducing the fiscal deficit was consistent with increasing the pool of savings and lower interest rates—steps that favor greater investment in new plant and equipment. The investment focus of the Omnibus Act, however, went well beyond plant and equipment to stress the importance of investing in technology, education, and training.

Perhaps even more important than the range of elements was the way Congress was thinking of how the elements supported one another to make a more prosperous, more competitive country. Technology and a well-trained workforce were viewed as critical to making high-quality products that could meet the test of global competition. In parts of Congress and the business community, trade and technology created their own synergy. In a later administration, officials would talk about how today's innovation was tomorrow's export.

Political and business leaders were beginning to develop a shared understanding of their necessary and complimentary roles. They were on their way to defining a New Growth Compact that further defined the roles of the public and private sectors. The Omnibus Act also shows the impact of public and private thinking about partnerships.

A series of congressional and commission reports had laid the basis for a competitiveness strategy. *Rebuilding the Road to Opportunity,* the Young Commission report, and the Bonker task force report all pointed in the direction of taking a comprehensive approach to the competitiveness challenge. Separate committees had their priorities and timetables, yet their collective effort forged an Omnibus Act with a clear and comprehensive set of policies that could help spur long-term growth and competitiveness. At about the same time, state governments were adopting a range of growth strategies that complemented and, in some cases, anticipated the new federal direction. As the 1980s drew to a close, industry was itself adopting new practices that helped create the basis for an economic resurgence.

When President George H. W. Bush took office in January 1989, the private and public elements for an effective competitiveness strategy were largely in place. The popular view is that the Bush presidency essentially ignored economic growth and focused instead on major foreign policy challenges. But that is far from the whole story. A combination of business pressure, congressional initiative, popular concern, and the efforts of some important figures in the Bush administration itself resulted in several key initiatives that also moved the country toward a more competitive future.

Notes

1. *Congressional Quarterly Weekly Report,* September 21, 1985, 1856.

2. Council of Economic Advisers, *1985 Economic Report of the President* (Washington, D.C.: U.S. Government Printing Office, 1985), as quoted in *Congressional Quarterly Weekly Report,* February 9, 1985, 266.

3. *Congressional Quarterly Weekly Report,* February 16, 1985, 317.

4. *Congressional Quarterly Weekly Report,* March 30, 1985, 609.

5. *Congressional Quarterly Weekly Report,* August 31, 1985, 1738.

6. Author's interview with former speaker of the House James Claude Wright Jr., July 9, 2002. The interview took place in the speaker's office at Texas Christian University in Fort Worth.

7. Interview with Wright.

8. Author's interview with Don Bonker, May 21, 2002. The interview took place at Bonker's office at APCO Associates in Washington.

9. For a brief discussion of Speaker O'Neill's decision to establish the ad hoc energy committee, see John A. Farrell, *Tip O'Neill and the Democratic Century* (Boston: Little, Brown, 2001), 466.

10. Interview with Bonker.

11. Interview with Wright.

12. Author's interview with Sally Ericsson, March 11, 2002.

13. Author's interview with Rufus Yerxa, April 21, 2002. I conducted the interview by telephone.

14. *Congressional Quarterly Weekly Report,* April 6, 1985, 647.

15. *Congressional Quarterly Weekly Report,* February 23, 1985, 358.

16. Susan C. Schwab, *Trade-Offs: Negotiating the Omnibus Trade and Competitiveness Act* (Boston: Harvard Business School Press, 1994), 69. The House bill was HR 3035, and the companion Senate bill was S 1449. See *Congressional Quarterly Weekly Report,* July 20, 1985, 1436–37.

17. Schwab, *Trade-Offs,* 69.

18. *Congressional Quarterly Weekly Report,* March 30, 1985, 609.

19. *Congressional Quarterly Weekly Report,* April 6, 1985, 645.

20. *Congressional Quarterly Weekly Report,* March 16, 1985, 501.

21. *Congressional Quarterly Weekly Report,* March 16, 1985, 502.

22. *Congressional Quarterly Weekly Report,* July 6, 1985, 1336.

23. *Congressional Quarterly Weekly Report,* August 10, 1985, 1606.

24. Interview with Wright.

25. Author's interview with Steve Charnovitz, April 15, 2002. The interview took place over coffee next to Charnovitz's law firm. Charnovitz served as a legislative aide on international trade and also wrote speeches for Majority Leader and Speaker James Wright.

26. *Congressional Quarterly Weekly Report,* September 14, 1985, 1793.

27. Prior to the Trade and Tariff Act of 1984 (TTA-84), there was a dispute over whether or not the U.S. trade representative could self-initiate investigations of trade barriers under Section 301 of the trade law. The TTA-84 amended Section 301 to make clear that the U.S. trade representative "may initiate investigations 'in order to advise the President concerning the exercise of the President's authority under Section 301.'"

See Stephen L. Lande and Craig VanGrasstek, *The Trade and Tariff Act of 1984: Trade Policy in the Reagan Administration* (Lexington, Mass.: D. C. Heath, 1986), 49.

28. *Congressional Quarterly Weekly Report,* September 14, 1985, 1785.

29. Schwab, *Trade-Offs,* 70. As Destler notes, the communiqué itself did not refer to a weak dollar. Instead, it called for "further orderly appreciation of the major non-dollar currencies against the dollar." I. M. Destler, *American Trade Politics,* 2nd ed. (Washington, D.C.: Institute for International Economics with the Twentieth Century Fund, 1992), 124.

30. The text of the president's remarks can be found in *Congressional Quarterly Weekly Report,* February 28, 1985, 1948–49.

31. Destler, *American Trade Politics,* 124.

32. Steve Dryden, *Trade Warriors: USTR and the American Crusade for Free Trade* (New York: Oxford University Press, 1995), 311–12.

33. Clyde V. Prestowitz Jr., *Trading Places: How We Allowed Japan to Take the Lead* (New York: Basic Books, 1988), 57.

34. Destler, *American Trade Politics,* 128–29.

35. Schwab, *Trade-Offs,* 71.

36. *Congressional Quarterly Weekly Report,* December 21, 1985, 2686.

37. Steve Pressman, "In Capital Market Place: Trade Expansion Bills," *Congressional Quarterly Weekly Report,* 557.

38. The six committees were Ways and Means, Foreign Affairs, House Banking and Currency, Energy and Commerce, Education and Labor, and Agriculture. The separate pieces of legislation included Ways and Means' HR 4750; Foreign Affairs' HR 4708; Banking, Finance, and Urban Affairs' HR 4574 and HR 2373; Energy and Commerce's HR 3131 and HR 3777; and Education and Labor's HR 4728. Agriculture did not report a separate bill or issue a report. See *Congressional Quarterly Weekly Report,* May 24, 1986, p. 1986.

39. Interview with Ericcson.

40. Steve Pressman, "Over Reagan's Protest, House Votes Trade Bill," *Congressional Quarterly Weekly Report,* May 24, 1986, 1154.

41. See Steve Pressman, "Panel Backs Trade 'War Chest'; Ex-Im Bank Bill," *Congressional Quarterly Weekly Report,* March 15, 1986, 597.

42. *Congressional Quarterly Weekly Report,* March 29, 1986, 689.

43. Schwab, *Trade-Offs,* 74. Schwab described the vote as a "second incident of spontaneous combustion" in response to the Administration's inaction on trade. See also Steve Pressman, "Larger Issues Almost Derail Canada Trade Talks," *Congressional Quarterly Weekly Report,* April 26, 1986, 905.

44. *Congressional Quarterly Weekly Report,* July 5, 1986, 1544.

45. Lou Cannon, *President Reagan: The Role of a Lifetime* (New York: Simon & Schuster, 1991), 826–28.

46. Prestowitz, *Trading Places,* 217–18.

47. Prestowitz, *Trading Places,* 218.

48. Schwab, *Trade-Offs,* 201, provides a brief discussion of the Garn initiative as well the complication it caused in the conference over the trade and competitiveness legislation.

49. A conglomerate is a rough approximation to the Japanese *keiretsu* structure. It does capture the sense that Toshiba sold an array of products to a variety of customers in the United States and elsewhere.

50. Jaqueline Calmes, "The Hill Leaders: Their Places on the Ladder," *Congressional Quarterly Weekly Report,* January 3, 1987, 6. Calmes quotes Wright as pointing to three bills he guided through the House in the preceding year (on trade, terrorism, and illegal drugs) as "valid models for [dealing with] important national problems. If several committees are involved, there needs to be some coherence" (p. 6).

51. Interview with Charnovitz.

52. Jim Wright, *Balance of Power: President and Congress from the Era of McCarthy to the Age of Gingrich* (Atlanta: Turner Publishing, 1996), 450.

53. Wright, *Balance of Power,* 450.

54. John M. Barry, *The Ambition and the Power: The Fall of Jim Wright—A True Story of Washington* (New York: Viking, 1989), 265.

55. Remarks of House Majority Leader Jim Wright to Council on Competitiveness, November 18, 1986.

56. Barry, *Ambition and the Power,* 103. See also Wright, *Balance of Power,* 450–51. Also see interview with Wright and author's interview with Alan Magazine, first president of the Council on Competitiveness, July 2, 2002.

57. Wright, *Balance of Power,* 451.

58. Steve Pressman, "Democrats Off Starting Blocks in Effort to Enact a Trade Bill," *Congressional Quarterly Weekly Report,* January 10, 1987, 82.

59. Pressman, "Democrats Off Starting Blocks," 82.

60. Pressman, "Democrats Off Starting Blocks," 82.

61. The legislation was introduced by the Senate minority leader, Robert Dole (as S 539), and by House Minority Leader Robert Michel (as HR 1155) on February 19. The same day, textile quota legislation was introduced by Hollings (as S 549) and Representative Butler Derrick (D-S.C.) (as HR 1154). See "Trade Bill Introduced," *Congressional Quarterly Weekly Report,* February 21, 1987, 335.

62. Schwab, *Trade-Offs,* 84.

63. Gephardt announced his candidacy on February 23, 1987.

64. For the text of the Gephardt amendment, see *Congressional Record,* April 29, 1987, H 2755–H 2757. The reference to the current account surplus appears under section j(1)(C) on H 2756. For a summary of the bill as reported by the House Ways and Means Committee and the way Representative Gephardt proposed toughening the bill, see Democratic Study Group, *Fact Sheet: The Trade Bill,* No. 100-6, April 26, 1987. For a side-by-side comparison of current law, the House passed version (HR 3) and Senate Finance Committee action see "Comparison of S 490 with HR 3 and Current Law," May 15, 1987.

65. Lee Iacocca, the chief executive of Chrysler Corporation, was a high-profile exception. He endorsed the Gephardt amendment in an April 15, 1987, letter to Congress and strongly endorsed the Gephardt approach in a letter to Chrysler employees cosigned by Owen Bieber, president of the Untied Auto Workers union. See "Special Report Eye on Washington" in the *Chrysler Motors Times,* Chrysler's in-house publication. The issue is undated but must have appeared in the spring of 1987 before the House vote on the Gephardt amendment.

66. See Richard A. Gephardt, "The New World of Foreign Trade," *Washington Post,* May 4, 1987. Gephardt argues that "protectionism abroad requires a firm yet measured response."

67. Schwab, *Trade-Offs,* 170.

68. Drew Douglas, "Trade Bill Heads to Floor Trailing Veto Threat," *Congressional Quarterly Weekly Report,* June 20, 1987, 1318.

69. Douglas, "Trade Bill Heads to Floor," 1321.

70. Author's interview with Pat Windham, October 25, 1999.

71. Douglas, "Trade Bill Heads to Floor," 1321.

72. Douglas, "Trade Bill Heads to Floor," 1321.

73. Author's interview with James Turner, professional staff member, House Committee on Science, June 10, 2002. The interview was conducted by phone.

74. Interview with Turner.

75. John Cranford, "Trade Bill Passes Senate, Heads for Conference," *Congressional Quarterly Weekly Report,* July 25, 1987, 1636.

76. Author's interview with Christopher T. Hill, vice provost for research and professor of public policy and technology, George Mason University, September 5, 2002. At the time, Hill was a senior specialist at the Congressional Research Committee who worked closely with the science committees on Capitol Hill.

77. Interview with Windham.

78. Schwab, *Trade-Offs,* 146.

79. Cranford, "Trade Bill Passes Senate," 1632–36. In *Trade-Offs,* Schwab discusses the administration pressure for no votes and the debate it triggered inside the weekly Republican policy lunch. See Schwab, *Trade-Offs,* 153–54.

80. For a brief description of Sematech, see Philip Webre, "Using R&D Consortia for Commercial Innovation: Sematech, X-Ray Lithography, and High-Resolution Systems," Congressional Budget Office, July 1990.

81. John Cranford, "House Passes Ban on PX Sales of Toshiba Goods," *Congressional Quarterly Weekly Report,* August 1, 1987, 1728.

82. Although the Senate acted on S 1420, the conferees considered HR 3 as amended in the Senate. The Constitution requires that revenue bills originate in the House. Tariffs are considered revenue measures and, as a result, tariff and related trade legislation is initiated in the House. In such cases, the Senate may act on its own bill but after completing action will substitute its language for the House bill, in this case HR 3, while retaining the original shell. As a result, the conference was considering HR 3 and not S 1420.

83. The full conference met first on August 7, 1987. See Schwab, *Trade-Offs.* The real bargaining took place in the various subconferences that dealt with different aspects of the legislation.

84. The conference on HR 3 was not, however, the largest. The omnibus budget reconciliation bill in 1981 involved 250 conferees meeting in 58 subconferences. See Walter J. Oleszek, *Congressional Procedures and the Policy Process,* 2nd ed. (Washington, D.C.: Congressional Quarterly Press, 1984), 207, as cited in Schwab, *Trade-Offs,* 157.

85. Elizabeth Wehr and John Cranford, "Crippled Market Spurs Budget Breakthrough," *Congressional Quarterly Weekly Report,* October 24, 1987, 2573.

86. For background on Bryant, see Michael Barone and Grant Ujifusa, *Almanac of American Politics, 1984* (Washington, D.C.: National Journal, 1983), 1131–32.

87. Barone and Ujifusa, *Almanac of American Politics,* 729–32.

88. Barone and Ujifusa, *Almanac of American Politics,* 693–96.

89. "Reagan Rejects Trade Bill, Calls for Better Alternative," *Congressional Quarterly Weekly Report,* May 24, 1988, 1476–77.

90. The Senate acted on June 8, 1988. Senator William Proxmire (D-Wis.) and Majority Leader Byrd were the only two Democrats to vote against the bill. Proxmire ob-

jected to proposed changes in the Foreign Corrupt Practices Act (which had established criminal penalties for the use of bribes to secure overseas business). In the case of Byrd, who was a strong backer of the bill, a no vote allowed him to move to reconsider the vote at some future date. See Elizabeth Wehr, "Senate Sustains Trade-Bill Veto," *Congressional Quarterly Weekly Report,* June 11, 1988, 1568.

91. See Elizabeth Wehr, "Senate OKs Advance Notice of Plant Closings," *Congressional Quarterly Weekly Report,* July 9, 1988, 1919.

92. Elizabeth Wehr, "Trade Plant-Closing Bills Win Strong House Backing," *Congressional Quarterly Weekly Report,* July 16, 1988, 1991.

93. Elizabeth Wehr, "Reagan Bows to Politics on Plant-Closing Bill," *Congressional Quarterly Weekly Report,* August 6, 1988, 2216. In writing about the president's decision, Wehr noted that Republican strategists and Democratic supporters were both surprised at the degree of popular support for the measure. Polls, media coverage, and influential commentators all pointed to its widespread popularity. Wehr passes on reports that George Bush "found the issue an embarrassment in his presidential campaign" (p. 2216).

94. Wehr, "Trade Plant-Closing Bills," 1991.

95. Elizabeth Wehr, "Senate Clears Trade Bill by Lopsided Vote," *Congressional Quarterly Weekly Report,* August 6, 1988, 2215.

96. Schwab, *Trade-Offs,* 218.

97. The author was the recipient of one of those calls.

98. Phil Kuntz, "Bill Creating Technology Clears," *Congressional Quarterly Weekly Report,* October 8, 1988, 2824.

99. Schwab, *Trade-Offs.*

Chapter 8

Building the Base for Future Prosperity: The Private Sector and the States

With the passage of the Omnibus Trade and Competitiveness Act of 1988, Congress and the country moved several steps toward forging a consensus on a new path for future growth. The strategy sought renewed income and productivity growth on the basis of an economic environment that encouraged private investment, key public investments, and a commitment to opening markets around the world.

The Private Sector Pushes Policy

As the 1980s progressed, the private sector called on Washington to adopt policies that would support private efforts to meet international competition. The Omnibus Act was, in no small measure, the product of a private sector that was seeking a new, cooperative relationship with the federal government. Private-sector voices helped develop the Omnibus Act and continued to call for federal action after its passage into law. By requiring a range of reports and creating commissions with significant private-sector participation, the Omnibus Act created its own momentum for change. Reports do not often lead to an immediate change in policy. As with the Young Commission report, however, they can help frame a debate and have significant influence over time.

The Private Sector: New Structure, New Strategy

Throughout the 1980s, the private sector underwent a dramatic change. International competition, in particular the challenge posed by Japan, was

204

forcing companies to adopt new production techniques and corporate strategies that were critical elements in laying the basis for renewed productivity growth. At the same time, U.S. businesses' corporate structure and corporate finance were rapidly evolving. Many companies began to focus on their core competencies rather than hedging against the business cycle by building a conglomerate of disparate activities. Many also felt caught between the need for long-term investment and stock market pressure for robust quarterly earnings. The combination of international competition, the advent of high-interest (or "junk") bonds, and the pressure for quick financial returns created an active market for management as companies were brought, sold, and taken from publicly traded to privately held.

The States Meet the Competitive Challenge

State governments were responding to the same economic forces that were buffeting the private sector and the federal government. By the time of the Omnibus Act, many governors were ahead of the federal government in focusing on technology, education, training, and trade as key elements in state-based growth strategies. States responded to the challenge and opportunity of global markets by establishing their own overseas offices to promote the sale of state-made products and to attract inward investment from Europe and Japan. While Congress was creating a new dialogue with the private sector, many states were already forming public–private partnerships to promote investment, innovation, and an improved skill base.

This chapter first looks at some of the important private-sector voices that spoke up before and after the Omnibus Act. The chapter then traces the changes in corporate structure and private practices that helped lay the basis for the prosperity of the 1990s. Finally, the chapter takes a brief look at how states were themselves responding to the competitiveness challenge in ways that made significant contributions to the country's competitive future.

The Private Sector: Calling for Competitiveness

The Young Commission's call for private as well as public initiatives hit a responsive chord among many leading American companies. In addition to speaking as individual companies, industrial America began to look to a variety of trade associations and other organizations with a significant business membership to address the question of America's declining international competitiveness.

One of the earliest voices came from the Business–Higher Education Forum, a nonprofit organization that fostered dialogue between the business and higher education communities. Even before the Young Commission report was issued, the Business–Higher Education Forum was focusing on the question of long-run growth and renewed American competitiveness. In seeking to make a thoughtful statement on competitiveness, the forum drafted Pat Choate, a specialist in regional development who had turned his attention to the performance of the national economy. The forum issued Choate's 1983 report as *America's Competitive Challenge: The Need for a National Response.*[1] The report was widely read and made its own contribution to the Young Commission, which started its work in mid-1983 (see chapter 5).

By the time the Young Commission's work was under way, a number of other influential groups had begun to speak out on national competitiveness. The list included such diverse voices as the Business Roundtable, representing many of America's largest companies, and the Labor–Industry Coalition on International Trade, which brought together labor unions, industrial firms, and the AFL-CIO.

Young Forms the Council on Competitiveness

In looking back at the Young Commission report, Young saw the September 1985 initiatives on trade and the dollar as being consistent with the direction that the report advocated.[2] In terms of the report's broader agenda, however, there was little action. Young saw the recommendations of the report as forming a complex whole that required private-sector initiative as well as a variety of public-sector policies. Because the report's recommendations did not fall easily into the purview of one or even two major departments, the competitiveness agenda advocated by the commission called for an administration-wide shift in thinking and coordinated action that involved virtually the entire government. In a late 1985 conversation with Alexander B. (Sandy) Trowbridge, the president of the National Association of Manufacturers, Young realized that President Ronald Reagan would have to take ownership of such a wide-ranging set of proposals. After waiting for much of a year, Young no longer hoped that the president would take up that particular challenge.

Instead, in August 1986, Young settled on creating the Council on Competitiveness to take ownership of the entire competitiveness agenda.[3] Young sought and successfully recruited a high-quality, diverse membership. His "executive committee was composed of business and labor leaders, university presidents, prominent scientists, and newspaper and magazine publishers."[4] The general membership included the chief executives of dozens of leading companies and the presidents of America's leading research universities.

In building the council, Young again drew on the talents of Tom Uhlman, who, following his work on the Young Commission, had joined Young at Hewlett-Packard. For the council's first executive director, Young and Uhlman chose Alan Magazine, then serving as the executive director of the Business–Higher Education Forum.

Technology and Competitiveness

Young had created the Council on Competitiveness to take ownership of a national growth strategy that required extensive private-sector initiative as well as public action that cut across traditional lines of bureaucratic responsibility. In its first policy statement, the council applied that crosscutting philosophy to the question of commercial innovation. In *Picking Up the Pace: The Commercial Challenge to American Innovation*, the council spelled out the policy steps needed to turn promising ideas into commercial products that would meet the test of international competition.[5]

In *Picking Up the Pace,* the council had an immediate hit. The report garnered wide press coverage and intense congressional attention. As is often the case with detailed reports, one item or another will crystallize a national thought or encapsulate a national anxiety. Dan Burton, the council's vice president and principal drafter of *Picking Up the Pace,* was looking for a compelling way of stressing the competitive challenge America faced in an array of high-technology products. He found it in a single table of the report titled "The Erosion of the U.S. Share of Technology Markets."[6] The table highlighted how U.S. firms had lost domestic market share in one product after another. In almost every case, the product had been invented and developed in the United States. In several cases, market share had not only declined but disappeared altogether. Two pages later, the reader found a chart that highlighted the loss of American leadership in memory chips and the related rise of Japan.[7] In tracing the decline of American sales and the rapid rise of Japanese market share, the chart showed a large X. It was an X that seemed to mark the very spot of American decline, an X that would be come very familiar as the debate on America's economic future moved into the Bush years.

By making its first policy statement in 1988, the Council on Competitiveness hoped that its priorities might find their way into the presidential debate. To some extent they did. At one campaign stop, then-vice president George H. W. Bush reportedly waved *Picking Up the Pace* and described it as his bible.[8] Bible or not, President Bush did at least take some verses from *Picking Up the Pace* and make them administration policy. Young himself notes that Bush created the position of presidential science and technology adviser, as urged by *Picking Up the Pace.* Young also stressed that it was Bush's science and technology adviser, Alan Bromley, who helped legitimize the federal role in fostering enabling technologies.[9]

Dreams and Deficits

The next policy statement of the Council on Competitiveness, published later in 1988, had a more complicated fate. In *Picking Up the Pace*, the council had promised its own comprehensive proposal for deficit reduction. It met that commitment in *Reclaiming the American Dream: Fiscal Policies for a Competitive Nation*,[10] in which it spelled out principals and specific recommendations that could lead to deficit reduction. The sheer breadth of the council's membership held out the possibility that its proposals might be politically palatable as well as economically compelling.

The council had produced a credible deficit reduction plan that might have started the country on the path toward a balanced budget.[11] With the successful example of the 1983 Social Security Commission behind it, Congress had created a deficit reduction commission that was to report shortly after the 1988 election. In effect, the council was offering the commission a useful starting point for deficit reduction that would command considerable support from the business world. By the time the council reported, however, then Vice President Bush had already made a "no tax" pledge that was widely credited with helping him win the New Hampshire primary. At the Republican convention, the vice president followed his New Hampshire commitment with his now-famous line "Read my lips, no new taxes." Facing a Democratic Congress, deficit reduction would require tax increases as well as spending restraint—deficit reduction would have to wait.

Calculating Competitiveness

The Council on Competitiveness also marked 1988 by issuing its first *Competitiveness Index*.[12] The council had asked Harvard Business School professor Michael Porter to chair its effort. Burton took the lead for the council staff and worked closely with Porter on the project.

Burton and Porter were both interested in finding a single "Dow Jones–like" number that would sum up the competitive standing of the United States. But the subject proved too complex and involved too many separate indicators that could not be readily compressed into one prominent number. Instead, they used four separate measures to compare the economic performance of the United States with that of the other major industrial powers. The ultimate measure of competitive success was the standard of living (output per capita). They also assessed U.S. performance in international markets (share of world exports), manufacturing productivity growth, and rate of investment (including spending on research and development, or R&D, and education as well as on new plant and equipment).

Burton and Porter both were adept at expressing complex ideas in clear, visual form. Burton had actually studied painting at one point in his career, and Porter had studied aeronautical engineering before focusing on business economics. In the case of the index, Porter and Burton adapted the image of a pyramid with investment as its base, supporting productivity growth, which, moving up the pyramid, is translated over time into global export share, which in turn contributes to a rising standard of living, shown at the very top.

The Economic Strategy Institute

The story of the Economic Strategy Institute starts with the same Clyde Prestowitz who had served as a counselor for Japan affairs to President Reagan's first secretary of commerce, Malcolm Baldrige.[13] Prestowitz brought considerable experience to his role at the Commerce Department. A former foreign service officer, Prestowtiz had also spent years working in Japan. He had developed a fluency not only in Japanese but also in his understanding of the Japanese approach to trade policy. At Commerce, Prestowtiz was in the middle of the 1980s debate over U.S. trade policy and the challenge of Japan. Among other issues, he was an active participant in the negotiations that led to the 1986 semiconductor pact with Japan.

Trading Places

At the Commerce Department, Prestowitz became increasingly concerned about the lack of an effective trade policy to help counter America's declining economic fortunes. In particular, he saw the United States as responding to Japanese strategy with no strategy of its own. After leaving Commerce, Prestowitz wrote his clarion call for U.S. action, *Trading Places: How We Allowed Japan to Take the Lead,*[14] which was published in 1988.

In *Trading Places,* Prestowitz spelled out differences between Japan and the United States, going well beyond business practices to also include national culture and national priorities. He added vivid detail on the challenge to the semiconductor industry and gave the reader the insider's perspective of a trade negotiator. *Trading Places* was designed to motivate as well as educate. He opens the book with a chapter titled "The End of the American Century," and in his final section he describes the United States as "a colony in the making."[15] Like Ezra Vogel's 1979 *Japan as No. 1,*[16] Prestowtiz's title, *Trading Places,* caught the public's imagination and seemed to crystallize popular concern.

Two years after publishing his book, Prestowitz founded the Economic Strategy Institute (ESI). In naming ESI, he highlighted his view of an America that lacked a strategy for dealing with Japan or for pursuing long-term growth. He attracted support from the AFL-CIO and a number of leading companies, including Chrysler, Motorola, and Milliken and Company.

Throughout the Bush administration, Prestowitz remained a powerful voice on U.S. trade policy generally and U.S. economic relations with Japan in particular. Through Prestowitz, key labor and business groups were pressing for an active response from the Bush administration to the economic challenges facing the country.

Climbing the Competitiveness Summit

In 1991, a group of chief executives of smaller businesses, chief technical officers, and concerned citizens came together to plan a Summit on Competitiveness. Many had been active in the Industrial Research Institute, a professional association for senior vice presidents and directors of research in major companies. J. Nelson Hoffman, chairman of Brice Manufacturing Company; Richard K. Lee, of Denver-based Rocklite, Incorporated; and a number of others took the lead in planning the summit.

The summit planners' work came together on July 18, 1991, when speakers and participants gathered at the Broadmoor Hotel in Colorado Springs. Their objective was to "develop a focused vision and action plan to reverse the trend of declining U.S. competitiveness in global markets and begin implementation of the plan."[17] They were intent on action as well as analysis.

The summit attracted prominent academics, including Lester C. Thurow, then dean of the Sloan School of Management at the Massachusetts Institute of Technology, and Harvard Business School professors Bruce R. Scott and George Cabot Lodge. In looking to Scott and Lodge, many of the conference participants were also looking to their business school roots. Prestowitz and I (I had succeeded Alan Magaziner as president of the Council on Competitiveness in 1990) spoke for the growing competitiveness community. The Bush administration was represented by Jack Kemp, then the secretary of housing and urban development.

The evening address was delivered by Craig Fields, the president and chief executive of Micro Electronics and Computer Technology Corporation, an Austin-based public–private partnership. Fields had earlier served as the director of the Defense Advanced Research Projects Agency (DARPA), the Pentagon-based agency that developed cutting-edge technologies for military applications. Fields had been an active proponent of government support for a fledgling American high-definition television system. While he was still at DARPA, a recent defense authorization bill had given DARPA the ability to take equity positions in companies developing needed technologies. Fields used the authority to invest "$4 million in a California high-speed-integrated circuit company rather than allow a Japanese firm to invest in the concern."[18] Fields was dismissed for his trouble. At least the investment was the specific act that precipitated Fields's dismissal. Many observers, however, saw Fields as being punished for his outspoken advocacy of government support for emerging technologies. At least in its early days, the Bush administration seemed to carry forward the Reagan-era antipathy to anything that could be characterized as industrial policy.

Hoffman, Lee, and the others were intent on turning the summit into a national movement. In a sense, the first summit was a clear sign that a national movement was already well under way. As the country moved into the election year of 1992, national concern over the country's economic future continued to build. Hoffman, Lee, and the others started to work on a second, even more ambitious summit.

The summits contributed ideas and energy to the effort to define and implement a competitiveness agenda. They were also a very American response to a major challenge. The country had responded in a similar fashion after the 1957 launch of Sputnik by the Soviet Union. It was a time when a thousand flowers were blooming—waiting for a national leader to harness the nation's energy and turn random flowers into a garden.

The Persistent Influence of the Omnibus Act of 1988

The hundreds of pages of legislative language that made up the Omnibus Trade and Competitiveness Act of 1988 had a lasting impact on American policy and American thinking about the future. Over the course of the Bush presidency, the act influenced the administration's approach to trade negotiations, export promotion and policy, civilian technology and, to some extent, training. As President Bush took office, popular pressure, key interest groups, the policy community, and the academic world all favored deficit reduction. In part, the Omnibus Act was a product of these same forces. But the act contributed its own impetus to deficit reduction—the act's emphasis on investment and a fairly valued dollar was, after all, built on the premise of declining deficits.[19]

In seeking to move the government and the country toward a national competitiveness strategy, the Omnibus Act imposed a wide variety of reporting requirements on the administration. The reports ranged from international economic and exchange rate policy[20] to the president's policies with regard to semiconductor research.[21] The act also created a number of commissions to provide advice to the administration and to Congress. Two of the commissions were particularly active and visible: The National Advisory Committee on Semiconductors[22] and the Competitiveness Policy Council.[23]

The National Advisory Commission on Semiconductors

The National Advisory Commission on Semiconductors (NACS) was specifically charged with analyzing the U.S. semiconductor industry. To head NACS, President Bush chose Ian M. Ross, the president of AT&T Bell Laboratories, which had been a font of inventions in the field of electronics and was widely respected for its scientific accomplishments. Ross was no stranger to the issue of competitiveness. He had served on the original Young Commission and had also joined the executive committee of the private-sector Council on Competitiveness.

The private-sector members of NACS read like a *Who's Who* of the semiconductor world of the 1980s. The list included Robert W. Galvin, then chairman of the board of Motorola; Jerry Junkins, chairman, president, and chief executive of Texas Instruments; Charles E. Spork, president and chief executive of National Semiconductor Corporation; and John A. Armstrong, vice president for science and technology at IBM. Also serving were Norman R. Augustine, chairman and chief executive of Martin Marietta Corporation (now Lockheed-Martin), a leading defense contractor. James G. Treybig, president and chief executive of Tandem Computers, came from the computer industry; and James C. Morgan, chairman and chief executive of Applied Materials, was from a leading supplier of equipment and material for the semiconductor industry. Three Cabinet secretaries sent senior representatives, including Thomas J. Murrin, deputy secretary of commerce. Murrin had also served on the Young Commission and would, after leaving government, join the executive committee of the Council on Competitiveness.

In its 1989 report, *A Strategic Industry at Risk,* Ross and his fellow committee members articulated the "vital national role" of the semiconductor industry, traced its decline, and described the "major root causes" of the industry's ills.[24] NACS portrayed a semiconductor industry that faced a double squeeze from its Japanese competitors. As U.S. firms lost their hold on the consumer electronics market, American semiconductor firms lost formerly reliable customers. Direct Japanese competition for global chip sales had further eroded the American position, especially in memory chips. In a statement that was reminiscent of the Young Commission's approach, NACS warned that "unless U.S. industry and government take coordinated, concerted and timely action," the industry, the economy and national security would all suffer.

In proposing remedies, the first NACS report was comprehensive and ambitious. In seeking to reduce the cost of capital, NACS not only called for deficit reduction but also proposed a series of tax changes that ranged from making the tax credit for research and experimentation permanent to a call for reinstating the investment tax credit. NACS also sought to foster the reentry of American firms into the consumer electronics business. Its proposed vehicle was the Consumer Electronics Capital Corporation (CECC), a multi-billion-dollar pool of patient capital that would be privately managed on a for-profit basis. The initial NACS report saw the CECC as playing three complimentary roles: providing equity finance for consumer electronic companies seeking to develop and commercialize advanced technologies, providing management assistance, and seeking out promising technologies in university or national laboratories.

NACS was just as ambitious in the trade arena. Access to the U.S. consumer market should be "contingent on reciprocal opportunity for U.S. companies" in foreign markets.[25] NACS demanded full access to foreign markets, with special emphasis on Japan. It also called on Japan to make immediate and significant steps to increase its purchase of American-made semiconductors. In NACS' view, "specific sectors in Japan's market should be segregated for increased purchases and the success of these efforts should be measured in terms of increased market share."[26]

In calling for added semiconductor purchases, NACS had a precedent on its side. Japan had, after all, already agreed to specific results in the 1986 semiconductor pact (see chapter 3). But the idea of results-based rather than rules-based trade remained controversial. NACS wanted to take the next step and designate added markets and specific market shares. Traditional free traders both within and outside the administration were likely to object. So were the Japanese.

NACS did not stop at the cost of capital or trade policy. It made sweeping recommendations to improve the workforce. Noting that early childhood education was a critical first step, NACS proposed "a nationwide, quality, comprehensive preschool for economically disadvantaged, at risk, 4-year-old children."[27] NACS also proposed higher standards for education and teachers and business sharing of managerial expertise with educational institutions. It described a workplace with 20 to 30 million adults suffering from literacy problems. NACS urged business and government to work on improving workplace literacy and called for state and federal support for literacy training. In higher education, NACS pointed to the need for "curricula stressing manufacturing and total quality concepts."[28]

The NACS report also made a host of recommendations focusing on the development of specific technologies critical to the future of the semiconductor industry. With an eye to what NACS saw as the Japanese ability to effectively mix competition and cooperation, it urged legislation to further liberalize the antitrust laws by allowing joint production as well as joint research.

Shortly after the first NACS report, there was more troubling news for the American electronics industry. In an effort to develop a significant American source of supply for memory chips, seven major users or makers of memory chips formed U.S. Memories in mid-1989.[29] "The idea was to develop a secure, stable U.S. source of advanced semiconductors by using IBM's 4-megabit DRAM technology and pooling the consortium members' financial resources with commitments to buy chips from the new venture."[30] The major companies were looking to Sanford Kane, a twenty-seven-year veteran of IBM, to recruit additional members and to raise a hoped-for $1 billion in capital.

Only seven months later, in January 1990, U.S. Memories closed its doors. Kane pointed to several causes. He noted that the mix of computer manufacturers and chip companies had no history of working together. By contrast, the 1987 formation of Sematech built on a history of cooperation among chip makers. Kane also pointed to bad timing. Shortly after U.S. Memories was launched, the market was flooded with imported low-cost DRAMS, making it more difficult to portray U.S. Memories as a profitable venture. "Kane also expressed surprise at the lack of support from the Congress and the Bush Administration, which, with the exception of an early statement by Commerce Secretary Robert Mosbacher, stayed on the sidelines."[31] Industry observers pointed to other causes as well. Sheridan Tatsuno, writing in *New Technology Week,* called Kane the wrong quarterback.[32] At IBM, Kane had worked in an essentially closed world, where IBM chips were produced for IBM products. He had no experience selling to other companies in what was generally referred to as the merchant market. Tatsuno also thought that Kane started with a plan that was overly ambitious. In scaling back to a more realistic starting point, Tatsuno thought that Kane lost time and credibility. Tatsuno also pointed to the risk that antitrust laws might be applied to a joint-production agreement like U.S. Memories. In its first annual report, NACS had called for allowing joint production on the same terms that applied to join research efforts. That change would come, but not until the first year of the Clinton presidency and far too late for U.S. Memories.

Timing was another problem. The idea for U.S. Memories had been born in 1987, when DRAMS were expensive and hard to come by. Market conditions had changed sharply by the time work began on U.S. Memories in mid-1989. They changed sharply again just after the collapse of U.S. Memories. Writing from Tokyo, *New York Times* correspondent David Sanger reported that on the very day that U.S. Memories collapsed "one by one, within hours, Japan's biggest chip makers announced plans to cut their production of one-megabit memory chips."[33] In discussing the Japanese action, Sanger points to several possible motives but clearly raises the question of cartel-like behavior to first eliminate U.S. Memories and then raise prices.

NACS' proposals were an alternative to U.S. Memories. But its ambitious initial agenda encountered predictable opposition. The call for CECC invoked memories of the industrial development bank proposed by Representative John La Falce (D-N.Y.) in the early 1980s and was attacked on industrial policy grounds. The proposal for market-sharing agreements with Japan was attacked as managed trade. By the time of their final reports in 1992, both proposals were gone.

Yet it would be a mistake to dismiss NACS or its work. The NACS reports themselves were read in the technology community, and some of NACS' specific recommendations were translated into legislative proposals. For instance, Senator Max Baucus (D-Mont.) became a champion of reducing the depreciable lives of semiconductor manufacturing equipment to three years. NACS also added its voice to those calling for deficit reduction, a more assertive trade policy, and the continued development of a national technology policy. Over time, the Bush administration moved in all these directions.

The Competitiveness Policy Council

If NACS was focused on a single, critical industry, the Competitiveness Policy Council (CPC)[34] was charged with developing "national strategies . . . to enhance the productivity and international competitiveness of United States industries."[35] The CPC was established by the Omnibus Act of 1988, in keeping with a specific proposal for it that had emerged from a Senate task force headed by Senator Jeff Bingaman (D-N.M.).[36] The roots of the CPC could also be traced back to the 1984 proposal by Representative La Falce for a Council on Industrial Competitiveness and *Rebuilding the Road*'s Economic Cooperation Council. There were also other House proposals for some type of forum that would bring together key elements of the private and public sectors.

In creating the CPC, Congress sought to bridge the gaps between itself and the executive branch, between the House and Senate, between the parties, and between the public and private sectors.[37] The other members of the council (the statute required a two-thirds majority) chose as its chair C. Fred Bergsten, one of the four CPC members chosen by the House. Bergsten had first come to Washington as an aide to the then-national security adviser, Henry Kissinger and had then risen to added prominence as the senior international financial official in President Jimmy Carter's Treasury Department. After the Carter administration, Bergsten founded the Institute for

International Economics (IIE), a highly regarded Washington-based think tank focused on, as its name suggests, international economic questions. From the start, IIE emphasized the complexities as well as the benefits of an open and integrated international economy.

By choosing Bergsten, the CPC also helped rebut the lingering charge that competitiveness was just another word for protectionism. Bergsten was clearly identified with open markets and full engagement with the international economy. He put the protectionist question to rest. Bergsten, in turn, strengthened his own hand by adding a Coalition), with a trade history that dated to the international division of President Carter's Labor Department, served as executive director. Steve Charnovitz, a top aide to then-Speaker Jim Wright and now a professor at George Washington University Law School, served as the policy director.

In March 1992, the CPC issued its first report, *Building a Competitive America*. Drawing on the Young Commission, the CPC defined competitiveness as the country's "ability to produce goods and services that meet the test of international markets while our citizens earn a standard of living that is both rising and sustainable over the long run."[38] The report covered important but familiar territory, detailing everything from a low saving rate to the mixed quality of America's elementary and secondary education system. To the four familiar areas of concern—investment, innovation, education and training, and trade policy—the CPC added corporate governance and the question of high and rising health care costs. Annual reports followed in 1994 and 1995, before the CPC wound up its work in 1996.

While NACS and the CPC were particularly prominent, they were not the only voices created by the Omnibus Act of 1988. The Treasury was directed to make periodic reports on any manipulation of exchange rates to garner a competitive edge in international trade. The Treasury was also charged with reviewing foreign direct investments that could threaten national security. In reviewing the Omnibus Act, Otis Graham counted "30 new federal offices or panels" and "100 new reports to Congress and the public."[39] NACS and the CPC stand out because of their comprehensive view of the competitiveness challenge and the attention they garnered in both the private and public spheres. NACS and the CPC also spoke of a national effort that required effective action by private enterprise, individual citizens and supportive public policies. They both emphasized public–private partnerships and on the need to coordinate federal efforts with state initiatives.

The Private Sector Works to Meet the Global Challenge

The 1970s had been a difficult period for the American economy and much of American industry. If anything, the 1980s proved even more daunting. International competition was an important part of the equation. Japan was the most visible variable. In the 1970s, Japan was challenging the automobile and steel industries with better prices and, in many cases, better quality. By the mid-1980s, Japan dominated the American consumer electronics market and was challenging American leadership in semiconductors and computers.

Corporate America responded to the Japanese challenge in a number of ways. In the 1970s and early 1980s, a number of steel and auto companies and their respective unions sought legislation that would provide trade protection for some embattled domestic industries. There was also a generally shared concern about the overvalued dollar in the early 1980s. As corporate leaders made the link between deficits and higher interest rates and the overvalued dollar, corporate opposition to the persistent budget deficits continued to build.

But as the quality of Japanese products continued to win the loyalty of American consumers, American companies paid more and more attention to the Japanese corporations themselves. Reluctantly, many companies came to concede the quality of Japanese products and the effectiveness of Japanese practices. Could Americans match the Japanese in quality, innovation, and price? At first, some auto industry leaders attributed the superiority of Japanese cars to the unique qualities of Japanese culture. In labor peace, they saw a Confucian acceptance of hierarchy; in quality, they saw a Japanese dedication to detail; in work teams, they saw the feudal heritage of the Japanese village; and in education and skills, they saw again the invisible but palpable influence of Confucius.

American companies were not, however, content to accept defeat or even gradual decline. In the auto industry, they set about adopting and adapting the production techniques developed by Toyota. The leaders of Ford made "Quality Is Job One" their company-wide motto. Hierarchies were flattened, workers' skills improved, and empowered work teams became the norm. Chrysler (as of 1999, DaimlerChrysler) shifted to platform teams, in which designers, engineers, and production specialists worked together to dramatically reduce the time it took to bring new models to market. The automobile industry as a whole emphasized the importance of high-quality manufacturing in service of the American consumer.

The shift in American electronics was, if anything, more dramatic. In the 1970s, Japanese firms had taken the lead in consumer electronics with a combination of quality, price, and focus on the customer. They also benefited from below-cost pricing (or dumping), a low (relative to the dollar) fixed exchange rate, and a protected Japanese market. American companies did seek government action but, in general, did not attempt to match the quality/price advantage of the Japanese firms. Instead, American companies often moved their facilities overseas or marketed Japanese products under their own brand names. American organized labor supported efforts to invoke the antidumping laws and continued its effort to secure at least temporary protection for workers and industries facing stiff import competition. Some unions encouraged companies to introduce competitive technologies. There were also the beginnings of broader union–management cooperation on the trade front, both in terms of slowing imports and in seeking greater access to the Japanese market.

By the mid-1980s, the Japanese were taking the lead on the memory (DRAM) chip business and threatening American preeminence in the computer field. This time, the American electronic companies fought back. By the end of the decade, leading American companies were emphasizing quality, concurrent engineering, and empowered work teams. Like their Japanese counterparts, many were also working more closely with key suppliers on design and quality.

American companies found themselves competing with Japanese companies that had a very different relationship with their government. They saw a system and a state that was focused on economic growth[40] with an intensity that matched America's commitment to national security. There were elements of "Japan, Incorporated," that could be emulated and others that could be attacked. In both cases, public action could make a significant difference.

In contrast to the United States, Japan, Germany, and a number of other countries produced high school graduates that were better prepared for the demands of competition focused on the use of technology and the commitment to quality. For most of the post–World War II era, Germany and some other European countries relied on a system that prepared some students for college-level academics while tracking others into an elaborate apprenticeship system. Japan adopted a different approach. The American occupation had imposed a familiar, American structure on Japanese education, with elementary, junior high, and senior high schools. As it evolved after World War II, the Japanese system came to rest on three pillars: classroom instruction, after-school study in classes known as *juku,* and the famous "education mother." Added to the three pillars were a national curriculum that pushed the average student and a dedicated teacher core that worked with parents and students to assure in-school success.

Neither the German nor the Japanese system could be easily imported into the United States, though both have influenced the course of educational reform and practice. They did set an example of how an effective public commitment to education contributed to economic growth and the competitive strength of a country's industrial base. The private sector looked to the federal government as well as local school districts to improve education. By the late 1980s, the private sector was already involved in a host of partnerships with individual school districts, colleges, and universities. The companies undertaking these efforts were slowly developing the outlines of a New Growth Compact that, at times, involved active public–private partnerships.

Technology Policy and Industrial Innovation

As the 1980s drew to a close, the elected policymakers and business leaders saw their international competitors actively encouraging the development and widespread use of new technologies. In Germany, the Fraunhoffer Institutes provided research support for small and medium-sized manufacturers and helped spread the use of new technologies throughout industry. In Japan, the Ministry of International Trade and Industry formed industrial consortia to help develop new technologies.

In national security, space, and health, the U.S. government was actively involved in research that supported the downstream efforts of American companies. With the notable exception of agriculture, in other parts of the economy, there was little explicit focus on developing new technologies. By the time of the Young Commission report, however, business leaders were calling on the government to develop a civilian technology policy.

Trade: Going Global

Because governments set global trading rules, American companies forged an early working relationship with the U.S. government on trade matters. In practice, the private sector had considerable say in setting national trade policies and establishing national negotiating priorities. As part of the Trade Act of 1974, Congress had established an elaborate system of advisory committees to allow industry to provide the executive branch with a steady stream of advice on trade problems and possibilities.[41] There were also trade advisory committees established for the Defense, Labor, and Agriculture Departments, and, in the late 1990s, for the environment.[42] In the late 1980s, however, it was industry that used the advisory committee process most actively.

The trade agenda also helped work a change in corporate thinking and strategy. Key parts of the business community were working closely with Washington—the legislative as well as the executive branch. It was a vivid and long-lasting example of how private-sector and public-sector initiatives could be effective complements in an overall growth strategy.

Investing for the Long Term

Even when Silicon Valley firms felt a kind of invincible dominance in the late 1970s, they pointed to the advantage Japan had in terms of ample capital. The lower cost of capital was important, but so was its patience. In comparison with American industries, German and Japanese firms had access to long-term investors who were willing to wait for a research project or other investments to bear fruit. As competition intensified during the 1980s, the question of patient capital received more and more attention. By the end of the decade, it was common to hear complaints about the focus of America's financial markets on each and every quarterly financial report. Many manufacturers felt they were faced with a Hobson's choice of canceling research projects, planned acquisitions, and long-term marketing plans or delivering a disappointing quarterly report that would translate into a fall in the value of their shares.

From Conglomerate to Core Competence

In the 1980s, American businesses were also rethinking the wisdom of the corporate conglomerates built in the 1960s. In that period of American industrial dominance, there was an emphasis on diversifying assets so that a company would not be caught by a downturn in the demand for a particular product or service. The key to effective management lay in mastering the financial details of these diversified holdings, not in knowledge of a particular product or how to make it. By the 1980s, corporate thinking had begun to change. Instead of unrelated activities, there was an emphasis on a company's core competence. There was a growing sense that the whole had become less valuable than the sum of its parts. As a result, unrelated holdings were sold off so that firms could concentrate on core activities. The same logic was applied to in-house services such as accounting, which increasingly were purchased from outside accounting firms.

There were many causes for the shift. Some conglomerates proved unwieldy. In other cases, management thought a clear focus would bring enhanced results. At times, outsourcing was a way of shifting work from union to nonunion facilities. International competition also played a part. German and Japanese managers were generally viewed as being more knowledgeable about their products and services. In the Japanese case, managers usually started on the assembly line before beginning a progression through the management ranks. Manufacturing or front-line customer service was at least as much a part of their formative experience as were financial spreadsheets.

Managers as Owners

There was a parallel concern that management had become too divorced from ownership. Stock options became a relatively common way to create clear incentives for professional managers who otherwise did not have an ownership stake in the company. In addition to using stock options to attract top technical talent to new companies, Silicon Valley firms granted a high percentage of total stock options to much of their workforce. A growing number of corporations were adopting a company-wide use of stock options as a way of aligning corporate and individual interests. In the 1980s, there were also small teams of managers who thought they could buy individual pieces of a conglomerate and dramatically improve their performance and profitability. This shift in corporate thinking away from conglomerate ownership and toward an emphasis on managerial ownership paralleled the creative use of the high-yield (or junk) bonds that facilitated both trends.[43]

Market for Management

By the end of the 1980s, American corporations were caught in the crosscurrents of intense international competition and turbulent financial markets. Matching German or Japanese performance demanded investments in new equipment or whole new facilities, a renewed emphasis on innovation and quality, added investments in worker training, and a commitment to develop new markets. At the same time, the financial markets often demanded quick financial results that would improve the next quarterly report.

A falling stock price was never a cause of celebration. Meetings with the board of directors would be unpleasant. The company's officers could expect angry calls from major shareholders. Now, however, the future of the company or at least its management might be at stake. In the financial climate of the late 1980s, international competition, the unwinding of the conglomerates, and the use of high-interest (or junk) bonds had created an active "market for management." In a contemporaneous development, boards of directors and institutional investors became more active. Some major chief executives were unceremoniously shown the corporate door. Institutional investors, especially the public (and increasingly the private) pension funds, demanded effective corporate management.

Both public and private sectors responded to the crosscutting pressures. Individual management teams adopted so-called golden parachutes to assure themselves of a soft landing should they lose their positions in a forced merger or hostile takeover. Others adopted "poison pills" that added significantly to the cost of any prospective hostile takeover. Many did both. State legislatures often acted to protect firms headquartered in their respective states. Congress debated legislation that would ban poison pills in the name of shareholder value and other legislation that would limit takeovers in the service of critical long-term investments.[44]

Not surprisingly, what Margaret Blair has dubbed the "Deal Decade" spawned considerable academic research.[45] Some economists saw the sharp spur of competition driving companies to improve their performance, while others saw a short-term mentality that was endangering America's economic future.

Again, the private-sector Council on Competitiveness played a significant role. Like much of American manufacturing, the council's members were facing the pressure of international competition and financial markets. Many members were in high-technology fields that demanded large investments in R&D coupled with the added costs of bringing a new product to a global market. Financial pressures or systemic differences that penalized long-term investment could put even the industrial leaders in the council at risk.

The Council on Competitiveness again turned to Michael Porter, a distinguished Harvard Business School professor and council executive committee member, who had served on the original Young Commission. Porter, in turn, assembled a top-flight group of academic economists and business school professors to look at different aspects of the question. Over time,

Porter broadened his research beyond the specific question of quarterly reports and the financial markets to take a systematic look at how corporate investment decisions were made in Germany, Japan, and the United States.

In his book *Capital Choices,* Porter painted a complex picture of investment decisions that depended on the structure of internal decision making as well as outside financial pressures.[46] He noted that some industries were characterized by persistent long-term investing. For instance, even after a new drug was discovered or developed, the testing required by the Food and Drug Administration could last a decade or more. Yet pharmaceutical companies were able to generate and attract long-term investments.[47] Venture capitalists, heavy investors in firms developing electronics and information technology, were also prepared to wait for a number of years before receiving a financial return.

For some industries and many companies, however, Porter did find that the financial pressures were real. In particular, the external emphasis on quarterly reports could interact with an internal investment committee in a way that penalized the so-called softer investments—research, training, or marketing. Because soft investments were expensed or totally written off when incurred, they caused a dollar-for-dollar reduction in reported profits, with obvious implications for quarterly reports. Structures or new equipment, however, were usually depreciated over a number of years and so did not pose the same threat to reported earnings.

America Adapts

American companies did adapt. Japanese manufacturing techniques were adapted to American needs and spread beyond manufacturing to affect services and even the public sector. Companies became adept at using more expensive and more impatient capital. The growth in outsourcing was one response. The shift to core competencies was another. In many cases, spending on R&D was transferred out of central laboratories to individual business units. At the same time, there was a shift from longer-term research to nearer-to-market projects. From a corporate point of view, research became more productive. The application of information technology to many research ventures has made R&D even more productive. Companies actively sought and developed a wide variety of public–private partnerships that helped respond to economic change and global competition.

Throughout the 1980s, American industry was transforming itself in a way that helped make possible the prosperity of the 1990s. When George H. W.

Bush entered the White House, however, corporate America was still struggling with that transformation. It was painfully aware of the challenges posed by international competition. Instead of a traditional adversarial relationship, it was looking for a federal government that would create a positive environment for growth and make needed investments in everything from technology to training. It and much of the American public wanted a government that would be an effective partner in responding to the global challenge to America's economic future.

The States Build a Competitive Future

Even during the decades immediately following World War II, some state governments had been actively involved in encouraging economic development. In the South, state governments added tax holidays to their low labor costs as a way of attracting textile and other labor-intensive industries from the North.

Until the 1970s, much of the state effort was concentrated on attracting or retaining investment. The 1970s brought a change to state development strategies, as states attempted to respond to the same economic challenges faced by the nation as a whole. The national debate over growth strategies and industrial policy had its state-based counterparts. The states, like the nation, became more focused on international trade and investment, the increased role of innovation, and the growing importance of an educated workforce.

In describing the state response to the economic turmoil of the 1970s, Peter K. Eisinger points to the rise of "an entrepreneurial state" that takes an active role in encouraging state-based growth.[48] Even some major cities developed their own strategies for economic development. By the early 1980s, virtually every state had an economic development office. State-based staffs devoted to economic development had tripled since the late 1960s.

Governors were also learning from the same examples that influenced the debate in academic circles and the broader policy community. German and particularly Japanese success had an independent impact on state thinking. The proliferating high-technology firms in Silicon Valley and along Route 128 near Boston were other success stories that had considerable influence. In both cases, large, research universities played a critical role in stimulating new technologies and new firms. Both areas had met the modern test of economic development by creating jobs and raising incomes at the same time.[49] At the end of the 1980s, Michael Porter's *The Competitive Advantage of Nations* linked sound national policies to the economic success of geographically based industrial clusters—confirming and influencing state strategies.

As outlined by Eisinger, the entrepreneurial state shifted from competition for mobile capital through low wages and taxes to an emphasis on creating a competitive advantage by using a variety of methods to grow nationally or globally competitive businesses within the state. Now, more than a decade after Eisinger, it is clear that competition for mobile capital remains an important element in state growth strategies. But the nature of that competition has changed. Instead of simply relying only on low wages, low taxes, and other financial concessions, states are luring high-technology and other investments by emphasizing "the availability of highly skilled labor and access to high-quality academic institutions."[50]

As competition among the states shifted to developing and attracting high-technology businesses, support for state-led efforts usually cut across partisan and community lines. In the early days of the Clinton administration, the Department of Commerce developed a Partnership for a Competitive Economy (PACE) program that highlighted successful public–private partnerships at the regional, state, or local level.[51] Many of the sessions included a fifteen-minute videotape on how technology improved the lives of Americans, with President Clinton serving as the moderator. In contrast to the angry congressional debates over various Clinton administration partnership initiatives, PACE found states pursuing a variety of public–private partnerships with little in the way of controversy. The support for these partnerships was driven by the broadly embraced goal of economic development and did not depend on whether the governor's mansion was occupied by a Democrat or a Republican, a liberal or a conservative.

State Initiatives and Federal Action

Just as the states were influenced by broad economic currents, national policy debates, and an industrial America struggling to adapt, they were also influenced by national initiatives that were designed to improve the American economy. In 1979, the Department of Labor issued new regulations to allow public pension funds to invest a "small portion of their assets in high-risk venture."[52] The change in the so-called prudent man rule allowed states to put a portion of their pension funds into higher-risk, higher-yield venture capital funds. In 1980, Congress passed the University and Small Business Patent Act.[53] Better known as the Bayh-Dole Act (after its principal Senate sponsors), the new law allowed universities and small businesses to license their federally funded inventions to industry. In addition to opening up new fields for university–industry collaboration, Bayh-Dole set a precedent that could be applied to state-funded research as well.

In education, training, and research, federal funds were often targeted at state institutions. Whether or not state matching funds were involved, state initiatives frequently paralleled or complemented the federal effort. Federal initiatives often looked to the states for administration or depended on state action to achieve national goals.

Financing Development

As the national focus shifted to high technology and an emphasis on encouraging the creation of new firms, states moved in a more entrepreneurial direction. Individual states used a variety of tools, which ranged from creating their own venture capital funds to making research grants to utilizing state tax incentives.[54] The move toward state venture capital funds dates to 1981, when the "state of Washington Investment Board began investing as a limited partner in . . . venture undertakings."[55] Ohio and Michigan took a more dramatic step in 1982, when they began "to earmark by statute a proportion of their public employee retirement funds for investment in local venture capital undertakings."[56]

States also became more adept at supporting the different phases of business development. As an example, Eisinger pointed to Illinois, which maintained an array of financing programs that supported start-ups, small businesses, and larger firms as well.[57] Michigan developed an even more integrated approach by linking finance to a "number of different high- and middle-risk stages of the business cycle."[58]

Fostering Innovation

In a number of cases, the states' development of a venture capital capacity was linked to its interest in attracting high-technology industries that would contribute to a state's innovative capacity. As early as 1983, the Congressional Office of Technology Assessment "described 150 state economic development initiatives" that were to some extent linked to high-technology development.[59] State initiatives ranged from fostering basic and applied research, to helping spread technology among small and medium-sized businesses, to supporting university incubators, to establishing entire research parks.

Visible progress in one state had a clear impact on the strategies in other states. For instance, the success of North Carolina's Research Triangle has spawned a number of imitators and likely competitors. Writing in 1984, Michael Peltz and Marc Weiss found eighteen states that had "or were planning research parks."[60] Weiss also points to the growing practice of states supporting the development of incubators on university campuses to encourage the commercialization of university research. With the example of garage-based inventions becoming major industries, states, universities, and many businesses saw considerable promise in the incubator idea.

In some cases, states created new research institutes to foster innovation and support the industrial use of advanced technology. Pennsylvania's Ben Franklin Partnership Centers are frequently cited as a model of what industry-oriented research institutes can do. Founded in 1982, the Ben Franklin Centers sponsor research, "provide financing and management assistance to new companies, run incubators, and provide training for workers in the new industries."[61] Congress did not create similar bodies until the Omnibus Act of 1988, and even then full implementation of the related portions of the act did not take place until the advent of the Clinton administration.

Promoting Exports

State interest in exports did not start in the 1980s. Eisinger points to a 1959 trip by state governors to Europe to pursue foreign trade that was led by North Carolina's governor, Luther Hodges.[62] By the 1980s, governor-led foreign trade missions were commonplace. A majority of states had opened commercial offices in major overseas markets and were actively involved in promoting agricultural and industrial exports.

The federal government had its own set of export promotion programs, but they were far from the centerpiece of U.S. trade policy. States were not content to wait for federal action. As part of the export promotion effort, states often partnered with private associations and supported the development of international trade centers.

States were quick to see exports as a way to make the most of their own comparative advantage. High-technology firms were already globally oriented and frequently looked to exports as a way of driving company quality as well as funding the next round of research. Effective export promotion programs often were part of a promising business climate that attracted, grew, and retained businesses. Agricultural states turned to exports as critical elements in maintaining prosperity in their farming communities. When federal attention lagged, states stepped in to master everything from Thai tastes to Japanese custom regulations.

Developing Skilled Labor

Rising international competition was driving many of the low-wage, labor-intensive industries offshore. Starting in the1960s, America began losing jobs in textiles, apparel, shoes, and consumer electronics. Europe, Japan, and then the developing world lured American industry and investment, much the way the low-wage, low-cost South had once competed for Northern industry.

Many high-technology industries were now demanding a more skilled and highly educated workforce. The assembly of semiconductor chips did not require highly developed skills and, as a result, chip assembly frequently migrated to Southeast Asia and other offshore locations. But research, design, engineering, and applications all put a premium on education.

In addition, established industries were starting to turn to information technology. Computer-assisted design and computer-assisted manufacturing became critical tools in improving quality, meeting the demands of specific consumers, and reducing costs. When companies looked for a machinist in the 1980s, they were often talking about someone who could reprogram a numerically controlled machine tool as well being able to repair the machine itself.

International competition was also driving American companies to change their internal structure in a way that demanded greater skills. The empowered work teams and flattened hierarchies associated with the best of Japanese production translated into a need for workers with a wider variety of skills. By the late 1980s, state-funded community colleges and universities were working to respond to the economic demands of the states and the nation. States were also starting the long process of demanding more from local school districts. In some cases, increases in state funding were linked to growing demands for local accountability.

Building the Base

By the late 1980s, the states were adopting a number of policies that were contributing to the nation's prospects for long-term growth. States created their own commissions to look at innovation, industrial development, and state competitiveness.[63] In virtually every case, these commissions proposed policies that paralleled and complemented those advocated by the Young Commission and adopted by Congress in the Omnibus Trade and Competitiveness Act of 1988. At the same time, the states were learning from and informing the national debate over America's competitive future.

State by state, governors were sorting out the respective roles of the states and the private sector. They were establishing state-based versions of what would become the national New Growth Compact. Part of every state's strategy was a wide variety of public–private partnerships that created their own variations on the emerging Partnership Nation at the national level.

Notes

1. Pat Choate, *America's Competitive Challenge: The Need for a National Response* (Washington, D.C.: Business–Higher Education Forum, 1983).
2. Author's interview with John Young, November 30, 1999.
3. Mark Potts, "Council on Competitiveness Formed: Leaders Seek to Improve Performance of American Industries," *Washington Post*, December 3, 1966.
4. John B. Judis, *The Paradox of American Democracy: Elites, Special Interests, and the Betrayal of Public Trust* (New York: Pantheon, 2000), 184.
5. Council on Competitiveness, *Picking Up the Pace: The Commercial Challenge to American Innovation* (Washington, D.C.: Council on Competitiveness, 1988). The material on *Picking Up the Pace* draws on a May 15, 2000, interview with Daniel F. Burton Jr. Burton came to the council from the United Nations Association, and he went on to become council president in 1993 and then vice president for government affairs at Novell, a major software company.
6. Council on Competitiveness, *Picking Up the Pace*, 15.
7. Council on Competitiveness, *Picking Up the Pace*, 17.
8. Author's interview with Alan Magazine, May 10, 2000.
9. April 17, 2000, letter from Young to the author.
10. Council on Competitiveness, *Reclaiming the American Dream: Fiscal Policies for a Competitive Nation* (Washington, D.C.: Council on Competitiveness, 1988).
11. At the time, there was relatively little talk in the Congress or in the Washington policy community of budget surpluses. Some academics, including Lawrence Summers —who become President Clinton's second secretary of the Treasury—were beginning to think, write, and talk about budget surpluses as one way of increasing the American savings rate.

12. Council on Competitiveness, *Competitiveness Index* (Washington, D.C.: Council on Competitiveness, 1988).

13. See Judis, *Paradox of American Democracy*, 185–88, for a brief history of the founding of the Economic Strategy Institute.

14. Clyde V. Prestowitz Jr., *Trading Places: How We Allowed Japan to Take the Lead* (New York: Basic Books, 1988).

15. Prestowitz, *Trading Places*, 308.

16. Ezra Vogel, *Japan as No. 1: Lessons for America* (Cambridge, Mass.: Harvard University Press, 1979).

17. This quotation is from the Summit 91 Agenda.

18. Michael Duffy and Dan Goodgame, *Marching in Place: The Status Quo Presidency of George Bush* (New York: Simon & Schuster, 1992), 240.

19. U.S. Congress, *Omnibus Trade and Competitiveness Act of 1988: Conference Report to Accompany HR 3* (Washington, D.C.: U.S. Government Printing Office, 1988), section 5301, pp. 376–77. The Omnibus Act called for a "Federal Budget Competitiveness Impact Statement" that would spell out "the budget's impact on the international competitiveness of the United States and the U.S. balance of payments position" (p. 376). Under section 5301, the government was called upon to report on the extent of government borrowing in the private credit markets and on the impact on interest rates and the "real effective exchange rate" (p. 377).

20. U.S. Congress, *Omnibus Trade and Competitiveness Act of 1988*, section 3005, p. 285.

21. U.S. Congress, *Omnibus Trade and Competitiveness Act of 1988*, section 5141, pp. 357–58.

22. U.S. Congress, *Omnibus Trade and Competitiveness Act of 1988*, section 5142, pp. 358–60.

23. U.S. Congress, *Omnibus Trade and Competitiveness Act of 1988*, section 5201, pp. 368–76.

24. National Advisory Committee on Semiconductors (NACS), *A Strategic Industry at Risk: A Report to the President and the Congress from the National Advisory Committee on Semiconductors* (Washington, D.C.: National Advisory Committee on Semiconductors, 1989), vi.

25. NACS, *Strategic Industry at Risk*, 24.

26. NACS, *Strategic Industry at Risk*, 28.

27. NACS, *Strategic Industry at Risk*, 27.

28. NACS, *Strategic Industry at Risk*, 28.

29. The seven were IBM, Digital Equipment, Hewlett-Packard, Intel, Advanced Micro Devices, LSI Logic, and National Semiconductor.

30. "Kane Reflects on Demise of U.S. Memories," *Challenges* (Council on Competitiveness, Washington), March 1990, 1, 4.

31. "Kane Reflects on Demise," 4.

32. Sheridan Tatsuno, "Life After U.S .Memories: Can the U.S. Re-Enter the Memory Chip Business?" *New Technology Week,* February 12, 1990, 1, 12–13.

33. David E. Sanger, "Contrasts on Chips, as a Joint Venture Collapses in U.S., Japanese Companies Act Like a Cartel," *New York Times,* January 18, 1990.

34. See subtitle C, Competitiveness Policy Council, section 5201, Omnibus Trade and Competitiveness Act of 1988, 368–76.

35. Subtitle C, Competitiveness Policy Council, Omnibus Act, 370.

36. Otis L. Graham Jr., *Losing Time: The Industrial Policy Debate* (Cambridge, Mass.: Harvard University Press, 1992), 218.

37. Subtitle C, 371.

38. Competitiveness Policy Council, *Building a Competitive America* (Washington, D.C.: Competitiveness Policy Council, 1992), 1.

39. Graham, *Losing Time,* 219.

40. These are elements of what Chalmers Johnson referred to as the Developmental State. See Chalmers Johnson, *MITI and the Japanese Miracle: The Growth of Industrial Policy, 1925–1975* (Stanford, Calif.: Stanford University Press, 1982), 17 et. seq.

41. The advisory structure was established by section 135 of the Trade Act of 1974 (19 U.S.C. 2155). Over time, the industry structure has evolved through amendment and executive order. In terms of industry, there are 17 Industry Sector Advisory Committees and 4 Industry Functional Committees, which give voice to some 400 industry representatives. The structure has adapted to changing circumstances and emerging industries. For instance, the E-Commerce Advisory Committee was established in 1999. The Department of Commerce Web site provides summary details of the committees, including membership. See http://www.ita.doc.gov/td/rep/hom.html.

42. The Office of the United States Trade Representatives cochairs the Agriculture, Defense, Labor, and Environment Committees with the relevant federal department or agency. The Agricultural, Defense, and Labor Committees were established in 1975. The Environment Committee is the newest—being established in 1999. All the advisory committees report to the top-level Advisory Committee on Trade Policy and Negotiations, which was also established in 1975. For detail, see http://www.ustr.gov/outreach/index.shtml.

43. For a discussion of the leveraged buyouts of the 1980s, see Margaret Blair, *The Deal Decade: What Takeovers and Leveraged Buyouts Mean for Corporate Governance* (Washington, D.C.: Brookings Institution Press, 1993).

44. For a discussion of state action and congressional inaction, see Mark J. Roe, "Takeover Politics," in *The Deal Decade: What Takeovers and Leveraged Buyouts Mean for Corporate Governance,* ed. Margaret M. Blair (Washington, D.C.: Brookings Institution Press, 1992), 321–62.

45. Blair, *Deal Decade.*

46. Michael Porter, *Capital Choices: Changing the Way America Invests in Industry* (Washington, D.C.: Council on Competitiveness, 1992).

47. It is true that the Japanese were not major competitors in the pharmaceutical field, but the Europeans certainly were.

48. Peter K. Eisinger, *The Rise of the Entrepreneurial State: State and Local Economic Development Policy in the United States* (Madison: University of Wisconsin Press, 1988).

49. In Eisinger's view, "policies of the entrepreneurial state reject the assumption that low wages constitute a competitive advantage. Economic development is increasingly understood as a process that involves not simply employment growth but also increasing incomes"; *Rise of the Entrepreneurial State,* 30. Note the parallels to the test for national competitiveness articulated in the Young Commission Report. The Young Commission ruled out meeting international competition in a way that lowered standards of living. In place of simple price competitiveness through a lower exchange rate, the Young Commission set a higher standard that demanded innovation and quality from private business and supportive policies and investments by the public sector.

50. Joint Economic Committee, U.S. Congress, *Location of High Technology Firms and Regional Economic Development* (Washington, D.C.: U.S. Government Printing Office, 1982), as cited in Michael Peltz and Marc A. Weiss, "State and Local Government Roles in Industrial Innovation," *APA Journal,* summer 1984, 271.

51. As part of the Partnership for a Competitive Economy (PACE), the Technology Administration published a PACE newsletter, the *Pacesetter.* Published between 1997 and 1999, copies of the *Pacesetter* can be found online in the Technology Administration's Archives. See http://www.technology.gov/Archives/p_Newsletters.htm.

52. National Commission on Entrepreneurship, *American Formula for Growth: Federal Policy and the Entrepreneurial Economy, 1958–1998* (Washington, D.C.: National Commission on Entrepreneurship, 2002), 27–28. The new regulation can be found at 29 C.F.R. 2550-404a-1.

53. P.L. 96-517 (35 U.S.C. 200–212).

54. Peltz and Weiss, "State and Local Government Roles," 276.

55. Eisinger, *Rise of the Entrepreneurial State,* 256.

56. Eisinger, *Rise of the Entrepreneurial State,* 256.

57. Eisinger, *Rise of the Entrepreneurial State,* 262.

58. Eisinger, *Rise of the Entrepreneurial State,* 263.

59. Peltz and Weiss, "State and Local Government Roles," 270. Peltz and Weiss cite Office of Technology Assessment, *Technology, Innovation, and Regional Economic Development: Census of State Government Initiatives for High-Technology Industrial Development*, Background Paper 1 (Washington, D.C.: U.S. Government Printing Office, 1983).

60. Peltz and Weiss, "State and Local Government Roles," 273.

61. Eisinger, *Rise of the Entrepreneurial State,* 286.

62. Eisinger, *Rise of the Entrepreneurial State*, 294.

63. See, for instance, Cuomo Commission on Trade and Competitiveness, *The Cuomo Commission Report* (New York: Simon & Schuster, 1988).

Chapter 9

President Bush Takes the Stage

The popular shorthand summary of George H. W. Bush's presidency is still: victory in the Persian Gulf, domestic neglect, and electoral disaster. Although there is some truth in this sketch of the Bush years, it is misleading in its simplicity. It understates the degree to which his administration made its own contribution to a more competitive America.

Bush faced his share of economic challenges. He assumed the presidency at a time of growing concern about the economy despite several years of uninterrupted growth. He inherited a budget deficit that threatened his political coalition, added to his economic problems, and limited the scope for domestic initiatives. The savings and loan crisis made credit harder to find —especially for smaller businesses. Bush's decision to take on the crisis was good for long-term growth but triggered federal guarantees that added to the near-term fiscal deficit.[1] During his presidency, American industry was continuing to downsize or restructure in a way that threatened the jobs of salaried middle managers as well as front-line workers. The Federal Reserve's tightening of monetary policy helped tip the economy into a brief recession—adding cyclical misery to structural pain. The final collapse of the Soviet Union led to swift and often painful downsizing in the defense sector of the economy. The Rodney King riots in Los Angeles highlighted the failure of the administration to develop an urban strategy.

The president and at least part of his team did respond to some of these challenges. They had some success in reducing the budget deficit, in defining and implementing an administration technology policy, and in bringing businesses together with the governors in an effort to improve the nation's schools. The Labor Department was working to strengthen the government's training programs. The Treasury Department was exploring the impact of financial markets on the investment horizons of American corporations. And the Treasury and Commerce Departments jointly explored the availability of capital to fund private-sector investments in research and development.

The Bush administration also made major strides toward completing the Uruguay Round of trade negotiations and the North American Free Trade Agreement. To help focus the government's export promotion efforts, President Bush used an executive memorandum to create the Trade Promotion Coordinating Committee,[2] bringing into one interagency body the government's many export promotion efforts. There were a variety of other specific initiatives that were generally consistent with the kind of national competitiveness strategy articulated in the report of the President's Commission on Industrial Competitiveness (or the Young Commission).

Another group, based largely in the White House, was developing a series of initiatives that focused on individual empowerment as a replacement for the welfare state. To foster individual empowerment, advocates proposed everything from individual incentives to enterprise zones. These kinds of empowerment ideas—often referred to as the New Paradigm—had considerable support within and without the administration. They were not, however, embraced by the president himself.

In a very real sense, the Bush administration was developing two separate but complementary domestic strategies: competitiveness and empowerment. It was not until late in his reelection campaign, however, that President Bush issued his own competitiveness strategy, the *Agenda for American Renewal*.[3] The *Agenda* was credible in the sense that it could point to specific administration initiatives. But to many observers, it was a dollar short and many days too late.

The Reagan Legacy and the 1988 Election

Bush won the 1988 election with a decisive electoral college victory (426–112) and with a narrower but still comfortable 54 percent of the popular vote.[4] It some respects, it had been a remarkable victory. Bush had lost to Bob Dole in the Iowa caucuses and trailed Dole going into the final weekend before the balloting in the New Hampshire primary. The strong support of New Hampshire governor John Sununu and Bush's willingness to sign a no-tax pledge turned the tide. After nailing down the nomination, Bush failed to turn his primary successes into broad popular support. By the end of the Democratic convention in August, he trailed his Democratic opponent, Governor Michael Dukakis of Massachusetts, by 17 percentage points.

Bush started his turnaround with a strong speech at the Republican convention. He wore the mantle of Reagan-era success but suggested a softening of its harsher aspects by promising a "kinder, gentler" America. He spoke of an America renewed by "a thousand points of light" without pointing to specific goals or the question of resources.[5] In his most memorable and most haunting line, he committed himself to Ronald Reagan's agenda of lower taxes. "Delivered with theatrical pauses that would have made Reagan proud,"[6] Vice President Bush "brought the convention to its feet: 'The Congress will push me to raise taxes, and I'll say no, and they'll push, and I'll say no, and they'll push again. And all I can say to them is: *Read my lips. No new taxes.*'"[7] (emphasis added)

If the phrase created subsequent political and economic problems for the administration, the phrase and the speech had immediate political benefits. "He had cut Dukakis' lead in half."[8]

Governor Dukakis had built his earlier seventeen-point lead by emphasizing his competence and pointing to his ability to bring a traditional industrial state back to economic health—the Massachusetts miracle. To a country still unsure about its economic future, the Dukakis campaign brought a message of hope. What had worked in Massachusetts might just work in other parts of the country.

Following the convention, the Bush campaign and its supporters set to work to paint Michael Dukakis as out of the American mainstream. Dukakis was portrayed as a "card-carrying member" of the American Civil Liberties Union and was pilloried for having vetoed (in 1977) a bill passed by the Massachusetts legislature requiring teachers to lead their classes in the Pledge of Allegiance. He was tarred for being soft on crime. The attack focused on Willie Horton, a convicted murderer who, "while on furlough from a Massachusetts prison in 1987 . . . made his way to Maryland, broke into a home, pistol-whipped the owner, cut him twenty-two times across the midsection, and then raped his wife."[9]

During the primary campaign, then-senator Al Gore raised the furlough issue without mentioning Horton by name. The case also came to the attention of James Pinkerton, the director of Bush's opposition research. Lee Atwater, Bush's campaign manager, was quoted as saying that he would win the election if he could make Willie Horton a household name.[10] The Bush campaign ran an ad titled the "Revolving Door" showing prisoners (actually young Republicans at Brigham Young University dressed in prison garb) "walking through a turnstile as they moved in and out of prison."[11] The more controversial ad was run by the National Security Political Action Committee (NSPAC), one of many independent groups that support one candidate or another without being an official part of the campaign. The NSPAC ad featured the threatening visage of Horton himself. Until the NSPAC ad appeared, the fact that Horton was an African American had not been an aspect of the debate. Many observers thought it was a conscious attempt by NSPAC to inject race into the 1988 election and accused the Bush campaign of having worked with NSPAC while still maintaining an official distance. The Bush campaign denied any involvement with NSPAC. In his biography of Bush, John Robert Greene notes that Andrew Card, Bush's New Hampshire campaign manager, "remembered that we didn't even want them to run it."[12]

In his acceptance speech at the 1988 Democratic convention, Dukakis spoke of an election that would be about competence rather than ideology. Having started to paint Dukakis as a liberal out of touch with American values, the Bush campaign went on to attack his competence as well. To make their point, Bush rode around Boston Harbor while attacking Dukakis for failing to clean up the sludge. They painted Dukakis's Massachusetts as more mess than miracle.

For most of the campaign, Dukakis neither launched his own attacks nor found an effective way to respond to the charges made by the Bush campaign. The result was a campaign more about symbols than substance. There was little effort to articulate a vision of the future, explain the challenges facing the country, or draw on the lessons of the past. Bush won a substantial Electoral College victory, but compared with the Reagan landslide of 1984, Bush "had received 5.4 million fewer Republican votes . . . lost 500 counties Reagan had won, and received less support from Independents and 'Reagan Democrats.'"[13] While losing the White House, the Democrats managed to pick up seats in both Houses of Congress. Nor had Bush built the kind of broad popularity achieved by Ronald Reagan. The electorate gave him only a 43 percent favorable rating on election day—enough to be beat the 32 percent favorable standing of Dukakis but not much of an endorsement by the voters. The public, it seemed, did not so much love Bush more as they loved Dukakis less.

In strictly political terms, Bush entered the White House without the groundswell of support that carried Reagan to victory in 1980 and 1984. His negative attacks proved so effective that the campaign never had to spell out a vision for the future or a national strategy of how to achieve it. He also relied on a Reagan coalition that was showing some strains. Under Reagan, social conservatives found a champion that brought their issues into the national dialogue. Reagan, however, had made little effort to push legislation that would make the values of social conservatives the law of the land. After eight years, they were likely to want more than rhetoric. Persistent national deficits created a different set of tensions. Supply-siders continued to press for added tax cuts and resist the idea of tax increases. Tax cuts, after all, had defined the Reagan revolution. That Reagan also had agreed to major tax increases was somehow ignored. At the same time, a growing number of Americans saw the deficits as a sign that the country was in trouble. Living beyond your means even suggested a kind of moral laxity. Many Republican-leaning business leaders saw the deficits as an economic burden that raised their cost of capital and weakened their ability to meet international competition.

President Reagan cast a long shadow in the Republican Party and in much of the country. Political commentators wrote less about gridlock and more about how Reagan had made the presidency work again. Reagan's optimism about the country had proven infectious. He managed to project a sense of American strength while seldom having to put it to the test. In what many saw as Reagan's third term, Bush ran the inevitable risk of seeming a second banana to America's first "acting president."[14]

Foreign Policy:
From the Persian Gulf to the End of the Soviet Union

The foreign policy of the Bush administration will fill books and dissertations for years to come. Here the focus is on the geopolitical context within which the early competitiveness strategy would have to develop. The foreign policy challenges that confronted the Bush administration were so varied and so daunting that they help explain why the president may have been less focused on the domestic economy. A brief detour into foreign policy also helps bring home how the president's successful management of many foreign crises raised expectations for domestic action and contrasted with what more and more Americans felt was the administration's failure to deal with the economy.

In looking back at the Bush presidency, almost everyone remembers his stunning success in the Persian Gulf War. In a relatively brief period of time, the president built a global coalition to oppose Iraqi leader Saddam Hussein's invasion of Kuwait. The American military mastered a major logistical challenge in bringing troops and matériel halfway around the world. Five weeks after the first Allied air strikes, the ground war began on February 24, 1991. By March 3, General Norman Schwartzkopf was dictating the terms of a cease-fire. The Persian Gulf dominated the nation's headlines and captured the national imagination. It was a tribute to American (and President Bush's) global leadership and determination.

President Bush's foreign policy challenges did not, however, start or stop with the Persian Gulf War. The first came on June 4, 1989, when tanks of the People's Liberation Army (PLA) rolled into Tiananmen Square in Beijing to crush a student-led demonstration that had begun to attract workers and the unemployed. The American public had been following the student demonstrations for days on live television broadcasts and watched as the PLA tanks and troops moved into position. The students chose a statue of lady liberty as the symbol of their call for freer speech and more open government—every American saw it as an invocation of the Statue of Liberty. The networks replayed the incident where a lone Chinese challenged a tank and seemed to turn it aside. It was David dominating Goliath. It was how John Wayne would have handled the situation.

The student demonstrations were taking place while the Chinese leadership was welcoming Soviet leader Mikhail Gobachev on a state visit.[15] The leadership was clearly embarrassed. Embarrassment turned to concern over the political potential of the demonstrations and to apprehension as unemployed workers began to join the students. Finally, the PLA moved decisively—tanks rumbled through Tiananmen Square, killing protesters and destroying their makeshift structures. The world was stunned.

Americans and Congress wanted near-term action, but President Bush feared the long-term consequences. In the end, the president, a former de facto ambassador to China, did impose some limited sanctions on China, including banning high-level contact with its government. Two weeks after his ban on high-level contacts, Bush dispatched national security adviser Brent Scowcroft and deputy secretary of state Lawrence Eagleburger on a secret mission to talk with the Chinese leadership.[16]

After China and while preparations were under way for the Persian Gulf War, American paratroops landed in Panama on December 20, 1990. Within hours, they had subdued the opposition and captured Manuel Noriega, the Panamanian strongman. It was a foretaste of the short, decisive war to come in the Persian Gulf.

Even more challenging was the gradual unraveling of first the Soviet empire and then the Soviet Union itself. The symbolic break with the Soviet era came on November 9, 1989, when the gates of the Berlin Wall were thrown open. Communist governments fell rapidly and peacefully with the exception of Rumania, where the longtime dictator Nicolae Ceaucescu and his wife were executed on Christmas Day.

Then came the collapse of the Soviet state. In seeking to rebuild the Soviet Union, Mikhail Gorbachev had pushed aside an established leadership, allowed Eastern Europe to move out of the Soviet orbit, and threatened the historic monopoly of the Communist Party. In doing so, he made enemies who waited for an opportunity to reassert their control and end his. When Gorbachev left for vacation in the Crimea in mid-August 1991, they moved. On August 18, Gorbachev was placed under house arrest and the coup leaders announced the formation of a new government. Days later, Gorbachev was back and the coup was over. Three days after his return, the parliament voted the Communist Party out of existence. The Soviet Union gave way to the Commonwealth of Independent States on December 21, when the eleven member republics accepted Gorbachev's resignation four days before it was formally submitted.[17] Bush continues to be praised for the conduct of the Persian Gulf War. If anything, he has received too little credit for his role in guiding American policy during the decline and fall of the Soviet Union.

Initially, at least, the president was rewarded for his foreign policy successes—particularly his stunning victory in the Persian Gulf. At the start of the Gulf War, the president's popular standing had fallen in the wake of his abandoning his "no new taxes" pledge as part of the November 1990 budget agreement. The Persian Gulf victory reversed his earlier decline and pushed his favorability rating to virtually unheard-of levels, even reaching 91 percent in one *USA Today* poll.[18]

In early 1991, Bush seemed unbeatable. Leading contenders for the Democratic presidential nomination decided not to run. Who, after all, could best Bush now? But the early success may have contained the seeds of Bush's eventual defeat. From the pinnacle of a 91 percent approval rating, the need for an aggressive domestic agenda may have seemed unnecessary. Governor Sununu, the president's chief of staff, suggested that Congress could simply go home—the administration had achieved its key goals.

Just as the Persian Gulf success and the attendant popularity lulled the Bush administration into a dangerous sense of electoral inevitability, it may have raised expectations for domestic action. If America could defeat a major army halfway around the world, could not something also be done to attack unemployment, dwindling competitiveness, and decaying cities? Success bred higher expectations, not popular complacency.

The Economy: Recession to Recovery without Renewal

In addition to the economic expansion, President Reagan had passed on a number of economic problems to his vice president. Productivity growth remained anemic during the Reagan expansion. As a result, for many Americans real wages had remained stagnant or actually fallen. American investment in new plant and equipment continued to lag behind the performance of other leading industrial countries, and Japanese firms began to dominate the list of new patent filings. Low domestic savings coupled with relatively rapid growth led to one record trade deficit after another. Even more confining were the persistent budget deficits and the resulting increase in the national debt. Interest payments on the federal debt were already becoming a major item in the federal budget, and projected budget deficits suggested they would continue to rise.

When President Bush came to office, the economic expansion continued. Even before his election, however, the Federal Reserve acted to tighten policy out of its concern over inflationary pressures.[19] Growth began to wane in the second half of 1989, and the "growth slowdown" continued during 1990.[20] Preliminary figures included in the *1991 Economic Report of the President* showed negative growth in the fourth quarter of 1990. Subsequent revisions showed that negative growth in the third quarter actually signaled the transition from slow growth into recession.

Early in his first term, the president's economic team was already concerned about the economic impact of the Fed's tightening. On March 3, 1989, Michael Boskin, chair of the President's Council of Economic Advisers, wrote a memo to the president noting that private economists were predicting a "slow-down or recession in late '89 or '90" because of earlier Fed tightening.[21] In his reflections on the politics and economics of the Bush era, Darman saw Fed tightening as an additional prod for eventual action on the budget deficit.[22]

Even before the economy actually slipped into recession, the Fed was beginning to reverse course by lowering interest rates and increasing the money supply. Despite the Fed's actions, signs of recovery in the spring of 1991 gave way to a sputtering economy in much of the rest of the year.[23]

"Sluggish" was the word that characterized a recovery that was much slower than other postwar recoveries.[24] The final Bush economic report noted that "the sluggish nature of the recovery was particularly evident in the labor market."[25] In other words, growth was slow and unemployment remained high. "By June 1991, the national unemployment rate had risen to 7.8 percent, the highest in eight years."[26] The unemployment rate would stay above 7 percent throughout the election year of 1992.[27]

The president's economists had foreseen the recession and anticipated a slow recovery. For a variety of reasons, however, his economic advisers did not urge the president to take action. Additional fiscal stimulus in terms of tax cuts or increased spending would require legislation and would not, therefore, have an immediate impact on the economy. Turning to fiscal policy would also risk overturning the 1990 budget agreement that had led the president to break his "no new taxes" pledge. Some saw virtue in inaction. Nicholas Brady, Bush's secretary of the Treasury, reportedly believed that recession "had a way of 'cleansing the economy' of underperformers."[28]

With his advisers predicting recovery and opposing economic intervention, the president initially chose to do nothing. In early 1991, he was still basking in the surge of popularity that came with the American victory in the Persian Gulf. Plaudits for the war effort, however, did not overwhelm popular concern about the economy. In the midst of the recession, many companies were also adjusting to international competition by eliminating an array of middle managers in a process referred to as "downsizing." Suddenly, secure jobs with America's top companies were simply being eliminated. The 1981–82 recession had hit blue collar workers in the industrial heartland. The 1990–91 recession also hit white collar jobs on both coasts. Overbuilding by developers and the collapse of the savings and loan industry had left the country with "years of excess commercial real estate."[29] By April 1991, the majority of voters had reversed their opinion and now saw the country as being on the wrong track.[30]

As the economy moved into a weak recovery, the president and his advisers continued to look to monetary policy to fuel faster growth. Before reappointing Alan Greenspan as chairman of the Board of Governors of the Federal Reserve System, President Bush and his team decided to seek a commitment for monetary growth that would allow a real growth rate of 2.75 percent. Given the rate of inflation, to achieve real growth of 2.75 percent, the money supply would need to grow at a 5 or 6 percent rate. According to Duffy and Goodgame's *Marching in Place*, Secretary Brady was tapped to strike the agreement with Greenspan, but when meeting with the

Fed chairman, Brady did not identify the higher nominal rate needed to meet the desired real interest rate target.[31]

Despite the sluggish recovery, Bush continued to resist economic intervention. In September 1991, he actually vetoed an attempt to add unemployment benefits on the grounds that it would "destroy the bipartisan budget agreement."[32] Throughout 1991, Bush continued to hear economic complaints from the Republican Party's business base. In November, the political news forced the president's team to look more closely at the economy. In a race for the Pennsylvania Senate seat, Democratic senator Harris Wofford "came from more than 40 points behind to defeat Bush's attorney general and former Pennsylvania governor, Richard Thornburgh."[33] National polls suggested that the president's troubles were not confined to Pennsylvania. In November's *Time*/CNN poll, only 18 percent approved of the president's handling of the economy.[34] By December, Bush changed course. The president's economic team told the House Ways and Means Committee that it was considering middle-class tax cuts. "Deficits, all of a sudden, did not matter. Reelection did."[35]

In early 1991, George H. W. Bush had looked so politically invincible that most Democrats decided not to seek their own party's nomination. But by the end of 1991, the economy and the polls both suggested his vulnerability. The president found himself challenged by Republican conservatives, by an independent promising to balance the budget, and a relatively unknown governor from Arkansas who was focused on the economy. In retrospect, President Bush's many supporters point to the economic improvement that came in the second half of 1992 as both justifying his strategy and laying the basis for the prosperity of the 1990s. In the heat of the presidential campaign, the growth rate averaged 3.8 percent for July, August, and September. In the last three months of year, growth jumped again to 5.7 percent. The figures are accurate but beside the political point. The recovery and the president's efforts were simply "too little, too late" to help his reelection effort.

During his term in office, President Bush did take some important and difficult economic steps. A wide spectrum of observers agreed that deficit reduction was necessary, and most thought that tax increases had to be an element of any agreement with the Democratic Congress. Like the budget deficit, the savings and loan system had gone from bad to worse over the course of a decade. Early in his administration, Bush faced up to the S & L crisis that Congress and President Reagan had avoided. The need to make good on insured deposits added to the budgetary pressure, and the unwinding of the crisis created added problems for parts of the real estate industry. The president or his team also undertook other initiatives that helped develop a long-run competitiveness strategy. The White House, however, did not seem to sense the extent of public anxiety about the country's economic future and individual economic prospects. Important speeches touched on the economic future, but the country lacked a sense of presidential engagement. The president's foreign policy successes seemed to highlight his relative lack of attention to domestic affairs. Even his positive economic steps were masked by a series of political mistakes.

Debts, Deficits, and Destiny

It is hard to overstate how much the deficit dominated the political debate in Washington. For Republicans who wanted to slow new spending initiatives or reduce the size of government, emphasizing deficit reduction gave them considerable leverage. At the same time, a growing portion of their business base was pushing for deficit reduction, even if that meant an increase in federal taxes.[36] Democrats were on the defensive—in many cases they wanted to increase spending as well as protect existing programs. In the 1980s, taxes did rise—in response to recommendations of a Social Security commission and bipartisan efforts to reduce the deficit.[37] But Democrats were still attacked as "tax-and-spend" liberals. The original phrase dated from the New Deal era—tax and tax, spend and spend, elect, elect. By the beginning of the Reagan era, however, many middle-class voters found inflation pushing them into higher tax brackets when their real income had not changed. There was added resentment that some of the spending was ineffective or spent on the "undeserving poor."

In the 1984 campaign, Democratic candidates for the presidential nomination had prepared their own, often-detailed plans for balancing the federal budget. By contrast, the 1988 campaign never came to terms with most key issues, including the budget deficit. The Bush political team's success in characterizing Dukakis as a Massachusetts liberal weak on crime, ineffective in government, and out of touch with American values did not create much of a policy mandate.

While the Bush political team was focused on winning the election, the prospective members of a Bush government were already wrestling with the challenge of reducing the deficit. Richard Darman, who would serve as Bush's director of the Office of Management and Budget (OMB), was one of those thinking ahead. In *Who's in Control: Polar Politics and the Sensible Center,* Darman recounts his effort to knock the "no new taxes phrase" out of Bush's speech accepting the Republican nomination for president. In Darman's telling, speechwriter Peggy Noonan insisted that the phrase was the one dramatic moment in the speech. The political team agreed. Yet this phrase would complicate the effort to achieve a deficit reduction agreement with Congress and would eventually create serious political problems for the president.

Historians of the George H. W. Bush presidency, including Darman, suggest that Bush was committed to deficit reduction. Bush had never been an easy convert to the economic claims of the supply-siders—views he had labeled as "voodoo economics" when he opposed Ronald Reagan in the 1980 primaries. Bush also seemed to have agreed with the business community that fiscal deficits were a burden on the capital markets that drove up interest rates and put American business at a competitive disadvantage. The retrospectives on Bush's administration also suggest that from the early days of his presidency, he accepted the necessity of tax increases as part of the process of reaching an agreement on deficit reduction with the Democratic Congress. Darman and others portray the president as focused not on whether but when to raise taxes. If the pledge had to be broken, he did not want to do it his first year in office.

In that first year, President Bush and his team made relatively modest changes to the budget prepared by President Reagan and submitted it as their own. This initial budget passed without breaking the president's pledge on taxes. As the administration moved into 1990, the president submitted his budget for fiscal 1991. (The federal fiscal year begins in the October of the preceding calendar year.) The proposed budget did include proposals for added user fees (i.e., charges for services provided by the federal government) but, again, it did not violate the president's pledge on taxes.

The president's budget team led by OMB director Richard Darman continued to feel the pressure for an agreement that would effectively deal with the deficit. He shared and articulated the view that tax increases would be a necessary part of any budget that reduced the deficit. There were a variety of factors weighing on the president and his budget director. On October 13, 1989, the Dow Jones Industrial Average dropped 130 points in its sharpest fall since the near collapse of October 1987. Inflation was marching upward and reached 5 percent for all of 1989. The deficit was widely viewed as part of the problem. Meeting the obligation of federally insured funds in collapsing savings and loan institutions threatened to add many billions to the federal deficit.[38] In addition, current budget rules required mandatory cuts in domestic and defense spending if deficit reduction targets were not met.

As negotiations over the fiscal 1991 budget continued, broad agreement was reached on the necessity of a tax increase. After a May 6 meeting with the congressional leadership, the White House issued a press release indicating that budget negotiations would begin "without pre-conditions."[39] At the session itself, the president reportedly assured Senate majority leader George Mitchell that he was willing to talk about taxes.[40] By late June 1990, that agreement appeared to include key elements of the Republican leadership on Capitol Hill. In *Who's in Control,* Darman quotes Gingrich as saying "I can imagine a five-year package where I try to sell taxes."[41] Top-level negotiations continued on June 26 between the president, his economic team, and the bipartisan congressional leadership. According to Darman's account, House speaker Thomas Foley took the lead in spelling out that any agreement would require "entitlement reform, defense and domestic discretionary spending reduction, budget process reform and tax increases."[42] He and Brady combined to encourage the issuing of a press release. Darman prepared a draft that Sununu quickly edited, adding a provision for growth incentives and changing Foley's tax increases to "tax revenue increases."[43]

The White House proceeded to release the agreed-on statement without any effort to prepare Congress, conservatives, or the country. Sununu attempted to persuade conservatives that the pledge still held, that "tax revenue increases" referred to growth initiatives, not new taxes. No one agreed. "The *New York Post* ran the headline, 'Read My Lips: I Lied.'"[44] When Sununu tried the same tack with Gingrich, Gingrich simply hung up.[45]

In retrospect, Darman was critical of himself for failing to lay the popular and political groundwork for an increase in taxes. By virtually all reports, "conservatives were furious, treating the announcement as the ultimate denial of Reaganism."[46] Bush and his team proceeded to strike an agreement with Congress, only to find Gingrich leading a successful charge to reject it. Ed Rollins, the director of the Republican Congressional Campaign Committee, urged Republican candidates to run away from the agreement rather than on it. When a final agreement was reached with Congress, it took the added step of raising marginal tax rates—striking at the real heart of the supply-side aspects of Reaganomics.

Bush reportedly looks back on the agreement as playing into the hands of the opposition and his right-wing critics.[47] Darman defends the overall agreement on economic and policy grounds but agrees that there were serious tactical errors in how the agreement was announced.[48] Some observers questioned the timing of the agreement, wondering if an earlier breaking of the pledge would have given the president more time to deal with the inevitable political fallout.[49]

It is hard not to be puzzled at how little political or policy ground had been laid for breaking the pledge. While the Bush administration could not easily clarify the record of the Reagan administration, there must have been friendly think tanks that could have highlighted the major tax increases signed into law by Ronald Reagan. Ways and Means Committee chairman Dan Rostenkowski had urged the president to link deficit reduction and tax increases to the competitive standing of the country. "Tell the people," said Rostenkowski, "that if we don't balance our budget, we're going to be number two."[50] There had been no series of speeches to key Republican or national groups spelling out the risks of mandatory budget cuts (a "sequester," in the budget language of the day) to national security—or the implications of drastic entitlement reform for veterans, the elderly, or the social safety net. It is hard not to agree with the observation of Charles Kolb, then working in the White House, that Bush "downplayed and virtually ignored two factors that had contributed mightily to Reagan's success: the importance of presidential rhetoric and the creation of a well-oiled propaganda machine for swaying public opinion."[51] Bush was surrounded by able, experienced, and, in several instances, genuinely brilliant advisers. What he did not have on his White House team was someone with the political instincts of James Baker or the media savvy of Michael Deaver.

At least as striking is the degree to which the background of the Bush agreement was a prologue to the Clinton economic strategy in 1993 and, to some extent, for the Gingrich charge for a balanced budget in 1995–96. At the very start of the Bush administration, Darman received a congratulatory call and invitation to lunch from Alan Greenspan, the chairman of the Federal Reserve Board. At the lunch, Darman reports, Greenspan called for a "major deficit reduction package. His polite implication was that he would not allow higher money supply growth or higher real economic growth without [Bush] first achieving a legislative solution to the deficit problem."[52] Instead, Bush delayed his action on deficit reduction. Early Bush action might have secured a more supportive monetary policy. Instead, Bush suffered through a brief recession (1990–91) and weak recovery that contributed to his electoral defeat in 1992. Greenspan would have a similar discussion with president-elect Bill Clinton on December 3, in Little Rock, a discussion that led to very different results. Clinton managed to achieve significant deficit reduction in his first year in office and appeared to have developed an effective working relationship between his administration and the Fed.

At a March 6, 1990, meeting of the budget team, Darman distributed a memorandum that, among other things, proposed taxes on alcohol and energy. According to Darman, "the energy tax had been especially recommended to me by Greenspan."[53] Earlier the same day, Rostenkowski had met with the president and his budget team to let them know that he was proceeding with his own deficit reduction proposal. When he introduced it on March 11, it included a fifteen-cent-per-gallon gasoline tax increase.[54] The energy (or "British thermal unit") tax included in President Clinton's initial budget proposal is often attributed to Vice President Gore's concern about global warming and the environment. It may have had a more complicated parentage.

Congress Continues the Push for National Competitiveness

During this same period, Congress continued to press for the policies embodied in the Omnibus Trade and Competitiveness Act of 1988. The act made Congress an active and often demanding partner in turning federal policy toward national competitiveness throughout the Bush administration. Congressional debates, committee hearings, ad hoc advisory groups, and new legislation were all part of the congressional arsenal.

In 1991, the Center for Strategic and International Studies (CSIS) entered the competitiveness fray. That CSIS—well known for its studies on national security and foreign policy—was venturing into competitiveness was another sign of how economic security was increasingly viewed as a critical element in supporting a country's military posture and foreign policy.

CSIS started by forming the Strengthening of America Commission (hereafter, the CSIS Commission). Senator Sam Nunn (D-Ga.) and Senator Pete Domenici (R-N.M.) served as cochairs of the commission, which also included other current and past members of Congress, veterans of past administrations, state and local elected officials, business and labor leaders, prominent academics, and specialists from Washington-based think tanks and associations. The CSIS Commission followed the broad outlines of the Young Commission by focusing on productivity growth and the country's standard of living.[55] Not surprisingly, the CSIS Commission stressed investments in science and technology and education and training. In addition to emphasizing the need for added saving, the CSIS Commission proposed a progressive consumption tax that, its members felt, would stimulate savings while preserving the fundamental fairness of the tax code. Like the Young Commission, the CSIS Commission called for a significant restructuring of the federal government by proposing the creation of a National Economic Council to stand on equal footing with the National Security Council.[56] In addition to the progressive consumption tax, the commission called for a reorganization of Congress that would create a joint committee on the budget, a two-year budget cycle, and the merging, where feasible, of the authorizing and appropriating committees.[57]

The CSIS Commission's report was published near the end of 1992, too late to have a direct impact on either the Bush administration or the presidential campaign. But the sheer prominence of its membership meant that many of the CSIS Commission's ideas were circulating in the administration, in Congress, and in both presidential campaigns well before the first report was issued. The congressional voices were part of a distinguished chorus and carried the added weight of potential legislation.

Other senior members of Congress developed their own competitiveness proposals. Senator Max Baucus (D-Mont.) was a prominent case in point. Baucus had been an early supporter of the competitiveness effort. He served as cochair of the Congressional Competitiveness Caucus and chairman of the Finance Committee's subcommittee on trade. Working through the Center for National Policy, a Democratic-leaning think tank, Baucus developed *The New American Economy: Building for the Long-Term.*[58] In broad terms, Baucus's proposals followed the competitiveness fundamentals of capital investment, education and training, supporting innovation, effective trade policy, and a modern infrastructure. But Baucus added the kinds of specific steps that could be easily translated into legislative language.[59]

Some new competitiveness-related proposals did take the form of legislation. Through a series of legislative steps, Senator Jeff Bingaman (D-N.M.) continued to push the administration to identify and pursue technologies that were critical for the nation's future.[60] Developing and releasing lists of these technologies became a source of debate and some controversy inside the Bush administration, which is discussed in more detail below.

The bipartisan, bicameral Competitiveness Caucus that Pat Choate had helped to form grew in numbers and activities. To help support the caucus, Choate and others formed the not-for-profit Congressional Economic

Leadership Institute (CELI). With the active support of her four cochairs, CELI executive director Nancy Leamond played an active and effective role in scheduling meetings, arranging programs, briefing members of Congress, and organizing trips that ranged from Silicon Valley to Japan.

Ways and Means Committee chairman Dan Rostenkowski (D-Ill.) had been a leading participant in crafting the Omnibus Trade and Competitiveness Act of 1988. In devising legislative answers to the competitiveness challenge, Rostenkowski's Ways and Means would play a critical role. In addition to being the principal committee on trade legislation, Ways and Means was the lead congressional committee on taxes. If deficit reduction (and hence increased national savings) was to involve added revenue, Ways and Means would have to act on tax increases. Advocates of a national competitiveness strategy also urged the use of tax incentives to spur research, increase training, or encourage specific types of investment. Ways and Means would have to act first. When the Competitiveness Policy Council called for changes in health care as a way to increase national saving and investment, Ways and Means would be the key committee.

To help build solid relationships as well as a consensus on key issues facing the committee, Rostenkowski held annual issue retreats. The topic for 1992 was international competitiveness.[61] On May 7, the committee and invited speakers gathered at the U.S. Naval War College in Newport, Rhode Island. In that setting, it was hard not to make the link between national competitiveness and national security. Rostenkowski's staff was careful to bring balance to the discussions that ranged from the computer's contribution to productivity growth to the appropriate role for government. But the competitiveness viewpoint was well represented. The opening overview of America's competitive position started with presentations by C. Fred Bergsten, the director of the Institute for International Economics, who also chaired the Competitiveness Policy Council, and by myself as the president of the private-sector Council on Competitiveness.

Rostenkowski had gotten to know President Bush when Bush represented Houston in the House. They had remained close and, according to press reports, talked frequently and candidly during the Bush presidency. Bush had appointed Rostenkowski's senior trade counsel, Rufus Yerxa, to be the senior delegate of the Office of the U.S. Trade Representative at the General Agreement on Tariffs and Trade in Geneva. Press reports also suggested that Rostenkowski was frustrated with President Bush's lack of engagement with domestic policy. The 1992 retreat was an education for the committee. It may also have been a message to the president.

Laying the Basis for a Competitive Future

The president seemed to be unaware that the country was going through a painful adjustment to international competition and the impact of new technologies. When the president marveled at a supermarket checkout scanner, it was widely viewed as showing how out of touch he was with the lives of everyday Americans. Even the luster of the Persian Gulf victory had faded with Iraqi leader Saddam Hussein still in power and still a potential threat. Books on the Bush presidency also paint a picture of a president only intermittently focused on domestic events. Retrospectives on the Bush years describe the president and his core team as resistant to broad initiatives.[62]

In terms of American competitiveness, the president and his team were often seen as unaware, out of touch, or actively dismissive. He seemed ready to take a different tack when, shortly after assuming office, he established his own, Cabinet-level Council on Competitiveness to be chaired by Vice President Dan Quayle. To avoid confusion, the private-sector Council on Competitiveness established by John Young had urged the president to choose a different name.[63]

The name may have been the same, but the mission was quite different. As vice president, Bush had been in charge of the Reagan administration's Task Force on Deregulation. Bush saw the Quayle council as continuing that work rather than pursuing the broader growth strategies emerging from the private-sector council and the growing competitiveness movement. In some cases, the president and his core team actively opposed specific competitiveness-related initiatives. In the first Bush budget, no funds were sought for the congressionally authorized Advanced Technology Program (ATP)—in budget parlance, it was zeroed out.

The administration was even slower to embrace the Competitiveness Policy Council (CPC). To some in the Bush administration, the CPC must have seemed like a thinly disguised effort to develop a national industrial policy. The roots of the CPC did, after all, date back to the Economic Co-operation Council proposed by the Democratic Caucus in its 1982 *Rebuilding the Road to Opportunity* and the 1984 efforts of Representative John La Falce (D-N.Y.) and others to create a Council on Industrial Competitiveness.[64] In creating the CPC, members of Congress sought a body that would help bridge the often-differing views of the legislative and executive branches. They sought to contribute to a national consensus by drawing individual CPC members from business, labor, the academic world, and state and local government. Four members of the CPC were to be appointed by the president, four by the leadership of the Senate, and four by the leadership of the House. The administration, however, waited until April 1991 to appoint its full complement of members and designate Secretary of Commerce Robert Mossbacher to specifically represent the administration.

In other cases, the president and his core team were viewed as being actively dismissive of the business sector's growing anxiety about national competitiveness. In meetings with Governor Sununu, the business community frequently heard a suggestion that they come back when they had a "long-range strategic" plan to ensure their competitive health.[65] In other cases, business delegations were dismissed without getting much of a hearing at all. The Advanced Technology Coalition (ATC), made up of key private-sector associations focused on technology development, met with just this kind of treatment. On October 23, 1991, the ATC scheduled a day of meetings with key administration officials. Although their agenda was modest—consisting of elements drawn largely from recent speeches by the president—it clearly favored an active technology policy. While waiting for Governor Sununu, the members of the ATC discussed technology and technology policy with Alan Bromley, the president's adviser on science and technology.

When Sununu finally arrived, he did not even feign interest in the ATC's modest, one-page agenda. Instead, he waved around the carefully crafted single page while telling the ATC members that the answer to their needs lay with the New York financial world and not the administration. The ATC members' attempts to explain their views, their support for recent presidential statements, and their concern about America's technological leadership all went unheard.

To more and more business leaders, the administration seemed unaware of and uninterested in the challenge of Japan. Michael Boskin, the chairman of Bush's Council of Economic Advisers, was widely quoted as seeing no difference between computer chips and potato chips.[66] Boskin, however, "firmly denies ever having said anything remotely resembling" the computer chips / potato chips statement. Certainly, Boskin was not an obvious candidate to dismiss the importance of technology. His own work emphasized the critical role of science, technology, and overall knowledge in fostering growth and raising living standards. In fact, the technology team in the Clinton administration frequently quoted a Boskin study on the role of technology in growth to buttress their own technology initiatives. Yet whatever the truth of the "computer chips / potato chips" quote, it was widely reported and widely believed.

The president's disengagement seemed to extend to symbols as well as substance. For instance, his January 1992 mission to Tokyo included a number of chief executives of leading high-technology firms. These were companies that bested Japan in third-world countries but often had difficulties gaining access to Japan's own market. It was a potentially effective way to show concern for America's economic future and, at the same time, highlight Japanese protectionism. At the last minute, however, the president and his team added the chief executives of the Big Three American automobile companies. The American auto producers had legitimate complaints. They had done much to reinvent themselves and were effectively shut out of the Japanese market. Still, many Americans thought the prospect of exporting cars to Japan was a little like the proverbial attempt to carry coals to Newcastle. Instead of a clear focus on America's future, the trip began to look more like a routine appeal to a traditional Republican constituency.

In other instances, presidential initiatives seemed to garner little budgetary support or to suffer from only intermittent presidential attention. His campaign promise to be the education president did lead to a historic meeting with state governors. But the complete lack of new funding left critics viewing the effort as an "empty public relations exercise."[67] When the president had first referred to his "thousand points of light," Senator Jim Sasser (D-Tenn.) was quick to comment that the batteries were not included. More and more Americans were thinking in similar terms about the entire Bush domestic agenda.

Dealing with the Deficits

As was noted above, Bush delayed acting on the deficit until his second year in office and did not reach a final agreement until November 1990. Instead of reducing the political damage, Bush was left with less time to repair it. Instead of reaping the late-term benefits of an economic recovery, Bush actually tightened fiscal policy after the economy had already slipped into recession. Nor was there an effective effort to explain deficit reduction to the American public.

Indeed, Bush seems to have had the worst of both the political and the economic worlds. But he did significantly reduce the budget deficit. Darman puts the five-year budget savings at $500 billion.[68] Current estimates are only slightly lower.[69] Subsequent deficit reduction packages in 1993 and 1996 built on the Bush agreement.

Deficit reduction was an important element in the long-term economic expansion under President Clinton. Most economic observers agree that deficit reduction freed capital for investment and contributed to lower interest rates by reducing the federal presence in the capital markets. Lower deficits also allowed the Federal Reserve to adopt a monetary policy that supported added investment. The work of Bush, his budget director Darman, and his economic team made an important contribution to the prosperity of the 1990s.

Discovering Technology Policy

The Omnibus Trade and Competitiveness Act of 1988 had created new institutions and new programs that forced the Bush administration to either act or resist. New technology programs and policy, however, created special problems for key members of the Bush administration, who saw them as little more than a veiled form of industrial policy. Particularly in the early years of the administration, there was considerable resistance to embracing Congress's call for an active technology policy.

The Advanced Technology Program became an early battleground.[70] Initially, the Bush administration did not seek any funds for the program. The program, however, was strongly supported not only by Alan Bromley, the president's science and technology adviser, but also by other key figures in the administration. At the Department of Commerce, which housed the ATP, deputy secretary Thomas Murrin, undersecretary Robert White and assistant secretary Deborah Wince-Smith were all strong advocates of funding the ATP. Both Murrin and White were from research-intensive industries—Murrin from Westinghouse and White from Control Data, then a major computer firm. This was the same Thomas Murrin who had served on the Young Commission and would go on to eventually join the Executive Committee of the Council on Competitiveness. Wince-Smith had a distinguished career at the Office of Science and Technology Policy (OSTP) before accepting a political appointment at the Commerce Department. In addition to her broad background in science and technology policy, Wince-Smith brought with her to Commerce a sense of how to make things happen in government. After leaving Commerce, she joined the Council on Competitiveness as a senior fellow and became its president in December 2001.

Although the ATP was part of a longer effort to shift federal support to the development of civilian technologies, it did highlight the departure from a past that had been dominated by federal support for defense, space, and specific missions such as health or energy. The ATP's proponents saw the economy, productivity growth, international competitiveness, and technological strength as an added federal mission. Unlike the traditional approach to scientific research, industry was viewed as a necessary partner in developing and commercializing new technologies. Federal funds were to be matched by industry, and federal support followed two peer reviews, one for technological excellence and one for commercial viability.

While the ATP's supporters gradually gained the upper hand in the Bush administration, influential voices in the administration and in the White House continued to oppose the philosophy and the programmatic thrust of the Omnibus Act of 1988. Opponents of industrial policy had strenuously argued that the market, not the government, should choose industrial winners and losers. When Congress pressed the federal government to identify critical technologies, the same objection was raised. How, the opponents asked, could the government do a better job of identifying critical technologies than American industry?

The economic case for public support for basic technologies was much the same as it had been for basic science. Companies would shy away from investing in research because of the inherent risks involved and the added uncertainty that no individual company would capture (or appropriate) enough of the benefit from the research to justify the cost. A variety of economic studies pointed to a high rate of overall (or social) return from investments in science and technology.[71] The greater emphasis on civilian research in German and Japanese budgets was an added spur to developing an American response.

In meetings with key Bush administration officials, John Young, who had chaired the President's Council on Industrial Competitiveness and now spoke for the private-sector Council on Competitiveness, added a different perspective to the question of picking winners. He noted that the National Science Foundation (NSF) and the National Institutes of Health (NIH) made thousands of decisions every year on national research grants. NSF and NIH relied on specialists in a particular field to evaluate the grant applications. The same approach could be readily adapted to work on basic technologies.[72]

Senator Jeff Bingaman (D-N.M.) and others continued to pursue their interest in critical technologies. After asking the Department of Defense to identify technologies that were critical for national defense, Bingaman then pressed the Department of Commerce to develop a similar list from the perspective of the overall economy. In 1989, Bingaman authored and helped pass legislation that required the OSTP to appoint a Critical Technologies Panel that would "come up with a definitive list of technologies that had broad potential applicability across civilian and military sectors."[73] Just as the list was about to be released in March 1991, key staff attached to Vice President Quayle's office strenuously objected to any report that would suggest that the government rather than the private sector was picking critical or "winning" technologies. As a result, the report did not carry the presidential seal or even the White House address.[74] The release came while Bromley was out of the country. In Bromley's *Reminiscences,* he blames the extensive coverage of the report in the national press and "various trade publications" for creating a "brouhaha . . . around the suggestion that OSTP was attempting to move the Bush Administration into industrial policy."[75] Whatever the role of the press, the incident revealed continuing tensions over technology policy and raised questions about the administration's commitment to competitiveness in both Congress and the private sector.

Young responded to the attack on federally identified critical technologies in a particularly creative way. Rather than defending the work of a specific department, he turned to the Council on Competitiveness. Putting aside the existing lists, the council surveyed "nine major technology-intensive industries," asking them to identify technologies that would be critical for their commercial success over the next ten years.[76] After generating individual industry lists, the council looked across industries to identify technologies that appeared on a number of lists. In its March 1991 report, the council could then point to a set of technologies that were generic as well as critical. Instead of relying on the federal government, the council was reporting from the front lines of industry. In some sense, it was the voice of the market much celebrated by the opponents of technology policy.

The Council on Competitiveness did not stop with a list of technologies. It also put them into an international context by measuring where America stood in various critical technologies relative to the international competition. The news was sobering. The council found that the "the U.S. position in many critical technologies" had slipped and in some cases had "been lost altogether." The council added a warning that "future trends [were] not encouraging."[77] In looking at Europe and Japan as well as the United States, the council found "a broad domestic and international consensus about the critical generic technologies driving economic growth and competitiveness."[78] It also found that Japan's Ministry of International Trade and Industry and the European Community had developed lists quite similar to those of the U.S. government.

The effort of the Council on Competitiveness had been led by Admiral Bobby Inman, the former director of the National Security Agency and former deputy director of the Central Intelligence Agency. To many eyes, Inman's presence helped stress the link between technology and national security. Inman's team (the council's Technology Advisory Committee) ranged from Arno Penzias, a vice president and Nobel Prize winner from AT&T's Bell Laboratories, to William Spencer, the president and chief executive of Sematech. The committee included representatives from America's top high-technology industries. In the context of the industrial policy debate, these were all sunrise industries. There was not a hint of sunset among them.

The Council on Competitiveness was not alone in its emphasis on technology. The two Competitiveness Summits mentioned in chapter 8 drew many of their participants from the Industrial Research Institute, a professional society composed of the senior executives who oversaw the laboratories and research activities of major industrial companies. The Institute of Electrical and Electronics Engineers, representing hundreds of thousands of American engineers, formed an active competitiveness committee. Individual reports from the Pentagon's Defense Science Board, from trade associations, from think tanks, and from advisory groups all stressed the importance of maintaining American preeminence in science and technology.

So when President Bush entered office in January 1989, there was already a growing chorus calling for a more active technology policy. Some of the voices in the choir were from his own supporters in high-technology industry and elsewhere in the private sector. There were ample opportunities to act. Unlike the situation in education, the federal government was an active player in the development of science and technology. At the time, the federal government accounted for more than half of all national spending on research and development. Congress had just (in 1988) passed the Omnibus Act of 1988 that created new technology programs that involved the private as well as public sectors.

In the end, Bush and his team made some significant contributions to the debate over technology policy and the actual development of a more activist approach. But it was a policy that seemed to advance by fits and starts. Some parts of the his team were moving to work with industry, while others were adamant about leaving the country's industrial future to the market. Alan Bromley, President Bush's adviser for science and technology, describes Bush as more than willing to support key initiatives in science and technology. Bromley reports that "shortly after [he] arrived in Washington, President Bush asked [him] to recommend a small number of areas in science and technology that were of particular national importance and to which he could give his personal support using the bully pulpit of the Presidency."[79] In reviewing his years as Bush's adviser, Bromley identified a number of initiatives that cut across the research activities of individual executive-branch departments.

Bromley spent some time and effort in building and expanding the reach of OSTP. The legislation establishing OSTP provided for four associate directors to be confirmed by the Senate but did not specify their responsibilities. Bromley proposed creating the post of associate director for industrial technology. According to Bromley, the president agreed that there were two reasons for the new post: "First, industrial technology was of great intrinsic importance to our entire economic competitiveness, and second, the appointment would send a real message to the industrial community that we in the Bush Administration were serious about the importance of this area."[80]

There are real accomplishments to be found in the Bush-Bromley record. While expanding the size and scope of OSTP, Bromley improved the flow of advice from outside the government by establishing the President's Council of Advisers on Science and Technology. Bromley managed to create several cross-cutting technology initiatives, including one in high-speed computing that helped lay the basis for more ambitious initiatives in the Clinton administration. It was under Bromley that the White House issued its first-ever white paper on technology policy, *U.S. Technology Policy*.[81] Even before the paper came out in September 1990, the president was delivering key parts of its message to the high-technology community. For instance, in a March 7, 1990, speech to the American Electronics Association, he stated that his administration was "committed to working with [them] in the critical pre-competitive development stage where the basic discoveries are converted into generic technologies that support both our economic competitiveness and our national security."[82]

In addition to proposing a series of steps that would improve the American innovation system, *U.S. Technology Policy* sought to draw the line between the appropriate public and private responsibilities for technology development. It was here that the White House spoke in favor of the federal government participating "with the private sector in *precompetitive research on generic, enabling* technologies that have the potential to contribute to a broad range of government and commercial applications" (emphasis added).

This phrase had first appeared in the March 7, 1990, presidential address to the American Electronics Association. Yet it had not been added to the White House lexicon without a struggle. Bromley added the phrase to the text of the address, only to find that his opposition in the White House had taken it out. Altogether, he had to put the phrase back in six times, the last shortly before the president gave the address.[83]

In many ways, Bromley was also successful in conveying his supportive message to industry. The President's Council of Advisers on Science and Technology was part of that effort. *U.S. Technology Policy* was particularly effective. The report was well received at the next meeting of the private-sector Council on Competitiveness, where George M. C. Fisher, chief executive of the electronics giant Motorola, had taken the reins from John Young. At a meeting of the council's Executive Committee, Fisher held up the Bromley report for all to see. In his view, the title *U.S. Technology Policy* itself was a victory. The council also paid attention to the president's March 7 speech on the appropriate federal role. It was not by accident that the council's March 1991 report, *Gaining New Ground,* pointed to technologies that were generic as well as critical.

Bromley drew support from other parts of the administration. Admiral James D. Watkins, serving as Bush's secretary of energy, issued an edict instructing the national energy laboratories that national competitiveness was a new priority. Watkins proposed applying the "the science and technology base of the Laboratories . . . [to] the question of the competitiveness of our industries and businesses . . . in partnership with business and universities."[84] The Department of Commerce was particularly active. Secretary Robert Mossbacher had been quick to weigh in on the side of a federal role in supporting the development of high-definition television but, after being solidly opposed by much of the administration, took a lower profile on technology issues. Others in the Commerce Department, however, continued to push for an active federal role in technology development. Working with Undersecretary Robert White, Assistant Secretary for Technology Policy Wince-Smith developed a 1992 National Technology Initiative designed to foster collaboration between the national laboratories and the private sector.[85]

Although Bromley tells an important part of the Bush story on technology and technology policy, it is not the whole story. While Bush was encouraging Bromley to identify key initiatives, OMB was refusing to fund the congressional initiatives for developing advanced technologies or creating a manufacturing extension service, an effort to bring up-to-date technology to small manufacturers. Bromley did support both programs and both were eventually funded by the Bush administration, though at relatively modest levels.

Yet, while Bromley was seeking to work with the private sector, John Young and others encountered a stubborn reluctance in some other parts of the Bush White House. The tensions among different camps persisted until almost the end of the Bush administration. Tom Murrin remembers some of the obstacles from his days as President Bush's deputy secretary of commerce. In college, Murrin had been a starting tackle at Fordham University when football great Vince Lombardi was the coach. At Fordham, they always looked back to an earlier, fearsome football line better known as the seven blocks of granite. Murrin brought a Lombardi-like dedication to the competitiveness movement and to his concern about the country's declining fortunes in the technology arena. Yet he found himself too often blocked by an indifferent and sometimes recalcitrant White House. Murrin continues to recount one meeting where he finally told Sununu that he had become like the seven blocks of granite standing in the way of improving the nation's competitiveness. The experience of Murrin, the Advanced Technology Coalition, and others spread through the business and political communities.

The role of the Quayle Council further muddied the private and public view of the Bush administration. When OSTP prepared the congressionally mandated list of critical technologies, as was noted above, the Quayle Council pushed to distance the White House from it. Instead of pursuing or even embracing an already-well-developed competitiveness strategy, the Quayle Council focused almost entirely on regulatory review. Although thinking about regulations was a potentially important element in fostering innovation and growth, the Quayle Council never made its reigning philosophy of regulations clear. Many Democrats saw the Quayle Council as little more than a back door for special interests to attack unwanted regulations.

Financing the Future:
Financial Markets and Long-Term Investment

The Bush administration came to power during an era of creative financing and corporate restructuring. Seemingly arcane financial terms—takeovers, leveraged buyouts, junk bonds—became the stuff of everyday conversations. The financial frenzy only fed fears about America's competitive future. "In its year end 1990 review on competitiveness, *Business Week* observed that 'you can feel America's eroding status in your bones.'"[86]

As Americans looked for differences between the currently troubled American system and those of its competitors, the role of the financial markets stood out. By the late 1980s, the business and policy communities were both talking about what was generally called the "time horizons" question —the idea that by focusing on the short term, America and American businesses were failing to invest in the long-term future.

Bush's secretary of the Treasury, Nicholas Brady, had come from the investment banking side of the financial markets and reportedly brought an interest in time horizons with him. As part of his team, Brady recruited David Mullins from Harvard Business School. One of Mullins's colleagues, Michael Porter, had repeatedly raised the time-horizons question in his 1990 *The Competitive Advantage of Nations.*[87] To pursue the interest in competitiveness, finance, and corporate governance issues, Brady and Mullins established a corporate finance group. Mullins, in turn, recruited Michael T. Jacobs to be the director of corporate finance.

Jacobs set to work synthesizing the best research and the best experience in both business and government on "the complex set of questions that formed under the general umbrella of 'time horizons.'"[88] Jacobs and his team developed a number of suggestions that were, however, not embraced by the broader administration. Many of them found their way into Jacobs's 1991 *Short-Term America,* in which he suggests reforms in the financial markets that would facilitate long-term investment.[89]

Jacobs also cochaired an effort with Wince-Smith of the Commerce Department to specifically explore ways of improving the flow of investment capital in support of developing new technologies. As part of their work, Jacobs and Wince-Smith reached out to the policy and business communities for ideas.[90] Although they issued a useful report, it seemed to have had little impact within the Bush administration. It was however, carefully read by the incoming technology team of the Clinton administration.

The Education President

When Bush came to office, education was still very much on the country's mind. It was not the first time in postwar America that the quality of education had been linked to the strength of the country. Following the 1957 Soviet launch of Sputnik, Americans insisted that their schools improve the teaching of mathematics and science. With the Soviet Union viewed as a global challenge, foreign languages took on a strategic importance along with science and mathematics. The focus on education began to fade in the

1960s as protests roiled university campuses. Foreign language instruction declined. The periodic tests administered by the National Assessment of Educational Progress traced a gradual decline in the performance of high school students in English as well as mathematics.[91]

In 1983, the country was jolted awake by *A Nation At Risk*, the report of a blue ribbon commission appointed by Reagan's education secretary, Terrence Bell. The report's stark condemnation of America's elementary and secondary schools is still quoted today: "If an unfriendly foreign power had attempted to impose on America the mediocre education performance that exists today, we might well have viewed it as an act of war."[92] Despite the dire warnings of *A Nation At Risk*, in the five years following the report American schools had shown only marginal improvement. During the same period, Germany, Japan, and others posed more and more of an economic challenge to the United States. In part, the academic and policy communities pointed to their more demanding and more effective education (as measured by coursework and scores on international examinations) as one source of their economic strength. The American business community agreed. In 1987, the Conference Board, a New York–based, business-supported organization, asked the community affairs officers of 260 major corporations to identify their top community concern. Sixty-four percent of the respondents "named elementary and secondary education."[93]

When Bush took office in 1989, he had many reasons to make education a priority. It was a national concern that had caught the attention of social conservatives and the business community—both parts of his electoral base. It was also consistent with the "kinder, gentler" philosophy he had stressed in his acceptance speech at the 1988 Republican convention. During the campaign, he had also pledged to meet "with the nation's Governors to discuss education."[94] At the same time, he faced a number of constraints. America's elementary and secondary schools were governed by thousands of local school districts.[95] Most of a school's budget came from the state or local government. By contrast, in 1989 the federal government accounted for barely 6 percent of the total spending on elementary and secondary public education, and much of that was targeted at university rather than primary and secondary education. Bush led a party that was generally wary of increased federal spending and generally suspicious of intruding on the prerogatives of local school boards. Even if the political limitations disappeared, Bush still faced the need to reduce the federal budget deficit.

From the start, Bush stressed the importance of education and education reform. In his inaugural State of the Union address, he called for action on education. In his February 9, 1989, "Building a Better America" speech to Congress,[96] he emphasized four broad education themes: excellence and success in American education, greater choice and flexibility, targeting scarce federal resources, and accountability. He proposed to recognize the best schools, create presidential awards for the best teachers, and encourage magnet schools. His initial steps were criticized by teachers for a lack of funding and by movement conservatives for putting too little emphasis on choice, values, and merit pay. In response, Bush moved to keep his pledge to meet with the nation's governors. At a July 31, 1989, speech to the National Governors Association, he invited the governors to meet with him in Charlottesville, Virginia, in the fall. "Only twice before in the country's history had the nation's governors met with a president to address an issue."[97] President Theodore Roosevelt had called the governors together to pursue conservation; President Franklin Roosevelt in response to the Great Depression.

The president and governors gathered at the University of Virginia in Charlottesville in late September 1989. Two days and six sessions of closed-door meetings almost foundered on the question of increased federal funding for education. The Democratic governors pushed for added spending, while the Bush administration wanted to keep the focus on the structural reforms that had been outlined in his February 8, 1989, speech to Congress. The Democratic view was pressed by the chairman of the National Governors Association's education committee, the young, still relatively obscure governor of Arkansas, Bill Clinton. In the end, Clinton and the other Democratic governors relented. The final communiqué stressed state-by-state restructuring, greater flexibility in using federal resources, and "creating a process for setting national education goals."[98] Four months later, the administration and the governors announced six national goals that were to be met by 2000. From making sure that every child is ready to go to school, to periodic assessments of educational progress, to the ambitious commitment to be first in the world in mathematics and science, these goals of Bush and the governors still help frame the expectations for American education reform.[99]

At the end of 1990, Bush fired his first secretary of education, Lauren Cavasos, and replaced him with Lamar Alexander—a former governor and now Senator from Tennessee and then president of the University of Tennessee—who had a reputation as an effective education reformer. As his deputy secretary, Alexander had David Kearns, the former chief executive of the Xerox Corporation and an active advocate of education reform.

Working with Kearns, Alexander developed a strategy to meet the national goals established by the administration and the governors. With the hard-won budget agreement still painfully fresh in the administration's mind, Alexander probably did not count on a major increase in federal spending. Instead, his "plan called for voluntary national tests to enforce higher standards."[100] Bush and Alexander also urged the creation of the New American Schools Development Corporation (NASDC). The corporation was to look principally to corporate America for up to $200 million to "finance revolutionary new 'break-the-mold' school designs that could then be . . . replicated by communities across America."[101] Kearns was to oversee the corporation's activities. "Membership in the New American Schools Development Corporation read like a *Who's Who* of corporate America," including Louis Gerstner, then the head of RJR Nabisco, and other top executives of *Fortune* 500 companies.[102]

In his *White House Daze,* Kolb points to the creation of NASDC as "a classic example of the Bush Administration's penchant for seizing a populist initiative and turning it topsy-turvy."[103] Kolb's comment adds an important insight into what may have been part of the administration's ultimate electoral undoing. From a competitiveness viewpoint, however, Bush was also redrawing the relationship between the public and private spheres. In this particular instance, he was emphasizing a kind of public–private partnership as a way of revitalizing what has long been a public responsibility in the United States.

Although NASDC did not become a major force for change, Bush's education initiatives continue to influence the debate and reinforced an existing trend of bringing the private and public sectors together in reforming public education. Gerstner himself emerged as a major corporate leader in the cause of improving education. As the chief executive of IBM, he published his own manifesto for educational reform,[104] and he now heads Achieve, a private organization devoted to improving the nation's schools.

Opening the Doors to Global Trade

Bush came to office with the prospect of continued trade deficits, a business community frustrated over foreign trade barriers, and a Congress demanding action. To steer around this Charybdis with two Schyllas, Bush nominated Carla Hills to become the U.S. trade representative, America's lead trade negotiator. Hills was an accomplished Washington lawyer who had already served as an assistant attorney general and as President Ford's secretary of housing and urban development.[105] In announcing Hills's appointment, Bush was photographed handing her a crowbar to pry open the foreign markets currently closed to American exports.

With the president's support, Hills became an active negotiator. During her tenure, the administration started and essentially completed negotiations with Canada and Mexico to establish the North American Free Trade Agreement. It also completed much of the work on the ambitious and complicated Uruguay Round of multilateral trade negotiations. Upon returning from negotiations in Geneva, she would regularly convene a group from the trade policy community to give her feedback on the current direction of the negotiations. At times, Hills used the Thumbs Group (for thumbs-up approval or thumbs-down rejection) to check her own thinking; in other cases, she would look for informal reports on trends in the private sector or Capitol Hill.

The president and Hills had to wrestle with the spirit and the letter of the trade mandates contained in the Omnibus Act of 1988. In no small measure, the new requirements were intended to put pressure on Japan to open its market to international competition. Under the Super 301 provision added by the 1988 act (after Section 301 of the 1974 Trade Act), she had to single out for action "priority countries" marked by the extent of their trade barriers and their impact on U.S. exports. Japan had been the principal congressional target and was one of three countries put on the Super 301 priority list. In addition, the administration launched separate Structural Impediments Initiative talks with Japan to look at broader barriers to the Japanese market, such as distribution systems or patterns of saving and investment.[106]

The New Paradigm: The Political and Policy Potential of Empowerment

The various strands of a competitiveness strategy were not the only domestic option open to the president. Inside the White House, a group was developing a series of ideas based on increasing individual opportunity and responsibility. The ideas were usually associated with White House aide Jim Pinkerton and marched under the unfamiliar label of the "New Paradigm." Pinkerton had managed opposition research in the Bush campaign before becoming part of the White House staff. At the time and in retrospectives of the Bush presidency, Pinkerton is usually referred to as an idea man.

The focus on enhancing individual opportunity and responsibility had

Cabinet-level support as well. The secretary of housing and urban development, Jack Kemp, and the drug czar, William Bennett, were both active supporters. In fact, some of the Reagan-era proposals developed by Kemp and Bennett anticipated and helped shape the New Paradigm thinking. Pinkerton also found support from William Kristol, Vice President Quayle's chief of staff.

The use of the term "New Paradigm" drew on the work of Thomas A. Kuhn, a noted philosopher of science. Charles Kolb—a deputy assistant to the president for domestic policy in the White House and an adherent of the New Paradigm approach—summed up Kuhn's thinking on scientific revolutions in Kolb's account of service in the Bush White House. "Kuhn's 1961 book, *The Structure of Scientific Revolutions*, argued cogently that scientific progress and the pattern of new scientific discovery often resulted from a fundamental rethinking of the status quo prompted by the need to respond to some new crisis that could not be properly or adequately addressed under the governing explanation, theory, or "paradigm."[107] Kuhn also notes the parallels between the impetus for scientific and political change. In Kuhn's view, "political revolutions are inaugurated by a growing sense . . . that existing institutions have ceased to adequately meet the problems posed by an environment that they have in part created."[108] Kolb also quotes Kuhn on the parallels between scientific and political change.

Pinkerton unveiled his thinking in a speech on the New Paradigm to the World Future Society. He struck similar themes in an April 23, 1990, speech on the New Paradigm to the Reason Foundation.[109] Kolb saw Pinkerton taking an approach to social policy that constituted a "revolutionary break with the New Deal–Great Society model."[110] In part, Pinkerton saw governments as much more subject to market forces than they had been in the past.[111] His New Paradigm was characterized by further decentralization, in part a familiar Republican theme of pushing funding and control to lower levels of government or the private sector. At the same time, Pinkerton saw an active role for government in broadening individual choice and working to "empower people" so that they can make "choices for themselves."[112] Finally, Pinkerton saw his New Paradigm as putting "an emphasis on what works." As Pinkerton put it, "we don't necessarily need more government or less government . . . we need capable government."[113] There were echoes of Gary Hart and parallels with Bill Clinton.

There were periodic attempts to push empowerment or the New Paradigm as an overall domestic strategy for the president. In *White House Daze,* Kolb summarizes several of the attempts to turn the New Paradigm into national policy. He also described a struggle between different factions in the administration. In *Marching in Place: The Status Quo Presidency of George Bush,* Duffy and Goodgame describe the warring camps as the Passivists (including Sununu, Brady, and Darman) versus the Activits (Kemp, Bennett, Kristol, and Pinkerton).[114]

In some sense, Darman had a foot in both camps. He did launch a damning and derisive attack on the New Paradigm in a November 16, 1990, speech to the Council on Excellence in Government. After touting the recent five-year budget agreement with Congress, Darman dismisses the New Paradigm as one more example of America's "chronic attraction to the new. Thus, we have had not only the New Deal, but the New Frontier, the New Federalism (twice), the New American Revolution, the New Realism, several New Partnerships, and two recent New Beginnings."[115] He ended his treatment of the subject by suggesting that others "might simply dismiss it by picking up the refrain, 'Hey, brother, can you paradigm.'"[116] White House activists were not the only target of Darman's speech. He also alluded to the House Republican whip, Newt Gingrich, by including a reference to the New-Newt-ism. At the same time, Darman was a brilliantly creative student of public policy. While placing him solidly in the Passivist camp, Duffy and Goodgame also recognize that Darman was himself the source of many policy ideas that could have been pursued by the president.

What Happened to the Domestic Agenda?

In a 2000 appearance at the Woodrow Wilson International Center for Scholars, Governor Sununu pointed to a long list of significant domestic legislation passed during the Bush presidency. He was calling for a reevaluation of a presidency that is often viewed as lacking in domestic interests and accomplishments.[117]

Some revisionism may already be under way. Jonathan Rauch's May 22, 2000, assessment of the Bush presidency pointed to solid domestic as well as international achievements.[118]

Yet it is hard to look back on the Bush presidency without wondering why there was no consistent domestic message. Why were genuine accomplishments either ignored or left unconnected to other initiatives or broader themes? Why did the president and parts of his team seem to either ignore or actively oppose the elements of a competitiveness strategy present in several parts of the Bush administration? Why did the president fail to embrace the empowerment agenda that proved to have considerable appeal in the 1992 campaign and as a governing principle in the Clinton administration? There are a host of usual suspects advanced to explain the Bush administration's apparent lack of engagement with domestic policy. The 1988 campaign never seemed to move beyond character attacks to spell out a clear direction for the country, the restrictions imposed by budget deficits, and the pressing demands of foreign policy.[119]

There were also many signs that the president did not take domestic policy seriously. There seemed to be little appreciation of the widespread anxiety about the future. Some of his critical choices—Dan Quayle as vice president, Clarence Thomas as Supreme Court justice—suggested to many Americans a lack of focus on the domestic side of government. Duffy and Goodgame note that both the "hyperpragmatic Darman" and the Activists suggested antibureaucratic programs, "but they could win no sustained support or interest from Bush."[120]

A Potential Competitiveness Agenda

Despite the Bush administration's reputation for domestic inertia, as noted above, it contained the seeds of a competitiveness strategy. Its macroeconomic policy was targeted at deficit reduction, as part of an emphasis on much needed investment. OMB director Darman pursued deficit reduction with a clear awareness that it was a necessary step toward a more supportive monetary policy that would help foster added capital investment.

Many of the other elements were present as well. Bromley made important strides in defining and developing a national technology policy. He also looked at innovation as a national system that included basic research and an environment that encouraged commercialization.

The Treasury Department was looking at the interaction of financial markets and corporate governance and the implication of both for long-term investments. There was the specific effort of the Treasury and Commerce Departments to assess the prospects for funding technology development.

The president periodically took the lead in pushing for educational reform. Most observers felt that the aversion to a federal role and the lack of new funding meant that the Bush education program was all symbol and no substance. Still, the administration could point to its historic summit with the governors, a useful focus on incentives to improve school performance, and the imaginative idea of "break-the-mold" schools to be funded by the private sector. In education and technology, the Bush administration was taking steps toward defining the separate but complementary roles of the public and private sectors in pursuing national growth. In many cases, the administration was specifically encouraging public–private partnerships.

The president was actively involved—in supporting deficit reduction, in supporting administration-wide technology initiatives, in pushing for trade negotiations, and in urging school reform. The president could have pointed to his initiatives as evidence that he heard the cries of concern, that he was focused on the future, and that he and his team had a strategy to build the American Dream. But he did not—at least not until near the very end of his administration, when his embrace of competitiveness was discounted as political panic and campaign calculus. It was largely viewed as another points of light—batteries not included.

If Bush ignored the policy and political potential of competitiveness and the New Paradigm, Governor Bill Clinton of Arkansas did not. With some frustration, Kolb comments on an October 1991 speech delivered by Democratic candidate Clinton on a "New Covenant." Not only did this New Covenant speech pick up on the New Paradigm themes of individual opportunity and responsibility but also, as Kolb notes, Clinton even spoke of "empowering" individuals to make choices among improved government services. It was, Kolb writes, a speech he would have been proud to deliver himself.[121] If anything, Clinton was even more aggressive in articulating and pursuing the competitiveness agenda as a way of responding to the economic challenges facing individual Americans and the country as a whole.

Notes

1. It was Professor Murray Weidenbaum of Washington University who focused my attention on the fiscal impact of resolving the savings and loan crisis.

2. George Bush, "Memorandum for the Economic Policy Council," White House, Washington, May 23, 1990.

3. George Bush, *Agenda for American Renewal,* Bush-Quayle '92 General Committee, September 1992. For press coverage, see Ann Devroy, "Bush Offers Agenda to Revive Economy," *Washington Post,* September 11, 1992. Also Ann Devroy "Bush Message Emerges: Less Government and Clinton Draft Issue," *Washington Post,* September 13, 2003. Hobart Rowen, the *Washington Post* economics columnist, was uncharitable in finding the Bush program "mostly a rehash of old themes." Hobart Rowen, "Ballyhoo Aside, Bush Isn't Acting Like a Global Leader," *Washington Post,* September 13, 1992. For a far more sympathetic review, see the Heritage Foundation, "A Guide to the Presidential Economic Plans," Background 918, Heritage Foundation, October 23, 1992.

4. John Robert Greene, *The Presidency of George Bush* (Lawrence: University Press of Kansas, 2000), 41.

5. In referring to the thousand points of light, Senator James Sasser (D-Tenn.) was widely quoted as saying that "apparently the batteries weren't included."

6. Greene, *Presidency of George Bush*, 37.

7. Greene, *Presidency of George Bush*, 37.

8. Greene, *Presidency of George Bush*, 37.

9. Greene, *Presidency of George Bush*, 38.

10. Greene, *Presidency of George Bush*, 39.

11. Greene, *Presidency of George Bush*, 39.

12. Greene, *Presidency of George Bush*, 39. The quote is based on a Greene interview with Andrew Card.

13. Greene, *Presidency of George Bush*, 42.

14. *The Acting President* was the title Bob Schieffer and Gary Paul Gates chose for their 1989 biography of President Reagan. See Schieffer and Gates, *The Acting President* (New York: E. P. Dutton, 1989).

15. Greene, *Presidency of George Bush*, 93.

16. See Michael Duffy and Dan Goodgame, *Marching in Place: The Status Quo President of George Bush* (New York: Simon & Schuster, 1992), 183. Duffy and Goodgame describe the Scowcroft-Eagleburger trip as a "secret mission to kowtow to the rulers of China" (p. 183). In *The Presidency of George Bush,* Greene quotes (p. 95) Scowcroft and Eagleburger as intent on making the Chinese understand that progress with the United States depended on an end to repression.

17. Greene, *Presidency of George Bush*, 161.

18. Jack Germond and Jules Witcover, *Mad as Hell: Revolt at the Ballot Box, 1992* (New York: Warner Books, 1993), 50.

19. Jonathan Rauch, "Testing the Fed," *National Journal,* June 18, 1988, 1612–15.

20. Council of Economic Advisers, *1991 Economic Report of the President* (Washington, D.C.: U.S. Government Printing Office, 1991), 49.

21. Richard Darman, *Who's in Control: Polar Politics and the Sensible Center* (New York: Simon & Schuster, 1996), 223.

22. Darman, *Who's in Control,* 223.

23. Council of Economic Advisers, *1992 Economic Report of the President* (Washington, D.C.: U.S. Government Printing Office, 1992), 40.

24. Council of Economic Advisers, *1993 Economic Report of the President* (Washington, D.C.: U.S. Government Printing Office, 1993), 58.

25. Council of Economic Advisers, *1993 Economic Report of the President,* 58.

26. Greene, *Presidency of George Bush*, 161.

27. Council of Economic Advisers, *1994 Economic Report of the President* (Washington, D.C.: U.S. Government Printing Office, 1994), 315.

28. Duffy and Goodgame, *Marching in Place,* 245.

29. Duffy and Goodgame, *Marching in Place,* 248.

30. Duffy and Goodgame, *Marching in Place,* 248.

31. Duffy and Goodgame, *Marching in Place,* 249.

32. Greene, *Presidency of George Bush*, 161.

33. Duffy and Goodgame, *Marching in Place,* 250.

34. Duffy and Goodgame, *Marching in Place,* 251.

35. Duffy and Goodgame, *Marching in Place,* 251.

36. See, for instance, Council on Competitiveness, *Reclaiming the American Dream:*

Fiscal Policies for a Competitive Nation (Washington, D.C.: Council on Competitiveness, 1988).

37. Herbert Stein, *Presidential Economics: The Making of Economic Policy from Roosevelt to Reagan and Beyond,* 2nd revised ed. (Washington, D.C.: Brookings Institution Press, 1988), 278.

38. For a brief summary of the series of policy mistakes that contributed to the savings and loan crisis, see Greene, *Presidency of George Bush,* 81–83.

39. Greene, *Presidency of George Bush,* 84.

40. Greene, *Presidency of George Bush,* 84.

41. Darman, *Who's in Control,* 255. See also Greene, *Presidency of George Bush,* 85.

42. Darman, *Who's in Control,* 262.

43. Darman, *Who's in Control,* 262–63.

44. Greene, *Presidency of George Bush,* 84.

45. Darman, *Who's in Control,* 264.

46. Greene, *Presidency of George Bush,* 84.

47. Greene, *Presidency of George Bush,* 84.

48. Darman, *Who's in Control,* 265.

49. Greene, *Presidency of George Bush,* 85.

50. As quoted in Duffy and Goodgame, *Marching in Place,* 229.

51. Charles Kolb, *White House Daze: The Unmaking of Domestic Policy in the Bush Years* (New York: Free Press, 1994), 3. In his *White House Daze,* Kolb is himself bitterly critical of Bush for repudiating Reaganomics while, at the same time, recognizing that Reagan himself raised taxes on a number of occasions.

52. Darman, *Who's in Control,* 202.

53. Darman, *Who's in Control,* 244.

54. Darman, *Who's in Control,* 245.

55. Center for Strategic and International Studies (CSIS), "The CSIS Strengthening of America Commission First Report," photocopy, Center for Strategic and International Studies, Washington, D.C., 1992.

56. CSIS, "CSIS Strengthening of America Commission First Report," 133–35.

57. CSIS, "CSIS Strengthening of America Commission First Report," 135–37.

58. Max Baucus, *The New American Economy: Building for the Long-Term* (Washington, D.C.: Center for National Policy, 1992).

59. Baucus outlined some of his thinking in a February 21, 1992, speech to the Center for National Policy. In the same speech, he called for a temporary Voluntary Restraint Agreement with Japan to limit U.S. auto imports from Japan.

60. See Lewis M. Branscomb, "Targeting Critical Technologies," in *Empowering Technology: Implementing a U.S. Strategy,* ed. Lewis M. Branscomb (Cambridge, Mass.: MIT Press, 1993), 48. In his essay, Branscomb traces the discussion of critical technologies to the mid-1970s exercise in controlling technology exports.

61. For the retreat agenda as well as background material used at the retreat, see "International Competitiveness," U.S. House of Representatives Committee on Ways and Means, U.S. Naval War College, Newport, R.I., May 7–9, 1992 (Congressional Research Service, Library of Congress, Washington).

62. See, for instance, chapter 7, "Empowerment and the 'New Paradigm,'" in Kolb, *White House Daze,* 185–230.

63. Author's interview with Alan Magazine, first president of the private-sector Council on Competitiveness.

64. For a brief discussion of the Council on Industrial Competitiveness, see Otis L. Graham Jr., *Losing Time: The Industrial Policy Debate* (Cambridge, Mass.: Harvard University Press, 1992), 159.

65. See Alan Bromley, *The President's Scientist: Reminiscences of a White House Advisor* (New Haven, Conn.: Yale University Press, 1994), 54–55.

66. Bromley includes the following quote in his retrospective on the Bush administration. "What's the difference? A hundred dollars worth of computer chips or a hundred dollars worth of potato chips. It's still a hundred dollars. Who cares?" Bromley, *President's Scientist,* 124.

67. Susan Chira, "Lamar Alexander's Self-Help Course," *New York Times Magazine,* November 23, 1991, 52; as quoted in Greene, *Presidency of George Bush,* 71.

68. Darman, *Who's in Control,* 273.

69. See, for instance, Jonathan Rauch, "Father Superior: Our Greatest Modern President," *New Republic,* May 22, 2000, 25.

70. See Omnibus Trade and Competitiveness Act of 1988, April 20, 1988, Conference Report, subtitle B—Technology, part 1—Technology Competitiveness, subpart C —Advanced Technology Program, section 5131, pp. 352–57. For a brief description of the early years of the ATP, see Lewis M. Branscomb and George Parker, "Funding Civilian and Dual-Use Industrial Technology," in *Empowering Technology* 91–92. For a more detailed history of the ATP that puts it in the context of Federal efforts to enhance civilian technology, see Christopher T. Hill, "The Advanced Technology Program: Opportunities for Enhancement," in *Investing in Innovation: Creating a Research and Innovation Policy That Works,* ed. Lewis M. Branscomb and James H. Keller (Cambridge, Mass.: MIT Press, 1998), 143–73.

71. For brief summaries of the link between research and development and the economy, see Bruce L. R. Smith and Claude E. Barfield, "Contribution of Research and Technical Advance to the Economy," in *Technology, R&D, and the Economy,* ed. Bruce L. R. Smith and Claude E. Barfield (Washington, D.C.: Brookings Institution Press and American Enterprise Institute, 1996), 1–4. Another brief summary can be found in Linda R. Cohen and Roger G. Noll, *The Technology Pork Barrel* (Washington, D.C.: Brookings Institution Press, 1991), 7–11.

72. I accompanied Young on this visit.

73. Bromley, *President's Scientist,* 131–32. See also Branscomb, "Targeting Critical Technologies," 48.

74. See *Report of the National Critical Technologies Panel* (Washington, D.C.:U.S. Government Printing Office, 1991). Even the transmission letter to the president carefully distances the work from the White House and the Office of Science and Technology Policy. Although the letter was signed by William D. Phillips, the associate director of the OSTP for industrial technology, he is only identified as the chair of the National Critical Technologies Panel, and the letterhead is that of the National Critical Technologies Panel as well.

75. Bromley, *President's Scientist,* 132.

76. Council on Competitiveness, *Gaining New Ground: Technology Priorities for America's Future* (Washington, D.C.: Council on Competitiveness, 1991), i.

77. Council on Competitiveness, *Gaining New Ground,* 2.

78. Council on Competitiveness, *Gaining New Ground,* 4.

79. Bromley, *President's Scientist,* 61.

80. Bromley, *President's Scientist,* 37–38.

81. Office of Science and Technology Policy, *U.S. Technology Policy* (Washington, D.C.: Executive Office of the President, 1990).

82. Text of remarks by the president during American Electronics Association luncheon, Washington, March 7, 1990.

83. Author's interview with Alan Bromley, May 30, 2002.

84. From a letter from Secretary James D. Watkins to Congressman George E. Brown Jr., chairman of the House Committee on Science. The quote from the letter appears in Lewis M. Branscomb, "National Laboratories: The Search for New Missions and New Structures," in *Empowering Technology,* 103.

85. See Bromley, *President's Scientist,* 137.

86. As quoted in Michael T. Jacobs, *Short-Term America: The Causes and Cures of Our Business Myopia* (Boston: Harvard Business School Press, 1991).

87. Michael Porter, *The Competitive Advantage of Nations* (New York: Free Press, 1990).

88. From David Mullins's introduction to Jacobs, *Short-Term America.*

89. Jacobs, *Short-Term America.*

90. U.S. Department of Commerce and U.S. Department of the Treasury, *Financing Technology: A Report of the Financing Technology Round Tables* (Washington, D.C.: U.S. Department of Commerce and U.S. Department of the Treasury, 1992).

91. The National Assessment of Educational Progress is on the Web site of the National Center for Education Statistics in the U.S. Department of Education. See http://www.nces.ed.gov/nationsreportcard/sitemap.asp.

92. As quoted in Ellen Hoffman, "Many American Schools Still at Risk," *National Journal,* April 23, 1988, 1082.

93. Hoffman, "Many American Schools Still at Risk," 1083.

94. Kolb, *White House Daze,* 133.

95. In 1999–2000, there were still slightly more than 14,000 school districts in the country. See National Center for Education Statistics (NCES), "Revenues and Expenditures in Public School Districts: School Year 1999–2000," NCES Statistics Brief; table 1; http://www.nces.ed.gov/pubs2003/2003407.pdf.

96. Kolb, *White House Daze,* 131–32.

97. Greene, *Presidency of George Bush,* 69.

98. Kolb, *White House Daze,* 135. After the summit, Clinton received a gracious and optimistic note from the President. See Greene, *Presidency of George Bush,* 70.

99. The list of six goals can be found in Kolb, *White House Daze,* 136.

100. Greene, *Presidency of George Bush,* 71.

101. Kolb, *White House Daze,* 16.

102. Kolb, *White House Daze,* 16. See also Greene, *Presidency of George Bush,* 71.

103. Kolb, *White House Daze,* 16.

104. Louis V. Gerstner Jr. with Roger D. Semerad, Denis Philip Boyle, and William B. Johnston, *Reinventing Education: Entrepreneurship in America's Public Schools* (New York: Dutton, 1994).

105. I. M. Destler, *American Trade Politics,* 2nd ed. (Washington, D.C.: Institute for International Economics with the Twentieth Century Fund, 1992), 131.

106. For a brief summary of the Structural Impediments Initiative, see Destler, *American Trade Politics,* 132.

107. Kolb, *White House Daze,* 186.

108. Thomas Kuhn, *The Structure of Scientific Revolutions,* 2nd ed. (Chicago: University of Chicago Press, 1970), 158, as quoted in Kolb, *White House Daze,* 186.

109. James Pinkerton, "The New Paradigm," a speech delivered to the Reason Foundation, Los Angeles, April 23, 1990.

110. Kolb, *White House Daze,* 187.

111. Pinkerton, "New Paradigm," 4.

112. The summary of "New Paradigm" is taken from Kolb, *White House Daze,* 187.

113. Pinkerton, "New Paradigm," 6.

114. Duffy and Goodgame, *Marching in Place,* 69.

115. Richard Darman, "Neo-Neo-Ism: Reflections on Hubble-ism, Rationalism, and the Pursuit of Excellence (After the Fiscal Follies)," speech at the Council of Excellence in Government, Washington D.C., November 16, 1990, 5.

116. Darman, "Neo-Neo-Ism," 6. Darman was, of course, adapting the Depression-era "brother, can you spare a dime" to modern-day purposes.

117. He stated this at a joint session of the Baker Institute and the Woodrow Wilson International Center for Scholars at the Wilson Center, June 15, 2000.

118. Rauch, "Father Superior."

119. Darman saw two problems that affected the popular view of Bush's domestic accomplishments. In part, Darman thought Bush was the victim of his foreign policy successes. "Just as the success of Project Apollo two decades before had led to insistent hopes for a 'domestic moonshot,' so demands for a 'domestic equivalent of Desert Storm' followed the televised techno-success in the desert." Darman did recognize the importance of the president's failure "to communicate a vision of the future that was sufficiently relevant and hopeful for the broad middle of the American electorate." Instead, Bush was widely known for simply dismissing what he called "the vision thing."

120. Duffy and Goodgame, *Marching in Place,* 211.

121. Kolb, *White House Daze,* 206–7.

Chapter 10

The 1992 Presidential Election:
The Campaign for Competitiveness

Memories of the 1992 presidential campaign often settle on a vivid moment in a debate, an awkward phrase, or a dramatic campaign advertisement that captured a candidate's strength or weakness. In the actual 1992 campaign, however, the candidates and the country focused much of their attention on strategies for improving the domestic economy. From the time of his October 1991 announcement speech in Little Rock through election day in November 1992, Governor Bill Clinton spelled out a set of economic ideas that would guide his campaign and the conduct of his presidency. He developed an economic strategy that focused on improving the opportunities of the middle class and the economic fortunes of the country. He focused on public and private investments that would increase opportunities for citizens and improve the prospects of businesses. He spoke in terms of a "New Covenant," under which the government would work to create opportunities and citizens would work to seize them. He used similar thinking to spell out the combination of federal support and private initiative that would lead to growth, innovation, and jobs.

In dealing with a series of international challenges, President George H. W. Bush and his administration were less focused on the economy and other domestic policies. The president's core economic team expected the recession to end and the country to start down the path to economic recovery. By the end of 1991, however, the White House began to turn toward domestic initiatives. For much of the 1992 election year, Bush sought to have Secretary of State James Baker leave the State Department to head the Bush reelection campaign. But Baker, having left the rough-and-tumble world of politics for the challenge of global diplomacy, was reluctant to return to the political fray. When he did leave the State Department, it was for a White

House post—had he actually left, the government ethics laws would have kept him from talking to the administration until well after the election. When Baker and his team finally arrived in the White House in August 1992, they quickly pulled together their own long-term growth or competitiveness strategy that promised individual opportunity as well as national renewal.

Ross Perot, the Texas billionaire, created an added challenge for the major parties' candidates. Perot's record of business success and his plain-spoken style hit a responsive chord with millions of voters. It is easy to forget that at the time of the August 1992 Democratic convention, Perot had made the election a three-man race. In the midst of the Democratic convention, Perot withdrew from the race, citing threats to his family that were unsubstantiated, only to reenter the fray in September. Despite his on-again, off-again candidacy, he garnered 19 percent of the popular vote, more than any third-party candidate since the 1912 vote for Theodore Roosevelt and his Bull Moose Party. Moreover, Perot's focus on the economy and his persistent emphasis on deficit reduction weakened President Bush and influenced the future course of fiscal policy.[1]

The Economic Context:
Recession, Recovery, and a Reluctant Administration

George H. W. Bush had entered office on a final upturn of Reagan-era prosperity. The economy slowed in 1989, and by the third quarter of 1990 had slipped into a recession. Recovery came in the second half of 1991 but was tepid enough that unemployment continued to rise, passing the 7 percent mark by the end of the year. When the voters went to the polls in November 1992, unemployment still registered 7 percent.

Bush proposed little in the way of a response either to the recession or its economic consequences. Worse, to preserve the budget compact, he had vetoed a September 1991 legislative effort to extend unemployment benefits. To many Americans, the president must have seemed actively indifferent to their plight. In *Mad as Hell,* Jack Germond and Jules Witcover, two highly respected political journalists, described a "deep recession [that] gripped the nation and held it fast, as the president first denied its severity, then denied its longevity, then prematurely proclaimed its end."[2]

The recession was only one of the economic problems facing the Bush administration. The *1992 Economic Report of the President* pointed to the impact of major structural changes in the economy. The widespread bank-ruptcies that hit much of the savings and loan industry disrupted credit markets. The post–Cold War slowing of defense spending was already forc-ing painful adjustments on defense industries and the workers and commu-nities that depended on them.[3]

The economy was still going through a painful adjustment to inter-national competition. Companies struggling to match the quality and agility of Japanese firms began to adapt and adopt the "lean production" techniques first developed by Toyota. Lean production meant flattened hierarchies—another way of saying that thousands of middle managers would no longer be needed. Past recessions had hit hardest at blue collar workers, who were often brought back to the same job as the economy recovered. The severe recession of 1981–82 had already broken that pattern to some extent as thousands of manufacturing workers saw their jobs disappear because of technological innovation and international competition. Now the fact and, even more, the fear of unemployment was sweeping through white collar ranks as well.

The Challenge of Japan

As the United States entered the 1990s, Japan loomed as an industrial colos-sus. Over the course of the 1980s, Japan had become a force in industries ranging from machine tools to advanced memory chips. The Japanese pres-ence was also highly visible in industries that America had once called its own—automobiles, steel, and an array of consumer electronics. In the *Com-petitiveness Index 1991,* the private-sector Council on Competitiveness reported that Japan was investing in new plant and equipment at almost twice the rate of the United States (23.4 vs. 12.6 percent of gross domestic product).[4] Japan, with an economy roughly half the size of that of the United States, was actually investing more *in actual dollars* than the American private sector.

In retrospect, it is clear that some of the Japanese investment was ill con-ceived. Many Japanese real estate "trophy purchases"—such as Rockefeller Center and Pebble Beach Golf Club—proved to be money losers as well. But at the time, the idea of Japan out-investing the United States hit a sen-sitive chord that seemed to capture and concentrate the national anxiety about slipping today and losing tomorrow.

The Policy Climate

As Republicans and Democrats began to shift their attention to the 1992 presidential campaign, the policy climate continued to change. The debate over Japan was tilting toward the revisionists, who argued that the Japanese economy worked differently than the American economy in ways that posed a challenge to public and private sectors alike.

The political and policy community began to refer to Paul Kennedy's 1987 *The Rise and Fall of Great Powers* as a warning about America's future.[5] Concerned congressional staff were also talking about Aaron L. Friedberg's *The Weary Titan*.[6] Friedberg pictured a late-nineteenth and early-twentieth-century Britain faced with challenges to its military and economic pre-eminence. The twin challenges triggered a British debate over economic policy that focused on free trade or a protective tariff and, in the end, missed the focus on measures that would have increased investment and improved the productivity of domestic industry. To contemporary eyes, the debate had an eerie similarity to the 1980s battle over the trade deficit and industrial policy. Was America, they asked, about to make the same mistake?

The Popular Mood

The mood of the country was so bleak that America's many strengths were often overlooked. The United States still had the highest standard of living of the major industrial powers, the highest level of manufacturing productivity, strong research universities, and a host of world-class industries. That was not, however, how the country saw it. In September 1991, the Council on Competitiveness sponsored a national poll to gauge popular attitudes on where the country stood relative to the international competition and what ought to be done about it. By a margin of seven to one, Americans thought that Japan was the number one economy in the world.[7]

Economic Strategy and the 1992 Campaign

The formal presidential campaign started with the April 30, 1991, announcement of former Massachusetts senator Paul Tsongas. He was not initially viewed as a formidable candidate. A bout of cancer had cut short his career in Congress, he was not well known nationally, and some political commentators thought that "after Michael Dukakis, the demand for 'another Greek from Massachusetts,'" would be limited.[8]

What Tsongas did have was a set of ideas. These were not just a random set of proposals designed to appeal to traditional Democratic interest groups. In a year when Americans were looking again for economic answers to a recession, the decline of defense industries, and the challenge of international competition, Tsongas proposed a comprehensive strategy in *A Call to Economic Arms: Forging a New American Mandate.*[9] He spelled out an economic strategy that encompassed much of the thinking developed in the earlier Bentsen–Joint Economic Committee reports, the *Rebuilding the Road to Opportunity* report of the House Democratic Caucus, and the more detailed prescription advanced by the President's Commission on Industrial Competitiveness (or the Young Commission) in 1985. And he called for deficit reduction and increased national savings. Investment would take precedence over consumption, with a clear commitment to research, education, and the development of a skilled workforce.

Tsongas was developing a view that regarded public policy and private initiative as important complements rather than hostile alternatives. He saw the American standard of living as "*totally* dependent" on the ability of American corporations "to compete and be profitable" (original emphasis).[10] He urged Americans to "think of government and industry as partners with the same level of enthusiasm, indeed patriotism, that the military-industrial complex generates for its joint mission."[11]

Clinton and Competitiveness

Four months after Tsongas entered the race, on October 3, 1991, Governor Bill Clinton of Arkansas threw his own hat into the ring. Speaking at the Old State House in Little Rock, Clinton promised to restore the American Dream with a change in direction that he described as neither "liberal or conservative. It's both," he said, "and it's different."[12]

Clinton linked opportunity to growth, and growth to a series of steps that included most of the elements of a long-term competitiveness strategy. His administration would "give people incentives to make long-term investments in America . . . invest more money in emerging technologies . . . [and] convert from a defense to a domestic economy."[13] He stressed the need for "world-class skill and world-class education . . . [and] pre-school for every child who needs it." He promised a college loan for everyone or an "apprenticeship program for kids who don't want to go to college."[14] And he put his growth strategy in a global context that recognized the economic challenge posed by Germany and Japan.

The politics and economics of Arkansas turned out to be a very good proving ground for the 1992 presidential campaign. Like many states in the post–World War II South, Arkansas had relied on low wages, the lack of strong unions, and tax incentives to lure manufacturing plants from the North. By the 1980s, however, these plants were subject to fierce international competition. In many cases, their owners had closed their doors and moved overseas in search of even lower wage rates. Campaigning in 1986, Clinton talked about the impact of foreign competition: "The people in our state whose livelihoods are subject to foreign competition and who can't compete are really suffering."[15] He responded to the economic challenge with a several-part strategy that combined technology, capital, and education.

During his 1992 run for the presidency and later as president, Clinton drew on many of the ideas developed by the Progressive Policy Institute, the think tank of the Democratic Leadership Council. Particularly influential on economic policy was the thinking of Rob Shapiro, the institute's vice president and chief economist, who had worked on Capitol Hill as Senator Daniel Patrick Moynihan's (D-N.Y.) budget specialist and had contributed to Moynihan's proposal to link reduced deficits with more expansive monetary policy as a way of maintaining growth and stimulating investment. Gary Hart had already put Moynihan's approach to work in calculating the impact of his 1984 "Budget for the Future."[16] In 1992, Shapiro's views were usually summed up as "cut and invest"—cut the deficit and increase needed public investments in education, training, research, and infrastructure.

Putting People First

In a June 22, 1992, speech to the U.S. Conference of Mayors, Clinton restated his growth strategy—*Putting People First.* He built an economic strategy around "encouraging private investment, . . . opening world markets . . . and supporting lifetime learning."[17] He saw an America that was not keeping pace with the growth of Germany and Japan because they "decided to invest in their people and Washington did not."[18] Clinton proposed $50 billion in additional spending in each of the next four years while promising to cut the deficit in half.

Clinton stressed the importance of public and private investment to the nation's future. To increase public investment, he promised a $20 billion "Rebuild America Fund" to build the "world's best communication, transportation and environmental systems."[19] The idea of rebuilding America had a strong appeal. It responded to the widely shared sense that America was slipping, while promising high-wage jobs that would help ease the transition from a defense-oriented to a civilian economy.

In calling for more private investment, Clinton and Gore contrasted America with a Japan that was investing twice as much as the United States. They proposed a targeted tax credit to stimulate investment in new plant and equipment. For small business, Clinton and Gore offered a 50 percent tax exclusion (i.e., half the income would not be taxed) for individuals who made long-term investments in new businesses. Clinton was not explicit about how long the investor needed to hold the stock to qualify for favored tax treatment. He may have had in mind proposals advanced by congressional Democrats and Republicans that offered a steady drop in the capital gains tax with, in at least one proposal, the rate reaching zero in the fifth year.[20]

Clinton and Gore continued to stress the importance of new technologies. Clinton built on his Arkansas experience and Gore on his active involvement with technology issues on Capitol Hill. Gore had been an early supporter of funding for the Internet and had also headed the Congressional Clearinghouse on the Future. They proposed making the research and experimentation credit permanent and creating a civilian "research and development agency to bring together business and universities to develop cutting-edge products and technologies."[21]

Putting People First also proposed an aggressive trade policy to open up world markets to the products of American workers and American business. It called for a "stronger, sharper" policy to open markets and promised that "if other countries refuse to play by our trade rules, we'll play by theirs."[22] To coordinate an effective trade and economic policy, it proposed the creation of an Economic Security Council that would be similar to the National Security Council. Clinton and Gore thus wanted an activist but reinvented government. They were intent in shifting "from top-down bureaucracy to an entrepreneurial government that empowers citizens and communities to change our country from the bottom up."[23]

On September 8, 1992, the Clinton-Gore team put a second plank in its economic platform, "Manufacturing for the 21st Century: Turning Ideas into Jobs."[24] In "Manufacturing," they proposed a national network of manufacturing extension centers to help small manufacturers, training initiatives, centers to ease the conversion from defense to the civilian economy, and the creation of a civilian agency that would invest in advanced manufacturing technologies. Throughout, the emphasis was on being "market driven" rather than government determined.

Putting People First proposed civilian research and development initiatives but did not provide much in the way of details. The "Manufacturing" campaign paper was a first step in adding some specifics. Ten days later, the campaign published the third element of its economic strategy, "Technology: The Engine of Economic Growth,"[25] which took a long step beyond the more familiar emphasis on research and development spending or specific tax incentives linked to research. The Clinton-Gore technology strategy promised initiatives involving some of the more than 700 national laboratories. In particular, there was considerable interest in drawing on the expertise of the national energy laboratories, whose mission had centered on nuclear weapons. Clinton and Gore also made a commitment to focus on critical technologies—an area where public- and private-sector studies had found the U.S. slipping relative to its international competitors.

"Technology," however was not confined to developing technologies in a narrow sense. In essence, "Technology" was an entire competitiveness or growth strategy seen through the prism of innovation. The document proposed investing in a twenty-first-century infrastructure, emphasizing the need for "a world-class business environment for private sector investment and innovation" and an education and training system that made sure American workers had "the requisite skills for a technology intensive workforce."[26]

"Technology" was also another example of how Clinton worked to combine policy and politics. Thirty Silicon Valley chief executives had endorsed the Clinton-Gore technology policy on September 15, three days before its formal release. Prominent among these chief executives was John Young, the head of Hewlett-Packard and chair of the Young Commission that had done so much to focus national attention on competitiveness and technology.

The endorsement was not a happenstance. In fact, Clinton had been seeking national business support since announcing his candidacy in October 1991. Clinton was right to sense an opportunity. At a fall 1991 dinner with corporate friends, Young found that "probably eight out of twelve" were going to vote for Clinton rather than Bush.[27] Young remembers being impressed by Clinton when the candidate made a late 1991 visit to Silicon Valley. At the time, Clinton was not seeking an active endorsement but wanted executives' consideration.

In seeking Silicon Valley's support, Clinton had at least one established ally, Dave Barram, a vice president of Apple Computer.[28] Before joining Apple, Barram had worked for Hewlett-Packard and Silicon Graphics. Although he joined Apple on the financial side, he quickly moved into a key role as an adviser on policy and politics to the company's chief executive, John Scully. With Apple's interest in serving the education market, it was not surprising that Scully was later asked to serve on the board of the National Center on Education and the Economy, which included Ira Magaziner as its director and included Hilary Clinton among its members.

Barram helped set up meetings for Clinton and worked to interest other chief executives in the Clinton (and then the Clinton-Gore) campaign. Barram also worked closely with Ellis Mottur, the director of the campaign's outreach to the business community.[29] This was not Mottur's first effort to bring the high-technology community into the Democratic fold. During Michael Dukakis's campaign, Mottur had lived in Silicon Valley while conducting his outreach to the high-tech business world.

Clinton continued to court the high-tech community during the course of his campaign. Young, Scully, Larry Ellison (chief executive of Oracle), and several other Silicon Valley chief executives began to listen seriously to Clinton. From the start, Young had been impressed with Clinton's "command of the issues and the similarity of their views."[30] In a meeting with interested chief executives, Clinton stressed the importance of technology and asked them if they had anything on technology that they thought he should say. After meeting with Clinton, a group of the chief executives gathered in Scully's kitchen. Young expected the group to gather around the kitchen table and come up with a few talking points. But Young had a different idea. "Do you want to do it right?" he asked, and then answered his own question by suggesting that they call the Council on Competitiveness. The next day, Young called the council and asked for its help in drafting the Clinton technology policy.[31]

The council staff jumped at Young's offer. A first draft was done by Dan Burton, the council's vice president; Erich Bloch, a distinguished council fellow, former head of the National Science Foundation, and Medal of Technology winner; and me. We then worked with Ira Magaziner to turn the draft into Clinton's campaign white paper, "Technology: The Engine of Economic Growth." With the release of this paper, Clinton had completed the last piece of his economic plan: deficit reduction as part of a climate to spur investment; public and private investments in research and development; high-quality education and skills for a high-technology economy; and opening global markets for American products. Clinton also tied these pieces together into a coherent whole that promised long-term growth for all Americans.

President Bush Responds: An Agenda for American Renewal

On August 23, Secretary of State James Baker returned to the White House to be chief of staff with clear responsibilities for putting the campaign on track. Almost immediately, Baker was confronted by more troubling economic news. In June, President Bush had made "a premature announcement of economic recovery."[32] The economy was growing, but the slow pace of growth was not enough to make a major dent in unemployment or raise incomes. Just before Labor Day, the Census Bureau announced that 35.7 percent of Americans were living in poverty—more than at any time since 1964.[33] At about the same time, the Commerce Department reported that private-sector earnings had fallen by 3.2 percent since 1989.[34] Although the Bush campaign continued to emphasize Clinton's supposed character flaws and to focus on family values, the central question became "whether George Bush could offer a coherent program to come to grips with that problem [the economy]."[35]

On September 10, Bush answered this question before the Economic Club of Detroit with his detailed "Agenda for American Renewal."[36] According to campaign insiders, Baker had directed his key aide, Robert Zoellick, to pull together "all the disparate parts of Bush's previous economic-recovery packages, legislation and ideas" into a coherent strategy.[37]

Bush surrounded his program with traditional conservative principles of small government, lower tax rates, and more competition. But his plan itself was a call for an activist government that would work with markets and the private sector. His approach included most of the elements of a comprehensive competitiveness strategy. Instead of a "leave it to the states" approach to education, Bush's proposals ranged from voluntary national standards to increased funding for child immunizations. After an almost ritual attack on industrial policy, he described an agenda that would "increase funding for basic research and complement that work with a focus on applied research and development."[38]

While Clinton continued to hone his economic message, Bush returned to attacks on Clinton's character. Bush's failure to emphasize his economic plan in the year of the economy almost surely contributed to his defeat.[39]

What was a loss for Bush was also a loss for the country. Instead of seeing two candidates explaining their "new paradigm" or fighting over the best competitiveness strategy, the message was muddied by the focus on the character issue. The press had seen the Bush plan as little more than a restatement of old policies. With a close and colorful horse race to cover, they had little time and less incentive to chart the emergence of a new approach to economic policy. That would wait until the first term of the Clinton presidency.

Notes

1. Ross Perot, *United We Stand: How We Can Take Back Our Country* (New York: Hyperion, 1992).

2. Jack Germond and Jules Witcover, *Mad as Hell: Revolt at the Ballot Box, 1992* (New York: Warner Books, 1993), 16.

3. Council of Economic Advisers, *1992 Economic Report of the President* (Washington, D.C.: U.S. Government Printing Office, 1992), 25–27. The report also points to demographic changes and the overhang of private debt as additional factors that contributed to "structural imbalances."

4. Council on Competitiveness, *Competitiveness Index 1991* (Washington, D.C.: Council on Competitiveness, 1991), 10.

5. Paul Kennedy, *The Rise and Fall of Great Powers: Economic Change and Military Conflict from 1500 to 2000* (New York: Random House, 1987).

6. Aaron L. Friedberg, *The Weary Titan: Britain and the Experience of Relative Decline, 1895–1905* (Princeton, N.J.: Princeton University Press, 1988).

7. Council on Competitiveness, *Looking for Leadership: The Public, Competitiveness and Campaign '92* (Washington, D.C.: Council on Competitiveness, 1991).

8. Council on Competitiveness, *Looking for Leadership*, 83.

9. Paul E. Tsongas, *A Call to Economic Arms: Forging a New American Mandate* (Boston: Foley Hoag & Eliot, 1991).

10. Tsongas, *Call to Economic Arms*, 11.

11. Tsongas, *Call to Economic Arms*, 16.

12. William Jefferson Clinton, Announcement Speech, as reprinted in Bill Clinton and Al Gore, *Putting People First: How We Can All Change America* (New York: Times Books, 1992), 191.

13. Clinton and Gore, *Putting People First*, 192.

14. Clinton and Gore, *Putting People First*, 192–93.

15. Quoted in David Osborne, *Laboratories of Democracy: A New Breed of Governor Creates Models for National Growth* (Boston: Harvard Business School Press, 1988), 83.

16. I drew up the initial budget in Ottumwa, Iowa. We used one of the major econometric models to adjust for a more expansive monetary policy and lower interest rates.

17. Clinton and Gore, *Putting People First*, 3–4.

18. Clinton and Gore, *Putting People First*, 6.

19. Clinton and Gore, *Putting People First*, 9.

20. Senator Dale Bumpers, a Democrat from Arkansas, had, as chairman of the

Small Business Committee, proposed a sliding-scale capital gains tax for new purchases of small company stock. Senator Robert Packwood, a Republican from Oregon, had proposed his own sliding-scale approach.

21. Clinton and Gore, *Putting People First*, 12.

22. Clinton and Gore, *Putting People First*, 13.

23. Clinton and Gore, *Putting People First*, 24.

24. Bill Clinton and Al Gore, "Manufacturing for the 21st Century: Turning Ideas into Jobs," National Campaign Headquarters, Little Rock, September 8, 1992.

25. Bill Clinton and Al Gore, "Technology: The Engine of Economic Growth—A National Technology Policy for America," National Campaign Headquarters, Little Rock, September 18, 1992.

26. This quotation is from the press release accompanying Clinton and Gore, "Technology: The Engine of Economic Growth."

27. James A. Barnes, "Where Are Those Gray Flannel Suits?" *National Journal*, September 23, 1995, p. 2370, as quoted in John Robert Greene, *The Presidency of George Bush* (Lawrence: University Press of Kansas, 2001), 162.

28. E-mail communication from David J. Barram, former deputy secretary of commerce and former administrator, General Services Administration.

29. Author's interview with Ellis Mottur, November 16, 2001. Mottur served in the Clinton administration as the deputy assistant secretary for technology and aerospace industries in the trade development arm of the Department of Commerce's International Trade Administration.

30. Max Holland, *The CEO Goes to Washington: Negotiating the Halls of Power* (Knoxville: Chief Executive Press, 1994), 21.

31. The details on the meeting in Scully's kitchen and the quotes are from the author's interview with John Young. Council vice president Daniel Burton did the initial drafting with the assistance of the author and Erich Bloch, the IBM veteran and former head of the National Science Foundation who had recently become a distinguished fellow at the council. The council staff also worked closely with Ira Magaziner from the Clinton campaign.

32. John Hohenberg, *The Bill Clinton Story: Winning the Presidency* (Syracuse, N.Y.: Syracuse University Press, 1994), 48.

33. Hohenberg, *Bill Clinton Story*, 104.

34. Hohenberg, *Bill Clinton Story*, 105.

35. Germond and Witcover, *Mad as Hell*, 416.

36. Germond and Witcover, *Mad as Hell*, 427.

37. Mary Matalin and James Carville, with Peter Knobler, *All's Fair: Love, War, and Running for President* (New York: Random House, 1994), 332.

38. Matalin and Carville, *All's Fair*, 16.

39. In their coverage of the 1992 campaign, Germond and Witcover quote the Bush campaign communications director, Jim Lake, as saying that despite elaborate plans to promote Bush's *Agenda for American Renewal*, "it lasted one day." Germond and Witcover, *Mad as Hell*, 428.

Chapter 11

Competitiveness as National Policy: Turning Ideas into Action

With the election of 1992, ideas that first emerged in the 1970s now took center stage. Throughout the 1992 campaign, the economy remained the key issue, although character questions kept intruding. From the announcement of his candidacy to the final day of the election, Bill Clinton maintained his emphasis on the economy, the forgotten middle class, and traditional American values, calling for greater opportunities along with renewed responsibilities.

The Clinton Competitiveness Strategy

Much of the Clinton strategy had been spelled out in his three campaign documents: *Putting People First,* "Manufacturing for the 21st Century: Turning Ideas into Jobs," and "Technology: The Engine of Economic Growth."[1] In all three, he stressed the need to create an economic climate conducive to private-sector investment. He also emphasized the importance of public-sector investment in infrastructure, technology, and training. Finally, he pursued a market-opening trade policy that put the spotlight on exports and the better (i.e., higher-paying) jobs they often brought.

Clinton articulated his policy in his first State of Union address and again in his budget message to Congress. In his first (1994) economic report to Congress, he spoke of his 1993 deficit reduction plan as "the principal factor in the dramatic decline in long-term interest rates."[2] The accompanying report of the Council of Economic Advisers spelled out a "Strategy for Growth and Change" that included separate sections on "Reducing the Deficit to Promote Capital Formation," "Investing in People," "Investing

287

in Public Infrastructure," and "Investing in Technology." There was also a section on the link between "Trade Policy and Living Standards."[3]

In his second (1995) economic report to Congress, Clinton talked about having taken steps to put America's fiscal house in order. In a section titled "Preparing the American People to Compete and Win," he again emphasized education, training, and new technologies. In the section on trade policy, he pointed to the administration's success in promoting American exports, which had "created and safeguarded tens of thousands of American jobs."[4] The accompanying report of the Council of Economic Advisers gave a midterm report on the administration's economic game plan. The report started with macroeconomic policy and pointed to deficit reduction as "the linchpin of the Administration's economic strategy."[5] "The second defining component of the strategy," continued the report, "is a set of policies to help American workers and businesses realize the opportunities that flow from rapid changes in technology and an increasingly global economy. The common theme of these policies is *investment, public and private*"[6] (emphasis added).

Coordinating Competitiveness Policy

In terms of structure, Clinton's major departure was the creation of the National Economic Council (NEC), a Cabinet-level body that was meant to parallel the structure and prominence of the National Security Council. Clinton and his team had adopted a long-term competitiveness strategy that was a puzzle of many interacting pieces. They sought to manage that complexity by linking the NEC to other institutions in the White House and throughout the government. On the international economic front, the NEC shared a staff member with the National Security Council. On technology, the NEC worked closely with the Office of Science and Technology Policy, as well as with several Cabinet agencies that shared responsibility for science and technology. On education, training, and lifelong learning, the NEC turned to the Departments of Education and Labor but also included the Department of Defense, which did more actual training than all the other government agencies combined. In addition, the NEC brought to the table the Department of Commerce, which worked more closely with the private sector that did much of the nation's training and was playing a growing role at every level of education.

People as Policy

When Clinton appointed his economic team, he turned to many individuals who had been active in shaping a national competitiveness strategy. Every administration brings in a variety of like-minded people. When Ronald Reagan took office, most of his economic team favored sharp reductions in marginal tax rates and the size of government. But the Clinton economic team was distinctive in that so many of them saw the need for a strategy that involved several elements working together to achieve long-term growth and competitiveness. In bureaucratic terms, this meant that the NEC would be more likely to seek to involve all the relevant departments and also increased the chances that each department would see its own mission enhanced by the actions of a sister department.

In the White House, Clinton chose Robert Rubin, the managing partner at the New York investment bank Goldman Sachs, to be his first director of the NEC. Rubin had been thoroughly exposed to the competitiveness debate through his service on Governor Mario Cuomo's Commission on Trade and Competitiveness.[7] Rubin's domestic deputy, Gene Sperling, played a major role inside the campaign in pulling together different aspects of what became Clinton's competitiveness strategy.[8] The NEC staff was also sprinkled with individuals who had been active in developing various aspects of the competitiveness agenda.

To head his Council of Economic Advisers, Clinton chose Laura Tyson from the Berkeley Roundtable on International Economics. Tyson and her roundtable colleagues had helped elaborate the competitiveness agenda in their work for the 1983–85 President's Commission on Industrial Competitiveness (or the Young Commission). In her 1992 book *Who's Bashing Whom? Trade Conflicts in High Technology Industries,* Tyson applied some of Paul Krugman's ideas on strategic trade to actual trade disputes involving high-technology industries.[9] As his science and technology adviser, Clinton chose John Gibbons, who had served as head of the Congressional Office of Technology Assessment. Bruce Reed, a veteran of the Democratic Leadership Council, took the reins at the Domestic Policy Council.

Much of the cabinet had the same strong competitiveness background. Clinton's first treasury secretary, Senator Lloyd Bentsen, came from his position as chairman of the Senate Committee on Finance. This was the same Lloyd Bentsen who, as chairman of the congressional Joint Economic Committee, had articulated a productivity growth strategy in the committee's

1979 and 1980 annual reports. As commerce secretary, Clinton chose Ronald Brown, then head of the Democratic National Committee and a partner at the prominent Washington law firm of Patton, Boggs, and Blow. Brown had not been active in developing a competitiveness strategy, but he surrounded himself with those who had been.

At the Labor Department, Clinton installed Robert Reich, his longtime friend and fellow Rhodes Scholar. During his many years at Harvard's John F. Kennedy School of Government, Reich had written extensively on the competitive challenge facing America. For secretary of education, Clinton turned to former governor Richard Riley of South Carolina. As governor, Riley had emphasized education and training as a key to individual opportunity and overall economic growth.

Al Gore, the newly elected vice president, had been active in competitiveness-related initiatives during his days in the House and the Senate. Gore had been a member of the Committee on Party Effectiveness, created in the early 1980s by the House Democratic Caucus chair, Gillis Long (D-La.). Although Gore had not been part of the task force developing a long-run growth strategy, he had served as vice chair of the committee's environmental task force. He would have been part of the group that reviewed the long-term growth strategy in *Rebuilding the Road to Opportunity* before it became a committee and then a caucus document.

Even more surprising is the degree to which key administration officials *outside the economic core* also shared a competitiveness perspective. At the Defense Department, Secretary Les Aspin had also been a member of Gillis Long's Committee on Party Effectiveness during his service in the House. Deputy Secretary William Perry was a veteran of the Carter administration who had built a career as a venture capitalist in Silicon Valley. Undersecretary John Deutch, a chemistry professor and provost at the Massachusetts Institute of Technology (MIT) had served on the MIT Commission on Industrial Productivity. The commission's 1989 report, *Made in America: Regaining the Productive Edge,* like the 1985 Young Commission report, spelled out complementary policy recommendations for industry, labor, and government.[10] Following the broad outlines of the Young Commission, the MIT Commission urged the government to emphasize science and technology, continuous education and training, and a market-opening trade policy. The MIT Commission also proposed "macroeconomic policies that reduce the cost of capital for private industry [that] will require measures to . . . reduce the federal budget deficit."[11]

Turning Promises into Performance

After the Democratic convention, James Carville, the campaign manager, hung his much-quoted sign in the "war room, where daily strategy and rapid response" to the campaign of George H. W. Bush were developed:

> Change vs. more of the same.
> The economy, stupid.
> Don't forget health care.[12]

For Clinton, bringing change to the economy involved turning his growth strategy into administration leadership and legislative action. Deficit reduction was central to the Clinton strategy for political as well as economic reasons. For better or for worse, Democrats had acquired a tax-and-spend label that suggested too much taxing and ill-considered spending. Part of the reaction dated from the inflation of the 1970s, which pushed more and more middle-class Americans into higher tax brackets. At the same time, the popular reaction to many Great Society initiatives left some voters with the sense that the taxes still applied to them but the spending was destined for someone else.[13] For many Americans, deficits also took on a decidedly moral tone. The sense that a country living beyond its means was heading for trouble created broad general support for deficit reduction. Ross Perot's surprisingly strong run for the presidency in 1992 had focused on the deficit as the problem that other leaders would not face.

Deficit reduction—if well-timed and carefully crafted—held out the promise of lower interest rates, higher levels of investment, and rising incomes. By increasing the pool of domestic savings, deficit reduction would also reduce the need to borrow overseas and thus lower the trade and current account deficits.

Following the election, Clinton and his economic team began to look at a budget that would meet their promises for a middle-class tax cut, short-term stimulus, added public investments, and halving the budget deficit in his first term. The president agreed that they could not keep all their promises. The middle-class tax cut was abandoned.

In his 1994 book *The Agenda,* the *Washington Post*'s Bob Woodward paints a detailed picture of how the president and his economic team arrived at a budget and worked to secure its passage.[14] It has become a familiar Washington cliché that no one wants to see how either sausage or legislation is made. Woodward adds the Clinton budget process to that list. In almost agonizing detail, Woodward describes the tensions between deficit hawks and investment advocates; between those urging a partnership with business and those urging a populist attack on the rich.

It is a tribute to Woodward's rich reportorial skills that he succeeded in talking in depth to so many people so early in an administration. In retrospect, however, Woodward's tale does appear to unfold from the perspective of those urging public investments and suggesting populist attacks. Looking at the president through their eyes, he is seen as shocked at the size of the deficit, unaware of congressional action putting caps on domestic spending, and stunned at the power of the financial markets. At other points, Woodward suggests a Clinton who saw the deficit and the overall economy with considerable clarity and sophistication. In a brusque exchange with Clinton political adviser Paul Begala, deputy Office of Management and Budget director Alice Rivlin "said bluntly [that] 'Bill Clinton knew where this deficit was going.'"[15] At another juncture, Woodward quotes Clinton as seeing his public investments as being one part of a much larger national economy.[16]

Woodward provides surprising detail on the interplay between Federal Reserve Board chairman Alan Greenspan and President Clinton. In his review of the book, Kevin Phillips suggested that "if *The Agenda* were to have a subtitle, it could fairly be 'The Greenspanning of America."[17] At Clinton's request, Greenspan flew to Little Rock for a December 3, 1992, meeting with the president. Clinton's briefing paper on Greenspan made clear what tightened monetary policy did to the reelection hopes of President Bush.

At the time of their meeting, Greenspan and the Fed had already brought short-term interest rates down to about 3 percent, but long-term rates remained 3 to 4 full percentage points higher. According to Woodward, Greenspan explained that the gap between short-term and long-term rates was usually not that high. In Greenspan's view, the higher long-term rates reflected expectations of future inflation that were driven by the prospect of continued large fiscal deficits. Greenspan suggested that a credible deficit reduction package would bring down long-term rates, triggering added investment in housing, increased consumer spending, and a rising stock market. Given the current economic circumstances, suggested Greenspan, deficit reduction "would actually increase employment.[18] With credible deficit reduction, the economy would grow "at a strong sustainable rate."[19] A short-term stimulus, Greenspan warned, "would result in a renewed recession in 1995 or so."[20] After the meeting, Clinton told his vice president that "we can do business" with Greenspan.[21]

The British journalist Martin Walker, the *Washington Post*'s Bob Woodward, and others portray Clinton as surprised at the power of markets. Walker refers to "the Keynesian views that Clinton instinctively upheld."[22] Woodward described a Clinton railing at the markets and expressing anger at what a deficit reduction package would do to his public investments or any thought of a stimulus package.

There is considerable reason, however, to think that as a governor seeking to attract investments to a small, poor state, Clinton had every reason to be aware of the power of the financial markets. In addition, many leading Democrats had been seeking to square the economic and political imperative of deficit reduction with the need to stimulate investment and growth. In 1983, Senator Daniel Patrick Moynihan (D-N.Y.) advocated a macroeconomic policy that combined fiscal tightening with faster monetary growth. In 1994, Senator Gary Hart carefully adjusted his "Budget for the Future" to allow for lower interest rates and faster monetary growth as deficits came down. Certainly, some New Democrats were familiar with the idea of shifting the macroeconomic mix. Clinton had served as the chairman of the Democratic Leadership Council, a bastion of New Democrat thought. Robert Shapiro, a key Clinton economic adviser in the 1992 campaign, had served on Moynihan's staff in 1983 and was now vice president of the Progressive Policy Institute, the think tank arm of the Democratic Leadership Council.

In subsequent chapters, Woodward continues to track Greenspan's influence on the decision to emphasize deficit reduction as part of the president's overall growth plan. According to Woodward, Bentsen kept Greenspan informed of the growing support for reduction inside the administration. At one point, Bentsen reported back to Clinton that Greenspan would not give them an actual deal on the budget but "short of that . . . it looked good."[23] While his budget was being developed, Clinton was working hard to bridge the gap that exists between any administration and the Federal Reserve. The unveiling of Clinton's plan was scheduled to take place at a February 17 speech to a joint session of Congress. At the suggestion of his chief congressional liaison, Howard Paster, Clinton invited Greenspan to sit in the first lady's box. After some deliberation, Greenspan came and was seated between Hillary Clinton and Tipper Gore. In a visually vivid way, the president was telling the country and the financial markets that his administration and the Federal Reserve Board would work to find common ground on economic policy. Woodward goes so far as to report that "the chairman of the Federal Reserve was in some ways the ghost writer of the Clinton Plan."[24]

Looking back at events can give them an aura of inevitability. Woodward's detailed reporting gives the reader a sense of how much less certain the world seems when looking forward. The professional economists on Clinton's team agreed that deficit reduction could bring down long-term interest rates but worried about whether these lower long-term rates would offset the immediate, contractionary impact of lower spending. Those members of the economic team with more business or market experience were generally more confident that long-term rates would come down but still had some disagreements over timing. In Woodward's picture, the political disagreements were even sharper. In brief, the populist advisers wanted to blame the rich and the economic advisers wanted to work with them.

Nor was there anything foreordained about the passage of Clinton's program. Along the way, Clinton saw further reductions in his proposed investments and actual rejection of his modest $16 billion stimulus package. The initial House-passed proposal contained a comprehensive energy (or "British thermal unit") tax that was eventually dropped in the Senate version of the bill. Congressional debate, threatened congressional defections, and intense lobbying continued up until the last minute in the House (on August 5) and the Senate (August 6). In the end, a switch of two votes would have defeated the program in the House. It took the vice president's vote to secure a 51–50 margin of victory in the Senate. Not a single Republican in either house voted for the Clinton plan.

In pursuing deficit reduction, Clinton had taken both economic and political risks. Would interest rates and, more fundamentally, the economy respond? How much ground had he lost with liberals because of his failed stimulus package? Had he lost credibility with the public as he reduced proposed investments and abandoned a middle-class tax cut? The legislative fight over deficit reduction had delayed decisions on health reform, a key campaign pledge. Why did he take the risk?

Clinton was, of course, responding to a number of political imperatives. Many voters saw deficit reduction as being as much a values as an economic question.[25] A country in debt was not a country headed in the right direction. Clinton's package also reflected some clear Democratic imperatives. Added taxes made up the bulk of Clinton's deficit reduction plan, but they were largely tailored to be acceptable to a Democratic majority.[26] Although the package eventually included a gasoline tax of 4.3 cents a gallon, the bulk of the new taxes were paid by those making more than $140,000 a year. In addition, Clinton sharply increased the Earned Income Tax Credit, a kind of negative income tax targeted to help working poor people.

There was also a clear economic rationale. In late October 1993 remarks, Alan S. Blinder, the lead macroeconomist on the Council of Economic Advisers, spelled out "The Strategy of Clintonomics."[27] Blinder started by pointing to the sharp differences in philosophy between the Reagan-Bush vision and that of President Clinton. "The Reagan-Bush vision was the 'invisible foot'—that government can only be an obstacle to growth," while Clinton saw government as a "helper and partner" or even a "catalyst in the process of economic growth."[28] Blinder particularly stressed the importance of the government in providing the "raw materials for economic progress—like technology, like an educated and well-trained labor force, like public infrastructure, and capital for private investment."[29] In some sense, Blinder was restating a consensus view among students of economic growth. But he was also articulating a view of the economy that could trace its public policy roots back to Bentsen's Joint Economic Committee reports, the long-term growth strategy of *Rebuilding the Road to Opportunity,* and the view articulated in the Young Commission report.

Blinder then poses the question of why deficit reduction, when "trimming spending and raising taxes, will not spur a single technological breakthrough, improve a single school, nor build a single road or bridge."[30] Blinder answered his own question by putting deficit reduction in the context of a growth strategy that included private as well as public investments. In particular, he stressed the "folly" of "cutting *public* investment to make room for more *private* investment"[31] (emphasis in original). He also stressed the importance of international trade—the administration was then working to pass the North American Free Trade Agreement—as a path to a stronger economy and better jobs.

Clinton's deficit reduction package was targeted at increasing the pool of investment capital and at lowering long-term interest rates. A larger pool of capital and lower interest rates would facilitate state and local public investment. Deficit reduction was part of a broader strategy that involved creating an economic climate that encouraged private investment. The vice president's efforts to "reinvent" government were also part of this strategy. Clinton actively courted the business community through a series of White House dinners and the efforts of key Cabinet members. In a sense, his entire growth agenda—public investments, pragmatic partnerships, and a multifaceted trade policy—contributed to a positive climate for private investment.

Not all the interest-rate cards were in Clinton's or even Greenspan's hands. In an age of global capital markets, the shift in European and East Asian monetary policies can have an affect on U.S. interest rates and the international value of the dollar. Clinton and his economic team experienced considerable variability in long-term rates despite their successful effort to reduce the budget deficit. At first, long-term rates came down as predicted and expected. By the end of the year, long-term rates were rising. They continued to rise. In Phillips's review of *The Agenda,* he reports that by April and May of 1994, "the whole Greenspan-Bentsen-Rubin notion that deficit reduction would bring and hold down long-term bond interest rates lay shattered as those rates soared back to pre-Clinton inauguration levels."[32] Fortunately for Clinton, they did not stay there. Clinton's Council of Economic Advisers explained the rise by linking it to an economy that had proven to be stronger than expected. Home mortgage rates also rose but remained well below the level of 1992. Economic strength could be found in unemployment rates that fell steadily throughout 1993 and 1994.[33] Business investment remained strong, and spending on business (or nonresidential) structures rose.[34]

Clinton was on the right long-term growth path. But his approach incurred some significant short-term political costs. The president made miscalculations in constructing his deficit reduction package and in learning how to deal with a powerful Congress rather than a relatively weak state legislature, as he had in Arkansas. Still, the saga of deficit reduction should remind economists how difficult it is to look even a year ahead, how global markets compound the complexity of prediction, and why political leaders need to think about the timing of economic benefits as well as their eventual magnitude.

Technology: The Engine of Economic Growth

Clinton had been the first president to give technology and technology policy a central role in his economic strategy. One of his three major campaign documents on the economy focused on his technology policy, and he had promised to give his vice president a lead role in translating campaign promises into actual policy. Clinton's emphasis on technology policy had also been an important element in securing the backing of leading chief executives from Silicon Valley.

Clinton moved quickly on the technology front. In late February, Clinton and Gore issued *Technology for America's Economic Growth: A New*

Direction to Build Economic Strength.[35] This was not a routine document issued by an obscure bureau in a distant department. It carried the presidential seal and the president's as well as the vice president's names. In it, Clinton and Gore laid out an ambitious agenda for a technology policy that reached far beyond the traditional focus on laboratory science. As in the campaign's "Technology: The Engine of Economic Growth," technology policy was put in the context of a broader growth strategy that required investments in twenty-first-century infrastructure, the education of a skilled workforce, and open global markets for new products.

Technology for America's Economic Growth was published just five days after Clinton unveiled his proposed budget for the future, which included added funding for investment in technology and also targeted a small slice of the $16 billion stimulus package at technology. But by the time the budget dust had cleared, the investments had been scaled back even more, and the stimulus package had failed altogether. Despite these fiscal limitations, Clinton still had considerable room to maneuver on the technology front. At the time, federal spending on research and development (R&D) was in excess of $70 billion. With that large a budget, Clinton had some ability to propose redirecting or refocusing funds without raising overall spending.

Clinton and Gore also thought of technology policy in broad terms that encompassed not only specific research funding but also an array of policies that contributed to a climate of innovation or that better coordinated the federal research dollar. They looked to the newly created National Economic Council to "coordinate technology policy with the policies of the tax, trade, regulatory, economic development and other economic sectors."[36] They also indicated a clear intent to build on Alan Bromley's work in the Bush administration to improve coordination of R&D programs throughout the federal government.

Bromley had reinvigorated the Federal Coordinating Council on Science, Engineering, and Technology. Clinton's science and technology adviser, John Gibbons, took the added step of creating a National Science and Technology Council with a subcommittee structure meant to help coordinate the entire federal R& D enterprise.

In the 1992 campaign, Clinton had emphasized the need for both traditional and twenty-first-century infrastructure. By the time his budget was put together, the emphasis on traditional infrastructure had faded. Some infrastructure spending was included in the stimulus package, and some of that was criticized as unneeded pork. The administration may have thought that traditional infrastructure spending was likely to take care of itself. Major transportation bills usually contained something for every state, if not every district. There was likely to be ample congressional support for transportation and other infrastructure-related bills. There was some precedent for leaving infrastructure aside. The Young Commission had made the same decision. Not, John Young said, because infrastructure was unimportant but rather because it was a more familiar and less pressing problem.[37] Traditional infrastructure was, however, incorporated in some of the president's technology initiatives. In addition to supporting funding already approved by existing congressional legislation,[38] the administration proposed investing in magnetic levitation transportation and funding research on "smart highways" and on new materials.

Clinton and Gore had also stressed the importance of a twenty-first-century infrastructure. In *Putting People First,* a significant portion of Clinton's special fund for needed investments was to be devoted to building twenty-first-century infrastructure, or what became known as the national information superhighway. After the election, Clinton and Gore maintained their broad commitment to an information superhighway and made it a key element of their technology policy. The government's role, however, was eventually shifted from constructing the information superhighway to working with the businesses that would actually build the system. The government would focus its efforts on encouraging universal access, developing new applications, and supporting next-generation technologies.

The Clinton-Gore technology policy posited three broad goals—long-term sustainable growth, more efficient and responsive government, and world leadership in science, mathematics, and engineering. To achieve these goals, they proposed a series of detailed initiatives ranging from a permanent tax credit for research and experimentation to improved education and training to a fuel-efficient, environmentally benign automobile. They fully embraced proposals to share the cost of developing high-risk technologies with business and to establish a nationwide manufacturing extension service. Both programs were part of the Omnibus Trade and Competitiveness Act of 1988. Both had been initially resisted and then only tepidly supported by the Bush administration's budgets.

The Clinton administration's statement on technology was followed by action on a number of fronts. The administration's pursuit of a comprehensive competitiveness strategy provided added support. Deficit reduction, export strategies, and an added emphasis on education and training were also part of creating a climate that encouraged the development and commercialization of technology. The administration understood that being the first to invent meant little if American industry was the last to market.

In setting trade policy, the Clinton administration built on the achievements of the Bush years but was very aware of the implications for technology development. U.S. Trade Representative Carla Hills had largely completed the Uruguay Round of multilateral trade negotiations by the time the Clinton team took office. Part of her effort had been directed at eliminating or severely restricting subsidies, including those targeted at R&D. Support for her position had come from three disparate camps. One group thought the government should not be involved in subsidizing industry, while a second group saw an economist's market failure rationale for federal subsidies but did not have confidence that the government would be effective in practice. A third group favored a more active government role but saw little prospects of effective action during either the Reagan or Bush years. In the view of the third group, if the United States would not work with industry, then the next best approach was to level the playing field by discouraging the technology initiatives of America's major economic competitors.

As the Clinton team took office, this alliance of "shouldn't, couldn't, and wouldn't" forces was about to carry the day. When the about-to-be-made decision on a subsidies code reached the White House Office of Science and Technology Policy, however, there was a sharp reaction. The office and Skip Johns, its incoming associate director for technology, took the lead in changing the American position so that R&D subsidies would be given a green light in terms of the trade laws.[39]

The end of the Cold War had led to sharp cutbacks in military spending. By the time Clinton came to office, the defense sector was laying off thousands of front-line workers, engineers, and senior managers. Communities heavily dependent on defense spending were reeling from a kind of triple whammy—recession and slow recovery, the restructuring that was affecting most manufacturing firms, and the pressures of the sudden end of the Cold War. Southern California and several other parts of the country were struggling to adjust. As part of his response, Clinton proposed using technology as a way of stimulating the creation of new firms and providing opportunities for people leaving the defense sector.

In the long run, science and technology would account for as much as half of economic growth and even more of expected increases in individual income. In pursuing a technology policy, Clinton and his technology team were applying much the same economic rationale that justified the massive federal investment in science. Markets were likely to underinvest in high-cost or high-risk technologies where they were uncertain about their ability to control or appropriate the benefits. Strategic trade theory had provided its own rationale for government action in key technology areas. An early inventor might have strong "first mover" advantages or an early developer might gain advantages through global economies of scale. Portions of the environmental movement were also looking to technology as at least a partial solution to an array of environmental problems. Where earlier industrial development had contributed to air and water pollution, newer technologies promised cleaner and greener growth.

An emphasis on technology also brought some political advantages. The relative decline of America's international standing had hit American pride as well as profits. An aggressive technology policy was an effective response to widely reported studies showing the United States losing its ranking in certain critical technologies. In some sense, technologies and high-technology industry were also associated with a brighter future that appealed to the optimism of the American people. Where technology promised clean growth, it held out the possibility of reducing the potential tensions between the industrial unions and the environmental movement—both important constituencies of the Democratic Party. In addition, Clinton had begun to forge closer ties with the high-technology community in Silicon Valley and around the country. His views on technology and his campaign statement on technology policy had been part of building that relationship. Now he needed to show clear progress.

In early November 1993, the Clinton technology team had an opportunity to report back to the leaders of Silicon Valley who had given Clinton such a critical boost in September 1992. The Berkeley Roundtable on International Economics scheduled a conference on the Clinton administration's technology policy. They saw the conference as a way for the administration "to detail its intentions to the high-tech community" and "to permit the leaders of the West Coast technology community to provide detailed feedback on the policy agenda to the relevant administration officials."[40] Campaign veterans also weighed in. In a memorandum to Secretary of Commerce Ronald H. Brown, campaign technology issues coordinator Richard Bradshaw pointed to growing skepticism in the high-tech community about "the Administration's commitment to the 'investment package.'"[41]

By late July, key Silicon Valley business leaders were committed to speak at the conference. The administration responded in force. Knowing Silicon Valley wanted results as well some reassurance of the administra-

Competitiveness as National Policy

tion's intent, the White House produced *Technology for Economic Growth: The President's Progress Report.*[42] In his introductory letter, President Clinton emphasized that he had "made technology policy a key element of my economic strategy." He also pointed to accomplishments in his first nine months; he had supported "tax incentives for investments in R&D and new businesses, liberalized export controls, shifted federal resources toward basic research and civilian technology, invested in worker skills, and aggressively promoted defense conversion." The president saw partnerships as critical to the success of his technology policy. "All of our initiatives," he continued, "will require a new partnership between government, industry, labor and academia."[43]

Secretary of Commerce Brown led the administration's delegation, which included key officials from the White House and the major agencies with responsibility for technology development. Brown's Commerce Department had been charged with taking the lead in developing a civilian technology policy. To help show that it was working to meet that responsibility, Commerce issued its own report to the conference, *Commerce ACTS: Advanced Civilian Technology Strategy.*[44] In his introductory letter, Brown made clear that *Commerce ACTS* was a draft strategy intended to elicit comments from business to help the department understand "what actions the government should take—or refrain from taking—to enable American business to meet and win the new global competition."[45] Again, Brown was stressing partnership, working together, and listening to industry.

Brown gave the keynote address after Vice President Gore had spoken to the summit via satellite link to Washington. In effect, Gore was showing how the administration would also put technology to work to help do the country's business. Over the two days of the conference, the administration's technology team joined industry leaders on a series of topical panels.

By Washington standards, the administration had already accomplished a great deal on the technology policy front. Silicon Valley, however, worked by a different, faster clock. Whole generations of semiconductor chips might come and go in the time it took to turn a public policy proposal into legislation. The government and the high-technology world still had much to learn about each other.

The administration's November report card was far from the end of the its technology initiatives. Throughout the rest of 1993 and 1994, the administration pushed to secure passage of the legislation needed to meet its goals. Two legislative bills took on particular prominence: the National Competitiveness Act and the Telecommunications Act.

The first bill was the National Competitiveness Act of 1993 (HR 820 in the House and S 4 in the Senate), which bundled together several of the technology initiatives based at the Commerce Department. The bill contained significant increases in funding for both the Advanced Technology Program and the manufacturing extension service program. The bill also included a loan program to help small and medium-sized firms apply or develop new technologies and a pilot program to provide venture capital to foster advanced or critical technologies.[46]

Despite the relatively small sums involved, the bill attracted a great deal of controversy. In the House and Senate, Republicans were quick to attack some elements of the bill as an attempt to resurrect an industrial policy that would involve the government in picking "winners and losers." Even the best of intentions could raise passionate objections. One House amendment was designed to assure that a percentage of the loans would go to "socially and economically disadvantaged individuals."[47] The Republicans on the Science, Space, and Technology Committee immediately attacked the amendment on the grounds that the Commerce Department might construe the amendment to "include homosexuals as a class of people to whom loans could be targeted."[48] The issue faded after the committee's counsel assured the objecting members of Congress that the amendment followed the Small Business Administration's definition of disadvantaged people, which did not include homosexuals as a class.

Senate opponents "complained that the bill's grant and loan programs would serve as a useful political tool for Commerce Secretary Ronald H. Brown, a former chairman of the Democratic National Committee."[49] In the Senate, there was a sharp clash over whether the new loan programs should be housed in the Small Business Administration or the Commerce Department.

Thomas J. Manton (D-N.Y.), however, proposed the most controversial amendment, which would "deny foreign-owned U.S. based companies from taking part in the bill's program unless the nation of the parent company offered similar programs."[50] Writing in *Congressional Quarterly,* Mike Mills reported that the "sponsors accepted the amendment to appease" John D. Dingell (D-Mich.), who chaired the powerful Commerce Committee and who threatened to "request that the bill be referred to his committee."[51] Dingell used his power to assert an expansive view of his committee's jurisdiction. Referral to his committee would at least slow passage of a prominent element of the president's technology strategy and might have lasting consequences for other technology initiatives.

While accepting the Manton amendment bought peace with Dingell, it brought harsh criticism from the business backers of the bill. Bruce Stokes, the *National Journal's* highly regarded economic reporter, saw the dispute as a clash between a trade perspective that saw technology programs as leverage to open markets and a technology perspective that emphasized cooperative ventures as the best way to speed technology development.[52] The debate over Manton continued throughout the 103rd Congress. Although funding for key technology programs went forward, the broader authority in the proposed National Competitiveness Act died with the end of the 103rd Congress. After the Republican victories in the 1994 election, the congressional supporters of technology policy succeeded in maintaining funding for the Manufacturing Extension Partnership and the Advanced Technology Program, but they had shifted to the defense of existing programs rather than attempting to resurrect the National Competitiveness Act.

The National Information Infrastructure

During the 1992 campaign, Clinton and Gore had initially envisioned the federal government constructing an information highway, much as it had built the national interstate highway system starting in the Eisenhower administration. After the election, the administration adopted a different role whereby the government promoted private-sector investment through tax incentives and regulatory policies.

To coordinate the administration's efforts, the president established the interagency National Information Infrastructure [NII] Task Force, to be chaired by Commerce Secretary Ronald H. Brown. The Commerce Department acted as the secretariat for the task force, and its key agencies and personnel were involved.[53] From the start, the initiative had the backing of the White House, with the vice president playing an active and prominent role.

On the research side, the NII built on and complemented the High Performance Computing and Communications (HPCC) program that had been established by President Bush. The HPCC was one of several initiatives that brought together the related research efforts of several departments (see chapter 6). The Clinton administration not only continued support for the HPCC but, in anticipation of its broader NII initiative, also added an Information Infrastructure Technology and Applications component to it.

Central to the vision of the NII was the deregulation of the domestic telecommunications system. In a 1984 antitrust ruling, Judge Harold Green had started the process by breaking up American Telephone & Telegraph into a long-distance company, several local telephone companies, and a separate manufacturing company. The famous Bell Labs continued to be part of the manufacturing arm, which was renamed Lucent, but gradually shifted its focus toward more applied research. The Regional Bell Operating Companies supported a separate research arm.

Since Judge Green's ruling, technology had continued to race ahead. Cable and power companies were laying the fiber-optic cable that would allow them to enter the telecommunications market. Satellites provided a third alternative, and the development of wireless technology created additional competitors. For several years, Congress had wrestled with developing its own set of rules to help govern a rapidly evolving market that now saw the convergence of formerly distinct industries, some regulated, some not.

By September 1993, the Clinton administration had settled on a strategy that assigned "to the private sector the lead role in developing and deploying the NII."[54] The administration looked to the elimination of regulatory hurdles and further deregulation as spurring competition that would drive rapid development of the NII. Congress was faced with a series of legislative proposals and caught in the crosscurrents of multiple interests ranging from the computer industry to the concerns of local government. Although the administration moved forward with several programs that supported the goals of the NII, reform of the telecommunications industry was delayed until January 1996.

The Continuing Debate over Industrial Policy

Most members of the Clinton economic and technology team had lived through the 1980s debates over industrial policy. They had seen the failures of various industrial policy proposals to gain political acceptance. The debate had also focused their attention on the myriad ways that the governments worked to stimulate industries. They had been impressed by the success of Sematech—the partnership between the Department of Defense and the leading American producers of semiconductors. In particular, they saw the joint effort as having significantly strengthened the semiconductor supplier chain, which included many small firms in the equipment and materials field. Some of them took strategic trade seriously and feared that Japan was proving more adept at the game than others. Most saw science, innovation, and the commercialization of technology as critical to long-term productivity and income growth.

Many opponents of industrial policy held their views with ideological certainty. For them, the government should never intervene in the market, while for others the government should not provide subsidies or corporate welfare to companies with ample profits. There were tensions in the Clinton administration as well. With his eye on the debate over welfare reform, Secretary of Labor Robert Reich leveled some harsh criticism at "corporate welfare." He was met, however, with swift and public disagreement by Secretaries Brown and Bentsen. Brown, for instance, saw Reich's remarks as undercutting his efforts to preserve funding for the Advanced Technology Program.

For the most part, however, the Clinton economic, trade, and technology teams came to office with a pragmatic view. In general, support for industry was focused on cases of market failure (e.g., the development of risky technologies) or the development of public goods. But there was also a shared sense that the United States was moving and would continue to move in the direction of high-technology industries. Few members of the economic team and none on the technology team were content with a traditional view of comparative advantage that depended on relatively fixed endowments. As John Young once put it, the question was not trading British cloth for Portuguese wine (the classic case cited by the nineteenth-century economist David Hume) but how to develop a comparative advantage in producing a video camera.

At the time, there was also a concern that America's highly segmented electronics industry was at a potential disadvantage when facing the large, vertically integrated Japanese companies and the closer corporate networks that characterized Japanese industry in the 1980s. Most worried about the future of high-technology industries such as semiconductors that provided the base for civilian industries as well as key weapon systems.

Despite the success of Sematech in strengthening the supplier chain for semiconductors, some critical links in the chain still had very few domestic suppliers. This was particularly true of the industry that made steppers—the machines that print the circuits on a silicon wafer. By 1993, there were two leading-edge manufacturers of steppers—GCA, a division of General Signal, and Silicon Valley Group Lithography—selling advanced tools to the merchant (or general) market. A third company, Ultratech, was successful but produced "non-leading-edge tools."[55] IBM also produced steppers, but only for its own use.

In January 1993, General Signal announced its intention to close its semiconductor operations, including GCA. Considerable federal money had been invested in technologies that were at risk because of the real possibility of financial failure. Losing another supplier would make American companies even more dependent on Japanese stepper manufacturers, which were closely aligned with the U.S. firms' principal competitors in the semiconductor market. The national energy laboratories that periodically purchased steppers for their own use faced the same risk of growing dependency.

On May 21, 1993, GCA ceased operations and closed its doors. Career civil servants in the Commerce, Energy, and Defense Departments and in the intelligence community feared the loss of the critical technology for manufacturing steppers. The Clinton team was also concerned and prepared to act. Four days after the closure of GCA, the National Economic Council organized a conference call with John Gibbons, the president's science and technology adviser; Laura Tyson, chair of the Council of Economic Advisers; and the "[chief executives] of various semiconductor firms." Gibbons and Tyson were exploring the possibility of a "purchase of GCA by the private sector."[56] On June 23, 1993, at the request of the National Security Agency, the Department of Commerce hosted an interagency meeting to discuss a possible sale of GCA. The next day, Bowman Cutter, deputy director of the NEC, and Tom Kalil (who followed technology matters on the NEC staff) announced a July 1 meeting of a "working group on U.S. competitiveness" that would report to the Deputies Committee on Science on Technology.[57]

What they found, however, was that the vehicles for supporting industry —even in the interest of national defense—had atrophied from a lack of interest and lack of use. Expected government demand for steppers was far too limited to assure the commercial viability of the firm even if the energy and other federal laboratories had been willing to concentrate their purchases on a single source. They then turned to seeking a corporate partner with an interest in preserving some competition in the supplier industry. The vice president himself made a call, but there were no takers. General Signal set early December as the date for auctioning off GCA's equipment. In late November, the Department of Defense asked for Commerce's help in delaying the auction.[58] In response, Mary Lowe Good, Commerce's undersecretary for technology, wrote asking Allied Signal to delay the auction for thirty to sixty days—to no avail.[59] A flurry of activity had not met with success but had highlighted the limited tools in the government's hands. (For more on the stepper case, see chapter 15.)

If saving an individual stepper company proved difficult, the government faced an even greater challenge in the field of flat-panel displays. Although flat-panel digital displays had been invented in the United States, the Japanese had taken the lead in what was then the most widely used technology, active-matrix liquid-crystal displays. The lack of an American presence had begun to worry the Pentagon. Flat panels were finding their way into cockpit and tank displays. Some strategists already saw individual flat panels in a soldier's helmet that would display real-time changes in the battlefield via overhead satellites. The United States did have a strong presence in flat-panel technologies. In some alternative flat-panel technologies, there was even a U.S. manufacturing presence. To encourage a domestic source of supply for active-matrix liquid-crystal displays, the Pentagon was supporting a single company. Because the production run was limited, the domestically produced panels were expensive and there was none of the constant innovation that characterized other parts of the electronics industry.

Why not go overseas? Aside from the general preference for at least some domestic supply, flat panels posed a particular problem. At the time, the principal supplier of the active-matrix liquid-crystal display flat panels was Sharp, a major Japanese electronics firm with more than 50 percent of the world market. The Japanese Constitution included a prohibition on the Japanese engaging in the export of arms. Sharp, not the Japanese government, had a particularly restrictive interpretation of the Japanese Constitution. As a result, they would not sell their flat-panel displays directly to the Defense Department, nor would they customize panels for prime defense contractors.

The leader of the flat-panel-display initiative was Kenneth Flamm, an MIT-educated economist who had come to the Defense Department by way of the Brookings Institution. At Brookings, Flamm had specialized in the economics of high-technology industries with a particular focus on electronics and computers—industries for which the government market or government research had been important at critical junctures in their development.[60] At the Defense Department, Flamm was the senior deputy assistant secretary for international and dual use (civilian and military) programs, as well as a special assistant to Undersecretary John Deutsch.

With the support of the NEC, Flamm headed an interagency task force to develop an administration-wide strategy to create a globally competitive flat-panel display industry. Flamm and his team developed a comprehensive approach that looked across the entire government for research and policy support. For instance, they hoped that the Commerce Department would provide needed export assistance as new companies sought global markets.

Flamm was constrained in his efforts by everything from the budget deficit to the global trading rules that limit industrial subsidies. The just-concluded Uruguay Round of trade negotiations had essentially precluded subsidies for industrial production while still permitting subsidies for R&D. In the end, Flamm crafted a clever plan that concentrated on subsidies for second-generation research. To qualify for the research funds, however, a company already would have to be producing flat panels. The hope was that the research carrot—all within the global trading rules—would be enough to bring an American flat-panel display industry to life. Then Flamm was hit by a congressional attack on industrial policy. Senator John Danforth (R-Mo.) was particularly vehement (he had also opposed the National Competitive-ness Act on anti-industrial-policy grounds) in opposition until he was per-suaded that there was a legitimate national security rationale for the program. The Flamm initiative has stimulated the development of new technologies but has not yet succeeded in creating a vibrant, United States–based active-matrix liquid-crystal display industry. It may, however, have accelerated the entry of other, overseas suppliers such as South Korea, Taiwan, and, more recently, China. The United States remains dependent on imports but at least now has a number of suppliers from several exporting countries.

In its first two years, the Clinton administration's technology policy met with some clear success as well as some serious obstacles. It continued to emphasize technology as a key element in economic policy and to recog-nize that trade, education, and macroeconomic policy were also important elements in an effective technology policy. In pursuing technology policy, the administration delineated more clearly the emerging New Growth Compact between government and the private sector. On paper and in prac-tice, the administration was learning how to form effective public–private partnerships. More and more key administration figures were developing a deeper understanding of technology and becoming more adept at explain-ing the everyday impact of new technologies. In effect, they were beginning to take technology out of the laboratory and make it part of those discussions that take place around the kitchen table.

Education, Training, and Lifelong Learning

In his 1992 campaign, Clinton made education and training key elements in his long-term competitiveness strategy for the country. In *Putting People First* and again in "Technology: The Engine of Economic Growth," Clin-ton stressed the importance of education and training. To put his priorities into practice, Clinton and his White House team expected close collaboration between Education Secretary Riley and Labor Secretary Reich. As South Carolina's governor, Riley had worked hard to improve the quality of education in his own state. In his 1991 *The Work of Nations,* Reich had stressed that a country's people were its ultimate source of comparative advantage.[61] Clinton had drawn on Reich's ideas in developing his 1992 campaign strategy. Reich had also played a key role in leading the Clinton transition team on economic policy. Now he had the opportunity to put some of his ideas into practice.

The Department of Labor had broad responsibility for the American worker, including workplace safety, insurance for private pensions, and an array of training programs. The department's training efforts, however, were largely focused on dislocated workers—unemployed workers caught with outdated skills in declining industries. Reich had a much broader vision for the department. He wanted to help prepare the American workforce for the new realities of global competition and rapid technical change.

As American companies sought to respond to international competition, many of them adopted and adapted the Japanese approach to manufacturing —often referred to as lean production or the high-performance workplace. In place of the traditional assembly line, the high-performance system gave workers more responsibility but also demanded higher skills. It was part of the American effort to respond to the Japanese system, which found that giving workers more discretion, responsibility, and training allowed them to build quality into the product while it was being made rather than attempting to correct mistakes at the end of the assembly line. American companies also began to emphasize lifelong training as a way of combining high skills with a flexible workforce that could move from one process or product to the next.

Reich saw the high-performance workplace as offering a win–win situation that could appeal to unions and businesses alike. Higher skills meant higher pay and more job security for the workers. Along with higher skills also came better quality and more rapid innovation—critical to company profitability and even survival. Reich wanted the practice to spread.

As a way of promoting the high-performance workplace, Reich enlisted the collaboration of Secretary of Commerce Brown. The Commerce and Labor Departments worked together to organize a conference that would explain and promote the concept of the high-performance workplace. On July 26, 1993, a wide array of large and small businesses, unions, and academic specialists gathered in Chicago for an all-day Conference on the

Future of the American Workplace. In addition to Reich and Brown, President Clinton not only came but also moderated one of the sessions. Just before the conference, Reich had established the Office of the American Workplace in the Department of Labor. Although the office had a limited budget and only a few staff members, it set about promoting the benefits of the high-performance workplace. The office was another good example of how the administration would use a kind of targeted bully pulpit to promote a New Growth Compact that saw business, labor, and government as effective partners in achieving long-term growth and greater opportunity.

In the end, the office had not only a limited budget but a limited life. It was one of the early casualties of the Republican Congress that took power in January 1995. The office became a double target—it was a Clinton administration initiative and it brought the government closer to working with the private sector. It finally closed its doors in July 1996.[62]

No single department was responsible for all the elements of a lifelong learning strategy. The Department of Health and Human Services was responsible for programs targeted at prenatal and early postnatal care. Health and Human Services also managed the Head Start program that provided early childhood education for millions of children living in families with incomes that fell below the national poverty line. In terms of the federal role, elementary and secondary education was largely the province of Riley's Department of Education. Although the federal role had grown slightly since 1989, it was still severely limited in financial terms, accounting for about 6.8 cents of every dollar spent in America's public elementary and secondary schools.[63] It was local and increasingly state governments that were the dominant funders of elementary, middle, and high schools. Worker training was largely the province of the Department of Labor but was targeted toward the unemployed. There was little provision for upgrading the skills of the still employed. College or postsecondary education was again the province of the Department of Education. To some extent, the Treasury Department was also involved in lifelong learning through key provisions of the tax code.

President Clinton and his team found a system for lifelong learning that was underfunded and ill equipped for a rapidly changing economy that was facing stiff global competition. In the first two years of his presidency, Clinton and various departments moved on both fronts. The early focus on deficit reduction and the congressionally imposed caps on domestic spending limited what could be done to increase funding. This was the pressure on "investments" that so frustrated the president and much of his team. They did succeed in securing added funding for Head Start, which provides health services, nutrition, and education for many children up to the age of five years. As a result of bipartisan support, funding for Head Start had more than doubled between 1989 and 1995.[64] Yet even with the added funding secured by the Clinton administration, only 40 percent of eligible families were being served by the end of 1995.

There was greater flexibility in redesigning programs or creating new programs that were catalytic in nature. The Clinton administration took both approaches. As governor of Arkansas, Clinton had fought a major political battle to require higher standards for teachers and schools. He had worked closely with President Bush and the National Governors Association to establish long-term goals for American education at the 1989 Charlottesville Summit. Early in his presidential administration, Clinton sought to enshrine these goals in legislation that would also provide funding to help states and school districts set and implement higher standards. There were eight goals that ranged from higher graduation rates to adult literacy. Improved performance in mathematics and science was one of the most visible goals carried forward from the work with President Bush. The Bush administration and the governors had set the bar high—America's children were to be first in the world in math and science by 2000. The United States had a long way to go.

In 1994, Congress passed the Goals 2000: Educate America Act to help states set and implement higher standards. The states were clearly ready to act. "In the first round of grants, every state but two applied for funding to support statewide systemic reform efforts as well as promising local initiatives."[65]

The bulk of federal spending on elementary and secondary schools is made up of grants to local schools to provide added educational resources to disadvantaged students. When Congress reauthorized the Education and Secondary Schools Act of 1965, there was an attempt to complement the move to higher standards.[66] For instance, the act now allowed state governments to intervene in failing schools and provided federal support for new experiments such as charter schools.

The administration took definite albeit limited steps to improve the world of training. The first step was to borrow the general idea of the German apprenticeship system and adapt it to American conditions while keeping within the limitations imposed by the budget. Under the School-to-Work Opportunities Act of 1994, the federal government would "act as a catalyst, providing venture capital to States for the development and implementation of school-to-work systems."[67]

There were also some early attempts to improve the opportunities of the incumbent work force. The Goals 2000 Educate America Act included a provision for the development of voluntary national skill standards. The administration envisioned a collaborative effort of "businesses [working] with labor, educators, human resource professionals, and community leaders" to identify and certify "higher-wage skills."[68] With a certificate to indicate acquired skills, the worker would have greater opportunity and more mobility. The certificate would also improve the ability of an employer to judge the skills of a prospective employee.

Reich sought a similar kind of flexibility in his proposed Reemployment Act of 1994.[69] In place of an existing set of categorical (or narrowly targeted) programs, he proposed a comprehensive program that would apply to all workers who lost their jobs. As in many other administration programs, Reich proposed working closely with business and unions so that the government would be "investing in putting people where the jobs are."[70]

During his presidential campaign, Clinton had proposed offering college scholarships to students who served the country by "addressing the nation's unmet human, education, environmental and public safety needs."[71] As a civilian version of the highly successful GI Bill, the National Service program was part of Clinton's broader emphasis on rights and responsibilities. It was also a first step toward making college education more accessible. For more than a decade, the cost of a college education had been increasing steadily, rising 70 percent for two-year colleges and 86 percent for four-year institutions. At the same time, "the maximum value Pell grant, the primary federal grant program for low-income students, fell by more than 25 percent."[72] National Service was a relatively small step in improving opportunities for a college education. It did, however, presage more serious attempts to come.

With the administration's emphasis on technology and technology policy, it is not surprising to see it proposing the application of technology to the challenge of educational reform. In developing and deploying technologies to the schools, the administration again acted as a catalyst. In the case of the national information superhighway, the administration challenged the private sector to link public schools to the Internet. The president and the vice president used their bully pulpits and high-visibility participation in so-called Net days to leverage millions of dollars in private investment.

The same kind of philosophy was evident in their development of the Technology Learning Challenge.[73] The new program provided "challenge grants to partnerships of schools, colleges and the private sector for the development and demonstration of educational technology."[74] The program was designed with the idea of stimulating voluntary, community-based efforts and leveraging private-sector investment with modest public-sector grants.

In interagency deliberations on the program, the vice president was frequently quoted as thinking in terms of the story about Dumbo the flying elephant and his magic feather. In the story made famous by Walt Disney, Dumbo's large ears gave him the capacity for flight but not the confidence to try. Only when his circus mouse friend gives him a "magic feather" does Dumbo take the plunge. Part way through his flight, Dumbo drops the magic feather but finds he can fly anyway. With only modest funding available, the vice president knew that few would be chosen from the many seeking grants. He hoped, however, that many communities—having formed partnerships to seek grants—would find they could fly without the magic feather of a federal stipend. Many did.

The administration was also successful in attracting considerable private resources to match federal funding. In the first year of operations (1995), there were 500 proposals for the 19 grants awarded. The $10 million in grants in turn leveraged some "$70 million in private sector contributions in the first year."[75]

The development of the Technology Learning Challenge also adopted the president's approach of looking across separate agencies to construct a coherent whole. Much of the day-to-day impetus for the program came from Paul Dimond, who served on the National Economic Council. From the start, Dimond and the NEC went beyond the Departments of Education and Labor to include representatives from the Departments of Commerce and Defense. Commerce had an interest in the development and deployment of technologies in general and also had a closer relationship with prospective partners in the private sector. By a substantial margin, Defense had the most government experience in developing and using learning technologies.

The NEC also played an integrating role on the broader questions of linking education and training to projected job trends in the American economy. Early in the administration, deputy NEC director Bowman Cutter pulled together an interagency group to further develop the administration's competitiveness strategy and assess the prospects for future job creation. The group included representatives from the major economic agencies and the White House. In general, they shared the view that the economy would continue to demand higher skills and that an administration emphasis on education and training would increase growth, improve opportunity, and reduce the growing disparities of income that were often associated with levels of education. Cutter and his key aide, Bonnie Dean, also helped build a network and a shared consensus on policy and problems across the entire administration. Many of the same group worked on subsequent administration initiatives, including the Technology Learning Challenge.

In its first two years, the Clinton administration took a number of steps to make investing in people a series of policies rather than just promises. In developing specific policies, the administration generally put government programs in the broader context of a national economy that was heavily influenced by activist governors and even more by a dynamic, rapidly changing private sector. In the field of lifelong learning, the Clinton administration was working to define the outlines of the evolving New Growth Compact between the public and private sectors. Some initiatives were designed to leverage or foster private investment. Many were catalytic in nature—linking the bully pulpit or federal leadership to state, local, and private action. In some cases, the federal government was looking to forge public–private partnerships as part of a developing Partnership Nation that was becoming a force in other aspects of economic policy.

International Trade: Growth, Innovation, and Better Jobs

As part of his campaign, Clinton advocated an aggressive trade policy that was very much part of his overall competitiveness strategy. In his principal campaign document, *Putting People First,* he supported ratification of the North American Free Trade Agreement (NAFTA) negotiated by the Bush administration. He pledged to complete the Uruguay Round of multilateral trade negotiations in a way that opened markets for U.S. industry and agriculture, protected intellectual property rights, and preserved American laws on health, safety, and the environment.[76] Clinton also promised an aggressive effort to open individual markets that kept American "farmers, workers and businesses from selling products abroad and creating jobs at home."[77] Clinton was promising a three-pronged approach that stressed multilateral, regional, and bilateral agreements.

The Clinton administration did not pursue trade policy in isolation. Particularly during Clinton's first term, trade was linked to an overall competitiveness strategy in which the separate elements complemented each other. In the *Putting People First* chapter on trade, Clinton included provisions on training, incentives to strengthen manufacturing, and a strong commitment to the development of civilian technology.

Open trade had been an article of economic faith for most of the post–World War II era, with intellectual and editorial opinion firmly in favor of open markets. An open trade policy also fit nicely with Clinton's efforts to bring the high-technology business community into the Democratic coalition. For high-technology industry, global markets were an essential element in their thinking. When Ira Shapiro, advising the Clinton campaign, suggested the campaign slogan "compete not retreat," he not only encapsulated Clinton's policy but also captured much of the American spirit. Shapiro, a Washington lawyer and former Capitol Hill staff director, went on to serve at the Office of the U.S. Trade Representative, where he earned the rank of ambassador.

Not all parts of Clinton's coalition shared his enthusiasm for open trade. Organized labor, environmental activists, and some human rights advocates were expressing reservations about new trade agreements, ranging from growing concern to outright hostility. Organized labor was most adamant about slowing the rush to further market opening. In particular, the industrial unions opposed NAFTA as a direct threat to their jobs either through imports or by the shift of United States–based production to Mexico.

If NAFTA was new, the challenge posed by Mexico was not. During the 1970s and 1980s, more and more companies had established assembly plants on the Mexican side of the U.S. border, known as maquiladoras. Labor linked the growing U.S. presence in Mexico to a provision of U.S. tax law that limited the duty American companies paid on imports from the Mexican assembly plants. (The value of U.S. parts included in the Mexican product was not subject to a tariff when exported back to the United States.) In labor's view, NAFTA posed an even greater threat.

While maintaining a commitment to open trade, NAFTA, and the completion of the Uruguay Round, Clinton attempted to respond to the concerns of labor, environmentalists, and human rights advocates. He conditioned his support for NAFTA on "adequate protections for workers, farmers, and the environment on both sides of the border."[78] He promised the leadership necessary to complete the Uruguay Round of trade negotiations but also stressed that they would raise rather than lower standards for the environment. For human rights activists, candidate Clinton criticized the Bush administration for extending most-favored-nation (now referred to as "normal trading relations") status to China "before it achieved documented progress on human rights."[79] While President Clinton did speak out on human rights, he and his administration continued to support most-favored-nation status for China.

In addition to political motives, Clinton had strong economic reasons for supporting open trade. Opposition to trade would have made it difficult if not impossible for Clinton to have forged an understanding on macroeconomic policy with Federal Reserve chairman Greenspan. International trade also added a powerful force for competition to the American economy. During the preceding decade, the deregulation of transportation, telecommunications, and the energy industries had introduced competition to three major sectors of the economy. The more rapid pace of innovation was adding even more new competitors. Together, trade, deregulation, and technology made it more difficult for companies to raise prices. That added check on inflation made it all the easier for Greenspan to keep interest rates low.

The combination of opening new markets and promoting exports offered Clinton an alternative way of stimulating the economy, raising productivity, and generating new jobs. Trade could easily be a more effective engine of short-term growth than the unsuccessful $16 billion stimulus package.

In its first two years, the Clinton administration took several important steps on trade. From the start, the administration adopted "an aggressive approach at opening foreign markets through negotiating multilaterally, plurilaterally and bilaterally."[80] The first challenge and opportunity was regional—NAFTA, which Congress finally approved, after an intense legislative struggle.

The administration took other steps to strengthen regional economic ties. It built on NAFTA to start laying the basis for a Free Trade Area of the Americas. In Asia, it worked to move the Asia-Pacific Economic Cooperation coalition from a forum focused on discussion to a body that would help lower tariffs and open markets in much of the Pacific basin.

The Clinton administration completed the Uruguay Round of trade negotiations that had started under President Reagan. Even with a Democratic Congress, the agreement did not meet with immediate approval. Several aspects of the agreement proved controversial. There were, for instance, serious reservations about a provision that would severely limit the ability of the United States to use trade sanctions as a way of securing market opening or enforcing agreements. The Uruguay Round agreement also included provisions for a World Trade Organization with enhanced enforcement powers. The combination led to inevitable questions about the erosion of U.S. sovereignty. With a largely open U.S. market, few economic interests were being exposed to a major increase in competition. The major exception was the textile and apparel industry. For years, country quotas established under the Multi-Fiber Arrangement (MFA) had governed apparel imports. The Uruguay Round agreements provided for the phasing out of these quotas and the MFA itself over a number of years. Not surprisingly, representatives and senators from major textile and apparel producing states raised strenuous objections.

The Uruguay Round agreements did eventually pass, but not until a lame duck congressional session after the 1994 congressional elections. The administration and the Democratic Congress had missed another opportunity to demonstrate progress on the economic front that could have partially offset the impact of the failed health care effort.

The first year of the Clinton administration put a trade spotlight on Japan. For much of the Clinton economic team, Japan had been the subject of study and concern during most of the 1980s. Shortly after taking office, a small group of senior Clinton administration officials began to develop a more determined approach to trade policy with Japan. It was very much an interagency effort, with representatives from the key economic agencies joining White House officials and representatives from the Office of the U.S. Trade Representative. The group faced two separate but related problems. By 1993, Japan's current account surplus had reached $125 billion a year.[81] At $50 billion a year, the U.S. trade deficit with Japan made up a significant portion of the Japanese surplus. Open markets coupled with faster Japanese growth would reduce their surplus and stimulate growth in the United States, Europe, and other parts of the world. Faster Japanese growth and increased U.S. exports also looked like an ideal way to boost the slowly growing U.S. economy while focusing on deficit reduction.

The Clinton Japan team was intent on opening Japanese markets to industries where the United States had a clear competitive advantage. Old allies like organized labor and potential allies in the high-technology community also wanted access to the Japanese market. Past experience suggested that traditional trade agreements would not work. Instead, the team pressed for results-oriented trade. At one point, the United States called for a series of numerical targets coupled with the threat of retaliation if the Japanese did not meet them.[82]

The United States did not, however, succeed in securing a series of results-oriented agreements or markedly influence the course of Japanese macroeconomic policy. There were times when Japan did stimulate its economy, but this was largely in response to domestic political and economic pressures rather than in response to the United States or the larger world community. The United States would continue to press trade disputes directly with Japan and in the dispute-settlement mechanism of the World Trade

Organization. The battle goes on, but the war has largely shifted to other fronts. A decade of stagnation in Japan and a decade of prosperity in the United States have muted popular concern over continued Japanese strengths in manufacturing, still-widespread barriers to trade and investment, and the slow pace of overall deregulation. The emergence of the information age has played to American strengths in flexibility and technology. Japan's more consensus-oriented society has been slower to adapt. However, in fields where innovation is a bit slower and the emphasis is on manufacturing quality, Japan still sets the standard.[83]

The Clinton team was aggressive and effective in promoting exports. In previous administrations, the commerce secretary had eventually clashed with the U.S. trade representative over trade priorities and trade strategy. Brown, however, did not attempt to supplant the role of the trade representative. Instead, he took the export promotion ball and ran with it.[84] His emphasis on exports came at a particularly propitious time. Recent legislation had made the secretary of commerce chair of the Trade Promotion Coordinating Committee (TPCC), which was composed of the nineteen departments or agencies with an interest in export promotion and thus gave Brown a vehicle to assert leadership over the entire U.S. export apparatus.[85]

Brown's and the administration's export initiatives made both economic and political sense. When Clinton entered office in January 1993, a slow recovery had left many workers unemployed and much industrial capacity underutilized. In these circumstances, additional exports should translate into new jobs. New export-related jobs would probably be concentrated in manufacturing—where organized labor still held considerable strengths. Export-oriented or internationally based industries—such as aircraft, automobiles, heavy equipment, and farm implements—were heavily unionized.

In talking about success in economics or politics, Brown often quoted Wayne Gretzky, the Canadian hockey star. The secret of success in hockey, according to Gretzky, was being where the puck was going to be. Brown applied the Gretzky philosophy to exports by focusing on parts of the world where rapid growth created opportunities and where foreign government policies made U.S. government support most helpful to American exporters. To Brown, that meant the rapidly developing economies that would need to invest hundreds of billions of dollars in infrastructure, power plants, and modern telecommunications—fields in which the United States had a strong competitive advantage. In much of the developing world, government departments and public funds still played a major role in infrastructure development. America's principal commercial rivals had been effective over the years in winning major contracts through the use of government-to-government contacts. At times, competing governments linked foreign assistance or other public policies to major export contracts. There were also frequent allegations that foreign-based private competitors had used bribes and other inducements to land a major contract—practices that were illegal under U.S. law.

From the start of his tenure, Brown worked to make the TPCC an action-oriented committee. Paul Rosenberg, the lead trade staff member in Brown's policy office, threw himself into the job of developing an interagency strategy to boost America's export performance. Under the title *National Export Strategy,* the first TPCC report spelled out Brown's broader vision and indicated the steps that the Commerce Department and other agencies were taking to achieve it.[86]

To translate his vision into programmatic terms, Brown brought in Jeffrey Garten to be his undersecretary for international trade. Garten was part of Peter Peterson's Blackstone investment group in New York and also taught international economics at Columbia University. (He stepped down from serving as dean of the Yale University School of Organization and Management in 2004.) At the International Trade Administration, Garten could call on his very able and widely experienced career deputy Timothy Hauser. Garten also persuaded Brown to add a second deputy to focus on Brown's export priorities. To fill that slot, Garten tapped David Rothkopf. Like Garten a New Yorker, Rothkopf had been the executive director of an organization of major corporate chief executives. In addition to running the organization and editing its publication, Rothkopf also organized overseas trips for his chief executive members.

Garten and Rothkopf used Brown's vision and his version of the Gretzky philosophy to design the Big Emerging Markets (BEMs) program.[87] The BEMs encompassed ten major emerging markets that held out the prospect of billions of dollars in sales for United States–based firms. The BEMs were intended to focus departmental resources and highlighted the determination of Brown and the president to support private efforts to improve U.S. standing in international competition.

Early in his tenure, Brown also led the first of several high-profile overseas trade missions. Brown was intent on helping to boost U.S. exports and on showing visible results. He focused on inviting businesses with pending contracts at a point where a boost from Brown or the president might help the company seal an agreement. In addition, Brown sought to include some small business chief executives on every mission. Encouraging diversity at the department was also a major priority for the secretary. Progress on diversity was added as a mandatory element to the annual job performance appraisal of every political appointee. Brown applied the same philosophy to the trade missions and sought to include chief executives from diverse backgrounds.[88]

By a number of measures, the trade missions were a success. In strictly economic terms, Brown announced multi-billion-dollar results that would support thousands of jobs, strengthen a number of major U.S. companies, and help build a more competitive economy. The missions were also effective in building bridges to the corporate community. They were one of many ways the president could say he was delivering on the technology policy he had developed with the Silicon Valley chief executives. When the new Republican Congress sought to eliminate the Department of Commerce in 1995 and 1996, major American companies became critical allies in a successful effort to maintain the department's mission and institutional existence.

The trade area had long lent itself to close consultation and collaboration with individual businesses. In developing the TPCC agenda, Brown was also active in "developing new partnerships with the private sector." Trade, like the other elements of the national competitiveness strategy, was also helping construct the Partnership Nation.[89]

Export Controls

As part of its effort to contain the influence and limit the power of the Soviet Union, the United States and its allies sought to limit the export of strategic materials and products to the Soviet Union and its allies. The effort led to the formation of the Coordinating Council for Multilateral Export Controls (COCOM), which included all the NATO members (except Iceland) and Japan. Through COCOM, the allies agreed to limit the export of civilian items that could strengthen the military base of the Soviet Union as well as actual weapons of war.

By the time Clinton took office, however, the military and economic landscape was very different. Although COCOM ended in 1993, not long after the end of the Cold War, the U.S. export control regime was still very much in place. Especially in the realm of computers, export controls usually lagged well behind the pace of innovation. In 1993, the degree of control was based on the speed with which chips could perform specific calculations. The pace of change was so rapid that items would become readily available in retail outlets while still being subject to cumbersome export-licensing requirements. Unless the speed bar for exports was raised, the Department of Commerce was facing the prospect of a flood of export licenses covering what had become everyday technologies.

As part of his strategies for technology, exports, and overall competitiveness, Clinton moved dramatically to raise the speed of computers eligible for normal export. The shift on export controls was partly a product of different economic and political circumstances. But it also fit the Clinton administration's broader philosophy of a regulatory regime that could support industry and kept pace with change. It was yet another step toward building the New Growth Compact.

Health Care

At least initially, there was an economic as well as social welfare interest in health care. When Clinton took office in January 1993, the United States spent more than 12 percent of its gross domestic product (GDP) on health care, considerably more than Germany or Japan. The spending gap was even wider on a per person basis because the United States had a considerably higher per capita GDP. Yet, despite the much higher level of spending, other industrial countries seemed to have superior results, at least in terms of access, universal coverage, life expectancy, infant mortality, and other similar measures. Initially, Clinton saw the possibility of achieving universal care and, at the same time, freeing up funds for deficit reduction, public and private investment, and higher wages.

The details of the Clinton health security proposal have already been extensively discussed in a number of volumes.[90] It is a subject well beyond the scope of the present book. Yet it should be noted that in approaching health care, the administration sought to blend the broader use of markets and competition with more traditional government controls. As part of the plan, there was also an active effort to forge an effective partnership with a number of industries. In that sense, the administration was seeking to adapt its approach to a growth strategy to the arena of health care.

The First Two Years

In his 1992 campaign, President Clinton articulated a comprehensive competitiveness strategy that focused on public and private investment as the key to long-term national prosperity. He had some notable successes in his first two years—deficit reduction, the effective working relationship with

Greenspan and the Federal Reserve, and the passage of NAFTA. And there was a host of other less publicly acclaimed achievements in everything from technology to training. Clinton's policies contributed to improved growth and reduced unemployment.

There were also clear failures in the first two years. Despite Democratic majorities in both houses, the president was unable to secure a vote on his health security proposal in either the House or the Senate. Less attention is paid to a number of other important economic initiatives. Democratic barons in the House and Senate played a significant role in preventing enactment of the proposed Competitiveness Act (focused on civilian technology), telecommunications reform, and the implementing legislation for the Uruguay Round. Nor was Reich successful in securing passage of his proposal to combine several training programs into a separate GI Bill for workers. Perhaps nothing could have overcome the health care defeat. But if these three or four bills had become law, the president could have pointed to added progress on his path to stimulating long-term prosperity and economic strength. There would have been less visible gridlock and more concrete accomplishments.

By the election of 1994, an impatient public seemed to focus more on the failures than the gains. Clinton and the Democratic Congress were about to be caught in a popular tide that swept Congress into Republican hands and left the president struggling to redefine his strategy and role.

Notes

1. Bill Clinton and Al Gore, *Putting People First: How We Can All Change America* (New York: Times Books, 1992); Clinton and Gore, "Manufacturing for the 21st Century: Turning Ideas into Jobs," National Campaign Headquarters, Little Rock, September 8, 1992; and Clinton and Gore, "Technology: The Engine of Economic Growth —A National Technology Policy for America," National Campaign Headquarters, Little Rock, September 18, 1992.

2. Council of Economic Advisers, *1994 Economic Report of the President* (Washington, D.C.: U.S. Government Printing Office, 1994), 4.

3. Council of Economic Advisers, *1994 Economic Report of the President*, 31–48.

4. Council of Economic Advisers, *1995 Economic Report of the President* (Washington, D.C.: U.S. Government Printing Office, 1995), 6.

5. Council of Economic Advisers, *1995 Economic Report of the President*, 20.

6. Council of Economic Advisers, *1995 Economic Report of the President*, 20.

7. Cuomo Commission on Trade and Competitiveness, *The Cuomo Commission Report* (New York: Simon & Schuster, 1988).

8. Author's interview with Ellis Mottur, November 16, 2001.

9. Laura D'Andrea Tyson, *Who's Bashing Whom? Trade Conflict in High Technology Industries* (Washington, D.C.: Institute for International Economics, 1992). Much of Krugman's thinking on international trade can be found in Paul R. Krugman, *Rethinking International Trade* (Cambridge, Mass.: MIT Press, 1990).

10. Michael L. Dertouzos, Richard K. Lester, Robert M. Solow, and the MIT Commission on Industrial Productivity, *Made in America: Regaining the Productive Edge* (Cambridge, Mass.: MIT Press, 1989). The recommendations can be found in chapter 11, pp. 147–55.

11. Dertouzos et al., *Made in America,* 152.

12. Jack Germond and Jules Witcover, *Mad as Hell: Revolt at the Ballot Box, 1992* (New York: Warner Books, 1993), 432.

13. See, for instance, Thomas Byrne Edsall and Mary D. Edsall, *Chain Reaction: The Impact of Race, Rights, and Taxes on American Politics* (New York: W. W. Norton, 1991).

14. Bob Woodward, *The Agenda: Inside the Clinton White House* (New York: Simon & Schuster, 1994).

15. Woodward, *Agenda,* 114.

16. Woodward, *Agenda,* 140.

17. Kevin Phillips, "The Troubled Soul of Clintonomics," *Washington Post,* June 8, 1994.

18. Woodward, *Agenda,* 70.

19. Martin Walker, *The President We Deserve: His Rise, Falls, and Comebacks* (New York: Crown Publishers, 1996), 169.

20. Walker, *President We Deserve,* 169..

21. Woodward, *Agenda,* 71. The British journalist Martin Walker emphasizes the same meeting in his 1996 biography of the president, *President We Deserve,* 168–69.

22. Walker, *President We Deserve,* 168.

23. Woodward, *Agenda,* 98.

24. Woodward, *Agenda,* 135.

25. As part of the preparation for a poll on popular attitudes on the American economy and how it compared with its major competitors, Geoffrey Garin of Peter D. Hart Research Associates talked with white collar and blue collar focus groups in Denver during September 1991. While most indicated that the deficit was a problem, only one person suggested that it might have something to do with interest rates. The poll was taken by Linda Divall of American Viewpoint and Geoffrey Garin. Results from the poll were published by the Council on Competitiveness, *Looking for Leadership: The Public, Competitiveness and Campaign '92* (Washington, D.C.: Council on Competitiveness, 1991).

26. The August 2, 2000, *Wall Street Journal* reported that in a recent study Robert Reischauer, former director of the Congressional Budget Office, found that increased taxes made up more than 60 percent of Clinton's 1993 deficit reduction plan.

27. Alan B. Blinder, "The Strategy of Clintonomics," photocopy, Council of Economic Advisers, October 1993.

28. Blinder, "Strategy of Clintonomics," 1–2.

29. Blinder, "Strategy of Clintonomics," 2.

30. Blinder, "Strategy of Clintonomics," 2.

31. Blinder, "Strategy of Clintonomics," 3.

32. Phillips, "Troubled Soul of Clintonomics."

33. Council of Economic Advisers, *1995 Economic Report of the President*, 83, 320.

34. Council of Economic Advisers, *1995 Economic Report of the President*, 52–53.

35. William J. Clinton and Albert Gore Jr., *Technology for America's Economic Growth: A New Direction to Building Economic Strength* (Washington, D.C.: U.S. Government Printing Office, 1993).

36. Clinton and Gore, *Technology for America's Economic Growth*, 4.

37. Author's interview with John Young, November 30, 1999.

38. The administration supported the funding already authorized by the Intermodal Surface Transportation Efficiency Act of 1991; see Clinton and Gore, *Technology for America's Economic Growth*, 18.

39. Under then-existing and current laws, one government can apply added or countervailing duties to offset another government's subsidies under specific circumstances. The OSTP was partly concerned that the United States was about to make an international commitment that would undercut the administration's commitment to an active technology policy.

40. June 22, 1993, conference invitation letter from Michael Borrus, codirector of Berkeley Roundtable on International Economics, and Harvey Stern, conference manager, University of California Extension.

41. Richard Bradshaw, memorandum to Ronald H. Brown, secretary of commerce, July 27, 1993.

42. White House, *Technology for Economic Growth: The President's Progress Report* (Washington, D.C.: White House, 1993).

43. William Jefferson Clinton, introductory letter, in White House, *Technology for Economic Growth*.

44. U.S. Department of Commerce, *Commerce ACTS: Advanced Civilian Technology Strategy for Jobs and Economic Growth* (Washington, D.C.: U.S. Government Printing Office, 1993).

45. Introductory letter from Secretary Ronald H. Brown, in U.S. Department of Commerce, *Commerce ACTS*.

46. The text of the National Competitiveness Act of 1993 (HR 820 and companion bills) can be found at http://www.house.gov/science_democrats/legis/lreps103htm.

47. Mike Mills, "Panel Approves Loan Money to Help Firms Compete," *Congressional Quarterly*, May 1, 1993, 1079.

48. Mills, "Panel Approves Loan Money," 1079.

49. Mike Mills, "GOP Filibuster Stalls Competitiveness Bill," *Congressional Quarterly*, March 12, 1994, 594.

50. Mike Mills, "Debate on House Floor Dulls 'Competitiveness' Luster," *Congressional Quarterly*. May 15, 1993, 1220.

51. Mills, "Debate on House Floor," 1220.

52. Bruce Stokes, "Focus: Two Sides of the Competitive Edge," *National Journal*, July 30, 1994.

53. For a more detailed discussion of the Information Infrastructure Task Force structure, see Brian Kahin, "Beyond the National Information Infrastructure Initiative," in *Investing in Innovation: Creating a Research and Innovation Policy That Works*, ed. Lewis M. Branscomb and James H. Keller (Cambridge, Mass.: MIT Press, 1998), 342.

54. White House, *Technology for Economic Growth*, 17.

55. Semiconductor Industry Association, "Report of the Economic and National Security Working Group on Lithography," photocopy, January 1994.

56. Memorandum by Michael Levitt, acting assistant secretary, Office of Legislative and Intergovernmental Affairs, June 20, 1993.

57. Bowman Cutter and Tom Kalil, Memorandum for the Departments of Commerce, Defense and Energy, the Council of Economic Advisers, National Security Council, and the Office of Science and Technology Policy, June 24, 1993.

58. The request came to me as the associate deputy secretary of commerce for competitiveness policy. Memorandum from Kenneth Flamm, principal deputy assistant secretary of defense, "Preservation of GCA Technology," November 24, 1993.

59. Letter from Mary Low Good, undersecretary of commerce for technology, to Stephen W. Nagy, senior vice president, General Signal Corporation, December 1, 1993.

60. Kenneth Flamm, *Targeting the Computer: Government Support and International Competition* (Washington, D.C.: Brookings Institution Press, 1987).

61. Robert B. Reich, *The Work of Nations: Preparing Ourselves for 21st Century Capitalism* (New York: Alfred A. Knopf, 1991).

62. The Department of Labor's Web site carries a brief note on its founding and demise. See http://www.fed.org/rescrib/articles/labor.

63. See http://www.NCES.ed.gov/pubs2003/digest02/ch_2 asp#6.

64. Council of Economic Advisers, *1996 Economic Report of the President* (Washington, D.C.: U.S. Government Printing Office, 1996), 210.

65. Council of Economic Advisers, *1996 Economic Report of the President,* 211.

66. The Improve America's Schools Act included the reauthorization of the Elementary and Secondary Education Act of 1965. See Council of Economic Advisers, *1996 Economic Report of the President,* 212.

67. Council of Economic Advisers, *1996 Economic Report of the President,* 215.

68. U.S. Department of Labor, *Investing in People and Prosperity: A Review of Key Clinton Administration Initiatives to Spur Creation of More and Better Jobs* (Washington, D.C.: U.S. Government Printing Office, 1994), 24.

69. For a brief summary of the act, see U.S. Department of Labor, *Investing in People and Prosperity,* 25.

70. U.S. Department of Labor, *Investing in People and Prosperity,* 25.

71. U.S. Department of Labor, *Investing in People and Prosperity,* 23.

72. Council of Economic Advisers, *1996 Economic Report of the President,* 216.

73. The Learning Technology Challenge was funded under Title III of the Elementary and Secondary Education Act. See Council of Economic Advisers, *1996 Economic Report of the President,* 213.

74. Council of Economic Advisers, *1996 Economic Report of the President,* 213.

75. Council of Economic Advisers, *1996 Economic Report of the President,* 213.

76. Clinton and Gore, *Putting People First,* 156–57.

77. Clinton and Gore, *Putting People First,* 156.

78. Clinton and Gore, *Putting People First,* 156.

79. Clinton and Gore, *Putting People First,* 157.

80. Robert Z. Lawrence, "International Trade Policy in the 1990s," in *American Economic Policy in the 1990s,* ed. Jeffrey A. Frankel and Peter R. Orszag (Cambridge, Mass.: MIT Press, 2002), 285. For Clinton's broad view of trade initiatives, also see Walker, *President We Deserve,* 285–87.

81. Hobart Rowen, "Tossing Aside a Stick Will Help U.S. on Trade," *Washington Post,* June 13, 1993.

82. Lawrence, "International Trade Policy in the 1990s," 304–6.

83. Author's interview with George M. C. Fisher, Chairman of Kodak, June 6, 2000.

84. See Steven A. Holmes, *Ron Brown: An Uncommon Life* (New York: John Wiley & Sons, 2000), 249–50.

85. The TPCC was initially established by President George Bush through an Executive Memorandum. Section 201 of the Export Enhancement Act of 1992 (P.O. 102-429) required the president to establish the TPCC. President Clinton formally did so by Executive Order 12870 on September 30, 1993. The first report under Brown was the product of an extensive and intensive interagency process; see Trade Promotion Coordinating Committee, *Toward a National Export Strategy: U.S. Exports = U.S. Jobs* (Washington, D.C.: U.S. Government Printing Office, 1993).

86. Trade Promotion Coordinating Committee, *National Export Strategy: Report to the United States Congress* (Washington, D.C.: U.S. Government Printing Office, 1993).

87. In his 2000 biography of Ron Brown, Steven Holmes includes a discussion of the development of the BEMs program. See Holmes, *Ron Brown,* 253.

88. Holmes beautifully captures the focus, energy and success Brown brought to a series of high-level trade missions. See Holmes, *Ron Brown,* 258–69.

89. Trade Promotion Coordinating Committee, *National Export Strategy: Report to the United States Congress* (Washington, D.C.: U.S. Government Printing Office, 1994), 8.

90. See, for instance, Theda Skocpal, *Boomerang: Clinton's Health Security Effort and the Turn against Government in U.S. Politics* (New York: W. W. Norton, 1996); David Broder and Haynes Johnson, *The System: The American Way of Politics at the Breaking Point* (Boston: Little, Brown, 1996); and Paul J. Quirk and William Cunion, "Clinton's Domestic Policy: The Lessons of a 'New Democrat,'" in *The Clinton Legacy,* ed. Colin Campbell and Bert A. Rockman (New York: Seven Bridges / Chatham House, 2000), 216–18.

Chapter 12

The Gingrich Revolution
and the Comeback President

The 1994 midterm elections were a stunning defeat for the congressional Democrats. They lost control of the Senate and the House. They had also lost control of the Senate in the Reagan victory of 1980, but the House had been in Democratic hands for four decades. The loss of the Senate was not a total surprise. By the time of the election, many analysts were predicting a Republican Senate. But virtually no one predicted the Democrats would lose the House—let alone by a significant margin.[1]

The one person prepared for victory was the House Republican whip (the number two position in the House Republican leaderships), Newt Gingrich. For years, he had pushed the party to reject its seemingly perpetual minority status. And he did more than talk. Through everything from developing college courses to preparing new candidates, he spread his vision of a conservative opportunity society to replace the welfare state.[2] According to his press secretary, Tony Blankley, Gingrich began planning in the spring of 1994 on the assumption that there would be a Republican House.[3]

As part of his strategy for victory, Gingrich prepared a ten-item *Contract with America* as a way of setting a future agenda and turning a series of local elections into a national referendum on President Bill Clinton and the congressional Democrats.[4] Most Republican sitting members and many candidates signed the contract. Gingrich promised a House vote on every item in the contract in the first hundred days of the next Congress. The first hundred days has become an almost ritual measure of presidential action that harkened back to the first year of Franklin Roosevelt's presidency. But according to Blankley, Gingrich was also thinking "of Napoleon's hundred-day regime when he returned from exile."[5]

Gingrich as Speaker

As speaker of the House, Gingrich moved aggressively to bring power back to the speaker's office. The Watergate "class of 1974" had pulled power away from the House leadership and the committee chairs. Gingrich moved in a very different direction. He often ignored seniority to push loyalists as chairs of major committees. A small circle around the speaker and his office made key decisions on policy and legislative strategy.[6]

Gingrich and his House allies started immediately to turn the contract into actual legislation. On the first day of the new Congress, the House adopted a series of changes in House procedure that had been promised in the contract. By the end of the first hundred days, the Gingrich House had not only voted on all ten items but actually passed most.

Gingrich and the new members of Congress did not share Clinton's vision of an activist government forging a new relationship with the private sector. For many, they were carrying on the Reagan tradition of lower taxes, strong defense, and a government that left business and markets alone. They were not content with a modest reduction in spending or the elimination of a few outmoded programs. Deficit reduction was not just an element in an economic strategy; it was a key tool in dismantling the welfare state and dramatically reducing the powers of the federal government.

The Battle over Deficits

The *Contract with America* did not set a specific timetable for deficit reduction. Instead, the focus was on a balanced budget amendment to the constitution. That measure passed the House and came within a single vote of passing the Senate. Senator Mark Hatfield (R-Ore.) cast the deciding vote against the amendment. After he voted no, several younger Republican members of the Senate wanted to strip Hatfield of his Appropriations Committee chairmanship.[7] How the amendment would have fared in the individual states is not clear. The vote in the Senate, however, was a clear proxy for how many political leaders felt a strong position on deficit reduction was either good for the country or critical for their reelection prospects. In fact, if several Democratic senators had not reversed their pro-amendment votes from the previous Congress, the amendment would have passed and been sent to the states for ratification.

Gingrich was not content, however, with passing a procedural amendment.

After wrestling with the figures, Gingrich and his allies settled on 2002, seven years in the future, as the target date for actually balancing the budget. At the time, the Congressional Budget Office estimated that balancing the budget in seven years would require some $1.2 trillion in spending cuts. In addition, the Republicans were committed to cutting taxes, increasing spending on defense, and leaving Social Security untouched.

The push for a balanced budget amendment and the growing congressional pressure for eliminating the deficit in seven years touched off a heated debate inside the Clinton administration. Dick Morris, the president's outside political consultant, Vice President Gore, and the deputy chief of staff, Erskine Bowles, all favored developing a Clinton deficit reduction plan.[8] The president's chief of staff, Leon Panetta, who was a veteran of Congress, feared the congressional reaction. The deputy chief of staff, Harold Ickes, and the senior policy adviser, George Stephanopolous, worried about the economic and social impact of the cuts needed to achieve budgetary balance. To some extent, the split paralleled the 1993 debate over deficit reduction versus the investments that were both promised in the 1992 campaign.

Clinton opted for a balanced budget and a specific date. In a June 13, 1995 address he announced his plan to balance the budget in ten years. "He said his plan was designed to help working people, avoid cuts in education, strengthen Medicare, save Medicaid, cut taxes for the middle class, cut welfare and protect the environment."[9] The Republicans rejected the president's proposal and continued to press for a balanced budget in seven years. The negotiations over the budget deficits were punctuated by the actual closing of the government. The first shut down came on November 13 and lasted for six days, ending with the passage of a continuing resolution and a Clinton commitment to balance the budget in seven years. The second came on December 15 and lasted for a full twenty-one days. Moderate Republicans were under pressure from their home constituencies, as were Republicans with large numbers of federal employees in their districts. The Senate majority leader, Robert Dole (R-Kans.), found the shutdown to be a handicap in his own aspirations for the Republican presidential nomination.

The Gingrich revolution slowed after the government shutdown that started on December 16, 1995. Gingrich and his freshman allies had exceeded their mandate and overplayed their hand. As the government shutdown lasted through first one week and then a second, media coverage and the public turned against the Republican effort. Most observers saw the Republicans engaged in a classic case of snatching a defeat from the jaws of a clear victory.

There was general agreement that the Republicans had forced Clinton into a balanced budget commitment against his will. Clinton had not only agreed to a seven-year deficit reduction timetable, but also a deficit scored, as Gingrich demanded, by the Congressional Budget Office. As Elizabeth Drew put it in *Showdown,* "The seven-year/C.B.O budget [was] the ticket to reopening the government and Clinton paid the price for the ticket."[10]

In the end, Clinton prevailed on some of the specific priorities in the budget in line with his emphasis on Medicare, Medicaid, education, and the environment. From Clinton's point of view, there may even have been some political and economic benefits from the seven-year timetable. Once the Republicans had won the battle over the general proposition on deficit reduction, a major Republican rallying cry was off the table. The battle shifted to the question of whether or how much to cut specific programs, territory more congenial to the Democrats. In strictly economic terms, the balanced budget commitment also reinforced the first Clinton budget initiative. The combination of deficit reduction policies and a booming economy would soon shift the budget into balance. That shift from deficit to surplus changed the political and economic landscape in a way more favorable to an activist government. Instead of being saddled with the "budget buster" tag, the Democrats were able to lead the debate over how to deal with an era of current and projected budget surpluses. Perhaps Clinton saw the Republicans' balanced budget effort as a way of being thrown into a difficult but still promising briar patch.

Dismantling Government

Dismantling government was not just a phrase for Gingrich and his freshman troops. Modest spending reductions or even wholesale repeal of existing programs were not enough. They were intent on dismantling the structure of a government that, in their view, had grown too large, too intrusive, and too inefficient. In mid-February, Sam Brownback, a freshman from Kansas, led a press conference of freshman to announce that they wanted to eliminate four Cabinet departments. Their four initial targets were the Departments of Housing and Urban Development (HUD), Commerce, Energy, and Education.

Their sweeping proposal met considerable opposition, including some in Republican ranks. In its budget resolution, the House targeted the Departments of Education, Energy, and Commerce. Senator Pete Domenici (R-N.M.), however, strongly objected to the elimination of Education and

Energy.[11] As a result of his strong stand, the Senate budget resolution (Domenici chaired the Senate Budget Committee) only targeted Commerce. Inside the administration, Alice Rivlin, the director of the Office of Management and Budget (OMB), had actually raised the possibility of Cabinet elimination as part of the post-1994 election budget deliberations. In a preemptive move, HUD secretary Henry Cisneros offered to "radically strip" down his agency.[12]

The attack on the Department of Commerce took almost everyone by surprise. The Washington expectation was that the probusiness Republican majorities would, if anything, look more favorably on a department housed in the Herbert Hoover Building. The freshman class in the House was also notable for including an unusually large number of members with prior experience in the business world. Their business world, however, was usually small business with roots in the service sector. Commerce's responsibility for export promotion, export controls, telecommunications, industrial technology, the weather service, and the census seemed distant if not irrelevant to many of the new members.

The attack on the Commerce Department also had at least some parallel to the Reagan administration's attack on the Export-Import Bank. Reagan's OMB director, David Stockman, was leading an effort to reduce welfare spending and the entire welfare state. To help make his point, he went after what he saw as "corporate welfare." With the bulk of Export-Import loans supporting exports from industrial giants such as Boeing and General Electric, he argued that there was no need for the government to subsidize the largest of America's corporations. The giants responded by taking their case to the Congress on economic and meeting-the-competition grounds. In the end, the Export-Import Bank survived Stockman's attack. But the concept of corporate welfare developed a life of its own.

When Gingrich and his freshman took power, they brought with them an antipathy toward big government. They had as well an almost populist suspicion of big business and what seemed like open hostility to large multinational firms. For this group of new members, the Commerce Department came to look like the perfect example of big government providing corporate welfare to big business. Commerce became three targets in one.

The Commerce Department was home to two of the president's signature programs—the Advanced Technology Program and the Manufacturing Extension Partnership (MEP) program. Commerce also had a lead responsibility for key parts of the president's competitiveness strategy. Some business publications had already labeled the emphasis on technology, training, and trade as Clinton's version of an industrial policy.[13] The very phrase was a red flag to the freshmen and many other Republicans. Finally, there was Secretary of Commerce Ron Brown. With his background as the head of the Democratic National Committee, they correctly saw Brown as one of the architects of President George H. W. Bush's defeat in 1992. As an African American and the 1988 Democratic convention manager for Jesse Jackson, Brown had a base in the African American community and the liberal wing of the party. He had also worked briefly for Senator Edward Kennedy (D-Mass.). In the election, Brown had been particularly effective at rallying the party's traditional base to support Clinton's New Democrat themes.

As Clinton took office, California was going through a wrenching adjustment to the downsizing of the defense sector of the economy that came with the end of the Cold War. In response, Clinton established an administration-wide task force to coordinate federal efforts to ease California's transition to a more civilian-based economy. He asked Ron Brown to head the California effort. Brown was an inspired choice. The Commerce Department had some institutional responsibility for local economic development and was well suited to play a coordinating role. Brown also had a clear understanding of the political pressures that came with economic dislocation. His choice, however, made him more of a target. Even before the Gingrich revolution, Republicans in Congress were attacking Commerce's new programs as Brown's "California slush fund."

To the extent that the new Republican majority was raising the question of reorganization, it had a point. Much of the current federal government structure had been built to respond to the Great Depression of the 1930s, World War II, or the early days of the Cold War. Even the newer executive-branch departments were viewed by some as having lived beyond their time. The Department of Energy had been created in response to the 1970s energy crisis, which had long passed. Many Republicans felt that the Education Department had been created as a sop to a loyal Democratic constituency rather than as a step toward meeting a pressing national need. By 1994, the economy, the nation, and the world had all changed dramatically. During the preceding two decades, corporate America had gone through a dramatic restructuring that saw the decline of some sectors, the emergence of new industries, and internal adjustments that came with the adoption of lean production and the high-performance workplace. There was little question but that the government's structure had lagged behind.

Over the years, the Department of Commerce had grown, shrunk, and changed. Relatively early in its existence, the Department of Labor was carved out of what had been part of Commerce. When a Department of Transportation was created in the 1960s, Commerce lost its responsibility in maritime matters. In the early 1970s, the Nixon administration was taking some steps toward departmental consolidation. As part of that plan, it had merged several independent agencies into the National Oceanographic and Atmospheric Administration (NOAA) and made it part of the department.

Commerce's responsibilities for trade and technology had also grown over the years. In most cases, the changes reflected congressional pressure to make the government more focused on economic growth and more responsive to industry. Congress and parts of the private sector felt that the Treasury Department had put foreign policy ahead of American economic interests by often failing to enforce the antidumping and countervailing duty laws. President Carter responded to these pressures by shifting responsibility for their enforcement to the Commerce Department. Congress and the private sector thought that the State and Defense Departments gave too little weight to America's economic interests in regulating U.S. exports of high-technology products. In response, Congress gave Commerce an enhanced voice by creating a separate Bureau of Export Administration within the department. (The bureau was renamed the Bureau of Industry and Security in 2002.) Commerce gained added responsibility for civilian technology development when, in 1988, Congress established the Technology Administration, changed the Bureau of Standards to the National Institute for Standards and Technology, and created new programs to spur the development and diffusion of industrial technology.

The Commerce Department had several other duties that ranged from export promotion to the census to telecommunications. There was an inner logic to Commerce. Trade and civilian technology fit neatly together. NOAA was, in part, a major environmental agency with responsibility for ocean fish, coastal marine sanctuaries, and atmospheric and oceanographic research. In an era when the country had begun to think about sustainable development, Commerce was one of the few federal agencies with important economic and environmental responsibilities. In addition to important trade and technology programs, Commerce also housed the Economic Development Administration (EDA), which focused on stimulating growth in economically distressed regions of the country. Many of Commerce's programmatic and regulatory functions were also very much part of the new economy. Its

Bureau of Economic Analysis was, in part, attempting to update the nation's statistics so that they would more accurately track the new economy.

The Commerce Department could have been a logical candidate for either growth or streamlining. For instance, export promotion programs or even most trade functions could have been consolidated in Commerce or a separate trade agency, as they are in most countries. With the end of the Cold War, one or more of the national laboratories might have been redirected toward civilian research and brought under the aegis of Commerce's Technology Administration. Commerce's statistical functions might have been made part of an independent statistical agency (the path chosen by Canada), or more statistical functions might have been transferred to Commerce.

Gingrich and his new majority were not, however, focused on streamlining. If government was part of the problem, as President Reagan had said, then destruction and not reconstruction was the proper path. It soon became clear that the House Republicans had chosen a target without making much of an effort to understand what the Commerce Department actually did. One anecdote illustrates the point. James Baker, a noted oceanographer, had become the undersecretary for Commerce's NOAA. With the Commerce Department under attack, Baker began to visit the Hill to explain what NOAA actually did. One of his visits was to newly elected Representative Richard Chrysler (R-Mich.), who was one of those leading the charge to eliminate the department. As Baker began to walk through the various responsibilities of NOAA, he came to the National Weather Service. Chrysler stopped him at that point and asked if the country needed a national weather service when all the weather forecasts he needed were readily available on television news reports.[14] It was the classic case of ignoring the cow because milk came from the supermarket.

Chrysler was not lacking in ability. He was a self-made millionaire who had come late to politics. But he was uninformed about government. Ideology took the place of information and analysis. The lack of understanding of the Commerce Department or the government as a whole led the Republican revolutionaries into a number of surprises. As they moved forward in their effort to dismantle the agency, they found strong support for its individual pieces in the Republican Conference. Harold Rogers (R-Ky.), chair of the House Appropriations Subcommittee responsible for Commerce was a strong supporter of EDA. Rogers's district had been a major beneficiary of EDA grants. Rogers was not alone in wanting to save all or part of Commerce. There were ten other House committees with jurisdiction over Commerce. None of them were interested in seeing the department eliminated.[15]

There was support in the business community for both the Commerce Department's export promotion and export control functions. The farm, transportation, and tourism industries were active users of the Weather Service. The Constitution itself mandated a census every ten years to allow the reallocation of House seats among the various states. Many businesses relied on the census for statistics to help guide their investment and production decisions. Commerce's Patent and Trademark Office was a critical element in facilitating and protecting intellectual property.

The effort to eliminate Commerce Department programs ran into one hurdle after another. Still, there was continuing pressure to eliminate the whole even if the parts had to be saved. At one point, the proponents of eliminating Commerce to save money found themselves faced with the need to create seven new independent agencies to house the separate pieces of the department. At that point, the question of real savings seems to have been replaced by the need to attain a symbolic victory.

While the Republican House and Senate were working to eliminate the Commerce Department and many of its programs, Secretary Brown was turning to the department's allies and asking them to call on their friends in Congress.[16] At first, Brown encountered only tepid business support for the department as an entity. Business did care about a number of the pieces of the department, but it was not yet committed to the department as a whole. As long as the pieces were preserved, where they were housed might not make much difference.

Gradually, business thinking began to change. There was no obvious alternative home for the export promotion activities. The export controls functions could be shifted to the State Department or Defense Department, but neither one would have Commerce's focus on the speed of innovation, international competition, or the growing technological capacity of Europe, Japan, and other emerging competitors. Finally, business began to think of Commerce as the one agency more familiar with the private sector and the intricacies of commercial markets. Brown was convinced that leading businesses and business organizations realized that Commerce was, in a sense, their institutional voice at the interagency table.[17] Brown was convinced that it was Commerce as an advocate of economic growth that turned business indifference into business support. As business was increasing its support for Commerce, Brown felt he needed to make the department a more effective advocate of progrowth policies that could fall under the jurisdiction of any individual department. He was in the process of designing this approach when he was killed in an airplane crash in Croatia in April 1996.[18]

At the time of Brown's death, the battle over the Commerce Department was largely won. President Clinton's decision to appoint U.S. Trade Representative Mickey Kantor as the next secretary of commerce was the final step in assuring Commerce's survival. Kantor was close to the president and was known as a fighter. The president was signaling his determination to keep Commerce alive.

When William Daley became secretary of commerce in early 1997, he moved quickly and effectively to further ensure the Commerce Department's long-term survival. There were costs. Daley cut back on the number of major trade missions and made them much lower-key affairs. In addition, Daley promised to eliminate 100 of the positions reserved for political appointees. The forced cuts were painful and to some extent limited the ability of the department to move in new directions. But Daley proved to be very adept at forging ties with Congress. His work with Congress was particularly important in his successful effort to secure House passage of permanent normal trade relations with China. Although trade was Daley's focus, he and his department were also lead players in developing the administration's policies on electronic commerce and information-technology workers.

The congressional effort to eliminate the Commerce Department bore relatively little fruit. Congress did eliminate the bureau that promoted tourism to the United States, but its function was transferred to Commerce's International Trade Administration. Commerce's budget was affected, principally with regard to the Advanced Technology Program. The scaling back of secretarial trade missions may have reduced a growing rapport with business leaders, but Daley's work on trade, electronic commerce, and information-technology workers kept overall private-sector ties strong.

From the standpoint of dismantling the government, the Republican effort was largely a failure. From the standpoint of restructuring the government or creating a government for the twenty-first century, the Republican effort was a lost opportunity. Effective reorganization almost always requires an adjustment of congressional jurisdiction as well as a shift of responsibilities within the executive branch. When Gingrich and his allies came to power, they had the will to make significant changes in House procedures and were intent on shaking up and reshaping the entire federal government. Although it was never seriously debated on the floor, they just might have been willing to go through the painful adjustment of congressional jurisdiction.

The Attack on Clinton's Priorities

In significant ways, Gingrich and Clinton saw the world changing in similar ways. Both talked about an information age and a global economy. Both stressed themes of renewing America—Clinton with his New Covenant and Gingrich by restoring American values. Clinton's emphasis on opportunity, responsibility, and community had some parallels with Gingrich's vision of an opportunity society.

But there were also stark differences. Gingrich saw his conservative opportunity society as replacing major parts of the New Deal. Clinton sought change but also considerable continuity. In addition to preserving major parts of the New Deal and Great Society safety net, Clinton saw government acting as a catalyst for national action or an effective partner with the private sector. Gingrich was committed to a smaller government that did less. For Clinton, the private sector working through markets was a critical element in any successful growth strategy. In addition, markets were often an effective way to achieve national and social goals. For Gingrich and his allies, markets were almost always seen as the principal answer, never the problem.

From the start of his speakership, Gingrich saw the budget as a way to redefine and redirect government. Instead of scaling back the size or cost of individual programs, Gingrich was intent in eliminating an array of programs as well as entire Cabinet departments. In Elizabeth Drew's book on the Clinton-Gingrich battle over the budget, she saw the greatest collision of "competing philosophies about the role of government" in the battle over "the appropriations bill for the Departments of Labor, Health and Human Services, and Education."[19] Altogether, the House Appropriations Committee eliminated 170 individual programs.

Not surprisingly, the Appropriations Committee also significantly reduced or in some cases eliminated altogether Clinton's investments and initiatives.[20] The House Appropriation's bill eliminated Clinton's Goals 2000 education program, his national service program, and the summer jobs program for low-income youth. In addition, the bill made significant cuts in education spending for schools with large numbers of poor students and for the preschool Head Start program. Other legislation took aim at Clinton's school-to-work initiative.

There was also a concerted attack on Clinton's effort to establish a civilian technology policy. In the House, funding for the Commerce Department's

Advanced Technology Program was eliminated altogether. Efforts to eliminate (or zero out) MEP failed after Republican governors expressed their support. MEP had already become an integral part of many state's efforts to improve their own manufacturing base.

Clinton Responds

There is little question that the Republican victories in the House and the Senate put Clinton and the Democrats on the defensive. In his January 23, 1996, State of the Union address, Clinton declared that the era of big government was over.

The Gingrich revolution certainly marked at least the temporary end of major new initiatives from the Clinton administration. It did not, however, mark the beginning of congressional government. Clinton found that there were still several tools at his disposal. The veto proved to be a powerful weapon. Eventually, the Republicans' efforts to both reduce the size of government and redirect spending priorities were limited by their inability to find veto-proof majorities.

Clinton also began the process of "governing alone."[21] Over time, he turned to the unilateral powers that a president can still exercise. In a 1998 *New York Times* article, Robert Pear notes that Clinton had "issued a blizzard of executive orders, regulations, proclamations, and other decrees to achieve his goals, with or without the blessings of Congress."[22] Over time, Clinton also used his power to waive regulations governing social programs to allow experimentation in the states.

Individual departments pursued their own efforts to preserve programs and to limit budget cuts. As the principal target for complete elimination, the Commerce Department had to be particularly agile. As was noted earlier in the chapter, Secretary Brown worked hard to convert his business constituency into active support for the department. Commerce also initiated programs designed to stress their philosophy of public–private partnerships in trade, technology, and training. Through its Partnership for a Competitive Economy (PACE) initiative, Commerce carried its message to a variety of localities across the country. PACE brought together community leaders from the business, labor, and academic communities, as well as government officials. The focus was on local partnerships to stimulate growth, jobs, and innovation.[23]

After the government finally reopened, Congress began to seek a working agreement with the president. The budget battle of 1995 and early 1996 had meant that Congress was months late in passing its appropriations bills. The 1996 consideration of the fiscal 1997 budget was a stark contrast. Congress acted in record time by enacting all of the appropriation bills before the September 30, 1996, deadline.[24] This was not just Republican accommodation. The Republicans also faced a "different Clinton," who had accepted the Republican demand for a balanced budget in seven years based on Congressional Budget Office economic assumptions. In achieving quick action on the budget, Clinton also accepted domestic spending that was "$22 billion below the 1994 level." Some of the cuts affected his own initiatives and priorities.[25]

Revolution and Response:
The Lasting Impact on Competitiveness

How much did the Gingrich revolution, the shutdown of the government, and the attack on Clinton's initiatives affect the overall thrust of the president's competitiveness strategy? The verdict is mixed. The Republican Congress did eliminate some Clinton programs, reduced the funding for others, and slowed the pursuit of new initiatives. In other instances, particularly those involving fiscal policy and international trade, the Republican Congress acted in ways that supported the president's strategy.

After the Republicans took control of Congress in the 1994 midterm election, Clinton did not propose added deficit reduction. The Republicans —particularly Newt Gingrich and his House allies—took the lead. They pressed for and achieved a commitment for a balanced budget in seven years. In macroeconomic terms, the move toward a balanced budget had created the potential for a larger pool of domestic savings, had further eased pressure on long-term interest rates, and may have earned added cooperation from the Federal Reserve as well. In strictly political terms, the president's commitment to a balanced budget shifted the national discussion from the widely supported question of fiscal balance to the arena of national spending priorities. The president's determination to protect spending on Medicare, Medicaid, education, and the environment proved popular with the public. Debating spending priorities instead of budget balance had put the president and the Democrats on firmer ground.

The president had already achieved key international trade goals before the 1994 elections. The North American Free Trade Agreement (NAFTA) passed in 1993, and the implementing legislation for the Uruguay Round trade legislation passed in a November 1994 lame duck session. Republican votes had been helpful in both instances, and they were critical in the approval of NAFTA in 1993. For the most part, Republicans would remain supportive of traditional trade agreements, including the May 2000 approval of permanent normal trading relations with China.

By and large, there was also continuing congressional support for the export promotion efforts of the president. Where Brown had led high-visibility missions on government planes with top-level chief executives, Daley substituted a lower-key approach that relied on commercial airlines and did not always involve the company chief executive. The change was a mixed blessing. The shift from frequent high-level contact may have made it somewhat more difficult for the administration to forge public–private alliances in the trade field. While virtually impossible to measure, the more limited chief-executive-level contacts may have contributed to the inability of the administration to secure a renewal of fast-track trade negotiating authority (now referred to as trade promotion authority) from Congress. At the same time, the change earned Daley respect and support in a Republican Congress. Clinton and Brown had already made the point that they were part of an administration that took exports and the jobs that came with them seriously. The lower-key trade missions were a Republican victory but one whose consequences may not have been far reaching.

It was in the field of public investments that Clinton suffered the biggest initial setbacks. To some degree, Clinton's efforts to develop a more ambitious technology policy were slowed by the Gingrich revolution. The original $750 million target for the Advanced Technology Program was scaled back to under $300 million. House Republican hostility to the program as an exercise in industrial policy continued throughout the Clinton presidency. MEP, the effort to make modern technology more available to small and medium-sized manufacturers, not only survived but thrived. By the end of Clinton's first term, there was a nationwide system of MEP centers or offices.

In more general terms, the shift to a Republican Congress almost surely slowed the pursuit of other technology initiatives. The Gingrich budget also slowed Clinton programs and policies in the field of education. Secretary Reich's Office of the American Workplace was eliminated. The school-to-work program survived the Gingrich onslaught but was subsequently eliminated. The initial effort to eliminate the Goals 2000 program failed, but the provision for establishing national education standards was repealed. Just as important, progress on Clinton's proposals was stalled. Reich's proposed GI Bill for Workers, involving the consolidation of existing training programs and the move to training vouchers, did eventually become law as part of the Workforce Investment Act—but not until 1998.

The Clinton Presidency: Life on a See-Saw

In President Clinton's first term, he went through three distinct periods. In his first two years, he pursued an active and ambitious agenda. During his first days in office, he issued a series of executive orders reversing several of President George H. W. Bush's policies. The still-Democratic Congress quickly passed a number of bills that had been vetoed by President Bush. In fairly short order, the president signed the "Family and Medical Leave Act, motor voter registration, and a gun control measure, the Brady Bill."[26] From the start, the president worked to put his competitiveness strategy into practice. He supported broad-based private-sector investment through deficit reduction, a cooperative relationship with the Federal Reserve, and a reinvented government. He emphasized public and private investments in training, education, and technology. Finally, he coupled aggressive export promotion with a wide-ranging effort to open markets on a multilateral, regional, and bilateral basis.

There were notable losses in the first two years, with health care at the top of the list. The failure of the Democratic Congress to pass the technology initiatives in the Competitiveness Act, telecommunications deregulation, and the implementing legislation for the Uruguay Round of multilateral trade negotiations reduced the president's economic accomplishments and helped build the case for Washington gridlock.

The political world changed in 1994 as the Republicans swept to power in the House and the Senate. Instead of setting the agenda, the president found himself "resisting revolution."[27] In response to Republican pressure, the president committed himself to a balanced budget in seven years as measured (or scored) by the Congressional Budget Office. The commitment translated into domestic spending well below the 1994 level. The president's political fortunes shifted again after the December–January shutdown of the government. The commitment to a balanced budget had shifted the national focus to spending priorities that generally favored the president and the Democrats. By overplaying his personal and political hand, Speaker Gingrich and to some extent the congressional Republicans had lost standing with the public. Instead of confrontation built on a frontal assault on government, there was "a period of relatively cooperative divided government."[28]

By September 1996, "Clinton was enjoying approval ratings of 60 percent, comparable to those of popular, easily reelected presidents such as Dwight Eisenhower and Ronald Reagan at the same stage."[29] Clinton went on to a clear victory over his Republican rival Bob Dole and the independent candidate Ross Perot. His second term saw a continuation of cooperation with the still-Republican Congress.

Then the political world changed again. In February 1998, reports and rumors began to spread in Washington about the president's involvement with a White House intern. The president was already the subject of a separate suit, essentially alleging sexual harassment, that dated from his days as governor of Arkansas (the Paula Jones case). According to the initial flurry of allegations, the president had also committed perjury by denying his relationship with the intern while testifying in the Jones case.

Seasoned Washington hands began to count the president's future in terms of weeks or even days. Speculation began over whom Vice President Gore would choose as vice president after he succeeded President Clinton. Clinton, however, had other plans. "In his 1998 State of the Union address, delivered days after the first revelations of the alleged perjury . . . Clinton attempted to forge ahead with his policy agenda."[30]

In August 1998, the president finally admitted to an improper relationship and apologized for misleading his colleagues, Congress, and the country. The president's public admission, however, did not put an end to either the work of Kenneth Starr, the independent counsel, or the congressional investigators. The question of impeachment hovered in the air. Under the constitution, the House acts as a combined prosecutor and grand jury. If the House votes to impeach the president, the Senate conducts a trial to determine whether the president should actually be removed from office. The constitutional test in both cases is "high crimes and misdemeanors." Despite polls indicating public opposition to impeachment, the House made President Clinton the first elected president to be impeached.[31] Without gaining a single Democratic vote, the Republican Senate majority failed to secure the two-thirds margin needed to actually remove the president.

Much of 1998 was consumed by the scandal. From the political talk shows to the late-night comics, the scandal and its aftermath were a constant topic. It was not a time for major new domestic initiatives. Instead, the president continued his strategy of "governing alone" through executive orders, proclamations, regulations, and a targeted use of the bully pulpit. He was determined to show that he was not distracted by the allegations but instead was doing the people's business. Individual departments were under constant pressure to develop initiatives that required only modest spending or did not depend on congressional action.

In economic terms, the president continued to pursue his long-term competitiveness strategy. He dealt with emerging budget surpluses with a call to save Social Security first, a tactic that slowed spending and deflected pressure for tax cuts. In setting current revenues aside for future Social Security and Medicare needs, the president was committed to paying down the national debt. In effect, he was maintaining his earlier policy of increasing the pool of capital available for long-term investment and fostering lower, proinvestment interest rates. He coupled his macroeconomic strategy with increases in spending on education and training. Working with the Republican Congress, he finally achieved the consolidation of training programs originally sought by Labor Secretary Reich in his first term.[32] The president also supported investment initiatives and essentially pursued what might be called an industrial policy in support of the spread of the Internet and electronic commerce. Again, drawing heavily on Republican support, the president continued to pursue his international trade agenda. Although he was unsuccessful in seeking to launch a new round of trade negotiations in late 1999, he did succeed in securing permanent normal trading relations with China in 2000.

Clinton as President: Five Phases with a Single Strategy

In the course of eight years, Clinton had several presidencies: the ambitious agenda of his first two years, the Gingrich revolution, a period of cooperative government, the Monica Lewinsky scandal, and the final period marked by several new initiatives. What is striking about Clinton's record, however, is not so much the changing circumstances but the persistence with which he pursued his original economic strategy. At times, pressures accelerated an aspect of the policy, as was the case with his promise to achieve a balanced budget in seven years. In other cases, he adapted to new pressures by scaling back his proposals—the Advanced Technology Program is a prime example.

Just as striking is the degree to which Clinton consistently articulated his strategy. One can draw a straight line from the announcement of his candidacy in late 1991 to his final economic report to Congress in early 2000. He struck similar notes in his 1996 reelection campaign book *Between Hope and History: Meeting America's Challenges for the 21st Century*. Although he did not specifically use the phrase "New Growth Compact," his reelection book used the concept. "Government," he wrote "doesn't create jobs; that's businesses' responsibility." Instead, "the federal government has another critical responsibility: creating the framework in which our economy can grow."[33] In the course of his book, he often illustrated a point with an example of private initiative, community involvement, or pragmatic partnership.

Much the same tack was taken in the 1995 and 1996 competitiveness reports from the Department of Commerce.[34] At the time, the Clinton administration was frequently talking about building a bridge to the twenty-first century. Commerce pursued the same theme and gathered administration initiatives into four clusters or pillars that supported a bridge that took the country from yesterday to a prosperous tomorrow.

The Commerce Department reports were explicitly about national competitiveness. Drawing on the work of the 1985 report of the President's Commission on Industrial Competitiveness (or the Young Commission) and the subsequent work of the private-sector Council on Competitiveness, the Commerce reports defined long-term competitiveness in terms of a widely shared national prosperity. Like the president's *Between Hope and History*, the Commerce reports saw the nation's economic future as a national challenge. As the first report put it, "If the American Dream is to survive, it will require the talents of its people, the innovations of its industries, and the cooperation of its government."[35]

The Competitiveness Strategy:
How Important to Today's Prosperity and Tomorrow's Promise?

The premise of this volume is that the competitiveness strategy made a significant contribution to the economy of the 1990s and that the strategy suggests a policy path for the future. Policy did not operate in a vacuum. By the time President Clinton took office, two decades of rising international competition had forced American companies and whole industries to go through a series of adjustments affecting millions of American workers and hundreds of communities.

Nor would one expect every element of a competitiveness strategy to have a major short-term effect. The focus on public and private investment as a key to productivity and income growth suggests a long-term perspective. The reservations of early commentators or the frequent skepticism of economists does not always look beyond the near-term impact of fiscal or monetary policy. The broader questions of long-term investments, partnerships, and a New Growth Compact often go unexplored. As pursued in the 1990s, the national competitiveness strategy emphasized everything from the importance of business confidence and expectations to the creation of a long-term framework for national economic policy.

What then was the impact of the broad-based competitiveness strategy on 1990s prosperity? To what extent does the competitiveness strategy point the way to the future? These are the questions that we will explore in chapter 13.

Notes

1. Charles Cook of *National Journal's Cook Report* may have been the only one of the major political prognosticators to have foreseen the Republican sweep, and even he saw it very late in the day.

2. Elizabeth Drew, *Showdown: The Struggle Between the Gingrich Congress and the Clinton White House,* Touchstone paperback ed. (New York: Simon & Schuster, 1997), 26.

3. Drew, *Showdown,* 29.

4. Representative Newt Gingrich and Representative Dick Armey, *Contract with America* (New York: Times Books and Random House, 1994).

5. Drew, *Showdown,* 28.

6. Drew, *Showdown,* 36—37.

7. Drew, *Showdown,* 163—66.

8. The account draws largely from Bob Woodward, *The Choice* (New York: Simon & Schuster, 1996), 206—8.

9. Woodward, *Choice,* 209.

10. Drew, *Showdown,* 369.

11. Drew, *Showdown,* 240.

12. Drew, *Showdown,* 71—72.

13. "Bill's Recipe: How He Plans to Help U.S. Business Cream Rivals," *Business Week,* October 18, 1993. In their October 1993 report, *Business Week* reporters describe an "industrial policy, Clinton-style."

14. I heard the story over a lunch with Undersecretary Baker at the Department of Commerce.

15. Drew, *Showdown,* 259.

16. Drew, *Showdown,* 259.

17. This is from my conversation with Secretary Brown.

18. See the memorandum from Secretary Ronald H. Brown to Department of Commerce senior staff, March 18, 1996.

19. Drew, *Showdown,* 268.

20. Drew, *Showdown,* 268.

21. Joel D. Aberbach, "A Reinvented Government, or the Same Old Government?" in *The Clinton Legacy,* ed. Colin Campbell and Bert A. Rockman (New York: Seven Bridges / Chatham House, 2000), 127.

22. Robert Pear, "The Presidential Pen Is Still Mighty," *New York Times,* June 28, 1998, as quoted in Aberbach, "Reinvented Government," 128.

23. Starting in the spring of 1997 and ending in the summer of 1999, the PACE program produced eight copies of its newsletter, the *Pacesetter.* They can be found in the archives of the Department of Commerce's Office of Technology at http://www.technology.gov.

24. Dilys M. Hill, "Domestic Policy," in *The Clinton Presidency: The First Term, 1992—96,* ed. Paul S. Herrnson and Dilys M. Hill (New York: St. Martin's Press, 1999), 112.

25. Hill, "Domestic Policy," 114.

26. Paul J. Quirk and William Cunion, "Clinton's Domestic Policy: The Lessons of a 'New Democrat,'" in *The Clinton Legacy,* ed. Colin Campbell and Bert A. Rockman (New York: Seven Bridges / Chatham House, 2000), 206.

27. Quirk and Cunion, "Clinton's Domestic Policy," 207.

28. Quirk and Cunion, "Clinton's Domestic Policy," 210.

29. Quirk and Cunion, "Clinton's Domestic Policy," 211.

30. Quirk and Cunion, "Clinton's Domestic Policy," 213.

31. Andrew Johnson was impeached by the House and survived a Senate trial by only one vote. Johnson, however, had been elected as Abraham Lincoln's vice president and came to office after Lincoln was assassinated.

32. Instead of Clinton's proposed GI Bill for workers, the eventual bill is known as the Workforce Investment Act.

33. Bill Clinton, *Between Hope and History: Meeting America's Challenges for the 21st Century* (New York: Random House, 1996), 95.

34. U.S. Department of Commerce, *Building the American Dream for the 21st Century* (Washington, D.C.: U.S. Government Printing Office, 1995); and U.S. Department of Commerce, *Building the American Dream: Jobs, Innovation and Growth in America's Next Century* (Washington, D.C.: U.S. Government Printing Office, 1996).

35. U.S. Department of Commerce, *Building the American Dream for the 21st Century,* 33.

Chapter 13

The Competitiveness Strategy: Explaining the Past and Forging the Future

How much difference did the competitiveness strategy make? Did the broad-based competitiveness strategy embodied in the Omnibus Trade and Competitiveness Act of 1988 set the stage for the record prosperity of the 1990s? As the country moved toward a New Growth Compact, how important was the revolution in corporate practice that started in manufacturing and eventually spread to many parts of the public sector? The thesis of this book is that policy did matter, that policy made a powerful contribution to the economic growth, and that the competitiveness strategy applied in the 1990s provides an effective framework for national economic policy in the twenty-first century.

But policies did not work in isolation. Not surprisingly, good public policies, good private-sector practices, good timing, and even good luck proved a powerful combination. The Clinton administration's policies preceded and then accompanied the longest unbroken economic expansion in the nation's history. What some now refer to as the "Roaring Nineties"[1] combined rapid growth, low unemployment, and stable prices. In the second half of the decade, the economy became the proverbial tide that was raising most if not all boats. In the present volume, the focus is on the good policies and their contribution.

When President Bill Clinton turned a competitiveness strategy into national economic policy, he acted in very favorable circumstances. Much of the American business community had gone through a painful restructuring in the 1980s and early 1990s that helped close the quality, price, and innovation gap that had existed between U.S. and Japanese industries. More than any single factor, the Japanese challenge forced a change in

347

America's approach to manufacturing, corporate structure, and, to a considerable degree, in the system of innovation that turned ideas into products or services. In the path-breaking *The Machine That Changed the World,* James P. Womack, Daniel T. Jones, and Daniel Roos trace the change in thinking and then practice that eventually swept through the U.S. automobile industry.[2] The emphasis on lean production spread quickly to other industries. In *The Productive Edge,* Richard K. Lester sorts through the successful renewal of several key American industries.[3] Drawing on the work of the Sloan Foundation Industry Centers that have been established at several universities, Lester emphasizes the importance of individual firms *"mastering the fundamentals of efficient, high-quality manufacturing operations"* (emphasis added).[4]

By the 1990s, much of corporate America had remade itself in response to changing technology and international competition. Michael Porter, Mariko Sakakibara, and Hirotaka Takeuchi make just this point in a recent book, *Can Japan Compete?*[5] In writing about Japan, Porter and his colleagues note that as American (and other) companies adopted Japan's best manufacturing practices, they eroded Japan's competitive advantage. Recent retrospectives on the 1990s point to the restructuring of U.S. business as an important element in setting a favorable context for the investment, innovation, and productivity growth that dominated much of the decade. In their take on the "Fabulous Decade," Alan Blinder and Janet Yellen note that when economic activity picked up, "American businesses were well positioned to capitalize on the new opportunities."[6]

The geopolitical and geoeconomic positions of the United States were also favorable. The fall of the Berlin Wall in 1989 marked the beginning of the end for the Soviet empire, and with the 1991 collapse of the Soviet Union the United States emerged as the sole remaining superpower. The German economy took on the challenge of absorbing the woefully inefficient industries and the degraded environment of the former East Germany. As the decade began, Japan experienced the bursting of its economic bubble as its securities and real estate markets crumbled, ushering in more than a decade of economic stagnation. Even before the rapid growth of the 1990s in the United States, America had reasserted itself as the world's dominant, largely unchallenged economy.

In addition to good timing, the Clinton administration had considerable good economic luck. During the 1990s, demands for wage increases were generally moderate.[7] Particularly in the second half of the decade, the economy benefited from a series of favorable trends (or positive supply shocks)—

energy prices, led by ample supplies of oil, fell, and the dollar strengthened against other major currencies. The decision of the Bureau of Labor Statistics to adjust the Consumer Price Index made its own modest contribution by more accurately reporting (and reducing) the reported level of inflation.[8]

By sharply increasing the supply of skilled and unskilled labor, the open-border U.S. immigration policy contributed to the pace of economic growth. The Internet added its own impact by allowing many companies to use electronic links to draw on skilled workers overseas. The resulting abundant supply of skilled and unskilled labor was another force limiting inflation that helped make a more expansive monetary policy possible. It also meant more competition for a wide range of American workers.

Other circumstances also conspired to keep monetary policy looser than it might have been. Federal Reserve Chairman Alan Greenspan was convinced that there was a "new economy," in the sense of increased productivity growth that allowed for faster growth without triggering inflation. Still, as economic growth persisted and unemployment continued to fall, Greenspan might have been tempted to tighten monetary policy. There are critics who think that the Fed should have tightened policy in response to asset inflation even though the price increases for goods and services remained moderate. In their view, an earlier tightening might have limited the financial bubble that finally burst in the spring of 2000. In December 1996, Greenspan warned against "irrational exuberance" in the financial markets but did not push to tighten policy or increase the margin requirement for stock purchases.[9]

Over the next two years, however, new challenges made tightening difficult. In July 1997, the Thai bhat fell to speculative attacks and was devalued. An unexpected contagion followed that affected several currencies of East and Southeast Asia, spread to Russia, and eventually, on January 19, 1999, forced Brazil to devalue and float the real.[10] In their essay on the "The Fabulous Decade," Blinder and Yellen note that "the Fed seemed poised to tighten further in the summer of 1997" when the Asian financial crisis hit.[11] When Russia partially defaulted, the Fed actually cut rates and then cut them again in response to the near collapse of Long Term Capital Management, a major hedge fund.

Even when the Federal Reserve did eventually tighten monetary policy, its move was almost surely tempered by concern about what was generally referred to as the "Y2K crisis." This was the widespread fear that computers might mistakenly read the "00" in the year 2000 as 1900 instead, which would wreak havoc throughout the economy, especially in the financial markets.

Y2K also accelerated spending on computers, related information technology equipment, and software as the private sector invested hundreds of billions of dollars in new equipment rather than risk Y2K disruption. After 2000 arrived with virtually no disruption to computer systems, the Fed did tighten enough so that the federal funds rate rose from 4.75 percent in June 1999 to 6.5 percent in May 2000.[12] The Fed's partially unintended experiment with loosening, resisting increases, and then loosening again showed that at least under the right circumstances the unemployment rate could fall below 4 percent without igniting inflation. Whether the combination of strong growth and low inflation is easily replicable is still very much under debate.[13]

President George H. W. Bush and President Clinton pursued elements of a competitiveness strategy. Bush is often remembered as the last Cold War president and as having fought a successful war in the Persian Gulf. He did not run on a competitiveness strategy for the country or fully embrace a competitiveness strategy until the waning days of his presidential campaign. Yet many key individuals in his administration pushed for policies that were consistent with and in some cases inspired by the same forces propelling change in the private sector and the development of a broader competitiveness strategy. In fiscal policy, technology, and education, Bush supported initiatives that provided an important base for the subsequent Clinton administration.

President Clinton ran on a competitiveness strategy that emphasized complementary public and private investments. He was the first modern president to make technology policy a major plank in his presidential campaign. At considerable political cost, he pursued deficit reduction in a way that also garnered the public commendation and support of the chairman of the Federal Reserve Board. Later in his first year in office, again at considerable political cost, he successfully shepherded the North American Free Trade Agreement (NAFTA) through Congress.

Fair or not, presidents generally get the political credit for a good economy and political blame for an economy gone sour. Most economists, however, stress the limitations on the modern presidency. The president may propose a fiscal policy, but Congress controls the purse strings and the independent Federal Reserve Board makes key decisions on monetary policy. Students of the presidency also point to other limiting factors, including a complex web of public institutions, universities, and the private economy. Context does matter. Even the immense U.S. economy is now increasingly affected by developments in the global economy. Two decades of rising international competition forced American companies and whole industries to go through a series of adjustments affecting millions of American workers and hundreds of communities.

The focus on public and private investment as a key to productivity and income growth requires a long-term perspective. For instance, the contribution of the Internet in the 1990s can be traced to investments made decades earlier by the Department of Defense. The basic infrastructure of the information age reaches back even further to the development of the transistor shortly after World War II. Some investments in people can take equally long to mature. For instance, a sharp improvement in preschool education will not affect the active workforce for another twelve or more years. And even then, the flow of new graduates would only slowly change the skill mix of the much larger stock of existing workers.

Early retrospectives on the Clinton presidency reflect some of the skepticism about a president's ability to influence the economy. In assessing Clinton's first term, Christopher Bailey noted the political benefits that flowed from a robust economy. As regards policy, however, he gives Clinton little credit. In his view, "the best that could be said is that Clinton's efforts to manage the economy did not do any short-term damage."[14] Writing in 1999, Paul Quirk and William Cunion shared the view that "presidents do not control the economy, except marginally."[15] They were, however, a bit more charitable than Bailey in concluding that "Clinton's policies, especially early in his term, probably contributed to the long-lived economic expansion."[16]

More recent studies are more nuanced in their judgments. Clinton's macroeconomic approach, his trade policies, and the comprehensive nature of his strategy are all noted and generally praised. At the same time, the studies point to the earlier steps taken during the George H. W. Bush administration, and they stress a series of events (usually referred to as favorable supply-side shocks) that contributed to a low rate of inflation.[17] The latest studies also have been done in a decidedly different economic and political context. By the end of 2002, the country had experienced a short recession, rising unemployment, and three years of declining financial markets.

Even more important than judging the past is setting a strategy that will lead to economic strength and broad-based prosperity in the future. The development of a New Growth Compact, the emergence of a Partnership Nation, and the emphasis on public and private investment were tested in the 1990s and, to a considerable extent, validated. The combination of tighter fiscal and a more accommodative monetary policy did have the initial, desired effect of bringing down long-term interest rates, improving business confidence, and contributing to conditions favorable to private-sector investment. The sustained impact of the information technology revolution, including the Internet, on productivity suggests that an ongoing commitment to policies favorable to improving and developing technology should be part of any future growth strategy. Open trade policies created new markets for American innovations and, by helping control prices, also supported a more expansive monetary policy. Public concern and continued private-sector pressure for improved education and training should keep the public focus on lifelong learning.

In the Clinton administration, the elements that are emphasized in growth accounting, development economics, and (at some level of abstraction) growth models had found their way into a politically sustainable set of policies that were contributing to growth today and laying the basis for growth in the future. In both the public and the private sectors, there was a growing sense of how the complementary roles of government and private markets added up to faster growth, better jobs, and increased innovation. A multitude of partnerships helped translate a general strategy into specific investments.

Seeking to judge the impact of past and future competitiveness strategies is not easy. Analysts must recognize the importance of the global context, domestic political currents, and sheer good or ill fortune. In making my own assessment, I come with a predisposition to give a strong positive grade to the competitiveness strategy for its impact on the 1990s and even more for its importance to the country's economic future. In staff positions on Capitol Hill, in presidential campaigns, at the private-sector Council on Competitiveness, and as a political appointee in the Clinton administration, a competitiveness strategy was my responsibility—and often my preoccupation. Still, in attempting to sort through the political and economic currents of the 1990s, I made every effort to winnow the grains of future policy from the chaff of good fortune.

Public Policies: Fiscal, Monetary, and Investment Strategies

Clinton's strategy for American competitiveness depended on public and private investments in education, training, and technology. That emphasis on investments dictated a policy of low interest rates that required the right mix of fiscal and monetary policies coupled with private-sector confidence.

The reality of a United States already deeply tied to the global economy led Clinton to pursue an aggressive policy of trade negotiations, export promotion, and global economic engagement.

The Fiscal and Monetary Mix

In 1990, President Bush accepted significant tax increases as part of an overall plan to reduce the long-term budget deficit. The economy did not, however, reap the real benefits of either faster growth or the visible victory of a lower fiscal deficit during Bush's tenure in office. In part, the potential impact on the deficit was masked by a recession and the need to deal with a savings and loan crisis that had been festering since the early 1980s. As the federal government closed many thrift institutions and acquired their assets, the government paid out billions of dollars to insured depositors. It was a direct addition to the fiscal deficit. Subsequent sales of the closed thrifts' assets would eventually reduce the deficit, but that came only after President Bush had left office.

By the time President Clinton entered office, a modest recovery was under way, although not one strong enough to make a major difference in the unemployment rate. The Federal Open Market Committee (FOMC), the body in the Federal Reserve that actually makes the decisions governing monetary policy, had brought short-term interest rates (the federal funds rate) down to 3 percent. Given the rate of inflation, the inflation-adjusted federal funds rate was effectively zero.

As chairman of the Federal Reserve Board, Greenspan had weathered a series of challenges that had given him credibility and, by all reports, considerable confidence. Greenspan's tenure had started with a storm. Shortly after he became chairman of the Fed in August 1987, he was faced with the stock market crash of Black Monday, on October 19, when the market fell 22.6 percent, or 508 points. That was almost twice the 11.7 percent decline on Black Tuesday, October 29, 1929.[18] The next day, as chair of the Fed and the FOMC, Greenspan issued a statement assuring the markets that they would "serve as a source of liquidity to support the economic and financial system."[19]

In the fourth quarter of 1987, the real growth of the gross domestic product hit 6.6 percent.[20] In December, unemployment fell to 5.7 percent.[21] Fearing an overheated economy, Greenspan reversed course later in 1987 and tightened monetary policy, a policy he pursued throughout 1988.[22] For a variety of reasons, Greenspan retained a relatively tight policy well into the early years of the Bush administration. At least in part as a result of Fed policies, the economy slipped into a recession starting in July 1990. Many in the Bush administration point to Greenspan and Fed policies as having caused the president's loss in 1992.

When Clinton came to office, there was the potential for a cooperative relationship with Greenspan. First, Alan Greenspan had proved his mettle as an inflation fighter who would tighten policy even at the cost of a recession. That would give him more latitude later when he resisted tightening monetary policy as unemployment fell to and beyond the point where most economists thought that inflation would accelerate. Second, the Fed had already reversed course and brought the federal funds rate (a good guide to short-term interest rates) down to 3 percent. Finally, Greenspan and Clinton had a similar sense of the power of the financial markets and the importance of credible policies in changing expectations and building confidence.

In the latter half of the decade, Greenspan saw through the inevitable fog of economic statistics to identify a new economy, in which technology and other factors were driving more rapid productivity growth. At the same time, trade, technology, and the Internet had created new competitors that made it difficult for firms to raise prices. Instead, they had to look for ways to become more productive and more innovative. As the 1990s progressed, Clinton's embrace of open trade, deficit reduction, and the new economy seemed to complement (and perhaps even reinforce) Greenspan's own analysis of the economy. Again, the timing was right.

Chapter 11 described the December 1992 meeting between president-elect Clinton and Federal Reserve Chairman Greenspan. In their conversation, Greenspan noted that longer-term interest rates had remained high while the Fed's FOMC had gradually lowered short-term rates essentially to zero in inflation-adjusted terms. Greenspan stressed that long-term rates remained high in expectation of future inflation, driven by large and persistent budget deficits. It was Greenspan's view that the relatively high long-term rates were deterring private-sector investment in plant, equipment, and housing. In his campaign, Clinton had stressed the importance of private as well as public investment. He had generally talked about deficit reduction but also promised a middle-class tax cut. Much higher postelection deficit figures, the conversation with Greenspan, and Clinton's sense of the country's investment potential all pointed to the importance of deficit reduction. In an after-the-fact conversation with Joe Klein, a Clinton biographer and then a reporter for the *New Yorker,* Clinton said he "believed there were vast flows of venture capital—confidence capital—that were out there ... waiting to happen."[23]

Clinton's choice of an economic team suggests that he already had policies in mind that would be sensitive to the bond market and fiscally prudent. At the Office of Management and Budget, both Leon Panetta, former chairman of the House Budget Committee, and his deputy Alice Rivlin, former director of the Congressional Budget Office, had strong deficit-reducing credentials. At the Treasury Department, Clinton had former Finance and Joint Economic Committee chairman Lloyd Bentsen—who had, a decade before, urged a combination of fiscal and monetary policies that would foster private investment. Robert Rubin, head of the newly created National Economic Council, had come straight from Goldman Sachs and an enormously successful career as a bond trader. With years of experience in the financial world, Rubin was keenly aware of the dangers of large deficits and the impact on markets of real or expected inflation.

For much of a decade, a number of economists and key Democrats had urged a combination of tighter fiscal policy and more accommodating monetary policy as a way of dealing with deficits while lowering interest rates and encouraging private investment. For these policies to work, there had to be some sort of effective dialogue, a meeting of the minds, and the adoption of policies that complemented the FOMC's action. There is considerable evidence that Clinton and his team managed to reach such an informal arrangement with Greenspan. There was Clinton's "we can do business" comment as he left his postelection meeting in Little Rock with Greenspan.[24] There was the reported shuttle diplomacy of Lloyd Bentsen as Clinton hammered together his first, deficit-reducing budget.[25]

In their summing up of the "Fabulous Decade," Blinder and Yellen note that "central bankers who abhor large budget deficits may want to reward politicians for good behavior. In some sense, both Greenspan and Paul Volcker before him had been 'offering' the politicians this deal for years."[26] In his retrospective on government service, Richard Darman, President George Bush's Office of Management and Budget director, reported receiving just such an offer from Greenspan.[27] Blinder and Yellen, however, found little evidence to support the idea of a formal agreement in the FOMC's minutes (Blinder served as vice chair of the Fed as well as on Clinton's Council of Economic Advisers).

Rubin, who was an active part of President Clinton's transition team that made the key decisions on the deficit reduction policy, reports that discussions centered on how a deficit reduction would affect the bond market "though the effect on the Federal Reserve Board also entered the discussion." He was firm in saying that the idea that there had been a deal between the president and Greenspan was "simply wrong."[28] Greenspan did not speak about a deal, but some years later in a conversation with Bob Woodward, he said he had told Clinton that "if you had not turned the fiscal situation around, we couldn't have had the kind of monetary policy we've had."[29] In *Greenspan: The Man Behind Money,* Justin Martin reports on a January 21, 1994, meeting with President Clinton and his aides at which Greenspan indicated he would have to raise short-term rates. According to Martin, "Clinton was furious and viewed the move as a betrayal. It seemed as though Greenspan was going back on his word."[30] Yet in February 1994, when rates were actually raised, Blinder and Yellen remember Greenspan working hard to limit the increase to 25 basis points (or a quarter of a percentage point). It appears that there was at least a tacit understanding on both sides, if not a more explicit arrangement.

Whether deal, understanding, or simply parallel cooperation, Congress did adopt the deficit reduction package—though by a single vote in each chamber. Did it work? At least Blinder and Yellen conclude that it did. In their view, "The 1993 budget agreement galvanized the bond market, and the thirty-year bond rate plummeted by more than 160 basis points from Election Day 1992 to October 1993."[31] In addition to deficit reduction per se, Blinder and Yellen point to five factors that added to the credibility of the package, including its larger than expected size.[32]

Not everyone puts the same emphasis on expectations. Joseph Stiglitz, a former chairman of Clinton's Council of Economic Advisers, also pointed to the way lower interest rates encouraged bank lending. After the savings and loan crisis, banks were forced to increase the capital they held to match the riskiness of their investments. Logically, the question of risk would extend to long-term government bonds—which, while safe from any danger of default, can lose or gain value as interest rates rise or fall. The Federal Reserve, however, allowed banks to treat long-term government bonds as if they carried no risk and thus did not require the bank to hold reserves against them. When interest rates were high, the government bonds provided substantial earning to the banks. As interest rates fell and bond prices moved in the opposite direction, the banks had a potential profit on their bond holdings. In *The Roaring Nineties: A New History of the World's Most Prosperous Decade,* Stiglitz saw lower long-term rates, by making bond holdings less attractive, as encouraging banks to shift from holding long-term bonds to more active lending—one way of putting the profits from earlier bond holdings to work.[33] Stiglitz did, however, see at least a "kernel of truth" in the focus "on confidence."[34]

In drawing their own lessons from the experience of the 1990s, Blinder and Yellen agreed that a contractionary fiscal policy (raising taxes or cutting spending) could be expansionary but did not suggest it as a general rule.[35] The broader point is that the competitiveness strategy as practiced by Clinton kept long-term investment in focus while seeking a boost in near-term economic growth. The Clinton team as well as Greenspan was carefully looking at the specifics of the situation and the developments in the economy.

The combination of tight fiscal policy and looser monetary policy was part of a decade that saw a sharp increase in private-sector investment in plant and equipment. It came as something of a surprise to many economists that tighter fiscal policy did not actually raise the national savings rate. As public saving rose (through a reduced deficit and eventually a surplus), personal and corporate saving declined. Foreign investment (and thus large trade and current account deficits) made up the difference. Without the added public saving, however, the United States would have had either higher interest rates and less investment and growth, or even larger and hence more potentially destabilizing current account deficits.

Macroeconomic policy did not function alone. As it created a climate that fostered private investment, the private sector was in a position to invest, and much of what it bought helped boost productivity growth. It was the right policy at the right time in the specific circumstances.

Trade, Finance, and International Integration: Adding to an Already Competitive Economy

From its early roots in the late 1979 and 1980 annual reports of the congressional Joint Economic Committee, the developing competitiveness strategy emphasized the importance of international commerce. The administrations of Ronald Reagan, George H. W. Bush, and Bill Clinton had all pursued policies that not only resisted restrictions on international trade but also sought to open markets around the world. In the 1990s, opportunities for trade were significantly expanded through the approval of NAFTA (1993), the implementation of a new multilateral trade agreement (1994), and the accession of China to the World Trade Organization (2000).

In terms of the competitiveness strategy legislated in the Omnibus Trade and Competitiveness Act of 1988, an increase in international trade and investment would contribute to growth in several ways. As was noted in chapter 2, since David Hume wrote in the early nineteenth century, economists have emphasized the doctrine of comparative advantage—that countries can each gain by producing and trading more of what they do best relative to the strengths of their trading partners. In addition, increased international trade often spurs innovation, creating pressures for companies and countries to improve their capacity to innovate. Competitive imports also put downward pressure on prices, allowing the Federal Reserve to follow a more accommodative monetary policy without risking an increase in inflation. By keeping interest rates low or lower than they would otherwise be, foreign investment can also act as an important complement to a macroeconomic policy that encourages investment.

Trade and investment grew rapidly in much of the 1990s. Some of the increase in 1990s trade was the product of trade opening agreements that came into force in the 1990s. Much of the increase in trade, however, resulted from the development of new products and the added demand for oil and other commodities, or was the product of earlier trade agreements. The full impact of trade and new trade agreements may not be felt until years or, in the case of a trade-induced innovation, for decades in the future.

In supporting open trade and greater integration with the world economy, the competitiveness strategy built on an American policy that started with the Reciprocal Trade Act of 1934. Under this act, the United States negotiated a series of bilateral trade agreements that, by 1945, had significantly lowered duties on a wide range of goods.[36] In the post–World War II era, the United States took the lead in negotiating a series of multilateral trade agreements that sharply lowered tariffs in the industrial democracies and started the process of dismantling nontariff barriers to trade as well.

In the late 1980s and the early 1990s, Presidents Reagan and Bush built on that legacy through multilateral and regional trade agreements. In the early 1990s, the George H. W. Bush administration was actively engaged in the Uruguay Round of multilateral trade negotiations that had been launched in Punta del Este in September 1986. The Bush administration also took the lead in proposing, negotiating, and signing NAFTA with Canada and Mexico.

If anything, the Clinton administration was even more active on trade. Despite considerable skepticism about the benefits of further trade concessions in his own party, then-candidate Clinton supported open trade as part of an overall growth or competitiveness strategy. Campaign aide Ira Shapiro suggested the phrase "compete not retreat," and the president made it his own. When Clinton gave his first major speech on international trade at American University in February 1992, the Shapiro phrase became his basic theme.[37]

The Clinton years were marked by early successes on trade, followed by some serious setbacks and then by added successes at the end of his second term. Clinton had endorsed the Bush administration's effort to forge NAFTA but demanded side agreements on labor rights and environmental protection. He got both, but faced stiff opposition in Congress. The first year of his administration also saw the development of a Framework Agreement with Japan[38] that sought to assess progress through a mix of quantitative and qualitative measures. In December 1993, the Clinton administration concluded the Uruguay Round of negotiations; it agreed on final details in April 1994, in Marrakech; and it worked successfully for congressional adoption of the implementing legislation after the midterm elections in November 1994. There were also other initiatives in particular regions or countries, the proposal for a Free Trade Agreement of the Americas, support for greater economic integration in the Asia-Pacific Economic Cooperation forum, and World Trade Organization membership for China. In the waning years of the Clinton presidency, the administration's trade team initiated bilateral trade negotiations with Chile and Jordan. Particularly in his first term, Clinton also coupled trade negotiations with an aggressive approach to export promotion.

There were setbacks, however. In the trade realm, the Clinton administration failed to achieve a Multilateral Investment Agreement that would have replaced the network of bilateral investment treaties among the industrial democracies. Nor was Clinton able to secure renewed "fast-track" authority (now also referred to as "trade promotion authority") or to launch a new round of multilateral trade negotiations at the 1999 Seattle meeting of the World Trade Organization.

The Clinton commitment to open markets and deeper international integration came at considerable political cost. NAFTA was strongly opposed by organized labor, an important constituency for the Democratic Party and for future Clinton initiatives. After his September 22, 1993, presentation of his health care proposal to a joint session of Congress, Clinton had a conversation with Lane Kirkland, then the AFL-CIO's president. "Mr. President," started Kirkland, "that was a terrific speech, and we have $10 million we'd like to spend on television promoting your health care plan. . . . Of course, if you insist on going ahead with NAFTA, we're going to take the $10 million and spend it in opposition to that."[39]

Since the 1970s, the United States had become ever more integrated into the world economy. Though international trade captured the bulk of attention, integrated capital markets and world financial flows were becoming increasingly important. With a competitiveness strategy that stressed low interest rates to foster public and private investment, the Clinton administration eventually adopted a rhetorical stance as well as growth policies consistent with a strong dollar.[40]

Clinton faced a serious financial challenge and significant domestic political risk when Mexico edged close to financial collapse in December 1994. The administration team feared that a financial default by Mexico would create a serious risk of contagion—the spread of financial panic to other emerging-market economies. Clinton sought congressional support for $50 billion in loan guarantees for the Mexican government. According to J. Bradford DeLong and Barry Eichengreen, "President Clinton was told that his reelection prospects could be effectively destroyed by this one issue if Mexico failed to pay the money back."[41] In their view, "nothing more than the decision to nonetheless go ahead could have made the commitment to globalization and openness more clear."[42]

But the real question is not policy intent or political courage but results. Did international trade and international integration contribute to job growth, foster rising incomes, stimulate productivity growth, and encourage innovation? Was trade a policy partner of a macroeconomic strategy based on encouraging investment?

The answer to both questions is yes. The same judgment would be made by large segments of the economics profession. In his overview of administration trade and international economic policy, Kennedy School professor Robert Lawrence points to sharp increases in trade and investment during the 1990s and concludes that the Clinton policy "surely . . . was" a success.[43]

Much the same can be said for the administration's approach to international finance. The commitment to a strong dollar and international capital flows allowed the United States to help finance the investment boom of the 1990s. There were also crises and, no doubt, some mistakes. In particular, the International Monetary Fund and the Clinton Treasury Department were premature in pressing a number of emerging-market countries to open their financial markets to short-term capital flows. In hindsight, these countries did not have the financial institutions, regulatory bodies, or experience to handle the mid-1990s surge in financial flows. Still, Lawrence Summers, the former secretary of the Treasury (and now president of Harvard University), is right when he argues that the crises are not the sole measure of success. Instead, Summers stressed the shift from a world where few countries had access to international capital to one where "a large number of countries could access capital from a large number of institutions."[44]

As the competitiveness strategy developed during the 1980s, there was a growing awareness that the whole was considerably larger than just the sum of its parts, that it was the synergy among its pieces that made the strategy dynamic. The Clinton Commerce Department had the lead responsibility for export promotion and the development of a civilian technology policy. In speeches, department officials would regularly use the phrase that has appeared above in several places about how today's innovation was tomorrow's export and how tomorrow's export helped fund the next round of innovation. Lawrence makes a complementary point in stressing that "U.S. trade policies . . . played an important role in creating an environment in which the U.S. and other economies could benefit from technology and innovation."[45]

Lael Brainard, a veteran of Clinton's National Economic Council, noted how "the course of trade policy over the 1990s was integrally shaped by the interaction with the overall state of the economy." She goes on to note that "trade developments were heavily conditioned by the Clinton Administration's commitment to fiscal discipline and the stunning performance of the information technology sector."[46]

Trade and the strong dollar policy also contributed to macroeconomic strength in the 1990s. By keeping direct price pressure on significant portions of the economy (tradable goods and services), open trade and the strong dollar made it all the easier for the FOMC to follow a policy of lower interest rates. Trade was also a very important part of a series of policies—deregulation, the emergence of new industries, and greater integration with the world economy—that made it difficult for many companies to raise prices. When companies could not raise prices, they turned to investment, adopted new technologies, or emphasized more rapid innovation. As a result, profits, wages, and income-raising productivity growth got a boost.

As applied in the 1990s, the emphasis on deeper international integration incurred costs as well as benefits. With an incomplete safety net, the incomplete portability of benefits, and a limited trade adjustment assistance

program in the 1990s, workers displaced by imports, the shift of plants overseas, and the decline of entire industries could face a difficult adjustment.
Despite the success in dealing with the 1994 Mexican financial crisis, the
administration and much of the financial community were unprepared for
the size and scope of the Asian financial crisis. The macroeconomic benefits
of a strong dollar and imports came at the cost of rising external debt and
large trade and current account deficits.

Still, the record of the 1990s is impressive. Foreign investment in the
United States did help keep interest rates lower and thus did contribute to
added private-sector investment. Inflation remained low throughout the
1990s and, at least in the financial press, there were persistent reports about
how trade was one of the factors that limited the pricing power of many corporations. In turn, the higher productivity growth that was, in part, spurred
by the added competition from trade did allow the Federal Reserve to pursue a more accommodative monetary policy that had a powerful influence
on growth in the 1990s. That decade also saw an increase in private spending on research and development and the rapid spread of the Internet and
other information technologies. What the 1990s do demonstrate is the impact both trade and trade agreements had on prosperity and the prospects for
long-term growth.

Technology: Harvesting the Past, Enabling the Present, and Strengthening the Future

In looking back at the 1990s, economists and most students of the economy
saw the development and adoption of new technologies as a critical element
in the mix of investment and productivity growth. The result was rapid growth
in the overall economy that, by the second half of the decade, brought rising prosperity to most Americans.

It was not just technology that changed. The 1990s also saw a growing
interest in an explicit technology policy that complemented the post–World
War II emphasis on scientific research. The two economic challengers of
the 1980s, Germany and Japan, had more active technology policies targeted at stimulating commercial innovations and the commercial application of existing technologies. Competition from Japan helped drive the
United States to adopt an explicit, active technology policy.

As was noted above, Clinton was the first modern presidential candidate
to make technology policy a major plank in his platform. He could build on

a significant base of past initiatives that provided tax incentives for research, encouraged commercializing federally supported research, and facilitated company-to-company collaboration on research. Having been authorized by the Omnibus Trade and Competitiveness Act of 1988, George H. W. Bush's administration took the first steps to fund the Commerce Department's Advanced Technology Program, expand the number of manufacturing extension centers, and support key research initiatives drawing on several agencies.

The Clinton administration increased efforts to spur new technologies, encouraged cooperative efforts between government laboratories and the private sector, and proposed sharp increases in funding for the Advanced Technology Program. President Clinton charged the Department of Commerce and its undersecretary for technology, Mary Lowe Good, with developing a comprehensive civilian technology policy. As part of that effort, the president secured increased funding for the Manufacturing Extension Partnership program to establish a nationwide system of manufacturing extension centers to speed the diffusion of technologies to small and medium-size businesses. The government focus on technology paralleled industry action to increase funding for near-to-market research, adapt the lean production technique to American conditions, and shorten the time between invention and the introduction of a new product to the commercial market.

In examining the 1990s, however, it is important to distinguish between the adoption of a more active technology policy and the long-term impact of technology. Although technology played a dramatic role in sharply increasing productivity growth, key technologies did not emerge overnight. The Internet, which became such a force in the 1990s and beyond, can trace its roots to innovations that, in some cases, date from World War II. The first general-purpose digital computer was created in 1946, and the transistor in 1948.

By speeding the diffusion of technology to small and medium-sized firms, the manufacturing extension centers made a contribution to the positive productivity trend of the 1990s. The Clinton administration also provided strong support for the Internet by encouraging its use, by supporting a freeze on Internet taxes, and by funding second-generation Internet research. The public and private emphasis on innovation in the 1990s created new technologies, but their impact during the decade was relatively small compared with that of earlier innovations.

Like deficit reduction, technology policy also contributed to business confidence. When President Clinton worked to deliver on candidate Clinton's technology-related promises, it was a decided boost for technology-based industries that had not been the focus of the preceding Bush administration.

The Internet and Information Technology

The Internet is a powerful example of how current policy can build on a stock of earlier innovations and investments. There were 313,000 Internet hosts in 1990. The number had jumped to 42,230,000 by 2000.[47] The explosive growth of the Internet is associated with the acceleration in productivity growth that characterized the 1990s.

The Internet, however, was not itself a product of the 1990s. Its history goes back to a 1974 paper by Vincent Cerf and Robert Kahn describing a possible network of networks. The idea was pursued by the Pentagon's Defense Advanced Research Projects Administration and was expanded to supercomputer centers by the National Science Foundation and eventually to the private sector in the mid-1990s.[48] In terms of growth, jobs, and productivity, the Internet offers many lessons. Three are important for setting future policy: public investments in technology are often critical for growth; today's investment may not fully blossom until sometimes years later; and the development, adoption, and diffusion of technologies depends critically on the active involvement of the private sector. The explosive growth of the Internet in the 1990s very much fit the outlines of the New Growth Compact, whereby the government developed a precompetitive technology and set investment fostering rules of the game. Forces outside of government did much of the rest.

Technology Policy

The Clinton administration's February 1993 statement on technology policy and the earlier campaign document on which it was based were really an articulation of growth strategies viewed through the prism of technology and technology policy. "The administration anticipated a broader role than simply public financing for research and development. Theirs was to be a strategy of investment—in technical knowledge, in human skills, and in research institutions—carried out through a variety of public–private partnerships."[49]

The president and his science and technology adviser, Jack Gibbons, created the National Science and Technology Council to broaden the ability of the administration to coordinate multiagency research projects.[50] Faced with congressional opposition to either higher energy taxes or mandated increases in mileage standards, the administration created a Partnership for a New Generation of Vehicles with Chrysler (now DaimlerChrysler), Ford, and General Motors.

Technology Policy: How Important in the 1990s?

How important was technology policy in the 1990s boom? Martin Baily, a member of the Council of Economic Advisers in President Clinton's second term, articulates a widely shared view that though fiscal and monetary policy had the greatest impact during the 1990s, explicit initiatives in technology, education, and training made complementary contributions. During that decade, federal research and development spending showed relatively little growth, with the exception of funding for the life sciences through the National Institutes of Health. Baily notes, however, that private-sector spending during the decade grew rapidly, so that the overall national commitment to research and development was much more pronounced. Initiatives in the field of education and particularly training also helped speed the adoption of new technologies, though much of the payoff from investments in education lies in the future.[51]

The rapid productivity growth of the 1990s grew from seeds that had been planted years or even decades before. Any technology policy will build on past policies and structures and complement the drive for innovation in the private sector. But the growth of the 1990s has three solid lessons for the future. First, investing in innovation today is critical for productivity growth in the sometime distant tomorrows. Second, today's technology policy can improve the overall innovation system, speed the adoption of new technologies, and bolster business confidence that feeds into investments in plant, equipment, and research. Third, the private sector has a powerful influence on the creation of new inventions, the diffusion of new process technologies, and the speed with which ideas move from the laboratory to the living room. The private sector may fund research in the university, conduct basic or increasingly applied research on its own, generate venture funds to support innovative ideas, and bring products to market. In the twenty-first century, America's competitiveness strategy must pay attention to the entire innovation system.

Education and Training:
Responding to Today and Preparing for the Long Run

Like technology, today's investments in education can take a long time to have an economic impact. For instance, the development and application of a new and highly effective approach to teaching reading would affect today's first-grade students, but this approach would not have an impact on the economy until the students graduated from high school or completed postsecondary education. When today's first graders enter the workforce, they will be a relatively small addition to a stock of workers trained under an older, hypothetically less effective system. More advanced training or education—whether inside a company, at a community college, or with individual effort—will make a more immediate contribution to productivity but still adds a relatively small flow to a stock of American workers that is approaching 150 million.[52]

The periodic focus on education is not new. Faced with past challenges, the country has often turned to education. In the wake of the Soviet launch of Sputnik in 1957, the United States responded by emphasizing mathematics and science and the mastery of critical foreign languages. Education became a national security question. In 1983, A Nation at Risk, released by Terrence Bell, President Reagan's secretary of education, described an educational system that was no longer keeping pace with the standards set by other countries.[53] The report pointed to the Japanese challenge in automobiles, a state-of-the-art steel mill in South Korea, and the growing prominence of German machine tools. Those developments, the report concluded, "signify a redistribution of trained capability throughout the globe."[54]

While work was being done on A Nation at Risk, thinking about national competitiveness was already taking shape. Competitiveness strategists made their own link to national security, arguing that the U.S. military edge often depended on technology and an innovative economy that produced it. The capacity for creating and adopting new technologies was, in turn, linked to a strong education system. When the House Democratic Caucus published its Rebuilding the Road to Opportunity, education (including technical and computer literacy) was already identified as a key element in a growth (or competitiveness) strategy that emphasized a variety of public and private investments.

In his 1988 campaign, President George H. W. Bush vowed to be the education president. In pursuit of education, Bush initiated one of the few summit meetings ever held with the nation's governors. Working with the

National Governors Association, Bush and the governors articulated six broad goals for education, including a growing emphasis on standards.

Goals and standards were part of the Clinton approach as well. As governor of Arkansas, Clinton had been one of two governors who worked closely with President Bush and his administration. In pursuing education goals and several other initiatives, Roger Porter, President Bush's assistant for economic and domestic policy, correctly points to "continuity in policy across administrations."[55]

But in embracing, articulating, and refining a national competitiveness strategy, the Clinton administration strove to move well beyond continuity. Alan B. Krueger and Cecilia E. Rouse provide a detailed overview of 1990s initiatives in the field of education and training.[56] Krueger and Rouse identify "four core principles that underlay most of the Clinton Administration's initiatives in the labor and education arena."[57] They point to efforts to reduce wage inequality, increase skills, streamline existing programs, and "make it easier for workers and students to cope with a volatile economy."[58]

Krueger and Rouse are positive about many of the changes initiated in the 1990s, but in the end they agree that the changes were "not an essential contributor to the record economic growth in the 1990s."[59] They note the relatively modest increases in federal investment in education and training and the expected rate of return on such investments. In their view, more ambitious plans by the Clinton administration were "side-tracked" by the emphasis on deficit reduction and further limited by the shift to a Republican-controlled House after the 1994 election.[60]

Yet, a strict focus on federal spending understates the impact of the competitiveness–Clinton approach. In addition to the four principles spelled out by Krueger and Rouse, it is important to remember three other factors at play. First, the competitiveness approach made education and training part of a much broader growth strategy. Second, the competitiveness approach and the Clinton version of it always put education policy in the context of the broader currents that were affecting the private sector as well as state and local governments. Third, there was a persistent emphasis on public–private partnerships tailored to specific regional needs.

The principal Clinton campaign document, *Putting People First,* had a separate section on education and education reform. The discussion of training and the proposal to require "every employer to spend 1.5 percent of payroll for continued education and training," however, came in the section on international trade.[61] In linking training, technology, and other investments to export performance, Clinton was following a path similar to the one articulated in the 1985 report of the President's Commission on Industrial Competitiveness (or the Young Commission). To meet the standards of international competition while raising national incomes required improved productivity growth, which in turn depended on an educated and well-trained workforce.

In *The Roaring Nineties: Can Full Employment Be Sustained?* editors Alan B. Krueger and Robert Solow bring together a series of studies that seek to explain why the 1990s achieved rapid growth, low unemployment, and low inflation.[62] The authors list several factors—including past investments in training, shifts in organizational technology widely adopted in the private sector, and the move to outsourcing. Other authors wondered if the unexpected productivity growth that brought lower inflation and wages that lagged behind productivity growth would erode as individuals adjusted their wage demands to the higher rate of productivity growth. There were also a number of favorable "supply shocks" that ranged from falling energy prices to the strong dollar. The broader point was that federal policy should always be set with an eye to trends in the private sector and, in the twenty-first century, in the world economy.

In several instances, the Clinton approach was designed to use small carrots, information, or the bully pulpit as a way to encouraging a large change in private-sector or individual choices. The small-carrot approach was used in the education technology program described above in chapter 11. The general idea was that though few would be chosen, the many who were called would continue to pursue the stated goal in any case.

Clinton set a tone for the administration when he stressed the new challenges facing America and Americans. He and others in the administration stressed the shift from a world of one job and one employer to a time when Americans could expect to have several jobs, some with different employers, and many requiring a constant upgrading of skills. In addition to training and education, the administration developed policies to foster lifelong learning. In describing the Clinton administration's efforts to promote the use of technology in education, Krueger and Rouse point to a number of specific programs but also to a number of "bully pulpit initiatives."[63]

How much did the first George H. W. Bush's and Bill Clinton's education policies contribute to the growth and rising incomes of the 1990s? As was noted above, we will not be able to fully evaluate the impact of the George H. W. Bush, Clinton, and George W. Bush administrations until well into the future. In assessing the primary and secondary school system, the performance of American schoolchildren in tests administered by the

National Assessment of Education Progress shows relatively little improvement since the 1960s. U.S. performance on international tests in mathematics and science demonstrate that the country has a long way to go to meet the top international standard.

There are enormous strengths in the highly decentralized American system. The average U.S. high school's performance is part of a system that offers a wide variety of advanced placement or honors tests. The American emphasis on participation, questioning, and developing an independent view contributes to political as well as economic strength. U.S. research universities still dominate the list of leading international institutions. Outside scientific fields, U.S. universities attract many of the world's best students in medicine, law, business, and a broad array of graduate studies.

As for lasting impact, Clinton mixed programs and tax incentives for added training with a frequently repeated message that in the 1990s (and beyond) many Americans would hold several jobs in their lifetime and would need to frequently upgrade their skills. Beyond specific public or private initiatives, the individual choices of millions of American workers will have an enormous future impact on everything from growth to individual opportunity.

Education, training, and the acquisition of new skills have been a critical part of past economic success and will be even more important in the future. The collapse of the Soviet Union, China's turn toward markets, and India's more outward-looking approach have added 2.5 billion people to the world economy since the late 1980s. China, India, and Russia all emphasize training in mathematics, science, and engineering. Their collective size and commitment to education create a growing challenge to the U.S. economy and the U.S. system of education. Long-term competitiveness in the twenty-first century will hinge on strengthening and adapting the American learning system to this new competition.

Even where employment involves human skills not usually taught in the classroom or a great degree of physical strength, education still is central to preparing informed citizens, meeting the country's commitment to equal opportunity, and opening doors for personal interests and growth. In no small measure, education is the future of the American Dream and America itself.

Business Confidence: The Return of Animal Spirits

Economists have long recognized the importance of psychology and often sought to measure intangibles such as a willingness to take risks or to plan ahead. When John Maynard Keynes talked about business leaders' willingness to invest, he noted that, in part, investments were the product of a buoyant optimism about the future—what Keynes referred to as "animal spirits." The question of business and market confidence is woven through former secretary of the Treasury Robert Rubin's *In an Uncertain World*, a reflection on his own professional life as well as his service in Washington.[64] Financial pages in newspapers now routinely contain reports on consumer or business confidence. Surveys attempt to plot future consumer demand and business plans for the purchase of equipment or commitments to research and development.

Even before taking office, President Clinton was moving to build credible economic policies and to buoy confidence in the economic future. The December 1992 gathering of economic specialists and private-sector leaders in Little Rock showed the nation a president focused on the economy, in command of the situation, and reaching out to many of the key actors who influence the course of the national economy. The by now famous lunch with Alan Greenspan dealt explicitly with business confidence. According to published reports,[65] Greenspan explained high long-term interest rates as the product of the markets' fear of deficit-driven future inflation and a lack of confidence in contemporary politicians. In these specific circumstances, Clinton's deficit reduction policy ran against expectations and did succeed in bringing down long-term rates in 1993 in a way that fostered investment and growth.

Confidence was a key element in the strategy. In his discussion of fiscal policy, Rubin recounted the efforts of Clinton's economic team to spell out the trade-off between a contractionary (i.e., reducing spending and or raising taxes) fiscal policy and the expansionary impact of the hoped-for reduction in long-term interest rates. It was only later that they realized "that even more important would be the effect on confidence."[66] Although "the increase in confidence and the effects of increased confidence are hard to capture, [they] were key to the whole period."[67]

Clinton and much of his economic team worked hard at bolstering private-sector confidence. As in many administrations, the secretary of commerce is a key link to the business community. As secretary of commerce in the first Clinton term, Ron Brown worked aggressively to reach out to the business community. His trade missions were not just focused at building commercial good will around the world. Invitations were targeted at companies that were close to landing overseas contracts and felt that the boost of a trade mission might just close the deal. At the same time,

Brown worked hard to tell the business world that its export success was part of the Clinton strategy and the country's prosperity.

Clinton had made technology and technology policy a centerpiece of his campaign. In late 1993, Brown led a delegation to Silicon Valley to report on the progress the administration had made in turning promises into policy. Following the lead suggested by Rubin's insight about confidence, the report to Silicon Valley was a clear indication that the administration took the Silicon Valleys of the country seriously; that the administration was listening and responding added to a general sense of business confidence.

The anxiety of the 1980s and early 1990s was not limited to the business community. Much of the country was concerned about the challenges posed by international competition, the impact of new technologies, and the pace of change in the economy. The Clinton administration talked ceaselessly about the realities of economic change and the country's ability to turn that change to its advantage. In his reflections on the Clinton administration and the new economy, Martin Baily, a member of the Council of Economic Advisers in the second Clinton term, noted how "President Clinton and Vice President Gore both embraced the new economy."[68] The Clinton administration was not just talking about new realities but also adopting policies— Baily points to the Earned Income Tax Credit "and increased education and training opportunities" that "made economic change and adjustment more acceptable to the population at large."[69]

Virtually all the political observers of the 1990s commented on how Clinton, like President Reagan, projected an optimism and confidence in the future that made Americans more confident about their own prospects. Though hard to measure, that confidence did matter.

The New Growth Compact and the Emerging Partnership Nation

From the late 1970s onward, the public and private sectors were looking for a combination of public policies and private initiative that would bring the country back to a path of rapid productivity growth and rising incomes. It took private initiatives, public investments, and a climate that encouraged private investment. It demanded public policies and private business practices that were adapted to the reality of global competition and global realities. Technology, technology policy (past, present, and future), and a capacity for innovation were all part of the story.

Over the course of the 1980s, there emerged something of a New Growth

Compact. There developed a shared understanding among the various components of the public and private sectors on what made for an effective long-term growth strategy. In addition to a focus on investments and innovation, there was a commitment to broadly shared benefits and to policies that helped individuals and the private sector adjust to a rapidly changing economy.

In many cases, the public and private sectors developed a wide variety of partnerships that facilitated investment or innovation. These partnerships were of many types—some involving different levels of government, others including educational institutions, and some limited to either the public or private sphere.

Looking back to a Decade of Success and a Half-Decade of Excess

From the perspective of the early twenty-first century, we can see more clearly the successes and the excesses of the 1990s. In part, the success can be read in the numbers—rapid and sustained productivity growth, low unemployment and significant employment gains, low interest rates and high rates of capital formation. In a word, it was prosperity today built on a range of investments that promised prosperity tomorrow.

The successes were built on a comprehensive long-term growth or competitiveness strategy coupled with a wide-ranging restructuring of the private sector. The emergence of an informal New Growth Compact and the proliferation of public–private and other partnerships was an important part of the story.

It was not just good policy or good corporate practice. Good timing and good luck also made major contributions to creating the best economic record in the history of the United States. Instead of a perfect storm, the 1990s, particularly the second half of the decade, seems like a perfect summer in which good policy was combined with all the right elements to create a widely shared prosperity.

After three years of declining financial markets, slow growth mixed with three quarters of recession, rising unemployment, and an uncertain economic future, the excesses of the 1990s come into starker relief. No one disputes the existence of an extraordinary financial bubble. When Alan Greenspan first warned of "irrational exuberance" in December 1966, there was an initial decline in market values that quickly gave way to a rapid increase. Individuals and institutional buyers were paying high prices for stocks with no reported earnings and untested business plans.

Part of the surge in demand for information technology equipment was the prudent corporate reaction to the possibility of computer-based disruption as the year 2000 approached. But the telecommunications and Internet equipment manufacturers went beyond hard orders and were themselves apparently dazzled by the promise of online prosperity. They started financing their own sales to what they believed were promising dot-coms. As one dot-com after another failed, the equipment manufacturers were left with unpaid bills and the telecommunications companies with an enormous base of unused fiber-optic capacity that suppressed near-term demand for their products. Just as the 1990s had seen an investment led boom, the early twenty-first century saw an investment-led slowdown.

Even more troubling were the rolling revelations about failures in the accounting profession, false statements by brokerage houses, duplicitous (albeit often legal) practices by investment banks, and the outright fraud found in a number of leading companies. More than a year after Enron's collapse in December 2001, revelations of questionable practices continued.

Lessons Learned, Lessons Forgotten

The public policies and private practices that were so important in the 1990s did not develop overnight. It took a decade and more to fully develop a national competitiveness strategy and to take it from idea to legislation to national policy. The same was true for corporate practices. Throughout the 1980s, one American company after another struggled to change its organization, its manufacturing process, and its service delivery to match or exceed the best in the world. To complement the public emphasis on basic technology as well as basic science, companies increased their own spending on research and development as a necessary element in maintaining a competitive edge.

With the end of the post–Cold War era, the war on global terrorism, and the emphasis on homeland security, there is a danger that the economic policy lessons of the 1990s will be neglected, perhaps even forgotten. In the 1990s, government policy consisted of a comprehensive competitiveness strategy that combined private investment, a commitment to open markets, and public investments in education, training, and technology. Now, much of economic policy seems to have turned back to the early Reagan years and to the supply-side theory that cuts in marginal tax rates will be the key to long-term prosperity. The tax cut aspect of fiscal policy seems to the most prominent if not the only arrow in today's economic quiver.

At the same time, a series of corporate, investment banking, brokerage, and accounting scandals have created a skepticism about the reliability of corporate America. Instead of a growth compact with the private sector, many Americans may be thinking about whom to sue over their record financial losses. A dramatic turning away from markets, an excessive dependence on government, or a rejection of public–private partnerships would be a costly mistake with long-term consequences.

Tomorrow's Promise:
Growth, Partnership, and the Future of America

Tomorrow's promise depends on adapting a competitiveness strategy to new circumstances, continuing to define the New Growth Compact, and developing effective public–private partnerships. In part, it will require developing new standards for corporate accounting and corporate governance that restore individual and community confidence in markets and corporate America. Some of the reforms have already taken legislative or regulatory shape. Others are under consideration. The stock exchanges are adopting their own set of new standards and institutional investors are rediscovering their ability to influence corporate governance. The U.S. Financial Accounting Standards Board and its international counterpart, the International Accounting Standards Board, are working to develop improved accounting standards. Less tangible but just as important, some business schools and leading corporate statesmen are putting renewed emphasis on corporate citizenship. Some academics are beginning to rethink the idea that corporations are only about near-term shareholder value.

The question of corporate and financial reform is critical to the country's future. An adequate treatment of the subject is, however, well beyond the scope of this volume. The future also depends on sound public policy and a federal government that is agile and innovative enough to be part of a New Growth Compact and, in many cases, an effective partner with the private sector, various levels of government, and other institutions. Government investments and growth strategies must be set with an awareness of global market forces and the growth strategies of other major economic powers.

The future is not just a simple story of public and private hands across a traditional divide. There are inevitable tensions between country and corporation. A purely financial calculus will often dictate concentrating research or production facilities in different locations around the globe. From a national point of view, that may create vulnerable supply lines or constitute a loss of the spillover effects from research. But the competitiveness movement's commitment to rising prosperity for all Americans will require investments in education and training as ladders of opportunity that will also involve the private sector. It is to all these challenges that we turn in the remaining chapters of the book.

Notes

1. See, for instance, Alan B. Krueger and Robert Solow, eds., *The Roaring Nineties: Can Full Employment Be Sustained?* (New York: Russell Sage Foundation and Century Foundation Press, 2001).

2. James P. Womack, Daniel T. Jones, and Daniel Roos, *The Machine That Changed the World: The Story of Lean Production* (New York: Macmillan, 1990).

3. Richard K. Lester, *The Productive Edge: How U.S. Industries Are Pointing the Way to a New Era of Economic Growth* (New York: W. W. Norton, 1998).

4. Lester, *Productive Edge,* 143.

5. See Michael Porter, Mariko Sakakibara, and Hirotaka Takeuchi, *Can Japan Compete?* (Cambridge, Mass.: Perseus Publishing, 2000).

6. Alan S. Blinder and Janet L. Yellen, "The Fabulous Decade: Macroeconomic Lessons from the 1990s," in *The Roaring Nineties,* ed. Krueger and Solow, 95.

7. Blinder and Yellen, "Fabulous Decade," 117–121.

8. Blinder and Yellen provide a useful overview of the favorable supply shocks in "Fabulous Decade," 121–28.

9. Greenspan first used the phrase in a December 5, 1966, speech to the American Enterprise Institute in Washington, when the bubble first began to appear.

10. Paul Blustein, *The Chastening: Inside the Crisis That Rocked the Global Financial System and Humbled the IMF* (New York: Public Affairs, 2001), 362.

11. Blinder and Yellen, "Fabulous Decade," 129.

12. Blinder and Yellen, "Fabulous Decade," 130.

13. Many of the essays in Krueger and Solow, eds. *Roaring Nineties,* are devoted to just this question.

14. Christopher J. Bailey, "Clintonomics," in Paul S. Herrnson and Dilys M. Hill, *The Clinton Presidency: The First Term* (New York: St. Martin's Pres, 1999), 86.

15. Paul J. Quirk and William Cunion, "Clinton's Domestic Policy: The Lessons of a 'New Democrat,'" in *The Clinton Legacy,* ed. Colin Campbell and Bert A. Rockman (New York: Seven Bridges / Chatham House, 2000), 214.

16. Quirk and Cunion, "Clinton's Domestic Policy," 214.

17. See, for instance, *American Economic Policy in the 1990s,* ed. Jeffrey A. Frankel and Peter R. Orszag (Cambridge, Mass.: MIT Press, 2002); Bob Woodward, *Maestro: Greenspan's Fed and the American Boom* (New York: Simon & Schuster, 2000); Blinder and Yellen, "Fabulous Decade"; and Justin Martin, *Greenspan: The Man Behind Money* (Cambridge, Mass.: Perseus Publishing, 2000). In his *The Natural: The Misunderstood Presidency of Bill Clinton* (New York: Doubleday, 2002), Joe Klein speaks to economic policy as part of his broader retrospective on the Clinton presidency.

18. Martin, *Greenspan*, 174.

19. Martin, *Greenspan*, 176.

20. Council of Economic Advisers, *1990 Economic Report of the President* (Washington, D.C.: U.S. Government Printing Office, 1990), 297.

21. Council of Economic Advisers, *1988 Economic Report of the President* (Washington, D.C.: U.S. Government Printing Office, 1988), 292.

22. In response to the sharp drop in the stock market on October 19, 1987, Greenspan had followed his announcement with policies that made ample credit available. However, as the economy continued to show signs of strength, the Federal Reserve adopted "a more cautious tack" and "took no further moves to ease policy." See Council of Economic Advisers, *1988 Economic Report of the President,* 45. In March 1988, the Federal Reserve effectively tightened monetary policy by allowing the money supply to come "closer to the mid-point" of its target range. In July, the Federal Reserve announced its "preliminary policy intentions" to lower its target ranges for 1989 as part of an ongoing policy to reduce the rate of inflation. See Council of Economic Advisers, *1989 Economic Report of the President* (Washington, D.C.: U.S. Government Printing Office, 1989), 280.

23. Klein, *Natural,* 50.

24. Bob Woodward, *The Agenda: Inside the Clinton White House* (New York: Simon & Schuster, 1994), 71; Martin Walker, *The President We Deserve: His Rise, Falls, and Comebacks* (New York: Crown Publishers, 1996), 169.

25. Woodward, *Agenda,* 98.

26. Blinder and Yellen, "Fabulous Decade," 107.

27. Richard Darman, *Who's In Control: Polar Politics and the Sensible Center* (New York: Simon & Schuster, 1996), 202.

28. Robert Rubin, "Comments" on "Fiscal Policy and Social Security Policy During the 1990s," by Douglas W. Elmendorf, Jeffrey B. Liebman, and David W. Wilcox, in *American Economic Policy in the 1990s,* ed. Frankel and Orszag, 131.

29. Woodward, *Maestro,* 231, as quoted in Blinder and Yellen, "Fabulous Decade," 107.

30. Martin, *Greenspan,* 204.

31. Blinder and Yellen, "Fabulous Decade," 101.

32. Blinder and Yellen believed that "five factors contributed to the [Clinton's] proposal's unusual and virtually instant credibility in the financial markets." Their five factors included the (1) size and boldness of the deficit reduction plan; (2) a seriousness of purpose demonstrated by proposing tax increases; (3) attacking some "budgetary sacred cows for slaughter" (Blinder and Yellen specifically mention the provision to make more social security benefits taxable); (4) avoiding the use of accounting gimmicks; and (5) basing the plan on the more pessimistic economic forecast of the Congressional Budget Office. Blinder and Yellen, "Fabulous Decade," 103–4.

33. Joseph E. Stiglitz, *The Roaring Nineties: A New History of the World's Most Prosperous Decade* (New York: W. W. Norton, 2003), 41–43.

34. Stiglitz, *Roaring Nineties,* 45.

35. Blinder and Yellen, "Fabulous Decade," 146–47.

36. I. M. Destler, *American Trade Politics,* 2nd ed. (Washington, D.C.: Institute for International Economics with the Twentieth Century Fund, 1992), 12.

37. Robert Z. Lawrence, "International Trade Policy in the 1990s," in *American Economic Policy in the 1990s,* ed. Frankel and Orszag, 285. In his "International Trade

Policy in the 1990s," Lawrence gives an insightful, comprehensive overview of the successes and failures of the Clinton administration's trade policies.

38. Lawrence, "International Trade Policy in the 1990s," 302–6.

39. Klein, *Natural,* 80–81.

40. See J. Bradford DeLong and Barry Eichengreen, "Between Meltdown and Moral Hazard: International and Financial Policies of the Clinton Administration," in *American Economic Policy in the 1990s,* ed. Frankel and Orszag, 197–204.

41. DeLong and Eichengreen, "Between Meltdown and Moral Hazard," 213.

42. DeLong and Eichengreen, "Between Meltdown and Moral Hazard," 213.

43. Lawrence, "International Trade Policy in the 1990s," 316.

44. Lawrence Summers, "Comments" on "Between Meltdown and Moral Hazard" by DeLong and Eichengreen, in *American Economic Policy in the 1990s,* ed. Frankel and Orszag, 260.

45. Lawrence, "International Trade Policy in the 1990s," 316.

46. Lael Brainard, "Comments" on "International Trade Policy in the 1990s" by Lawrence, in *American Economic Policy in the 1990s,* ed. Frankel and Orszag, 342.

47. Pamela Samuelson and Hal B. Varian, "The 'New Economy' and Information Technology Policy," in *American Economic Policy in the 1990s,* ed. Frankel and Orszag, 365. On page 364, Samuelson and Varian given a thumbnail sketch of the Internet's history.

48. Samuelson and Varian, "'New Economy,'" 364.

49. Lewis M. Branscomb and James H. Keller, eds., *Investing in Innovation: Creating a Research and Innovation Policy That Works* (Cambridge, Mass.: MIT Press, 1998), 2.

50. See David M. Hart, "Managing Technology Policy at the White House," in *Investing in Innovation,* ed. Branscomb and Keller, 445–47. I served as the Commerce Department's representative on the National Science and Technology Council subcommittee on transportation.

51. Martin N. Baily, "Comments" on "International Trade Policy in the 1990s" by Lawrence, in *American Economic Policy in the 1990s,* ed. Frankel and Orszag, 416–17.

52. The *2004 Economic Report of the President* reports a 2003 civilian labor force of 146.5 million. See Council of Economic Advisers, *2004 Economic Report of the President* (Washington, D.C.: U.S. Government Printing Office, 2004), table B 35, p. 327.

53. On April 26, 1981, Secretary of Education Terence Bell established the National Commission on Excellence in Education. Two years later, in April 1983, the commission delivered *A Nation at Risk* to the secretary. The text of the report can be found at http://www.ed.gov/pubs/NatAtRisk/risk.html.

54. National Commission on Excellence in Education, *Nation at Risk,* 2.

55. Robert Porter, "Comment" on "Putting Students and Workers First? Education and Labor Policy in the 1990s" by Alan B Krueger and Cecilia E. Rouse, in *American Economic Policy in the 1990s,* ed. Frankel and Orszag, 739.

56. Alan B Krueger and Cecilia E. Rouse, "Putting Students and Workers First? Education and Labor Policy in the 1990s," in *American Economic Policy in the 1990s,* ed. Frankel and Orszag, 663–728.

57. Krueger and Rouse, "Putting Students and Workers First?" 666.

58. Krueger and Rouse, "Putting Students and Workers First?" 666.

59. Krueger and Rouse, "Putting Students and Workers First?" 719.

60. Krueger and Rouse, "Putting Students and Workers First?" 663.

61. Bill Clinton and Al Gore, *Putting People First: How We Can All Change America* (New York: Times Books, 1992), 159.

62. Krueger and Solow, *Roaring Nineties,* xvii–xivi.

63. Krueger and Rouse, "Putting Students and Workers First?" 685.

64. Robert E. Rubin and Jacob Weisberg, *In an Uncertain World: Tough Choices from Wall Street to Washington* (New York: Random House, 2003).

65. See Woodward, *Agenda,* 69. Also see Walker, *President We Deserve,* 168–69. Walker reports that Greenspan referred to a "crisis of confidence; the markets did not trust the politicians" (p. 168).

66. Rubin, "Comments," in *American Economic Policy in the 1990s,* ed. Frankel and Orszag, 131. Rubin again stressed the impact on confidence in his own *In an Uncertain World.* "In retrospect, the effect of the Clinton economic plan on business and consumer confidence may have been even more important than the effect on interest rates," in Rubin and Weisberg, *In an Uncertain World,* 122.

67. Rubin, "Comments," in *American Economic Policy in the 1990s,* ed. Frankel and Orszag, 132.

68. Baily, "Comments," in *American Economic Policy in the 1990s,* ed. Frankel and Orszag, 417.

69. Baily, "Comments," in *American Economic Policy in the 1990s,* ed. Frankel and Orszag, 417.

Chapter 14

Competing for the Future

In the first decade of the twenty-first century, the economy is again becoming a priority. In thinking about the economy, today Americans face a new set of economic conditions and new challenges at home and abroad. This chapter will assess the changed economic landscape, describe some of the economic challenges facing the country, and suggest how a strategy for competitiveness or long-term productivity growth might be developed for the twenty-first century. In particular, this chapter will examine policies that will create an environment that fosters public and private investment. Subsequent chapters will emphasize strategies for stimulating innovation, expanding the nation's commitment to lifelong learning, and broadening the country's approach to global engagement. The concluding chapter will link a twenty-first-century competitiveness strategy to an American Dream for the twenty-first century and the future of America's global mission.

How can the United States build its economic strength in the twenty-first century? What policies and initiatives should the country pursue? The 1990s pointed to the success of a competitiveness strategy that fostered public and private investment, strengthened the nation's ability to innovate, took many steps toward a system of lifelong learning, and sought new opportunities through active competition in global markets. As the country pursued a competitiveness strategy, it developed an informal New Growth Compact that stressed the complementary roles played by the public and private sectors. During the past two decades, the country also became something of a Partnership Nation as the private and public sectors sought economic progress through a variety of partnerships—often with each other. Finally, the competitiveness strategy of the 1990s was built on the premise that the goal of economic policy was to raise the standard of living and the economic opportunities of every American and not just those who are already successful.

The broad outlines of a twenty-first-century competitiveness strategy are clear, but the specific policies pursued with so much success in the 1990s need to be adapted to the economic and political circumstances of the early twenty-first century. Both the domestic and global economies have changed. The United States again faces a host of challenges that will call on its economic resources.

The Challenges Ahead

The list of global challenges is long and growing. Since the tragic terrorist attacks on the World Trade Center and the Pentagon on September 11, 2001, national attention has shifted to questions of security—at home and abroad. By mid-2004, America had embarked on a costly and decades-long effort to bring enduring democracy and market-based prosperity to Afghanistan, Iraq, and the Middle East. Working in conjunction with the European Union, Russia, and the United Nations, the United States has been seeking to establish, by 2005, a secure Israel and an independent, democratic Palestinian State. Any final settlement will require significant investments in Palestine to create the infrastructure for sustained prosperity. In July 2003, President George W. Bush sent a small contingent of American forces to Liberia to help restore order and keep the peace. With serious conflicts in other parts of Africa, pressure for further interventions is likely to grow. Military intervention and long-term democracy building will put added demands on the American military and on the U.S. Treasury.

In a world where hundreds of millions struggle merely to survive, simple morality as well as national security demand a commitment to global growth. The continuing technological advancements in communications and the ease of world travel have brought the picture of industrial-world living standards to the most remote villages. Rapid increases in population and repressive governments create their own pressures for change. Both are often found in economies that grow enough to upset traditional structures but not enough to satisfy modern ambitions. The result is a volatile combination that can breed terrorism.[1]

There are a host of other global challenges. Successful completion of the

George W. Bush administration's ambitious set of bilateral, regional, and multilateral trade negotiations will, over the long-term, foster growth in the United States and around the world. The inevitable pain of economic adjustment can be eased by a growing economy and effective adjustment assistance. In addition to fighting the global pandemic of AIDS, the United States and other prosperous nations are placing more emphasis on developing vaccines and cures for a growing list of tropical diseases. The 2003 outbreak of Severe Acute Respiratory Syndrome (SARS) temporarily slowed economic activity in Asia and could have had broader economic consequences. The quick global response to SARS also points to the value of continuing to build a global monitoring capacity to stop diseases before they spread.

The prospect of global warming was already driving a search for alternatives to hydrocarbon fuels. In the wake of September 11, 2001, there is again a renewed emphasis on reducing American dependence on overseas energy supplies. The Bush administration and private industry are both investing in fuel cells powered by hydrogen.[2] In addition to perfecting the manufacture of hydrogen-powered engines, research will be directed at clean, energy-efficient means of producing and distributing hydrogen. The adjustment to new fuels holds enormous promise but will require protracted economic investment and significant economic adjustment.

At home, the country is facing the impending retirement and growing medical needs of the baby boom generation. Educating the children of the baby boom, the so-called baby boom echo, is already straining the country's higher education system. President Bush's call "to leave no child behind" is sure to require added resources as well as higher standards for the country's primary and secondary school system. More than 40 million Americans still lack health insurance. Continued population growth through immigration brings benefits, but it also demands more spending on education, health care, and other social services.

In the twenty-first century, as in the twentieth, American success and leadership will build on the long-term strength of the country's economy as well as the enduring appeal of its ideals. The pace, nature, and equitable distribution of global growth will affect American morality, future economic growth, prospects for U.S. leadership in the world, and the state of international security. The competitiveness challenge did not end with the prosperity of the 1990s. Building a competitive economy at home and abroad is very much a twenty-first-century project.

The Changing Economic Context

From the stagflation of the 1970s to what some refer to as the "Roaring Nineties,"[3] the U.S. economy has gone through a series of changes. Now, as America enters the twenty-first century, the domestic economy and the international context continue to evolve. Where inflation had been the concern in the late 1970s, in 2003 financial anxiety briefly turned to a falling price level or deflation[4]—a reality that had already affected the manufacturing sector. Rapid productivity growth, slow growth abroad, and new competitors everywhere combined to erode the pricing power of whole sectors of the economy.

The question of deflation largely disappeared by 2004, as rapid growth in Asia and concern about geopolitical risks drove commodity and overall price levels upward. If Asia continues its rapid growth, there will be persistent pressure on the price of oil and other key commodities. But the existence of excess global manufacturing capacity, large pools of unemployed labor, a rapid pace of innovation, and the growth in global competition for online digital services are all forces that should limit the prospects for resurgent inflation.

The U.S. economy has become ever more closely tied to the world economy. Relative to the size of the American economy, imports and exports have grown by more than 50 percent over the past twenty years, and in 2003 imports and exports of goods and services amounted to roughly 22 percent of the country's output.[5] Except for a few firms in the defense sector, virtually every manufacturing enterprise and a growing array of services face international competition. More and more trade consists of parts rather than products, and a large and growing percentage of international trade takes place among the various branches of large multinational companies.

With global integration has come added prosperity and increased vulnerability. The combination of international sourcing of parts and the practice of just-in-time inventory has made firms more vulnerable to disruptions of supply. Tightened border controls in the wake of September 11, a West Coast longshoreman's strike, and the 2003 SARS outbreak all had consequences for international trade.

As the competitiveness strategy developed in the 1980s, the focus was on matching the price, quality, and speed of innovation in Germany and Japan. Today, U.S. firms and workers face increasingly global competition. Brazil has become a major competitor in moderate-sized commercial aircraft. South Korea and Taiwan are a force in semiconductors and flat-panel displays.[6] Korea is also becoming a factor in the North American car market. China is rapidly moving up the learning curve from toys and textiles to automobiles and advanced electronics. Starting from a base of telemarketing and customer service call centers and simple software coding, India has come to provide a growing array of computer and business services. China and a number of other countries are following India's lead by developing the communications infrastructure and highly educated workforce that allow them to enter the world of online competition.

It is not just a matter of new competitors. The entire nature of global competition is shifting. The industrial democracies and a growing array of middle-income countries are actively competing for global investments in new factories and new laboratories. When Japan was starting its industrial drive after World War II, delegation after delegation came to study American management—viewed as the best in the world. In the 1980s, America's public and private sectors looked abroad for policies and practices that would make their economy or their firm more competitive. The industrial democracies and middle-income countries are now carefully studying each other to adopt and adapt the policies and private-sector practices contributing to growth and innovation.

The world has entered a stage of "Nationopoly," in which many nation-states are carefully monitoring and responding to the competition—something along the lines of a private-sector oligopoly. For instance, the United States' successful use of Section 301 of its trade law (the 1974 Trade Act) to open foreign markets was eventually copied by the Europeans. The American practice of annually publishing a list of foreign trade barriers to U.S. exports was also copied by the European Commission, and, eventually by Japan. The United States has been a successful policy borrower as well—the Advanced Technology Program was inspired by Japanese policies, and the Manufacturing Extension Partnership program echoes successful systems in both Germany and Japan.

Even before the end of the Cold War, cutting-edge technologies were increasingly being driven by commercial rather than defense considerations. After the end of the Cold War, the defense-oriented industrial base downsized, consolidated, and in some cases merged with its European counterparts. While the Pentagon continued to look to technology for improved weapons, overall procurement fell. In the post-9/11 world, defense and homeland security needs are again likely to drive the development of new technologies. The private-sector Council on Competitiveness has initiated a project focused on seeking commercial as well as defense applications for many of the new technologies.[7]

The development and implementation of a competitiveness strategy has itself helped change the American economy. To some extent, institutions and individuals are adapting to the need for lifelong learning. Although K-12 education has not shown much improvement, state governments are actively working to measure results and provide early intervention where students fail to meet basic standards in reading and mathematics. State governments continue to seek their own versions of Silicon Valley.[8] Like its two predecessors, the George W. Bush administration is pursuing a policy of deepening U.S. economic integration with the rest of the world.

Popular attitudes toward the balance between government and the market continue to evolve. During the Great Depression and the prosperous years following World War II, the federal government was viewed with considerable confidence. Many economic studies were focused on how the government could stabilize the economy or correct the imperfections of the marketplace. Academic thinking had already begun to emphasize the power and efficiency of markets when first Vietnam, then Watergate, and finally the stagflation of the 1970s eroded popular confidence in government. When, in the 1980 presidential campaign, candidate Ronald Reagan called government the problem and not the solution, large numbers of Americans nodded their heads and voted accordingly.

During the 1980s and early 1990s, business rediscovered the importance of government and many Americans acquired a new appreciation for markets. The emergence of an informal New Growth Compact developed in parallel with a proliferation of partnerships that moved the country toward being a partnership nation. At the start of the twenty-first century, attitudes may shift yet again. Grover Norquist—the president of the Americans for Tax Reform, a Washington-based advocacy group—speaking for important elements in the Republican coalition, is intent on reducing the size and scope of government. While the federal government is under attack in some quarters, the collapse of Enron in late 2001 and the series of corporate scandals that followed have raised public skepticism about corporate America. The idea of "a few bad apples" has given way to the realization of a system-wide failure encompassing everything from boards of directors to government regulators to the financial press. The government and the private sector will need to work hard to restore lost public confidence.

And then there is the global war on terrorism, U.S. troops fighting on two fronts, and the emergence of new diseases. The good times of the late 1990s left the country with a burst financial bubble and an overhang of excess capacity. The combination of an overvalued dollar, slow growth overseas, and unused capacity in many parts of the world has exacted a serious toll on U.S. manufacturing. The United States has entered a kind of symbiotic relationship with much of the world. Asia in particular depends on exports to the United States to maintain growth at home, and the United States depends on a steady inflow of foreign capital, a growing percentage from Asian central banks, to finance its imports. To finance the 2003 current account deficit of $546 billion, the United States needed to attract more than $1.4 billion in foreign investment every day of the year.

In sum, U.S. economic policymakers in the twenty-first century must address a constantly changing world that is at least as challenging as the one they faced in the 1970s. How should the United States respond to slow economic growth at home, an embattled manufacturing sector, and serious financial imbalances while continuing to focus on long-term productivity growth?

Fostering Public and Private Investment

In creating a pro-investment environment, government policy will continue to target stable prices, low interest rates, and high levels of demand. Fiscal policy remains an important regulator of short-term demand and the degree of long-term debt. The competitiveness movement added an emphasis on the content of fiscal policy—how much spending is devoted to key public investments that make a direct contribution to growth and complement critical private investments in plant, equipment, training, and innovation. Encouraging a competitive dollar, smaller current account deficits, and more open markets around the world can, over time, make a powerful contribution to long-term productivity growth.

The focus on long-term investment does not suggest ignoring the state of the day-to-day economy. A corporation focusing only on long-term developments while ignoring profits or liquidity could find itself in financial difficulties or even bankruptcy court. Policymakers know that a full order book is a powerful incentive for the private-sector investment that supports long-term productivity growth. Many economists and even more politicians are quick to quote John Maynard Keynes's famous maxim that in the long run we are all dead. Political and economic considerations will often combine to drive short-term action. From the perspective of long-term competitiveness, the important consideration is to adopt monetary and fiscal policies with an eye to future investment, innovation, and job-creating, income-raising growth.

Policies need to be adapted to the context and economic nature of the short-run challenge. In 1993, deficit reduction in the face of a weak recovery, a restructured corporate sector, and inflationary expectations worked very well.[9] The Clinton administration team that crafted the deficit reduction package was careful to backload or delay the fiscal tightening so that lower, long-term interest rates could stimulate investment. In reflecting on the 1993 deficit reduction, Alan Blinder (who served on Clinton's Council of Economic Advisers and as vice chairman of the Federal Reserve) saw it as fitting a specific set of circumstances and not as a policy for all occasions (see chapter 13).

The situation in 2001 was quite different. As was noted above, inflation had largely disappeared as a threat, the private sector had restructured in response to international competition and new technologies, and the U.S. economy had become ever more integrated into a global economy that was itself becoming more competitive. The first years of the twenty-first century added other challenges. Starting in March 2000, the air started to come out of an enormous financial bubble, erasing trillions of dollars in financial assets. The related sharp drop in investment spending reached near-depression levels in the telecommunications industry, and a global slowdown left a large overhang of unused manufacturing capacity. The 9/11 terrorist attacks shocked the country, as did (in a different way) the series of corporate and financial market scandals that started with the late 2001 collapse of the energy giant Enron.

In response, monetary and fiscal policy shifted to stimulate the economy. After the bursting of the financial bubble in the spring of 2001, the Federal Open Market Committee (FOMC) steadily reduced short-term interest rates. By July 2003, the overnight federal funds rate (the rate banks pay each other to borrow funds held by the Federal Reserve) stood at 1 percent—the lowest rate since 1958. As long-term interest rates also trended downward, the housing market flourished. As millions of Americans refinanced their mortgages to take advantage of lower rates, many took out larger mortgages to finance added consumption. Fannie Mae (formerly the Federal Home Loan Mortgage Corporation) estimates that homeowners took out $96 billion in added equity in 2002 and another $50 billion in the first half of 2003. The president's Council of Economic Advisers estimates that roughly half the cash-out was spent on consumption, which boosted economic growth by 0.4 percent in 2002.[10]

Tax cuts in 2001, 2002, and 2003 and sharp increases in spending for domestic as well as national security goals provided significant fiscal stimulus. In fulfilling his campaign promise to cut taxes, President Bush's 2001 tax cut was very well timed but not well structured. Too little of the tax cut was concentrated on immediate spending, and the cuts were targeted at upper-income groups that were less likely to spend. The initial tax cut included little in the way of direct incentives for investment, and, over time, the tax cut will contribute to a long-term structural deficit that could eventually raise interest rates, erode business confidence, and slow investment.

As part of its tax cut initiatives, the administration did allow a short-term window for businesses to write off a significant percentage of the cost of new equipment. In terms of investment incentives, the administration also points to the 2003 tax cut, which reduced to 15 percent the maximum tax on dividends and capital gains. A relatively small portion of the added spending on national and homeland security will find its way into research and new technologies that may make a future contribution to overall growth. While spending on other domestic priorities also grew rapidly in the early 2000s, little of it was in pursuit of an explicit long-term competitiveness strategy.

In a series of steps and statements, the Bush administration moved away from the Clinton-Rubin policy of consistently endorsing a strong dollar.[11] Secretary of the Treasury John Snow and President Bush both traveled to Asia with a message urging China, Japan, and other countries in the region to allow their currencies to rise in value relative to the dollar. At the 2003 meetings of the Group of Eight (G-8) heads of state and subsequent meeting of the G-8 finance ministers, the United States sought and secured statements endorsing greater reliance on flexible exchange rates and a greater role for markets in determining the international value of currencies. This was widely seen as yet another message to China, Japan, and other Asian economies to allow their currencies to appreciate. Whether because of a market reaction to high current account deficits, shifting economic trends, or the change in administration posture, the dollar did decline by almost 20 percent in 2002 and early 2003.[12] In any case, as U.S. exports became more competitive on world markets, the domestic economy did receive an added boost.

The president sought and secured congressional approval for his "No Child Left Behind Act" a major federal effort to reform and improve the elementary and secondary education system. The act is unprecedented in the scope of its incentives and its degree of federal involvement in local education. Over the next few years, the states, local school boards, and the Department of Education will be adjusting to the challenge of improving education, measuring results, and restructuring failing schools. Despite high overall domestic spending, the requirements of the No Child Left Behind Act are often viewed as another only partially funded mandate from Washington.

With regard to the long term, however, the administration has largely returned to the supply-side economics of the early Reagan years. The administration dismisses the lack of academic support for supply-side economics and minimizes the impact of long-term budgets on future investment. Tax cuts have taken the place of public and private investments as a driver of long-term productivity growth. Nor has there been much in the way of efforts to help the fiscally beleaguered states that account for much of the nation's spending on education, a significant portion of spending on traditional infrastructure, and increasingly active efforts to stimulate innovation and encourage the use of new technologies. There has been no recognition of the complementary pieces of the competitiveness puzzle, nor of a New Growth Compact in which both public and private sectors play critical, complementary roles. The administration has continued to seek public–private partnerships—for instance, in homeland security or in the development of the hydrogen car—but has not connected them to a broader growth strategy.[13]

Policies for the Long Term

With an eye to long-term investment as well as short-term recovery, what steps might we take next? In looking ahead to the rest of the first decade of the twenty-first century and beyond, a number of policies can strengthen the long-term economic future of the country. The policies briefly described in the following subsections are illustrative, not exhaustive. These policies will also have to adjust to fit the shifting sands of economic circumstance. Again, the fundamental idea is to keep future economic prosperity and strength in mind when crafting policies for today.

Announcing a Comprehensive Growth Strategy

So far, the administration's economic strategy has relied almost entirely on a variety of tax cuts. The U.S. economy requires a broader policy that includes a strategy to reduce long-term budget deficits, strengthen the innovation system, and improve education, training, and lifelong learning. The George W. Bush administration has been very active in seeking to open new markets through bilateral, regional, and multilateral trade agreements but has left them largely unconnected to a broader growth strategy. A credible long-term competitiveness strategy would build business and consumer confidence in the economic future.

Targeting Investment as Well as Consumption

Unlike many past recessions, during which Federal Reserve tightening led to a fall in consumption, the 2001 recession was led by a decline in corporate investment with a near collapse of investment in the information-technology sector. At some point, time will deal with excess capacity and corporations will begin to replace or upgrade their computer and communications systems.[14] The George W. Bush administration, however, has done relatively little to directly attack the overcapacity created by the financial bubble and dot-com craze. Innovative policies could have helped speed the needed adjustments. Tax credits could have stimulated the linking of unused fiber-optic capacity to homes and businesses. The administration could also have brought modern communications, whether cable or wireless, to a number of developing nations—stimulating growth and helping to use the manufacturing capacity of the information-technology sector.

Recognizing the Risk of Long-Term Deficits

If expectations matter, then the markets and investors must be concerned about the return of large and rising deficits. Tax policy has compounded the fiscal challenge posed by the retirement of the baby boom, which will sharply increase spending on Social Security and health care. Some investors may believe the long-term challenge will be met through changes in policy—raising the retirement age, means testing Medicare, or shifting the cost and risk to individuals through the partial privatization of both programs. Or they may think that taxes will rise as the public's demand for extensive benefits clashes with limited federal revenues.

The Bush administration has largely dismissed deficits, arguing at different times that tax cuts will stimulate so much economic activity that deficits will be considerably smaller than currently predicted or that deficits have little impact on interest rates and thus long-term investment. In a recent study, Michael Boskin, the former chairman of the Council of Economic Advisers, pointed to the taxes that will be paid on 401(k)s, Individual Retirement Accounts, and other tax-deferred retirement accounts, when funds are withdrawn—sharply reducing the projected deficits.[15] Not everyone shares Boskin's optimism. As baby boomers start to retire, they may also push to reduce the tax bite on withdrawn retirement income. Most observers expect that at least some of the recent tax cuts will be made permanent, though deficit estimates assume that they will all end after their ten-year life. Discounting deficits is a risky business.

Not Forgetting the States

Like the federal government, the states have experienced a sharp fall in revenue. The three years of decline in the financial markets, a recession, and slow growth have all contributed to the drop in revenue. With many state tax systems tied to the federal tax code, the Bush administration's tax cuts have had the indirect effect of reducing state revenues as well.

Unlike the federal government, however, most states must balance their budget. Some estimates put the combined state deficit at $80 billion in 2003. A Goldman Sachs economist, William Dudley, estimated that state-level tax increases or spending cuts would total $50 billion in 2003—essentially offsetting the 2003 stimulus of the latest Bush tax cut.[16]

In addition to providing (or preserving) stimulus, some state spending is critical to long-term growth. States provide important support for elementary and secondary schools as well as higher education and fund basic infrastructure investment. Many states are working with industry to encourage training and innovation as part of statewide development strategies.

Continuing to Target Expectations

In 1993, deficit reduction was aimed at lowering inflationary expectations as well as freeing up capital for investment. In 2003, the prospect of the first deflation since the Great Depression created its own set of fears. Deflation was already a reality in Japan, and there was speculation that Germany might suffer the same fate. At the time, short-term interest rates were so low that the FOMC had limited room to make further cuts. To avoid fueling fears that the FOMC would then be powerless to fight deflation, Federal Reserve Chairman Greenspan raised the possibility of driving down long-term interest rates by buying long-term federal bonds.

By 2004, the domestic focus had shifted yet again to the question of rising prices driven by rising costs in some sectors and a spike in energy prices. The broader point is that the FOMC needs to keep a credible and creative eye on a price level that threatens either deflation or resurgent inflation. A presidential administration can provide a powerful complement to actual or potential action by the Federal Reserve. Faced with the prospect of deflation, an administration could seek global cooperation to stimulate growth. Or if faced with possible inflation, an administration could take similar steps to restrain demand and put added emphasis on productivity.

Growing Together

In the late 1970s, the Group of Seven (G-7) countries faced a similar period of inadequate global growth. At the London Summit in May 1977, the G-7 countries agreed to "monitor progress" toward domestic economic goals. When German and Japanese growth appeared weaker than expected, the summit commitment "reinforced domestic considerations" and encouraged each government to take additional steps to stimulate its respective economy.[17] At the July 1978 Bonn Summit, the United States promised to curb inflation, reduce the current account deficit, and adopt an energy policy ambitious enough to reduce oil imports. Germany and Japan made complementary commitments to stimulate growth and "thus reduce the current account surplus."[18] Just a month later, however, revolutionary currents in Iran were beginning to reach full tide. By January 1979, the shah of Iran left his country with a pledge to return only as a constitutional monarch.[19] Iranian oil production, then 10 percent of the world supply, had already fallen, and spot and official oil prices moved rapidly upward.[20] In the end, the intended coordination of macroeconomic policies foundered on resurgent inflation and the reluctance of several countries to push growth policies in the face of rapidly rising prices.

In today's current decidedly slow-growth environment with few inflationary pressures, it is time to try G-7 cooperation again. By agreeing to act in concert, the industrial democracies may make it easier for individual countries to make growth-, employment-, and productivity-raising structural changes. Most observers see the need for Europe to make significant changes in its labor markets and for Japan to right its bad-loan-burdened financial system—changes that would be much more easily made in the context of steady growth that brought rising employment.

Recent economic developments also make it easier for Europe to shift its monetary policies. Higher European productivity growth and the recent appreciation of the euro should lower inflationary expectations in Europe and could encourage the European Central Bank to lower interest rates. Fiscal policy has been constrained by the Maastricht Treaty's (which created the euro) agreement to limit fiscal deficits to 3 percent of gross domestic product (GDP)—regardless of the economic circumstances. A pan–G-7 commitment to growth might also make it easier for Europe to rethink its limit on short-term deficits in favor of fiscal balance achieved over a longer period. A change in policies could trigger a virtuous circle, with full order books driving the investments and innovations that foster long-term productivity growth. The impact will be even greater if key emerging markets such as China, India, and Brazil are added to the mix.

Adjusting Currencies and Current Accounts

Slow growth is not the only challenge facing the global economy. During the past few years, the United States has been running large current account imbalances with its 2002 deficit approaching $500 billion, or 5 percent of GDP, and rising to $530 billion in 2003. There are several possible paths to righting the imbalance in trade and current accounts. Increased U.S. saving (discussed below) and continued global engagement (discussed in the next chapter) are two possibilities.

More rapid growth abroad would translate into greater demand for U.S. exports. But with a slow-growth global economy, a decline in the international value of the dollar has be to a near-term alternative. By making U.S. exports more competitive and raising the price of imports in the United States, the declining international value of the dollar will, over time, help reduce the trade and current account deficits. Starting in early 2002, the dollar began to decline in value (relative to other key currencies), and by the spring of 2003, it had fallen roughly 20 percent against the euro, about 10 percent against the yen, and about 10 percent against a basket of all currencies weighted by their importance in U.S. trade. By September 2003, however, the dollar had strengthened as the U.S. economy showed signs of a recovery. That again raised the specter of large, or perhaps even rising, current account deficits.

To finance the current account deficit, the United States has had to depend on a steady flow of foreign capital. For much of the 1990s, Europeans were major direct investors, establishing or purchasing factories, laboratories, and retail concerns as well as purchasing securities. In 2003, Europeans are investing less but Asian central banks became major buyers of dollars in an effort to keep their own currencies down and their exports up. Japan is often quite open in its willingness to buy dollars to keep Japanese exports competitive in the American market.[21] The same is also true of other East and Southeast Asian countries.

Large current account deficits and the resulting increase in the U.S. external debt may continue for some time because of the U.S. appetite for foreign capital and the combination of slower (than U.S.) growth abroad and the dependence of a number of foreign economies on exports to the U.S. market. The shift to shorter-term, more liquid foreign investments, however, brings an added risk. Though direct investments are relatively stable, U.S. Treasury bonds and other securities are easily traded. The risk is that a sudden change in investor sentiment could lead to a precipitous fall in the value of the dollar, which could slow growth in many parts of the world— including the United States.[22] The current account deficits are not ultimately sustainable. The unsettled question is whether the adjustment of currencies and trade flows will come suddenly in a way that will disrupt economies around the world or will take place gradually in a way that would allow governments, industries, and workers to adjust.

Again, the past suggests a possible approach. In 1985, the finance ministers of the five largest industrial democracies (France, Germany, Japan, the United Kingdom, and the United States) met at the Plaza Hotel in New York to discuss the strength of the dollar and the large U.S. trade deficit.[23] Political considerations were also at play. The trade deficit had become a political issue in the United States that threatened the Reagan administration and raised the possibility of trade-restricting legislation in Congress. In September 1985, the finance ministers announced an agreement to work together to gradually lower the value of the dollar and reduce the global imbalance in trade.

At the time of the 1985 Plaza Accord, the U.S. dollar had already begun to retreat from the highs recorded earlier in the year. In *Managing the Dollar: From the Plaza to the Louvre,* Yoichi Funabashi described the Japanese proposal for intervention as "leaning with the wind."[24] With the international financial markets already reducing the value of the dollar relative to the euro and the yen, it could be a propitious time for controlled intervention or coordinated macroeconomic policies or both. Given the current distribution of current account surpluses and deficits, the G-7 structure may not be sufficiently broad. Japan still has a large trade surplus with the United States, but a significant share of the U.S. trade and current account deficits are with other East and Southeast Asian countries. In some cases, China is a prominent example; its currency is linked to the dollar to prevent any appreciation that would erode the price competitiveness of its exports. Some countries, like Japan, intervene in the international currency markets to keep their currency from appreciating. Even though China's overall 2002 current account surplus was a relatively modest $30 billion, China's prominence in international trade suggests that it should have a seat at the bargaining table. The G-7 took the first step in that direction by meeting with China's finance minister on October 1, 2004, on the eve of the annual meeting of the World Bank and the International Monetary Fund.

Securing an appreciation of Asian currencies will not be easy. During his September 2003 trip to China and Southeast Asia, Secretary of the Treasury John Snow met with little success beyond a vague Chinese commitment to floating its currency sometime in the future. President Bush had a similar response during his own trip to the region in October 2003. As in the Cold War era, however, Snow's and the president's hands were partially tied by geopolitical considerations that ranged from the war on terrorism to dealing with the nuclear posture of North Korea.

Encouraging Saving

The overall rate of American saving remains low by international standards and has more or less fallen steadily since the 1950s.[25] The same is true of the personal saving rate (i.e., what individuals save out of personal disposable or after-tax income). In the early 1980s, the personal saving rate was still over 10 percent, whereas by 2003, it had fallen to below 2 percent. For much of the last two decades, the federal government has run significant budget deficits, another way of saying that the public has subtracted rather than added to overall American saving. Even when the budget shifted to a surplus in the late 1990s, private (corporate and personal) saving declined in a way that left overall saving essentially unchanged. During the past twenty years or more, the gap between domestic consumption and investment and national savings has been reflected in the current account deficit. In effect, the country as a whole is borrowing from abroad to maintain its current standard of living and investing.

Fears about the national saving rate are nothing new. The leading voices on competitiveness added their concern about national savings to a large and growing literature. The second report of the private-sector Council on Competitiveness (COC), *Reclaiming the American Dream: Fiscal Policies for a Competitive Nation,* addressed the federal deficit (what economists call public dissaving) as well as the composition of federal spending.[26] From its inception, the congressionally created Competitiveness Policy Council (CPC)[27] focused on the low level of American saving and investing. In *Saving More and Investing Better: A Strategy for Securing Prosperity,* the CPC devoted its entire fourth report to the question of increasing saving and improving the allocation of capital to high-productivity uses.[28]

With mounting budget deficits and low private saving, we have returned to one of the major economic challenges that confronted the COC, the CPC, and public officials in the early 1990s.[29] Many of the proposals of the COC, CPC, and many others apply today. The surest approach to increasing national saving is to increase public saving (or decrease public dissaving) by reducing the budget deficit and, if conditions permit, moving back into a budget surplus. In making their earlier recommendations, the COC, the CPC, and a host of others combined a call for eliminating the budget deficit and shifting the composition of federal saving to favor research and development, infrastructure, education, training, and other investments. Cutting the budget deficit by reducing the very public investments that encourage private investment would be decidedly counterproductive.

Over the years, the economics profession and political leaders have debated a number of other possibilities. In the past, moving from an income tax to a value-added tax[30] or a progressive consumption tax[31] have been proposed by key legislators. The *2003 Economic Report of the President* briefly discusses the advantages of a consumption tax as opposed to an income tax for promoting saving.[32]

For more than two decades, Congress has adopted proposals to create tax incentives such as Individual Retirement Accounts (IRAs) to increase savings for retirement and some other purposes. Economists disagree on the impact of IRAs on saving but most think that individuals simply shift existing savings to IRAs rather than actually increasing their saving. If, as many think, individuals are target savers—focused on housing, education, or retirement—the greater return on savings because of tax advantages may actually lower the rate of saving. Some economists point to the late 1990s to make this point—returns in the stock market were rising rapidly but, rather than save more to acquire additional stocks, the personal saving rate fell to near zero.[33]

There are also a variety of proposals to change the tax code to encourage productive investment. For instance, the CPC and others have argued for the gradual reduction of the tax deductibility of mortgage interest as a way of shifting saving and investment from housing toward a pool that could be invested in new plant and equipment, research and development, or education and training. Congress has taken a modest step in that direction. Mortgage interest remains deductible, but not interest paid on the portion of a mortgage that exceeds a million dollars. In the early twenty-first century, however, the rising price of housing has partially offset the enormous financial losses due to the three-year decline in stock prices. With mortgages rising in tandem with housing prices, it is unlikely that there will be strong political support for further limiting the deductibility of mortgage interest.

The supply-side school of economics that arose in the late 1970s still promotes the view that lowering marginal tax rates will increase the pool of overall savings. The George W. Bush administration shares the supply-side view and urged it as one of the reasons to adopt its 2001, $1.3 trillion tax cut to be phased in over ten years. In proposing to make the later-year tax cuts effective in 2003, the administration contended that they would add short-term stimulus and encourage long-term investment at the same time. The administration continued to dismiss the lack of academic support for supply-side economics and still downplayed the impact of long-term budget on future investment. During the 1980s and 1990s, lower marginal tax rates and increased opportunities for tax free saving corresponded with a declining personal saving rate.

As was noted above, some of the Bush tax cuts are targeted at investment. There is the short-term window for businesses to write off a significant percentage of the cost of new equipment and the reduction in the tax on most dividends and capital gains to 15 percent. The change amounts to a 5-percentage-point reduction for capital gains income and an even sharper drop for dividends (assuming that dividend payments are concentrated among individuals in higher income tax brackets) that were taxed as ordinary income. The administration contends that the drop in capital gains and dividend taxes will drive up the value of stocks, encourage investment as the cost of capital falls, and stimulate consumption as stock owners become richer. The timing and magnitude of the impact on investment and consumption are both subject to debate.

In terms of income distribution, the benefit from the reduction in taxes on dividends and capital gains will, as with the other administration tax cuts, be concentrated among upper-income families. The lower tax on dividends, however, should not be looked at as solely or even principally as either short-term stimulus or a long-term incentive to investment. Two other factors are important. Under current law, companies are allowed to deduct from taxable revenue the cost of interest but not dividends. That creates a bias toward debt financing that may not be desirable over the long term. In the wake of the Enron and other corporate scandals, some analysts also stress the value of a regular dividend as a discipline on management. No amount of accounting gimmicks can provide the earnings needed for actual dividend payments.

The administration has also proposed simplifying and expanding the tax incentives for individual saving. If adopted, President Bush's plan would replace the current tax-favored saving with two new accounts. Every year any individual, regardless of income, would be able to contribute $7,500 (indexed for inflation) to a Lifetime Savings Account (LSA). Earnings would not be taxed and could be withdrawn tax free at any time for any purpose. Individuals would also be able to contribute $7,500 to a Retirement Savings Account (RSA). There would be no tax on earnings while in the RSA or on withdrawal, but tax-free earnings could only be withdrawn after reaching the age of fifty-eight years. In addition, the administration has proposed creating Employer Retirement Savings Accounts (ERSA) that would consolidate tax-favored retirement plans while following a simplified version of the current rules applicable to 401(k) plans.[34] As was noted above, most economists remain skeptical about how much tax-favored vehicles such as IRAs have actually raised savings. In addition, the combination of tax-free accumulation and withdrawal will add to a long-term deficit that itself poses a challenge for long-term investment and productivity growth.

The 2003 tax cuts took another step toward a wage rather than income tax with the reductions in taxation on dividends and capital gains to 15 percent. As for long-term savings and investment, the administration is shifting income to individuals and households that are likely to save the most. For instance, individuals in the top 1 percent of the income distribution save ten times as much as individuals in the lower 20 percent and three times the rate of saving of the average American. From the administration's point of view, the change has the added attraction of adding to the income of the upper-income Americans who tend to support and contribute to the Republican Party. In any case, the country, political leaders, and policy advisers will need to continue struggling with the question of a low overall rate of saving, persistent federal deficits, and rising external debt.

Stimulating Investment

The 2001 recession was an investment-led, not consumption-led, recession, and policymakers need to think about how to stimulate investment. Creating a larger potential pool of savings, however, does not seamlessly translate into a larger capital stock. In addition to a general policy climate that favors long-term investment, Congress and the administration can take four other steps.

First, the public sector needs to maintain its commitment to public investments in research and development, education and training, and traditional (as well as newer) information-technology infrastructure. These public investments (discussed in the next chapter) complement private investment and make private investment more likely and more profitable.

Second, the public sector needs to work with the private sector to develop methods of corporate accountability that resolve the unintended consequences of the fraud-inducing tyranny of the quarterly report. For many—though clearly not all—industries, the focus on the quarterly report may deter investment in research and development, training, supply-chain management, and export development.[35]

Third, the private and public sectors need to develop better tools to measure and manage intangible assets that encompass everything from patents to the intellectual capital represented by an innovative team of researchers. For investors, financial analysts, and corporate leaders, intangibles are often the critical investments that can determine a company's future. The same can be said of national economies, where the ability to generate and effectively use intellectual property, skilled professionals, and other intangible assets will be important to long-term national strength. Considerable work is under way within the American private sector, but in terms of official standards, the United States is lagging behind the London-based International Accounting Standards Board, which sets accounting for the European Union and is followed by much of the world outside the United States.[36] The risk is that U.S. corporate managers and individual American investors will not match the investment decisions and hence the competitive edge developed by their international counterparts.

Fourth, at times those concerned will need to adopt investment strategies for specific sectors of the economy. Economists, policy analysts, and political leaders are often forced to deal with the failures of markets in dealing with externalities or spillover effects, public goods (e.g., national security), and national goals that include a more equitable distribution of opportunity and income. Yet they are also often wary of government intervention on behalf of a firm, industry, or even a broad sector of the economy. They point out that government may be slow to respond, that private interests may capture public action, that helping one firm or industry may come at the expense of another, and that public officials may pursue private rather than public means.

In thinking about sector-specific responses, it is important to recognize the limits of both markets and government intervention. Like macroeconomic policy, sector- or industry-specific steps have to be taken with care and with an eye to the long-run strength of the American economy.

Limits to Markets

Markets are a powerful and usually efficient way to allocate resources. Yet markets are often imperfect and sometimes irrational. For instance, market prices usually will not include either the costs of pollution or the benefits of basic research. Whether smoke from a factory or waste dumped in a river, neither individuals nor companies have an incentive to take on the added cost of eliminating or reducing pollution.

The story of basic research is just the opposite. A single company investing in research will often find that the results are not useful to the company or industry in question. The costs of a major research project may simply be too high. There is the added risk that the results of the research will be used by a company's competitors in the United States and around the world. The added cost of research can put the company at a competitive disadvantage if it pays the full cost of research while the whole industry shares the benefits. Without government funding, we may find that there is significant underinvestment in research.

Markets can also be guilty of "irrational exuberance," as was highlighted by Federal Reserve Chairman Greenspan. The late 1990s were one of many such instances in financial history. Recent economic work has focused on how imperfect information will affect and distort the decisions made by markets. Enron and the related scandals are a reminder that the goals of a chief executive may deviate from those of the profit-maximizing corporation.

In a global context, markets may dictate the growth of overseas production and the emergence of a global just-in-time inventory system but may leave a nation-state vulnerable to supply disruption or create a dependence on overseas production that could affect national security. The national response may be as obvious as the strategic petroleum reserve, guarding against a major disruption in oil supplies, or as complicated as public support for Sematech, to help strengthen a domestic semiconductor industry.

Limits to Government Action

As noted above, government action can be slow, influenced by special interests, subject to the private goals of public officials, or put Peter at risk by intervening to save Paul. Government, particularly the American government, was set up to " secure the blessings of liberty" as well as "to promote the general welfare." The checks and balances of the federal government and the entire federal system were not designed with either speed or corporate-like efficiency in mind.

Many analysts fear that a government program or agency will be captured by special interests. Action targeted at regulating prices, allowing the use of public lands, or even ensuring quality can, at times, be turned to an industry's advantage. The result can be added costs to the consumer, lost public revenue, or the creation of a monopoly. In other cases, the government may itself lack the knowledge to make a sound decision or lack some of the tools needed to deal with a particular problem.

Just as a chief executive may favor his or her own interest rather than that of the corporation, there is a school of thought (the public choice school) that emphasizes the risk that a government official will pursue private ends rather than public purposes. While instances are relatively rare, there are examples of actual corruption or favoring a specific private contractor with the hope of future, postgovernment employment. At times, a public servant may seek greater size or influence for a particular office or agency whether or not that serves the broader public interest.

Even if the public intervention is well informed and well executed, government support for one sector or one industry may come at the expense of another. For instance, when Congress decided to provide loan guarantees to Chrysler in January 1980, there was fear in some quarters that the Chrysler rescue would put Ford at risk. In other cases, there is a concern that a successful intervention might harden into a lengthy commitment as interests form to preserve federal action or federal support. In *The Technology Pork Barrel*, Linda Cohen and Roger Noll focus on three major initiatives (the supersonic aircraft, the nuclear breeder reactor, and the Synfuels Corporation) that they argue lived past their natural lives because of political influence.[37]

Beyond the Industrial Policy Debate

The proposals of the late1970s and early 1980s for a coherent industrial policy foundered on generic hostility to government intervention in the market, skepticism about the government's capacity to improve on the market, and the specific proposal for an industrial bank. At the time, it was common to characterize industrial policy as a potential form of the central planning that helped drive the Soviet Union to economic collapse. Although bureaucratic and industrial Japan were respected in the 1980s, the powerful Ministry of International Trade and Industry was viewed as commanding Japanese industry in a way that was unimaginable and undesirable in the United States.

The past two decades suggest a more nuanced view. Government intervention is often part of a complex process that combines public and private elements. In the case of the National Institutes of Health, the public and private sectors are intertwined in a way to facilitate rapid innovation. The rapid spread of the Internet was fostered by industry-specific efforts to limit the taxation of Internet commerce at home and abroad. When the country sought to build the so-called information superhighway, it was private capital that built it. Government provided support through intelligent regulation, next-generation research, and an effort to make access to the Internet universal.

Industry- or Sector-Specific Challenges

In the early twenty-first century, a number of industries or sectors came under significant pressure. The collapse of the dot-com bubble left the telecommunications sector in dire straits. In the wake of the terrorist attacks on 9/11, many of the nation's airlines suffered huge financial losses. The combination of an overvalued dollar and the economic slowdown put pressure not only on the steel industry but also on much of the manufacturing sector as a whole.

Telecommunications. The challenges facing individual industries are not uniform. During the Internet boom, the manufacturers of telecommunications equipment financed many of their own sales to Internet based firms (the much-ballyhooed dot-coms). When the financial bubble burst and many dot-coms shrank or fell into bankruptcy, the manufacturers found themselves holding bad debt, faced with little demand for their product.

Many telecommunications companies had rapidly expanded their capacity but had not found a comparable demand for their services.

Airlines. The post-9/11 fall in air travel hit an industry that was already saddled with considerable debt and an archaic route structure. The airlines, which were grounded for a period after 9/11, feared a significant loss of traffic while facing the potential of added security-related costs. As the airlines went through painful adjustments—including bankruptcy—they put added pressure on the firms that made aircraft and aircraft parts as well as other major suppliers.

The steel industry. The integrated steel industry (i.e., which makes steel from coke and iron and does not just reuse it) has been under pressure from domestic and international suppliers for three decades. Its latest wave of adjustment has been marked by a wave of bankruptcies and consolidation. In many cases, the consolidation occurs as steelmaking assets are purchased from bankrupt firms without the obligation to meet the legacy costs—the health and pension benefits that had been promised to retired workers.

Manufacturing. Manufacturing has been under multiple pressures. The bursting of the financial bubble in 2000 triggered an investment-led recession that left high-technology and other capital-goods producers with dwindling orders. While consumer spending and home building remained healthy, three years of slow overall growth provided little demand for new capital spending. The overvalued dollar has worked as a tax on manufactured exports and a subsidy to manufactured imports, and many manufacturing firms are competing in industries with considerable excess capacity at home and abroad. Deflation or generally falling prices have already hit the manufacturing sector. While falling prices hit profits, they did nothing to relieve the value or burden of existing debt.

International competition for high-skill services. Multiple pressures have forced a broad-based adjustment in the manufacturing sector. Firms ranging from automobile manufacturers to semiconductor chipmakers are transferring production facilities overseas. Research and development facilities are, to some extent, following the shift of manufacturing facilities. The Internet now poses a new challenge. The popular press has focused on back office operations for financial firms or call centers to provide information or technical advice. But the challenge is much broader. A growing array of tasks that can be digitized can also be analyzed anywhere in the world—financial accounts, chip design, or reading an X-ray. The structural shift in manufacturing and services is real and poses a significant adjustment challenge for large swathes of the American economy.

The Bush Administration's Responses

In thinking about sector-specific initiatives and long-term growth, it is instructive to examine the industry- or sector-related initiatives of the Bush administration. Early on, the president took specific steps with regard to the airlines and steel industry. More recently, the president has proposed initiatives in manufacturing and in telecommunications. Beyond indicating that offshoring is simply another form of international trade, the administration has not taken any steps with regard to the offshoring phenomenon or the growing international competition for highly skilled talent.

Telecommunications. In 2004, the president set a goal of 2007 for broadband technology to reach "every corner of our country."[38] As the country moves toward that goal, the country will take advantage of some of the excess fiber-optic cable that has already been installed but left unused. As broadband usage increases, it should stimulate the development of new services and related products.

Airlines. In the wake of the 9/11 attacks, the administration successfully backed the creation of an emergency loan fund for struggling airlines. The government also federalized much of airport security with the creation of the new Transportation Security Administration. With Boeing's civilian aircraft business in the doldrums, defense business became all the more important. The Pentagon proposed leasing a hundred refueling tankers over the next several years to replenish an aging fleet. While modernizing the stock of tankers, the arrangement also promised significant benefits to Boeing. Under congressional and public scrutiny, however, the tanker-leasing proposal has undergone considerable criticism and will probably be significantly amended or superseded by another approach.

Steel. The Bush administration also decided to grant temporary import relief to much of the steel industry. In part, the decision was seen as a necessary compromise to secure congressional agreement for expedited consideration of trade agreements, currently known as trade promotion authority, or fast-track authority. But it was also seen as inspired by reelection politics, which have been focusing on steel-producing, battleground Midwestern states that would be crucial in the 2004 election.

A World Trade Organization panel found the steel tariffs to be in violation of the organization's rules. The tariffs have also been widely criticized by trade experts and leading editorial pages. Steel users have complained that higher prices for domestic steel have put them at a disadvantage at home and abroad. The temporary tariffs have provided the industry with the time to consolidate and rationalize—both of which seem to be taking place while shifting the costs of supporting retirees onto the federal insurance scheme for private pensions and to the retirees themselves.

Manufacturing. In response to complaints from the manufacturing sector, the Bush administration has gradually moved away from former Treasury secretary Robert Rubin's mantra of always endorsing the strong dollar. Instead, the president and Secretary of the Treasury John Snow both made trips to Asia, where they urged the Chinese and others to allow their currencies to rise against the dollar. The expectation was that a more competitive dollar would boost manufactured exports and, by raising the price of imports in dollars, give domestic manufacturers more breathing room.

In an August 2004 recess appointment, the president made Albert A. Fink the manufacturing "czar" in the form of a new assistant secretary for manufacturing in the Department of Commerce. Fink is cofounder and executive vice president of Fabrica International, a California-based manufacturer of luxury carpets. The president also proposed restoring some funding to the manufacturing extension centers that had been scheduled for significant budget cuts.

International competition in high-skill services. The Bush administration has not yet taken any significant steps intended to slow, accelerate, or adapt to the increase in response to the spread of telecommunications and the digital revolution that permit international competition for an array of services that formerly faced largely domestic competitors (see below). The administration (and much of the economics profession) sees the phenomenon as another form of international trade. As the administration put it in the *2004 Economic Report of the President,* "When a good or service is produced more cheaply abroad, it makes more sense to import it than to make or provide it domestically."[39]

Although not focused on either offshoring or the international competition for scientific and engineering talent, the security-driven steps taken in the wake of 9/11 may have an impact on both. Though no definitive study has yet been done, universities and businesses have related many stories about their difficulties in attracting employees, students, or instructors because of the strict application of existing and the adoption of new visa procedures.

Alternative Steps for Troubled Sectors

How might the government have dealt with specific sectors with long-term economic strength in mind? Are there approaches that manage to avoid the

Scylla of ignoring market failure and the Charybdis of government-induced inefficiency? Below, I spell out some possibilities, which are meant to be illustrative. Some policies would require structural adjustment that would point more directly to a long-term future.

In the case of airlines, the administration responded to the impact of 9/11 on what was an already financially troubled industry. In the case of telecommunications and manufacturing, the steps have been limited, and in steel created tensions with U.S. trading partners. As was noted above, the international competition in services did not trigger any significant response.

Telecommunications. I, and a host of other observers—including the president's Council of Advisers on Science and Technology,[40] have urged the administration to make regulatory changes or adopt incentives to encourage the use of the massive amounts of fiber-optic capacity that already exists.[41] In the past, consumers and businesses have found effective and creative ways to use added speed and capacity. The United States has already fallen behind some countries in broadband usage; taking advantage of installed capacity will help build a competitive base for the future.

Airlines. The airlines were such an integral part of the country's infrastructure and faced such an unexpected and unprecedented challenge in the post-9/11 world that some government action was called for. The focus was on keeping the country in the air rather than dealing with the structural challenges facing the industry. In practice, the airlines have not been quick to seek or secure the loan guarantees. At the least, the program signaled the public and the airlines that the government was concerned and would provide some kind of support for the industry. The move to federal rather than private-sector airport security personnel also probably helped restore public confidence in air travel. The administration and Congress had to respond quickly, and they did. The larger question of financial stability, however, is being worked out through the entry of new low-cost airlines; major airlines creating low-cost affiliates; new collective-bargaining agreements that, in general, lower wages; outsourcing and offshoring of repair services; and the occasional bankruptcy.

The federal government should take the lead in fostering a long-term discussion about how air travel will fit into future U.S. and international transportation systems. Past legislation has taken the step of providing an integrated approach to surface transportation. The next step is to more formally link all modes of transportation with an eye to ongoing technological innovation. Telecommuting already affects travel patterns and will do so more in the future. Another significant development is the 2004 decision by

Boeing to build a medium-sized jet (rather than a new jumbo jet) that is designed to allow long-distance destination-to-destination travel without such heavy reliance on changing planes in major airports—the current hub-and-spokes system.

Steel. Steel and other established manufacturing industries developed the equivalent of a private welfare system during and after World War II. While Europe and Japan developed publicly funded pension and health care systems, the United States depended on an employer-based system. When the mini-mills (which generally reuse scrap rather than turning iron into steel) came into being, they contributed to retirement programs—such as 401(k)s —but did not promise specific pension payments in the future. They had shifted from a defined (or promised) benefit to a defined (or specific) contribution. As the integrated steel industry adjusted to productivity gains and rising competition, fewer and fewer employees essentially carried the responsibility of meeting commitments to retirees. The search for import protection, bankruptcy, or consolidation is, at least in part, a response to the attempt to shift away from the existing private retirement system. Some industry observers expect the automobile industry to face a similar challenge by the end of the first decade of the twenty-first century.

Government insurance provides partial protection for some pensions, but there is little provision for covering the health care of the already retired until they qualify for Medicare. In place of piecemeal protectionism or serial bankruptcy, the federal government needs to deal directly with the mismatch between the private retirement system in the United States and the publicly supported systems of its major competitors.

Manufacturing. In its 2003 proposal to create a new assistant secretary of commerce for manufacturing and services and a new Office of Manufacturing and Services in the Department of Commerce, the Bush administration focused on renaming an existing assistant secretary and building on the existing Office of Trade Development, whose principal focus has been identifying export opportunities. Trade Development is filled with talented civil servants, a number of whom have considerable understanding of specific industries. But over time the mission of the agency had shifted from a focus on industry competitiveness (particularly by Secretary Malcolm Baldrige in the early and mid-1980s) to an emphasis on export markets.

In the future, the country can build on the Bush administration's initiative through a number of other steps. The Commerce Department should create a separate division focused on manufacturing with its own under-secretary. Backed by his expanded staff and under the aegis of the National

Economic Council, the secretary of commerce should lead a Cabinet-level interagency team that would coordinate analysis and manufacturing initiatives for the entire government.

There are more ambitious proposals. The National Association of Manufacturers has advocated a much more extensive competitiveness-like agenda that encompasses taxes, trade, technology, and training.[42] Candidates vying for the 2004 Democratic presidential nomination proposed a broad-based approach to strengthening manufacturing,[43] as has the Progressive Policy Institute, the think tank arm of the Democratic Leadership Council.[44]

International competition for high-skill services. It was not until 2003 that the phenomenon of outsourcing of software and other business services struck a national nerve. The academic community, policy analysts, and the business community have made varying estimates of how far and how fast the phenomenon will extend. The sheer scale of change, however, is staggering. In fifteen years, 2.5 billion new workers have joined the global market economy. China, India, and the countries of the former Soviet Union all emphasize education in engineering, science, and mathematics. Together, they are annually graduating multiples of the number of engineers produced by the American education system. Other countries are already emphasizing the physical and educational infrastructure needed to offer online services in an increasingly digital world.

Serious structural change lies ahead. The country should move now to begin the process of adjusting to that change. In the near-term, service workers should be brought under the ambit of the improved Trade Adjustment Assistance (TAA) program, which was adopted as part of the Trade Act of 2002 to provide opportunities for retraining, wage insurance, and partial support for the cost of health insurance premiums. At present, TAA is limited to manufacturing workers. With the prospect of shifting positions, employers, and perhaps skills, the country should take added steps to complete the transition to a fully portable safety net. Improved gathering and dissemination of international trends will help individuals and businesses make the right decisions about education and careers. Targeted tax or other incentives can help businesses and universities adapt to the need for new specialties and flexible skills.

In continuing to foster a climate that favors investment, monetary and fiscal policy remain the most forceful tools. The interest rate and the exchange rate are the two prices that can affect virtually every aspect of the economy. But the government should not stop at broad macroeconomic policies. In some special cases, sector-specific initiatives will be needed to deal with excess capacity, the impact of an overvalued dollar, or the opportunity posed by a new technology.

As economic conditions change, so will the need for specific policies. Whatever the conditions, policymakers should be thinking about long-term productivity growth, the changing domestic landscape, developments in the global economy, and the economic strategies of other major industrial powers.

Notes

1. Jennifer Bremer and John D. Kasarda, "The Origins of Terror," *Milken Institute Review,* fourth quarter 2002, 34–48.

2. Dan Baum, "GM's Billion-Dollar Bet," *Wired Magazine,* August 2002.

3. *The Roaring Nineties: Can Full Employment Be Sustained?* was the title used by editors Alan B. Krueger and Robert Solow for their 2001 look at the 1990s. The volume was published by the Russell Sage Foundation and the Century Foundation Press, New York, in 2001. Nobel Prize–winning economist Joseph E. Stiglitz also chose *The Roaring Nineties* as the title of his most recent book. See Stiglitz, *The Roaring Nineties: A New History of the World's Most Prosperous Decade* (New York: W. W. Norton, 2003).

4. See, for instance, Alan Beattie, "Fed Holds Rates but Warns of Inflation Risk," *Financial Times,* May 7, 2003.

5. U.S. Department of Commerce, Bureau of Economic Analysis, International Statistics and Current Dollar Gross Domestic Product, at http://www.bea.gov.

6. For instance, Don Clark, "Samsung Closes Flash-Chip Gap on Intel," *Wall Street Journal,* September 11, 2003.

7. The council launched its initiative in 2002 after its National Symposium on Competitiveness and Security; see http://www.compete.org.

8. For the challenges in creating a Silicon Valley, see Michael S. Fogarty and Amit K. Sinha, "Why Older Regions Can't Generalize from Route 128 and Silicon Valley: University–Industry Relationships and Regional Innovation Systems," in *Industrializing Knowledge: University–Industry Linkages in Japan and the United States,* ed. Lewis M. Branscomb, Fumio Kodama, and Richard Florida (Cambridge, Mass.: MIT Press, 1999), 473–509.

9. Fed chairman Alan Greenspan argued that relatively high long-term interest rates were a product of fears that large and growing budgets would eventually lead to inflation. Deficit reduction would reduce those fears. The decision also reinforced the impression of Bill Clinton as "a different kind of Democrat" who could work with business. Not everyone, however, shares the view that the deficit reduction worked by targeting expectations. In his recent *Roaring Nineties,* Nobel Prize–winning economist Joseph Stiglitz argued that lower long-term interest rates raised the value of the government bonds held in bank reserves. And with interest rates low, the banks shifted from investing in bonds to seeking more profitable investments. See Stiglitz, *Roaring Nineties,* 42–44.

10. These figures were cited in Tom Buerkle, "Betting the Ranch," *Institutional Investor,* September 2003, 74–84.

11. See Robert E. Rubin and Jacob Weisberg, *In an Uncertain World: Tough Choices from Wall Street to Washington* (New York: Random House, 2003), 182–85.

12. Buerkle, "Betting the Ranch," 81.

13. President Bush announced the Freedom CAR program in his January 2002 State of the Union message. As with President Clinton's clean car initiative, the Department of Energy will be working with DaimlerChrysler, Ford, and General Motors. For details, see "Freedom CAR & Vehicle Technologies Program" at http://eere.energy.gov/vehicleandfuels.

14. For some sign of hope, see Greg Ip, "Long a Drag on the Economy, Capacity Glut Begins to Ebb," *Wall Street Journal*, September 8, 2003.

15. Jodie T. Allen, "Found Treasure?" *U.S. News & World Report,* July 14, 2003, 35.

16. Buerkle, "Betting the Ranch," 83.

17. Council of Economic Advisers, *1978 Economic Report of the President* (Washington, D.C.: U.S. Government Printing Office, 1978), 115.

18. Council of Economic Advisers, *1979 Economic Report of the President* (Washington, D.C.: U.S. Government Printing Office, 1979), 142.

19. Burton I. Kaufman, *The Presidency of James Earl Carter* (Lawrence: University Press of Kansas, 1993), 123–24.

20. Robert Solomon, *The International Monetary System: 1945–1981* (New York: Harper & Row, 1981), 317.

21. See Akio Mikuni and R. Taggart Murphy, *Japan's Policy Trap: Dollars, Deflation and the Crisis of Japanese Finance* (Washington, D.C.: Brookings Institution Press, 2002).

22. For a useful discussion of the possibilities of a soft landing and the costs of a hard landing, see U.S. Trade Deficit Commission, *The U.S. Trade Deficit: Causes, Consequences and Recommendations for Action* (Washington, D.C.: U.S. Trade Deficit Review Commission, 2000), 168–96.

23. Yoichi Funabashi, *Managing the Dollar: From the Plaza to the Louvre* (Washington, D.C.: Institute for International Economics, 1989), 9–42.

24. Funabashi, *Managing the Dollar,* 11.

25. For gross savings, see Council of Economic Advisers, *2003 Economic Report of the President* (Washington, D.C.: U.S. Government Printing Office, 2003), 315.

26. Council on Competitiveness, *Reclaiming the American Dream: Fiscal Policies for a Competitive Nation* (Washington, D.C.: Council on Competitiveness, 1988).

27. The Competitiveness Policy Council was created by the Omnibus Trade and Competitiveness Act of 1988.

28. Competitiveness Policy Council, *Saving More and Investing Better: A Strategy for Securing Prosperity,* Fourth Report to the President and Congress (Washington, D.C.: Competitiveness Policy Council, 1995).

29. See, for instance, Alan Murray, "Bush's Talk About Spending Discipline Is So Much Hot Air," *Wall Street Journal,* September 9, 2003; and John D. McKinnon and Greg Ip, "Deficit Passes $500 billion Mark," *Wall Street Journal,* September 9, 2003.

30. In the 1970s, former representative and Ways and Means Committee Chairman Al Ullman (D-Ore.) and Senator Russell Long (D-La.) proposed a variant of the value-added tax commonly used in Europe. Coming from a state that had long resisted the imposition of a sales tax, Ullman may have paid a political price. He was defeated for reelection, in part on the grounds that he had become out of touch with his home state.

31. As noted in an earlier chapter, former senator Sam Nunn (D-Ga.) and Senator

Pete Dominici (R-N.M.) proposed the adoption of a progressive consumption tax. In its simplest form, individuals would fill out a form much like that used for the current income tax, list their income, subtract saving, and pay a progressive tax on consumption.

32. Council of Economic Advisers, *2003 Economic Report of the President*, 208.

33. For a recent discussion of individual retirement accounts, see Jane G. Gravelle, "Individual Retirement Accounts (IRAs): Issues and Proposed Expansion," Congressional Research Service, March 11, 2003.

34. For a summary of the proposal, see the press release by the U.S. Treasury, January 31, 2003, "President's Budget Proposes Bold Tax-Free Savings and Retirement Security Opportunities for All Americans," which can be found on the Treasury Web site at http://treasury.gov.

35. Michael Porter, *Capital Choices: Changing the Way America Invests in Industry* (Washington, D.C.: Council on Competitiveness, 1992).

36. See Jonathan Low and Paul Cohen Kalafut, *Invisible Advantage: How Intangibles Are Driving Business Performance* (Cambridge, Mass.: Perseus Publishing, 2002), for a broad overview of the growing importance of intangibles to business decisions.

37. Linda R. Cohen and Roger G. Noll with Jeffrey S. Banks, Susan A. Edelman, and William M. Pegram, *The Technology Pork Barrel* (Washington, D.C.: Brookings Institution Press, 1991).

38. Remarks by the president at the American Association of Community Colleges Annual Convention, Minneapolis, April 26, 2004. The text of the speech can be found at http://www.whitehouse.gov/news/rleases/2004/04/20040426-6.html.

39. Council of Economic Advisers, *2004 Economic Report of the President* (Washington, D.C.: U.S. Government Printing Office, 2004), 229.

40. President's Commission of Advisers on Science and Technology, "Report on Building Out Broadband," photocopy, Washington, D.C., December 13, 2002.

41. Kent H. Hughes, "R&D Can Keep America Competitive Amid New Challenges," *Chronicle of Higher Education*, November 30, 2001.

42. See Franklin J. Vargo, Testimony before the U.S.-China Economic and Security Review Commission, Washington, D.C., September 25, 2003.

43. See, for instance, "Making America Stronger: A Report with Legislative Recommendations on Restoration of U.S. Manufacturing," photocopy, Office of Senator Joseph I. Lieberman, Washington, D.C., September 2003.

44. See Robert D. Atkinson, "The Bush Manufacturing Crisis," Policy Report, photocopy, Progressive Policy Institute, Washington, D.C., October 2003.

Chapter 15

Competing for the Future: Strengthening the American Innovation System

As the United States moves through the first decade of the twenty-first century, policymakers and private strategists alike confront domestic and international economies that have changed significantly during the past two decades. The broad outlines of the competitiveness strategy that developed in the 1980s continue to provide the best framework for public policy or private initiative directed at long-term prosperity. However, whether developing remedies for elementary and secondary education or stimulating innovation, a twenty-first-century competitiveness strategy must be adapted to the emergence of new technologies, the rise of new competitors, and the adoption of new national priorities.

The preceding chapter focused on steps to recreate a climate that fosters and sustains public and private investment. The current chapter emphasizes another essential element of a long-term competitiveness strategy: innovation.

The Changing American Innovation System

During the past two decades, public and private research have both grown and changed in character. Private research and development spending has grown more rapidly and now accounts for roughly two-thirds of the national total. As private-sector research has grown, it has shifted away from basic science and technology to emphasize nearer-to-market development. Many of the great industrial laboratories of the past have been closed or sold or have moved away from fundamental research. Public funding has continued to grow but with a concentration on the life sciences. The 1990s decline in defense spending had the unintended affect of limiting funds for research

411

in the physical sciences and engineering. Innovation has also gone global—with American firms doing research overseas and foreign-based multinationals establishing research arms in the United States.[1]

The United States has taken many steps to strengthen the technology base of the civilian economy during the past two decades. In part, the greater emphasis on research and development targeted at the civilian economy has been driven by the growing importance of commercial innovation to national security needs. From the end of World War II through the 1970s, advocates of spending on defense and space research emphasized their contribution to the civilian economy as well as to national security. Technologies developed for weapon systems or advanced rocketry were eventually "spun off" to a commercial use. By the 1980s, however, it became common to speak of commercial technologies being "spun on" or adapted to defense needs rather than defense technologies always being spun off to benefit the civilian economy.[2]

In addition to a direct contribution to national security, the public and private sectors emphasized the importance of long-term prosperity to American goals and America's international leadership. The move to focus on the civilian economy dates back to the early 1980s, when Congress took steps to increase the economic impact of spending on federal mission-oriented research, such as research on space, health, and national security. Since then, Congress has created a structure to facilitate the commercial use of technologies developed by universities[3] and by the national laboratories,[4] and to encourage industry to work in partnership with the national laboratories.[5] On a parallel track, Congress adopted legislation to support private research and development through tax credits[6] and by facilitating joint research[7] and production.[8] During the past twenty years, the federal government also shared the costs and risks of developing new high-risk technologies through grants to small businesses[9] and matching grants to companies.[10] The federal government is also sharing the costs of developing a new generation of safe, efficient, and environmentally benign vehicles.[11]

Steps toward an Innovative Future

The innovation system will continue to change. The post–September 11, 2001, focus on terrorism, the continued development of a more agile military, and securing homeland defense are already pulling the development of technologies in one direction—just as new diseases will drive it in another.

In setting policies to strengthen the national capacity for pursuing basic science and developing new technologies, policymakers must keep their focus on the innovation system as a whole. Public funding and popular attitudes toward science will both influence the future course of the American innovation system. Established and emerging national research missions from health to homeland security will create new opportunities and inevitably limit others. Private-sector profits, the availability of venture capital funds, and their shifting focus will also influence the future capacity of the country to innovate. So do international trends, which affect everything from the state of global knowledge to the pace of technological development overseas.

The U.S. government must regularly inform the country on the state of America's innovation system in relation to meeting and anticipating the needs of national security and domestic prosperity. The country needs to measure the current innovation system against past performance, the international competition, and national goals. The following recommendations will help the United States evaluate its current national innovation system and take steps to improve it. As circumstances change, policies must also change. What will not change is the central role that innovation will play in America's future.

This chapter makes six broad recommendations to strengthen the American innovation system. First, provide periodic assessments of the innovation system to the country and Congress backed by regular administration reports, speeches, and testimony. Second, build sustained political support for science and technology by linking them to economic growth, environmental protection, national security, and individual opportunity. Third, support basic or high-risk, high-payoff technologies as well as basic science. Fourth, shore up weaknesses in the existing innovation system by expanding funding for research in the physical as well as life sciences and by broadening the availability of venture capital. Fifth, promote great missions that will drive innovation and build popular support—a new source of energy, fighting new diseases, or responding to the challenge of an aging population. Sixth, do not neglect the importance of improving the climate for commercialization, paying attention to the many factors that help move ideas from the laboratory to the marketplace, the classroom, or the doctor's office.

Regularly Assessing the American Innovation System

The government must have a clear sense of how federal support for research and development fits into the larger national system and how both are linked to an increasingly international process of innovation. Over the years, a number of useful reports have brought a historical perspective to science and technology and put both in the broader context of national security and economic growth. During the post–World War II period, a number of federal reports also took a broad look at the United States' innovation system. There were the 1967 Charpie Report (*Technology Innovation: Its Environment and Management*)[12] and the 1978 report from President Carter's Advisory Committee on Industrial Innovation.[13] The next year, President Carter proposed legislation that would strengthen the U.S. innovation system and "included funding for 'generic' R&D [research and development] of value to industry." The Carter R&D initiative "stalled under [President] Reagan," but industry-focused R&D became part of the Omnibus Trade and Competitiveness Act of 1988.[14] Prompted by slow productivity growth and international competition, it was in the 1980s that public and private America really focused on innovation as a complex system.

In the 1990s, the White House Office of Science and Technology Policy issued a series of reports: *Science in the National Interest;*[15] *National Security, Science and Technology Security;*[16] and *Technology in the National Interest.*[17] The Commerce Department's Technology Administration provided insights on a variety of related topics.[18] Leading competitiveness voices from the private and public sectors, the Council on Competitiveness, and the Competitiveness Policy Council added their own perspectives.[19]

The White House should build on this past work to provide a *quadrennial report* on innovation that would be linked to the federal budget cycle. The report should be prepared by the White House Office of Science and Technology Policy and should cover federal science and technology policy, the broader national innovation system, and international trends in science and technology. Much of the needed data is already collected by the federal government[20] or available through private-sector surveys.[21] The reports of foreign governments and international bodies will provide a useful overview of international trends. The federal government can gain added insights into overseas trends by emphasizing science and technology reporting by the State Department's Foreign Service officers and the Department of Commerce's Foreign Commercial Service.

The quadrennial report should be released early in the first year of a president's term. If a president is entering a second term, the results of the quadrennial study will already be influencing the preparation of the next fiscal year's budget. A president elected in November, however, will have little more than two months to modify a budget that has been prepared by the outgoing president before submitting it to Congress in January for a fiscal year that will begin in October. If copies of the draft quadrennial report are given to the incoming president's transition team immediately after the election, the report might retain some impact on the budget. And at the least the quadrennial report would be fully available for work on the budget for the next fiscal year.

Congress should add force to the report by giving it a legislative mandate, requiring periodic testimony by the president's adviser on science and technology, and using oversight hearings to encourage government wide coordination of research efforts. Congress should also add an "innovation impact statement" requirement to major pieces of legislation and important international agreements. Impact statements have a mixed history—powerful in the environmental arena, largely ignored with regard to inflation, and enacted but never really tried in relation to competitiveness.[22] At least a requirement might have an initial heuristic value. The point is to find vehicles that will focus presidential and congressional attention on policies that determine the long-run strength of the economy.

Building Sustained Political Support for Science and Technology

The key test for government support is whether important benefits flow from research that markets are unlikely to pursue. It is a case of the government cautiously walking (not rushing) in where markets fear to tread. In his insightful 1998 essay, Louis Branscomb (of the John F. Kennedy School of Government at Harvard University) makes this point by emphasizing the need for a research policy rather than a science policy.[23]

At times, science and particularly technology policy have proved to be controversial territory. For instance, President Clinton's ambitious technology policy came under severe political attack in 1995 and 1996 as being little more than another version of industrial policy or a disguised form of corporate welfare. The attack extended to the Technology Reinvestment Programs (TRP) established in 1992 and housed in the Defense Advanced Research Projects Agency.

In part, TRP was designed to help the defense sector of the economy make the transition to a post–Cold War world.[24] Because California was home to so many defense contractors as well as being the high-technology capital of the country, many firms seeking support from TRP or other technology programs were California based. Although TRP was a Department of Defense program, the overall effort to help California make the transition from defense to civilian production was coordinated by the Commerce Department. Commerce was also home to some of the president's major technology initiatives. For some in Congress, the technology programs were just adding to a "slush fund" that then-commerce secretary Ron Brown could use to win political points in California.

The attack came despite TRP's competitive process for making awards and its cost-sharing element. To competition and cost sharing, the Advanced Technology Program (ATP), also housed at the Commerce Department, added a double peer review (i.e., for both technical merit and to commercial viability) to set even more demanding standards. Both effective planning and local partnerships were required by the Manufacturing Extension Partnership (MEP), another Commerce program. As presidential priorities, the ATP and MEP commanded White House attention and attracted congressional criticism. Although some of the political firestorm over technology policy has abated, the George W. Bush administration initially sought to eliminate or sharply reduce funding for both the ATP and the MEP.[25]

There remains the urgent need to articulate a clear rationale for technology policy that garners sustained political support. Several steps need to be taken. First, the president and other leaders interested in technology policy must emphasize the importance of technology to growth, the full nature of the U.S. innovation system, and how the system is changing. The president should give an annual or at least a periodic "State of the Innovation System" address.

Second, the president and other leaders need to respond to the two most frequent attacks on technology policy—that it is just a veiled form of industrial policy and that it is an exercise in corporate welfare. The economic case for basic technologies is much the same as it is for basic science. When markets are not going to invest, then the government is responsible for deciding whether, when, where, and how to invest. For instance, the ATP has looked for high-risk, high-payoff research proposed by the private sector. In deciding whether to provide research support, the ATP borrowed the technical peer review approach used by both the National Science Foundation and the National Institutes of Health (NIH) to make thousands of individual research grants and added a second peer review to judge the prospects for commercial success.

Questions are often raised about grants made to major companies that already conduct ample research. It is not that the company in question lacks profits or the capacity. But, in many cases, the company avoids pursuing a technology because the cost is too high or the benefits too distant. The company also may be unsure of its ability to fully capture the results of the research, fearing that it may undertake the cost of development only to see benefits going to its competitors. The prospect of sharing the costs with other partners including the federal government can lead to an innovation that fosters industry-wide or economy-wide as well as specific corporate benefits.

Third, the economic benefits of peer-reviewed federal research in material science or information technology must be emphasized just as they are in the medical field. Linking some research grants to their industrial payoff or their regional impact can and should be done without endangering the peer-review process. Making the ATP or other grant awards to the company and chief executive as well as the research department will raise the profile of the program and build private-sector support. Inviting the local U.S. representative, the mayor, and an administration official to a ceremony marking a peer-reviewed grant will build political support as well. Fourth, periodic programmatic reports and an ongoing dialogue with Congress will also contribute to a long-term political constituency.

Supporting High-Risk, High-Payoff Technologies

During the past twenty years, the federal government has successfully intervened to strengthen or foster the development of new technologies. In other instances, it has ignored competitive developments overseas or intervened too late to save a domestic industry or maintain a promising technology. The country needs to track critical industries and technologies here and abroad so that policy is informed by a clear sense of global developments. Industry-specific knowledge on a global basis will allow for targeted intervention before an industry is in competitive difficulty. Alternatively, the United States must be prepared to manage dependence where either maintaining an existing industry or stimulating a new one is judged to be too difficult, too late, or too expensive either financially or diplomatically. In those cases, the United States can increase its degree of independence by keeping on the technological edge and seeking to diversify international sources of supply.

There are many examples of how federal research support has helped stimulate the development of new technologies, which in turn have fostered new industries, spurred growth, and created new job opportunities. For instance, the biotechnology revolution has been fostered and supported through government-sponsored basic research, intellectual property laws, and the presence of a large and growing demand for health care that is also, to a significant degree, publicly funded.

The government also played a critical role in the efforts to develop electronic commerce. The Internet is a direct descendent of a Defense Department program initially designed to link major federal research facilities. In the 1990s, the government encouraged the spread of electronic commerce by working to develop a global legal structure that protects intellectual property and privacy while limiting intrusive regulations or taxation. The government's 1990s emphasis on wiring schools, the deregulation of the telecommunications industry, and the search to make Internet access a new kind of universal service have added further stimulus to the industry's development.[26]

The federal government has also intervened to help key industries regain their strength. A compelling example came in the mid-1980s response to the Japanese challenge to the American semiconductor industry (this is described in detail in chapter 3). In part, the American response was the familiar effort to temporarily slow imports and make the most of the resulting "breathing room." There was also something new. A consortium of major chip makers formed Sematech, which—with the Department of Defense bearing 50 percent of the costs—facilitated the sharing of technology among its members and significantly strengthened the material and equipment industries that supply chip makers. Particularly with regard to the equipment makers, it was an example of America successfully making up a good deal of lost ground.

Even where it proves too difficult or too costly to maintain or develop an American-based industry, government support can add technological strengths and help manage the risks of global interdependence. The cases of the effort to develop or retain an American presence in flat-panel displays and advanced lithography (used to print transistors on semiconductors) are instructive.

Having become concerned about the almost total U.S. dependence on imports of flat-panel displays, the Department of Defense made several efforts to create (not just save) an American-based source of supply. The initial reliance on a single domestic captive supplier proved expensive and did not bring with it the innovative dynamism of a globally competitive industry. Although Defense was constrained by World Trade Organization rules on subsidies and limited by a congressional aversion to industrial policy, it relied on research and development grants to create a commercially viable industry. It has succeeded in stimulating new technologies, but the program has not yet resulted in significant domestic production. It is still possible, of course, that some of the new technologies—coupled with America's venture capital market and entrepreneurial culture—may yet carry the day.[27] The American initiative may also have helped accelerate the entry of South Korean and Taiwanese producers, which at least reduced U.S. dependence on Japanese production, dominated by a single firm, Sharp.

In the case of advanced lithography, the United States was trying to retain rather than create a presence. In the late 1990s, Intel took the lead in forming a consortium composed of the Silicon Valley Group, chip makers, and two national energy laboratories. The Silicon Valley Group was one of America's few remaining producers of advanced lithography tools (or "steppers") used in printing semiconductor circuits.[28]

The consortium was focused on turning the extreme ultraviolet technology developed by the national laboratories (Lawrence Livermore and Sandia) into a new tool for printing ever-finer circuits on a silicon wafer. From the start, Intel and other chip makers wanted to include either Nikon or Cannon, Japanese firms that dominated the stepper field. They were concerned about Silicon Valley Group's ability to meet the expected volume of steppers and, in any case, were reluctant to be dependent on a single supplier, whether American based or not. There was immediate resistance to the sale by some in the Clinton administration and by many members of Congress, for fear that a publicly funded technology would be lost to overseas development. In the end, ASM Lithography Holding, NV, a Dutch company that ranks third (behind Nikon and Cannon) in global stepper production, entered the picture. After considerable debate within the Department of Defense, the George W. Bush administration finally approved the sale of the Silicon Valley Group in 2001.[29]

The result may not be harmful to long-term American competitiveness. Three major competitors can still provide the kind of competition that drives stepper prices down and stimulates future innovation. The United States remains a major customer for stepper sales, is an important source of technology, and still has some domestic production. At least, however, an important degree of control has passed into Dutch hands. (For more on the stepper case, see chapter 11.)

Shoring Up Weaknesses in the Innovation Chain

The post–Cold War decline in defense spending had an unintended result: Overall federal support for research in the physical sciences has been stagnant. Not only are the physical sciences important in themselves, but they also help meet needs in the life sciences where federal support has continued to grow. Had the United States monitored the innovation chain more carefully, the administration or Congress could have funneled needed support through the National Science Foundation or other federal agencies as well through the Department of Defense itself. The federal government must move quickly to provide adequate funding for the physical sciences.

Venture capital has been one of the great strengths of the American approach to innovation. It is, however, volatile. At times, venture capital will concentrate on a specific industry—say, biotechnology—at the expense of other fields. The availability of venture capital has also fluctuated widely, ballooning in the late 1990s and shrinking dramatically after the financial bubble burst in 2000. Can the government help act as a balance wheel, providing a steadier flow of risk capital to a variety of industries? In 1993 and 1994, the Clinton administration supported a competitiveness bill that included provision for a venture capital fund. It failed to pass, in part because of insistence by key House members that any grants include a requirement that resulting innovations be commercialized in the United States. It is time to create a National Institute of Innovation (NII) that, like NIH, would provide a more predictable flow of funds to support the development of innovative products and processes. Like NIH, NII will need to set broad priorities, draw on peer review for making awards, and forge effective partnerships with universities, public and private research laboratories, and private industry.

Supporting Great Missions That Drive Innovation

In the world of science and technology, great and demanding goals drive innovation. Twentieth-century examples of such goals include the Manhattan Project that built the atomic bomb, the Apollo Project that took America to the moon, and the defense-driven demand for ever greater computing power. There are many other missions or goals that would have enormous impact on the future of the nation. Three are touched on here.

First, make a national effort to develop a *new source of energy* that will support economic growth, protect the environment, and achieve energy independence for the country. After the first energy crisis in 1973, the United States took several steps toward a new national energy policy. By the end of the decade, there was a new Cabinet-level Department of Energy, a strategic petroleum reserve to guard against future oil embargoes, and an emphasis on conservation. There were also a number of initiatives to develop new sources of energy, with both environmental improvement and energy independence as goals.

Since the 1970s, successes in conservation and the growing importance of services—as opposed to more energy-intensive industrial production—have combined to sharply reduce the amount of energy required to produce a dollar of national output. At the same time, continued economic growth, the shift to light trucks (including sport utility vehicles), and the limits to significantly increasing the domestic production of oil and gas have steadily increased the nation's dependence on imported oil. During the next twenty years, rapid growth in Asia and elsewhere around the world will put added pressure on oil supplies that are still concentrated in the Middle East, the Caucasus, and Central Asia. A history of turmoil in the Middle East and the growing concern about global warming give added impetus to the pursuit of energy independence and to developing new, more environmentally benign sources of energy.

Today, much of the energy focus is on fuel cells and hydrogen. The Clinton administration's Partnerships for a New Generation of Vehicles (PNGV) focused on hydrogen as a long-term possibility, as well as emphasizing interim steps that could improve fuel economy during the next decade.[30] While not maintaining a number of the PNGV initiatives, the Bush administration has continued the effort to develop a hydrogen car. Before becoming a hydrogen-based economy, researchers will be pushed to develop nonpolluting and safe methods of generating, distributing, and using hydrogen. Hydrogen need not be the only target—there have been recent advances in wind, solar, and even fusion power. There is also renewed interest in clean coal technology linked to research on how to sequester carbon dioxide emissions. The achievement of a new, clean, domestically generated source of energy would contribute to everything from a reduction in global warming to the conduct of U.S. foreign policy. Pursuing such a source of energy would also result in the development of many other technologies and pose new puzzles that would stimulate basic scientific research. Americans need to return to a national energy strategy that funds research on alternative sources of energy, supports pilot projects, and introduces alternative approaches to energy use into everything from the design of manufacturing equipment to the pattern of metropolitan growth.

Second, *attack new and existing diseases on a global basis.* Between the invention of penicillin in the 1940s and the start of the spread of HIV/AIDS in the 1980s, much of the industrial world lived a moment in history that was often free of the fear of disease. Even the 1950s rise of polio was met by the relatively rapid development of an effective vaccine. That era is now passing. There is a growing sense that every nation is only one plane ride away from any disease. In addition to HIV/AIDS, there has been the discovery of Ebola, the sudden emergence of Severe Acute Respiratory Syndrome (SARS), and the more recent fears about a virulent form of a bird virus. To nature's diseases have been added the threat of human-made pathogens.

Long-standing diseases create their own challenges. In some cases—tuberculosis and polio—the challenge is education, effective distribution of remedies, and assuring proper use of the medicine. There is already a nearly successful international effort to eliminate polio. But there are a host of other tropical diseases often ignored by the research laboratories of the advanced economies.

The new diseases and the threat of global bioterrorism all call for accelerated efforts directed at very early detection, added research, and the development of vaccines or other treatments. Had there been a global early warning system in place, the HIV/AIDS epidemic might have been caught and contained. As the global cooperative response to SARS has shown, partnership can contain diseases and, it is to be hoped, speed discoveries of cures.

Some imaginative steps have been taken to spur the development of cures and vaccines for established diseases. The Bill and Melinda Gates Foundation is helping to create a market that will attract the innovative talents of the major pharmaceutical companies to work on tropical diseases. Trade negotiations are on the path toward easing developing countries' access to lower-cost generic drugs. The Bush administration has committed itself to help fight the major diseases that afflict many poor countries. Creating Gates Foundation–like incentives focused on tropical diseases is an important initiative. America needs to take the added step of building a global early warning system and helping to create research outposts in the developing world. The United States must work with the World Health Organization and other countries with research capabilities to institutionalize the rapid worldwide response to the threatened recurrence of SARS. Research by itself is not enough. The United States, Europe, and Japan should work with the World Bank and national governments in the developing world to create networks that can administer vaccines, deliver medicines, and monitor treatments. By leading the global struggle against new and existing diseases, the United States will not only serve a higher morality but also stimulate basic scientific understanding and the development of new technologies.

Third, *apply technology to the challenge of an aging population* facing the United States and the other major industrial powers.[31] The industrial world is growing older. While not a panacea, technology can provide part of the answer. For instance, the spread of broadband technology will increase the type of work and range of meetings that can be held online, allowing employees to combine partial retirement while continuing to work from home. Japan has already moved ahead of the other industrial democracies in developing robots to substitute for human labor,[32] and recent developments suggest similar developments that could even affect the demand for low-skill labor.[33] A concerted focus on technologies targeted at an aging workforce will support more active lives, facilitate partial retirement, and ease the financial burden for individuals and the fiscal burden for democratic societies. And there will be the added benefit of stimulating breakthroughs in material science, electronics, and information technology.

Technology can also play an enormous role in containing the rise of health care costs that are squeezing individual paychecks, limiting corporate profits, and making demands on public budgets. At almost 15 percent of gross domestic product (GDP), the United States spends far more on health care (in percentage of GDP as well as in absolute terms) than any other major industrial democracy, despite leaving tens of millions of Americans without adequate health care.

Why does the United States manage to spend so much on health care and yet fall so far short of universal coverage? There are many explanations— failure to effectively apply information technology, lack of a public health emphasis on diet and routine care, and the steady parade of expensive new technologies for diagnosis and treatment. Research should focus on all three elements. For instance, information technology is still used in only a limited way to allow off-site consultations. Broader application of information technology to standardized record keeping could provide enormous saving. Reducing the cost of portable diagnostic devices that can be used at work or at home will help in the detection and monitoring of easily treated diseases such as hypertension. We need to allocate research funds targeted at reducing the cost of effective but expensive procedures. The focus on research targeted at costs must not take the place of efforts to develop new cures and treatments. But targeted research should reduce costs, facilitate broadening insurance coverage, and improve national health.

There are many other national goals that will drive innovation. President Bush has announced a new vision for future missions to the moon and, eventually, to Mars.[34] Although the president did not mention the new missions in his State of the Union address on January 20, 2004, space exploration still has the potential for capturing the imagination of the American people. As with some of the other missions mentioned above, the human exploration of Mars will drive innovations and science in many new directions. The challenge of eventually modeling human life through time will drive biological understanding and enormous improvements in information technology.

In the developing world, there is a tremendous need for clean water and crops adapted to tropical conditions. There are already some new innovations with promise. For instance, DEKA, the company of inventor/entrepreneur Dean Kamen, has invented a machine the size of a packing crate (a cube measuring 4 feet on each side) that will turn a dirty or diseased stream into potable water. A similar-sized machine that can be powered by virtually anything provides the needed electricity. There are others working to develop cheap, effective means of delivering clean water. Kamen's individual effort and those of other inventors need to be elevated to the status of a national mission.

Some of these ventures would not require a major increase in spending. Other goals—for instance, a mission to Mars—would require substantial, multiyear funding. Budgetary consideration will always be an element in setting priorities and deciding on initiatives to pursue. To develop the science and technology that will save lives, strengthen the economy, improve the environment, and increase national security, the United States must chose major goals, provide sufficient funding, and make sure that the effort has sustained popular and political support.

Continuing to Improve the Climate for Commercialization

The public role in fostering a favorable climate for commercialization requires a philosophy that encompasses the entire innovation system, including commercialization and a government that is agile in responding to changing economic circumstances. Sensible regulation is an important part of fostering a climate that favors innovation. Abdicating regulatory responsibilities is not. As part of the New Growth Compact, the government must be in constant communication with consumer organizations, business groups, industrial innovators, labor leaders, environmentalists, and others to be able to respond quickly and adapt regulations to new scientific knowledge and changing economic circumstances.

Throughout the 1980s, the United States continued to be strong in basic science and the generation of new technologies. Though first in the laboratory, however, the country was too often second to reach the living room, failing in the race to turn an innovation into a marketable product. A comprehensive competitiveness strategy itself contributes to a climate conducive to commercialization. Steady growth, low interest rates, stable prices, adequate financing, innovation-oriented regulations, and a reinvented government are all important pieces of the commercialization puzzle, as they are for competitiveness generally.

For innovation, however, two elements of our competitiveness strategy stand out as deserving special treatment: trade and training. Trade negotiations over technical standards and access to global markets are critically important to the success of new products. America must focus on emerging technologies and the shifting policies of its trading partners to anticipate the need for negotiations before standards-based barriers impose an economic penalty. Just as fundamental is access to overseas markets. As noted in earlier chapters, access allows greater sales and profits, forces American firms to match the best in terms of quality and prevents U.S. trading partners from using domestic sanctuaries to gain an edge in the American or third-country markets. In many cases, effective access must include opportunities for direct investments. Firms may not be able to provide a service or effectively support a product unless they can invest in overseas facilities. As industrial and industrializing countries develop more and more technologies of their own, an overseas American presence will facilitate the adoption of these technologies by American firms and speed their introduction in the American economy.

Education, training, and lifelong learning are also critical to the entire system of innovation. Whether the inventor in a laboratory, the front-line worker in an assembly plant, the technically proficient salesperson, or the knowledgeable person who provides follow-on service, skills and continued training are critical. It is an area in which both the emerging growth compact and a multitude of public–private partnerships are at play. The public sector provides an education that emphasizes personal growth and citizenship, as well as general, marketable skills; the private sector must complement public education with job-specific training. The public and private sectors must effectively share their own teaching techniques and technologies with each other. There are few areas where partnerships are more necessary or more promising. It is to the question of education, training, and the American system of learning that we turn in chapter 16.

Notes

1. Council on Competitiveness, *Going Global: The New Shape of American Innovation* (Washington, D.C.: Council on Competitiveness, 1998).

2. See John Alic, Lewis M. Branscom, Harvey Brooks, Ashton B. Carter, and Gerald K. Epstein, *Beyond Spinoff: Military and Commercial Technologies in a Changing World* (Boston: Harvard Business School Press, 1992). The first chapter discussed the paradigm of seeing commercial technologies being spun off of defense needs and traces four fundamental changes that have changed the paradigm; see pp. 8–13.

3. The Bay-Dole Act of 1980 (Patent and Trademark Amendments Act, PL 96-517).

4. The Stevenson Wydler Act of 1980 (the Technology Innovation Act, PL 96-480).

5. The Federal Technology Transfer Act of 1986 (PL 99-502) created the authority for the federal laboratories to enter into cooperative research and development agreements with the private sector. See Lewis M. Branscomb, "National Laboratories: The Search for New Missions and New Structures," in *Empowering Technology: Implementing a U.S. Strategy,* ed. Lewis M. Branscomb (Cambridge, Mass.: MIT Press, 1993), 103–31.

6. The Research and Experimentation Tax Credit was first adopted in 1981.

7. The National Cooperative Research Act of 1984 sought to facilitate private-sector collaboration in research by reducing the risks and costs of violating the antitrust laws.

8. In 1993, Congress amended the National Cooperative Research Act to reduce the risks of joint production.

9. In 1982, Congress adopted the Small Business Innovation Development Act, which required federal agencies to devote a small percentage of their research dollar to small innovators.

10. Created as part of the Omnibus Trade and Competitiveness Act of 1988, the Advanced Technology Program shared the cost with industry of developing high-risk, high-payoff technologies.

11. The Reagan administration's Defense Department provided half the funding for Sematech, the consortium of major American semiconductor producers. The Clinton administration worked with Chrysler (now DaimlerChrysler), Ford, and General Motors in the Partnership for a New Generation of Vehicles. Though the Bush administration has dropped the PNGV label, it is building on the PNGV's work on fuel cells and hydrogen in its own hydrogen car effort.

12. Robert Charpie chaired a panel convened by the secretary of commerce, hence the Charpie Report. Department of Commerce, *Technological Innovation: Its Environment and Management* (Washington, D.C.: U.S. Government Printing Office, 1967).

13. White House Office of Science and Technology Policy and Department of Commerce, *Domestic Policy Review of Industrial Innovation* (Washington, D.C.: U.S. Government Printing Office, 1978).

14. See Lewis M. Branscomb and George Parker, "Funding Civilian and Dual-Use Industrial Technology," in *Empowering Technology,* ed. Branscomb, 72.

15. President William J. Clinton and Vice President Albert Gore Jr., *Science in the National Interest* (Washington, D.C.: Office of Science and Technology Policy, 1994).

16. Committee on National Security of the National Science and Technology Council, *National Security, Science and Technology Strategy* (Washington, D.C.: Office of Science and Technology Policy, 1995).

17. Committee on Civilian Industrial Technology of the National Science and Technology Council, *Technology in the National Interest* (Washington, D.C.: Office of Science and Technology Policy, 1996).

18. See, for instance, Technology Administration, U.S. Department of Commerce,

International Science and Technology: Policies, Programs and Investments (Washington, D.C.: U.S. Department of Commerce, 2000).

19. Council on Competitiveness, *Endless Frontier, Limited Resources: U.S. R&D Policy for Competitiveness* (Washington, D.C.: Council on Competitiveness, 1996); and Erich Bloch, "Technology Policy for a Competitive America," Report of the Critical Technologies Subcouncil of the Competitiveness Policy Council, in *Reports of Subcouncils* (Washington, D.C.: Competitiveness Policy Council, 1993).

20. National Science Foundation, *Science and Engineering Indicators 2002* (Washington, D.C.: U.S. Government Printing Office, 2002).

21. For instance, the Industrial Research Institute, a professional organization representing the vice presidents for R&D in major corporations, conducts an annual survey of its members projected R&D spending. The National Commission on Entrepreneurship tracks the availability of venture capital.

22. Section 5421 of the Omnibus Trade and Competitiveness Act of 1988 requires the administration to include in "any legislation which may affect the ability of United States firms to compete in domestic and international commerce a statement of the impact of such legislation . . . on the ability of United States' firms engaged in the manufacture, sale, distribution or provision of good or services to compete in foreign domestic markets." See U.S. Congress, *Omnibus Trade and Competitiveness Act of 1988: A Conference Report to Accompany HR 3* (Washington, D.C.: U.S. Government Printing Office, 1988).

23. See Louis M. Branscomb, "From Science Policy to Research Policy," in *Investing in Innovation: Creating a Research and Innovation Policy That Works*, ed. Lewis M. Branscomb and James H. Keller (Cambridge, Mass.: MIT Press, 1998), 112–42. Branscomb is the Aetna Professor (Emeritus) of Public Policy and Corporate Management at Harvard University's John F. Kennedy School of Government.

24. For background on the Technology Reinvestment Program, see Linda Cohen, "Dual-Use and Technology Reinvestment Project," in *Investing in Innovation,* ed. Branscomb and Keller, 174–93.

25. As part of the Bush administration's January 2004 manufacturing initiative, they propose restoring some but not all the funding for the Manufacturing Extension Partnership program. See Mike Allen, "Commerce Dept. Plans More Help For Industry," *Washington Post,* January 16, 2004.

26. See Brian Kahin, "Beyond the National Information Infrastructure Initiative," in *Investing in Innovation,* ed. Branscomb and Keller, 339–60.

27. For a more detailed assessment of the Clinton administration's Flat Panel Display Initiative, see Jeffry A. Hart, Stefanie A. Lenway, and Thomas P. Murtha, "Technonationalism and Cooperation in a Globalizing Industry: The Case of Flat-Panel Displays," in *Coping with Globalization,* ed. Aseem Prakash and Jeffrey A. Hart (New York: Routledge, 2000), 117–47.

28. The stepper derives its name from the printing process. It *steps* across the silicon wafer as it prints the circuits.

29. The bare bones of the agreement are covered in Optics.org at http://optics.org/articles/news/7/5/9/1.

30. See Daniel Roos, Frank Field, and James Neely, "Industry Consortia," in *Investing in Innovation,* ed. Branscomb and Keller, 407–11.

31. See, for instance, statements by Martha Farnesworth Riche and U.S. Comptroller General David Walker at an April 24, 2003, meeting jointly sponsored by the

Woodrow Wilson International Center for Scholars and AARP. The statements and a summary of the meeting can be found on the Wilson Center's Web site, http://www. wilsoncenter.org.

32. See, for instance, James Brooke, "Japan Seeks Robotic Help in Caring for the Aged," *New York Times,* March 5, 2004.

33. Rodney Books, "The Robots Are Here," *Technology Review,* February 2004, 30.

34. George W. Bush, "President Bush Announces New Vision for Space Exploration Program," Remarks by the President on U.S. Space Policy at NASA Headquarters, Washington, January 14, 2004. The text of the president's remarks can be found at http://www.whitehouse.gov.

Chapter 16

Competing for the Future: Building a Better American Learning System

As political and private-sector leaders began to develop a national compet-itiveness strategy in the late 1970s, they emphasized education and training to foster growth and increase opportunity at the same time. The link between education and American economic performance was not new. Scholars still see America's early adoption of free, universal education in the nineteenth century as speeding the country's economic growth. The 1862 Morrill Act's creation of land-grant colleges for the agricultural and industrial arts was another important step in the development of both agriculture and industry. There was also a similar return-to-education reaction to the 1957 launch of Sputnik, the Soviet satellite.

In the past two decades, elements of the American learning system have changed. The elementary and secondary school system has put considerable effort into increasing opportunities for children with special needs. In the past decade, there has been an effort to increase the number of minorities in honors classes and the number of women and minorities continuing in mathematics and science classes. Both President George W. Bush and Pres-ident Bill Clinton have pushed for higher academic standards that would improve elementary and secondary academic performance and help prepare students for a future that demands stronger analytical and communication skills. Community colleges now play multiple rolls—a stepping stone to a four-year degree, an opportunity to acquire a specialized skill, and a venue for the already employed to improve their skills. The number and percent-age of high school graduates seeking some kind of postsecondary education have risen significantly.

During the 1990s, the federal government took a number of steps to make college education and the acquisition of added skills more available.

Responding to the growing importance of education and training, the private sector has increased its own commitment to training, created high-school-to-work programs, and even company-based universities. Leading companies have been a major force for education reform and have formed a wide variety of public–private partnerships with elementary and secondary schools and universities.

Thinking about education has gradually broadened to encompass a lifelong learning system that starts with prenatal care and extends throughout an individual's working life. The American learning system, however, has not kept pace with that reality and is, at present, more a set of disparate pieces than a well-oiled machine. It starts with families and medical professionals, continues through a mix of nursery schools, and includes everything from universities to on-the-job training.

Despite the shift in thinking and more than two decades of work at reform, the system faces multiple challenges. The "grown-like-Topsy" nature of the system even makes it difficult for the various parts to communicate or work with each other. The lack of universal health insurance creates an added hurdle for many lower-income families seeking prenatal and early childhood health care. The elementary and secondary school system continues to struggle with two learning gaps among its students. Considerable national attention is periodically focused on the troubling reality that, on average, African American and Latino students lag behind their Asian American and white peers. Less attention is paid to the sobering reality that, on average, American students lag behind many of their foreign counterparts in mathematics and science. At the university level, while the pool of college-bound applicants continues to grow because of the children of the baby boom (the so-called baby boom echo), postgraduate enrollment in mathematics, science, and engineering depends heavily on students from overseas.

The twenty-first century has posed yet another challenge to the American learning system. Since the end of the 1980s, more than 2.5 *billion* people left national isolation to become part of the global economy. With the spread of digitization and the Internet in the 1990s, a growing portion of those billions can provide sophisticated online services to the United States and any other part of the world. The new challenge came with the collapse of first the Soviet empire in 1989 and then the Soviet Union itself in 1991. By the end of the 1980s, China had clearly opted to become an outward-looking market economy linked to the economic world around it. China's national strategy emphasizes the move to high-technology manufacturing and investments in education that will provide an ever greater array of on-line services. The 1980s also saw India begin to turn away from central direction and the much maligned "red tape Raj" toward the world market in goods and even more in services. Building on strong educational institutions, India is creating a growing comparative advantage in sophisticated services that can be delivered by temporary immigrants to the industrial world or via broadband Internet links.

The growing talent pool around the world, new technology, and the sheer pace of change will force the United States and its educational institutions to adjust and adapt undergraduate and graduate education to these still changing economic realities. It will be a decades-long challenge to higher education while the United States must continue to wrestle with many deficiencies in elementary and secondary education.

The Public Role in Education

The public role in education is enormous. Although many children are home-schooled or attend parochial and private schools, most American children are in publicly funded elementary and secondary schools. Most of the funding for these schools comes from state or local sources, with much of the federal support targeted at children with special needs or at schools with significant numbers of low-income students. Private institutions are more of a force in colleges and universities, but the majority of students attend state-funded community colleges, four-year public colleges, or state universities. Direct federal support and indirect support through the tax code are important sources of funding for many college students. Major public and private universities look to federal grants to fund a significant share of their research activities. Other parts of the American learning system depend on families, social welfare agencies, and the private sector.

With a system that extends from before the cradle to beyond formal retirement, there is an enormous array of potential initiatives. What follows is just a small sample of needed steps. First, the president and Congress need to highlight the full, complex, multipart nature of the American learning system. Second, the federal government needs to make increased expenditures on elementary education that target improved physical plant, at-grade-level reading by the third grade, and the development of new educational technologies. Third, all parts of the learning chain from parents to the private sector need to stimulate the demand for learning as well as the supply of new classrooms, better books, and improved computers. Fourth, a new structure needs to be developed to guide federal learning policy, including the possibility of a new Department of American Learning.

The President Must Highlight the Existing System

By giving a periodic "State of the American Learning System" address, the president will raise awareness among seemingly disparate parts of the system that they form part of an important whole. The speech also will validate the myriad efforts of leaders across the country and provide guidance for individual action, public spending, and private initiative.

Many participants in the system of lifelong learning are only vaguely aware of how their role may affect an individual's future and the economic potential of the nation. Doctors, nurses, social workers, and many school-teachers are motivated by a love of education, concern about children, or a dedication to social equity. Understanding that early education is not only effective care giving but also helps prepare a child for the world of work ahead can help caregivers think about a new set of potential allies, including the business community. By thinking about the entire system, business leaders—who already are active in promoting improved elementary and secondary education—will be even more aware of the economic benefits of what are often viewed as largely social policies.

By describing the nature and stressing the importance of the American learning system, presidents, cabinet secretaries, and congressional leaders will provide direction and impetus to the existing efforts to improve the system. One of the lessons of the decade-long battle to develop a national competitiveness strategy is that businesses, labor unions, schools and universities, state governments, and local communities were all responding to recession, slow productivity growth, and international competition. They were already working to borrow lessons from overseas, learn from America's own past, and adopt new, more effective ways of operating. When the administration or Congress highlighted the importance of encouraging innovation, improving worker training, or seeking new export markets, it added strength and a sense of national purpose to myriad state and local initiatives.

The bully pulpit can be a powerful path to reaching individual Americans. Over the course of his eight-year presidency, President Clinton frequently described a world in which people could expect several jobs, several employers, and several skills over the course of a working lifetime. Much more important than specific public or private training programs are the individual choices made by millions of Americans responding to a new reality and a presidential call for a new direction.

The president and other leaders must also explain the importance of the American learning system in achieving key national goals and why the system requires complementary public and private roles. Start with democracy —it depends on an educated electorate. Emphasize the link to individual opportunity—which, in an increasingly knowledge-based economy, requires added education and steady improvement in skills. Education leads to new innovations and the better use of new technologies—which are critical for everything from health care to the high-technology weapons that help preserve the country's national security.

Improved education and greater educational opportunity will drive long-term economic growth and reduce income inequality at the same time. In addition to significantly expanding the Earned Income Tax Credit, which is targeted at low-income working Americans, the Clinton administration also emphasized achieving greater equity by increasing individual opportunity. Today's income gap narrows as an individual's education grows; education contributes to equity and a rising middle class as well as long-term economic growth.

Leave No Child Behind

In 1983, the Reagan administration published *A Nation at Risk,* a scathing assessment of America's elementary and secondary education system.[1] It is sobering and saddening that, with only light editing, the report could be reissued today.

Building on the earlier work of Presidents George H. W. Bush and Clinton, with the No Child Left Behind Act, President George W. Bush has taken the first federal step toward *requiring* national education standards that respond to a national economy and a highly mobile population. Using the carrot of federal dollars, he has encouraged states and school districts to set academic standards and periodically measure student progress toward them. If a school fails to improve over a three-year period, its students will have the right to transfer to a school that is meeting its goals.

Not surprisingly, the act has proven controversial. Its critics note that it adds a considerable financial burden to local schools without providing sufficient federal resources—in budget parlance, it is often viewed as an "unfunded mandate." Other critics are concerned that the education standards set by the act are too rigid, failing to adjust for the number of students who speak English as a second language or who have specific learning disabilities. In early 2004, the program was changed to recognize just such problems. Still other critics are concerned about the straitjacket of teaching to a test. But whatever the fate of the act itself, the president has set a rhetorical standard—leave no child behind—that will live on as a test of national resolve and commitment long after specific programs have been modified or superseded.

Along with the act, there are ambitious proposals to remake the education system and dramatically change the teacher corps.[2] What follows are much more modest proposals that involve targeted increases in federal funding for elementary education. Because financial support can lead to greater federal involvement, proposals for added funding have often triggered controversy in a country that cherishes local control. Still, the president can and should take four critical steps that would have a limited impact on the federal budget or local control.

First, the nation must set a standard for the quality of the physical plant used by elementary schools and see that it is met nationwide. Construction budgets are sufficiently removed from classroom content that federal contributions would do little to endanger local control. By itself, a new or renewed physical plant does not make a good school, any more than "clothes make the man." But a new plant will improve the climate for learning and raise the expectations of teachers, parents, and students alike.

Second, to make sure every child is reading by the third grade, the country must set a standard for class size in the first three grades. As communities and teachers become more aware of the potential for tutoring through technology (see below), class size may become less essential for many students. Visions for the potential of technology in education are nothing short of revolutionary, with everything from virtual classrooms to global online mentoring,[3] but the technology, classrooms, and teachers are not yet quite ready.

Third, reading skills must be emphasized outside as well as in the classroom. Many parents, particularly recent immigrants still struggling to learn English, may not be able to provide much help with reading outside the classroom. Schools should offer English literacy programs for adults that are linked to their children's education as well as the skills needed for employment and citizenship. Weak readers often fall further behind during a book-free summer. School districts need to have summer reading programs—perhaps linked to once-a-month mini-camps where reading assessment is woven into games, sports, or other activities.

By requiring community service for high school students, many school districts are creating an enormous pool of potential tutors for aspiring readers. Given the pressures on the federal budget from national defense, homeland security, and other priorities, the country will want to target its spending to meet the greatest need—not an impossible task. The federal government has considerable experience in designing formulas for allocating funds that take into account local effort and adjust for local income.

Fourth, the federal government should take the lead in providing online support and educational technologies for use by teachers, students, and parents. The Clinton administration took a number of steps in this direction with programs that, for example, encouraged technical literacy and the effective use of educational technology.[4] By systematically drawing on existing government training programs—some Department of Defense educational programs are already being used in high schools—the federal government can accelerate the development and diffusion of learning technologies.

Building a Demand for Learning

All layers of government, universities, labor unions, businesses, and community groups need to help nurture the demand for learning. So much in the way of educational reform emphasizes the supply side of education—new schools, smaller class sizes, the latest computer, or an Internet connection. They are all important, but buying a new trough does not make the horse any more thirsty.

One model for stimulating the demand for learning is a national robot contest sponsored by the Foundation for the Inspiration and Recognition of Science and Technology (FIRST), which was established by Dean Kamen, the same New Hampshire–based inventor/entrepreneur who wants to bring clean water to the developing world.[5] FIRST pairs teams of high school students with teams of engineers from universities or businesses. Together, they build a robot that will play a game. The aim of the program is to create that thirst for learning by exposing students to the world of technology, the excitement of problem solving, and the appreciation of teamwork and "gracious professionalism" in the pursuit of common goals. The broader vision of FIRST is to create a national culture that celebrates achievement and recognizes the inventor as well as the sports hero or the movie star.[6] Kamen may be on his way. The 2004 FIRST final hosted hundreds of teams in Atlanta's Georgia Dome—a major site for the 1996 Olympics.

Creating a Federal Dialogue with the American Learning System

The American learning system has a host of parts that often have little direct contact or communication with each other or with the federal government. The elementary and secondary school system alone depends on active parents, thousands of local school boards, state regulators, several federal programs, and a growing number of public–private partnerships. Hundreds of thousands of schoolchildren are now home-schooled and use yet another set of networks. With such a large and variegated structure, the federal government needs a new approach to maintaining a regular dialogue with all parts of the American learning system.

Some existing federal structures serve as possible models. In the field of trade, every administration has an extensive set of advisory committees to provide private-sector views on the course of trade negotiations. Although the system concentrates on business, there are voices from organized labor, consumer interests, and the environmental community. In the field of technology, the President's Council of Advisers on Science and Technology is cochaired by the president's science and technology adviser and a leading figure from the private sector. The president needs to establish similar institutions that allow the president and his administration to keep abreast of new developments, emerging problems, and the latest thinking about education.

A new mechanism is also needed to coordinate the current and potential federal initiatives that will strengthen the American learning system. In the field of technology, the National Science and Technology Council and the earlier Federal Coordinating Council for Science, Engineering, and Technology have been successful in coordinating the research activities of a number of executive-branch departments in pursuit of a shared priority.

The president should also create, by executive order, a Cabinet-level Skills for Life Coordinating Committee to bring together the work of agencies ranging from the Department of Health and Human Services to the Department of Defense. This new interagency body would help coordinate crosscutting initiatives that include improvements in prenatal care, the accelerated use of technology in elementary schools, and a commitment to make algebra a standard requirement for the eighth grade and combine them all in a single legislative proposal. The interagency group could stimulate the development and use of learning technologies by bringing together the many learning technologies already used by the Department of Defense. Added power will come by including the research capacity of the national energy laboratories, coupled with the experience of the Commerce, Education, Health and Human Services, and Labor Departments. The interagency group should encourage public–private partnerships that can help adapt the many learning technologies used by industry to the needs of schools or the training needs of communities.

Should the country take the next step and create a federal Department of American Learning? In 1995 and 1996, Representatives William Goodling (R-Pa.) and Steve Gundeson (R-Wis.) proposed doing just that by merging the Departments of Education and Labor. The Goodling-Gundeson proposal, however, came in the midst of a congressional move to reduce the size of government and eliminate whole departments—including the Department of Education. Consolidation of the Education and Labor Departments would avoid some of the pitfalls that usually come with government consolidation. They are overseen by the same authorizing committee and the same appropriations subcommittee. There are good relations among some of the key interested parties—for instance, the AFL-CIO–affiliated American Federation of Teachers, and the unaffiliated National Education Association.

Yet creating or consolidating departments does not happen often. The 2003 creation of the Department of Homeland Security as a response to the ongoing threat of terrorism is a measure of Congress responding to a sense of crisis, not a precedent for frequent reshuffling of departmental responsibilities to meet changing circumstances. The match between the Education and Labor Departments is not perfect. Each has a distinct regulatory mandate, ranging from Labor's responsibility for pension security to Education's concern with special education. A merger would bring the usual clash of institutional cultures. It is also important to remember that the powerful message of the 1985 report of the President's Commission on Industrial Competitiveness (or the Young Commission) was partially obscured by its proposal to create a new federal department for science and technology and one for international trade. Still, creating a Department of American Learning would be a powerful way in both symbol and substance to highlight the importance of the American learning system.

Preparing America and Americans for
Global Leadership and Citizenship

In the post–September 11, 2001, war on terrorism, the United States is again launched on a global struggle. American combat troops, peacekeepers, and military trainers are now scattered across the globe. There is a renewed awareness that in some sense the roots of terror lie in societies that are struggling with poverty and where tradition is clashing with modernity. Great aspirations are fed by ubiquitous communications, the ease of global travel, and, often an overseas education—only to be thwarted by stagnating economies and corrupt governments. Dealing with world poverty and failing states is again a question of national security as well as a moral imperative.

In the economic realm, American workers, American business, and the American economy are ever more tightly tied to a complex, rapidly changing global economy. Emerging economic powerhouses such as Brazil, China, and India create new opportunities and new challenges for twenty-first-century America. Disease, ocean pollution, global warming, and the search for energy are all global challenges that will require an international response. In meeting the challenges of the twenty-first century, America must have an education system that prepares its citizens for a global role.

It is not the first global challenge that called for improved education. In 1957, the Soviet Union shocked and challenged the United States by launching Sputnik, the first satellite in space. The Soviet advance was a potential threat to American national security but it was also a blow to American pride. The U.S. response included a sense of urgency about improving American education, including an emphasis on foreign languages. Congress's global focus showed in its design of postgraduate education.[7] While encouraging study in a number of disciplines, Congress included provision for National Defense Foreign Language (NDFL) fellowships. By the time of Sputnik, the Cold War had already become a global struggle for influence in key parts of the world where people spoke dozens of different languages. Under the NDFL program, a student might study, for instance economics, and at the same time study one of a group of designated critical languages.

Some students shun foreign languages, pointing out that, since 1957, English has become more and more of a lingua franca in the worlds of scientific research, business, and tourism. Technology promises to develop universal translators that will allow two speakers with different languages to communicate with considerable ease. Although these things are true, knowledge of other languages and their implicit cultural worldviews still will help the American student see the world through, say, Brazilian, Chinese, or Egyptian eyes. And conversational mastery helps build informal contact and lasting ties that can be good for business and critical for peace.

Languages or even area studies are not enough. The United States must return to the NDFL approach of linking language facility to other key skills. If, for instance, the country wants to follow the Chinese electronics industry, it needs people who know how to make semiconductors as well as understand Chinese. The Bush administration has made a commitment to bring democracy, human rights, and market-based prosperity to the Middle East; yet only a relative handful of Americans are fluent in Arabic or Farsi. Even fewer can combine a foreign language with the needed technical skill.

Although the NDFL is a promising model for graduate study, the philosophy and funds need to be applied at the undergraduate level as well. The same could be said of community colleges, where key technical skills are often acquired. Even these steps fall short of the challenge. A second language study should be introduced in kindergarten. The United States will be a global leader, often *the* global leader, for much of the twenty-first century. In light of that long-term reality, the United States needs to dramatically expand existing efforts to offer key languages in the early elementary years of schooling and add opportunities to continue during the high school years. As schools express an interest, federal support should be offered for today's version of the 1960s list of critical languages.

Beyond languages, mathematics, science, engineering, and other key disciplines also are in short supply. Although American universities still set the global standard, it is striking that international students make up a significant percentage of students in U.S. graduate programs in engineering (41 percent) and in mathematics and computer science (39 percent).[8] The country has benefited enormously from the presence of foreign students in undergraduate and graduate programs. Learning with students from around the world is an added education for American students. In the past, many of the world's best students stayed in the United States and made major contributions in academic and business life. The growth of manufacturing, services, and research facilities in a number of emerging-market countries, however, is now luring many of the best foreign students back to their home countries. In the future, the United States must draw more and more on home grown talent.

In the 1990s, high pay in other professions and the rush to Wall Street no doubt had some effect on the relative decline of U.S. students in particular graduate fields. The cultural bias that consigns too many bright children to

the status of nerds and geeks is an ongoing challenge. The recent phenomenon of offshoring (i.e., using the Internet to send digitized, analytic work
offshore) has made the future of some technical careers less certain. As the
global supply of scientists and engineers grows, the United States will have
to develop a strategy that adapts higher education and career opportunities
to that reality. Global competition for scientific and engineering talent also
puts a spotlight on the failure of American elementary and secondary
schools to prepare enough students for technical careers. The United States
needs to identify the causes of dwindling engineering and scientific enroll-
ments and respond accordingly.

Notes

1. In discussing the congressional role in forging the final No Child Left Behind
Act, see Andrew Rudalevige, "No Child Left Behind: Forging a Congressional Compromise," in *No Child Left Behind? The Politics and Practice of School Accountability,*
ed. Paul E. Peterson and Martin R. West (Washington, D.C.: Brookings Institution Press,
2003), 23–54.

2. Matthew Miller, *The 2% Solution: Fixing America's Problems in Ways Liberals
and Conservatives Can Love* (New York: Public Affairs, 2003). See, for instance, chapter 6 on millionaire teachers and chapter 7 on vouchers even liberals can love.

3. U.S. Department of Commerce, *2020 Visions: Transforming Education and
Training Through Advanced Technologies* (Washington, D.C.: U.S. Department of Commerce, 2002).

4. For a brief summary see Alan B. Krueger and Cecilia E. Rouse, "Putting Students
and Workers First? Education and Labor Policy in the 1990s," in *American Economic
Policy in the 1990s,* ed. Jeffrey A. Frankel and Peter R. Orszag (Cambridge, Mass.: MIT
Press, 2002), 683–87.

5. Details about FIRST can be found at http://www.USFIRST.org.

6. For Kamen's take on changing the national culture, see the October 30, 2003,
interview at http://www4.gartner.com.

7. Robert A. Divine, *The Sputnik Challenge: Eisenhower's Response to the Soviet
Satellite* (New York: Oxford University Press, 1993), 164–66.

8. National Science Board, *Science and Engineering Indicators—2002* (Washington, D.C.: U.S. Government Printing Office, 2002), 2–27.

Chapter 17

Competing for the Future: Global Engagement in the Twenty-First Century

The trade- and finance-focused initiatives of the twentieth century form an important part of foreign economic policy in the early twenty-first century. But U.S. policy must move well beyond an emphasis on trade and trade agreements to a period of broad global engagement. Future U.S. policy will involve everything from a renewed commitment to economic growth in the developing world to effective policies that smooth adjustment at home and abroad to the costs and the benefits of deeper international integration.

To build long-term American prosperity and lasting economic strength in the twenty-first century, the United States must adapt the competitiveness framework developed in the 1980s and applied in the 1990s to rapidly changing international and domestic circumstances. The United States must develop a series of twenty-first-century policies that are crafted from a truly global perspective. Six are proposed here—sketched in the next paragraphs and explained in detail in the rest of the chapter.

First, the United States must continue to pursue international trade and financial policies that support American prosperity, aid growth in the developing world, and improve the environment. Second, where geopolitical priorities are pursued at the expense of domestic industry or innovation, the country needs policies that maintain the strength of a particular industry or encourage development of new technology. Third, America needs to respond to the emergence of new global competitors and the reality of worldwide, online competition. Fourth, the country needs policies that help make globalization work for everyone. At home, that will mean not only continuing to broaden trade adjustment assistance to include services but also taking steps that foster mobility, flexibility, and opportunity. Fifth, the public and private sectors need to continue to develop ways of managing the risks of disruptions in international supply chains, the need for foreign capital to fund trade and current account deficits, and the growing dependence on overseas suppliers for key parts and products. Sixth, the country needs to develop a capacity to set a future economic course that adjusts for global trends, new technologies, and the growth strategies of other countries. In sum, the United States must develop a capacity for geoeconomic strategy with the same dedication it applied to geopolitical strategy over the course of the Cold War.

Looking ahead in the twenty-first century, a competitiveness strategist must consider an even more complex set of international challenges. Since the 1970s, the United States has become more deeply intertwined with the global economy. Exports and imports have grown dramatically in importance relative to the size of the American economy. The 1993 adoption of the North American Free Trade Agreement, the 1994 legislation implementing the Uruguay Round of multilateral negotiations, and several other trade initiatives have only made the American market more open to international competition. The investment strategies of multinational firms have created truly global companies that increase trade, speed the diffusion of new technologies, and spread managerial expertise. In twenty years, international capital markets have grown in size and now have a truly global reach.

In the early twenty-first century, U.S. international economic policy faces a series of new challenges. The current global war on terrorism has, like the Cold War, brought about an era in which national security and foreign policy will significantly influence the conduct of foreign economic policy. China, India, Brazil, and other countries have joined Europe and East Asia as formidable competitors. The spread of digital technologies and broadband links has also created new global competition for a wide array of analytic services. Increased global interdependence has created risks as well as benefits. The international sourcing of parts, coupled with a global approach to just-in-time inventory, has made U.S. firms more vulnerable to supply disruptions. To finance record trade and current account deficits, the United States must attract more than $1.4 billion in foreign investment every day. Since the peak of the financial bubble in March 2000, foreign investment has shifted from more stable direct investments (i.e., in land and factories) to less stable portfolio investments (stocks and bonds). Instead of relying on large private investors, the country is now heavily dependent on the purchase of dollars and dollar-denominated assets by Asian central banks.

Negotiating Our Twenty-First-Century International Economic Future: Trade, Finance, and the Dollar Dilemma

The late-twentieth-century competitiveness strategy had an internationalist, open market bent. Competitiveness strategists looked at comparative advantage in dynamic terms—seeing it as the product of public and private investments, the strategies of other countries, international policies, and competitive market forces. Public- and private-sector leaders agreed that opening global markets created added opportunities.

The 1990s competitiveness strategy aimed to actively support opening markets abroad and keeping markets open at home. Building on that approach, President George W. Bush and his chief trade negotiator, Robert Zoelleck, are pursing an ambitious agenda that embraces bilateral, regional, and multilateral negotiations. The current multilateral negotiations have added a focus on the developing world and are referred to as the Doha Development Agenda (they were launched in Doha, Qatar). At the insistence of Congress, the Bush administration is also seeking to add provisions protecting the environment and ensuring labor rights in future trade agreements.

The focus on bilateral negotiations is part of the Bush administration's "competitive liberalization" strategy. The general idea is that if one country receives preferential access to the U.S. market, other countries will seek the same or even enhanced access. Each new bilateral agreement will, however, erode the advantages gained through earlier agreements. As the erosion proceeds, the Office of the U.S. Trade Representative expects that more and more countries will turn to the multilateral negotiations, which remain the stated U.S. priority.

For the United States, the European Union, Japan, and some other large economies, bilateral negotiations can more easily be used as "laboratories of agreement," where negotiators can try different approaches to protecting the environment, establishing or enforcing labor rights, and softening the adjustments expected from greater trade. With an eye on development as well as trade, it will be easier to combine bilateral agreements with separate initiatives, including investment incentives, technical assistance, and government-to-government support, that help make participation in the global economy more effective and more equitable. What the United States must keep in view is that the bilateral agreements must be made with the ultimate multilateral agreement in mind.

Agriculture

Success in the multilateral trade negotiations will depend on an agreement on agriculture. It is the key question. Agriculture has been largely left outside the realm of international trading rules. In Europe, Japan, and the United States, agriculture benefits from a host of domestic subsidies, protective tariffs and quotas, and export subsidies that have been largely negotiated away in the realm of manufactured goods.

Many developing countries see their own export opportunities in agricultural crops. They have often been unable to exploit their comparative advantage in agriculture because of the export subsidies and other practices of the advanced industrial economies. Several advanced and emerging-market economies that are already major exporters of agricultural products are also seeking better access to markets currently closed by a variety of trade barriers. The United States sits uncomfortably on this divide, with major agricultural exporters and many subsidized and protected crops.

In September 2003, the multilateral talks stalled at the World Trade Organization Ministerial in Cancún, Mexico. The many issues on the table ranged from proposals to harmonize antitrust (or competition) policies to demands for new rules governing investment. But agriculture was the key. There were new demands from the developing world for the unilateral dismantling of barriers to agricultural trade in the advanced economies. Four West African cotton-producing countries actively sought compensation for the damage done by U.S. cotton subsidies. Resistance to opening these markets will be fierce in the United States and elsewhere.

There are at least three steps the United States should take to ease adjustment to future market opening in agriculture. First, Congress should act now to establish a commission to explore a variety of means to deal with agricultural import competition. The commission should include a variety of members—representatives from the federal government, state and local elected officials, policy specialists, and academics. The members could start by examining the efforts to develop alternatives to tobacco as possible precedents for adjustment in other crops. The proposed commission will, among other questions, have to consider biotechnology as a source of new competitive crops; the shift to environmental payments rather than crop supports; and even the public purchase of farmland.[1]

Second, any decline in farming will affect neighboring communities that essentially exist to provide services to local agriculture. Communities as well as farms need an adjustment plan that will be influenced by the pace of future import penetration.

Third, whatever happens in the context of the Doha Development Agenda, new technology and new agricultural competitors will continue to affect American agriculture. Private and public institutions concerned with agriculture must be looking ahead a decade or more to prepare for opportunities or possibly further painful adjustments.

Environment, Labor, Corporate Responsibility, and Human Rights

Trade negotiators will be challenged to think through approaches to the environment, labor rights, and other issues relatively new to the trade agenda.[2] The Trade Act of 2002 granting trade promotion (or fast-track) authority to the president would not have been adopted by Congress without some commitment on labor and environmental standards.

Throughout the twentieth century, the industrial world sought to find the right balance between the role of markets and the protection of labor. Starting in the second half of the twentieth century, there was a similar effort to balance markets and the environment. In the twenty-first century, the same struggle will take place on the global stage.[3]

In seeking a new global balance for markets, growth, improving the environment, protecting labor, and securing human rights, advocates on all sides will need to think in terms that may go beyond the specific confines of a trade agreement. For instance, inveighing against child labor may simply drive visible, factory-based misery back into less visible but even more severe rural poverty. Instead, agreements banning child labor must be linked to foreign assistance to build schools. Programs should follow the pioneering effort by state governments in Brazil that in effect compensates parents for keeping their children in school and out of the field or factory.

Dollars and Deficits: Debts and Default

U.S. international economic strategists need to focus on the international value of the dollar, the stability of exchange rates, and the ongoing state of the international financial system—or what is often referred to as the international financial architecture.

The Dollar's Decline

Beginning in 2002, the American dollar began to decline. By the spring of 2003, the dollar had declined by about 10 percent against the yen and 20 percent against the euro. At a May meeting of the Group of Eight (G-8) finance ministers, Secretary of the Treasury John Snow termed the recent decline in the dollar a "modest realignment."[4] The next day, the dollar fell further, reaching the "same level at which the euro was born."[5] With Europe already poised for slow growth and Japan still struggling to avoid recession, the weakening dollar poses a dilemma for these and many other countries focused on the U.S. market. The dollar, the current account, and the long-run international balance were discussed in chapter 14. In the future, the United States, the G-8 industrial powers, and the broader Group of Twenty finance ministers (formed after the 1997 Asian financial crisis) need to work together to avoid the kind of imbalances that have emerged in the past ten years. For the United States, there will be the added imperative of dealing with a low personal savings rate and long-term fiscal deficits that are major factors in generating U.S. trade and current account deficits.

Dealing with Sovereign Debt

In its first two years, the George W. Bush administration was confronted with severe debt problems in Turkey as well as Argentina's default on more than $100 billion in sovereign debt. The Argentine default in particular has triggered yet another debate over how to improve the process of restructuring debt when default seems imminent or even likely. In response, the United States and the International Monetary Fund (IMF) started to develop separate proposals to improve the process of restructuring sovereign debt. The IMF proposed a sovereign-debt-restructuring mechanism (SDRM), a kind of international bankruptcy proceeding for countries. Pressured by its Executive Board, the IMF put aside its work on the SDRM in the spring of 2003. Instead, some middle-income countries began to include collective action clauses in new debt issues[6]—an approach favored by the U.S. Treasury.[7] A collective action clause in one bond issue, however, will not bind owners of earlier or subsequent issues. No one knows if the collective action clause will work or not. At the least, while the U.S. Treasury monitors their use, other alternatives, including refinements of the SDRM, should be explored. Neither approach deals with the more far-reaching proposals for a stand still on debt payment, the use of capital controls, or imposing added adjustments on lenders as well as borrowers,[8] alternatives that should also be analyzed.

Short-Term Capital Flows

In retrospect, many observers agree that the IMF and the U.S. Treasury were wrong to press many countries to open their capital markets to short-term, often speculative flows of capital.[9] Many countries did not have the financial regulatory institutions, the banking experience, or the private-sector practices to avoid problems that came with premature market opening. The almost blind confidence in markets is particularly surprising for Americans who had seen firsthand the nearly $200 billion loss involved in the savings and loan scandal in 1980s America. Despite the best markets in the world, decades of experience with financial regulation, and a political system with multiple checks and balances, a combination of economic trends, partial deregulation, and political influence led to an economic and financial disaster. Why should less experienced economies have been immune?

In the future, whether pursuing democracy or a market system, the lessons of the 1990s should caution the United States and international financial institutions to remember the importance of institutions and to think in evolutionary terms. The problem for the next decade, however, is unlikely to be too much capital flowing to the developing world but too little. As part of "getting globalization right," the industrial democracies will need to combine incentives for private investment in the developing world with an approach to foreign assistance that also creates incentives for effective public governance. The Bush administration has already taken a step in that direction with its Millennium Challenge Account, which links foreign assistance to, among other factors, improved governance.[10]

Geopolitical Priorities, Foreign Economic Policy, and the Domestic Economy

During the Cold War, foreign policy was often pursued at the cost of the domestic economy—containing the Soviet Union was the overriding priority. With the end of the post–Cold War era, the United States has again entered a period in which there will often be tensions between pursuing economic and foreign policy interests. President George W. Bush's recent decision to seek a free trade agreement with the Middle East by 2013 is driven by foreign policy rather than traditional trade concerns—except for oil, the level of Middle East exports falls below those of Finland. China is another prominent but not isolated example. China is a very important partner in the global war on terrorism and in seeking to stop North Korea's stated intention to develop nuclear weapons. Too much pressure on the Chinese to float or revalue their currency,[11] adjust rapidly to their World Trade Organization commitments, or actively prevent the piracy of intellectual property might not only alienate the Chinese government but also destabilize an economy that already has tens of millions of unemployed or only partially employed workers.[12]

When agreements are not enforced, when we turn a blind eye to the infringement of intellectual property rights, or when we fail to press for market access, the impact on domestic innovation and the domestic economy must be explicitly recognized and compensatory action taken. For instance, if rights to intellectual property are not enforced so that the United States can cement a political alliance, the federal government should increase its research budget, create added incentives for private innovation, or pursue some combination of the two.

Responding to New Competitors and Global Online Competition

China, South Korea, Taiwan, and the countries belonging to the Association of Southeast Asian Nations have joined Japan as major exporters of manufactured goods. Latin America, Brazil, Mexico, and other nations have also become a growing factor in global markets for specific manufactured products. As technologies and skills spread, other countries will join the global competition for global markets.

In the digital age, it is increasingly difficult to protect U.S. intellectual property. Whether in records, movies, or software, the digital era makes copying (or theft) extremely easy. Some voices in the academic world are already suggesting that many U.S. firms may have to think of a new business model that relies less on protecting intellectual property and more on the use of open source property combined with the provision of a specialized service.[13]

The many highly skilled and well-paid Americans who provide specialized services—from reading X-rays, to chip design, to financial analysis—face an even bigger challenge. Anything that can be digitized for individual evaluation can be analyzed anywhere in the world. The spread of high-speed, high-capacity, high-resolution communications will allow many domestically provided services to be offered anywhere that communications and qualified personnel come together. Already, many firms are moving portions of their software development, product design, and financial analysis to India. Argentina is yet another country following a path blazed by Ireland, India, and China.[14] There will be more online competition to come.

The rise of new competitors is not a product of simple, autonomous market forces. More and more countries are adopting education, investment, innovation, and the global economy as the four pillars of their own long-term growth strategy. Countries now link education, investment, and trade-negotiating strategies to create a new comparative advantage. India is a particularly interesting example. It has combined a strong educational system and the growing power of information technology to create a substantial domestic service sector linked electronically to the United States and other industrial countries.

India also sends a large number of well-educated undergraduate and graduate students to work and study in the United States. Indians trained and working in the United States can also help capture online service business for India-based businesses. India has already carried this philosophy into the Uruguay Round of multilateral trade negotiations. As a result, the adoption of the General Agreement on Trade in Services as part of the Uruguay Round binds the United States to admit at least 65,000 workers under its H-1B visa program designed for skilled workers.[15]

A simple faith in markets and passive inaction are not acceptable. The familiar pattern of individual U.S. states competing to attract investment is now being utilized on a global scale. As countries around the world adopt tax and other incentives to attract production and research facilities, the United States must either adopt offsetting or countervailing incentives or successfully negotiate (and enforce) international economic rules limiting the use of such incentives. In the twenty-first century, the United States will also have to focus on the global labor market—patterns of immigration, skill development, and the targeted use of education—to create a comparative advantage that will create new opportunities and new challenges for the American economy.

In a number of scientific and engineering disciplines, a high percentage of the graduate students come from overseas. Higher education has become an important service export of the United States and, in the past, many international students have stayed to contribute a great deal to America, its economy, and its capacity to innovate. We may not be able to count on the international graduate student forever. More and more of the graduates are returning to their home countries, which offer ever-greater opportunities for their talents. More overseas universities are becoming world class and keeping students at home. The tightened U.S. visa requirements in response to the September 11, 2001, attacks may also make it more difficult for foreign students to pursue their education in the United States. The prospect of a dwindling supply of foreign researchers adds impetus to the need to sharply improve the American learning system and attract more students into the fields of science and engineering.

Current U.S. immigration policy raises its own mix of challenges and opportunities. Despite laws limiting legal immigration and increased enforcement at the U.S. border, the combination of legal and illegal immigration has created a virtually unlimited supply of relatively low-wage workers who have become very important for a number of American industries, service providers, and many families. As part of his 2004 State of the Union address,[16] President Bush proposed allowing currently illegal or undocumented immigrants to achieve a limited legal status. He built his proposal on some existing legislative proposals, and others will follow in the wake of his speech. At the very least, the president's proposal will trigger a national debate that will encompass whether and how to limit future illegal immigration, how to integrate long-term but undocumented immigrants, and the impact of current patterns of immigration on everything from wages to social spending to education. The broader point is that U.S. policy and economic strategy must reflect a global perspective that includes the impact of the international flow of labor and the education and skill-based strategies of major U.S. trading partners.

Getting Globalization Right

Since the end of World War II, U.S. policy has played an active role in fostering global economic growth. In the immediate aftermath of that war, the United States focused on reconstruction in Europe and Japan and established international institutions to support reconstruction, support stable exchange rates, and foster international trade. Toward the end of the war, Britain and the United States had worked together to create an international system that would avoid the ruinous mistakes of the Versailles Treaty that ended World War I and the destructive form of international competition that took place during the interwar years. In place of reparations imposed on the losing powers, there would be reconstruction. During the interwar period, countries had sought to gain an economic edge by devaluing their currencies and raising trade barriers. The post–World War II system created institutions to support reconstruction (today's World Bank),[17] maintain stable exchange rates linked to the American dollar (the International Monetary Fund), and encourage lower trade barriers (the General Agreement on Tariffs and Trade).[18]

By the late 1940s, the United States and the Soviet Union were engaged in the Cold War. Reconstruction in Europe and Japan became part of that global struggle. The Cold War took on a global character as the United States and the Soviet Union contended for influence in Latin America and newly independent African and Asian countries. As the Cold War came to be defined, at least in part, as a competition between economic systems, both domestic growth and development abroad took on added urgency.

In addition to working with the World Bank and the IMF, the United States sought to foster developing countries' growth through foreign assistance, although this assistance was often given with an eye to national security and foreign policy as well as emergency relief and long-term development. Starting in the 1970s, the United States also sought to foster development and forge closer ties through a series of trade agreements granting favorable access to the American market. President Richard Nixon signed the first Generalized System of Preferences,[19] and subsequent presidents supported the Caribbean Basin Initiative, the Andean Pact, and the African Growth and Opportunity Act. Under the Generalized System of Preferences and subsequent trade preference agreements, low income countries were allowed tariff free access to the U.S. market. The preferences could be limited by dollar value of a country's export, or by the share of imports held by a single country in a particular product. The United States also took various steps toward closer North American trade ties, including the 1993 ratification of the North American Free Trade Agreement linking Canada, Mexico, and the United States. Over the course of the Cold War, several multilateral agreements reduced tariffs and trade barriers for all the countries that were members of the General Agreement on Tariffs and Trade. The various steps to reduce global barriers to trade have eroded the advantages offered to the developing world through a variety of trade preferences.

In the 1990s, several trends affected the U.S. approach to the developing world. The collapse of the Soviet Union and the end of the Cold War had made it difficult to secure support for foreign assistance strictly on grounds of national security. The Soviets were no longer there to rush in where America refused to tread. The adoption of the new trade rules adopted as a result of the Uruguay Round of trade negotiations increased developing countries' opportunities but also added often burdensome trade law commitments.

There are trends, however, that work to increase U.S. interest in development. The steady spread of U.S.-based multinationals has increased U.S. interest in the stability and growth of overseas markets. In the early twenty-first century, several forces have also made the United States more focused on "getting globalization right" at home and abroad. The post–Cold War decade-long interregnum of peace and prosperity came to a dramatic end on September 11, 2001. President Bush responded by declaring a global war on terrorism. American troops fought and won quick victories in Afghanistan (2002) and Iraq (2003), although both have been followed by difficult occupations. In a pattern reminiscent of the Cold War, U.S. troops and trainers are again active in a host of countries.

The war on terror has also taken on an economic dimension. Thomas Friedman, the influential *New York Times* columnist, argues that the Muslim Middle East has failed to share in the kind of rapid economic growth that has taken place in many parts of Asia and, to a lesser extent, in Latin America.[20] He saw at least the possibility of the war in Iraq being a kind of shock therapy that might help jar the Middle East into taking a more global direction. Economics is far from the whole story—nationalism, values, and ideology are also part of the equation. Yet the combination of economic deprivation and high levels of unemployment fuels a mix of envy and resentment. As the *Financial Times* columnist Michael Prowse wrote in 2003, "If terrorism is to be countered, the U.S. and its allies must do more to promote the economic development of the Islamic world, while also prevailing in a contest of philosophies."[21] With the prospect of having a significant economic, political, and military presence in the Muslim world for decades to come, the United States has an enormous stake in finding the right policies.

During the past decade, Congress and much of the country have become more aware of and more sensitive to the domestic costs as well as the benefits of global economic integration. As that sensitivity has grown, the country, academia, and the policy community are increasingly evaluating trade proposals in much the same way they assess tax legislation, looking at the distribution of benefits as well as the contribution to overall growth.

Since World War II, trade policy and tax policy have been approached in very different ways. At least in the United States, tax proposals are quickly evaluated for their detailed distributional consequences. While analysts recognize that certain sets of workers, industries, and communities will be adversely affected by trade agreements, gains are usually expressed in terms of the overall nation. That is beginning to change. In *Globalization and Its Discontents,* the Nobel Prize winner and former World Bank economist Joseph E. Stiglitz stresses that the benefits of trade liberalization depend crucially on the pace of market opening and the degree to which compensating policies are put in place.[22] Murray Weidenbaum—a Washington University professor, former chair of Ronald Reagan's Council of Economic Advisers, and ardent free trader—has also stressed the importance of recognizing and ameliorating the costs of open markets.[23] In *World on Fire,* the Yale University law professor Amy Chua argues that simple market opening and the introduction of majoritarian democracy can increase the wealth and power of already economically dominant ethnic minorities with often destabilizing political results.[24] The feminist approach to political economy looks at the impact of globalization from the standpoint of gender rather than class but is nonetheless focused on questions of distribution and the impact of globalization on the economic and social well-being of women.[25]

In the early twenty-first century, the thinking about deeper global economic integration has become more complicated and less reflexively optimistic. If the 1990s saw globalization as inevitable and overwhelmingly positive, the 2000s see globalization as holding out enormous benefits but also creating significant risks and imposing real costs. The 1997 Asian financial crisis, the difficult transition in Russia, and the record-setting Argentine default all point to the importance of institutions, regulatory structures, and private-sector experience. In the narrowly adopted Trade Act of 2002, Congress insisted on expanding trade adjustment assistance to secondary workers (workers who supply a company that has lost business due to international trade), added benefits in terms of health insurance, and a pilot program for wage insurance.[26]

The United States must again lead a global effort to foster growth and prosperity in the developing world. It cannot live safely in a world ever more tightly linked by communications and transportation yet divided by wealth and opportunity. Global development must be a national priority for both national security and economic reasons. In his second inaugural address, President Franklin Delano Roosevelt called the country to action when he pointed to "one-third of a nation ill-housed, ill-clad, ill-nourished."[27] The global challenge is much greater. The United States cannot be morally content to live in a time where *"two-thirds* of the world is ill-housed, ill-clad, and ill-nourished."

The United States has already started to take some important steps in the right direction. The decision to make the latest multilateral trade negotiations a development round has translated into an effort to complement trade agreements with foreign assistance, development bank loans, and incentives for private investment.

In responding to the inevitable dislocations from international trade, the U.S. president must take steps to broaden trade adjustment assistance to include services. Beyond the focus on trade, Congress and the president need to work on a series of measures that will ease adjustment to economic change—whether caused by trade, technology, or shifting consumer tastes. Portable universal health care will ease the path of change and also encourage the kind of risk taking that supports so much entrepreneurial activity in the United States. Whether through tax incentives or public matching grants, pensions need to become universal and portable. As much as possible, public and private institutions need to encourage the development of an American learning system that creates the kinds of portable skills that can lead to new opportunities in the face of economic dislocation.

Managing Interdependence in the Global Economy

Whether thinking in terms of oil, key electronic components, or investment capital, the United States is deeply tied to the global economy. Barring a cataclysmic event on the order of the World War I or World War II, the dependence will only grow. Some leading members of Congress have already expressed growing concern about the impact of dependence on the defense sector of the economy. In 2003, concern about growing U.S. dependence triggered a debate over Representative Duncan Hunter's (R-Calif.) proposal to add significant "Buy American" provisions to the 2003 Defense Authorization Act, despite the objections of President Bush and the European Union.[28] Legislative compromise limited the impact of Hunter's proposal, but debate over dependence and national security is likely to return in the future.

The United States can take several steps to manage that dependence, guard against disruptions of supply, and limit the loss of influence that often comes with interdependence. For years, America has created major stockpiles for commodities deemed essential for national security. Stockpiles can be expensive, difficult to manage, and disruptive of markets when they are reduced. But they do provide a kind of security. After the oil shocks of the 1970s, the United States adopted a strategic petroleum reserve to guard against another oil embargo. A more fundamental change would come with the development of technologies that would bring the kind of energy independence discussed above as an innovation-driving national goal.

At times, the efficiency of global supply chains may run counter to U.S. national security needs. International specialization in electronics and machine tools reduced the independence of an important portion of the civilian sector of the economy that also supported national security. For older systems, the Pentagon or defense contractors could stockpile specific parts. But technological edge often comes from the dynamism of commercial industry. Innovation cannot be stockpiled. A dedicated, single-source supplier cannot ensure the dynamism of a competitive industry.

The United States needs to respond with a flexible strategy that includes several elements. First, the Department of Defense should be aware of where key imported parts are manufactured, assembled, and shipped. Second, Defense—with the support of other relevant agencies—should encourage domestic production. Where that is uneconomical or unfeasible, Defense should strive for a variety of suppliers. Third, where there is a single international supplier for a particular key component, the United States should seek to offset that potential leverage by being a key customer, an important part of the foreign supplier's supply chain, or by being a key supplier to other firms in the same country.

Technology is not the only vulnerability. Continued dependence on international capital to consume and invest beyond U.S. domestic savings, creates another set of risks. Over time, America needs to adopt policies— whether running a budget surplus or encouraging domestic savings—that bring better balance to its international accounts. For domestic as well as international stability, the country needs to continue searching for an improved international financial architecture[29] that was triggered by the Asian financial crisis.[30]

Nor can America neglect domestic vulnerabilities. The combination of the Asian financial turmoil and the partial Russian default almost forced Long Term Capital Management, a major U.S. hedge fund, into bankruptcy.[31] A major infusion of private funds orchestrated by the Federal Reserve Bank of New York averted what might have been a global financial calamity. At the very least, the country needs to have the capacity to monitor the domestic and international financial structure, which includes greater knowledge about hedge fund activities.

Developing a National Capacity for Geoeconomics

There is a broader challenge. If the United States defines the economic future, there are many countries that want to follow the same path. In the 1980s, American eyes were concentrated on Germany and Japan. In the twenty-first century, a host of other countries are building their basic infrastructure, improving education, and investing in the ability to create as well as use technology.

To prepare for the twenty-first century, the United States needs a capacity for "geoeconomics" that matches its long-standing strength in geopolitics. The federal government needs a single agency that will track the economic strategies of countries that are both allies and competitors, overseas investments in key industries, and the emergence of promising new technologies. At home, the federal government must commit to monitoring the emergence of new technologies as well as the economic health and innovative capacity of established industries.

The Commerce Department is a logical candidate. It has a base for tracking industry and technology, an overseas commercial service, and responsibility for widespread data collection and analysis through the Bureau of the Census and the Bureau of Economic Analysis. It will need added resources, increased expertise, and the clear backing of the White House. The Department of Defense offers some useful precedents—employees have a career path that provides new challenges while building on their broad expertise. The National Defense University, with its War College and its Industrial College of the Armed Forces, provides future leaders with a broad view as well as advanced knowledge. A similar approach for geoeconomics should combine a new curriculum with national fellowships.

Some of the building blocks for geoeconomics are in individual governmental agencies, and others can be found in institutions outside the government. For instance, an independent body—the Board on Science, Technology and Economic Policy of the National Academies of Science—has done studies assessing the competitiveness of American industries in light of global trends.[32] While widely read, these studies are not linked to the policy cycle or done as a part of an ongoing assessment. The Sloan industry centers established at a number of universities could provide useful insights for economic policymakers, much as the RAND Corporation and similar institutions have for the U.S. military.[33]

Large U.S. corporations already practice a kind of geoeconomics as they assess risks and opportunities on a global scale. An ongoing dialogue with the private sector will significantly enrich the understanding of global developments in fast-moving, highly innovative markets. But their strengths are no substitute for a national strategy that adjusts policies to global trends, new technologies, and the growth strategies of other countries. Even the largest companies are focused on just a few industries. They will pay close attention to their own vulnerabilities to international events but will generally not take account of the full range of national strengths and weaknesses. Nor can they be expected to respond to externalities or side affects that do not have an impact on their own economic fortunes. In most cases, a corporate time horizon does not match that of the nation. Nor can most workers match the global mobility of investment capital. Global involvement may also divide corporate interests from the interests of many Americans more dependent on the geographically defined United States.

War games have been a long-standing tool for the Department of Defense. Sandia, one of the major national energy laboratories, has created another useful tool for geoeconomics by adapting that approach to the civilian economy in a series of prosperity games. Elected officials, political appointees, and public servants need to be aware of the potential tension between a global economy and national goals. Much can be learned from global companies that must adjust their own strategies to the development priorities of host governments and the strategies of their competitors.

Developing a capacity for geoeconomics will benefit all Americans. Authoritative information on global developments will help guide private and public investments. Trade negotiators will be better able to anticipate the strategies they will face across the bargaining table, and individuals will adjust their own education and training plans to evolving global economic conditions.

Global engagement must be part of the twenty-first-century competitiveness strategy, much as it was in the late twentieth century. In addition to the focus on immediate U.S. economic opportunity and strength, there will need to be a commitment to sustained and sustainable global growth as part of a century-long effort to get globalization right. At the same time, the United States needs to be strategic in its approach to globalization and interdependence. It will need to develop a sharpened sense of geoeconomics and the ability to manage the risks and opportunities that inevitably come with globalization.

Notes

1. See, for instance, David Minge, *Coordinating Colors: The WTO Green Box and Green Payments in Farm Programs* (Washington, D.C.: Woodrow Wilson International Center for Scholars, 2004).

2. I. M. Destler and Peter J. Balint, *The New Politics of American Trade: Trade, Labor and the Environment*, Policy Analysis in International Economics 58 (Washington, D.C.: Institute for International Economics, 1999).

3. See Kent H. Hughes, "American Trade Politics: From the Omnibus Act of 1988 to the Trade Act of 2002," Project on America and the Global Economy, Woodrow Wilson International Center for Scholars, November 17, 2003. A copy of the paper can be found under the Project on America and the Global Economy, http://www.wilson center.org.

4. Ed Crooks, "Snow Adds to Pressure on Dollar," *Financial Times*, May 19, 2003.

5. Christopher Swann, "Dollar Slips to Euro Launch Level," *Financial Times*, May 20, 2003.

6. Rescheduling bonds generally requires the unanimous agreement of the bondholders. With collective action clauses, a specified majority could bind all the bondholders and allow rescheduling to proceed.

7. Faced with an impending default, a single bondholder could prevent an agreement by other bondholders to reduce or reschedule debt payments. With a collective-action clause, a specified majority of bondholders can bind all and force an agreement on rescheduling. Mexico and Brazil have both successfully sold new bond issues with collective-action clauses on the international market. A simple collective-action clause in one bond issue, however, will not affect the holders of bonds issued in the future. In seeking to avoid default, Uruguay is proposing to substitute new bonds for old. With several different bond issues involved, they are proposing a kind of collective-action clause that will allow a large majority of the bondholders to bind the holders of specific issue of bonds.

8. See Joseph E. Stiglitz, *Globalization and Its Discontents* (New York: W. W. Norton, 2002).

9. Joseph E. Stiglitz is one of the most prominent critics. See Stiglitz, *Globalization and Its Discontents*.

10. Council of Economic Advisers, *2003 Economic Report of the President* (Washington, D.C.: U.S. Government Printing Office, 2003), 249–53.

11. Alan Beattie and Christopher Swann, "Greenspan Warns over China's Dollar Peg," *Financial Times*, July 17, 2003. An undervalued currency pegged to the dollar has helped China achieve a 2002 bilateral trade surplus of more than $100 billion with the United States. Although its overall surplus is only about $30 billion, it has accumulated more than $300 billion in hard currency reserves.

12. Comments by Lawrence C. Reardon in *China in the WTO: Domestic Challenges and International Pressures,* by Kent Hughes, Gang Lin, and Jennifer Turner (Washington, D.C.: Woodrow Wilson International Center for Scholars, 2004), 15.

13. Woodrow Wilson International Center for Scholars, "The Coming Bust of the Knowledge Economy: A Policy Forum on Owning and Counting Intangible Assets in the Post-Enron Era," Project on America and the Global Economy, Event Summaries. Available at http://wwics.si.edu/index.cfm?topic_id=1408&fuseaction=topics.event_summary&event_id=31236.

14. Michael Casey, "Argentina's High-Tech Chance," *Wall Street Journal,* July 24, 2003.

15. In the late 1990s, the limit on H-1B visas was raised and then raised again in response to the rising demand for information-technology workers. The change, however, was driven by U.S. companies and domestic politics, not India.

16. The text of the 2004 State of the Union address is available at http://www.whitehouse.gov.

17. The World Bank was originally referred to as the International Bank for Reconstruction and Development, which is still its official name.

18. The General Agreement on Tariffs and Trade paralleled and was developed at the same time as the commercial chapter of the more ambitious International Trade Organization that was never adopted by the U.S. Congress. With the adoption of the Uruguay Round Agreement in 1994, the United States approved the creation of the World Trade Organization.

19. The Generalized System of Preferences was first adopted as part of the Trade Act of 1974. See I. M. Destler, *American Trade Politics,* 2nd ed. (Washington, D.C.: Institute for International Economics with the Twentieth Century Fund, 1992), 84.

20. Thomas L. Friedman, "War of Ideas, Part 6," *New York Times,* January 25, 2004. See also Friedman, "Cursed by Oil," *New York Times,* May 5, 2004.

21. Michael Prowse, "A Show of Force Meets an Outbreak of Terrorism," *Financial Times,* May 24, 2003.

22. Stiglitz, *Globalization and Its Discontents.*

23. Murray Weidenbaum, "Weighing the Pros and Cons of Globalization," photocopy, Woodrow Wilson International Center for Scholars, Washington, D.C., 2004.

24. Amy Chua, *World on Fire: How Exporting Free Market Democracy Breeds Ethnic Hatred and Global Instability* (New York: Doubleday, 2003).

25. Mary Osirim, ""Carrying the Burdens of Adjustment and Globalization: Women and Microenterprise Development in Urban Zimbabwe," *International Sociology* 18, no. 3 (2003): 535–58. Also Lori Nitschke, "Women Demand Role in Trade Talks," *Women's eNews,* December 2, 2003.

26. See the Trade Act of 2002, PL 107-210. For a discussion of the Trade Act of 2002, see Hughes, "American Trade Politics."

27. The text of Roosevelt's second inaugural address delivered on January 20, 1937, can be found at http://www.newdeal.ferri.org/speeches/1937a.htm.

28. In early October 2003, the European Union threatened to lodge a World Trade Organization complaint if the Hunter proposal should become law.

29. Council on Foreign Relations, *Safeguarding Prosperity in a Global Financial System: The Future International Financial Architecture,* task force report (Washington, D.C.: Institute for International Economics, 1999). Carla A. Hills and Peter G. Peterson

served as cochairs of the independent task force. Morris Goldstein from the Institute for International Economics served as project director.

30. Paul Blustein, *The Chastening: Inside the Crisis That Rocked the Global Financial System and Humbled the IMF* (New York: Public Affairs, 2001). Capital markets throughout the world have become more closely linked through both information technology and policy as more and more middle-income countries have removed their capital controls. Flows of trade, technology, and capital fueled global growth, but the decade was also a reminder of how volatile global financial markets can be. In 1997, when Thailand was forced to cut the link to the dollar and allow the Thai baht to float against other currencies, it triggered a financial crisis of global dimensions. Currency difficulties spread to other parts of Asia, led to a default on some Russian bonds, and eventually forced Brazil to devalue its own currency. The Asian crisis stimulated an ongoing discussion on how to avoid future crises with a general consensus in favor of floating rather than pegged exchange rates and reservations about opening capital markets to short-term financial flows until proper institutions and regulations are in place.

31. Roger Lowenstein, *When Genius Failed: The Rise and Fall of Long-Term Capital Management* (New York: Random House, 2000).

32. See, for instance, David C. Mowery, ed., *U.S. Industry in 2000: Studies in Competitive Performance,* Board on Science, Technology, and Economic Policy (Washington, D.C.: National Academies Press, 1999).

33. Background on the Sloan centers can be found at http://www.Sloan.org/main .shtml.

Chapter 18

America in the Next American Century

America's late-twentieth-century competitiveness strategy was born in the midst of the Cold War when the country's economy was struggling with inflation, periodic recessions, and slowing productivity growth. From its inception, long-term competitiveness was also linked to strengthening the American Dream by broadening the opportunities and increasing the standard of living of all Americans.

In the Cold War, the United States offset the Soviet numerical advantage in people and matériel by maintaining a technological edge. By the 1980s, more and more of the critical technologies were being developed in the civilian rather than the defense sector of the economy. By making technology and technology policy key elements in the country's economic future, the competitiveness strategy promised to support and strengthen its high-technology sector.

The Cold War was also a contest of ideas and of economic systems. Where Nikita Khrushchev had once promised to "bury" the capitalist West, the 1960s American economy had outproduced and outperformed its Soviet rival. In contrast, the faltering economy of the 1970s had the potential of reducing the country's comparative standing relative to the communist East. The competitiveness strategy of the 1980s and the competitiveness policies of the 1990s helped restore that sense of American economic leadership.

Over seventeen chapters, this volume has traced the development of a national competitiveness strategy, assessed its contribution to the strong economy of the 1990s, and outlined a twenty-first-century competitiveness strategy adapted to new conditions and new challenges. Like its twentieth-century counterpart, the twenty-first-century competitiveness strategy is closely linked to expanding the reach of the American Dream. As the country

461

has grown and prospered, the dimensions of this dream have expanded to include a clean environment, greater equality of opportunity, broader access to higher education, and universally accessible health care. A strengthened innovation system, an improved American learning system, and a faster pace of productivity growth create the potential for achieving those aspects of the twenty-first-century American Dream. But Americans will also need to recapture a sense of national purpose, rediscover their commitment to shared gains and shared sacrifices, and renew their identity as Americans while becoming committed citizens of the world.

Like the Cold War, the twenty-first-century battle against religious extremists is a battle of ideas. Though the extremists do not articulate an economic system, as did the Soviet Union, the economy remains important. A growing economy and widely shared prosperity has its own universal appeal. In a sense, by continuing to build that Shining City on a Hill, the United States will strengthen an important element of global leadership.

U.S. global engagement will not stop at building a better America. National security and deep ties to the global economy both point to an active international role. America's lasting commitment to democracy, human rights, and global prosperity will not end because of the war in Iraq, the scandal of prisoner abuse, and the precipitous drop in U.S. popularity around the world. Wilsonian ideas and ideals will not die because of failure to pursue them in an effective manner.

The Rise and Fall and Rise of the First American Century

In 1941, Henry Luce began the talk of an American Century,[1] but that confidence began to wane just short of four decades later. In 1979, Ezra Vogel's *Japan as No. 1: Lessons for America* caught the country's attention by pointing to rising Japanese economic strength.[2] In the mid-1980s, concern grew that a stagnating American economy would be unable to sustain the American Dream or support America's global commitments. By 1988, Clyde Prestowitz saw America *Trading Places* as "we allowed Japan to take the lead."[3] At the end of the 1980s, the United States still led the West as the military superpower containing the Soviet Union, but it was increasingly Germany and Japan that were described as the coming economic superpowers. Playing off Henry Luce's 1940s statement, at least one author referred to America's as the "shortest century." The next century, we were told, belonged not to America but to Asia.

Then, during the 1990s, the pendulum of power and prosperity swung again. At the end of the twentieth century, America forcefully demonstrated that it was again the world's premier economy. Germany and Japan had encountered economic difficulties in the early 1990s and were still struggling to regain their earlier pace of economic growth. The collapse of the Soviet Union in 1991 had left the United States as the world's sole remaining superpower. The U.S. economic resurgence did not happen by accident. In significant measure, the prosperity of the 1990s was due to the application of a national competitiveness strategy targeted at long-term productivity growth.

Will There Be a Second American Century?

As America entered the twenty-first century, its economic fortunes turned, and its sense of security gave way to the new terrorist threat. Many began to fear that the confident prediction of Francis Fukuyama's *The End of History* had been overwhelmed by S. P. Huntington's arguments in *The Clash of Civilizations*.[4] Economic trouble came first with the bursting of the financial bubble in April 2000, a recession in 2001, a slow recovery, and employment growth that initially lagged when the recovery did take hold.[5] The economy suffered added blows from a series of corporate scandals at home and slow growth abroad.

Not surprisingly, the early twenty-first-century policy debate has focused on economic recovery. The long-term has been largely ignored. When Congress added a prescription drug benefit to Medicare in late 2003, there was little discussion of the long-term fiscal impact. Books, articles, and newspaper reports periodically point to the looming retirement costs of the baby boom generation, but they are just beginning to trigger a major national conversation. Discussion of the eventual impact of fiscal deficits on future investment is still largely confined to academic studies and policy journals.[6]

There are two recent exceptions to the general complacency. In his 2004 book *Running on Empty,* former Nixon administration commerce secretary Peter G. Peterson calls for major policy changes to deal with the fiscal and current account deficits.[7] And Martin Wolf, the well-known economic columnist for the *Financial Times,* has sounded his own clarion for action. Writing in the August 11, 2004, *Financial Times,* Wolf warns that America is "being driven along a road of ever rising deficits and debt that risk destroying the country's credit and the global role of its currency."[8]

There is a danger that the United States will again take long-term growth for granted, as it largely did from World War II through the economic challenges of the 1970s. In the 1980s, the Cold War continued to dominate foreign policy, often including economic policy. But in the 1980s, the spur of slowing productivity growth and rising international competition stimulated public and private efforts to build up the long-term economic strength of the country.

Terrorism poses a new foreign policy challenge, but without a major international economic competitor. The war on terrorism is a contest of ideas, but not of economic systems; there is no elaborate socialist economy or Soviet central planning that contends for the world's allegiance. Europe and Japan are still powerful and innovative economies but have faded as serious economic rivals. China and India are prompting greater concern but have only just begun to stimulate some thoughtful analysis. As American multinational firms adopt a truly global perspective, they draw on innovations, human talent, and growing economies around the world—with the result that they are less dependent on the domestic economy and domestic institutions. Indeed, they are more likely to press the federal government for assistance in building up their strength here and abroad rather than for a 1980s-like strategy that focused almost exclusively on improving United States–based competitiveness.

Resting on current laurels is always a risky strategy. It is hard to see how the United States will win the contest of ideas in the twenty-first century without continued economic growth, technological innovation, improved education, and broad-based equality of opportunity. Without a continued capacity to innovate, it is hard to see how America will meet its environmental responsibilities and aspirations. The growing realization that disease anywhere is a threat everywhere demands an even stronger U.S. commitment to biomedical research. Global engagement and international economic integration are now daily facts of economic life.

Twenty-First-Century American Dreams

The twenty-first-century competitiveness strategy spelled out in earlier chapters is designed to respond to the challenges and the changing political and economic realities of the new century. Securing long-term productivity growth will provide a critical base for American Dreams and American global leadership. But, as has been noted above, the country will need to take steps to restore national trust in key institutions, rediscover a sense of national purpose, restore its commitment to shared gains and shared sacrifices, and renew its sense of American identity.

Restoring Trust in Markets and Government

As the competitiveness strategy developed, the public and private sectors become aware of the complementary roles they played in fostering long-term competitiveness. In an earlier chapter, I referred to the public sector setting the stage (creating the infrastructure, making key investments, and maintaining the institutions that support growth) while the private sector put on the play. It was not so much a formal contract as a kind of shared understanding or a conscious parallelism.

During the last two decades of the twentieth century, the public and private sectors became ever more entwined in a complex of partnerships that went beyond the shared understanding of the New Growth Compact. Particularly where the public and private sectors shared an interest in education, training, technology, and trade, government and private companies often turned to explicit public–private partnerships.

However, as the prosperity and peace of the 1990s first blossomed and then faded at the turn of the century, nothing has changed more than the mutual trust and confidence needed for the New Growth Compact. Public as well as private failures have been involved. A series of corporate scandals, starting with the 2001 collapse of Enron, have seriously eroded the public's confidence in the financial markets and the state of corporate governance.

Much of the excess seems to have taken place during the period between December 1996, when Federal Reserve Chairman Alan Greenspan warned of "irrational exuberance,"[9] and 2001, when he looked back on a period of "infectious greed."[10] As it turned out, some cold and lumpy porridge came with the many economic blessings of the "Goldilocks" economy in the second half of the 1990s.

The corporate accounting scandals cast a spotlight on a systemwide failure in the private use and public oversight of financial markets. It was not a case of just a few bad apples but rather of barrels filled with questionable investment bankers, stockbrokers, and financial conglomerates. None of the checks seemed to work. Weak corporate governance allowed chief executives to garner large salaries, bigger bonuses, enormous stock options, and even million-dollar loans. Instead of carefully keeping the corporate books, accounting firms were both establishing and then supposedly auditing tax shelters that misled directors and shareholders alike. Neither the official regulators nor Congress provided effective oversight. Even the financial press seemed more focused on the exuberance of the markets than their irrationality and virtually missed the story of financial market fraud. To hidden financial sleight of hand was added the public concern over corporations shifting their headquarters overseas to avoid domestic taxes, increasing the sense that American companies had become footloose citizens of the world.

The story is less bleak in terms of pragmatic partnerships. The economics and risk of research and production still drive strictly private partnerships, and shared public and private interests continue to create incentives for public–private cooperation. With regard to innovation, the public and private sectors are so tightly interwoven at various stages of research, development, and even commercialization that partnerships are routinely pursued. The same is true for higher education and training, where public grants, loans, and tax incentives often complement the efforts of private institutions. There is, however, a serious danger that the erosion of trust in major corporations will obscure their role as a positive force for education reform and technological innovation.

Since the start of the George W. Bush administration, there has been little rhetorical support for the critical, complementary roles played by the public and private sectors, perhaps because the current congressional majority and the administration share a deeply held preference for smaller government. The tax cuts of 2001, 2002, and 2003 and the prospect of long-run deficits echo the approach of the early Reagan years, when tax-cut-driven deficits were designed, in part, to force a reduction in government spending. President Reagan's first director of the Office of Management and Budget, David Stockman, described the approach and its partial failure in *The Triumph of Politics.*[11] The small-is-beautiful approach to government has a historic and almost visceral appeal to most Americans. But, it does not square with either the growing security-related commitments of the Bush administration or with the expectations of the American people, which include everything from national parks to effective health care. It is the desire for large benefits and yet small government that creates much of the tension in modern politics.

For the most part, the war on terrorism, the challenge of bringing democracy to the Middle East, and an economic policy dominated by tax cuts have left little room or interest in focusing on a New Growth Compact. Faced with a mix of indifference, or, in some parts of Congress, outright hostility to government, the private sector has little incentive to sing a solo on the virtues of a supportive government.

Despite the change in national rhetoric, tone, and interest, there are ways in which the private and public sectors could help to create the conditions in which the New Growth Compact would continue to develop. Regulators, prosecutors, and many corporate boards are working to improve corporate governance and restore confidence to the financial markets. Pension funds and other major shareholders are forcing some of the right changes, demonstrating growing resistance to chief executive pay and overgenerous severance packages and strengthening the hand of boards of directors. The national press is considerably more vigilant than it was. Still, there is much to do. Chief executive pay remains excessive by historical standards, accounting firms resist further restrictions on their activity, and mutual funds are reluctant to report publicly on how they use their voting power in elections of boards of directors.

The elements of a long-term competitiveness strategy, a New Growth Compact, and development of a Partnership Nation are still very much in place. They need rediscovery, support, and adaptation to the challenges of the twenty-first century.

Renewing a Sense of National Purpose

There is an American dynamism that exists separate from great national challenges. With children raised on lemonade stands, paper routes, and cookie sales, America is blessed with an endless stream of striving entrepreneurs who bring new life to public as well as private enterprise. Still, there has always been something more about America: a belief that the future is America's unending frontier. There is an often unstated confidence that America has a special purpose—that America will arise to meet great challenges and pursue great goals.

In World War I, the United States fought the "war to end wars," the "war to make the world safe for democracy." In World War II, it fought to end fascism in Europe and militarism in Asia. In fighting the Cold War, it was striving to preserve freedom and democracy as well as to secure its own national security. Challenged by the Soviet Union's launch of Sputnik, the United States responded by putting the first human on the moon. Challenged by Germany and Japan in the economic sphere, public and private America responded with new policies and new private practices. Although there were many challenges in the 1990s, as the decade wore on, however, water cooler talk was more likely to turn to the stock market or the latest initial public offering.

National unity, purpose, and a renewed sense of country all returned on September 11, 2001. From a cautious, narrow definition of national interest that looked warily at overseas entanglements and explicitly turned away from nation building, President George W. Bush responded by leading the country into a global war on terrorism. Military victories have been swift. In Afghanistan, a mix of American air power and Special Forces working with the indigenous Northern Alliance defeated the ruling Taliban government in a matter of weeks. Just over a year later, American, British, and Australian troops teamed up to rout the Iraqi military and topple the Baathist regime of Saddam Hussein.

Yet the American people have not been asked to join in the global effort in any concrete way. There have been no war bond sales, no call to learn Arabic or study Islamic culture. Nor has the president focused the country on other major goals—energy independence, or national health care—that could unify the nation and drive innovation at the same time. Chapter 15 suggested a number of major goals that, if pursued, have the potential to solve major problems, create new technologies, and provide an added sense of national purpose.

The Bush administration, however, failed to prepare for the aftermath of major conflict in Iraq. Instead of stability, there was widespread looting, the destruction of everything from ministries to hospitals, intermittent sabotage, and eventually a spreading insurgency. By many measures, rather than striking a blow against a terrorist group, the war in Iraq has been a major recruiting tool for al Qaeda and similar groups. While several governments continue to support the American effort in Iraq, popular hostility to the war and to the United States has grown rapidly in virtually every country. In May 2004, pictures of prisoner mistreatment at the Abu Gharib prison were front-page news on newspapers around the world. Early attempts to explain away hooded prisoners, threats of electrical shocks, and sexual humiliation fell on ever more skeptical ears as evidence mounted that the treatment was the product of the need for greater intelligence and as reports surfaced of prisoner mistreatment elsewhere in Iraq and Afghanistan. By mid-2004, more and more American voters were questioning the wisdom of the war and the effectiveness of its execution.

Losing Our Sense of Shared Gains and Shared Sacrifices

Although the war on terrorism has brought a shared sense of vulnerability and renewed patriotism, the Bush administration lost the opportunity to call the country to a shared mission or shared sacrifice. Shortly after the terrorist attacks of September 11, the president urged the country to keep traveling by plane and to go shopping.

The lack of emphasis on shared sacrifice or shared gain is a sharp departure from the great struggles of the twentieth century. When the country entered World War I, it relied on a draft and on taxes. In the Great Depression, most Americans remembered hard times and the shared challenge they provided. The country was swept by demands for a greater sharing of the national wealth. Francis Everett Townsend called on the government to give "every person over sixty and free of criminality a monthly stipend of $200 of scrip" that had to be spent within the month.[12] Townsend clubs sprang up all over the country.[13] Huey Long, first the governor of and then a senator from Louisiana, rallied millions to his populist Share the Wealth Society, in which "every man was a king, but no man wore a crown."[14] Roosevelt led with relief and responded with Social Security—still a key element in the American safety net.

The country saw World War II as another era in which most Americans shared the sacrifice of war and the joy of victory. The Cold War saw continued defense spending at the cost of civilian programs or consumption. The global search for allies and influence in what was then called the Third World highlighted the contradiction between American ideals and the treatment of African Americans as second-class citizens. The Cold War made its own contribution to the civil rights movement. When the Soviet Union's Sputnik satellite beat the United States into space, it prompted a national commitment to improve education for all. The same "all hands are important" philosophy was echoed by the Reagan administration's 1983 *A Nation at Risk,* which described a failing education system that threatened national security. During the Cold War, there was a clear sense that every American counted.

The 1970s competitiveness challenge of slow growth, rising prices, and international competition also called for a nationwide response. From the start, there was an emphasis on growth and fairness or growth with equity.[15] The emphasis on equity was clear in the 1985 report of the President's Commission on Industrial Competitiveness (or the Young Commission), which defined competitiveness as a country's ability to meet the standard of international competition "while simultaneously maintaining or expanding the real incomes of its citizens."[16] By measuring ultimate success in terms of raising the income of all Americans, national competitiveness took on the mantle of the American Dream.

During the 1990s, there was consistent support for using tax rebates to supplement the income of the working poor. In the early years of the twenty-first century, national policy has moved in contradictory directions. In principle, President Bush's "leave no child behind" policy should, over time—if adequately funded and effectively implemented—expand opportunities, raise incomes, and reduce current income inequality. Tax policy, however, has taken a decidedly different tack by favoring the already well off with significant cuts in marginal tax rates and by shifting the tax burden away from capital and toward earned income.

Strengthening American Identity in a Global Economy

Popular and even scholarly history has come to focus on the gap between American ideals and the too-often-disappointing reality. The effort to write more accurate and inclusive histories became part of a broader effort to recognize and value the enormous ethnic diversity that still exists in the United States. Some academics took an added step and came to emphasize and value the variety of cultures in the United States while labeling mainstream American culture as irredeemably racist, sexist, and homophobic.

At one extreme, a different group conceived of a United States that was simply a geographic area occupied by disparate peoples and cultures—a shared space would take the place of a community of shared ideals. What had been the United States would become simply a pleasant place to live in North America, merely a particularly attractive place to do business. Yet over the course of America's history, the idea of America and its ideals have often been a force for moving the country forward toward those ideals. The dream of a more perfect America has been a powerful force in helping move all Americans toward the American Dream.

The pull of America and American Dreams remains strong. Many immigrants find themselves speaking English, supporting a favorite football team, and working their way up the economic ladder. Still, there are steps that the United States can take to strengthen American identity, broaden the path to greater inclusiveness, and renew Americans' shared ideals.

Unum as well as Pluribus

Public discourse has tended to emphasize the reality and importance of diversity to the United States. The "pluribus" has always been part of the American fabric. What has tended to get lost is the union Americans form out of that diversity. From the president to the Cabinet to other key officials, there needs to be a renewed emphasis on the "unum" as well as the pluribus. Political leaders need to speak again of the shared ideals that define the nation.

The bitter battles over the public display of the Confederate battle flag in South Carolina and Georgia are pointed reminders of how divisive the past can be. The Balkans is a frequently cited example of how holding onto history can bring tragic repetition. Still, many small towns have learned to celebrate the diverse heritage of their citizens in a unifying way. While visiting Port Jervis, New York, in the 1990s, I learned how one small town had found a way to give history a full and positive voice. Every summer's Heritage Days allowed the town's residents to celebrate their own heritage— there was everything from Caribbean food to Russian *piroshki* to a Civil War campsite with townspeople dressed as Union soldiers. It was history, it was education, and it was inclusive. Heritage Days that celebrate history and build community at the same time should join baseball as the nation's summer pastime.

Celebrating Progress

One can judge America from at least three points of view. Where did the country start, and how far has it come from the highly imperfect past? How close is it to meeting those ideals today? And how does America compare with other countries in democracy, human rights, equality of opportunity, and other ideals that Americans think of as typically American?

A prison scandal in Iraq, a lack of planning that has led to the loss of Iraqi as well as American life, and the spreading international anger toward the United States together will force another painful awareness of the gap between American ideals and American action. But it is wrong to ignore the progress that has occurred during the past fifty years. Civil rights, women's rights, and increasingly gay rights are now facts of everyday American life. Popular thinking, public behavior, and public policies have all changed. In the shadow of a difficult war and a prisoner abuse scandal, it is easy to ignore decades of progress. Many would agree that while Americans have a long way to go to fulfill the ultimate promise of America, we have come some distance toward meeting our ideals. Yet, too often, the judgment focuses only on the gap between the present and the ideal. In taking about America—"warts and all"—political leaders also need to celebrate the parts without the warts. The shared ideals that first took shape in the Declaration of Independence still provide the base for the ongoing drive for greater equality of opportunity and equality of respect. In a country that celebrates the football touchdown, it is important to celebrate progress as well as pointing to a scoreboard that reminds the country that it has not yet won the game.

The American Dream and American Leadership
in the Twenty-First Century

After a brief pause in the post–Cold War era of the 1990s, America is again thoroughly engaged in a global mission. The increasingly broad-based war on terrorism mixes a renewed concern about national security with America's long-standing commitment to spreading democracy and human rights.

In the wake of the Iraq war, there is a risk that Americans will turn away from that mission because of the way the Bush administration has pursued it. The administration's approach has often been to act alone and rely almost exclusively on military force—a policy that is at once unilateral and unidimensional. The contrast with the conduct of the Cold War is striking. Military readiness was coupled with broad international alliances. Analysis of Soviet military doctrine was matched by an emphasis on knowing Russian history and the Russian language. As the Cold War became truly global, the United States fought the battle of ideals and economic systems with radio broadcasts, foreign assistance, overseas libraries, foreign visitor programs, and an attempt to understand the many languages and cultures of the world outside the communist bloc.

Many factors have thrust America into a position of world leadership. World War II, the Cold War, the collapse of the Soviet Union, and the decline in military spending in Europe have left the United States with superior military strength. During the past few years, there have been various attempts to describe the degree of American military might—last remaining superpower or the sole hyperpower.[17] What Joseph Nye has termed American "soft power"—the ideals and culture of the country—also became a force in the world.[18]

This volume has focused on the past and future of the American economy. It traced the emergence of a new set of economic policies that proved politically sustainable and economically effective. The economy is and will remain a key source of American strength. Continued prosperity will help expand opportunity at home, fund the research to improve the environment and fight disease, undergird U.S. military strength, and finance American efforts to help bring peace and prosperity to a still-troubled world.

The American economy, however, does not exist in a vacuum. It is embedded in the values, goals, and aspirations of the country. Beyond rates of investment, levels of education, and new discoveries, the country and its economy both depend on strengthening American identity and community, renewing a sense of national purpose, and pursuing a twenty-first-century American Dream at home and abroad.

Leading by Example and Engagement

Before World War I, Britain helped provide global economic prosperity and a kind of international stability. It was an era when the world did think of Pax Britannica, when the sun never set on the British Empire. It was part of an earlier age of globalization, in which the Bank of England backed the gold standard, facilitated a growing exchange of goods, capital, and people, and supported considerable growth in Europe and the United States.

The United States is a distinctly different country. There is no popular interest in empire, but there is a long-standing post–World War II commitment to global leadership. Though Americans are sharply divided either about the wisdom of the war in Iraq or the quality of planning for postwar stability and reconstruction, Americans are broadly united behind the importance of spreading freedom and democracy around the world. Throughout more than 200 years of history, America has sought to lead by example and, in much of the twentieth century, by active engagement. Today, it must do both.

In pursuing its twenty-first-century global mission to include soft as well as hard power, the United States can lead by example and by active engagement. Sailing toward America in 1630, John Winthrop, a future governor of Connecticut, spoke of being "as a City upon a Hill" with "the eyes of all people . . . upon us."[19] The preamble to the American constitution spoke of an American people creating a constitution to form "a more perfect union." That sense of being a City on a Hill and the drive to create an ever more perfect union have influenced American values, policy, and politics throughout the nation's history. It is, again, the source of much of the soft power that Nye pointed to in his recent book *The Paradox of American Power.* That city, of course, is only partially built. Many Americans are left behind in inner-city slums or the impoverished hollows of Appalachia. Too many are in prison, too many were killed by guns, and too many are dying from drug abuse. There is much unfinished business. Eliminating the digital and other divides that keep some Americans from fully participating in the country's life would also be a beacon to a world rapidly following the United States down the same technological path.

Progress toward building the City on a Hill and perfecting the union have come only with time and painful effort. The Civil War, the battles over civil rights, the movement to protect labor, and the women's suffrage effort—all these struggles have helped define and strengthen the nation.

In the late 1990s, the U.S. Army's recruiting ads linked military service to the opportunity to "be all" that an individual can be. More Americans are now applying the same standard to America itself. Americans look forward to a country that will achieve its founding ideals, that will open the door of opportunity to all, and that will become a truly universal nation. Americans look forward to a country that will lead the world by example and by engagement. Americans want America to be all that it can be.

Notes

1. Luce first used the phrase in a 1941 *Life* editorial written before the December 7, 1941, attack at Pearl Harbor.

2. Ezra Vogel, *Japan as No. 1: Lessons for America* (Cambridge, Mass.: Harvard University Press, 1979).

3. Clyde V. Prestowitz Jr., *Trading Places: How We Allowed Japan to Take the Lead* (New York: Basic Books, 1988).

4. See Francis Fukuyama, *The End of History and the Last Man* (New York: Simon & Schuster, 1992); and S. P. Huntington, *Clash of Civilizations and the Remaking of World Order* (New York: W. W. Norton, 1997). Huntington's original essay on the clash appeared as "Clash of Civilizations" in the summer 1993 edition of *Foreign Affairs.*

5. Despite growth and a decline in the rate of unemployment, the December 2003 job figures indicated that the U.S. economy had produced only 1,000 new jobs. See Bureau of Labor Statistics, "The Employment Situation: December 2003," at http://www.bls.gov/schedule/archives/empsitnr.htm#2003. The *Financial Times* reported some puzzlement among professional economists, some of whom thought the jobs would come and others of whom thought business intentions to add jobs may have translated into added overseas employment. See Christopher Swann, "No End in Sight for America's 'Jobless Recovery,'" *Financial Times,* January 10, 2004.

6. For an early 2004 treatment of the question, see Martin Muhlstein and Christopher Tow, eds., *U.S. Fiscal Policies and Priorities for Long-Run Sustainability* (Washington, D.C.: International Monetary Fund, 2004). For initial reactions to the study, see Elizabeth Becker and Edmund L. Andrews, "I.M.F. Says Rise in U.S. Debts Is Threat to World's Economy," *New York Times,* January 8, 2004.

7. Peter G. Peterson, *Running on Empty: How the Democratic and Republican Parties Are Bankrupting Our Future and What Americans Can Do About It* (New York: Farrar, Straus, and Giroux, 2004).

8. Martin Wolf, "America Is Now on the Comfortable Path to Ruin," *Financial Times,* August 11, 2004, 11.

9. Alan Greenspan, "The Challenge of Central Banking in a Democratic Society," speech given at the Annual Dinner and Francis Boyer Lecture of the American Enterprise Institute, Washington, December 5, 1996.

10. Testimony of Chairman Alan Greenspan before the Committee on Banking, Housing, and Urban Affairs, U.S. Senate, July 16, 2002.

11. David Stockman, *The Triumph of Politics: Why the Reagan Revolution Failed* (New York: HarperCollins, 1987).

12. Jerome Agel, *We the People: Great Documents of the American Nation* (New York: Barnes & Noble, 1997), 160.

13. Townsend's ideas survived World War II. During the summer of 1961, I worked as a college intern in the office of Senator Wayne Morse of Oregon. I remember helping draft a response to correspondence calling for the adoption of the Townsend plan.

14. For an overview of Huey Long and his Share the Wealth movement, see David M. Kennedy, *Freedom from Fear: The American People in Depression and War, 1929–1945* (New York: Oxford University Press, 1999), 238–43. For Long's own words, see "Every Man a King," delivered on February 23, 1934, at http://www.americanrhetoric.com/speeches/hueyplongkind.htm.

15. House Democratic Caucus, *Rebuilding the Road to Opportunity: Turning Point for America's Economy* (Washington, D.C.: House Democratic Caucus, 1982), 2.

16. President's Commission on Industrial Competitiveness, *Global Competition: The New Reality* (Washington, D.C.: U.S. Government Printing Office, 1985), vol. 1, p. 6.

17. In February 1999, French foreign minister Hubert Vedrine referred to the United States as a "hyperpower." See William Safire, "Hyperpower," *New York Times,* June 22, 2003.

18. Joseph Nye, *The Paradox of American Power: Why the World's Only Superpower Can't Go It Alone* (New York: Oxford University Press, 2002).

19. See John Winthrop, "A Model of Christian Charity," written onboard the ship *Arbella* somewhere on the Atlantic Ocean, 1630; available at http://history.hanover.edu/texts/winthmod.html.

Timeline of Significant Events Affecting Competitiveness

The Competitiveness Timeline focuses on many of the policy changes that have contributed to America's long-run economic strength. The timeline reaches back to the beginning of the Republic and Alexander Hamilton's Report on Manufactures, a report that regained some prominence in the 1980s debate over America's economic future. The timeline also includes the 1862 Morrill Act establishing the land-grant college system. In the early 1980s, Senator Gary Hart proposed a High Technology Morrill Act to help prepare the country for the information age.

Where a specific date is less important, the timeline often reports the year rather than the actual date of congressional or presidential action. To help keep the competitiveness initiatives in context, the timeline also includes some significant dates in terms of economic, political, and foreign policy developments. Because a competitiveness strategy builds on so many elements, the timeline should be thought of as a rough guide and not an encyclopedic summary of all the relevant policy steps.

Pre–World War II

1787	The new Constitution of the United States gives Congress the power to protect intellectual property.
1791	On December 5, 1791, Alexander Hamilton submits his *Report on Manufactures* to the U.S. Congress. In his report, Hamilton makes the case for developing industry in the United States.
1862	The Morrill Act establishes the land-grant college system as part of fostering national agricultural development.

1901	Congress creates the National Bureau of Standards (now the National Institute of Standards and Technology).
1914	Congress adopts the Agriculture Extension Act to help disseminate improved agricultural practices.
1930	President Hoover signs the Smoot-Hawley Tariff Act.
1934	Congress enacts the Reciprocal Trade Agreements Act of 1934 giving the president the authority to negotiate reciprocal reductions in tariffs.

1941

December 7	Japan attacks Pearl Harbor.
December 8	The U.S. Congress declares war against Japan.
December 11	Germany and Italy declare war on the United States.

1944

July 1–22	The Bretton-Woods International Monetary and Financial Conference of the United and Associated Nations agrees to establish the International Monetary Fund (IMF) and the International Bank for Reconstruction and Development (IBRD or World Bank).
1944	GI Bill of Rights.

1945

April 25	The United Nations Organizational Conference meets in San Francisco.
May 8	Victory in Europe Day (VE day) declared after German unconditional surrender on May 7, 1945.
July 28	The U.S. Senate approves the UN Charter 89 to 2.
August 15	Victory in Japan Day (VJ day). Official surrender ceremonies are conducted by General Douglas MacArthur on the battleship Missouri on September 2.
1945	Vannevar Bush publishes *Science—The Endless Frontier,* which leads to the formation of the National Science Foundation in 1950.

1947

June 5	Secretary of State George C. Marshall proposes American help to reconstruct Europe.

| November 21 | The Havana Conference to consider formation of an International Trade Organization (ITO) opens in Havana, Cuba. |
| | President Truman agrees to have the United States sign the General Agreement on Tariffs and Trade (GATT). |

1948

January 1	GATT comes into force.
March 18	The U.S. House Committee on Ways and Means votes down a resolution supporting U.S. membership in the ITO.
June 28	President Truman signs bill appropriating $4 billion for European reconstruction as the first step in what becomes known as the Marshall Plan.

1950

May 10	Congress creates the National Science Foundation to support basic research (42 USC 1861 et. seq.).
June 25	The North Korean army crosses the 38th parallel and attacks South Korea.
	The UN Security Council (the Soviet Union was absent) labels North Korea the aggressor and calls on all its members to aid the United Nations in restoring peace.
June 27	President Truman orders American air and naval forces to support South Korea.
November 7	Republicans make significant gains in Congress.
December	President Truman indicates he will not resubmit the ITO Charter for congressional approval.

1952

| | GI Bill of Rights (Korea) |
| November | General Dwight David Eisenhower elected president. |

1953

| March 5 | Josef Stalin, the Soviet dictator, dies. |
| July 27 | North Korea signs an armistice agreement with the United Nations. |

1957

October 4   The Soviet Union launches Sputnik, the first artificial satellite to circle the Earth. The United States is stunned.

1958

August   Congress passes the National Defense Education Act.

1958   Congress passes the Small Business Investment Company Act allowing banks to form subsidiaries that could make equity investments in small companies.

1960

November 8   Senator John Fitzgerald Kennedy elected president.

1961

May 25   President Kennedy announces his intent to send an American to the moon.

1962

June 28   The U.S. House of Representatives passes the Trade Expansion Act of 1962 by a margin of 293 to 125.

September 19   The U.S. Senate passes the Trade Expansion Act of 1962 by a margin of 78 to 8. The act gave the president significant tariff negotiating authority. It also removed responsibility for trade negotiations from the State Department and created a new entity for trade negotiations, the Office of Special Trade Representative in the Executive Office of the president.

          The Trade Expansion Act provided the authority for what became the Kennedy Round of trade negotiations and established the first Trade Adjustment Assistance Program.

November 14   Christian Herter agrees to become the first special trade representative.

1963

January   In his 1983 State of the Union address, President Kennedy calls for a "substantial reduction in federal taxes." He proposed lowering the individual income tax rate from a range of 20 to 91 percent to a range of 14 to 65 percent. He also proposed reducing the corporate tax from 52 to 47 percent.

July 18   President Kennedy proposes an interest-equalization tax on American purchases of foreign securities (to deter the outflow of capital).

November 22   Lee Harvey Oswald assassinates President Kennedy in Dallas.

Vice President Johnson is sworn is as president.

1964

February 27   The U.S. Congress passes the Kennedy tax cuts proposed in 1962.

November 3   President Johnson wins the presidential election.

1965

February 10   President Johnson extends restraints on U.S. capital outflows.

December 31   *Time* magazine puts a portrait of John Maynard Keynes on its cover in recognition of the influence of Keynesian economics. It is the first time that the magazine has so recognized a deceased individual.

1965   Higher Education Act of 1965 (PL 89-329).

1966   GI Bill of Rights (Vietnam).

1968

January 1   President Johnson announces balance-of-payments program including mandatory capital controls.

March 31   President Johnson announces his decision not to seek the presidential nomination of the Democratic Party.

June   Johnson signs a bill imposing a temporary income tax surcharge and limits on spending.

July   Congress broadens the mission of the National Science Foundation to include applied research and technology (Daddario-Kennedy Amendment, PL 80-407).

November 5   Richard M. Nixon defeats Vice President Hubert H. Humphrey and Alabama Governor George C. Wallace to win the presidency.

1969

April 4   The United States eases controls on capital outflows.

1971

January   President Nixon establishes the Council on International Economic Policy (CIEP).

August 15   President Nixon announces a wage-price freeze and a 10-percent import surcharge, and ends the convertibility of dollars into gold, breaking with the fixed exchange rate regime established by the Bretton-Woods agreement.

August 15   Senator Vance Hartke (D-IN) and Congressman James Burke (D-MA) introduce the Foreign Trade and Investment Act of 1972.

1972

November 7   President Nixon re-elected president.

1973

February 12   Secretary of the Treasury George Shultz announces a 10-percent devaluation of the dollar.

March 16   The international monetary system adopts a floating, rather than fixed, dollar.

                        Soviet crop failure drives up world food prices.

October   OPEC imposes an oil embargo during 1973 Arab-Israeli war.

December   OPEC quadruples price of oil from its October 1973 level.

1974

April   President Nixon ends wage and price controls.

August 9   President Nixon resigns from office in wake of the Watergate scandal. Vice President Gerald Ford takes the oath as the president of the United States.

October 8   President Ford issues WIN (Whip Inflation Now) buttons, as part of his anti-inflation policy.

December 20   Congress passes the Trade Act of 1974.

1975

November 15–17   Six heads of state (from France, Germany, Italy, Japan, the United Kingdom, and the United States) meet at the first economic summit in Rambouillet, France. Canada joined the next year to make it the Group of 7.

November   Former Georgia Governor Jimmy Carter elected president.

1977

September   The Republican National Committee endorses the proposal of Senator William Roth (R-DE) and Congressman Jack Kemp, the "Kemp-Roth" bill, to cut marginal tax rates on individual income by 30 percent over three years.

1978

October 15   Congress passes the Revenue Act of 1978, which includes a reduction in the capital gains tax promoted by Congressman Steiger.

October 27   President Carter signs the Full Employment and Balanced Growth Act (Humphrey-Hawkins Act) (PL 95-423).

1978   Department of Labor issues regulations allowing pension funds regulated by ERISA to invest a portion of their holdings in venture capital funds (29 C.F.R. 2550.404a-1).

1979

Inflation (December 1978 to December 1979) climbs to 13.3 percent.

January 16   The Shah of Iran goes into exile, leaving Iran on the verge of revolution.

February 9   Ayatollah Ruhollah Khomeini returns to Iran.

January–March   Iranian revolution sparks a sharp increase in oil and gas prices.

March 22   The Congressional Joint Economic Committee releases its first unanimous annual report putting an emphasis on long-term productivity growth.

November	Paul R. Krugman publishes "Increasing Returns, Monopolistic Competition, and International Trade," in the November issue of the *Journal of International Trade.* It was an early step toward what became known as strategic trade theory.
1979	Ezra F. Vogel publishes *Japan as No. 1: Lessons for America.*

1980

January	Congress and President Carter adopt legislation approving loan guarantees for the Chrysler Corporation.
March 4	The Congressional Joint Economic Committee releases *Plugging in the Supply Side,* its second unanimous annual report.
April 2	The prime rate charged by U.S. banks reaches 20 percent.
October 1	President Carter signs the Stevenson-Wydler Act of 1980, the Technology Innovation Act (PL 96-480), promoting technology transfer from federal labs.
November 4	Ronald Reagan is elected president.
November 10	The International Trade Commission rejects a United Auto Worker petition seeking Section 201 (temporary import) relief.
December 12	President Carter signs the Bay-Dole Act of 1980, the Patent and Trademark Amendments Act (PL 96-517), designed to encourage the licensing of federally funded inventions to industry.
December	The House Democratic Caucus elects Gillis W. Long as chair.

1981

January– February	Gillis Long forms the Committee on Party Effectiveness, bringing together the various wings of the Democratic Party in the House.
April 27	U.S. Treasury Secretary Donald Regan announces that the United States will not intervene regularly in the foreign exchange markets.

June 26	The U.S. House passes the Gramm–Latta II deficit reduction bill.
August 13	President Reagan signs the Economic Recovery Tax Act of 1981. The act includes a provision for a Research and Experimentation Tax Credit.
November 11	The December 11, 1981, issue of *The Atlantic* includes William Greider's "The Education of David Stockman."

1982

July 22	President Reagan signs the Small Business Innovation Development Act, creating the Small Business Innovation and Research Program (PL 97-219).
August 4	Mexico draws on a Federal Reserve swap line for $700 million.
August 12	The Mexican exchange market is closed.
September	U.S. House Democratic Caucus releases *Rebuilding the Road to Opportunity*.
Books:	Ira Magaziner and Robert Reich, *Minding America's Business;* Richard Bolling and John Knowles, *America's Competitive Edge;* Chalmers Johnson, *MITI and the Japanese Miracle*.

1983

June 28	President Reagan establishes the president's Commission on Industrial Competitiveness (the Young Commission).
June	Congressman John LaFalce starts 35 days of hearings on industrial policy.
November 16	Senate Democratic Conference releases *Jobs for the Future*.
1983	The National Science Foundation establishes university-based engineering research centers.
	The Business Higher Education Forum publishes "America's Competitive Challenge: The Need for a National Response."

1984

January	National House Democratic Caucus releases *Renewing America's Promise*.

January	Trade and Tariff Act of 1984 (PL 98-573).
October 11	President Reagan signs the National Cooperative Research Act allowing industry collaboration on pre-competitive research with reduced risk of antitrust penalties (PL 98-462).
November	President Reagan reelected in a 49-state landslide.
December	John Young presents the findings of the president's Commission on Industrial Competitiveness to the Reagan cabinet.
1984	The National Research Council establishes the Government-University-Industry Research Roundtable.

1985

February 4	James A. Baker III becomes U.S. Secretary of the Treasury. Former Treasury Secretary Donald Regan takes Baker's role as White House Chief of Staff.
February	The dollar reaches its highest 1985 value on foreign exchange markets.
April	Democratic Trade Task Force chaired by Representative Don Bonker (D-WA) is launched.
July 17–18	Congressman Dan Rostenkowski, Congressman Richard Gephardt, and Senator Lloyd Bentson introduce bills to impose a surcharge on imports from countries that limit U.S. exports and have large trade surpluses with the United States.
August 3	Democrat Jim Chapman raises concerns about the impact of imports and the trade deficit on jobs. Chapman defeats the favored Republican, Edd Hargett in the first district of Texas.
September 22	The G5 (France, Germany, Japan, the United Kingdom, and the United States) agree to an orderly adjustment of "non-dollar currencies," the Plaza Accord, at a meeting at New York City's Plaza Hotel.
October 17	The House Democratic Trade Task Force Reports.
November 20	S 1860, a bipartisan trade bill, is introduced in the Senate.

1986

May 9   The House Democratic Trade Task Force Report is translated into legislation as HR 4800, the Trade and International Economic Policy Reform Act.

July 22   The Federal Technology Transfer Act (PL 99-502; 15 USC 3710-3714) amends the Stevenson-Wydler Act to allow government owned and operated laboratories to form cooperative research and development agreements (CRADAs) with private companies.

August   The United States and Japan sign a trade agreement to open the Japanese market to non-Japanese semiconductor imports.

August   John Young and other members of the president's Commission on Industrial Competitiveness (Young Commission) establish the privately funded Council on Competitiveness to continue the work of the Commission.

September 15   The members of GATT meet in Punte del Este, Uruguay, which leads to the launch of the Uruguay Round of Multilateral Trade Negotiations.

October 22   President Reagan signs the Tax Reform Act of 1986 (PL 99-514).

November 4   Democrats win control of the U.S. Senate.

1987

January 6   Democratic Majority Leader Jim Wright becomes speaker of the House.

January 6   HR 4800 reintroduced as HR 3, the Trade and International Economic Reform Act of 1987.

February 5   S 490, the Omnibus Trade Act of 1987 is introduced in the Senate.

February 19   The Reagan Administration proposes the 1,600-page Trade, Employment, and Productivity Act.

February 22   The Group of Six (the Italian minister of finance was absent) agrees to stabilize the value of the U.S. dollar in the Louvre Accord.

March 4	America's major manufacturers of computer chips announce plans to form Sematech (Semiconductor Manufacturing Technology), a research and development consortium.
March 7	More than 150 House and Senate members form the Congressional Caucus on Competitiveness.
Spring	Major American producers of semiconductors form a consortium, Sematech, to strengthen the industry.
April 30	The House passes HR 3, as amended.
June 24	Senate Majority Leader Robert C. Byrd places S 1420, the Omnibus Trade and Competitiveness Act of 1987, on the Senate calendar.
July 21	The U.S. Senate passes S 1420, including the Gephardt amendment and adding an amendment offered by Senator Byrd, requiring advance notice to workers of planned plant closings.
July	The U.S. Senate adopts an amendment to the Omnibus Trade and Competitiveness Act imposing sanctions on the Toshiba Corporation of Japan and Kongsberg Vaapenfabrikk for violating an international agreement by selling a highly advanced machine tool to the Soviet Union.
August 7	The full conference on trade and competitiveness legislation meets for the only time. The conference eventually includes 199 members from 9 Senate committees and 14 House committees.
August 20	President Reagan signs the Malcolm Baldrige National Quality Improvement Act of 1987 establishing the Baldrige award to recognize high-quality companies (PL 100-107).
October 19	The stock market suffers a dramatic 508 point decline on "Black Monday." The 22.6 percent decline in a single day contrasts with 12.8 percent on "Black Tuesday," October 28, 1929.
December 4	President Reagan signs the Fiscal 1988 Defense Authorization Act (H.R. 1748, P.L. 100–180), which included the authority (see Part F) to fund the Semi-

conductor Cooperative Research Program for fiscal years 1988 and 1989. The act allowed the Department of Defense to share the funding for public–private partnerships with Sematech, a consortium of the major U.S. semiconductor manufacturers.

Book: Paul Kennedy, *The Rise and Fall of the Great Powers.*

1988

April 21   The U.S. House passes trade and competitiveness legislation.

April 27   The U.S. Senate passes trade and competitiveness legislation.

May 24   President Reagan vetoes the trade and competitiveness bill.

May 24   The U.S. House overrides the president's veto.

June 3   The U.S. Senate fails to override the president's veto (61–37).

July 6   The U.S. Senate passes S 2527 (72–23), a separate plant-closing bill.

July 13   The U.S. House passes plant-closing legislation S 2527 (286–136).

The U.S. House passes HR 4848, the Omnibus Trade and Competitiveness Act of 1988, absent plant-closing legislation (376-45).

August 2   President Reagan announces intent to allow plant-closing legislation to become law without his signature.

August 3   The U.S. Senate approves HR 4848 by a veto-proof margin (85–11).

August 23   President Reagan signs the Omnibus Trade and Competitiveness Act of 1988 (PL 100-418).

October 5   The Fiscal 1989 reauthorization for the National Bureau of Standards establishes the Technology Administration in U.S. Department of Commerce.

November 15   Congress passes the National Defense Authorization Act for Fiscal 1989, which requires the U.S. Defense

Department to provide Congress with an annual critical technologies plan (PL 100-456, section 823).

Books: Clyde V. Prestowitz, Jr., *Trading Places: How We Allowed Japan to Take the Lead;* Benjamin M. Friedman, *Day of Reckoning: The Consequences of American Economic Policy under Reagan and After;* Aaron L. Friedberg, *The Weary Titan: Britain and the Experience of Relative Decline, 1895–1905.*

1989

January 20 George H.W. Bush is sworn in as president of the United States.

May James Fallows publishes "Containing Japan: Japan's Runaway Economy Will Harm the Rest of the World if Some Limits Aren't Set" in the May 1989 issue of *The Atlantic.*

November 1 National Advisory Committee on Semiconductors issues its first report, *A Strategic Industry at Risk.*

November 9 The Berlin Wall falls.

November 28 President Bush signs the National Competitiveness Technology Transfer Act of 1989 allowing government-owned but contract-operated national laboratories (includes the major energy labs) to form CRADAs with nongovernmental entities.

November 29 President Bush signs the Fiscal 1990 Defense Authorization Act (PL 101-189) establishing and funding the National Critical Technologies Panel to be created by the White House Office of Science and Technology Policy. The panel made its reports in March of 1991.

1989 The United States becomes a debtor nation as measured by market value of direct investments. In terms of current cost, the United States had become a debtor nation in 1987.

Book: Akio Morita, president of Sony, and Shintaro Ishihara, a leading Liberal Democratic Party politician, *The Japan That Can Say No.*

1990

July 1   East and West Germany agree to monetary unification.

October 3   East and West Germany unite.

                    The Technology Administration issues a list of emerging technologies.

                    The Defense Authorization Act for Fiscal 1991 (41 USC 6686) establishes the Critical Technologies Institute.

Book: Joseph S. Nye Jr., *Bound to Lead: The Changing Nature of American Power.*

1991

March 1991   The Council on Competitiveness (private sector) publishes *Gaining New Ground* listing industry-defined critical technologies and assessing the U.S. position in these critical technologies relative to its major international competitors.

July 18   The First Competitiveness Summit convenes in Colorado Springs.

August 19   Attempted coup in Moscow. Gorbachev placed under house arrest. The coup fails, the Communist Party is abolished, and, by the end of the year, the Soviet Union dissolves into the Commonwealth of Independent States.

October 3   Governor Clinton announces his intention to seek the presidency.

December 10   At a meeting in Maastricht, The Netherlands, the European Council agrees to the Treaty on European Union.

December 1991   The Commonwealth of Independent States replaces the Union of Soviet Socialist Republics.

1992

February 20   H. Ross Perot appearing on the *Larry King Live* show hints that he might accept a presidential draft.

March 1   The Competitiveness Policy Council issues its first annual report, *Building a Competitive America.*

June 1   Russia joins the IMF.

June 21   Governor Clinton announces his economic plan.

July 16	Perot withdraws from the race. Later in the summer he publishes his plan for balancing the budget in *United We Stand: How We Can Take Back Our Country.*
September	Governor Clinton publishes *Putting People First,* his campaign platform.
September 8	Governor Clinton publishes "Manufacturing for the 21st Century: Turning Ideas into Jobs."
September 10	President Bush unveils *Agenda for American Renewal* at the Detroit Economic Club.
September	Silicon Valley CEOs endorse Governor Clinton for president.
September 18	Govern Clinton publishes "Technology: The Engine of Economic Growth."
October 1	Perot reenters the presidential race.
November	Governor Clinton wins the presidency from George H.W. Bush.
December 3	President-elect Clinton meets in Little Rock, Arkansas, with Alan Greenspan, chairman of the Board of the Federal Reserve System.
December 14–15	President-elect Clinton hosts an Economic Summit in Little Rock.
1992	The Defense Conversion, Reinvestment and Transition Assistance Act (PL 102-484) creates the Technology Reinvestment Program.

1993

February 22	President Clinton and Vice President Gore spell out the Clinton Administration's technology policy in "Technology for American Economic Growth: A New Direction to Build Economic Strength."
June 10	President Clinton signs the National Cooperative Research and Production Act of 1993 allowing research venture participants to apply technologies with reduced anti-trust risk (PL 103-42).
August 10	President Clinton signs the Deficit Reduction Act (PL 103-86).

September 15	The Administration releases the National Information Infrastructure Agenda for Action.
September 29	The Administration establishes the Partnership for a New Generation of Vehicles (PNGV), a partnership among the federal government, academia, and the Big Three U.S. auto manufacturers.
November 17	The North American Free Trade Agreement (PL 103-182) passes the Congress.

1994

January 1	The North American Free Trade Agreement comes into effect.
February 4	The Federal Reserve raises the federal funds rate. The increase is followed by further increases on March 22 and May 17.
March 31	President Clinton signs the Goals 2000: Educate America Act (PL 103-227; 20 USC 5801 et. seq.).
May 4	President Clinton signs the Federal School to Work Opportunities Act of 1994 (PL 103-239; 20 USC 6101).
July 21	Congress decides against further action on the Clinton health care plan.
September	Newt Gingrich, Republican House colleagues, and Republican candidates unveil the Contract with America on the Capitol Steps.
November 8	The Republicans win majorities in the U.S. House and Senate.
December 1	The Congress adopts legislation to implement the Uruguay Round of trade negotiations agreement, which establishes the World Trade Organization (PL 103-465).

1995

| November 14 | The battle over the federal budget forces a three-day shutdown of the federal government. |
| December 15 | The federal budget battle shuts the federal government for two weeks. |

1996

January 23	In his State of the Union address, President Clinton says "The era of big government is over."
February 8	President Clinton signs the Telecommunications Act of 1986.
November 5	President Clinton reelected president.
December	Negotiators at the Singapore Ministerial of the WTO adopt the Information Technology Agreement eliminating tariffs (by January 1, 2000) on a large number of information technology products.

1997

July 2	Thailand moves to a managed float and triggers the Asian financial crisis.
July	Administration releases "A Framework for Global Electronic Commerce."
August 5	Congress passes the Taxpayer Relief Act of 1997, which includes the HOPE Scholarship and Lifetime Learning tax credits (PL 105-35).

1998

August 7	The Workforce Investment Act of 1998 (PL 105-226) becomes law.
August 17	Russia devalues its currency and defaults on its treasury bills.
September 23	The New York Federal Reserve Bank helps orchestrate a private sector bail-out of giant hedge fund Long-Term Capital Management.

1999

January 17	Brazil floats its currency, the real.
November/ December	WTO Ministerial in Seattle fails to launch a new round of multilateral trade negotiations. Europe and the United States had failed to agree on the dimensions of a new round, and emerging market and developing countries objected. The failure came amidst strong protests and anti-WTO street demonstrations.

2000

January 14	The Dow Jones Industrial Index peaks at 11,723.
March 10	The NASDAQ peaks at 5,048.62.
April	Unemployment falls to 3.9 percent and averages 4.0 percent for the year.
October 10	President Clinton signs law granting Permanent Normal Trade Relations status to China.

2001

January 20	George W. Bush is sworn in as president of the United States.
March	The United States economy falls into a recession.
June 7	President Bush signs $1.35 trillion, 10-year tax cut, the Economic Growth and Tax Relief Reconciliation Act (EGTRRA) (PL 107-16; 26 USC 1).
	President Bush signs the No Child Left Behind Act.
September 11	Al Queda terrorists crash hijacked airliners into the two World Trade Center towers and the Pentagon. A fourth hijacked plane crashes in Pennsylvania when the passengers attempt to retake the plane from the terrorists.
	The post–Cold War era and America's sense of security come to an end.
September 9	The *New York Times* reports a "growing credibility gap between [Enron] and Wall Street." Enron proves to be the first of a number of corporate accounting and tax scandals.
September 17	The New York Stock Exchange Reopens.
	The Federal Reserve cuts interest rates by 50 basis points.
October 2	The Federal Reserve cuts the federal funds rate to 2.5 percent, marking the ninth cut in 2001.
October 7	The president announces that the United States is bombing the Taliban regime in Afghanistan.
October 15	The office of Senator Thomas Daschle receives an anthrax-infected letter.

October 16	Bethlehem Steel files for Chapter 11 bankruptcy protection.
November	Kabul falls to the Northern Alliance backed by U.S. troops.
November 26	The National Bureau of Economic Research announces that the United States slipped into a recession in the second quarter of 2001.
December 11	China formally joins the World Trade Organization.

2002

March 9	The president signs the second tax-cut bill (PL 107-147).
August 8	President signs the Trade Act of 2002, granting the president trade-negotiating authority and trade-promotion or fast-track authority. The act includes a major expansion of trade-adjustment assistance.

2003

March 20	U.S. troops attack Iraq.
May 1	The president declares the end to major combat operations.
May 23	The House and Senate approve the Jobs Growth and Tax Relief and Reconciliation Act (JGTRRA, PL 108-27), which provides $320 billion in tax reductions over a 10-year period.
June	Unemployment reaches 6.3 percent but falls to 5.7 percent by December.
December	2003 trade deficit reaches $489.4 billion.
	2003 current account deficit reaches $541.8 billion.
	The net external debt (at market value) of the United States exceeds $2.6 trillion.

2004

January 4	Secretary of Commerce Evans releases "Manufacturing in America: A Comprehensive Strategy to Address the Challenges to U.S. Manufacturing."
April 26	The Bush Administration releases "Promoting Innovation and Competitiveness: President Bush's Technology

Hughes: Building the Next American Century

Errata:

On the copyright page, the ISBN line in the Library of Congress Cataloging-in-Publication data should read:

ISBN 0-8018-8204-4 (cloth: alk. paper)
ISBN 0-8018-8203-6 (pbk.: alk. paper)

On p. 217, the first full paragraph should read:

By choosing Bergsten, the CPC also helped rebut the lingering charge that competitiveness was just another word for protectionism. Bergsten was clearly identified with open markets and full engagement with the international economy. He put the protectionist question to rest. Bergsten, in turn, strengthened his own hand by adding a strong staff. Howard Rosen (now the director of the Trade Adjustment Assistance Coalition) with a trade history that dated to the international division of President Carter's Labor Department, served as executive director. Steve Charnovitz, a top aide to then Speaker Jim Wright and now a professor at George Washington University Law School, served as the policy director.

	Agenda: A New Generation of American Innovation," which calls for universal affordable-access for broadband technology by 2007.
April 26	The administration releases "Promoting Innovation and Competitiveness: President Bush's Technology Agenda."
June 5	President Reagan dies at the age of 93.
June 30	The FOMC raises the federal funds rate by 25 basis points to 1.25 percent.
July 22	The 9/11 Commission releases its report calling for sweeping changes in the organization of U.S. intelligence agencies.
July 29	Senator John F. Kerry accepts the Democratic nomination at the Democratic convention in Boston.
August 8	The FOMC raises the federal funds rate by another 25 basis points to 1.50 percent.
September 2	President Bush accepts the Republican nomination at the Republican convention in New York.
September 3	The Bureau of Labor Statistics announces a 5.4 percent unemployment rate for August and the creation of 144,000 jobs. From January to August, the economy generates 1.7 million jobs.
September 14	The Commerce Department announces a record current account deficit for the second quarter of 2004: $166.2 billion.
September 21	The FOMC raises the federal funds rate by another 25 basis points to 1.75 percent.
September 23	Congress passes a bill extending provisions from the 2001 tax cut (marriage penalty relief, child tax credit) to 2010. Bill includes extension of the research and experimentation tax credit for one year.
	Iraqi Prime Minister Ayad Allawi addresses a joint session of Congress.
October 4	President Bush signs the Working Family's Tax Relief Act of 2004, the fourth tax cut of his presidency.
October 11	Congress passes the American Jobs Creation Act of 2004 (H.R. 4520), the fifth tax cut passed during the

presidency of George W. Bush. The act eliminated an export susidy that was not in compliance with WTO rules and liberalized the rules for the taxation of foreign source income.

Glossary

absolute advantage. When a country (or economy) can use fewer scarce resources to produce a good than another country.

administrative guidance. The Japanese practice of the government strongly advising rather than specifically regulating specific decisions.

Advanced Technology Program. A U.S. federal government program that matches funds spent by university and private-sector partners to foster the development of high-risk, high-payoff technologies.

budget deficit or surplus. A shortfall or excess of revenue compared with expenditures.

comparative advantage. When a country can use fewer scarce resources to specialize in the production of one good and trade for another good than if it produced both goods internally—even if it has an absolute advantage in producing all goods.

cooperative research and development agreement. An agreement between a private entity and a national laboratory to conduct agreed-upon research.

critical technology. Depending on the context, a technology that is critical for national defense, private-sector prosperity, or overall national welfare.

current account balance. A comprehensive measure of international transactions. The balance on current account is equal to the sum of the value of imports of goods and services and net returns on foreign investment (including dividends and royalties), minus the value of exports of goods and services, and unilateral transfers such as foreign assistance.

disposable income. The total after tax-income received by persons; the income available to persons for consumption, saving, or investment.

dumping. Selling an export at a lower price than charged in the exporting country or at a price below the cost of production.

economies of scale. The situation whereby the average cost of an economic activity or function falls as volume increases.

elasticity. The measure of relative responsiveness of one variable to a change in another. For example, the elasticity of supply measures how much supply changes in response to a change in price.

exchange rate. The market price of one currency in terms of another currency.

external debt (net). The excess of international claims on a country's assets over its liabilities.

externality. The impact of one activity or decision on another individual, private entity, country, or the international community. Research often creates a positive externality, whereas pollution is a negative externality.

fast-track procedures. Congressional rules applied in the case of trade agreements that limit debate in both houses of Congress and forbid amendments.

General Agreement on Tariffs and Trade (GATT). The multilateral agreement that defined rules for international trade in goods established in 1948. (Now part of the World Trade Organization Agreement.)

gross domestic product (GDP). The market value of the goods and services produced by labor and property in a particular country.

Group of Eight (G-8). The **Group of Seven** plus Russia.

Group of Five (G-5). The group of finance ministers and central bankers from France, Germany, Japan, the United Kingdom, and the United States.

Group of Seven (G-7). The chief executives of the governments of Canada, France, Germany, Italy, Japan, the United Kingdom, and the United States.

human capital. The accumulation of knowledge, skill, and know-how in an individual or an economy, which is generally the product of education, training, and experience.

industrial policy. Government policies designed to achieve specific goals that usually discriminate in favor of or against specific industries or sectors of the economy.

internalizing an externality. Creating incentives or requiring action that induces or forces people to take account of their impact on others.

Laffer curve. A hypothesized curve that shows a trade-off between tax rates and revenue collected.

macroeconomics. The study of national economic relationships and trends, such as the causes and affects of inflation, unemployment, and growth.

Manufacturing Extension Partnership. An extension service in the United States that is designed to spread manufacturing technologies and techniques to small and medium-sized manufacturers.

microeconomics. The study of the economic relationships and choices affecting individuals, households, and private entities.

monopoly. Where a single firm is the only seller of a particular product.

Multifiber Arrangement. The multilateral agreement that established individual country quotas limiting imports of apparel into the United States and other industrial countries.

oligopoly. A situation in which only a few firms sell a particular product.

opportunity cost. The value forgone to make one choice rather than another. For example, with limited income, purchasing a new car may come at the expense of a planned vacation.

Partnership for a New Generation of Vehicles (PNGV). A partnership between the big three American automobile manufacturers (Daimler-Chrysler, Ford, and General Motors) and the national energy laboratories to develop fuel-efficient vehicles.

Phillips curve. A curve that shows the trade-off between higher inflation and lower unemployment.

productivity (labor). A measure of the economic efficiency of labor expressed as output per hour; the amount of goods and services produced by an hour of labor.

productivity (total). A measure of the economic efficiency expressed as output per unit of labor, land, and capital. Productivity is often a measure of technological progress and the basis for increasing the standard of living.

rational expectations. The adjustment individuals make to their economic behavior based on the expected effects of government policy. For instance, in theory, government deficit financing might lead to an expectation of future taxes and a consequent increase in individual savings that would tend to offset the impact of added government spending.

stagflation. Stagnant growth combined with rising prices.

supply-side economics. A school of economic thought that emphasizes the study of the causes of increased supply. Examples of "supply-side" propositions are that (1) a reduction in marginal tax rates will significantly increase saving and investment, work effort, and growth; and (2) a reduction in marginal tax rates will increase growth so much that tax revenues will actually increase.

trade balance. A measure of the value of the exports of goods and services minus the value of the imports of goods and services.

trade promotion authority. See **fast-track procedures**.

voluntary export restraint. A situation in which an exporting country voluntarily agrees to limit exports.

voluntary restraint agreement. Similar to a **voluntary export restraint**.

Bibliography

Abernathy, William J., and Robert B. Hayes. "Managing Our Way to Economic Decline." *Harvard Business Review,* July–August 1980, 67–77.

Agel, Jerome. *We the People: Great Documents of the American Nation.* New York: Barnes & Noble, 1997.

Albertine, Jack. Interview by author, March 1, 2002.

Alic, John, Lewis M. Branscom, Harvey Brooks, Ashton B. Carter, and Gerald K. Epstein. *Beyond Spinoff: Military and Commercial Technologies in a Changing World.* Boston: Harvard Business School Press, 1992.

Allen, Jodie T. "Found Treasure?" *U.S. News & World Report,* July 14, 2003, 35.

Bailey, Christopher J. "Clintonomics." In *The Clinton President: The First Term, '92–96,* ed. Paul S. Hernson and Dilys M. Hill. New York: St. Martin's Press, 1999.

Bailey, Thomas A. *The American Pageant: A History of the Republic.* Boston: DC Heath & Company, 1956.

Barley, Robert L. *The Seven Fat Years and How to Do It Again.* New York: Free Press, 1995.

Barnes, James A. "Where Are Those Gray Flannel Suits?" *National Journal,* September 23, 1995, 2370.

Barnett, Corelli. *The Pride and Fall: The Dream and Illusion of Britain as a Great Nation.* New York: Free Press, 1986.

Bartlett, Bruce. Interview by author, May 24, 2002.

Baucus, Max. *The New American Economy Building for the Long-Term.* Washington, D.C.: Center for National Policy,1992.

Baum, Dan. "GM's Billion-Dollar Bet." *Wired Magazine,* August 2002.

Baumol, William J., Sue Anne Batey Blackman, and Edward N. Wolff. *Productivity and American Leadership: The Long View.* Cambridge, Mass.: MIT Press, 1989.

Bhagwati, Jagdish. *In Defense of Globalization.* New York: Oxford University Press, 2004.

Biemiller, Andrew J. Statement before the House Ways and Means Committee. *Tariff and Trade Proposals.* Washington, D.C.: U.S. Government Printing Office, 1970. Quoted in *Trade Taxes and Transnationals: International Economic Decision Making in Congress,* by Kent H. Hughes (New York: Praeger Publishers, 1979).

"Bill's Recipe: How He Plans to Help U.S. Business Cream Rivals." *Business Week,* October 18, 1993.

Blair, Margaret M., ed. *The Deal Decade: What Takeovers and Leveraged Buyouts Mean for Corporate Governance.* Washington, D.C.: Brookings Institution Press, 1992.

Blank, Rebecca M., and David T. Ellwood. "The Clinton Legacy for America's Poor." In *American Economic Policy in the 1990s,* ed. Jeffery A. Frankel and Peter R. Orszag. Cambridge, Mass.: MIT Press, 2002.

Blinder, Alan S., and Janet L. Yellen. "The Fabulous Decade: Macroeconomic Lessons from the 1990s." In *The Roaring Nineties: Can Full Employment Be Sustained?* ed. Alan B. Krueger and Robert Solow. New York: Century Foundation Press, 2001.

Bloch, Erich. "Technology Policy for a Competitive America" (Report of the Critical Technologies Subcouncil of the Competitiveness Policy Council). In *Reports of Subcouncils.* Washington, D.C.: Competitiveness Policy Council, 1993.

Blustein, Paul. *The Chastening: Inside the Crisis That Rocked the Global Financial System and Humbled the IMF.* New York: Public Affairs, 2001.

Boggs, Lindy, and Katherine Hatch. *Washington Through a Purple Veil: Memoirs of a Southern Woman.* New York: Harcourt Brace, 1994.

Bolling, Richard, and John Bowles. *America's Competitive Edge: How to Get Our Country Moving Again.* New York: McGraw-Hill, 1982.

Bonker, Don. Interview by author, May 21, 2002.

Branscomb, Lewis M. "From Science Policy to Research Policy." In *Investing in Innovation: Creating a Research and Innovation Policy That Works,* ed. Lewis M. Branscomb and James H. Keller. Cambridge, Mass.: MIT Press, 1998.

———. "National Laboratories: The Search for New Missions and New Structures." In *Empowering Technology: Implementing a U.S. Strategy,* ed. Lewis M. Branscomb. Cambridge, Mass.: MIT Press, 1993.

———. "Targeting Critical Technologies." In *Empowering Technology: Implementing a U.S. Strategy,* ed. Lewis M. Branscomb. Cambridge, Mass.: MIT Press, 1993.

Branscomb, Lewis M., and Richard Florida. "Challenges to Technology Policy in a Changing World Economy." In *Investing in Innovation: Creating a Research and Innovation Policy That Works,* ed. Lewis M. Branscomb and James H. Keller. Cambridge, Mass.: MIT Press, 1998.

Branscomb, Lewis M., and George Parker. "Funding Civilian and Dual-Use Industrial Technology." In *Empowering Technology: Implementing a U.S. Strategy,* ed. Lewis M. Branscomb. Cambridge, Mass.: MIT Press, 1993.

Bremer, Jennifer, and John D. Kasarda. "The Origins of Terror." *Milken Institute Review,* fourth quarter of 2002, 34–48.

Broder, David, and Haynes Johnson. *The System: The American Way of Politics at the Breaking Point.* New York: Little, Brown, 1996.

Bromley, Alan. Interview by author, May 30, 2002.

Buerkle, Tom. "Betting the Ranch." *Institutional Investor,* September 2003, 42–44.

Burstein, Daniel. *Yen! Japan's New Financial Empire and Its Threat to America.* New York: Simon & Schuster, 1988.

Business–Higher Education Forum. *America's Competitive Challenge: The Need for a National Response.* Washington, D.C.: Business–Higher Education Forum, 1983.

Cannon, Lou. *President Reagan: The Role of a Lifetime.* New York: Simon & Schuster, 1991.

Caves, Richard E., Jeffrey A. Frankel, and Ronald W. Jones. *World Trade and Payments: An Introduction.* 9th ed. Boston: Addison Wesley, 2002.

Centre for Economic Policy Research. "Strategic Trade Policy: Is There a Case for Intervention?" *Bulletin,* February 19, 1987, 4.

Chandler, Lester V. *America's Greatest Depression, 1929–1941.* New York: Harper & Row, 1970.

Charnovitz, Steve. Interview by author, April 15, 2002.

Cheney, David W., and William W. Grimes. *Japanese Technology Policy: What's the Secret?* Washington, D.C.: Council on Competitiveness, 1991.

Chernow, Ron. *The House of Morgan: An American Banking Dynasty and the Rise of Modern Finance.* New York: Simon & Schuster, 1990.

Chira, Susan. "Lamar Alexander's Self-Help Course." *New York Times Magazine,* November 23, 1991, 52. Quoted in John Robert Greene, *The Presidency of George Bush* (Lawrence: University Press of Kansas, 2001).

Choate, Pat, and J. K. Linger. *The High-Flex Society: Shaping America's Economic Future.* New York: Alfred A. Knopf, 1986.

Choi, Woondo. "Japanese Bargaining Behavior and U.S.–Japan Relationship: FSX Co-Development Project." *2001 Global Economic Review* 30, no. 1.

Chua, Amy. *World on Fire: How Exporting Free Market Democracy Breeds Ethnic Hatred and Global Instability.* New York: Doubleday, 2003.

Clinton, William Jefferson. "Announcement Speech." In *Putting People First: How We Can All Change America,* by Bill Clinton and Al Gore. New York: Times Books, 1992.

Clinton, William J., and Albert Gore Jr. *Science in the National Interest.* Washington, D.C.: U.S. Office of Science and Technology Policy, 1994.

Cohen, Linda. "Dual-Use and Technology Reinvestment Project." In *Investing in Innovation: Creating a Research and Innovation Policy that Works,* ed. Lewis M. Branscomb and James H. Keller. Cambridge, Mass.: MIT Press, 1998.

Cohen, Linda R., and Roger G. Noll. *The Technology Pork Barrel.* Washington, D.C.: Brookings Institution Press, 1991.

Cohen, Stephen D. *Cowboys and Samurai: Why the United States Is Losing the Battle with the Japanese, and Why It Matters.* New York: Harper Collins, 1991.

———. *The Making of United States International Economic Policy: Principles, Problems and Proposals for Reform.* New York: Praeger Publishers, 1977.

Committee on Civilian Industrial Technology of the National Science and Technology Council. *Technology in the National Interest.* Washington, D.C.: U.S. Office of Science and Technology Policy, 1996.

Committee on National Security of the National Science and Technology Council. *National Security, Science and Technology Strategy.* Washington, D.C.: Office of Science and Technology Policy, 1995.

Competitiveness Policy Council. *Saving More and Investing Better: A Strategy for Securing Prosperity,* Fourth Report to the President and Congress. Washington, D.C.: Competitiveness Policy Council, 1995.

Congressional Budget Office. *The Industrial Policy Debate.* Washington, D.C.: U.S. Government Printing Office, 1983.

Council of Economic Advisers. *1978 Economic Report of the President.* Washington, D.C.: U.S. Government Printing Office, 1978.

————. *1979 Economic Report of the President.* Washington, D.C.: U.S. Government Printing Office, 1979.

————. *1980 Economic Report of the President.* Washington, D.C.: U.S. Government Printing Office, 1980.

————. *1984 Economic Report of the President.* Washington, D.C.: U.S. Government Printing Office, 1984.

————. *1988 Economic Report of the President.* Washington, D.C.: U.S. Government Printing Office, 1988.

————. *1989 Economic Report of the President.* Washington, D.C.: U.S. Government Printing Office, 1989.

————. *1990 Economic Report of the President.* Washington, D.C.: U.S. Government Printing Office, 1990.

————. *1992 Economic Report of the President.* Washington, D.C.: U.S. Government Printing Office, 1992.

————. *1993 Economic Report of the President.* Washington, D.C.: U.S. Government Printing Office,1993.

————. *1994 Economic Report of the President.* Washington, D.C.: U.S. Government Printing Office, 1994.

————. *1995 Economic Report of the President.* Washington, D.C.: U.S. Government Printing Office, 1995.

————. *1996 Economic Report of the President.* Washington, D.C.: U.S. Government Printing Office, 1996.

————. *2003 Economic Report of the President.* Washington, D.C.: U.S. Government Printing Office, 2003.

Council on Competitiveness. *Competitiveness Index 1988.* Washington, D.C.: Council on Competitiveness, 1988.

————. *Competitiveness Index 1991.* Washington, D.C.: Council on Competitiveness, 1991.

————. *Endless Frontier, Limited Resources: U.S. R&D Policy for Competitiveness.* Washington, D.C.: Council on Competitiveness, 1996.

————. *Gaining New Ground: Technology Priorities for America's Future.* Washington, D.C.: Council on Competitiveness, 1991.

————. *Going Global: The New Shape of American Innovation.* Washington, D.C.: Council on Competitiveness, 1998.

————. "Kane Reflects on Demise of U.S. Memories." In *Challenges.* Washington, D.C.: Council on Competitiveness, 1990.

————. *Looking for Leadership: The Public, Competitiveness and Campaign '92.* Washington, D.C.: Council on Competitiveness, 1991.

————. *Picking Up the Pace: The Commercial Challenge to American Innovation.* Washington, D.C.: Council on Competitiveness, 1988.

————. *Reclaiming the American Dream: Fiscal Policies for a Competitive Nation.* Washington, D.C.: Council on Competitiveness, 1988.

Cramer, Richard Ben. *What It Takes: The Way to the White House.* New York: Random House, 1992.

Cuomo Commission on Trade and Competitiveness. *The Cuomo Commission Report.* New York: Simon & Schuster, 1988.

Darman, Richard. "Neo-Neo-ism: Reflections on Hubble-ism, Rationalism, and the

Pursuit of Excellence (After the Fiscal Follies)." Speech at the Council of Excellence in Government, Washington, November 16, 1990.

———. *Who's in Control: Polar Politics and the Sensible Center.* New York: Simon & Schuster, 1996.

DeLong, Bradford, and Barry Eichengreen. "Between Meltdown and Moral Hazard: International and Financial Policies of the Clinton Administration." In *American Economic Policy in the 1990s,* ed. Jeffrey A. Frankel and Peter R. Orszag. Cambridge, Mass.: MIT Press, 2002.

Dertouzos, Michael L., Richard Lester, Robert Solow, and MIT Commission on Industrial Productivity. *Made in America: Regaining the Productive Edge.* Cambridge, Mass.: MIT Press, 1989.

Destler, I. M. *American Trade Politics.* 2nd ed. Washington, D.C.: Institute for International Economics with the Twentieth Century Fund, 1992.

———. *Making Foreign Economic Policy.* Washington, D.C.: Brookings Institution Press, 1980.

Divine, Robert A. *The Sputnik Challenge: Eisenhower's Response to the Soviet Satellite.* New York: Oxford University Press, 1993.

"DOD Technology Advisory Group Says Military Capability Is in Doubt Due to Loss of Electronics Industry." *Manufacturing & Technology News,* May 16, 2003, 1, 4–5.

Drew, Elizabeth. *Campaign Journal: The Political Events of 1983–84.* New York: Macmillan, 1985.

———. *On the Edge: The Clinton Presidency.* New York: Simon & Schuster, 1994.

———. *Showdown: The Struggle Between the Gingrich Congress and the Clinton White House.* New York: Simon & Schuster, 1996.

Dryden, Steve. *Trade Warriors: USTR and the American Crusade for Free Trade.* New York: Oxford University Press, 1995.

Duffy, Michael, and Dan Goodgame. *Marching in Place: The Status Quo Presidency of George Bush.* New York: Simon & Schuster, 1992.

Eisenhower, Dwight David. *Crusade in Europe.* New York: Doubleday, 1949.

Eisinger, Peter K. *The Rise of the Entrepreneurial State: State and Local Economic Development Policy in the United States.* Madison: University of Wisconsin Press, 1988.

Eizenstat, Stuart E. Speech at *Business Week* Corporate Planning 100 Senior Planner's Roundtable, Phoenix, November 18, 1982.

Entin, Steve. Interview by author, February 8, 2002.

Ericsson, Sally. Interview by author, March 11, 2002.

Etzkowitz, Henry. "Bridging the Gap: The Evolution of Industry-University Links in the United States." In *Industrializing Knowledge: University–Industry Linkages in Japan and the United States,* ed. Lewis M. Branscomb, Fumio Kodama, and Richard Florida. Cambridge, Mass.: MIT Press, 1999.

Fallows, James. "Containing Japan." *Atlantic Monthly,* May 1989, 40–54.

———. "Getting Along with Japan." *Atlantic Monthly,* December 1989, 53–64.

———. "The Japanese Are Different from You and Me." *Atlantic Monthly,* September 1986, 35–41.

———. "Playing by Different Rules." *Atlantic Monthly,* September 1987, 22–32.

———. "The Rice Plot." *Atlantic Monthly,* January 1987, 22.

Farb, Warren. Interview by author, December 10, 2003.

Farrell, John A. *Tip O'Neill and the Democratic Century.* Boston: Little, Brown, 2001.

Flamm, Kenneth. *Targeting the Computer: Government Support and International Competition.* Washington, D.C.: Brookings Institution Press, 1987.

Flesch, Rudolph Franz. *Why Johnny Can't Read, and What You Can Do about It.* New York: Harper & Row Perennial Library, 1955.

Fogarty, Michael S., and Amit K. Sinha. "Why Older Regions Can't Generalize from Route 128 and Silicon Valley: University–Industry Relationships and Regional Innovation Systems." In *Industrializing Knowledge: University–Industry Linkages in Japan and the United States,* ed. Lewis M. Branscomb, Fumio Kodama, and Richard Florida. Cambridge, Mass.: MIT Press, 1999.

Frankel, Jeffery A., and Peter R. Orszag, eds. *American Economic Policy in the 1990s.* Cambridge, Mass.: MIT Press, 2002.

Friedberg, Aaron L. *The Weary Titan: Britain and the Experience of Relative Decline, 1895–1905.* Princeton, N.J.: Princeton University Press, 1988.

Friedman, Benjamin M. *Day of Reckoning.* New York: Random House, 1988.

———. "Must We Compete?" *New York Review of Books,* October 10, 1994.

From, Alvin. Interview by author, February 28, 2002.

Fukuyama, Francis. *The End of History and the Last Man.* New York: Simon & Schuster, 1992.

Funabashi, Yoichi. *Managing the Dollar: From the Plaza to the Louvre.* Washington, D.C.: Institute for International Economics, 1989.

Garfinkle, Eric. *Roadmap for Results: Trade Policy, Technology, and American Competitiveness.* Washington, D.C.: Council on Competitiveness, 1993.

Germond, Jack, and Jules Witcover. *Mad as Hell: Revolt at the Ballot Box, 1992.* New York: Warner Books, 1993.

Gerstener, Louis V., Jr., Roger D. Semerad, Denis Philip Boyle, and William B. Johnston. *Reinventing Education: Entrepreneurship in America's Public Schools.* New York: Dutton, 1994.

Goldman, Peter, and Tony Fuller. *The Quest for the Presidency 1984.* New York: Bantam Books, 1985.

Granat, Diane. "Democratic Caucus Reviewed as Forum for Policy Questions." *Congressional Quarterly,* October 15, 1983, 2115.

———. "Rep. Long's Death a Blow to Democratic Leadership." *Congressional Quarterly,* January 26, 1985, 145.

Graham, Otis L., Jr. *Losing Time: The Industrial Policy Debate.* Cambridge, Mass.: Harvard University Press, 1992.

Greene, John Robert. *The Presidency of George Bush.* Lawrence: University Press of Kansas, 2001.

Greenspan, Alan. "The Challenge of Central Banking in a Democratic Society." Francis Boyer Lecture of the American Enterprise Institute for Public Policy Research, Washington, December 5, 1996.

Gregg, Gail. "Democrats Score on Budget in House and Senate Panels." *Congressional Quarterly,* April 11, 1981, 619.

———. "House Outlook Grim for Budget Conference." *Congressional Quarterly,* May 24, 1980, 1387.

Greider, William. "The Education of David Stockman." *Atlantic Monthly,* December 1981, 27–54.

———. *Secrets of the Temple: How the Federal Reserve Runs the Country.* New York: Simon & Schuster, 1987.

Grossman, Gene M., and J. David Richardson. *Strategic Trade Policy: A Survey of Issues and Early Analysis.* Special Papers in International Economics 15. Princeton, N.J.: Princeton University, 1985.

Hamrin, Robert. Interview by author, April 4, 2002.

Hansen, Katie, and Daniel F. Burton. *German Technology Policy: Incentive for Industrial Innovation.* Washington, D.C.: Council on Competitiveness, 1992.

Hart, David M. "Managing Technology Policy at the White House." In *Investing in Innovation: Creating a Research and Innovation Policy That Works,* ed. Lewis M. Branscomb and James H. Keller. Cambridge, Mass.: MIT Press, 1998.

Hart, Gary. *A New Democracy: A Democratic Vision for the 1980's and Beyond.* New York: Quill, 1983.

Hart, Jeffrey A., Stephanie A. Lenway, and Thomas P. Murtha. "Technonationalism and Cooperation in a Globalizing Industry: The Case of Flat-Panel Displays." In *Coping with Globalization,* ed. Aseem Prakash and Jeffrey A. Hart. New York: Routledge, 2000.

Harper, Edwin L. Interview by author, June 21, 2002.

Hill, Christopher T. "The Advanced Technology Program: Opportunities for Enhancement." In *Investing in Innovation: Creating a Research and Innovation Policy That Works,* ed. Lewis M. Branscomb and James H. Keller. Cambridge, Mass.: MIT Press, 1998.

———. Interview by author, September 5, 2002.

Hill, Dilys M. "Domestic Policy." In *The Clinton Presidency: The First Term, '92–96,* ed. Paul S. Herrnson and Dilys M. Hill. New York: St. Martin's Press, 1999.

Hoffman, Ellen. "Many American Schools Still at Risk." *National Journal,* April 23, 1988, 1082.

Hohenberg, John. *The Bill Clinton Story: Winning the Presidency.* Syracuse, N.Y.: Syracuse University Press, 1994.

Holland, Max. *The CEO Goes to Washington: Negotiating the Halls of Power.* Knoxville: Chief Executive Press, 1994.

Holmes, Steven A. *Ron Brown: An Uncommon Life.* New York: John Wiley & Sons, 2000.

Horrigan, John. "Cooperation Among Competitors in Research Consortia: The Evolution of MCC and Sematech." Ph.D. diss., University of Texas, 1996.

House Democratic Caucus. *Rebuilding the Road to Opportunity: Turning Point for America's Economy.* Washington, D.C.: House Democratic Caucus, 1982.

Hout, Thomas M., Michael E. Porter, Eileen Rudden, and Eric Vogt. "Global Industries: New Rules for the Competitive Game." Working Paper HBS 80-53, Graduate School of Business Administration, Harvard University.

Hughes, Kent H. "R&D Can Keep America Competitive Amid New Challenges." *Chronicle of Higher Education,* November 30, 2001.

———. *Trade Taxes and Transnationals: International Economic Decision Making in Congress.* New York: Praeger Publishers, 1979.

Huntington, Samuel P. *Clash of Civilizations and the Remaking of the World Order.* New York: W. W. Norton, 1997.

Industrial Union Department, AFL-CIO. *Software & Hardhats: Technology Workers in the 21st Century.* Washington, D.C.: Industrial Union Department, AFL-CIO, 1992.

International Trade Administration. An Assessment of U.S. Competitiveness in High Technology Industries. Washington, D.C.: U.S. Department of Commerce, 1983.

Ishihara, Shintaro, and Akio Morita. *The Japan That Can Say "No."* Unofficial translation, 1989.

Jacobs, Michael T. *Short-Term America: The Causes and Cures of Our Business Myopia.*
Boston: Harvard Business School Press, 1991.

Jaffe, Jim. Interview by author, April 9, 2002.

"Japan's Strategy for 1980s," *Business Week,* December 14, 1981, 65–87.

Johnson, Chalmers. *MITI and the Japanese Miracle: The Growth of Industrial Policy,
1925–1975.* Stanford, Calif.: Stanford University Press, 1982.

Joint Economic Committee, U.S. Congress. *Industrial Policy, Economic Growth and the
Competitiveness of U.S. Industry: Part 1.* 98th Cong., 1st Sess., 1983, pp. 92, 24–30.

———. *Joint Economic Report, 1978.* Washington, D.C.: U.S. Government Printing
Office, 1978.

———. *Report of the Joint Economic Committee on the January 1977 Economic Report of the President.* Washington, D.C.: U.S. Government Printing Office, 1977.

———. *Special Study on Economic Change,* vols. 1–10. Washington, D.C.: U.S. Government Printing Office, 1978.

———. *The Supply Side Revolution: 20 Years Later.* Washington, D.C.: U.S. Government Printing Office, 2000.

Josephy, Alvin M., Jr. *The American Heritage History of the Congress of the United
States.* New York: American Heritage Publishing Company, 1975.

Kaiser, Robert G., "Congress-s-s-s. That Giant Sound You Hear Is Capitol Hill Giving
Up Its Clout," *Washington Post,* March 14, 2004.

Katz, Richard. *Japan: The System That Soured—The Rise and Fall of the Japanese Economic Miracle.* Armonk, N.Y.: M. E. Sharp, 1998.

Kaufman, Burton I. *The Presidency of James Earl Carter.* Lawrence: University Press
of Kansas, 1993.

Kennedy, David M. *Freedom from Fear: The American People in Depression and War,
1929–1945.* New York: Oxford University Press, 1999.

Kennedy, Paul. *The Rise and Fall of the Great Powers: Economic Change and Military
Conflict from 1500 to 2000.* New York: Random House, 1987.

Keynes, John Maynard. *The General Theory of Employment, Interest and Money.* New
York: Harcourt Brace, 1936.

Kindleberger, Charles P. *The World in Depression: 1929–1939.* Rev. ed. Berkeley: University of California Press, 1986.

Klein, Joe. *The Natural: The Misunderstood Presidency of Bill Clinton.* New York:
Doubleday, 2002.

Kodama, Fumio, and Lewis M. Branscomb. "University Research as an Engine for
Growth: How Realistic Is the Vision?" In *Industrializing Knowledge: Univer-
sity–Industry Linkages in Japan and the United States,* ed. Lewis M. Branscomb,
Fumio Kodama, and Richard Florida. Cambridge, Mass.: MIT Press, 1999.

Krueger, Alan B., and Cecelia E. Rouse. "Putting Students and Workers First? Education and Labor Policy in the 1990s." In *American Economic Policy in the 1990s,* ed.
Jeffery A. Frankel and Peter R. Orszag. Cambridge, Mass.: MIT Press, 2002.

Krueger, Alan B., and Robert Solow, eds. *The Roaring Nineties: Can Full Employment
Be Sustained?* New York: Russell Sage Foundation and Century Foundation Press,
2001.

Krugman, Paul. "Competitiveness: A Dangerous Obsession." *Foreign Affairs,* March–
April 1994, 24–28.

————. *Peddling Prosperity: Economic Sense and Nonsense in the Age of Diminished Expectations.* New York: W. W. Norton, 1994.

————. *Rethinking International Trade.* Cambridge, Mass.: MIT Press, 1990.

Krugman, Paul R., and Richard E. Baldwin. "Market Access and International Competition: A Simulation Study of 16K Random Access Memories." In *Rethinking International Trade,* by Paul Krugman. Cambridge, Mass.: MIT Press, 1990.

Kuhn, Thomas. *The Structure of Scientific Revolutions,* 2nd ed. Chicago: University of Chicago Press, 1970.

Labor Policy Institute. *Software & Hardhats: Technology Workers in the 21st Century: A Report of Two Conferences.* Washington, D.C.: Labor Policy Institute, 1992.

Lawrence, Robert Z. "International Trade Policy in the 1990s." In *American Economic Policy in the 1990s,* ed. Jeffrey A. Frankel and Peter R. Orszag. Cambridge, Mass.: MIT Press, 2002.

Lester, Richard K. *The Productive Edge: How U.S. Industries Are Pointing the Way to a New Era of Economic Growth.* New York: W. W. Norton, 1998.

Lew, Jack. Interview by author, April 5, 2002.

Liberatore, Rob. Interview by author, June 7, 2002.

Lodge, George C. *The American Disease.* New York: Alfred A. Knopf, 1984.

Long, Gillis W. "Preface." In *Rebuilding the Road to Opportunity: Turning Point for America's Economy, by House Democratic Caucus.* Washington, D.C.: House Democratic Caucus, 1982.

Lowenstein, Roger. *When Genius Failed: The Rise and Fall of Long-Term Capital Management.* New York: Random House, 2000.

Magazine, Alan. Interview by author, May 10, 2000.

————. Interview by author, July 2, 2002.

Magaziner, Ira C., and Robert B. Reich. *Minding America's Business: The Decline and Rise of the American Economy.* New York: Harcourt Brace Jovanovich, 1982.

Martin, Justin. *Greenspan: The Man Behind Money.* Cambridge, Mass.: Perseus Publishing, 2000.

Matalin, Mary, and James Carville, with Peter Knobler. *All's Fair: Love, War, and Running for President.* New York: Random House, 1994.

McCulloch, Rachel. Interview by author, May 1, 2002.

————. "Point of View: Trade Deficits, Industrial Competitiveness, and the Japanese." *California Management Review* 27, no. 2 (1985): 140–56.

Merrill, Stephen A. "The Politics of Micropolicy: Innovation and Industrial Policy in the United States." In *Government Policies for Industrial Innovation: Design, Implementation, Evaluation,* ed. J. David Roessner. Tarrytown, N.Y.: Associated Faculty Press, 1984.

Mikuni, Akio, and R. Taggart Murphy. *Japan's Policy Trap: Dollars, Deflation and the Crisis of Japanese Finance.* Washington, D.C.: Brookings Institution Press, 2002.

Milbergs, Egils. Interview by author, August 5, 1999.

Mills, Mike. "GOP Filibuster Stalls Competitiveness Bill." *Congressional Quarterly,* March 12, 1994, 549.

————. "Panel Approves Loan Money to Help Firms Compete." *Congressional Quarterly,* May 1, 1993, 1079.

Minge, David. *Coordinating Colors: The WTO Green Box and Green Payments in Farm Programs.* Washington, D.C.: Woodrow Wilson International Center for Scholars, 2004.

Mobley, Sybil. Interview by author, June 7, 2002.

Morita, Akio, and Shintaro Ishihara. *The Japan That Can Say No: The New U.S.–Japan Relations Card.* Tokyo: Kobunsha, 1989.

Morita, Issei. "Japanese Explode the Myth of MITI Economic Growth: Once-Revered Ministry Hindered Industrial Progress, Say Financial Officials." *Financial Times* (London edition), June 27, 2002, 10.

Mottur, Ellis. Interview by author, November 16, 2001.

Mowery, David C., ed. *U.S. Industry in 2000: Studies in Competitive Performance.* Board on Science, Technology, and Economic Policy. Washington, D.C.: National Academies Press, 1999.

Muhlstein, Martin, and Christopher Tow, eds. *U.S. Fiscal Policies and Priorities for Long-Run Sustainability.* Washington, D.C.: International Monetary Fund, 2004.

Mundell, Robert A. *Monetary Theory: Inflation, Interest, and Growth in the World Economy.* Pacific Palisades, Calif.: Goodyear Publishing Company, 1971.

Murrin, Thomas. Interview by author, April 4, 2002.

Nasar, Sylvia. "The New Case for Protectionism." *Fortune,* September 16, 1985, 33–38.

National Advisory Committee on Semiconductors. *A Strategic Industry at Risk: A Report to the President and the Congress from the National Advisory Committee on Semiconductors.* Washington, D.C.: National Advisory Committee on Semiconductors, 1989.

National Center for Education Statistics. "Revenues and Expenditures in Public School Districts: School Year 1999–2000." NCES Statistics Brief. http://www.nces.ed.gov/pubs2003/2003407.pdf.

National Center for History in the Schools. *National Standards for History: Basic Education.* National Center for History in the Schools, University of California, Los Angeles, 1996. http://sscnet.ucla.edu/nchs/standards/preface/html.

National Commission on Entrepreneurship. *American Formula for Growth: Federal Policy and the Entrepreneurial Economy, 1958–1998.* Washington, D.C.: National Commission on Entrepreneurship, 2002.

National Commission on Excellence in Education. *A Nation at Risk.* 1983. http://www.ed.gov/pus/NatAtRisk/risk.html.

National Science and Technology Council, Committee on Civilian Industrial Technology. *Technology in the National Interest.* Washington, D.C.: Office of Science and Technology Policy, 1996.

National Science Board. *Science and Engineering Indicators—2002.* Washington, D.C.: U.S. Government Printing Office, 2002.

National Science Foundation. *International Economic Policy Research: Papers and Proceedings of a Colloquium Held in Washington, D.C., October 3, 4, 1980.* Washington, D.C.: National Science Foundation, 1980.

———. *Science and Engineering Indicators 2002.* Washington, D.C.: U.S. Government Printing Office, 2002.

Nitscke, Lori. "Women Demand Role in Trade Talks." *Women's eNews,* December 2, 2003. http://www.womensnews.org.

"No Child Left Behind Act of 2001" (PL 107-110). January 8, 2002. http://ed.gov/legislation/ESEA02/.

Norquist, Grover. "In Half-Still: No Cease Fire on Big Government." *American Spectator,* December 2001.

Nye, Joseph S., Jr. *Bound to Lead: The Changing Nature of American Power.* New York: Basic Books, 1990.

———. *The Paradox of American Power: Why the World's Only Superpower Can't Go It Alone.* New York: Oxford University Press, 2002.

Ohtawa, Yoshiyuki. "Public Financing of University Research in Japan." In *Industrializing Knowledge: University–Industry Linkages in Japan and the United States,* ed. Lewis M. Branscomb, Fumio Kodama, and Richard Florida. Cambridge, Mass.: MIT Press, 1999.

Okubo, Sumiye. "Introduction and Summary of the session on Changes in Comparative Advantage." In *International Economic Policy Research: Papers and Proceedings of a Colloquium Held in Washington, DC, October 3, 4, 1980,* ed. National Science Foundation. Washington, D.C.: National Science Foundation, 1980.

Oleszek, Walter J. *Congressional Procedures and the Policy Process,* 2nd ed. Washington, D.C.: Congressional Quarterly Press, 1984.

Osborne, David. *Laboratories of Democracy: A New Breed of Governor Creates Models for National Growth.* Boston: Harvard Business School Press, 1988.

Osirim, Mary. "Carrying the Burdens of Adjustment and Globalization: Women and Microenterprise Development in Urban Zimbabwe." *International Sociology* 24 (2003): 35–58.

Packer, Arnie. Interview by author, June 10, 2002.

Peltz, Michael, and Marc A. Weiss. "State and Local Government Roles in Industrial Innovation." *APA Journal* 50, no. 3 (1984): 271–79.

Pempel, T. J. *Regime Shift: Comparative Dynamics of the Japanese Political Economy.* Ithaca, N.Y.: Cornell University Press, 1998.

Perot, Ross. *United We Stand: How We Can Take Back Our Country.* New York: Hyperion, 1992.

Peterson, Peter G. *Running on Empty: How the Democratic and Republic Parties Are Bankrupting Our Future and What Americans Can Do about It.* New York: Farrar, Straus and Giroux, 2004.

Pinkerton, James. "The New Paradigm." Speech at the Reason Foundation, Los Angeles, April 23, 1990.

Polanyi, Karl. *The Great Transformation: The Political and Economic Origins of Our Time.* Boston: Beacon Press, 1957.

Policinski, Mark. Interview by author, April 5, 2002.

Porter, Michael E. *Capital Choices: Changing the Way America Invests in Industry.* Washington, D.C.: Council on Competitiveness, 1992.

———. *The Competitive Advantage of Nations.* New York: Free Press, 1990.

———. "The Competitive Advantage of Nations." *Harvard Business Review,* March–April 1990, 73–93.

———. Interview by author, May 17, 2002.

Porter, Michael, Mariko Sakakibara, and Hirotaka Takeuchi. *Can Japan Compete?* Cambridge, Mass.: Perseus Publishing, 2000.

Porter, Roger. Interview by author, April 24, 2002.

———. *Presidential Decision Making: The Economic Policy Board.* New York: Cambridge University Press, 1980.

President's Commission on Industrial Competitiveness. *Global Competition: The New Realtity.* 2 vols. Washington, D.C.: U.S. Government Printing Office, 1985.

Prestowitz, Clyde V., Jr. *Trading Places: How We Allowed Japan to Take the Lead.* New York: Basic Books, 1988.

———. *Trading Places: How We Are Giving Our Future to Japan and How to Reclaim It.* Paperback edition. New York: Basic Books, 1989.

Rauch, Jonathan. "Father Superior: Our Greatest Modern President." *New Republic,* May 22, 2000, 25.

———. "Testing the Fed." *National Journal,* June 18, 1988, 1612–15.

Regan, Edward. Interview by author, August 19, 2002.

Reich, Robert B. *The Work of Nations: Preparing Ourselves for 21st Century Capitalism.* New York: Alfred A. Knopf, 1991.

Rhode, David W. *Parties and Leaders in the Postreform House.* Chicago: University of Chicago Press, 1991.

Roberts, Paul Craig. *The Supply-Side Revolution: An Insider's Account of Policymaking in Washington.* Cambridge, Mass.: Harvard University Press, 1984.

Roe, Mark J. "Takeover Politics." In *The Deal Decade: What Takeovers and Leveraged Buyouts Mean for Corporate Governance,* ed. Margaret M. Blair. Washington, D.C.: Brookings Institution Press, 1992.

Rohatyn, Felix. "The Coming Emergency and What Can Be Done About It." *New York Review of Books,* December 4, 1980, 20–26.

———. "Reconstructing America." *New York Review of Books,* March 5, 1981, 16–21.

Roos, Daniel, Frank Field, and James Neely. "Industry Consortia." In *Investing in Innovation: Creating a Research and Innovation Policy That Works,* ed. Lewis M. Branscomb and James H. Keller. Cambridge, Mass.: MIT Press, 1998.

Rosen, Howard. Interview by author June 8, 2000.

Rubin, Robert. "Comments." In *American Economic Policy in the 1990s,* ed. Jeffery A. Frankel and Peter R. Orszag. Cambridge, Mass.: MIT Press, 2002.

Rubin, Robert E., and Jacob Weisberg. *In an Uncertain World: Tough Choices from Wall Street to Washington.* New York: Random House, 2003.

Samuelson, Pamela, and Hal B. Varian. "The 'New Economy' and Information Technology Policy." In *American Economic Policy in the 1990s,* ed. Jeffrey A. Frankel and Peter R. Orszag. Cambridge, Mass.: MIT Press, 2002.

Schlosstein, Steven. *The End of the American Century.* New York: Congdon & Weed, 1989.

Schwab, Susan C. *Trade-Offs: Negotiating the Omnibus Trade and Competitiveness Act.* Boston: Harvard Business School Press, 1994.

Scott, Bruce R., George C. Lodge, and Joseph Bower, eds. *U.S. Competitiveness in the World Economy.* Cambridge, Mass.: Harvard University Press, 1985.

Servan-Schreiber, Jean-Jacques. *The American Challenge.* New York: Avon, 1969.

Sinclair, Barbara. *Legislators, Leaders and Lawmaking: The U.S. House of Representatives in the Postreform Era.* Baltimore: Johns Hopkins University Press, 1995.

———. *Majority Leadership in the U.S. House.* Baltimore: Johns Hopkins University Press, 1983.

Skocpal, Theda. *Boomerang: Clinton's Health Security Effort and the Turn Against Government in U.S. Politics.* New York: W. W. Norton, 1996.

Smith, Bruce L. R., and Claude Barfield. "Contribution of Research and Technical Advance to the Economy." In *Technology, R&D, and the Economy,* ed. Bruce L. R. Smith and Claude Barfield. Washington, D.C.: Brookings Institution Press and American Enterprise Institute, 1996.

Smith, Hedrick. *Rethinking America: A New Game Plan from the American Innovators: Schools, Business, People, Work.* New York: Random House, 1995.

Solomon, Robert. *The International Monetary System: 1945–1981.* New York: Harper & Row, 1981.

———. *Money on the Move: The Revolution in International Finance since 1980.* Princeton, N.J.: Princeton University Press, 1999.

Stein, Herbert. *Presidential Economics: The Making of Economic Policy from Roosevelt to Reagan and Beyond.* 2nd ed. Washington, D.C.: American Enterprise Institute, 1988.

Stern, Robert M. "Changes in U.S. Comparative Advantage, Issues for Research and Policy." In *International Economic Policy Research: Papers and Proceedings of a Colloquium Held in Washington, DC, October 3, 4, 1980,* ed. National Science Foundation. Washington, D.C.: National Science Foundation, 1980.

Stiglitz, Joseph E. *Globalization and Its Discontents.* New York: W. W. Norton, 2002.

———. *The Roaring Nineties: A New History of the World's Most Prosperous Decade.* New York: W. W. Norton, 2003.

Stiglitz, Joseph E., and Shahid Yusuf, eds. *Rethinking the East Asian Miracle.* Washington, D.C.: Oxford University Press, 2001.

Stokes, Bruce. "Economic Interests: The Culture Clash at Cancún." *National Journal,* September 20, 2003.

———. "Focus: Two Sides of the Competitive Edge." *National Journal,* July 30, 1994.

Tate, Dale. "Rep. Jones Beleaguered Budget Chairman." *Congressional Quarterly,* June 19, 1982, 1449.

Tatsuno, Sheridan. "Life After U.S. Memories: Can the U.S. Re-Enter the Memory Chip Business?" *New Technology Week,* February 12, 1990.

Technology Administration, U.S. Department of Commerce. *International Science and Technology: Policies, Programs and Investments.* Washington, D.C.: U.S. Department of Commerce, 2000.

Terkel, Studs. *Hard Times.* New York: Avon Books, 1971.

Thurow, Lester C. "The Case for Industrial Policies." Photocopy, Center for National Policy, Washington, D.C., 1984.

———. *Head to Head: The Coming Economic Battle among Japan, Europe, and America.* New York: William Morrow, 1992.

Trade Promotion Coordinating Committee. *National Export Strategy: Report to the United States Congress.* Washington, D.C.: U.S. Government Printing Office, 1985.

———. *National Export Strategy: Report to the United States Congress.* Washington, D.C.: U.S. Government Printing Office, 1994.

———. *Toward a National Export Strategy: U.S. Exports = U.S. Jobs.* Washington, D.C.: U.S. Government Printing Office, 1993.

Ture, Norman B. "Supply Side Analysis and Public Policy." In *Essays in Supply-Side Economics,* ed. David G. Raboy. Washington, D.C.: Institute for Research on the Economics of Taxation, 1982.

Turner, James. Interview by author, June 10, 2002.

Tyson, Laura D'Andrea. *Who's Bashing Whom: Trade Conflict in High-Technology Industries.* Washington, D.C.: Institute for International Economics, 1992.

———. *The Yugoslav Economic System and Its Performance in the 1970s.* Berkeley: University of California Press, 1980.

U.S. Congress. *Omnibus Trade and Competitiveness Act of 1988: A Conference Report to Accompany HR 3.* Washington, D.C.: U.S. Government Printing Office, 1988.

U.S. Department of Commerce. *Building the American Dream: Jobs, Innovation and Growth in America's Next Century.* Washington, D.C.: U.S. Government Printing Office, 1996.

————. *Building the American Dream for the 21st Century.* Washington, D.C.: U.S. Government Printing Office, 1995.

————. *Technological Innovation: Its Environment and Management.* Washington, D.C.: U.S. Government Printing Office, 1978.

————. *2020 Visions: Transforming Education and Training Through Advanced Technologies.* Washington, D.C.: U.S. Department of Commerce, 2002.

U.S. Department of Commerce and U.S. Department of the Treasury. *Financing Technology: A Report of the Financing Technology Round Tables.* Washington, D.C.: U.S. Department of Commerce and U.S. Department of the Treasury, 1992.

U.S. Department of Education. *Japanese Education Today.* Washington, D.C.: U.S. Government Printing Office, 1987.

U.S. Department of Labor. *Investing in People and Prosperity: A Review of Key Clinton Administrative Initiatives to Spur Creation of More and Better Jobs.* Washington, D.C.: U.S. Government Printing Office, 1994.

U.S. Department of the Treasury. *Federal Credit Programs: An Overview of Current Programs and Their Beginning in the Reconstruction Finance Corporation.* Washington, D.C.: Office of Corporate Finance, U.S. Treasury Department, 1982. Quoted by Stuart E. Eizenstat, speech at *Business Week* Corporate Planning 100 Senior Planner's Roundtable, Phoenix, November 18, 1982.

U.S. Trade Deficit Review Commission. *The U.S. Trade Deficit: Causes, Consequences and Recommendations for Action.* Washington, D.C.: U.S. Trade Deficit Review Commission, 2000.

van Wolferen, Karel. *The Enigma of Japanese Power.* New York: Alfred A. Knopf, 1989.

————. "The Japan Problem." *Foreign Affairs,* winter 1986–87, 288–303.

"Vision for the 1980s: Basic Course of MITI's Trade-Industrial Policy." *The Oriental Economist* 47 (November 1979): 12–16.

Vogel, Ezra. *Japan as No. 1: Lessons for America.* Cambridge, Mass.: Harvard University Press, 1979.

Waldman, Raymond J. *Managed Trade: The New Competition Between Nations.* Cambridge, Mass.: Ballinger Publishing Company, 1986.

Walker, Martin. *The President We Deserve: His Rise, Falls, and Comebacks.* New York: Crown Publishers, 1996.

Wessner, Charles W., ed. *Securing the Future: Regional and National Programs to Support the Semiconductor Industry.* Board on Science, Technology, and Economic Policy of the National Research Council. Washington, D.C.: National Academies Press, 2003.

White House Office of Science and Technology Policy and U.S. Department of Commerce. *Domestic Policy Review of Industrial Innovation.* Washington, D.C.: U.S. Government Printing Office, 1978.

White, Mary. *The Japanese Educational Challenge: A Commitment to Children.* New York: Macmillan, 1987.

Wills, Garry. *Reagan's America: Innocents at Home.* Garden City, N.Y.: Doubleday, 1987.

Windham, Patrick. Interview by author, October 25, 1999.

Winthrop, John. "A Model of Christian Charity." 1630. http://history.hanover.edu/texts/winthmod.html.

Wolf, Martin. "America Is Now on the Comfortable Path to Ruin." *Financial Times,* August 18, 2004, 11.

Woodward, Bob. *The Choice.* New York. Simon & Schuster, 1996.

———. *Maestro: Greenspan's Fed and the American Boom.* New York: Simon & Schuster, 2000.

World Bank. *The East Asian Miracle: Economic Growth and Public Policy.* New York: Oxford University Press, 1993.

Wright, Jim. *Balance of Power: President and Congress from the Era of McCarthy to the Age of Gingrich.* Atlanta: Turner Publishing, 1996.

———. Interview by author, July 9, 2002.

Yergin, Daniel, and Joseph Stanislaw. *The Commanding Heights: The Battle between Government and the Marketplace That Is Remaking the Modem World.* New York: Simon & Schuster, 1998.

Yerxa, Rufus. Interview by author, April 21, 2002.

Young, John. Interviews by author, November 30, 1999, and September 15–16, 2000.

Zysman, John. Interview by author, April 10, 2002.

Zysman, John, and Laura D. Tyson. *American Industry in International Competition: Government Policies and Corporate Strategies.* Ithaca, N.Y.: Cornell University Press, 1984.

Index